RESEARCH METHODS & METHODOLOGIES IN EDUCATION

2ND EDITION

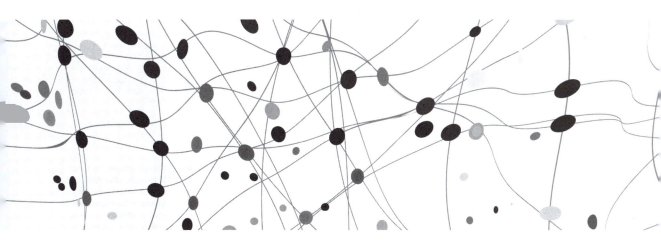

EDITED BY

ROBERT COE, MICHAEL WARING, LARRY V. HEDGES & JAMES ARTHUR

Los Angeles | London | New Delhi
Singapore | Washington DC | Melbourne

Los Angeles | London | New Delhi
Singapore | Washington DC | Melbourne

SAGE Publications Ltd
1 Oliver's Yard
55 City Road
London EC1Y 1SP

SAGE Publications Inc.
2455 Teller Road
Thousand Oaks, California 91320

SAGE Publications India Pvt Ltd
B 1/I 1 Mohan Cooperative Industrial Area
Mathura Road
New Delhi 110 044

SAGE Publications Asia-Pacific Pte Ltd
3 Church Street
#10-04 Samsung Hub
Singapore 049483

Editor: James Clark
Assistant editor: Robert Patterson
Production editor: Tom Bedford
Copyeditor: Aud Scriven
Proofreader: Elaine Leek
Indexer: Cathy Heath
Marketing manager: Lorna Patkai
Cover design: Sheila Tong
Typeset by: C&M Digitals (P) Ltd, Chennai, India
Printed and bound by
CPI Group (UK) Ltd, Croydon, CR0 4YY

First edition published in 2012 and reprinted in 2013 and 2015 (twice)

This second edition first published 2017

Library of Congress Control Number: 2016951255

British Library Cataloguing in Publication data

A catalogue record for this book is available from the British Library

ISBN 978-1-4739-6979-7
ISBN 978-1-4739-6980-3 (pbk)

RESEARCH METHODS & METHODOLOGIES IN EDUCATION

2ND EDITION

Praise for the first edition

Contents

List of figures and tables

Figures

Tables

About the editors

Professor Robert J. Coe, Durham University, Professor of Education and Director of the Centre for Evaluation and Monitoring. His research interests include evaluation methodology, evidence-based education and the involvement of practitioners in research, school effectiveness and improvement, including the methodology of school effectiveness research, the use and effects of feedback especially in performance monitoring information systems, and the statistical comparability of examinations in different subjects and over time.

Dr Michael Waring, Director MSc Education (QTS) Physical Education, School of Sport, Exercise and Health Sciences, Loughborough University. He sits on the executive of the Society for Educational Studies, and is on the editorial board of the *British Journal of Educational Studies and Higher Education Pedagogies*. His research interests focus on the development of a personal learning styles pedagogy and the use of learning technologies as part of distance and blended learning in higher education and initial teacher education contexts. Generally and as part of the exploration of this personalised learning agenda, he is interested in the use and innovative development of qualitative research methodology.

Professor Larry V. Hedges, Northwestern University, Professor of Statistics and Social Policy. A national leader in the fields of educational statistics and evaluation, his research is in the fields of sociology, psychology and educational policy. He is best known for his work to develop statistical methods for meta-analysis in the social, medical and biological sciences.

Professor James Arthur, Deputy Pro-Vice-Chancellor, Professor of Education and Civic Engagement, University of Birmingham. He is Director, Jubilee Centre for Character and Virtues, an inter-disciplinary research centre focusing on character, virtues and values in the interest of human flourishing. He has written widely on the relationship between theory and practice in education, particularly the links between communitarianism, social virtues, citizenship, religion and education. He is Secretary to the Society for Educational Studies.

Notes on the contributors

Dr Michael Atkinson, University of Toronto, Professor. He is co-editor of *Qualitative Research in Sport, Exercise and Health*, and past editor of the *Sociology of Sport Journal*. His research interests include health, youth masculinity, bioethics, violence, suffering, existentialism, and physical cultural studies.

Dr Greg Benfield (retired), formerly Oxford Brookes University, Educational Development Consultant. His work focused on supporting technology-enhanced learning. His research interests included learner experiences of technology-enhanced learning, computer-aided assessment, and computer-mediated communication in student group work.

Dr Ghazala Bhatti, Bath Spa University, Senior Lecturer at the Institute for Education. She is a founding member of the Network for Social Justice and Intercultural Education of the European Conference on Educational Research. Her research interests include social justice, ethnographic research, bilingualism in schools, comparative education research, and the educational achievements of children from minority ethnic backgrounds.

Professor Gert Biesta, Brunel University London, Professor of Education and Director of Research. He is associate editor of the journal *Educational Theory*. He conducts theoretical and empirical research on a range of topics, with a particular interest in education, democracy and citizenship, and the theory and philosophy of educational and social research.

Michael Borenstein is a researcher who specialises in statistical power analysis and meta-analysis. He has been funded by the NIH and the IES in the United States for the purpose of developing computer programs for statistical power analysis and meta-analysis, and lectures widely on these topics.

Professor Paul Connolly, Queen's University Belfast, Dean of Research. He is Professor of Education and Dean of Research for the Faculty of Arts, Humanities and Social Sciences. He is also Director of the Centre for Evidence and Social Innovation (www.qub.ac.uk/cesi). His research interests include diversity and social inclusion in early childhood, early intervention and prevention, evaluations of social interventions, and evidence synthesis.

Dr Laura Day Ashley, University of Birmingham, Lecturer, School of Education. She has a background in social anthropology and education and a particular interest in international and historical approaches to the study of education. She teaches research methods, international education and the history of schooling, and supervises dissertations and theses at undergraduate, Master's and doctoral levels. She has led research on private school outreach in India (funded by the Economic and Social Research Council), private and non-state schooling in developing countries (funded by the Department for International Development, UK), and Indian influences on progressive education in Britain in the early twentieth century (funded by the British Academy).

Dr Anita Gibbs, University of Otago, Associate Professor. She supervises postgraduate research related to social work research methods, disability and family practice areas. Her research interests are in mainstream, alternative and indigenous social work theories and methodologies, adoption and fostering, transcultural parenting, and fetal alcohol spectrum disorders.

Dr Graham R. Gibbs, University of Huddersfield, Reader in Research Methods. He is course coordinator for MSc Social Research and Evaluation (Distance Learning) and is a National Teaching Fellow of the HEA. His research interests include the use of technology in teaching and learning and the use of computers in qualitative research. He has published on computer-assisted learning and qualitative data analysis and he currently runs a YouTube channel on research methods.

Professor Stephen Gorard, Professor of Education and Public Policy, Durham University. He is author of over 1,000 pieces, and has conducted studies of primary education, early childhood, secondary education, FE, HE, adult and continuing education, and informal learning in the home. His research approach is multimethod, combining large-scale surveys, focus group work, complex statistical modelling and historical archive analysis, among others. He is the editor of *Review of Education*, and author of *Research Design* (Sage, 2013).

Ms Jill Hall, University of Edinburgh, Research Fellow. She works as a Research Fellow in the Usher Institute of Population Health Sciences and Informatics, and has written and co-written numerous publications around her research interests in telehealth systems, complex wounds, patient involvement in patient safety, clinical trials in fracture prevention and podiatry, and systematic reviews of the effectiveness of interventions.

Professor Ronald K. Hambleton, University of Massachusetts Amherst, Distinguished University Professor and Executive Director of the Center for Educational Assessment. He is a Fellow of Divisions 5 and 15 of the American Psychological Association (APA), a Fellow of the American Educational Research Association (AERA), and a Fellow of the International Association of Applied Psychology. He is the author or co-editor of nine books in the psychometric methods area, author or co-author of more than 700 research papers, and he has received several career achievement awards including awards from the National Council on Measurement in Education, the AERA, the APA, the International Test Commission, and the European Association of Methodology. He has been awarded honorary doctorates from the University of Umea in Sweden and the University of Oviedo in Spain.

Professor Martyn Hammersley, The Open University, Emeritus Professor of Educational and Social Research. He has carried out research in the sociology of education and studied the role of the media in reporting research findings. However, much of his work has been concerned with the methodological issues surrounding social enquiry. He has written several books, including (with Paul Atkinson) *Ethnography: Principles in Practice*, 3rd edition (Routledge, 2007) and (with Anna Traianou) *Ethics in Qualitative Research* (Sage, 2012).

Professor Steve Higgins, Durham University, Professor of Education. His research interests include the areas of effective use of digital technologies in schools, understanding how children's thinking and reasoning develop, and how teachers can be supported in developing the quality of teaching and learning in their classrooms. He has a particular interest in the use of evidence from education research to support improvement, and is the lead author of the *Sutton Trust-Education Endowment Foundation Teaching and Learning Toolkit*.

Professor Harvey J. Keselman, University of Manitoba, Professor of Psychology. He is Professor Emeritus in the Department of Psychology at the University of Manitoba. His current research program involves developing statistical tests that will be insensitive (robust) to non-normality and variance heterogeneity in independent and correlated groups designs. He would like to initiate in the future testing of social scientists' use of statistical tests to assess whether or not the effect of an experimental manipulation is significant.

Mrs Kate Lewis-Light, Information Specialist. She is an information specialist with over fifteen years' experience gained at the Centre for Reviews and Dissemination (CRD), University of York. At CRD she was responsible for contributing to systematic reviews, mainly through the design and running of complex search strategies. She also contributed to the production of CRD's DARE, HTA and PROSPERO databases, and taught on systematic review training courses run by CRD.

Dr Lisa M. Lix, University of Manitoba, Professor of Biostatistics. She is also a Manitoba Research Chair in the Department of Community Health Sciences at the University of Manitoba, Director of the Data Science Platform in the George and Fay Yee Centre for Healthcare Innovation, and Senior Scientist at the Manitoba Centre for Health Policy. Her research interests include analysis of longitudinal/repeated measures data, multivariate analyses of quality of life, risk prediction models, and behavioural health outcomes.

Professor Gary McCulloch, UCL Institute of Education, Brian Simon Professor of History of Education. He teaches History of Education and Research Methods. He is a member of advisory boards for *History of Education, History of Education Review, Journal of Educational Administration and History*. His research interests are in the history of education, including curriculum history, the history of secondary education, and documentary research methods. He is currently President-elect of the British Educational Research Association and editor of the *British Journal of Educational Studies*.

Dr Carolyn L. Mears, University of Denver, Affiliated Faculty and Guest Lecturer. She holds a research appointment and is dissertation advisor and adjunct faculty at the University of Denver. She is a noted author, consultant, and speaker on issues related to trauma and crisis recovery. Her research interests include the effect of trauma on communities following mass casualty events and prevention of school violence. Her dissertation, 'Experiences of Columbine Parents', won the 2006 AERA Outstanding Dissertation of the Year Award for its innovative contributions to qualitative research practice. Her book *Reclaiming School in the Aftermath of Trauma* won the Colorado Book of the Year Award for anthology, and her text *Interviewing for Education and Social Science Research: The Gateway Approach* was a finalist for the AERA Outstanding Qualitative Book of the Year Award.

Professor Claudia Mitchell, McGill University, Professor of Education. She is a professor in the McGill University Department of Integrated Studies in Education. Her research interests include youth, gender and AIDS, visual and arts-based research methodologies, girls' education in development studies, and teacher identity.

Professor Carol Munn-Giddings, Anglia Ruskin University, Professor in the School of Education and Social Care. She joined ARU in 1995 after many years as a social researcher and research manager in various health and social services settings. Her research focuses on ways in which citizens and citizen groups with a direct experience of a health or social situation can inform the development of appropriate health and social care services.

Jordan Rickles, American Institutes for Research, Principal Researcher. He specialises in research design and quantitative methodology. His research explores the intersection of multilevel modelling, causal inference and propensity score methods, with a particular interest in heterogeneity across educational settings.

Professor Michael Seltzer, University of California, Los Angeles. He is a Professor in the Advanced Quantitative Methods program in the Graduate School of Education and Information Studies at the University of California, Los Angeles. He specialises in multilevel modelling, particularly its use in multi-site evaluation studies and in analysing longitudinal data. A related facet of his work focuses on the use of Bayesian statistical approaches in specifying and estimating multilevel models in complex modelling settings.

Professor Rhona Sharpe, Oxford Brookes University, Head of Oxford Centre for Staff and Learning Development. She has directed a number of projects investigating learners' experiences of technology. These projects received national recognition in pioneering innovative research methods and techniques for eliciting students' expectations and experiences of using technology in their learning. The culmination of these projects was the creation of ELESIG – a special interest group for those interested in evaluations of learners' experiences of e-learning. Her interests in designing for learning and learner experience are well represented in two books co-edited with Helen Beetham: *Rethinking Pedagogy for a Digital Age,* 2nd edition (2013) and *Rethinking Learning for the Digital Age* (2010).

Professor Emma Smith, University of Leicester, Professor of Education. She researches issues of educational equity and the role that educational policy can play in reducing inequalities and closing achievement gaps in both the national and international context. Recent and on-going work has been in the following areas: shortages in the STEM workforce, special education and school accountability, inequalities in participation in post-compulsory science programmes, and school policy in England. She has a general interest in research methods and has led research methods courses at both undergraduate and postgraduate level. Her particular

area of interest is in the use of numeric secondary data, and she has co-edited the new two-volume BERA/Sage *Handbook of Education Research*.

Eve Stirling, Sheffield Institute of Art, Sheffield Hallam University, Senior Lecturer in Design. Her research interests include the use of social media within society and more specifically within higher education and the pedagogical impacts of this. She uses practice-based and visual research methods to explore the everyday lives of her participants.

Dr Michael Tedder, University of Exeter, Research Fellow. He has taught Liberal Studies and been responsible for teacher education for many years. His research interests include life history and biographical research, adult and community learning, the experiences of young people on vocational courses in FE, and notions of professionalism in post-compulsory education.

Professor Carole Torgerson, Durham University, Professor of Education. Previously, she held a Chair in Experimental Design at the University of Birmingham and a Readership in Evidence-based Education at the University of York. Her main methodological research interests are in experimental methods (randomised controlled trials and quasi-experiments) and research synthesis. She is particularly interested in applying methodological work in experimental research previously undertaken in the field of health care to the field of education.

Professor Peter Tymms PhD, Durham University. He is Director of the iPIPS project in the Centre for Evaluation and Monitoring and also part of the School of Education. He is a member of the Leibniz Institute for Educational Trajectories Scientific Advisory Board, the Sutton Trust's Education Advisory Group, the Advisory Board for The Learning & Psychology Centre, and an Academician of the Academy of Social Science. His main research interests include monitoring, assessment, performance indicators, ADHD, reading and research methodology.

Dr Elaine Vaughan, University of Limerick, Lecturer. She lectures in various areas of applied linguistics, and is programme director for the MA TESOL at the School of Modern Languages and Applied Linguistics. Her key areas of expertise are corpus-based discourse analysis, language teacher education, corpus linguistics, pragmatics, and Irish English. She has published on teacher professional talk in the workplace, the pragmatics of humour and laughter, teaching and learning in higher education, Irish English, and representations of Irish English in the media.

Anna Vignoles, University of Cambridge, Professor of Education and Director of Research at the Faculty of Education, and a trustee of the Nuffield Foundation. She has extensive experience of using large-scale administrative data to study factors relating to pupil achievement and students' outcomes from education. She has published widely on widening participation into higher education and on the socio-economic gap in pupil achievement. Her research interests include issues pertaining to equity in education, school choice, school efficiency and finance, higher education, and the economic value of schooling.

Rob Walker, University of East Anglia, Professor of Education. He teaches and researches in the area of higher education practice, dealing both with the practicalities of day-to-day teaching in lecture theatres, seminars and on websites, and acknowledging the growing debates about research, teaching and curriculum in universities. He is a member of the Centre for Applied Research in Education (CARE) and also the Centre for Staff and Educational Development.

Acknowledgements

SAGE would like to thank the following people whose comments have helped to shape this new edition:

Jean Conteh, University of Leeds

Alaster Scott Douglas, University of Roehampton

Loes Houweling, University of Applied Sciences, Leiden

Rory du Plessis, University of Pretoria

Linzi McKerr, University of Worcester

Liane Purnell, Newman University

Ben Tan, Sheffield Hallam University

List of abbreviations

AIDS	acquired immune deficiency syndrome
ANCOVA	analysis of covariance
ANOVA	analysis of variance
APA	American Psychological Association
AR	action research
ASC	Annual Schools Census
BECTA	British Educational Communications and Technology Agency
BERA	British Educational Research Association
CA	conversation analysis
CAQDAS	Computer-Assisted/Aided Qualitative Data Analysis
CHASS	Council for Humanities, Arts and Social Sciences (Australia)
CMC	computer-mediated communication
CONSORT	Consolidated Standards of Reporting Trials
CoPE	Certificate of Personal Effectiveness
CPD	continuing professional development
CSDP	Comer's School Development Program
DCSF	Department for Children, Schools and Families
ECLS	Early Childhood Longitudinal Study
Edna	Education Network Australia
ELESIG	Evaluation of Learners' Experiences of e-learning Special Interest Group
EPPI	Centre Evidence for Policy and Practice Information and Co-ordinating Centre
ERA	Excellence in Research for Australia
ERIC	Education Resources Information Center
ESDS	Economic and Social Data Service
ESL	English as a Second Language
ESRC	Economic and Social Research Council
FSM	free school meals
GNVQ	General National Vocational Qualification
GPA	grade point average
GPS	global positioning system
GT	grounded theory
GTCE	General Teaching Council for England
GTM	grounded theory method
HE	higher education
HEFCE	Higher Education Funding Council for England
HIV	human immunodeficiency virus
HSB	High School and Beyond
ICC	intra-class correlation
IDeA	Improvement and Development Agency
IEA	International Association for the Evaluation of Educational Achievement
IPRN	ITT Professional Resource Networks
IRF	Initiation, Response, Feedback/ Follow-up
ITT	initial teacher training
IWB	interactive whiteboard
LTE	language teacher education
NFER	National Foundation for Educational Research

NHST	null hypothesis significance testing
OECD	Organisation for Economic Cooperation and Development
ONS	Office for National Statistics
PAR	participatory action research
PICOS	participants, interventions, outcomes, study designs
PISA	Programme for International Student Assessment
PRISMA	Preferred Reporting Items for Systematic Reviews and Meta-Analyses Statement
QCA	Qualifications and Curriculum Authority
QCDA	Qualifications and Curriculum Development Agency
QUOROM	Quality of Reporting of Meta-analyses
RAE	Research Assessment Framework
RCT	randomised controlled trial
RDI	Researcher Development Initiative
RSA	Royal Society of Arts
SDM	standard mean deviation
SDQ	Strengths and Difficulties Questionnaire
SES	socio-economic status
SETT	Self-Evaluation of Teacher Talk
SIVS	strategically important and vulnerable subject
STEM	science, technology, engineering and mathematics
TDA	Training and Development Agency for Schools
TESL	Teaching English as a Second Language
TM	Transition Mathematics
UCAS	Universities Central Admissions Service
VLE	virtual learning environment
VSFG	very small focus group

Companion website

A companion website to the book can be found at https://study.sagepub.com/coe2e. This includes a range of free-to-access SAGE journal articles exemplifying the varied research methods and tools discussed in the book.

Introduction

Robert J. Coe

1

Aim of the book

Whether you are a postgraduate student on an education-related course or an early career researcher, this book is for you. It offers a broad introduction to core principles that underpin rigorous research and a pragmatic overview of the varied approaches to research design, data collection and data analysis that are used within educational research. It combines clear conceptual and theoretical coverage with a strong practical edge to give you an understanding of the intellectual tools available to you as an educational researcher and how these are used in practice. We aim to give you the knowledge and confidence to design, plan and carry out informed educational research using methods appropriate to your initial research question. Chapter authors are drawn from a geographically diverse group of international academic experts who discuss their respective topics in universally accessible language, avoiding any of the context-specific issues that relate to education in different parts of the world.

One consequence of inviting authors who are world-leading scholars and methodologists in such a broad range of topics is that they do not all agree. Educational research is a diverse and contested area, and anyone who reads the book as a whole will notice quite specific contradictions and inconsistencies in the advice given. This is both a strength and a weakness. For a student looking for simple, clear advice it may feel confusing and unhelpful to be confronted with such obvious inconsistencies. But

for anyone who wants to understand the true complexity of doing, evaluating and applying educational research, reconciling these discrepancies is part of the job. We could have sanitised these differences by inviting only contributors with a particular set of perspectives, or by strong editing to downplay or hide obvious anomalies. However, I am glad we did not do this; the challenge of a multi-voiced, eclectic text is deliberate, authentic and necessary, even if not comfortable.

Structure of the book

The book is divided into five parts. Part I sets the wider context for the book, exploring the nature of educational research and the fundamental 'building blocks' of research; ontology, epistemology, methodology and methods. Part II discusses the basic principles and practice in conducting research, including an introduction to research design and research ethics, and planning and conducting research. Part III begins the exploration of different educational research methods, by looking at specific examples of common approaches to research design, encompassing qualitative, quantitative and mixed-methods approaches. These include: grounded theory, visual methodologies, case study research, statistical and correlational techniques, the use of secondary data and systematic reviews. This is complemented by Part IV which covers a range of data collection tools including interviews, questionnaires and documentary methods, and Part V which explores a range of data analysis methods including software-based tools for qualitative and statistical data analysis, analysis of variance, multiple linear regression, multilevel analysis, a thorough discussion of effect sizes and meta-analysis.

The separation of these last three parts into archetypal research designs, data collection methods and data analysis methods is to some extent an artifice. Some topics, such as grounded theory, could have fitted into any of these and others could happily sit in more than one. Nevertheless, we hope the distinction is useful in separating the different stages of research and the different dimensions of choice in planning and design. While the novice researcher may find it helpful to think in terms of selecting a research design from a menu, then choosing an approach to data collection and finally deciding how to analyse the data, a sophisticated and experienced researcher is likely to consider all these aspects simultaneously, and creatively build new combinations from elements of each rather than sticking to the menu.

Chapter features

Each chapter has a consistent structure. It begins with a broad introduction and overview of the research methodology or approach covered which discusses the applicability of a given methodology. This includes clear practical guidance on how to carry out different types of research and an awareness of the strengths and limitations inherent in different approaches.

The second half of each chapter then explores a real-life research project that has used that method of research with a short commentary on how the research was undertaken, giving you an insight into how the general principles discussed in the first half of each chapter can be applied in the real world. It ends with 'questions for further investigation' – a set of reflective questions that ask you to engage with what you have read and consider some crucial issues that would apply to any research you may do using the methods and tools covered in any given chapter. Further reading suggestions will point you in the direction of more specialist literature on each chapter's topic, selected by chapter authors as high quality sources for gaining a more detailed understanding.

What's new in the second edition?

For this second edition chapter authors have carefully revisited their contributions to ensure that chapters are aware of key literature and methodological innovations that have appeared since the first edition. Greater depth to the general discussion of each research method has been added across the book, in particular the coverage of different types of research design has been expanded considerably to give you a deeper understanding of this crucial part of the research process. You will also find a greater degree of cross-referencing between chapters, highlighting where important concepts and principles apply across different types of education research.

There are two wholly new chapters in the second edition. Martyn Hammersley's chapter on research ethics offers a smart and pragmatic introduction to an aspect of research that is particularly important for research carried out in educational settings, and a topic that as researchers we must engage with fully. Eve Stirling's chapter on doing social media research discusses a rapidly evolving area of research that has expanded considerably since the publication of the first edition, and explores how Facebook can be used for ethnographic study.

Of course there are many more chapters that we should have included, and more detail that would ideally have enhanced those we have. The constraints of length have required us to make some difficult judgements. We are delighted that the first edition has been so well received and look forward to hearing any feedback about how the book could be improved still further.

Companion website

A companion website to the book can be found at https://study.sagepub.com/coe2e. This includes a range of free-to-access Sage journal articles exemplifying the varied research methods and tools discussed in the book.

Part I

Introduction to research methods and methodologies in education

The nature of educational research

Robert J. Coe

2

Introduction

Many books on research methods start with a section that describes a range of different views about what research is. For some, understanding these different views is a prerequisite to thinking about doing any kind of research: you cannot do or understand research unless you are clear about the fundamental philosophical issues of ontology, epistemology and axiology. Moreover, these issues really are fundamental in the sense that the philosophical position you adopt determines the kinds of research that are worth doing, the kinds of questions you can ask and the methods you will use. The different positions are often presented as a package, with a collection of apparently coherent views about different aspects of research combining to form a 'paradigm' – a world-view or perspective – being shared by groups of researchers who adopt the whole paradigm as the one true way and defend it in opposition to any other set of views.

My approach here is pragmatic and eclectic. Whether or not the philosophical positions determine the research approach, it is important for researchers to understand their own and others' views about the nature of reality (ontology), how we can know about it (epistemology) and the different values (axiology) that may underpin enquiry, along with a number of other differences. It probably is true that certain views tend to go together

and will influence choices about what kinds of questions a researcher believes to be interesting and important, as well as the methods they adopt to answer them. It may be important for researchers to understand how alternative positions have arisen as a reaction to what was seen as the constraining dominance of a particular view. It is true that researchers are influenced by each other and tend to gravitate towards common understandings across a range of issues. However, it is also true that in practice many researchers are often not as consistent as the philosophers might exhort them to be – although allegiance to a particular 'paradigm' may be a fundamental commitment for some, others can see the merits of both sides of an argument about opposing views, and may be willing to move between positions and back again. Different researchers differ in their perspectives on these issues: for example, even within this volume you will find different views presented in Chapter 3 by Waring and Chapter 19 by Biesta.

The next section offers an outline of some of the different positions researchers may take along a number of dimensions. Next we discuss different views about how, if at all, these positions can be reconciled. A third section discusses different aims for educational research. The last two sections of this chapter present, respectively, an attempt to define what distinguishes research from other forms of enquiry and what distinguishes good research from bad.

Dimensions of difference: paradigms?

In Table 2.1 each row represents a dimension or aspect of difference in views about the nature of research. The two columns present the extreme or opposing views on this dimension. A simplistic

interpretation would be to identify the positions outlined in the left-hand column with 'positivism' and quantitative research, while those on the right present the 'constructivist', qualitative paradigm. However, as we discuss below, the whole notion of a 'paradigm' is problematic and should probably be treated somewhat more critically than it often is.

Table 2.1   Differences in views about the nature of research

The world and phenomena are real and exist independent of perception.	Social phenomena are always perceived in a particular way; they have no 'reality' independent of perception.
There is truth and objective knowledge about the world.	All knowledge is subjective and socially constructed.
It is possible to find universal laws and knowledge that are generalisable.	Individual social contexts are unique; generalisation is neither desirable nor possible.
Research should aim to discover general (generalisable) explanations for phenomena and to make generalisable predictions.	Research should aim to understand individual cases and situations and to focus on the meaning that different actors bring to them.
The kinds of objective knowledge and facts discovered by research are not dependent on the values and beliefs of particular researchers.	Understanding the values and beliefs of researchers is crucial to understanding their claims.
Power relationships are not relevant to the truth.	Power, and particularly imbalances of power, are central to understanding social phenomena. A key purpose of research is to emancipate and transform.
Research aims to develop and test hypotheses. Hypotheses must be clearly stated before a study can be designed to test them.	Research is inductive, following an unending dialectical cycle of thesis, antithesis, synthesis. Hypotheses and theory emerge in the course of researching; they are critically tested and refined against data and theory. Researchers aim to avoid making assumptions before collecting data.
The world is fundamentally mechanistic and deterministic, in which human behaviour is governed by general laws and is capable of manipulation.	Human beings are active participants in the researched world, interacting with rather than reacting to their environment, constructing situations by bringing their own meanings and acting freely.
Phenomena can be understood by analysis of their component parts (reductionist).	Social phenomena are more than the sum of their parts and can be understood only holistically.
Causal laws exist, determine behaviour and can be discovered by the methods of science (e.g. experiments).	The complexity, level of interactivity, situational specificity and contextual dependence of social phenomena prevent the traditional concept of causation from being useful or appropriate.
Constructs must be operationalised to be used in research. Many constructs can be quantified and treated as having measurement properties. Characteristics such as validity and reliability are crucial.	Many constructs cannot usefully be quantified; only rich qualitative description can capture their essence. Representations of phenomena must be authentic, based on studying things in their natural settings.
Generalisation from observed samples to wider populations is justified in terms of statistical representativeness and probability sampling.	Observed cases can be a basis for generalisable theory and understandings, even where the number of cases is small (perhaps even one) and they are selected for some particular characteristics.
Quantitative.	Qualitative.
Positivist, neo-positivist, post-positivist.	Anti-positivist, constructivist (constructionist), interpretivist (interprevist).

What is a paradigm?

The use of the word 'paradigm' to describe a particular way of seeing the world derives from the work of the philosopher of science Thomas Kuhn. Kuhn (1970) explained the development of new ideas in science in terms of shared understandings or 'paradigms' within the social community of scientists. At any time there are known inconsistencies, but these are generally treated as 'puzzles' to be worked on within the rules of 'normal science'. Periodically, they become 'anomalies' that are so troublesome they trigger a 'scientific revolution' in which the dominant paradigm is replaced by a new one, generally as an older generation of scientists is replaced by a new generation rather than as a result of individuals being persuaded. The old and new paradigms are 'incommensurable' in the sense that they offer wholly different ways of understanding the world and there is no higher set of values or logic by which their relative merits can be easily or objectively compared.

Although it had not always been the case, by the time Kuhn was putting forward these ideas in the 1960s and 1970s the dominant view of educational research in countries like the UK and USA was essentially a scientific perspective, with most research adopting statistical, experimental and hypothesis-testing approaches (Nisbet, 2005). Kuhn's work was seen as supporting a challenge to this hegemony – a challenge which also drew on established qualitative traditions in anthropology and sociology, and new (or newly applied) ideas from other disciplines, such as phenomenology, poststructuralism, postmodernism and critical theory. These new approaches were (and still are) often presented as new paradigms, though the use of this word is not really consistent with Kuhn's original use (Hammersley, 2012). Moreover, Kuhn argued that his account of scientific revolution did not apply to the social sciences which are characterised by a lack of consensus on the appropriateness of different procedures, theories and metaphysical assumptions, and hence may more appropriately be seen as an immature science in a 'pre-paradigm' period (Bird, 2009).

Despite this distortion of Kuhn's use of the word, it is still common to see particular collections of philosophical and methodological preferences for educational research described as paradigms. Hammersley (2012) describes a number of different ways of classifying educational research, including a standard two-paradigm typology (quantitative/positivist vs. qualitative/interpretive/constructivist), a three-paradigm typology (the previous two, with the addition of a critical/emancipatory paradigm), and various typologies that subdivide further into multiple paradigms (including participatory research, mixed-methods, human ecology, ecological psychology, holistic ethnography, (cognitive) anthropology, ethnography of communication, symbolic inter-actionism, sociolinguistics, ethnomethodology, qualitative evaluation, neo-marxist ethnography and feminist research – see Jacob, 1987; Atkinson et al., 1988; Tashakkori and Teddlie, 2003; Hammersley, 2012).

Reconciling the different views

There are a number of different possible ways of dealing with the existence of different paradigms.

Incommensurability

The first is to accept the fundamental nature of these paradigms along with the need for consistency within each, and to see them as basically incommensurable. Under this view it is not possible to pick and mix from the available options; a philosophical commitment to a particular way of seeing the world necessarily implies the adoption of certain approaches and the rejection of others. If you believe, for example, that our knowledge of social phenomena is inevitably subjective and socially constructed then it makes no sense to seek general laws to describe the world. Nor is it possible to compromise between these discrete, defensible positions. Either you believe the world exists independent of our knowledge of it, or you don't; there is no middle way.

One consequence of the belief that different paradigms are incommensurable is that there is no way to compare or evaluate the relative merits of the approaches and results of research conducted under different paradigms. The choice to adopt, or believe the findings from, one particular paradigm over another cannot in principle be justified logically, since by definition such a logical argument can only be made within a particular paradigm (Pring, 2000).

Compatibility

A second approach allows that researchers must take a philosophical stance on fundamental issues such as the nature of reality and knowledge and on core values, but that these do not necessarily constrain other choices about the kinds of questions and methods they adopt. In this view the differences are real and important, but in the words of Gage (1989) 'Paradigm differences do not require paradigm conflict'. For example, one may believe in a realist ontology but still emphasise an interpretive approach, focusing on the meanings that participants bring to a situation and using naturalistic observation with qualitative data to study them. Or a feminist/emancipatory researcher may adopt the use of randomised controlled trials (e.g. Mertens, 2005; Oakley, 2006).

There is arguably some asymmetry in this perspective, however, since it may be harder to imagine a researcher who believes all knowledge is subjective and personal wanting to conduct large-scale surveys involving statistical analysis of quantitative data. For this reason, this perspective might be seen as a kind of positivism, albeit softened by the adoption of qualitative methods and the inevitable acceptance of subjectivity they imply, but in which those qualitative methods are essentially subservient to the quantitative. Certainly, an acceptance of compatibility is likely to depend on an environment in which researchers with different perspectives are able to respect the differences of others and feel confident enough of the security of their own position to be tolerant of others.

Pragmatism

A third perspective adopts the philosophical stance of pragmatism, rejecting the traditional philosophical dichotomies of realist vs. idealist ontology and subjective vs. objective epistemology. Some have linked pragmatism with an explicitly mixed-methods approach and even argued that the use of mixed methods is a paradigm in its own right (e.g. Johnson and Onwuegbuzie, 2004). However, another reading of the pragmatic approach is to see the whole notion of paradigms as problematic and unhelpful. In this sense, pragmatism is not just another philosophy, but is itself an anti-philosophy – not another paradigm, but a challenge to the whole notion of paradigms. According to this view, research may be conducted for particular reasons, for example to find answers to certain questions or to redress key inequities or injustices. The choice of those reasons is likely to be influenced by the values and beliefs of the researchers (including their, perhaps implicit, metaphysical beliefs); the particular questions or aims they select will also influence the research methods they use.

There are therefore practical and logical reasons why philosophy and methodology are not independent. However, it is an oversimplification – and unnecessary constraint – to see all research as having the characteristics of one of a small number of paradigms.

Different aims for educational research

Alongside the different paradigms and approaches to reconciling these, it is important to recognise that research is conducted for a range of very different reasons. As mentioned above, in some presentations of the different paradigms these reasons or research aims are combined with the philosophical and methodological differences outlined above to form further paradigms, such as the emancipatory paradigm or feminist research. Identifying a particular research aim with its own paradigm may be a way of emphasising the importance of that aim, since for those who adopt it, it fundamentally transforms everything they do. However, it is also clear that a single piece of research often has a mixture of aims of different kinds, and that different research studies with very different approaches may nevertheless overlap in their aims. For this reason we see the aims of a piece of research as a separate dimension from its values, assumptions and methodology, and present the following typology of different aims for educational research.

Scientific

The first set of aims for research may be described as scientific, in the broadest sense. This kind of research sets out to understand the world, to build, test and support theory, to discover or create knowledge. 'Scientific' here is not meant to imply a preference for a particular approach, such as quantification, or even a preference for empirical enquiry, but simply a search for knowledge. It is probably unusual for any educational research not to include some scientific aims.

Political

A second category of research aims is essentially political, in the sense that the research aims to change the world. If we hope our research may be used to help improve education in some way then it has at least partially political aims. Although research may not have explicitly political aims, it is perhaps unusual for these not to be at least implied; research funders increasingly call for research to have 'impact'.

Therapeutic

A third class of aims covers research that sets out to help individuals. The distinction between this and the previous category is that the individuals are in some sense participants in the research. This would be the case, for example, in action research, in which a practitioner-researcher works in a particular context alongside other actors to help address particular problems in that context.

Aesthetic

A final category of research aims may be described as aesthetic. Research with this kind of aim attempts to express, affirm or represent human experience, to 'engage, surprise, attract, shock, delight, connect the unconnected, stir the memory and fertilise the unconscious', or to 'communicate something ultimately unsayable' (Saunders, 2003). The research may have a poetic or literary quality, setting out to tell a story, perhaps using arts-based forms to present its messages, and aiming to connect with readers on an emotional or spiritual level (Barone and Eisner, 2006).

Other ways of classifying different types of educational research

There are a number of other distinctions that can be made and it may be helpful to understand these differences.

Applied vs. basic

This distinction is made by many writers. Applied educational research is focused on questions of practice or policy, with the intention of informing or improving some aspect of them and often containing explicit recommendations for action. Reports are likely to be publicly available and may be written for a lay audience. Applied research is sometimes commissioned by a particular agency with a specific agenda and is governed by an explicit contract with the researchers.

Basic research, by contrast, is conducted for the advancement of knowledge, with no concern about whether the research is directly or immediately useful in any way. This kind of research is typically conducted within an academic community, often within a particular disciplinary structure; reports of the work are written primarily for other scholars and there is less direct accountability for the delivery of any specific, pre-determined outcomes.

Empirical vs. theoretical

Empirical educational research is grounded in observation. It takes phenomena (things that exist or happen), or at least our perceptions of phenomena, as its starting point, and attempts to represent them as data which can then be analysed. In this way, empirical research aims to represent, describe and understand particular views of the educational world.

Theoretical research focuses on ideas rather than phenomena, though of course both kinds of research require both. Theoretical educational research may present, for example, a philosophical argument, a critique or a methodological advance.

Nomothetic vs. idiographic

Nomothetic educational research seeks understanding of the general case (*nomos*, 'the law' in Greek). It aims to discover general (and explicitly generalisable) explanations for phenomena and to make generalisable predictions to further cases. Theory consists of sets of such rules, together with the conditions under which they apply. Idiographic research, on the other hand, focuses on the individual case (*idios*, 'belonging to an individual' in Greek). It aims to describe and understand what is unique and distinctive about a particular context, case or individual.

Intervention vs. descriptive

A final distinction is less commonly made but is perhaps at least as important as any of the others listed here. Intervention research actively sets out to introduce some change into the educational world, then studies the reaction. It includes types of research that may traditionally not usually have been put together, such as action research (which often has a critical, emancipatory emphasis – see Carr and Kemmis, 1986) and randomised controlled trials (generally advocated from a scientific, positivist perspective). Nevertheless, these approaches share a belief in the importance of change and the

view that we can really only fully understand the world if we understand how to change it.

Descriptive research simply describes what is, without directly attempting to change it. Again, diverse approaches may be grouped together here, from ethnography (with a focus on natural settings and rich description) to large-scale surveys (characterised by generalisable, quantified measures). Of course, much apparently descriptive educational research actually has an (explicit or implicit) intention to provoke or support changes in the educational world. The point of making the distinction between intervention and descriptive research is to emphasise that we should not underestimate the difficulties of inferring implications for making changes from research that has not itself involved changing anything.

Characteristics of research

Given the variety of different kinds of educational research, the different reasons for doing it, the beliefs underpinning it and methods employed to conduct it, we may question whether there are any common elements that distinguish research from other kinds of activity. We would argue that research generally has the following characteristics, though we would also acknowledge that not all educational research will necessarily exhibit all these qualities (for other attempts to define or discuss the characteristics of research, see, for example, Kerlinger, 1970; Bridges, 2006).

Critical

Educational research is critical in the sense that it actively seeks to question its own claims, assumptions and methods, and those of others. Where explanations are offered, the research process seeks to verify them, generating and testing alternatives. Obvious and popular perceptions or explanations are treated with caution and subjected to scrutiny. Attempts are made to identify and remove extraneous influences and confounded explanations.

Systematic

Educational research is a deliberate, planned, intentional activity. It takes a specific question or questions which provide its focus and direction. Questions may be pre-determined or emergent. Research sets out to exhaust those questions, providing answers that are as full as possible. Research aims to consider all the evidence that may be relevant to its questions, not just what is easy to access or supports a particular view.

Transparent

Educational research is transparent in the sense that its aims, methods, assumptions, arguments, data and claims are stated explicitly and clearly. Results, and their supporting justifications, are disclosed fully, taking care to minimise the danger of misinterpretation, and made widely available. Prior beliefs, conflicts of interest and biographies of researchers are disclosed, where appropriate. Sufficient information is given that the work could be replicated or checked by another researcher.

Evidential

Educational research appeals to evidence, not opinion, authority or common sense, as the basis of its justification. Empirical research is grounded in phenomena and their authentic representation as data. Clear, logical arguments link those phenomena, or other premises, to their interpretations and the claims made.

Theoretical

Educational research is guided by theory, but also seeks to build and test theory. Theory attempts to help make sense of phenomena, to allow predictions to be made, to clarify thinking, to provide conceptual tools, and to enable subsequent research to build cumulatively on what has been done before.

Original

Educational research aims to add to existing knowledge in some way, be it through a new discovery, confirmation of previous findings, new theory or enhanced understandings. Research does more than simply re-present existing ideas, even if communicated in new or more effective ways.

How is educational research different from other kinds of research?

Defining what makes educational research different from any other research is not straightforward. Indeed, the most defensible answer may be that it is not different in any fundamental way. The notion of an academic discipline – a community of scholars who share common methods of investigation of particular types of questions, with agreed rules and criteria for judging the strength and quality of their claims – may be employed to try to define the discipline of education. Yet, as has been discussed above, such agreement about methods, questions, rules and criteria may be hard to find among those who would describe themselves as educational researchers.

We might try to avoid these differences by identifying as 'educational' any research that seeks to understand, inform or improve the practice of education. But education itself is hard to define in a way that is broad enough to include all the different kinds of activity that might come under this heading, while still retaining some common set of distinguishing characteristics.

Ball and Forzani define education as 'the deliberate activity of helping learners to develop understanding and skills' (Ball and Forzani, 2007: 530). Where this occurs in schools or similar institutions they say it is characterised by interactions among four elements: teachers, students, content and environments. These multiple interactions ('active processes of interpretation') constitute the 'instructional dynamic', which is the defining feature of education.

One problem in defining educational research is that research questions that relate to education can be found in many other, generally longer-established, disciplines. For example, significant parts of psychology are concerned with learning and much psychological research addresses questions on this issue. Claiming this research as educational might be seen as an unnecessary and unwelcome attempt to appropriate something that already had a perfectly good disciplinary home. Similar arguments could be made about the existence of educational research questions in older disciplines such as sociology, philosophy, history, economics, anthropology, geography, linguistics, political science, business and health sciences. Ball and Forzani (2007) make a distinction between 'research related to education' that adopts a perspective from another discipline, and 'research in education' that focuses on the 'instructional dynamic' of education by considering the multiple interactions among all four elements. Even if this definition is useful, however, it seems likely that it might include quite a small proportion of the research that is conducted by people who would describe themselves as educational researchers or that is published in educational research journals.

When education began to stake its claim to be seen as a discipline in its own right in the 1960s it became common to present it as built on the four 'foundation disciplines' of philosophy, history, psychology, and sociology. The development of education as a university subject was, in the UK at least (according to Simon, 1983), a response to a political drive to establish teaching as a graduate profession, and hence to locate the professional training of teachers in universities. In a search for academic respectability beyond what R.S. Peters (cited in Bridges, 2004) had described as the 'undifferentiated mush' of existing teacher education, education studies drew on these more established disciplines. In the 1970s, a focus on the curriculum as an object of study, the rise of classroom action research and the flourishing of new research methodologies (Bridges, 2004) contributed to a weakening of the foundation disciplines. Later developments – such as the growing demands of research funders (including governments) for educational research

to have direct applications in policy or practice, the increasingly instrumental focus of teacher training, and the influence of a much wider repertoire of methodologies and theories on educational research – have further displaced the original four disciplines. Today, whether education is itself a discipline and, if so, what differentiates it from other disciplines is very much open to debate.

Research quality

Perhaps an even harder task than defining educational research is defining good research. Given the breadth of approaches to doing educational research, it seems unlikely that there will be any universal criteria. We present here a list of questions that it may be appropriate to ask in evaluating the quality of a piece of research:

- What are the research questions/aims?
- Are they clearly stated?
- Are they relevant/important?
- Does the research actually address them?
- Is the methodology appropriate to them?
- Could the research add to existing knowledge?
- Does the research build systematically on what is already known?
- Are any of the assumptions or beliefs of the researcher(s) made clear?
- Is it clear who funded or supported the research and whether there are any potential conflicts of interest?
- Are any definitions of terms or constructs clear?
- Are these definitions appropriate (not too broad/ narrow)?
- Is it clear how phenomena have been represented?
- Are any constructs operationalised appropriately?
- Is any interpretation of constructs (e.g. measures, scores, variables) supported by a convincing validity argument?
- How realistic or representative are the contexts in which the research was done? Are they described adequately?
- Are any samples adequate? In what sense are they representative?

- Is there enough information about the participants? Who were they? Are we told what the study meant to them?
- How were participants chosen? Who is included/excluded? Is any non-response disclosed?
- Are the claims clear and explicit?
- Are there implicit causal claims?
- Does the evidence support the claims?
- How far are the claims generalised? Is any generalisation justified?
- Are alternative explanations offered/challenged?
- What is arbitrary? How might things have been done otherwise? Are the choices made by the researchers transparent?
- Has there been any selection in what is reported?
- If the data might have been interpreted or analysed differently, could this have led to different conclusions?

Questions for further investigation

1. In each row of Table 2.1 we have presented two opposing views. Is it helpful to see these as simplistic, caricatured extremes rather than strongly defensible, alternative positions? Is it possible to agree with both positions in a row, or are they mutually contradictory?
2. To what extent should researchers be consistent in their adoption of the views presented in either column of Table 2.1? Is it possible to mix elements from the right- and left-hand columns and still be philosophically coherent?
3. Is it possible to define research in a way that distinguishes it from other forms of enquiry or writing? What distinguishes educational research from other research?
4. Of the questions listed under 'research quality', which are the most important?

Suggested further reading

Hammersley, M. (2012) 'Methodological Paradigms in Educational Research', British Educational Research Association on-line resource. Available on-line at www.bera.ac.uk/wp-content/uploads/2014/03/Methodological-Paradigms.pdf

Lincoln, Y.S., Lynham, S.A. and Guba, E.G. (2011) 'Paradigmatic Controversies, Contradictions, and Emerging Confluences, Revisited', in N.K. Denzin and Y.S. Lincoln (eds), *The SAGE Handbook of Qualitative Research*, 4th edn. Thousand Oaks, CA: Sage.

Schwandt, T.A. (2000) 'Three Epistemological Stances for Qualitative Inquiry', in N.K. Denzin and Y.S. Lincoln (eds), *Handbook of Qualitative Research,* 2nd edn. Thousand Oaks, CA: Sage, pp. 189–213.

References

Atkinson, P., Delamont, S. and Hammersley, M. (1988) 'Qualitative research traditions: a British response', *Educational Researcher,* 58(2): 231–50.

Ball, D.L. and Forzani, F.M. (2007) 'What makes education Research "educational"?', *Educational Researcher,* 36(9): 529–40.

Barone, T. and Eisner, E. (2006) 'Arts-based Educational Research', in J. Green, G. Camilli and P. Elmore (eds), *Complementary Methods in Research in Education*. Mahwah, NJ: Lawrence Erlbaum Associates.

Bird, A. (2009) 'Thomas Kuhn', in E.N. Zalta (ed.), *The Stanford Encyclopedia of Philosophy.* Available at http://plato. stanford.edu/archives/fall2009/entries/thomas-kuhn (last accessed 12 March 2011).

Bridges, D. (2004) 'The disciplines and discipline of educational research'. Paper presented at the Annual Conference of the British Educational Research Association, Manchester Metropolitan University, September.

Bridges, D. (2006) 'The disciplines and discipline of educational research', *Journal of Philosophy of Education,* 40(2): 259–72.

Carr, W. and Kemmis, S. (1986) *Becoming Critical: Education, Knowledge and Action Research*. Lewes: Falmer.

Gage, N.L. (1989) 'The paradigm wars and their aftermath', *Educational Researcher,* 18(7): 4–10.

Guba, E.G. (2005) 'Paradigmatic Controversies, Contradictions, and Emerging Confluences', in N.K. Denzin and Y.S Lincoln (eds), *The SAGE Handbook of Qualitative Research,* 3rd edn. Thousand Oaks, CA: Sage.

Hammersley, M. (2012) 'Methodological Paradigms in Educational Research', British Educational Research Association on-line resource. Available on-line at www.bera.ac.uk/wp-content/uploads/2014/03/Methodological-Paradigms.pdf

Jacob, E. (1987) 'Qualitative research traditions: a review', *Review of Educational Research,* 57(1): 1–50.

Johnson, R.B. and Onwuegbuzie, A.J. (2004) 'Mixed methods research: a research paradigm whose time has come', *Educational Research,* 33(7): 14–26.

Kerlinger, F.N. (1970) *Foundations of Behavioral Research.* New York: Holt, Rinehart & Winston.

Kuhn, T.S. (1970) *The Structure of Scientific Revolutions* (2nd edn). Chicago: University of Chicago Press.

Kuhn, T.S. (1991) 'The Natural and the Human Sciences', in D. Hiley, J. Bohman and R. Shusterman (eds), *The Interpretative Turn: Philosophy, Science, Culture.* Ithaca, NY: Cornell University Press, pp. 17–24.

Mertens, D.M. (2005) *Research Methods in Education and Psychology: Integrating Diversity with Quantitative and Qualitative Approaches* (2nd edn). Thousand Oaks, CA: Sage.

Nisbet, J. (2005) 'What is educational research? Changing perspectives through the 20th century', *Research Papers in Education,* 20(1): 25–44.

Oakley, A. (2006) 'Resistances to "new" technologies of evaluation: education research in the UK as a case study', *Evidence and Policy,* 2(1): 63–87.

Pring, R. (2000) 'The "false dualism" of educational research', *Journal of Philosophy of Education,* 34(2): 247–60.

Saunders, L. (2003) 'On flying, writing poetry and doing educational research', *British Educational Research Journal,* 29(2): 175–87.

Simon, B. (1983) 'The study of education as a university subject in Britain', *Studies in Higher Education,* 8(1): 1–13.

Tashakkori, A. and Teddlie, C. (eds) (2003) *Handbook of Mixed Methods in Social and Behavioral Research.* Thousand Oaks, CA: Sage.

Finding your theoretical position

3

Michael Waring

Introduction

This chapter highlights the relationship between the four 'building blocks' of research (ontology, epistemology, methodology and methods) (Grix, 2002, 2010). It begins with an exploration of the nature of educational research, presenting various ways in which the researcher might see the world. It then links those assumptions with how the researcher sees what is possible with knowledge of that world. The text will then explore how this relates to certain procedures or logic to be followed in association with their views of the world and notions of knowledge within it. Having linked the first three building blocks of research, the relationship with the final block is made: the process of selecting and using appropriate techniques to collect data are outlined.

Fundamentally, research is about disciplined, balanced enquiry, conducted in a critical spirit (Thomas, 2013). However, the nature of educational enquiry and subsequently those attempts to define educational research have been and continue to be problematic (see Phillips, 2005, 2006, 2011; Morrison, 2007; Lingard and Gale, 2010; Whitty, 2016). The debate revolves around a number of issues but mainly relates to the complexity of the educational context, conceptual confusion, inappropriate adoption of positivistic interpretations of 'scientific' method and notions of rigour, as well as the dichotomy between practice and theory. Cohen et al.'s (2011: 1) definition of educational research is an acceptable one in that it acknowledges and accommodates many of the contentious issues: 'The systematic and scholarly application of the principles of a science of behaviour to the problems of teaching and learning within education and the clarification of issues having a direct and indirect bearing on those concepts'. Importantly, the use of the term 'science' here is taken to imply both normative and interpretive perspectives.

Over recent decades there have been, and continue to be, a debate and competition over the foremost set of beliefs which will inform and guide enquiry over and above all others (Entman, 1993; Guba and Lincoln, 1994; Lincoln et al., 2013). The debate will not be continued or reiterated to any great extent here – others offer more comprehensive accounts of this (see McNamara, 1979; Bradley and Sutton, 1993; Denzin and Lincoln, 2013). The purpose here is to identify the fundamental set of assumptions that underpin all research and to make clear their interrelationship and implications.

Ontology, epistemology, methodology and methods

All researchers need to understand that their research is framed by a series of related assumptions. These assumptions can be framed around four key questions, as identified in a simplistic fashion in Figure 3.1. These questions have an order.

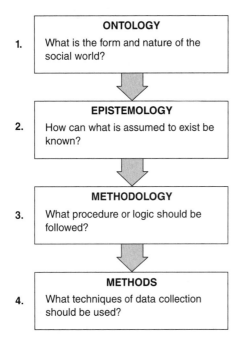

1. **ONTOLOGY**
What is the form and nature of the social world?

2. **EPISTEMOLOGY**
How can what is assumed to exist be known?

3. **METHODOLOGY**
What procedure or logic should be followed?

4. **METHODS**
What techniques of data collection should be used?

Figure 3.1   The relationship between ontology, epistemology, methodology and methods

Question 1

The first question that a researcher needs to ask relates to 'ontology'. That is 'what is the nature or form of the social world?' These assumptions will form the starting point for all research. Ontological positions can be seen to exist in a simplistic fashion along a continuum from left to right from realism to constructivism. In realism there is a singular objective reality that exists independent of individuals' perceptions of it. At the other end of the continuum, under constructivism reality is neither objective nor singular, but multiple realities are constructed by individuals. It is on the basis of the answers to the ontological question that the epistemological question can be asked and assumptions are made.

Question 2

Epistemology relates to knowledge and the researcher should ask the question 'how can what

is assumed to exist be known?' Taking the same continuum and extreme positions as identified above, the corresponding epistemological positions to realism and constructivism would be positivism and interpretivism respectively. Existing within a realist ontology, positivism sees it as possible to achieve direct knowledge of the world through direct observation or measurement of the phenomena being investigated. At the other end of the continuum, existing under a constructivist ontology, interpretivism does not see direct knowledge as possible; it is the accounts and observations of the world that provide indirect indications of phenomena, and thus knowledge is developed through a process of interpretation.

Question 3

Methodological assumptions are a reflection of the ontological and epistemological assumptions. Methodology asks 'what procedures or logic should be followed?' Developing the notion of the continuum, to the left (under realist ontology/positivist epistemology) the answer 'is nomothetic and experimental in nature'. To the right (under constructivist ontology/interpretivist epistemology) it is 'ideographic, dialectical and hermeneutical in nature'.

Question 4

Often confused with methodology is the final question associated with method. This asks 'what techniques of data collection should be used?' These will be the techniques or procedures used to gather the data. They will take various forms from questionnaires, interviews, observations, video and still images, etc. As part of Grix's (2002: 179) illustration of the interrelationship between the building blocks of research, he identifies that the method(s) are closely linked with the research questions posed and the sources of data collected.

He also considers that methods are free of ontological and epistemological assumptions, which relate to the researcher. The immediate relationship determining the methods to be used should be (but is not always) with the research question.

What data need to be gathered that will allow you to address the research question? When asking this, the researcher needs to consider not just what methods/procedures can be employed to gather appropriate data, but also whether those data can be collected. However Sparkes (1992), acknowledging the confusion over terminology and the way in which it exacerbates a fundamental misunderstanding with regard to epistemological assumptions underpinning the researcher and the research, considers the researcher's ontological and epistemological assumptions to influence all aspects of research. Consequently, to say that the nature of the problem of the research will determine the overall approach and the methods of investigation, he would consider misguided.

Any researcher should fully appreciate the research process and so should be able to understand and acknowledge the fundamental relationship between the ontological, epistemological and methodological assumptions that underpin their research and inform their choice of methods. Grix (2002: 176), in his paper about the need for clarity in the use of generic research terminology, reinforces this when he says that

> … a clear and transparent knowledge of the ontological and epistemological assumptions that underpin research is necessary in order:
>
> (1) to understand the interrelationship of the key components of research (including methodology and methods);
>
> (2) to avoid confusion when discussing theoretical debates and approaches to social phenomena; and
>
> (3) to be able to recognise others', and defend our own, positions.

The nature of paradigms: making sense of reality

Kuhn (1962) is commonly associated with the notion of the paradigm and believed it to be a set of interrelated assumptions about the social world which provided a philosophical and conceptual framework for the organised study of that world. Over time numerous authors have similarly defined it as a set of 'belief systems' (Guba and Lincoln, 1989), a 'world view' (Patton, 1978; Guba and Lincoln, 1994) and a particular 'lens for seeing and making sense of the world' (Sparkes, 1992), all of which emphasise the many definitions that mark out a paradigm.

A paradigm represents a person's conception of the world, its nature and their position in it, as well as a multitude of potential relationships with that world and its constituent parts. Therefore, as that person brings along with them the 'baggage' of their previous life experiences and knowledge base to any research context, it is this very amalgamation which constructs their competence and credibility as a member of any given research community, as well as their answers to certain fundamental questions which will determine such acceptance in and of that community. Proponents of any given paradigm can summarise their beliefs relative to their responses to those ontological, epistemological, methodological and methods questions identified.

Table 3.1 outlines those basic responses which proponents located at either end of a continuum of paradigms (from positivist to interpretivist) would make in reaction to those fundamental questions. This table is intended to be a basic framework/continuum which offers extreme positions (responses) to assist the reader in their discussion to locate themselves.

It is important to note that while the identification of paradigms at either end of a continuum is convenient in terms of clarifying the relationship between the fundamental assumptions and allows for familiarisation with key terminology, such a simple and clinical distinction is an incomplete and artificial one. As Silverman (2014: 27) highlights, dichotomies or polarities of this fashion can be dangerous if they are allowed to create a siloed mentality of 'armed camps'. Therefore, when considering Table 3.1 and the many others like it that you will come across in the research methods literature (see Creswell, 2013: 36; Lincoln et al., 2013: 208), it is important to focus on the process of enquiry and

Table 3.1   Basic assumptions fundamental to the positivist and interpretive paradigms

Assumptions	Positivism		Interpretivism[1]	
Ontology	**External realist**	Basic posture is reductionist and deterministic. Knowledge of 'the way things are' is conventionally summarised in the form of time- and context-free generalisations, some of which take the form of cause-and-effect laws.	**Internal-idealist, relativist (local and specific constructed realities, holistic and dynamic)**	Realities are apprehendable and mind-dependant.[2] There are multiple realities with the mind playing a central role by determining categories and shaping or constructing realities. We cannot see the world outside of our place in it. There is no separation of mind and objective since the two are inextricably linked together – the knower and the process of knowing cannot be separated from what is known and the facts cannot be separated from values.
Epistemology	**Dualist objectivist**	The investigator and investigated 'object' assumed to be independent entities; enquiry takes place as if in a one-way mirror. Investigator does not influence or is not influenced by the object. Replicable findings are 'true'.	**Subjectivist, transactional, interactive**	The investigator and the object of the investigation are assumed to be interactively linked so that the 'findings' are literally created as the investigation proceeds. Therefore, the conventional distinction between ontology and epistemology dissolves.[3]
Methodology	**Nomothetic, experimental, manipulative: verification of hypotheses**	Questions and/or hypotheses are stated in proportional form and subjected to empirical test to verify them; possible confounding conditions are carefully controlled (manipulated) to prevent the outcome from being improperly influenced.	**Ideographic, dialectical, hermeneutical**	The variable and personal nature of social constructions suggests that individual constructions can be elicited and refined only through interaction between and among investigator(s) and respondent(s). Conventional hermeneutical techniques are used in interpretations and compared and contrasted through a dialectical interchange. It is not a matter of eliminating conflicting or previous interpretations, but to distil a more sophisticated and informed consensus construction.
Enquiry aim	**Explanation, prediction and control**	Over time attempt to increasingly explain so that ultimately one can predict phenomena be they human or physical.	**Understanding, interpretation and reconstruction**	Over time, everyone formulates more informed and sophisticated constructions and becomes more aware of the content and meaning of competing constructions.

1. The term 'interpretivism' has been chosen because, as Sparkes (1992) has identified, it refers to a whole family of approaches which are in direct contrast to a positivist sense of social reality.

2. Mind-dependence here does not mean that the mind 'creates' what people say and do, but rather how we interpret their movements and utterances; the meaning we assign to the intentions, motivations and so on of ourselves and others becomes social reality as it is for us. In other words social reality is the interpretation (Smith, 1989, in Sparkes, 1992: 27).

3. The dashed line represents the challenge which such a posture represents between ontology and epistemology; what can be known is inextricably linked with the interaction between a particular investigator and a particular object or group.

Based upon Guba and Lincoln (1994) and Sparkes (1987, 1992)

not to isolate thoughts to just one paradigm or another. Instead be prepared to question and explore those 'shady' areas between research paradigms where the boundaries shift (see Grix, 2010: 62). Lincoln et al. (2013: 207) identify how those who are '… familiar with several theoretical and paradigmatic strands of research will find that echoes of many streams of thought come together …' and create dialogue and the dynamic shifting and blurring of paradigms. However, such evolution has to be set within a research methodologies landscape in which there has and continues to be contestation and confrontation over what research is valued and what criteria are used in judgement of its quality.

Hammersley (1992: 131) commented that 'There is no doubt that the 1980s and early 1990s have seen growing debates among educational researchers about methodology, sometimes taking the form of conflicts between incommensurable paradigms in which philosophical terms have been used as weapons'. Sparkes (2013) also highlights this by recounting Sage's (1989) description of what was named the 'paradigm wars' of the 1980s and Denzin's (2009) contention of the continuation of such wars, the associated conflict between quantitative and qualitative researchers, and the need to be mindful that such a dialogue and blurring of paradigms is challenged and confined by methodological fundamentalism, as well as notions of power and politics on many different levels. Lincoln et al. (2013: 257) also recognise the dynamic and tensions between the 'positivist and new-paradigm forms of enquiry' as well as within and between new and emergent paradigms as they 'either look for common ground or to find ways in which to distinguish their forms of enquiry from others'.

As part of the broader paradigmatical debate being rehearsed here it is important to acknowledge the increasingly popular and influential use of mixed-methods research (see Johnson and Onwuegbuzie, 2004; Bryman, 2008, 2016). Biesta (see Chapter 19 in this book) provides a very useful account of mixing methods in education in which he outlines the context and nature of mixed-method research, and different mixed designs. In relation to the paradigm debate it is helpful here to highlight the fact that the combination of qualitative and quantitative research approaches which basically defines mixed-methods research and its pragmatic approach can create confusion and problems in terms of meaning and application. In response to the ambiguity of what is actually being mixed, Biesta (2010) provides seven dimensions at which mixing might take place: Data; Methods; Designs; Epistemologies; Ontologies; Research Purposes; and Practical Orientations. The questions asked particularly in relation to the last four of these dimensions (*Epistemologies; Ontologies; Research Purposes; and Practical Orientations*), their relationship with each other and the associated implications are seen as complicated and potentially controversial. For example, considering if it is possible to combine different ontological and epistemological views, and given the response to that, how does it inform the possibility of combining an intent to generate interpretive understanding and causal explanation, and then ultimately how does all this connect with the researcher's intended achievements for the research and its contribution to the field and practice, which are associated with the potential for combining a critical understanding and analysis with the production of solutions? As part of considering your response to the potential of such combinations and understanding your theoretical location, see Coe (Chapter 2 in this book) who highlights dimensions of difference and paradigms, along with the reconciliation of different views and different ways of dealing with the existence of different paradigms. Hammersley (2012) is also helpful with a succinct outline of key divisions, issues and debates in educational research and the place of paradigms.

It is discerning while at the same time encouraging to know that many researchers experience and acknowledge confusion over the terminology employed in this whole paradigmatical debate (Cohen et al., 2011). A host of authors (Smith, 1989; Guba, 1990; Tesch, 1990; Blaikie, 2007; Grix, 2010; Hammersley, 2011; Weed, 2013) have identified a multiplicity of labels which have been attached to research, resulting in a confusion over the meaning and conceptual level of such terminology:

'Sometimes it is difficult to distinguish clearly labels that denote an epistemological stance and those that refer to method' (Tesch, 1990: 58). One other point on terminology relates to the use of the terms 'qualitative' and 'quantitative research'. These do not actually exist. 'Qualitative' and 'quantitative' refer to data which can be gathered and used in combination or singularly in any form of research.

Conclusion

Educational research is complex and there continue to be a host of debates about the nature of the educational enquiry and associated terminology. However, regardless of the definition of educational enquiry adopted, all researchers should appreciate how the research process and their research are framed by a series of fundamental questions associated with ontology, epistemology, methodology and methods. Having ownership of the process of generating assumptions allows researchers to be informed about the interrelationship between the key components of research, to minimise confusion, and to enhance their ability to critique and appreciate their own research position and that of others. Such an ability promotes understanding and in so doing the potential for 'intellectual, theoretical and practical space for dialogue, consensus, and confluence to occur' (Lincoln et al., 2013: 207), and a transparency in what research is done and why it is done.

Questions for further investigation

1. Where do you stand as an educational researcher between the different paradigms? What philosophical standpoints inform your position?
2. Why are research paradigms relevant in thinking about research processes and methods in education?

3. With regard to epistemological and ontological assumptions, what differences and commonalities underpin various research paradigms?

Suggested further reading

Conrad, C.F. and Serlin, R.C. (eds) (2011) *The SAGE Handbook for Research in Education: Pursuing Ideas as the Keystone of Exemplary Inquiry*, 2nd edn. Thousand Oaks, CA: Sage. This is a comprehensive text and offers a major revision of the first edition of the book. It identifies the different issues an educational researcher faces in their research endeavours, and explores the multiple purposes and challenges of enquiry by offering many examples of how researchers have addressed the key questions in their research.

Denzin, N.K. and Lincoln, Y. (eds) (2011) *The SAGE Handbook of Qualitative Research*, 4th edn. Thousand Oaks, CA: Sage. This book rehearses at length the paradigm debate, offering the reader an illustration of critical issues associated with a host of differing research perspectives.

Thomas, G. (2013) *How to Do Your Research Project: A Guide for Students in Education and Applied Social Sciences*, 2nd edn. London: Sage. This is an accessible text which addresses many of the fundamental questions and issues facing the researcher conducting a research project. It provides an engaging and practical source of information for any researcher.

References

Biesta, G. (2010) 'Pragmatism and the Philosophical Foundations of Mixed Methods Research', in A. Tashakkori and C. Teddlie (eds), *The SAGE Handbook of Mixed Methods in Social and Behavioral Research*, 2nd edn. Thousand Oakes, CA: Sage, pp. 95–118.

Blaikie, N. (2007) *Approaches to Social Enquiry: Advancing Knowledge*, 2nd edn. Cambridge: Polity.

Bradley, J. and Sutton, B. (1993) 'Reframing the paradigm debate', *Library Quarterly,* 63(4): 405–10.

Bryman, A. (2008) 'The End of the Paradigm Wars?', in P. Alasuutari, J. Brannen and L. Bickman (eds), *The SAGE Handbook of Social Research Methods*. Thousand Oaks, CA: Sage, pp. 13–25.

Bryman, A. (2016) *Social Research Methods*, 5th edn. Oxford: Oxford University Press.

Cohen, L., Manion, L. and Morrison, K. (2011) *Research Methods in Education*, 7th edn. London: Routledge.

Cresswell, J.W. (2013) *Qualitative Inquiry and Research Design: Choosing Among Five Approaches*, 3rd edn. Thousand Oaks, CA: Sage.

Denzin, N.K. (2009) *Qualitative Inquiry Under Fire*. Walnut Creek, CA: Left Coast Press.

Denzin, N.K. and Lincoln, Y.S. (2013) 'The Discipline and Practice of Qualitative Research', in N.K. Denzin and Y.S. Lincoln (eds), *The Landscape of Qualitative Research*, 4th edn. Thousand Oaks, CA: Sage, pp. 199–265.

Entman, R.M. (1993) 'Framing: toward clarification of a fractured paradigm', *Journal of Communication,* 43(4): 51–8.

Grix, J. (2002) 'Introducing students to the generic terminology of social research', *Politics,* 22(3): 175–86.

Grix, J. (2010) *The Foundations of Research*, 2nd edn. Basingstoke, Hampshire: Palgrave Macmillan.

Guba, E. (ed.) (1990) *The Paradigm Dialog*. Newbury Park, CA: Sage.

Guba, E. and Lincoln, Y. (1989) *Fourth Generation Evaluation*. Beverly Hills, CA: Sage.

Guba, E. and Lincoln, Y. (1994) 'Competing Paradigms in Qualitative Research', in N.K. Denzin and Y.S. Lincoln (eds), *The SAGE Handbook of Qualitative Research*. Thousand Oaks, CA: Sage, pp. 105–17.

Hammersley, M. (1992) 'The paradigm wars: reports from the front', *British Journal of Sociology of Education*, 13(1): 131–43.

Hammersley, M. (2011) 'Objectivity: A Reconceptualisation', in M. Williams and W.P. Vogt (eds), *The SAGE Handbook of Innovation in Social Research Methods*. Thousand Oaks, CA: Sage.

Hammersley, M. (2012) 'Methodological Paradigms in Educational Research', British Educational Research Association on-line resource. Available on-line at www.bera.ac.uk/wp-content/uploads/2014/03/Methodological-Paradigms.pdf

Johnson, R.B. and Onwuegbuzie, A.J. (2004) 'Mixed methods research: a research paradigm whose time has come', *Educational Researcher*, 33(7): 14–26.

Kuhn, T. (1962) *The Structure of Scientific Revolutions*. Chicago: University of Chicago Press.

Lincoln, Y.S., Lynham, S.A. and Guba, E.G. (2013) 'Paradigmatic Controversies, Contradictions, and Emerging Confluences, Revisited', in N.K. Denzin and Y.S. Lincoln (eds), *The Landscape of Qualitative Research*, 4th edn. Thousand Oaks, CA: Sage, pp. 199–265.

Lingard, B. and Gale, T. (2010) 'Defining educational research: a perspective of/on presidential addresses and the Australian Association for Research in Education', *The Australian Educational Researcher*, 37(1): 21–49.

McNamara, D.R. (1979) 'Paradigm lost: Thomas Kuhn and educational research', *British Educational Research Journal*, 5(20): 167–73.

Morrison, M. (2007) 'What Do We Mean by Educational Research?', in A.R.J. Briggs and M. Coleman (eds), *Research Methods in Educational Leadership and Management*, 2nd edn. Thousand Oaks, CA: Sage, pp. 13–36.

Patton, M. (1978) *Qualitative Evaluation Methods*. Beverly Hills, CA: Sage.

Phillips, D.C. (2005) 'The contested nature of empirical educational research (and why philosophy of education offers little help)', *Journal of Philosophy of Education,* 39(4): 577–97.

Phillips, D.C. (2006) 'Exploring the Multiple Purposes of Inquiry and Key Stake Holders: Introductory Essay', in C.F. Conrad and R.C. Serlin (eds), *The SAGE Handbook for Research in Education: Engaging Ideas and Enriching Inquiry.* Thousand Oaks, CA: Sage, pp. 3–5.

Phillips, D.C. (2011) 'Exploring the Multiple Purposes of Inquiry and Key Stakeholders', in C.F. Conrad and R.C. Serlin (eds), *The SAGE Handbook for Research in Education: Pursuing Ideas as the Keystone of Exemplary Inquiry*, 2nd edn. Thousand Oaks, CA: Sage.

Sage, N. (1989) 'The paradigm wars and their aftermath: a "historical" sketch of research and teaching since 1989', *Educational Researcher*, 18(1): 4–10.

Silverman, D. (2014) *Interpreting Qualitative Data*, 5th edn. Thousand Oaks, CA: Sage.

Smith, J.K. (1989) *The Nature of Social and Educational Inquiry: Empiricism versus Interpretation*. Norwood, NJ: Ablex.

Sparkes, A.C. (1987) 'The Genesis of an Innovation: A Case of Emergent Concerns and Micropolitical Solutions'. PhD, Loughborough University.

Sparkes, A.C. (ed.) (1992) *Research in Physical Education and Sport: Exploring Alternative Visions*. London: Falmer.

Sparkes, A.C. (2013) 'Qualitative research in sport, exercise and health in the era of neoliberalism, audit and new public management: understanding the conditions for the (im)possibilities of a new paradigm dialogue', *Qualitative Research in Sport, Exercise and Health*, 5(3): 440–59.

Tesch, R. (1990) *Qualitative Research: Analysis Types and Software Tools*. London: Falmer.

Thomas, G. (2013) *How to Do Your Research Project: A Guide for Students in Education and Applied Social Sciences*, 2nd edn. London: Sage.

Weed, M. (2013) 'Research Quality Considerations for Grounded Theory Research in Sport and Exercise Psychology', in A.E. Clarke and K. Charmaz (eds), *Grounded Theory and Situational Analysis*. Thousand Oaks, CA: Sage, Volume 2.

Whitty, G. (2016) *Educational Research and Policy in an Imperfect World*. London: UCL IOE Press.

Part II

Basic principles and practice in conducting research

Design of empirical research

Larry V. Hedges

4

Introduction

Research design is the organisation of data collection so that the data collected will support unambiguous conclusions about the problem being studied. This definition focuses on empirical studies. There are other forms of research that do not centrally involve empirical evidence, such as deductive mathematical or statistical research or philosophical research, but this chapter does not speak to the issues of that research. The perspective adopted here is that empirical research studies are designed to support arguments. The data collected are linked to the conclusions by a warrant that gives a logic explaining why the empirical evidence collected supports the validity of those conclusions.

A crucial objective of empirical research designs is to ensure the transparency of the research process. That is, research designs help make explicit what research data are considered relevant, the process by which that evidence is collected, and the relation between that evidence and how it is organised in the analysis to support research conclusions. Transparency helps other scholars understand one another's work, enables it to be subjected to public scrutiny, and enables future research to build on that work.

Many different research designs are used in various traditions of educational research, so many that it would be difficult to adequately characterise them. Instead, we will focus on general principles that may be relevant to the research designs that arise in many research traditions.

Problem formulation

Research design cannot be conceived in isolation from the problem the research is intended to investigate. Sound research design proceeds from an understanding of the question, problem or issue that the study addresses. Such an understanding of the problem situates that problem in a relevant context and relevant intellectual traditions. Such situation of the problem suggests what kinds of empirical evidence might be relevant, and what kinds of logics of enquiry might be employed.

Some research traditions require rather extensive specification of problems in terms of contexts, relevant empirical evidence and logics of enquiry. Other traditions frame problems in a broader context and relevant empirical evidence. For example, experimental traditions often have a rather detailed specification of how the data collection will be organised, what will be measured, and how data collected will be analysed. On the other hand, ethnographic traditions offer much more flexibility in how the data collection is organised, what evidence may be relevant, and how it will be organised in analysis.

Different problems require different research designs. The problem of understanding the normal development of certain intellectual skills (e.g. language development in pre-school children) may suggest research designs that passively observe development over time. The problem of determining if a particular intervention has a causal effect might suggest quite different research designs, such as an experiment. Much of wise research strategy involves matching the research design to the question or research problem.

Logic of enquiry

While it is essential that research designs be well suited to the research problem, they must also be well suited to the way in which the empirical evidence will be used to draw conclusions – to the logic of enquiry used in the research. The logic of enquiry for a particular problem will be shaped by the intellectual traditions in which the researchers are working and by how they conceive the particular problem being studied. This will determine what kinds of evidence might be relevant in supporting the conclusions of the research, as well as how they might be organised in analysis.

Many logics of enquiry involve implicit or explicit comparisons of units being studied (which may be individuals or collectives such as classrooms, schools or even countries). Some logics of enquiry involve comparisons of a unit or units with external standards, conventions, or ways of understanding. This is most obvious in studies like experiments or quasi-experiments that compare one group of individuals with another as an essential feature of their logic of enquiry. Such studies compare groups that are intended to be the same in every important respect except the intervention or treatment they are evaluating, arguing that any difference observed must be caused by the treatment or intervention.

A similar logic of enquiry involving comparisons motivates some kinds of research that do not manipulate or intend to draw causal conclusions. For example, survey research that attempts to describe populations often involves comparisons of one part of the population to another to give meaning to both or to define new comparative concepts, like the gaps between societal groups in academic achievement. Another kind of comparison that gives meaning in logic of research arises in studies of a single unit, where the comparison is with the unit itself at a different point in time, for example a single subject time series that traces behaviour over time using comparison of the unit with itself over time to gauge the progress or decline in desired behaviour. The same logic applies to time series representing the performance of aggregate units like schools over time.

Even studies that investigate a single unit (whether individual or aggregate) like intensive case studies use comparisons to give meaning to the evidence about that unit. Such studies often use internal comparisons as part of their logic of enquiry. They may also use comparisons to external standards or broader experience to give meaning to the evidence, even if it is never explicitly compared to another unit. Such use of comparisons with external standards is also part of the logic of other research designs, such as surveys (e.g. assessments) that include measures with externally referenced performance standards.

In many quantitative research traditions, the logic of enquiry involves highly specific logics involving statistical methods for data analysis and hypothesis testing. For studies in these traditions, important considerations in research design involve ensuring that the data collected will support the validity of inferences drawn using the statistical analyses, for example statistical power analysis to ensure that the sample size is adequate for the hypothesis tests to have a high likelihood of detecting effects if they are present. In survey research methods for drawing probability samples are highly specified to ensure that the findings will be generalisable to the appropriate population (see, for example, McGrath, 2011).

In many qualitative research traditions, the logics of enquiry are less specifically technical but are none the less highly evolved. For example, some logics of enquiry used in ethnography involve the idea that the process of developing descriptions, claims and interpretations must be based on evidence, subject to searches for alternative interpretations and attempts at disconfirmation.

Varieties of research designs

There are many kinds of research designs, but they differ on at least two dimensions. One dimension is whether a research design involves the manipulation of putative independent variables or passive observation. The other dimension is whether a research design involves a single unit (which may be a person or an aggregate unit such as a classroom or school) or multiple units. While there are sometimes ambiguities (such as designs that involve multiple intensive case studies), these dimensions are useful as principles to subdivide research designs for the purposes of discussion. This classification of research designs is summarised in Table 4.1.

Single units no manipulation

Some research designs are organised to study single units. Sometimes the purpose of the study is simply to describe the unit at one point in time. More often, designs study single units over time. For example, passive developmental studies might study the behaviour of a single individual over time, observing language or other behaviour over time in order to understand the development of cognitive skill or other concepts thought to generate behaviour. No intervention or manipulation (other than the observation) might be used nor would it be appropriate if the purpose of the study was to understand how 'normal' development unfolded. Similarly, some studies focus on an aggregate unit such as a school as it changes over time.

Intensive case studies, both contemporaneous and retrospective, fall into this category of designs. Quantitative studies such as time series designs that observe one or more variables over time for a single unit also fall into this category.

Single units with manipulation

Some research designs focus on a single unit but involve an attempt to determine if manipulating one (or more) putative independent variables will have a causal effect on another variable. For example, classic studies of single subject behaviour (often grounded in behavioural psychology) observe the behaviour of a single individual over time, but do so as different interventions are applied to try to influence that behaviour. The timing of the application of different interventions may be arbitrary or it may be highly formalised, even determined under a random allocation scheme.

Table 4.1   A typology of types of research design and some prominent examples of each type

	Focus of study			
	Single unit		**Multiple units**	
	Type of design	**Objective**	**Type of design**	**Objective**
Passive observation	Case study	Describe	Survey	Describe
	Time series	Describe	Cross-sectional comparative	Describe
			Longitudinal/panel study	Describe
Manipulated treatment	$(AB)^k$ designs	Infer causal effect	Natural experiments	Infer causal effect
			Randomised experiments	Infer causal effect
	Interrupted time series	Infer causal effect	Assignment by covariate (RDD)	Infer causal effect
			Quasi-experiments	Infer causal effect

Interrupted time series where outcome variables are measured over time both before and after an intervention is introduced fall into this category. The simplest of these interrupted time series designs is when there is only one observation before and one observation after the intervention is introduced (this is often called the pre-test/post-test design). In behavioural psychology, interventions are typically different reinforcement conditions. A common single subject design emphasises the differential response of outcomes to treatments, tracking the outcome under one reinforcement condition, then introducing an intervention, then removing the intervention and returning to the original reinforcement condition, then returning to the intervention. This is called the $(AB)^2$ design, a mnemonic for the idea that condition A is followed by condition B and that this sequence is repeated twice. If this sequence is repeated k times, it is called an $(AB)^k$ design.

Multiple units no manipulation

Several research designs focus on *multiple* units but involve no attempt to determine if manipulating one (or more) putative independent variables will have a causal effect on another variable. These designs can be described as using passive observation, although the data collection itself may involve questionnaires, interviews, the collection of administrative or even biologic data (such as blood or saliva samples). However, the more intrusive the measurement process, the more likely it is to have effects of its own, and the notion that these designs do not involve manipulation becomes more questionable (see, for example, Hill, 2012).

Cross-sectional surveys focus on the measurement of a collection of units at one point in time, supporting logics of enquiry that focus on comparisons between individuals at one point in time. Longitudinal surveys (also known as panel studies) collect data on the same units at several points in time to allow comparisons not only between different units at one point in time, but also the same units across time.

While surveys are among the most common research designs in this category, there are other important designs. Natural experiments are one of the most important. A natural experiment arises when existing differences in policies or practices create a situation in which naturally occurring groups that are quite similar on many variables except a key policy or practice (herein labelled the 'treatment') that is the focus of the research problem. Such natural experiments often occur when similar administrative entities adopt different policies or practices, such as when adjacent schools or school districts that are similar in other ways adopt different curricula or programmes. Natural experiments are so named because they resemble artificial experiments that (randomly) assign units to different interventions, policies or practices.

Natural experiments are difficult to distinguish from quasi-experiments using a comparison group that did not arise from manipulation by the researcher (sometimes called the non-equivalent control group design or an observational study). In both designs, the logic of enquiry is to try to deduce whether the causal effect of an intervention differs from that of another (the comparison condition) by comparing the groups on one or more outcome variables. The fundamental validity problem is to ensure that the groups being compared are alike in every way that might cause differences in outcome other than the intervention itself.

Validity claims require that extensive information be collected on the individuals in both the treated group and the comparison group on variables that could not be affected by the treatment. Variables that could not have been affected by the treatment are called *covariates*. Covariates are typically variables that have been measured before the treatment group receives the treatment (such as pre-tests), but can also be measured after the treatment has begun if they are unlikely to change (such as gender or social class). Naturally occurring comparison groups (even in natural experiments) are rarely sufficiently similar enough to the treated groups to support treatment effects without further refinement of the project's design.

The most important refinement in design is to use covariates to evaluate the equivalence of the treated and comparison groups and to use measured values of the covariates to improve the matching of the groups. One strategy for improving the matching of groups is to construct a more closely matched comparison group by explicitly matching (on covariate values) units in the comparison group with units in the treated group. Such matching can substantially improve the pre-treatment equivalence of the comparison group to the treated group and consequently strengthen validity claims. Explicit matching works best if the distribution of covariate values in the treated and comparison groups overlaps considerably and if there are considerably more potential comparison units than treated units. Even then, technical tools to facilitate multivariate matching (such as propensity scores) are often needed because units are being matched on not one but several covariates at the same time (see, for example, Shadish et al., 2012). Another strategy to improve matching of groups, which is often used in conjunction with explicit matching, is the use of statistical adjustment using the covariate values. While statistical adjustment is technically straightforward, it is viewed by many statisticians as inferior to explicit matching because it relies strongly on modelling assumptions that are often difficult to falsify empirically.

Multiple units with manipulation

Research designs in which the researcher manipulates the value of an independent variable so that different units have different values of that independent variable can provide strong evidence about the causal effects of independent variables on outcomes. There are principally two kinds of designs that rely on manipulation of independent variables by the researcher. The most prominent designs are experiments with random assignment. A lesser known alternative is the class of designs in which treatment assignment is based strictly on the value of a covariate, but where there is no random assignment.

Randomised experiments have a distinctive role in scientific enquiry because, in principle, they can provide valid inferences about the causal effect of treatments without requiring any statistical modelling assumptions. Natural experiments and other study designs that involve matching provide valid causal inferences only if all of the covariates that affect outcome have been measured and properly matched between the treatment and comparison groups. Randomisation achieves (on average) matching on all the covariates that a researcher may have imagined, and all the covariates the researcher *has not* imagined as well. Consequently, randomisation is a powerful tool for assuring the validity of causal inferences.

There are many varieties of experimental designs involving the random assignment of units to different treatments. Individual persons can be randomly assigned to treatments, but so can aggregate units such as classrooms or schools. Random assignment of groups such as classrooms or schools to treatment often has advantages in educational studies. For example, it may be practically difficult to assign different treatments to individual students in the same classroom. It may be politically difficult to assign different treatments to different individuals or classrooms within the same school, particularly if one of the treatments seems more desirable (regardless of whether there is any actual evidence that it is superior). In some cases the theory of the treatment is that it functions through the entire unit (e.g. whole-school reforms such as school-wide positive behaviour support programmes). In such cases, assignment of treatments to aggregate units such as classrooms or schools may be desirable or even essential.

Designs that assign treatment strictly on the basis of a covariate are an alternative to randomised experiments that can also provide very strong evidence about causal effects. The most prominent of such designs in education and the social sciences is the regression discontinuity design. The regression discontinuity design with two treatments involves assignment to one treatment of individuals with a covariate score less than a certain cutpoint and assignment to the other treatment of those whose scores exceed the cutpoint. This design was first used to evaluate the effects of fellowships and prizes (which were assigned according to a score used for selection), however it is well suited to other situations in which allocation decisions are made via a formula involving an explicit score (such as sorting into curricula or programmes).

Validity considerations

The principle function of research design is to support validity claims about the findings of research studies. The dominant perspective on the validity of research designs in quantitative social science grew out of an important paper (later published as a small book) by Campbell and Stanley (1963) that has been elaborated on since then (see Shadish et al., 2002). The key to this framework is the idea that conclusions reached from research design are subject to potential threats to their validity. If we think of the research process as developing an argument supporting conclusions, these threats to validity are like counter-arguments. While their framework was developed in the quantitative domain, the general thrust of their analysis is quite general.

In the Campbell–Stanley–Cook–Shadish framework, there are four classes of threats to the validity of research designs, which we have generalised slightly below to stress their general applicability.

Data analysis validity

Cook and Campbell (1978) originally called this class of threats to validity 'statistical conclusion validity', but the idea is clearly more general. All empirical research designs involve the collection of empirical materials which are organised by the analysis in order to draw conclusions. If the design does not assure that the empirical materials used in the analysis are adequate to draw conclusions, or if the analysis is not organised to permit drawing valid conclusions even if the materials collected are sufficient to do so, then the conclusions drawn from the research design will be invalid.

The specific threats to data analysis validity include:

- unreliable data elements (which might include measurements, notations of occurrences from field notes, incorrect observations of participants). Often this will occur due to too few observations, too little time spent observing, or poor choices as regards what to observe (e.g. intrinsically variable as opposed to more stable characteristics);
- incorrect analysis, meaning an invalid summary of data elements (which could include the use of improper statistical methods, relying on impressions or memory when more verifiable means are available, such as counting instances in field notes);
- incorrect data elements (including using invalid measurements, focusing data collection on the wrong participants or being deceived by informants).

Internal validity

This was one of the two original classes of threats to validity mentioned by Campbell and Stanley (1963). It refers to the issue of whether the relation observed between putative independent and dependent variables is a causal relation as opposed to just an association that is not causal. Obviously this class of threat applies only to research designs that are seeking to identify causal relations. Research designs or research traditions that seek just to identify associations are not subject to threats to internal validity. For research traditions that do make claims about cause and effect, achieving internal validity is a fundamental (and often daunting) validity challenge.

There is a long list of threats to internal validity in quantitative studies. Some of these threats apply only to specific types of designs, others apply more generally. For example, consider the threat of maturation given below. The threat is that individuals may have changed as part of a natural process over the period of the study and this might undermine the validity of causal claims made based on the design. Clearly this threat is more serious in a design such as the pre-test/post-test design (where it is completely indistinguishable from a change caused by the treatment) than in a design with a comparison group (where the comparison groups would also be subject to maturation and so could provide an indication of any maturation effects). Moreover, these threats are more important when a design is used to study some types of problem than when it is used to study others. For example, consider the threat of maturation again. Clearly this threat is more serious over a year-long study than a two-week study, and more serious when the outcome being measured is one that is changing rapidly in the natural development of individuals like those in the study.

Important threats to internal validity include the following:

- *Ambiguous temporal precedence.* Because causes must precede their effects, any claims of causality in which the putative cause does not unambiguously precede the putative effect are suspect.
- *Observation effects.* The act of observing (or measuring or interviewing) changes the phenomenon being observed in substantial ways. This presents a threat to internal validity when observation effects might be confused with relations between putative independent and dependent variables.
- *Maturation.* Individuals grow older, wiser and more experienced over time for reasons that have nothing to do with interventions. This presents a threat to internal validity when maturation effects might be confused with relations between putative independent and dependent variables.
- *Selection.* When groups are being compared that are not randomly assigned it is possible that those groups will differ in ways other than the putative independent variable which is the presumed cause of group differences in outcomes. This presents a threat to internal validity when the pre-existing differences between groups induced by selection could cause one of the groups to have higher outcome scores irrespective of the treatment.

- *Mortality.* Often, not every unit (e.g. person, classroom, or school) that begins the study persists throughout the study. This presents a threat to the internal validity of the study if the units that drop out do so in ways that are related to the putative independent variable. For example, in studies comparing two groups receiving different treatments, if the more able individuals tend to drop out of one group more frequently, and those who drop out differ from those who persist, this is a threat to the internal validity.

Generalisability

This was one of the two original classes of threats to validity mentioned by Campbell and Stanley (1963), where it was described as external validity. It refers to the issue of whether the relation observed between independent and dependent variables can be generalised from the settings, persons and contexts studied to those that are part of the scope of application intended by the researcher. Representative (that is probability or random) sampling can ensure external validity, but this is seldom a viable option outside survey research. Probability sampling requires the precise specification of the sampling frame that is the intended scope of generalisation. While external validity is often discussed in rather vague terms, the concept can be sharpened by a specific explication of the intended scope of applicability of the study results.

In the absence of probability sampling, one line of argument supporting external validity is based on the similarity of the study sample to the intended scope of application. Within this scope of application, it is helpful if the research design can provide information about whether there are variations in findings across subgroups (that is interactions) (see, for example, Hedges, 2013). Another line of argument supporting generalisability is based on the mechanism by which the independent variable has an effect on the dependent variable. To the extent that a research design can provide any information to support the mechanism, it may also support the generalisability of the findings.

Construct validity of explanation

Cook and Campbell (1978) called this threat to validity 'construct validity of cause and effect' because they focused on empirical studies of causal effects, but the idea is clearly more general. This validity threat concerns whether the explanation of the study has correctly identified the constructs in the interpretation. This concept of validity draws its inspiration from the measurement concept of construct validity and in some ways it resembles the measurement concept of consequential validity (whether the interpretations of a measurement 'as used' are correct). For example, a research design might identify a generalisable causal relation between an intervention and an outcome, but misinterpret the construct causing the effect. Hawthorne effects or novelty effects, where the actual cause of the effects is attention or a change in routine rather than the attributed type of attention or the particular attributed change in routine, are examples of how explanations can lack construct validity. Construct validity of explanation is not a property of designs, but of the interpretation of evidence from designs, which inevitably involve the theoretical framework in which the research is embedded. However, certain design features can support the construct validity of explanations. For example, having several variations of the treatment in the design can make it possible to determine whether the effects of particular variations of the treatment are consistent with an explanation in terms of treatment constructs.

Questions for further investigation

1. How does the articulation of threats to validity of research designs help to select research designs that will lead to more valid education research?
2. Are there examples of different research designs that are vulnerable to the same threats to validity, but where one design is probably more valid than the other?
3. In what ways is the evaluation of research designs a form of qualitative research?

Suggested further reading

Kirk, R.E. (1995) *Experimental Design*, 3rd edn. Belmont, CA: Brooks-Cole.

Kratochwill, T. (ed.) (1978) *Single Subject Research*. New York: Academic Press.

Rosenbaum, P.R. (2002) *Observational Studies*, 2nd edn. New York: Springer-Verlag.

Rubin, D.B. (2006) *Matched Sampling for Causal Effects*. Cambridge: Cambridge University Press.

Rubin, D.B. and Imbens, G. (2015) *Causal Inference for Statistics, Social and Biomedical Sciences*. New York: Cambridge University Press.

Shadish, W.R., Cook, T.D. and Campbell, D.T. (2002) *Experimental and Quasi-Experimental Designs for Generalized Causal Inference*. New York: Houghton Mifflin.

References

Campbell, D. and Stanley, J. (1963) *Experimental and Quasi-experimental Designs for Research*. Chicago, IL: Rand McNally.

Cook, T.D. and Campbell, D.T. (1978) *Quasi-experimentation*. New York: Houghton Mifflin.

Hedges, L.V. (2013) 'Recommendations for practice: justifying claims of generalizability', *Educational Psychology Review*, 25: 331–37.

Hill, C.E. (2012) *Consensual Qualitative Research: A Practical Guide for Investigating Social Phenomena*. Washington, DC: American Psychological Association.

McGrath, R.E. (2011) *Quantitative Models in Psychology*. Washington, DC: American Psychological Association.

Rubin, D. (1977) 'Assignment to treatment on the basis of a covariate', *Journal of Educational Statistics*, 2: 2–16.

Shadish, W., Cook, T.D. and Campbell, D.T. (2002) *Experimental and Quasi-experimental Designs for Generalized Causal Inference*. New York: Houghton Mifflin.

Shadish, W., Steiner, P. and Cook, T.D. (2012) 'A case study about why it can be difficult to test whether propensity score analysis works in field experiments', *Journal of Methods and Measurement in the Social Sciences,* 3: 1–12.

Thistlewaite, D.L. and Campbell, D.T. (1960) 'Regression-discontinuity analysis: an alternative to the ex post facto experiment', *Journal of Educational Psychology,* 51: 309–17.

Planning your research

Laura Day Ashley

5

Why is planning important?

Embarking on a research project can be over-whelming, particularly if it is the first time you have ever done such a thing. Planning is an important skill which can help you progress your research from the initial inception of an idea through to the collection and analysis of data and writing up your project. Rather than simply approaching the project in a linear fashion undertaking one task at a time in sequence, planning can encourage you to think ahead to future stages of your research and conceptualise your project as a whole. It can also enable you to anticipate potential problems you may face during the research process and consider potential resolutions to those problems in advance – as the old saying claims, 'forewarned is forearmed'. Through the process of planning you can start to take ownership of your research and realise that effectively *you* are the 'manager' of your project. As Jennifer Mason has argued, research demands 'a highly active engagement from its practitioners' (Mason, 2002: 4) as opposed to a 'passive following of methodology recipes' (ibid.) and '[i]t is vital … that researchers are fully conscious of the decisions they are making, and that these are informed and strategic rather than *ad hoc* or straightforwardly reactive' (ibid.: 5). By planning you can start to prepare and equip yourself for the difficult decisions you may have to make along your research journey.

Starting to plan early on

Planning is especially relevant in the early stages to help you think about the range of tasks you will need to complete before you actually start collecting your data. This section details a number of 'prestudy tasks' (Glesne, 2011) that you may need to consider, and suggests some strategies and techniques to aid your planning activities. There is some logic to the sequence in which these tasks are presented, however they may not be carried out in this precise order. As each element of research connects with the next, you may find that you need to consider tasks further down the list before you can adequately plan for earlier ones.

Being strategic about choosing your topic

Since you will be spending a considerable amount of time investigating your research topic it will help enormously if you choose a topic that interests and motivates you. You might additionally consider how it relates to your previous experiences or future plans, perhaps in terms of your career development. It is also important that your topic not only interests *you* but is also of interest, relevance and significance in wider terms.

To help you decide on your research topic you may consider discussing your ideas and plans with various people, such as colleagues in your institution or fellow students on your course, your tutor or supervisor, or practitioners and specialists in your potential field of study. Listening to their comments and questions and responding to these can be useful to help you clarify what you are planning to research and why.

Mapping out your research: research design and research questions

While it may be relatively easy to decide on a broad topic to research, it is a far more difficult task to develop focused research questions relating to your topic and design a research project that can address and answer them (Mason, 2002). Clearly defining specific research questions is a key part of planning; this set of research questions will express what you

are researching and how, and will serve as an important guide for your research project. Once you have a clear idea about the type of research questions you will be asking, you will then be able to think about the type of research design that is most suited to answer them (e.g. action research, ethnography, case study, historical research, survey, evaluation etc.). Conversely, it is possible that you already had a type of research design in mind when you decided on your topic – in this case your research questions will need to be consistent with that type of design. It is this issue of research design that is 'concerned with turning research questions into projects' (Robson, 2011: 70).

Brainstorming using mind maps and spider diagrams (see Figure 5.1) is a useful technique for moving from your broad topic to starting to think about

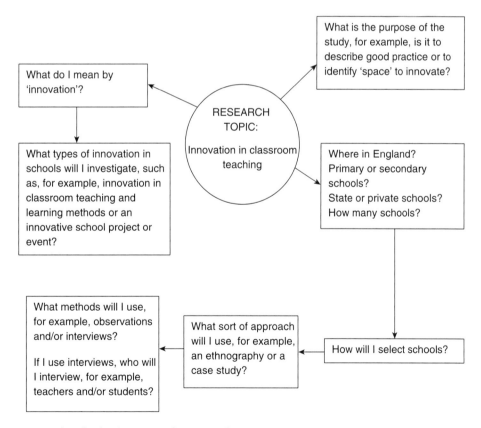

Figure 5.1 Example of a brainstorm of a research topic

designing your research project. This can allow you to interrogate your topic from different angles, consider various possible routes, and also decide which paths you definitely do not want to pursue. It can also help you refine your focus and lead you towards starting to think about the different elements of your research design, for example its purpose, selection and sampling strategies, and methods of data collection and analysis. You could do this brainstorming on your own or perhaps with a peer who can bring a different perspective to your research plans by asking questions and making suggestions that you may not have considered (Blaxter et al., 2006).

This brainstorming exercise can also provide a launch pad from which to start formulating relevant research questions. One approach to getting started with drafting research questions is detailed in Figure 5.2. This exercise may help you generate an initial set of research questions, however it is important to recognise that arriving at a set of research questions that can effectively articulate and guide your research may take time, and it is likely that you will continue to refine your research questions as you plan your research and read around your topic. You should also attempt to compose a single overarching research question which encompasses your set of research questions and encapsulates your research project; this research question might then become the basis of the title for your dissertation, thesis or research report.

Planning your literature review

It is likely that you will have already read about your topic before you sit down to plan your literature review. For example, you may have originally become aware of, or interested in, your topic through reading, and it is likely that reading helped you develop your research questions. When conducting a literature review you are concerned with two key questions:

(i) What is already known about my topic (i.e. what has already been researched)?
(ii) How will my research project contribute to existing knowledge?

Planning your literature review can help you identify fields of research that relate to your topic; it can also enable you to see how these fields and sub-fields interrelate. Again, visual displays such as mind maps can help you start to plan your literature review. Figure 5.3 illustrates how a research project might draw on broader fields of research to inform the specific topic and how the topic relates to sub-fields. It also shows that it might be useful to look at research literature surrounding similar topics which, although not directly related to your topic, might be of interest to compare with your own. You may additionally consider the role that theory will play in your

---

Activity for drafting research questions
1. Write a long list of questions that you would like to ask about your research project – don't limit the list at this stage.
2. Go through the list and underline the questions you think are the most important.
3. Use the following checklist – based on Keith Punch's criteria for good research questions (2014: 76) – to consider whether your questions are:

  • 'Clear'?
  • 'Specific'?
  • 'Answerable'?
  • 'Interconnected'?
  • 'Interesting and worthwhile' researching?

4. Adapt, refine and eliminate questions accordingly until you have a set of approximately two to five research questions (depending on the size of the project).

Figure 5.2   Drafting research questions

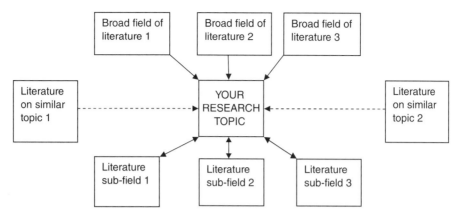

Figure 5.3   A mind map of a literature review

research and the theoretical literature you could draw on. In this way you will be able to build up a picture of the existing body of knowledge in relation to your topic and identify gaps. In the early stages of research, carrying out such an activity might lead you to revisit your original research ideas and refine your research focus; it may also help you justify your research rationale – for example, that your research project will fill a gap in the existing literature, or build on what is known from previous studies.

Planning the literature review also helps you consider the sources available to you; typically these will include books, chapters in edited books, journal articles, and unpublished theses and dissertations. You may also decide to look at other media in which research is disseminated (e.g. newspaper articles, radio programmes and websites). Searching for research literature today invariably involves using online resources, such as online library catalogues or electronic databases, to look for relevant books and journal articles or theses and dissertations. Key to the success of this process of searching is the identification of appropriate search terms related to your topic that will enable you to access the relevant materials.

You might plan your literature search by first listing the key terms related to your research – these may be terms you are using to articulate your research questions and plans. When listing

these terms you should consider the following: *Are they widely used by the public/research community? Are there alternative terms that you could use?* Searching is a process of trial and error – you may try a key word or combination of key words that will yield very few titles or even none; alternatively, your initial search might result in far too many titles to browse through. In such cases you would need to adapt and refine the key words you are using in your searches accordingly, or as Luker (2008) suggests, concentrate on the intersection between sets of relevant search terms.

When you do have a reasonable selection of titles relating to the various aspects of your research, you should then read through their abstracts to judge whether or not they are relevant to read in full. As part of your planning process you might consider printing the abstracts you have selected and cutting and pasting them onto a larger version of your mind map of your literature review. This will help you see the existing research related to your topic at a glance. It will also enable you to see in more detail the interrelationships between existing research fields and identify where your research project fits into this picture.

This process of planning your literature review will help you considerably when you come to write it up in your dissertation, thesis or research report. As Gary Thomas (2013) stresses, a good literature review should not just be a summary of the existing literature but also an analysis (i.e. indicating how the parts relate to one another) and a synthesis (i.e. bringing the parts together to create something new). The mind-mapping processes described in this section should help you in this endeavour.

Anticipating ethical issues

As part of your planning tasks it is important to give some thorough forethought to the ethical issues you may face at different stages in the research process. When designing your research and framing your research questions, you may ask yourself: *What is the purpose of my research in ethical terms? What are the implications of my research – is it likely to be of benefit to a particular group of people or wider society?* Ethical considerations are particularly important if your research involves people. You will need to gain the *voluntary informed consent* of all the participants in your research. This involves ensuring that you provide them with adequate information about the nature of your research, how it will be used and reported, its benefits, as well as any potential harm that could arise from it, to enable them to decide whether or not to agree to take part. It also involves specifying what participating in the research means (for example, being interviewed or observed and whether or not this will involve audio or video recording), why it is important, and clarifying that participants have the right to withdraw themselves (or data relating to them) from the study at any time.

During the process of data collection you will need to continue to engage with the ethics of what you are doing; for example, you might find yourself considering:

- How can I observe this classroom with minimal disruption to the lesson?
- How can I ask questions about a potentially sensitive topic without causing distress and anxiety to interviewees?

- If I introduce this educational intervention to one group of students, should I ensure that the control group also benefit from the intervention after I have collected my data?

Finally, you should continue your ethical thinking and practice through to the appropriate handling and storage of data and their analysis, and during the writing and dissemination of your research. An ethical matter particularly relevant to these research processes is respect for the privacy of your research participants, paying special attention to issues of confidentiality and anonymity.

Thinking ahead about the potential ethical issues that may arise in your research project can help you address these appropriately. It is also crucial to build ethical considerations into the early planning stages of your research as it is likely that you will be required by your institution and/or funding body to complete a formal ethical review process before commencing your research. As part of your early planning tasks you will need to find out what the process requires you to do, and the timescales you will need to meet. You may well need to go through an ethical review process before you make contact with your research site(s) and/or participant(s). You should also familiarise yourself with the ethical guidelines of your institution as well as those of the professional organisations in your subject area, such as the British Educational Research Association's *Ethical Guidelines for Educational Research* (2011). This topic is discussed in greater depth in Chapter 7.

Giving forethought to access considerations

It is likely that you will have already considered some of the issues around access when you decided on your research topic. However, it is important to give this more thought at the planning stage, not least because your project may well depend on your gaining access to appropriate research sites, participants, documents etc.

The first task is to identify the key individuals (often referred to in research methods literature as 'gatekeepers') who are in a position to give you the access you need for your research. It will be beneficial if you have some prior knowledge of these individuals, for example you may have been put in contact by a colleague, a friend or your supervisor. If this is the case, you could ask them what they think might be an appropriate way to make initial contact with the individual – for example, by letter, telephone or email – and whether you could use their name in your first communication to indicate your existing connection.

The purpose of the initial contact with the gatekeeper(s) should be ideally to arrange a face-to-face meeting (Walford, 2001). Such a meeting can be important in building trust as it enables the gatekeeper to find out who you are and ask questions about your research and the access you require. It can also prove beneficial for you to learn more about the site, participants and/or documents you are seeking to access which may help to inform your selection and sampling decisions. This meeting, and indeed the initial contact, should be carefully planned. Such investment of time and effort in planning is likely to pay off by increasing your chances of securing access. Figure 5.4 lists some points worth considering when planning your first contact or meeting with gatekeepers.

Preparing for data collection and analysis

Jennifer Mason draws our attention to an important, but sometimes neglected, point in planning research – that early decisions about research design and methods involve, to a degree, 'anticipating the process of data analysis' (2002: 37). Data analysis, then, should not be a process that is only thought about and carried out after the data collection has occurred. Instead, the analysis of data is central to the research process, with a main focus being: *How to collect data that can be meaningfully analysed to build descriptions and explanations that answer the research questions?*

A necessary point to make here is that planning should involve checking the internal consistency of your proposed research project so that the mode of data analysis that you intend to use is coherent with your methods of data collection, which in turn are appropriate given your research design and research questions. Jennifer Mason

---

- Have a clear idea of how you are going to introduce yourself and your research project succinctly; if necessary, write notes that you can look over beforehand.
- Plan to listen to gatekeepers; anticipate concerns and questions that they may have and consider how these might be addressed. You might also ask what aspects of your topic interest them or would be useful from their perspective to find out more about (Blaxter et al., 2006) and then consider incorporating this into your research plans.
- Consider how you can 'sell' your research project (Walford, 2001); for example, you might already have good reason to believe that your topic is something your gatekeeper is interested in – if so, share your interest and talk about the research purpose and possible outcomes. You can also offer to share research products, such as copies of research reports and publications, or you may be able to offer to provide a workshop (Blaxter et al., 2006). However, you should be realistic and not offer anything you will not be able to deliver. You should also be mindful of ethics: attempting to gain access should not involve either coercion or concealing aspects of your research.
- Find out in advance what you can about the site, documents, etc. you are seeking to access. This can help you to ask informed questions and gauge what sort of access would be reasonable to request.
- Be prepared to negotiate the access you need. You might be granted partial access and you will need to decide whether or not this would be sufficient – and what you plan to do if it is not, e.g. identify other research sites, participants and gatekeepers to approach, or adapt the focus of your study (Glesne, 2011).
- Finally, be aware at this early stage that access is an ongoing process (Blaxter et al., 2006). Even if you have been granted initial access, it is likely you will need to maintain and renegotiate it throughout the process of research.

Figure 5.4 Planning your communication with gatekeepers

(2002: 30) suggests an activity to help with this which involves drawing up a grid in which you list your research questions and then match each of these research questions to the data sources and methods you intend to use, as well as justify why these methods and sources will help you answer the research questions.

Once you are happy with your selection of methods of data collection and analysis, a *pilot study* can help you refine the techniques and tools you plan to use. You should plan to conduct the pilot study in a situation as close as possible to that of the actual research (Glesne, 2011), and preferably where participants are willing to play an active role in suggesting improvements to research instruments. This process will take you away from the 'drawing board' and bring you closer to the research context, enabling you to fine-tune your research plans to the realities of the research situation. You may also decide to pilot your intended data analysis methods by conducting analysis on a section of the data collected during the pilot study.

Carefully planning your data collection and analysis can prevent you making a common research error – collecting more data than you will have time to analyse. Planning can help you remain focused on collecting data that will directly address your research questions and also helps you keep in mind what you will be doing with those data in terms of analysis.

Planning your writing

During the research process it can be easy to lose sight of the fact that the research project in which you are absorbed will actually need to be written up. How you will present your research project and findings in your research report, dissertation or thesis (as well as journal articles, book chapters and conference papers) is of paramount importance. Therefore, it is good practice to engage with the idea of writing at the planning stage. This will enable you to consider how you will translate your project into words on a page, and to whom you will be communicating your research, e.g. your dissertation examiners, commissioners of the research project,

practitioners, policy makers and/or the wider research community.

Starting to write about your project at an early stage will help you articulate and develop your ideas. It will also enable you to consider when is the most productive time for you to write. This could depend on whether you feel you have more energy in the morning or later on in the day, or it may be a case of finding time in the day or week when you can write undisturbed, perhaps in the evening or at the weekend. Whichever you decide upon will depend on your particular circumstances and preferences. By engaging with writing early on, you will also gain an indication of the time you will require for writing; do remember to factor in the time it takes to draft, redraft, proofread, edit, provide a list of references and arrange for printing/binding processes – all of which can take longer than anticipated.

A number of research methodology books demonstrate how a dissertation might be structured in terms of the content to include and the percentage of the finished written product to allocate to each section (see, for example, Blaxter et al., 2006: 236 [citing Barnes]; Edwards and Talbot, 1999: 17; and Thomas, 2013: 31). Although these differ slightly in terms of the content and written percentages, they are really variations on a theme. However, all stress that their suggestion is a basic guide only and should not be rigidly adhered to. The final structure is likely to be modified in accordance with (a) the nature of your research project and (b) regulations or guidelines provided by your institution.

Managing your time and resources

The time and resources available to you will shape both the scale of your study and your research design. You will need to give consideration to both at the very beginning of your research. Resources include books and journals; equipment such as computers, digital voice recorders and cameras; consumables such as office supplies, postage, photocopying; services such as transcription or administrative assistance; travel expenses etc. Your first job will be to find out what is available for your use in your institution (Bryman, 2008) – both those resources that are freely available (perhaps as a loan service) and those which require additional payment. You will then need to identify any gaps: consider the costs of the resources you require and the funds available to you – perhaps funds that you have secured from a funding body; you may even consider identifying funding bodies to whom you could apply. However, if there is a gap between the resources you need and those which you have, and you cannot be certain to secure the funding required to cover their costs, you should be prepared to adapt your research design so that it depends on fewer resources.

The time you will have for your research project will be constrained by its submission date as well as the other demands on your time. When conducting educational research you should also be aware of the time constraints of your research participants, such as teachers and students whose activities and availability are shaped by school timetables. When you are planning the timescale for your research project – and particularly the data collection phase – you will need to accommodate these time limitations within your schedule.

It cannot be emphasised enough how important it is to draw up a timetable for your research – this is a useful tool that you can use and modify throughout your project to help you keep on track and meet your deadline. A useful place to start is with your submission date and to then work backwards, plotting the big tasks you will need to achieve perhaps on a month-by-month basis. There are many ways of doing this; my preferred approach is simply to draw up a table that lists the months of the year in the first column with the tasks I plan to carry out in the second column. I prefer to organise my table in this way on the basis that the months will not change but the activities might (e.g. as the project becomes more focused and defined over time, the order of tasks may change, new tasks may be added and others discarded, some may take longer than anticipated

and others surprisingly less time). This timetable should be regarded as a working tool that is regularly revised and updated.

It is important to note that while these practical issues require careful consideration, your project should not be led by them. Research decisions should be made first on sound academic grounds, but you may need to make realistic compromises in the face of obstacles. You should therefore ensure that you are able to justify why your research design was the best available option given the practical circumstances.

The research proposal or plan

The culmination of your planning processes in the early stages of research should be to write a research proposal or plan that sets out what your research is about and how you intend to carry it out. A research proposal is a very good preparation for research: it can help you identify weaker areas to work on, check the internal consistency of the design, justify your research decisions, and start to take ownership of the project. It will also get you writing and you might even use relevant sections of your proposal as starting points for chapters of your dissertation, thesis or research report.

If writing a research proposal is a requirement of your course, or if you are writing a research proposal for a prospective funder, you will probably be required to follow guidelines provided by your institution or funding body about the structure and content of the proposal. These may cover similar points to those set out in Figure 5.5, and you may also notice that these points broadly relate to issues and tasks we have discussed so far in the chapter.

While the proposal serves as an excellent basis for your research project, you should not feel overly constrained by it – it should incorporate some flexibility to enable appropriate tailoring to the research context as necessary. However, it is necessary here to warn against making too many changes after you have written your proposal, as this will entail the loss of precious time for carrying

- Your research topic and your rationale for choosing this topic.
- The purpose of your research.
- The research questions you are seeking to answer (or research problem you are aiming to solve).
- The literature that already exists on your research topic and/or fields of research related to your topic and how your research project will contribute to this existing body of knowledge.
- The research design you will use to address your research questions and why this is the most appropriate design for your project.
- Your methods of data collection and analysis and the rationale for your selection.
- The practical (e.g. access) or ethical issues you might face in your research and the measures you intend to put in place to address these.
- The resources your research project will need and how you will fund them.
- The outputs you plan to generate from your research in terms of publications or other forms of dissemination.
- The timescale for completing the different phases of your research project.

Figure 5.5   Points to consider in a research proposal or plan

out your research (Bryman, 2008), and you should check if you need to gain approval from your course tutor or supervisor and/or funding body to do so. An important message is this: the more you have done in terms of planning tasks *before* you write your proposal, the closer your proposal will be to what you will actually end up doing.

Planning as an ongoing activity

Planning is not something that you do once before you actually start your research and never again. You will need to draw on this key skill throughout the research process and it will come in particularly handy when you arrive at junctures in your research where you face new dilemmas and need to make new decisions. You can draw on and adapt some of the strategies and techniques suggested in this chapter to help you with this process. The last section of this chapter sets out questions for further investigation to consider as you conduct your research.

For first-time researchers in particular, the perceived enormity of the task of conducting a research project can feel overwhelming at times; often there will be several different elements of the project to keep an eye on and different tasks to juggle at the same time, many of which you may

not feel in complete control of. During my doctoral research I learnt to live with this feeling and began to welcome it, as I saw it as my being alert to the possibility of things not always going exactly to plan! This chapter has highlighted the importance of careful planning for research. However, it is also vital to be aware that even with the best-laid plans you may not always be able to anticipate every problem that may arise. Being aware of this may help you be ready to respond and draw on your planning skills to decide on an appropriate resolution should an unexpected problem occur. As Blaxter et al. (2006: 150) remark, 'Research is really about getting misdirected, recognising this as such, understanding why it happened, then revising our strategy and moving on.'

Questions for further investigation

1. Pose yourself 'difficult questions' (Mason, 2002) about your research as you carry it out. Such questions should be probing and critical to encourage you to think about the very things that you might prefer to brush under the

carpet! This will help you anticipate potential problems or inconsistencies in your research and address them sooner rather than later. You may also consider meeting with peers on a regular basis to discuss each other's research.

2. Keep a research diary in which you can note down these difficult questions along with other reflections on your research progress, including any new ideas or doubts you are having about the direction of your research or a particular research tool. You might use this diary to start to form arguments in relation to a key issue, or even to make some tentative interpretations about what appears to be going on in your research.

3. Each month revisit your timetable and the tasks you have set yourself. How long is each of these likely to take? How many days do you have available this month? Plot your tasks in a diary, setting yourself targets and mini-deadlines for the month.

Suggested further reading

Robson, C. (2011) *Real World Research: A Resource for Users of Social Research Methods in Applied Settings*, 3rd edn. Chichester: Wiley. A comprehensive book that focuses on the processes of applied research.

Thomas, G. (2013) *How to Do Your Research Project: A Guide for Students in Education and Applied Social Sciences*, 2nd edn. London: Sage. An important,

accessible and clear text on beginning a research project. Well structured and insightful.

Walford, G. (2001) *Doing Qualitative Educational Research: A Personal Guide to the Research Process*. London: Continuum. A reflection on the trials and tribulations and the problems and promises of conducting research – and also on the links between the idiosyncrasies and circumstances of researchers and what is possible in research from a respected scholar.

References

Blaxter, L., Hughes, C. and Tight, M. (2006) *How to Research*, 3rd edn. Maidenhead: Open University Press.

British Educational Research Association (2011) *Ethical Guidelines for Educational Research*. Available at www.bera.ac.uk/researchers-resources/publications/ethical-guidelines-for-educational-research-2011 (accessed 26 April 2016).

Bryman, A. (2008) *Social Research Methods*, 3rd edn. Oxford: Oxford University Press.

Edwards, A. and Talbot, R. (1999) *The Hard-pressed Researcher*, 2nd edn. Harlow: Pearson Education.

Glesne, C. (2011) *Becoming Qualitative Researchers: An Introduction*, 4th edn. Boston, MA: Pearson Education.

Luker, K. (2008) *Salsa Dancing into the Social Sciences: Research in an Age of Info-Glut*. Cambridge, MA: Harvard University Press.

Mason, J. (2002) *Qualitative Researching*, 2nd edn. London: Sage.

Punch, K.F. (2014) *Introduction to Social Research: Quantitative and Qualitative Approaches*, 3rd edn. London: Sage.

Robson, C. (2011) *Real World Research: A Resource for Users of Social Research Methods in Applied Settings*, 3rd edn. Chichester: Wiley.

Thomas, G. (2013) *How to Do Your Research Project: A Guide for Students in Education and Applied Social Sciences*, 2nd edn. London: Sage.

Walford, G. (2001) *Doing Qualitative Educational Research: A Personal Guide to the Research Process*. London: Continuum.

Inference and interpretation in research

6

Robert J. Coe

Introduction

This chapter addresses an important issue in the conduct of research: *How can we establish the strength and applicability of claims about interpretations and inferences?* The somewhat cumbersome wording of this question to include these four elements (strength, applicability, interpretations and inferences) allows it to encompass a wide range of issues, including those often considered under headings such as validity, reliability, generalisability (in the quantitative tradition); credibility, authenticity, trustworthiness, transferability (in the qualitative tradition); sampling and representativeness (in both traditions). This attempt at unification is deliberate: although the words used in different traditions may be different, the fundamental issues broadly overlap. Of course, the kinds of claims made, justifications given, importance attributed to different qualities, types of threats, etc., will vary greatly in the different traditions. But research of all types involves making interpretations and inferences whose validity (or credibility) must be established, along with some justification for the nature and extent of the domains to which those interpretations and inferences are, and are not, applicable.

The previous two chapters have dealt with questions about research design and planning, but they both make it clear that it is important to think about analysis and interpretation as part of these processes if the research is to end up supporting the kinds of claims we are likely to want to make. Anticipating such claims, and optimising their strength and applicability, are features of good design and planning.

Confusion over 'validity'

Validity is one of the fundamental concepts in research, yet also one of the most often confused. Within the quantitative tradition, some writers list a number of different types of validity, such as 'internal validity', 'statistical conclusion validity', 'face validity', 'criterion-related validity', 'construct validity' and many others. Textbooks and courses on quantitative research often present definitions and discussion of validity alongside reliability, sometimes presenting reliability as an aspect of validity, sometimes as a necessary but not sufficient condition for validity, sometimes arguing that they operate in tension: that more of one is achieved at the expense of the other. The widely quoted commonsense definition of validity as telling us 'whether an instrument measures what it is intended to measure' has often been seen by assessment experts as naïve in failing to capture a crucial aspect of validity: that it applies not to tests, assessments, questionnaires or other data collection instruments, but to particular interpretations or uses of them, since scores from the same assessment process may be interpreted or used in different ways. However, more recently some experts appear to have come to the defence of the 'naïve' view (Newton and Shaw, 2014). Furthermore, measures of internal consistency such as Cronbach's alpha, which are the most commonly used indicators of reliability in quantitative research, are widely interpreted as indicating the extent to which items in a test measure a common, unidimensional construct; this is properly an aspect of validity, not reliability. The novice researcher can be forgiven for being somewhat confused about exactly what 'validity' means and how it relates to other aspects of quality.

In the qualitative tradition, many writers (e.g. Lincoln and Guba, 1985) have eschewed the word 'validity' altogether as tainted with a legacy of positivistic thinking, and put forward alternatives that better capture the equivalent idea for qualitative data and an interpretive or naturalistic view, such as credibility, transferability or authenticity. Some have presented these alternatives as direct translations of each concept from the quantitative paradigm into the qualitative. Others have added to this list of alternatives to quantitative validity additional concepts (e.g. catalytic validity or paralogical validity) that do not have equivalents in the quantitative tradition but capture important quality concerns in at least some parts of the qualitative tradition.

Nevertheless, there is a core idea – that interpreting data in particular ways should be explicitly justified – which is essentially common to both traditions and a requirement for any good research, whatever its paradigmatic stance. Whether more is gained in emphasising the different traditions than is lost in the confusion engendered by using different words for broadly the same thing may be open to argument.

Teddlie and Tashakkori observe that, 'With so many types of validity, the term has lost meaning … validity has become a catch-all term that is increasingly losing its ability to connote anything. When a term is used with other words to connote so many meanings, it essentially has none' (2003: 12, 36). To illustrate this they provide a list of different types of validity in both qualitative and quantitative traditions (2003: 13), which is reproduced here in Table 6.1. As an alternative to the word 'validity', they suggest use of the general term 'inference quality' as a way of emphasising the fact that all the different types of validity relate to different

Table 6.1 Types of validity

Quantitative	Qualitative
Internal validity (causal, relationship definitions)	Catalytic validity
	Crystalline validity
Statistical conclusion validity	Descriptive validity
External validity	Evaluative validity
Population	Generalisability validity
Ecological	Interpretive validity
Construct validity (causal)	Ironic validity
Consequential validity	Neopragmatic validity
Validity (measurement)	Rhizomic validity
Face content	Simultaneous validity
Criterion related	Situated validity
Predictive	Theoretical validity
Concurrent	Voluptuous validity
Jury	Plus terms associated with authenticity:
Systemic	
Construct validity (measurement)	Educative
Convergent	Ontological
Divergent	Catalytic
Factorial	Tactical

Source: Teddlie and Tashakkori (2003: 13)

aspects of the quality of inferences that can be made from a collection of data.

In the following sections we draw on this attempt to unify the language of 'QUAL' and 'QUAN' in the context of mixed-methods research. We focus on particular types of claims that researchers make and the threats or challenges that may undermine those claims as a way of structuring an analysis of the different kinds of inferences and interpretations that can be made and the arguments that can be used to support them. Focusing on claims, and on the justifications that must be given to support them, we identify two general types:

• *Interpretation claims.* These include simple descriptive claims, but also the issue of 'interpretive validity' (ensuring that interpretations are consistent with the understandings of research participants). Interpretation claims also incorporate the idea of 'construct validity' in quantitative research, which addresses the kinds of arguments that are required to justify interpreting quantified measures (such as test scores, grades, ratings or scales) in particular ways.

- *Transfer claims*. These include any claims that a particular result, interpretation or inference is applicable to a setting other than the one in which it has been directly evidenced. Arguments about the representativeness of samples (generalisation), the theoretical applicability of particular explanations or understandings (transferability), and the extent to which findings may be sensitive to particular arbitrary or contingent features of the research (which includes the concept of reliability in quantitative research) are relevant here.

Interpretation claims

All empirical research involves the interpretation of data and a good deal of reporting of research can be classified as making interpretation claims. These may be simple descriptive claims, such as a verbatim transcript of words spoken or the presentation of a written answer given in response to a test question. The claim here is 'this is what happened' and the kinds of warrant or justification for the claim are generally fairly straightforward. Slightly more problematic would be interpretation claims that depend on an analysis, reduction or interpretation of the original data. For example, if part of a transcript is claimed as an example of a person expressing a particular view, or if answers are coded as right or wrong, the process of analysis must be understood before the reader can accept this interpretation as legitimate. At this point all data are essentially qualitative, even if subsequent analysis may involve quantification.

As the analysis becomes more complex, so too does the argument required to justify its interpretation. To continue our first example, if an analysis of a series of interviews is claimed to show that a person's strength of feeling about an issue is related to their past experience, we would need to follow a complex argument which would include more extensive data (such as multiple excerpts of text), details of methodology (how the text was coded),

context (where and when the research was conducted), and no doubt many other things, in order to be convinced of such a claim. In the second example, right/wrong codings of a series of questions might be combined to assign an overall score to a person and this score might then be interpreted as a measure of their 'intelligence'. Before accepting this interpretation as valid, we would need to consider a range of supporting evidence, including procedural details about the kinds of questions asked, the context in which they were asked, and how they were coded and combined. Evidence about the defensibility of interpreting responses to the different questions in the test as indicating a single trait would be needed. Evidence that the trait, or more appropriately the claimed interpretation of that trait, is fully represented by the set of questions asked and that the score being interpreted as a measure of that trait is not affected by other spurious factors, biases or confounds would also be required. Finally, in judging the appropriateness (validity) of the claim that a score represents a person's 'intelligence', we might want to examine the intended and unintended consequences of this interpretation and the ways it may be used. If we judge that its use brings worthwhile benefits without significant harm, then the validity will be endorsed; if the risk of harm is judged to be a concern, the validity of this interpretation is more problematic.

Establishing these kinds of interpretation claims may be seen as a process of answering a number of questions, each of which raises a particular concern about the interpretation. Examples are considered in further detail in the sections which follow.

Is the interpretation plausible?

This question is a major focus for justifying interpretation claims in the qualitative tradition. For example, Guba and Lincoln define 'credibility' as the match between an evaluator's representation and the 'constructed realities' of respondents or stakeholders (1989: 237). They offer a range of techniques the evaluator can use to verify this, including *prolonged engagement* ('substantial involvement at the site of enquiry'), *persistent observation* ('to add depth to the scope which prolonged engagement affords'), *peer debriefing* (discussing the work with another disinterested researcher), *negative case analysis* (revising hypotheses to account for all known cases), *progressive subjectivity* (checking developing ideas against what was believed at the outset to demonstrate responsiveness to the data) and *member checks* ('testing hypotheses, data, preliminary categories and interpretations with members of the stakeholding groups from whom the original constructions were collected' [1989: 238]). Other methods of verifying the plausibility of interpretations include providing full and explicit *audit trails* of the processes of data collection, analysis and interpretation.

In the quantitative tradition, the plausibility of interpretations of scores and scale measures comes under the heading of *face validity*. At its simplest this means looking at a test or instrument and making a judgement about how appropriate it would be to interpret responses to it as a measure of the intended construct. Related to face validity is *content validity* – indeed sometimes these terms are used interchangeably. A tighter definition of content validity restricts it to situations where the judgements are made by 'subject-matter experts' and/or when systematic procedures are used to examine individual questions or test items for suitability and relevance to the intended construct. Subject-matter experts may be asked to rate each item for its alignment with the construct and its suitability for inclusion in the measure. This practice may include examining the process by which responses are coded and the codes combined to form an overall score (the mark scheme). Another aspect of content validity relates to whether the whole of the target domain is covered by the assessment process. If some parts of the intended construct are not assessed, that interpretation cannot be said to have content validity (see the discussion of construct under-representation below).

Is the interpretation corroborated by other evidence?

A second question looks for convergence with other evidence. The word *triangulation* is widely used here, borrowing a metaphor from the world of surveying in which the precise location of a geographical feature such as a mountain can be found by observing it from two distinct fixed points. In a research context these two views may come from different methodologies, sources of data, methods of analysis, theoretical perspectives or observers, among other differences (Denzin, 1978). For example, in a study of bullying we might observe children in a playground and interpret one individual's behaviour as an instance of bullying, but then triangulate by asking the children for their interpretations, or getting another observer to give an interpretation. Or we might use member checks, sharing the transcripts or analyses of interviews with the participants to verify that researchers' interpretations are appropriate.

The method of *constant comparison* may also be seen as an example of this kind of corroboration of interpretations. In this process, newly collected data are constantly compared with existing data and theory. In this way theory is built on data, and both theory and interpretations of data (codings) are revised to ensure overall consistency.

In the quantitative tradition, the extent to which a measure corresponds with other things that we would expect it to correspond with is known as *convergent validity*. The process of *construct validation* (leading to evidence of *construct validity*) consists of making predictions, ideally based on explicit and defensible theory, about other measures with which we would expect the new measure to correspond, and estimating the strength of the expected correlation. These predictions are then tested empirically. If the measure behaves as we expected a measure of the intended construct should, then we can say it has construct validity. In the full construct validation process we would look for evidence not only of convergent validity, but also of *discriminant validity* – the extent to which the measure is distinct from (i.e. not correlated with) other measures that might be expected to be confused or confounded with it, but which logically and theoretically should not be (Campbell and Fiske, 1959). This aspect of the process is described in more detail below.

A specific form of the quantitative corroboration of the agreement between a new measure and its intended interpretation is known as *criterion-related validity*. If we want to be able to interpret scores from some instrument (such as a test or questionnaire) in a particular way and already have an existing validated measure of the target construct (the criterion measure) then the correlation between the putative measure and the criterion measure is an estimate of the criterion-related validity of the former. In this case it is common to express the strength of validity as a number: a validity coefficient, which is the correlation coefficient between the measure and the criterion. There are a number of different kinds of criterion-related validity, including *concurrent validity* (where the putative measure and the criterion are measured at the same time) and *predictive validity* (where the new measure is used to predict a criterion that is measured later). An example would be a selection examination that is used by universities to decide which applicants should be offered a place. If the selection examination is found to correlate well with later performance at university then it may be judged to have good predictive validity: it helps to predict who will do well and hence to decide who should be offered a place.

Of course the whole idea of criterion-related validity begs the question of how we know the criterion measure is valid. If claims about the interpretation of one measure can only be supported by presupposing the validity of another, we are left with a chain of claims that are dependent on each other and hence at best conditionally valid, but for which full validation could only be achieved by drawing on some additional source of support. Furthermore, in many cases there is no suitable criterion measure.

Is the interpretation based on an adequate range of supporting data, methods and contexts?

This question is often a high priority in the qualitative tradition, with its focus on naturalistic settings,
'thick description' and rich data. Qualitative researchers often adopt strategies such as prolonged engagement and persistent observation (see above) and approaches to data collection that are detailed, intensive and set out to be exhaustively comprehensive within a particular setting or group, rather than to sample a wider range of settings but treat them more superficially. The limits of applicability of interpretations are determined by theoretical sampling strategies that actively seek potential counter-examples or negative cases, and regard the continuing generation of significant new categories, themes or theoretical explanations as an indication that the breadth of the evidence-base still needs to be extended (*saturation sampling*).

In the quantitative tradition this question addresses the issue of *construct under-representation*. For example, if a mathematics test contains only questions involving numerical calculations it might be appropriate to interpret the score as a measure of arithmetic, but not as a measure of general mathematical understanding, since most interpretations of mathematics would include aspects other than just arithmetic (for example, algebra, geometry, statistics, modelling, etc.). Similarly, if the test contained only short-answer questions we might argue that it failed to reflect a candidate's ability to solve more extended problems, which could be seen as a vital element of mathematics. If we judged that the test questions could be answered by a candidate who had simply memorised a set of procedures, we might challenge the interpretation of test performance as an indication of 'understanding'. Further, we might object if the test used only written questions and answers and we took the view that mathematical understanding should encompass the ability to speak about mathematical ideas or solve problems in your head without writing anything down. We might also argue that the context of a school mathematics classroom imposes constraints on the ways children think about problems (for example, seeking simplistic right/wrong answers and drawing on a range of unstated conventional assumptions) which we might want to transcend in making claims about a person's 'mathematical understanding' that we hope would be applicable to a wider range of contexts. In all these cases the full construct is under-represented in what is measured and interpreting these test scores as an indicator of 'mathematical understanding' would not be appropriate.

It is also clear that in all these cases there is a considerable role for judgement, creativity and critical thinking in the validation process. Validating the interpretation of a measure requires us to start by thinking hard about what that interpretation should mean. We then need to think creatively and critically about possible ways in which we might have failed to capture some aspect of the intended interpretation in the process we have actually followed. We may, for example, have inadvertently narrowed the range of knowledge, skills, attitudes or behaviours from what was intended to what has actually been assessed. Often this will have been for compelling pragmatic reasons: some aspects may be much easier to assess than others.

We will also have used particular methods to capture the intended knowledge, skills, attitudes or behaviours, the results from which would not generalise to, or correspond with, the results we would have achieved by other methods. For example, if we have used multiple-choice tests, self-completion questionnaires or responses to simulated situations, we might find that had we used open-response questions, peer ratings or naturalistic observation, our results might have been quite different. If we want to be able to interpret a measure as indicating 'knowledge' without having to qualify it as 'knowledge (as demonstrated in a multiple-choice test)', we must either ensure that the measure incorporates a broad range of methods or show that the different methods agree well enough to be interchangeable.

This importance of demonstrating that quantitative measures represent some quality that transcends a particular method of collecting them is often overlooked in the validation process. The analysis of a range of different measures shows, rather disturbingly, that the correlations between measures of completely unrelated traits that have been collected using the same method are often about as high as the correlations between the same trait measured using different methods (Cote and Buckley, 1987). In other words, *method variance*

(the spurious correspondence between measures of unrelated constructs that are assessed using the same method) is often at least as large as *trait variance* (the extent to which the measure is actually determined by the trait it is intended to measure).

For example, suppose we want to measure two traits of children in schools that we believe should not be strongly related: their learning motivation and social connectedness. We might decide to use two methods to capture each: a self-report questionnaire and teacher ratings based on observation. What we would hope to find is that the two measures (self-report and teacher ratings) of the same trait would correspond well, while measures of the two traits (learning motivation and social connectedness) should correlate weakly, if at all. In practice what we often find is rather different – that measures of what is supposed to be the same trait captured using different methods correlate only moderately well, while theoretically unrelated traits, when measured using the same method, are found to be correlated. For example, the average cross-method, same-trait correlation found by Cote and Buckley (1987) in educational studies was only 0.35, hardly bigger than the average (0.31) for same-method, cross-trait correlations.

Could the interpretation have been influenced by other spurious or inappropriate features of the research process?

Again, this question is relevant in both qualitative and quantitative traditions, though the approach will differ.

In qualitative research the focus is often on the processes by which an interpretation has been made and on the researcher's awareness of the features that may influence that interpretation. The words 'spurious' or 'inappropriate' may not really apply here, since it is recognised that there is not necessarily any 'correct' (or incorrect) interpretation. Different perspectives or beliefs may lead to different interpretations, and in order to make sense of a particular interpretation we may need to understand the perspectives and beliefs that led to it and how they might have been influential. One of the approaches used to do this is *bracketing*. Here the researcher attempts to identify, state, suspend or dissociate from the research process aspects such as their own ontological and epistemological positions and theoretical frameworks, suppositions based on the researcher's personal knowledge, history, supposition culture, assumptions, beliefs, experiences, values and viewpoints, suppositions based on their academic and scientific theoretical orientations and theories, and pre-existing assumptions about the phenomenon being investigated. Approaches to bracketing may differ in the extent to which it is aimed to remove these aspects, which aspects are chosen, how permeable the brackets are around them and when in the research process bracketing is applied (Gearing, 2004).

Other methods used in qualitative research to identify or eliminate unwanted influences on interpretation have already been mentioned above. These include peer debriefing and progressive subjectivity. Audit trails also focus on the data collection and interpretation processes and may identify such influences.

In the quantitative tradition the influence of these spurious or inappropriate features is characterised as *construct-irrelevant variance*. If values of a score or measure are influenced by something other than the intended construct then we might say that the measure is biased or contaminated by another construct. For example, if we want to interpret scores on a written mathematics test as measuring mathematical ability, it might be a problem if we found that performance on the test was determined partly by a candidate's reading ability. This kind of problem would be harder to detect if we believed, as seems likely, that in general even a true measure of mathematical ability would be correlated with reading: people who are good at maths are often good readers too.

Test bias would be diagnosed if people who should have the same measure on the intended construct (i.e whose underlying mathematical ability is the same), but who differ on the contaminating construct (one is a good reader, the other less good) were found to have different scores on the test. This means that bias can only ever be identified relative to something else – a criterion measure. Unless we already have a pure, unbiased measure of mathematical ability against which to compare a new instrument, we cannot say whether two people whose test scores differ should really have the same measure on the construct.

In practice, we can estimate the relative biases of different items in a test, or the relative biases of different tests for different groups. There might also be cases where the equality of measures across groups was part of the definition of the construct. For example, empirically we might find that some items in a mathematics test are easier for females while others are easier for males. If we were developing a new test we might find it easier to generate the latter kind of items, so a lazy test developer might conclude that males were better at maths than females. On the other hand, we might incorporate in the definition of the construct of 'mathematical ability' the principle that on average the two groups should perform equally. Such a definition would allow us to identify test bias without requiring an additional 'unbiased' criterion measure.

Establishing that a measure is independent of things that it should not be related to provides evidence of its *discriminant validity*. To investigate this, we need to have a clear and detailed theory that allows us to predict how we would expect the construct that we are hoping to measure to be related to other things. Testing these predictions is the process of construct validation that establishes, if the predictions are confirmed, the *construct validity* of the interpretation.

Does the interpretation, or its likely uses, lead to any desirable or undesirable consequences?

This question relates to the issue of *authenticity* in the qualitative tradition. As well as responding to traditionally quantitative concerns of reliability and validity by developing equivalent notions more applicable to their aims, qualitative researchers have initiated a further list of quality criteria 'which spring directly from constructivism's own basic assumptions' (Guba and Lincoln, 1989).

Guba and Lincoln (1989) list five quality criteria under the heading of authenticity. The first is *fairness*, which concerns whether the research represents and honours the beliefs, values and understandings of all participants appropriately. To do this it must actively seek the constructions of all potential stakeholders and conduct an open, balanced negotiation of the whole evaluation process. The second is *ontological authenticity*. This is the extent to which involvement in the research enhances the way participants experience the world, by enabling them to better assess and situate their own experiences and awareness. *Educative authenticity*, the third criterion, is the extent to which participants are helped by the research to understand and appreciate how others see the world. The fourth criterion, *catalytic authenticity*, concerns whether the research stimulates action or decision making by participants. Finally, *tactical authenticity* relates to 'the degree to which stakeholders and participants are empowered to act' (Guba and Lincoln, 1989: 250).

In the quantitative tradition, the equivalent notion is captured by the idea of *consequential validity*. Championed by Messick (1989), this idea is still controversial, with some quantitative researchers arguing that it is not properly an aspect of validity (Newton and Shaw, 2014). Messick – and others since – argued that if validity relates to a particular interpretation or use of a score rather than to the instrument itself, then a judgement about the appropriateness of that interpretation or use must include a consideration of its consequences. If we want to use test scores in particular ways then we must provide evidence of the relevance and utility of the scores for those purposes. But interpretations themselves have consequences: different ways of interpreting the same test score may rest on different values and have different implications. For example, if we produce an intelligence test which is biased against candidates from a particular ethnic, racial or cultural minority, to describe this as a test of 'intelligence' would involve making the implicit assumption that the kinds of intelligence (and methods of assessing it) valued by the majority are more important than those that might be more appropriate for that minority. To interpret performance in that test as a measure of 'intelligence (as valued by the majority)' would be more honest – hence more valid – and makes its value-dependence clearer. Whether or not we think it would be appropriate to use that test score to make selection decisions among applicants from both majority and minority groups for employment or higher education opportunities depends crucially on how we interpret the meaning of the score.

Transfer claims

If a particular researcher conducts a study with a particular group of participants in a particular context on a particular occasion, then the claims that can be made about the interpretation of what was observed must be validated according to the processes described above. However, if we claim that a phenomenon, interpretation or inference has applicability or meaning beyond the particular occasion, context or persons that have been directly studied, then we are making a transfer claim. Some of the key points of disagreement between researchers in the qualitative and quantitative traditions concern the extent to which such transfer claims are appropriate and desirable (or even possible), and if they are how they may be justified.

If we want to make these kinds of transfer claims, there are broadly two kinds of errors we could make. On the one hand, if we underestimate the importance of the differences that distinguish contexts and the individual human beings that conduct and participate in research, we may make sweeping over-generalisations, stretching too far beyond what our evidence can safely support. On the other hand, if we overstress these differences, we will be limited to reporting what a specific researcher subjectively perceived to have happened on a unique occasion in a particular context with a precise set of individuals, with no basis on which to claim that this reflects any more than the idiosyncrasies of an individual researcher or that it has any relevance to any other situation.

Rejecting generalisation

Within the qualitative tradition some have argued that it is not appropriate for researchers to make generalised claims about the applicability of their work to other contexts. For example, Lincoln and Guba (1985) state that 'the only generalisation is: there is no generalisation', since the classical concept of generalisability depends on unwarranted assumptions of determinism and reductionist and inductive logic, and because of the impossibility of time- and context-free understandings and the difficulties of applying probabilistic generalisations to specific cases.

According to Lincoln and Guba (1985) it may be possible for research conducted in one context to be applicable to another, but at best this can be in the form of a 'working hypothesis', not a generalised claim. Moreover, the work of applying a working hypothesis from one context to another must often be done by the reader, not the original researcher. The latter can only provide sufficient 'thick description' to enable the former to judge whether the two contexts are sufficiently congruent. Only a person who has detailed knowledge of a particular context can make a judgement about whether what has been studied in another context has any relevance to it. Hence, in reporting the research that was conducted in one context, the researcher must resist the temptation to make any kind of general claims about its relevance or applicability, and must limit any specific claims of transferability to contexts that have been described in similar levels of detail to the originally studied context.

Naturalistic generalisation, which develops within a person as a product of experience, is a process of assimilating new experiences and knowledge with existing ones, expanding and accommodating existing constructions and understandings to incorporate the new. This kind of

'generalisation' is conducted by the reader of research and their reading can be seen as a form of learning. Research connects with the reader to provoke new insights, understandings, connections and explanations, which the reader may apply to their past experiences, their constructions of reality and their explanations of phenomena.

It follows that the selection of cases and contexts for study in qualitative research is guided not by their representativeness of some wider group, but for their potential to contribute information in their own right: their ability to provoke new insights, understandings, connections and explanations. Purposive sampling strategies, such as *intensity sampling* (choosing the most information-rich cases), *maximum variation sampling* (choosing cases to illustrate a wide range of the dimensions of interest), *critical case sampling* (choosing cases that deliberately test the theory), *extreme or deviant case sampling* (choosing unusual, extreme or exotic cases) or *typical case sampling* (choosing cases to illustrate what is normal), are likely to be the methods of choice (Patton, 1990). The sample may also be selected *contingently,* with each new case chosen in the light of what has been gained from existing cases. Although many authors suggest otherwise, strategies such as *snowball sampling* (identifying new cases from recommendations of those already chosen) or *convenience sampling* (using cases that are easy to identify, access or co-opt) are not really purposive in the same sense; they are simply pragmatic ways of achieving a sample.

Types of transfer claims

For the kinds of research that do set out to claim that interpretations and inferences from a particular context can be transferred to a range of other contexts, it is important to identify quality criteria for judging these claims. For transfer claims in general the question we need to address is this: *Is the claim dependent on particular choices of appropriate, but arbitrary or contingent, features of the research?* If the interpretations and inferences that have been made in relation to the particular context studied are appropriate, we still need to know whether they would be equally appropriate in other contexts. The research we carried out took place on particular occasions, made use of particular data collection methods and observers, and was conducted with particular participants in particular contexts. There may be no reason to challenge the use of these particular features, but if we want to be able to claim generalisability or transfer to what might be expected to happen on other occasions, using different methods or data collection instruments, observed by different researchers, carried out with different groups of participants or in different contexts, we must provide evidence that our interpretations and inferences are not sensitive to these particular choices. These five elements of arbitrariness in the research enable us to differentiate five different kinds of transfer claims relating to the transfer across occasions, instruments, observers, participants and contexts.

In the quantitative tradition, the first three of these forms of generalisability (transfer across occasions, instruments and observers) are conventionally listed under the heading of *reliability*, while the last two (transfer across contexts and participants) relate to the issue of sample *representativeness,* sometimes referred to as *external validity* or just *generalisability*.

Transfer across occasions

Evidence that some observed phenomenon, such as a performance or score on some test or assessment, is not just a 'one-off' but would be expected to be replicated on future occasions, is an important part of justifying interpreting it as a characteristic of the person who took the test. If we want to be able to claim that what has been measured is a stable trait rather than just a temporary state, we must provide evidence of its stability and consistency over time.

The stability over occasions of a measure is referred to as its *test-retest reliability*. It is generally estimated as the correlation between the same candidate's scores on a test or measure on successive occasions. The shorter the time interval between testing occasions, the higher the correlation is likely to be, since there is less time for the trait to genuinely change. On the other

hand, the correlation may be spuriously affected by the candidate's memory of having taken the same test a short time ago. One way round this is to use two versions of the test instead of repeating the identical test. The correlation between scores on these similar versions is known as *parallel-forms (or equivalent-forms) reliability*.

Transfer across instruments

If two parallel forms of the same test are given in quick succession then we are no longer assessing stability over time but are effectively estimating the equivalence, or interchangeability, of two different versions of the same instrument. Hence *parallel-forms reliability*, if taken on the same occasion, provides evidence of the consistency of scores across different versions of the instrument. More generally, we might want to be able to claim that a candidate's score on a test was not just a reflection of the particular questions asked, but could be interpreted as indicative of their likely performance on similar tests containing different questions. If the two parallel forms of the test are constructed by creating a larger item-bank of questions and then randomly allocating items to one or other version, we may interpret the correlation between their scores as an indicator of the robustness of the measure to arbitrary choices of particular items, taken from a universe of all the possible questions we could have asked on the same topics.

A clever way to estimate this without having to go to the trouble of creating two parallel forms of the test would be to treat the two halves of the test as if they were two parallel forms of a shorter test, administered in quick succession. Because shorter tests are less reliable than longer, we must apply a correction (the Spearman-Brown formula) to the correlation between the two halves if we want an estimate of what the correlation would be between two tests of twice the length. This would be the *split-half reliability*.

We might realise that there are many other ways we could split the test into two halves, for example counting all the odd-numbered items as one half and the even-numbered the other. If we were to calculate the average of all the possible split-half correlations we would have arrived at perhaps the most commonly cited estimate of reliability, *Cronbach's alpha* (in practice there is a much simpler formula to calculate it). Cronbach's alpha can therefore be interpreted as an indicator of how sensitive the overall test score is to the particular choice of items in the test. High values of alpha (close to 1) indicate that replacing the actual test items with equivalent items (e.g. items from a bank from which the actual items were a random sample) would not make much difference to the overall scores: the particular items are highly interchangeable.

If the test construction process had consisted of listing all the possible questions that could be used to assess the intended construct and then putting a random sample of them into the actual test, Cronbach's alpha could be interpreted as an indicator of the adequacy of that sample to be used as an estimate of what a candidate's score would have been across all the questions. In particular, if we use Cronbach's alpha to calculate the standard error of measurement of the test score, we can interpret this as an indication of the precision implied in using the observed test score as an estimate of the score that would have been achieved if the candidate had been able to answer all the possible questions.

Another way to interpret Cronbach's alpha is as an indicator of how well correlated all the test items are with each other. For this reason, it is often referred to as a measure of *internal consistency.* High values of alpha (close to 1) indicate that the items are highly inter-correlated, hence they are all measuring the same thing. This is sometimes taken as evidence that the construct being measured is unidimensional, though this is far from a guarantee: it is possible to get very high values of alpha in a test in which the main construct is confounded with one or more other constructs.

Transfer across observers

The third aspect of reliability relates to measures that depend on the judgement of an observer or rater. Some tests, such as an objectively marked multiple-choice test, may require no judgement at all. Others, such as a closed-answer mathematics test, may require minimal judgement. Still others, such as a test containing short-answer factual questions, may require some judgement. And some, such as essay questions, may require considerable judgement to mark. Other measures, such as ratings of behaviour by observers, may also depend on judgement.

If we want to be able to claim that a score based on such a judgement is not just a feature of the subjective perceptions or idiosyncratic marking of that particular rater, then we need to provide evidence that scores are consistent across observers. Getting two raters to rate the same behaviour or performance independently would allow us to demonstrate this consistency. The correlation between scores derived from different raters is known as *inter-rater reliability*, and this provides evidence of the transferability of the interpretation of those scores across observers.

Transfer across participants

The fourth kind of claim that we can transfer interpretations from what was specifically studied to some wider set of cases or situations relates to research participants, and takes us out of what is traditionally labelled as reliability into *generalisability* and sampling. How do we know that what we found with a particular sample of respondents or research participants can be applied to a wider group that we have not directly studied?

Most textbook discussions of sampling make a distinction between *probability sampling* and *non-probability sampling*, with the latter including purposive and pragmatic approaches, as discussed above. What is not always clear is that the approach to sampling we choose should depend on the aims for our research and the kinds of claims we want to be able to make. If our aim is to describe a particular context in rich detail, to make sense of the interpretations and constructions that people in that context make and to analyse them in ways that promote insightful and deep understanding, then a purposive sample is likely to be best. On the other hand, if our aim is to use the sample that we can access for study to make claims about a wider group that is of interest to us, then it is vital that the sample is representative of that wider group.

The starting point for thinking about sampling in the latter case is defining that wider group or *population* about which we want to find out. Unless we know who we want to be able to make claims about, we cannot choose a sample that is representative of them. Once that population is defined, we can then list its members: the *sampling frame*. A statistically representative sample is achieved by using some kind of random sampling, such as *simple random sampling* (each member of the population has an equal chance of being selected), *stratified random sampling* (the population is first subdivided to ensure that all important subgroups are captured adequately) or *cluster sampling* (sampling first clusters, such as schools, and then sampling individual students from each).

If we achieve a random sample, then we can use the information we collect from that sample to estimate the equivalent parameters for the whole population and apply some standard statistical analyses to indicate the precision of those estimates. Hence we can make precise claims about the population in which we were interested, with known levels of confidence. In practice, quantitative researchers often apply those analyses without worrying too much about the fact that they did not actually achieve a random sample. Even if a full sampling frame, which listed every unit in the population, was available (and it often isn't), as soon as a single person declines or fails to take part in the research we can no longer claim to have a random sample. Response rates to invitations to take part in educational research are often disappointingly low – or not even reported – which makes any kind of inference about the population quite problematic.

Transfer across contexts

The final type of transfer claim relates to the context in which the research was done and the contexts to which we want to claim its applicability. In educational research the issue of contexts is often subsumed under the issue of sampling participants, on the assumption that if we get an adequate, representative range of participants, the contexts from which they come will also have been sampled adequately. Sometimes a cluster or *multi-stage sample* will be used to sample context units (such as schools or neighbourhoods) and then participants (e.g. students, teachers, families) are selected from these. Provided the analysis respects the multilevel structure of the data and the sample size is adequate for both contexts and participants, this kind of approach is appropriate.

Questions for further investigation

1. Do you agree with Teddlie and Tashakkori (2003) that the word 'validity' has 'lost meaning'? How can clarity and precision of meaning be restored to discussions of 'validity'?
2. This chapter has tried to integrate qualitative and quantitative perspectives on issues like validity, credibility, triangulation and generalisation. How far do you think it has succeeded in arguing that the same issues arise in both types of approach?
3. Think of a study you are planning to (or could) conduct. Can you think of examples of the kinds of claims you expect – or hope – to be able to make? What kinds of evidence would you need to collect to support these? What kinds of alternative interpretations, counter-claims or critical challenges might arise? Will the evidence you collect allow you to address these challenges?

Suggested further reading

Kane, M.T. (2006) 'Validation', in R.L Brennan (ed.), *Educational Measurement*, 4th edn. Westport, CT: American Council on Education and Praeger. Traces the history of the development of thinking about validity from a quantitative perspective and gives a clear account of modern ideas within this tradition. In particular, he stresses the process of validation and the kinds of arguments and evidence that are likely to be required. This is a long chapter and hard going in parts, but a key reference.

Kemper, E.A., Stringfield, S. and Teddlie, C. (2003) 'Mixed Methods Sampling Strategies in Social Science Research', in A. Tashakkori and C. Teddlie (eds), *The SAGE Handbook of Mixed Methods in Social and Behavioral Research*. Thousand Oaks, CA: Sage. Provides an accessible overview of sampling strategies in both quantitative and qualitative traditions, together with arguments for their combination in mixed-methods approaches and illustrative examples.

References

Campbell, D.T. and Fiske D.W. (1959) 'Convergent and discriminant validation by the multitrait–multimethod matrix', *Psychological Bulletin*, 56(2): 81–105.

Cote, J.A. and Buckley, R. (1987) 'Estimating trait, method, and error variance: generalizing across 70 construct validation studies', *Journal of Marketing Research*, 24(3): 315–18.

Denzin, N.K. (1978) *The Research Act: A Theoretical Introduction to Sociological Methods*. New York: McGraw-Hill.

Gearing, R.E. (2004) 'Bracketing in research: a typology', *Qualitative Health Research*, 14(10): 1429–52.

Guba, E.G. and Lincoln, Y.S. (1989) *Fourth Generation Evaluation*. Newbury Park, CA: Sage.

Lincoln, Y.S. and Guba, E.G. (1985) *Naturalistic Enquiry*. Newbury Park, CA: Sage.

Messick, S. (1989) 'Validity', in R.L Linn (ed.), *Educational Measurement*, 3rd edn. Washington, DC: American Council on Education/Macmillan.

Newton, P.E. and Shaw, S.D. (2014) *Validity in Educational and Psychological Assessment*. London: Sage.

Patton, M.Q. (1990) *Qualitative Evaluation and Research Methods*, 2nd edn. Newbury Park, CA: Sage.

Teddlie, C. and Tashakkori, A. (2003) 'Major Issues and Controversies in the Use of Mixed Methods in the Social and Behavioral Sciences', in A. Tashakkori and C. Teddlie (eds), *Handbook of Mixed Methods in Social & Behavioral Research*. Thousand Oaks, CA: Sage, pp. 3–50.

Research ethics
Martyn Hammersley

7

Introduction

There is now a very substantial literature on social research ethics, some of it dealing specifically with educational research (for guidance in relation to this literature see Hammersley and Traianou, 2012b). In large part this literature has been generated by researchers reflecting on the ethical issues that arose in their own studies, and their problems in dealing with them. In addition, there have been flurries of literature surrounding particular investigations that have been criticised on ethical grounds. There are also some general introductions to research ethics, alongside the ethical guidelines produced by scholarly associations (for example, the British Educational Research Association, the British Psychological Society, the British Sociological Association), by universities, and by some funding bodies (for instance the Economic and Social Research Council). Finally, in recent years there has also been literature concerned with the spread of ethical regulation, a development which has transformed the ways in which ethical issues are addressed, and whose effects many researchers regard as pernicious.

The ethical issues discussed in the literature range across many aspects of the research process, from whether there are some sensitive topics or particular methods (for example, covert observation) that should be avoided, to how findings can be published without placing those who participated in the research at risk by making public what they have said or done. However, the boundaries around what counts as an ethical issue, and how these issues relate to other aspects of the research process, are not very clear, so it is necessary to begin with an attempt at clarification.

What is ethics?

There is a considerable philosophical literature concerned with the general field of ethics, and many discussions of research ethics draw on this to some degree. This literature is quite diverse in orientation, and involves several fundamental disagreements. There are even those who put forward forms of 'anti-ethics', rejecting any kind of ethical theory (for a discussion and response see Louden, 1992). Aside from this, there are a variety of views about how we should go about reaching conclusions and decisions about ethical matters (Hammersley and Traianou, 2012a: Chapter 1).

I suggest that a useful starting point for thinking about the nature of ethics, in general terms, is to recognise that it concerns one of several sorts of evaluative consideration that human beings employ. Others include what one enjoys or likes, what would best serve one's personal interests, and what is the most effective means for achieving some end. Generally speaking, ethical considerations are seen as in competition with these other grounds for judgement, and as relating to how we should deal with other people, and/or to what is in the general interest (already here I am at odds with the arguments of some writers on ethics, including Louden).

Most ethical judgements evaluate actions (ones that have already taken place, or are being contemplated), and are concerned with what it would and would not be right or good for someone to do in some specified type of situation. Here, two modes of argument are often distinguished: between evaluating actions in terms of *rules* about which intentions are right and wrong in principle (for example, 'it is wrong to lie') or in terms of actual, likely, or foreseeable *consequences* that are beneficial or detrimental to others or the common good. These are often given the label 'deontological' and 'consequentialist' approaches, respectively. However, ethical judgements are also sometimes made about *people*, rather than about specific actions, and here the concern is with virtues and vices, or with what is and is not a good way of life for a human being. This is often referred to as virtue ethics.

Some philosophical discussions of ethics assume that there are universal principles: principles that apply similarly to everyone – whoever they are, whenever or wherever they live. It is worth remembering that there are particularistic as well as universalistic values, focused on families, local communities, peer groups, organisations, ethnic groups, nation states, regional identities, etc. While these are weaker in modern societies than more traditional ones (by definition), they are by no means absent in Western societies today. Furthermore, there are modes of ethical thinking that emphasise some of these (an example would be feminist care ethics). However, there are writers on ethics who deny the existence or value of universal principles, while others argue that any principles must be qualified according to who is doing the evaluating, and/or whose action is being evaluated. For example, it is often recognised that certain roles, such as parent or teacher, impose special obligations. And there are some categories of person, for example children, who are often thought to have distinctive characteristics that alter judgements about what would be ethical treatment of them – for example, it may be thought that they are more vulnerable than adults in some respects, or that they are less capable of making decisions for themselves (interestingly, the latter claim has come under increasing challenge in recent years in the context of Childhood Studies).

While the term 'ethics' picks out an important family of evaluative considerations, there is no absolute dividing line between these and the other sorts of consideration that inform the judgements and decisions we all make in life, and the same is true in the context of research. Furthermore, it is important to remember that there are other legitimate considerations that should be taken into account in doing research besides those usually listed under the heading of 'ethics', and that all these considerations are intertwined together. A question that arises out of this, to which we will return, is whether it is possible for a researcher to give too much emphasis to ethics, as well as too little.

Research ethics is a form of occupational ethics, analogous to those found in relation to other occupations, notably in the fields of health care, education, social work, law, and business. So the focus is on the distinctive ethical issues that arise in the context of research, though to a large extent this is done by drawing on the more general ideas discussed in the philosophical literature, which have just been briefly outlined.

What is *research* ethics?

Just as there is some ambiguity about what the term 'ethics' means, so too the meaning of 'research ethics' can vary. One interpretation is that it refers to all of the *values* that ought to inform the work of researchers. We can divide these values into two categories: epistemic and practical. Epistemic values are concerned with knowledge: it can be argued that since the goal of research is to produce knowledge, researchers must be committed to discovering the truth and disseminating knowledge. Truth is therefore the central epistemic value, but also under this heading would come a commitment to honesty in presenting evidence, and in providing information about how the research was carried out. Interestingly, commitment to these epistemic values is by no means uncontroversial amongst social and educational researchers. One cause of this is the influence of sceptical arguments that question whether we can ever know the truth. Another is arguments which deny that the pursuit of knowledge is of value in itself, this leading to the conclusion that researchers should aim their work at practical goals, whether this is 'improving education', 'serving public policy', 'challenging inequality', or 'empowering the oppressed'.

However, even those who insist that the production of knowledge can be the only legitimate goal of research recognise that researchers must take account of practical as well as epistemic values in doing their work: these place constraints on how enquiries should be pursued (on the *means* employed). Among these practical values are several that would fall under the heading of 'ethics'. Discussions of these focus to a large extent on how researchers should deal with the people they encounter in their work, particularly those who are the focus of study and/or from whom data are obtained. Some attention may also be given to researchers' relations with research organisations (including universities and funding bodies), with fellow researchers (within the same research team and beyond), with gatekeepers who control access to research sites or to informants, and with audiences for the research findings.

In discussing relations with the people being studied, most discussions of research ethics identify a small number of principles that are of particular importance. In the next section I will outline these.

Ethical principles

As I have indicated, there are those who reject the idea of principles, but to a large extent their objection is to the idea that principles can tell us exactly what ought, or what ought not, to be done in any situation. It is better to think of ethical principles as pointing to particular considerations that should be *taken into account* in the course of action. Viewing principles in this way leaves open the question of whether in any particular situation what a principle implies is the right decision to make. The bedrock of ethics is particular judgements about what would and would not be ethically acceptable in particular situations. Nevertheless, principles provide useful resources in making those judgements.

Discussions of research ethics usually discuss a relatively standard set of principles, and foremost amongst these are minimising harm, protecting privacy, and respecting autonomy. As we shall see, none of these principles is entirely straightforward in meaning, and they may generate conflicting requirements, as well as being at odds with the researcher's commitment to producing knowledge as effectively as possible (for a more detailed discussion of these principles see Hammersley and Traianou, 2012a; on the nature of principles and the debates surrounding them see Hammersley, 2015b).

Minimising harm

The risk of harm, or actual harm, may arise from the research project itself. Equally, though, a researcher may become aware of harm being done to or by the people being studied. Both are matters that need to be taken into account. Furthermore, there are different kinds and different degrees of harm: generally speaking, we would treat serious physical injury as more significant than embarrassment at being asked a personal question – indeed it might be questioned whether the latter counts as harm. Equally important, often, what is at issue is the level of *risk* that a particular kind of harm will arise. For instance, one type of harm that can arise from research is damage to people's reputations, perhaps because they are reported as doing things that are at odds with what they say they do or with their declared principles. However, whether this damage occurs will depend on whether these people can be identified by readers of research reports, whether readers will interpret what is written in the way assumed, and who the readers are and perhaps also how many of them there are. Hence assessments must be made of the likelihood of various consequences, of whether these would constitute harm, and of how serious that harm would be.

Concern about the harm that research can do to participants is particularly central in the field of medical research, where much of the initial discussion of research ethics took place. In that context, the research itself often involves administering treatments and carrying out tests which may themselves cause pain and negatively affect people's health, but equally important may produce benefits. Given this, some assessment of the likelihood of various kinds of harm and benefit, and of their significance and distribution, is especially important.

There are some kinds of educational research where the issue of benefit and harm arises in an analogous way. This can be true, for example, where an experimental approach is adopted that involves randomly allocating children (or school classes) to groups receiving different 'treatments'. For example, randomised controlled trials (RCTs) in education, such as those concerned with the effectiveness of different ways of teaching reading or arithmetic, may involve children in the classes studied being treated differently from previously, and certainly being treated differently from one another. It must be asked whether these variations are likely to enhance or damage their learning, and whether some are being benefited at the expense of others (for example those being taught by the method whose effectiveness is being tested, or those taught by a more common method that is being used as a benchmark).

The central ethical guide relating to benefit and harm used in RCTs is the notion of 'equipoise'. This requires that there be no reliable evidence that one of the treatments is more beneficial (or involves more risk of harm) than the others involved in the trial. Generally speaking, 'evidence' here is taken to mean 'research evidence', but one of the problems is that teachers, parents, and perhaps children themselves, may judge that one 'treatment' is better than others, and might therefore conclude that the trial involves unjustified harm or unfairness. Aside from the fact that achieving equipoise is often not straightforward, there are further complications where what is being assessed in a trial is the degree of benefit of some treatment as against other ways of allocating the funds that would be entailed in 'rolling out' the treatment to a whole population. Here, as elsewhere, ethical judgements can be contentious.

Educational action research also involves the introduction of an intervention (or a series of interventions) into a situation, and here too the benefits and costs of this intervention, as compared with alternatives, and how these vary across those involved, need to be taken into account. It is tempting to assume that interventions will always be beneficial, but in fact all interventions involve costs as well as benefits, and these need to be addressed. Action research aims at a spiral of improvement, and it may be argued on this basis that all participants will gain in the long run. However there may be significant costs along the way, and these could be differentially distributed in ways that might be judged unfair.

Other kinds of educational research, whether involving surveys or qualitative investigations of some kind, do not usually involve any intervention whose benefits and costs need to be assessed. Nevertheless, it is still possible for this research to cause harm. Questions asked in interviews or on questionnaires may be distressing, observation in classrooms may be intrusive in the sense of causing problems for teachers or students, and reporting findings may have harmful consequences.

While potential or actual harm is an important ethical consideration in all educational research, it is important not to exaggerate either its severity or its likelihood. These are, of course, matters of judgement, and may be open to disagreement, but as we shall see exaggerated judgements are themselves not without costs.

I mentioned earlier that researchers must also be aware of the possibility that they will discover harm being done to or by the people they are studying. Here too judgements must be made about the severity of this, and the consequences of reporting it (not just for the researcher but also for the people involved). In some kinds of research it may be judged necessary to make clear in negotiations with gatekeepers, or in securing informed consent for interviews, that any evidence of serious law-breaking or highly unethical behaviour would have to be reported. However, doing this can sometimes have negative consequences that need to be taken into account.

Protecting privacy

A second principle frequently discussed in the literature on research ethics is the importance of protecting privacy. There are private places and there is private information, and if either are treated as if they were public then, arguably, privacy has been breached. However, we should note that what counts as private is a matter of judgement, and of degree, it can change over time, and it is subject to variable assessments. Furthermore, the value of the knowledge likely to be produced by the research may need to be weighed against any invasion of privacy that could be involved. For example, educational organisations frequently want to keep information about some matters, for example their finances, secret, and there may be good reasons for this, but it could be argued that where these organisations are receiving public funds there is a public right to know about their operation.

There are two ways in which issues regarding privacy arise in research. One concerns the collection of data: there are settings, such as homes, that may be declared private areas and therefore not open to observation by researchers, even were permission to be granted. And there are topics and information that could be regarded as private matters about which questions should not be asked in interviews, or perhaps even in questionnaires. While the boundaries involved have been subject to erosion, there are still live ethical concerns here.

The second major respect in which privacy issues arise concerns what information is made public via the research process or in research reports. In group interviews or focus groups, questions may be asked or topics opened up that will lead participants to disclose private information, for example about their sexual preferences or their financial circumstances, in a context that is relatively public. Researchers can often exercise only partial control over this at best, so this is a consideration that must be taken into account when deciding to employ such methods, and in the course of using them.

Researchers have more control, in principle at least, over what data or information is presented in research reports, and made public in that way. One of the ethical problems involved here is that it may be possible for readers to identify the people, organisations or places studied, and this may breach privacy as well as perhaps carry a risk of harm. One of the strategies used by researchers to avoid this, and maintain confidentiality, is anonymisation (i.e. using false names for people, organisations, places and so on). We should perhaps note that attempts to keep research participants anonymous do not always succeed: they may be identified despite researchers' best efforts. This has sometimes happened in case study and ethnographic research where a media agency has followed up on the findings of the research and identified the research site. There may be particular problems in protecting anonymity where visual data are being used, since people are often easily identifiable in photographs or videos. Various techniques have sometimes been used to make faces 'fuzzy' in order to maintain anonymity, but there are conflicting arguments about the desirability of this (see Flewitt, 2005; Nutbrown, 2011).

However, organisations and people will sometimes wish to be named, and some researchers will ask people their preferences about this, although it is important to remember that those at risk may not anticipate all of the consequences of exposure, and anonymising some people and not others may be impossible (once one person is identified, it may be possible to work out from this who are the people whose names have been anonymised). Even aside from this, anonymisation will not always offer much protection. For example, in the case of life history or biographical research, or where a very distinctive organisation or community is being studied, the identity of the people involved may be difficult to disguise.

There are also privacy issues about the storage and preservation of data. It is common today for data to be anonymised soon after collection, and stored separately from any key that would allow real and false names to be linked. This is to avoid confidentiality being breached should any attempt be made to access the data, whether illegally or under legal injunction. The same issue arises in the context of archiving data. Today, it is a common requirement on the part of funders that data be lodged in an archive after the research has been completed, but here too measures must be taken to preserve anonymity and thereby confidentiality.

One of the areas where concern over privacy has led to considerable debate is online research. Some argue that anything available via the Internet that is accessible without payment and is not password protected (and even some that is) should be deemed public, thus potentially including blogs and tweets, social media posts, discussions in forums, photographs and videos. By contrast, others insist that the restrictions which apply to any research with human participants offline should be applied online, that it should not be assumed that just because material is accessible that it is public in the sense of being usable for research purposes without obtaining permission.

A related issue here is copyright. This is not usually applied to what people say as part of their ordinary activities (which may be recorded by a researcher), or to what they say in interviews or write on questionnaires. However, the producers of some of what is available online may see themselves as creative writers and claim copyright for what they have produced. For this reason too it may be argued that permission to quote it for research purposes is required.

While there can be disagreements about what is public and what is private, sensible judgements about what constitutes an invasion of privacy, and about when this is and is not legitimate for research purposes, must be made on a case-by-case basis. Furthermore, while it is important to take account of people's views about privacy, these should not trump all other considerations. Complaints about invasion of privacy can be mobilised for ulterior purposes, and on the other side people may sometimes underestimate the effects of making what previously had been private public. In this area, as in others, it is the researcher who must take primary responsibility for deciding what is and is not ethically acceptable.

Respecting autonomy

The final principle I will discuss is respecting autonomy or freedom. It is often argued that people should be in control of their lives, and the implication of this is that they must be free to decide whether or not to participate in a research project. This is what underpins the widely stated requirement that there should be informed consent on the part of research participants: they ought to know they are being researched, be fully informed about what this involves, and be able to withdraw at any time.

The idea that people should be able to make decisions for themselves and thereby exercise considerable control over their own lives is a widely accepted principle, and most researchers would adhere to it. At the same time, it is usually recognised that there must be limits to freedom, because one person's exercise of freedom may infringe another's, because this value may come into conflict with others, and because there are practical constraints on people's actions. There is also socio-cultural variation in the emphasis given to this value: it has been argued by critics of Western liberalism that it is at odds with obligations to the community, or with caring for others. All of this needs to be taken into account when applying this principle in the context of social and educational research.

The concept of informed consent also involves some more specific issues, whose significance varies across research methods. These centre on what it means for a person to be informed, and what it means for them to consent.

As regards the first of these issues, there may sometimes be doubt about the capacity of particular types of participant sufficiently to understand information about the research and/or to make judgements that are in their own best interests. Examples would include adults with some kinds of mental health problem or learning difficulty, or young children. In recent years it has increasingly been argued that every effort should be made to explain the research even to those falling into these categories, and that their consent should be obtained wherever possible, perhaps alongside that of relevant caregivers. This is sometimes formulated in terms of human rights or the rights of children (however, there are problems with the appeal to rights; see Hammersley, 2015a).

More generally however there are questions about what it would mean for *anyone* to be *fully* informed about a piece of research. Here, too, there may be issues about whether participants can gain an adequate understanding of what the research involves (e.g. where people have no knowledge of methodology or no familiarity with the particular kind of research to be carried out). Equally, people may not wish or be able to spend the time it would take to become fully informed.

There can also be problems in informing people that arise from uncertainty in the early stages of a research project about what the data collection will entail, and it will be impossible to anticipate with certainty what findings will result, and therefore what the costs of publishing them might be. Furthermore, there is always potential uncertainty about the possible benefits or risks of harm involved in research. It is therefore never possible to put a potential participant in the position of full and certain knowledge of the consequences of consenting to participate in a research project. This means that if participants are to be able to make sensible judgements they must tolerate uncertainty and assess probabilities. However, their capacity to do this will probably vary.

Turning to the issue of consent, there may be doubts about whether people are free to decide whether to participate (e.g. if they work in an organisation that has already agreed to the research going ahead). Of course, if an organisation has refused access, then its members have been prevented from making the decision to participate, in a way that is beyond the researcher's control. Similarly, in some communities leaders are treated as empowered to make decisions about contacts with outsiders, so that seeking individual consent may be seen as breaching the local cultural norms. Whether these norms should be respected is the ethical issue that arises here, but there is also a practical considera-tion: the researcher may not be granted access unless those norms are respected. People may also feel under pressure from peers to consent or refuse to consent. There are also problems surrounding what are legitimate and illegitimate forms of persua-sion on the part of the researcher. One focus here is on the use of payments to research participants, or rewards offered to them for participation.

Another issue is the means by which informed consent is secured. It is common for ethics commit-tees to require signed consent forms, but there are cultural contexts where seeking *written* consent is not possible or desirable. This is not just because people may be unable to read or write, but also because where verbal agreement is prevalent any demand for written consent would be regarded as insulting or suspicious.

The requirement to secure informed consent has different implications for different methods. In the case of questionnaire surveys or interviews, we should note that gaining consent is, to a large extent, an unavoidable practical requirement irre-spective of any commitment on the part of the researcher to respecting people's autonomy. If one asks people to fill in a questionnaire or take part in an interview, they are usually in a position to refuse: gaining their participation requires telling them at least something about the research. Furthermore, it is usually possible for people to withdraw from an interview or from filling in a questionnaire if they decide to. Of course, they may feel under an obli-gation to continue, so that here the principle of respecting their autonomy may require the researcher to emphasise that withdrawal is allowed. Equally, a researcher could gain their agreement by giving them a false impression about the research, so it is here, above all, that ethical considerations play a role in these kinds of research.

If we turn to the case of observational research, it should be clear that applying the requirement of informed consent is rather more complex, and open to greater challenge. In the case of public settings, it might reasonably be argued that con-sent to observe is not required, perhaps even that there is no need to inform people that research is taking place. However, as I noted earlier, there can be disagreement about what is and is not public, and this is true offline as well as online. For instance, is a privately owned shopping centre that is open to the public a setting in which research can be carried out without prior agreement? The owners may well believe that permission is neces-sary, and there could be legal regulations that require this to be secured. Even in public streets or parks, is it legitimate, say, to video or even photo-graph people, including children, without having secured their permission? Interestingly, media organisations frequently do this. Similar questions may be relevant as regards audio-recording in settings often deemed to be public. It seems less clear, though, that observing and taking notes would require informed consent.

With many settings the researcher will have to negotiate access, unless a covert strategy is to be employed (e.g. taking a job in a college or becoming a student there). The ethics of covert observation has been the focus of considerable dispute (see, for example, Bulmer, 1982), but problems concerning informed consent arise in observational research even when access is negotiated. The source of the problem here is that rather than the researcher dealing with each participant separately, as in administering a questionnaire or carrying out an interview, access to a setting is usually obtained through one or more gatekeepers (e.g. a head-teacher or college principal). Furthermore obtaining gatekeeper agreement is rarely the result of a democratic decision by all participants. And even if it were, could we assume that the minority who voted against had nevertheless consented?

Of course, having secured access to an organisation, it may be necessary to negotiate access to particular settings within it (e.g. to particular class-rooms) and this may be judged to be ethically required. However, often in each of these settings a number of people will be open to observation simultaneously: must they all consent to involve-ment in the research before it can go ahead? What if the headteacher, college principal, teacher or lecturer believes that it is within their authority to grant access? Should this be challenged? And what if some participants consent but others do not (if the research does not go ahead the preferences of those who gave consent will not have been respected)?. Further complications may be added in the case of schools, since it may be felt necessary to obtain parental consent, or the school may insist on this. Here the likelihood of explicit consent being obtained for all participants is reduced fur-ther. Similar problems are introduced by the right

of individual participants to withdraw their consent at any time, and to have all data relating to them expunged from the record.

There is also the problem that in some settings it is simply not possible to obtain individual consent from *all* participants because there is rapid turn-over in the population or because seeking consent from individuals would be highly disruptive. This problem often arises in online settings, but also in more conventional kinds of ethnographic research. For example, research concerned with young peo-ple's eating habits could involve observation in the various places where they have lunch, but these are likely to be busy places in which there is a continual flow of people. Gaining the informed consent of all who could be observed may not be practicable.

While researchers must make judgements about what is ethically necessary and practically possible, they will also have to take account of others' judge-ments about these matters, such as those of gate-keepers, with which they may disagree. This is another respect in which ethical and practical con-siderations are often balanced against one another.

Ethics in practice

Most social and educational researchers would probably agree that the three ethical principles I have discussed should be taken into account when doing their work, though there are other principles that could also have been mentioned, such as 'rec-iprocity', 'equity', and 'social justice'. But it needs to be reiterated that these principles cannot tell us what to do, or even what not to do, in particular situations. One reason for this is that they are sub-ject to different interpretations. Another is that they may conflict with one another in their implications, leading to significant dilemmas. For example, respecting people's autonomy can sometimes open them up to potential harm. Furthermore, as I indicated earlier, ethical issues to do with how we treat participants are only one of several sorts of consideration that researchers need to take into account in doing their work. And these others may conflict with ethical ones (e.g. commitment to what I referred to earlier as epistemic values, concerned with what is necessary to produce worthwhile findings, will sometimes be at odds with some interpretations of privacy).

Against this background, a general question we might ask is 'how ethically sensitive should we be as researchers'? Should we seek to avoid all harm, completely respect privacy, and try to ensure fully informed consent? Or is it possible to be too ethical, to give ethical matters too much weight? I suggest that the answer to this last question is 'yes'. On some interpretations of the ethical principles I have outlined, full adherence could result in little or no empirical research being practicable, or only a few types of research. Similar problems arise in other aspects of our lives. For example, when we do our shopping we may well have a commitment to fair trade, organic production methods, animal welfare, minimising carbon footprints, etc. But fully living up to these commitments would make it difficult for us even to meet our basic needs: much of the time we simply will not have the information necessary to make a decision that respects those commitments, and even when we have the information we may find that none of the products available meets the requirements. In the case of research ethics, my view is that we should certainly keep a close eye open for potentially important ethical issues, and try to avoid acting in ethically unacceptable ways. However, we must not exaggerate the degree to which educational research is ethically problematic.

Of course today's researchers not only need to come to their own judgements about what would be ethically acceptable, the rise of ethical regulation has meant that they must also persuade ethics committees that what they propose to do meets ethical requirements.

Ethical regulation and ethics committees

Most research proposals must now be submitted for approval to an ethics committee, whether located in a university or some other organisation that controls access to research funds or to data. There are questions about the legitimacy and wisdom of ethical regulation of this kind, and indeed about the capacity of ethics committees to evaluate research proposals soundly (Hammersley, 2009). However, here I will focus on issues surrounding how researchers should deal with ethics committees. My point is that this, in itself, involves both practical and ethical considerations.

A first question here is whether researchers should acknowledge the authority of these committees by submitting proposals to them, even if they believe that their effects are detrimental or that they interfere with the proper exercise of researcher responsibility. This is clearly a matter of principle, but it also raises questions of what we might call prudence. Failing to submit research proposals to an ethics committee may well result in funding not being obtained, or in sanctions being applied to the researcher by a university or other research organisation. These are outcomes that researchers would generally wish to avoid, and indeed that may make it impossible to do research.

For this reason at least, most researchers accept that they must usually submit their research proposals to a relevant ethics committee. But they are wise if they treat this committee with caution: not as an enemy but nor entirely as friendly. A wary attitude of cooperation is usually the best strategy. To a large extent what ethics committees wish to see is detailed information about how the research will be done, and clear indications that attention has been given to potential ethical issues and to how these will be dealt with. Given that much will not be known at the start of a research project, what is required here is a reasonable outline of what is likely to be involved, what ethical issues could arise, and how they might be handled: perhaps presented with a little more certainty than it warrants.

Ethics committees can provide valuable feedback on a research proposal, not least in highlighting issues that had not been recognised. Dealings with ethics committees may also stimulate more thought about alternative ways of carrying out the research. Such benefits should be capitalised upon, but the dangers and problems of dealing with ethics committees must also be recognised. It is often the case that they are more reluctant to give certain types of research the go-ahead than others – particularly those where it is difficult, or impossible, to obtained written, informed consent. Here, there may well be a clash between what the researcher believes to be necessary in epistemic terms, and the ethical requirements that an ethics committee lays down. Of course, the decisions of ethics committees are usually open to considerable negotiation, but time needs to be allowed for this. And there is often the potential for major obstacles to be put in the way of some research projects, perhaps even a complete roadblock.

Finally, it is necessary to emphasise that the fact that a research proposal has been approved by an ethics committee does not imply that, subsequently, a researcher no longer needs to be concerned with ethics issues. It is the responsibility of individual researchers, or research teams, to pursue their work in ways that are ethically acceptable, as judged by themselves.

Conclusion

In this chapter I have sought to provide an overview of the nature of research ethics, and of some of the principles and problems involved. I emphasised that while ethics is important, if we confine it to the issue of how researchers should deal with the people being studied, or from whom data are obtained, it is only one of several types of consideration that must inform the practical decisions that researchers make about what to investigate, what funding to rely on, what data to collect, how to analyse these, and how to report and disseminate the findings. I indicated that ethical principles are always open to interpretation and can conflict in their implications. Furthermore, researchers will take decisions in circumstances involving considerable uncertainty: all that can reasonably be expected is that they will make the best judgements they can. I illustrated how the nature of the ethical problems that researchers face vary across different types of

research, and are always affected by the particular circumstances in which the research is being carried out. Finally I examined the significance of ethical regulation, and some of the practical issues to which it gives rise for researchers.

Questions for further investigation

1. If you are currently planning, or engaged in, a piece of research, what are the most important ethical questions you face or anticipate? How have similar problems been dealt with by other researchers?
2. What sorts of harm can educational research cause? How would you assess their seriousness?
3. Is there anything so private that it should not be the focus, or serve as data, for educational research?
4. In what circumstances, if any, would it be legitimate to carry out research without gaining informed consent from the participants?
5. Are there any funding sources in your field from whom you would not accept support? If so, what are your grounds for this?
6. Is it ever justified to withhold relevant information from an ethics committee, a funder, a gatekeeper, people being observed or interviewed, or readers of a research report? If so, what would be the grounds for this?

Suggested further reading

Hammersley, M. and Traianou, A. (2012a) *Ethics in Qualitative Research: Controversies and Contexts*. London: Sage. While this book only covers qualitative research, it provides a detailed discussion of key ethical principles relevant to social research generally, examines dilemmas to which they can give rise, emphasises that they are not the only values relevant to research, and relates them to the practicalities of social inquiry.

Hammersley, M. and Traianou, A. (2012b) 'Ethics and Educational Research', available at www.bera.ac.uk/wp-content/uploads/2014/03/Ethics-and-Educational-Research.pdf?noredirect=1
This provides an overview of ethical principles and issues, and a guide to relevant literature.

Israel, M. (2015) *Research Ethics and Integrity for Social Scientists*, 2nd edn. London: Sage. This is an excellent introduction to research ethics, covering all forms of social research.

Macfarlane, B. (2009) *Researching with Integrity: The Ethics of Academic Enquiry*. London: Routledge. In this book Macfarlane develops an illuminating perspective on research by drawing on a particular form of philosophical thinking called virtue ethics.

References

Bulmer, M. (ed.) (1982) *Social Research Ethics: An Examination of the Merits of Covert Participant Observation*. London: Macmillan.

Flewitt, R. (2005) 'Conducting research with young children: some ethical considerations', *Early Child Development and Care*, 175(6): 553–65.

Hammersley, M. (2009) 'Against the ethicists: on the evils of ethical regulation', *International Journal of Social Research Methodology*, 12(3): 211–25.

Hammersley, M. (2015a) 'Research ethics and the concept of children's rights', *Children and Society*, 29(6): 569–82.

Hammersley, M. (2015b) 'On ethical principles for social research', *International Journal of Social Research Methodology*, 18(4): 433–49.

Hammersley, M. and Traianou, A. (2011) 'Moralism and research ethics: a Machiavellian perspective', *International Journal of Social Research Methodology*, 14(5): 379–90.

Hammersley, M. and Traianou, A. (2012a) *Ethics in Qualitative Research: Controversies and Contexts*. London: Sage.

Hammersley, M. and Traianou, A. (2012b) 'Ethics and Educational Research', available at www.bera.ac.uk/wp-content/uploads/2014/03/Ethics-and-Educational-Research.pdf?noredirect=1

Louden, R. (1992) *Morality and Moral Theory*. New York: Oxford University Press.

Nutbrown, C. (2011) 'Naked by the pool? Blurring the image? Ethical issues in the portrayal of young children in arts-based educational research', *Qualitative Inquiry*, 17(1): 3–14.

Part III

Research designs

Action research

Carol Munn-Giddings

8

What is action research?

Action research (AR) has a long history in education and community development and is becoming increasingly popular in a range of other disciplines including health, social care and business studies. Trying to get an agreed definition can be very frustrating for students as there are many, in large part due to the number of disciplines involved. However, if we look a little more closely at a number of abridged definitions we can see some common themes that will help us discern both its core characteristics and distinction in relation to other research approaches.

For example, Kurt Lewin (a psychologist) first described it as a way of generating knowledge about a social system while at the same time attempting to change it (Lewin, 1946). John Elliott (an educationalist) described it as 'the study of a social situation with a view to improving the quality of action within it … providing the necessary link between self evaluation and professional development' (1991: 69), while Ernest T. Stringer (in relation to community action research) defined it as 'an approach to research that potentially has both practical and theoretical outcomes … in ways that provide conditions for continuing action – the formation of a sense of community. It is … rigorously empirical and reflective and engages people who have traditionally been called "subjects" as active participants in the process …' (1996: xvi).

We can see from these definitions that action research is considered to be based in practice or a community and not separate from it – it is the antithesis of 'ivory tower' research. Rather than a 'technical' activity that is carried out by 'expert researchers', it is a form of research that can be undertaken by practitioners such as teachers, social workers and community development workers, as well as by students and service users.

A key feature of the above definitions, as the term suggests, is that the research is action not description orientated. This distinguishes AR from purely quantitative and qualitative approaches since the purpose of AR is to work towards practice change during the research process, not merely to explore and describe a situation 'as it is' (e.g. involving teachers and students or mental health service users in a process of change to their practice or community). This is why AR is claimed to bridge the theory–practice gap, as there is technically no problem in having to implement findings because the process is educative for all those involved and learning and change occur within the AR process.

Although AR studies can be carried out by a single teacher or community worker the research process generally aims to be collaborative. Sometimes the term 'co-researcher' is used to describe collaborators on the project. Some writers make a distinction between 'action research' and 'participatory action research' (PAR), where the former is primarily seen as being about practice change and not necessarily involving participants throughout the research process, whereas PAR aims towards broader social or systemic change and more consciously involves participants in each stage of the research process. Other authors, however, use these terms interchangeably, and Hart and Bond have set out a useful typology of types of AR in their 1995 text.

Many traditional models of research locate the researcher as 'outside' the situation being studied and looking in – almost as if they were peering down a microscope at the situation and actors. By contrast, in action research the researcher or action researchers are part of their context or a catalyst/facilitator with people facing the immediate situation. For example, in educational action research the context is most often the teacher-researcher's classroom or organisational setting. As Townsend (2012: 32) puts it ' … importantly, they are part of the situation they want to understand and change'. This is sometimes termed 'insider' research, defined as research led by those facing the situation or trying to develop their practice, as opposed to an external 'outside' research expert who does research 'on' other people's problems or practices. However, in many contexts (e.g. health, social care and community development) a model exists whereby social researchers will act as 'facilitators' in the action research process, bringing a knowledge of research methods to the enquiry process but working alongside people who have lived experience of the situation being enquired into. In this latter mode the role of the researcher is more like that of a catalyst and coordinator of projects (Winter and Munn-Giddings, 2001).

Inherent to the ethos of action research is that being an 'insider' brings both a unique and rich knowledge base to their research and a commitment to improve the practice they are involved in studying. However, the very thing that enriches action research – the insider knowledge of the practitioner doing the research – also holds some dangers, and prompts us to ask how does an experienced practitioner in education, social work, community development etc. 'look outside' a practice they have been involved with for (sometimes) many years, and unearth the assumptions they might inadvertently have also developed over that time and genuinely engage in learning about their practice? Here the importance of reflection and

reflexivity in the research process becomes particularly important.

Locating ourselves 'in' our research should be a key part of any research process. We do not enter a research project as a neutral vessel, rather we take with us our values, politics, gender, ethnicity etc. We also take our assumptions, categories, feelings and previous experiences. This is inevitable but it is important that we should reflect on and be transparent about the way this impacts on our research. Action research itself should be a form of learning for those involved – in educational settings teachers are researching with their students and/or colleagues about the processes and structures of learning in which they are jointly engaged. Critical self-questioning therefore becomes a particularly necessary part of the action research process (Cook, 2009).

As Winter and Munn-Giddings (2001) point out, a significant dimension of action research is its link with the concept of reflective practice (Schon, 1991), based on the continuous reflection required by the complexities and uncertainties of professional practice. Being reflexive takes the process deeper and asks us to examine our own assumptions and judgements about why we categorise and make sense of things the way we do. Townsend (2012: 50) describes it as a concept (not exclusive to research) that emphasises the social processes of meaning making … suggesting that it is critical we understand that similar experiences might be interpreted differently based on the differences in people's experiences and resulting preconceptions.

The above suggest that to be open and transparent about research processes it is important to find mechanisms for building in reflection and reflexivity at every stage of the research process. One way to note and later challenge assumptions is for the researcher(s) to note down in a project what they already think is known about the topic (from practice experience and existing literature) as well as expectations about the likely outcome of the project. Doing that exercise with a team of co-researchers can be particularly enlightening in terms of illuminating how people with the same interests might work together but how their perspectives on the situation might differ.

Enlisting a 'critical friend' – someone outside the research team who can give an alternative and sometimes constructively challenging perspective on the key issues in the data – is really helpful, and a 'check' against an AR team of researchers only seeing what they want to see in the findings. The inherent collaboration in action research helps to avoid this but there is space for an outsider to 'look in' (Kember et al., 1997; Bambino, 2002).

AR therefore does not fit neatly into academic debates about 'paradigms'. It shares some features with the interpretivist paradigm in that the value base of AR would always have a commitment to understanding the meanings that participants and groups in the research attach to events and situations (i.e. the way in which individuals and groups construct their world). Some might locate AR in what Ernest (1994) defines as the 'critical theoretic paradigm', which goes beyond finding out and understanding but is also concerned with the search for improvement in aspects of social life or social institutions. Heron and Reason (1997) suggest that all forms of participatory research (including AR) can be seen as fitting into a 'participatory paradigm' that is always concerned with a 'participative reality' co-created with others, such as knowing in conceptual terms that something is the case (propositional knowing) and the knowledge creation that comes with actually doing what you propose (practical knowing).

The above discussion suggests that AR is a developmental process and research questions in AR reflect this, for example:

- How can I improve the way I work with large groups of students?
- How do we create a culturally sensitive online forum?
- In what ways do postgraduate students become each other's critical friends and how can this process be developed?

Research design

Typically the AR process is one that continually alternates between enquiry and action. This is often conceived of and illustrated as a series of stages, spirals or cycles. For example, Zuber-Skerritt (1992) outlines four stages in an AR cycle: planning, acting, observing and reflecting. There may be many cycles in any one project. Unlike most other forms of research, data collected in one stage/cycle will inform the development of the next stage of the project (as illustrated in the example below), although (as with all forms of research) the process is never as neat and linear as a diagram may suggest. The most significant aspect to note is that an AR design is iterative by design and as such changes and develops over time in response to new insights from the data. As Townsend (2012: 104) notes, it is the willingness to work in this complex and uncertain way which provides the greatest potential for achieving significant change. Although AR is rooted in the improvement of a situation and therefore based on an ethic of care, this type of design can be challenging to some standard ethics committee processes which seek to ensure participants in a research process are clear from the outset about exactly what the research will involve (Gelling and Munn-Giddings, 2011).

Action researchers will use any methods that are relevant to their research question. It is very common therefore to use a mixed-method approach combining both quantitative and qualitative data. Because AR is based in or close to practice, often the existing practice materials/resources are incorporated into the research design as 'data' (e.g. minutes from meetings). A number of researchers use methods from the creative arts as part of their studies to collect data (e.g. dance, collage work and poetry).

When we are 'analysing' the data within an AR project, we are concerned with learning and implementing change rather than (as in most other forms of social research) description or with constructing an interpretation. So we need to think about the data in terms of new possibilities for action. In terms of design, the cyclical nature of AR requires analysis and reflections on data collected at each stage of the project to be used to inform the next stage and practical step in the research process.

It can be easier to understand these characteristics through a concrete example, so the following sections provide a synopsis of a cross-disciplinary project that involved academics, practitioners and managers in a workplace setting; the principles would readily translate into an education setting.

Example: Stress in the workplace

In the project a team from Anglia Ruskin University worked with two large-scale organisations that had shown an interest in attempting to address the negative consequences of stress in their workplaces. These organisations were a healthcare trust and a social services organisation in the United Kingdom (England). Workplace stress and burn-out are recognised phenomena which impact negatively on the delivery of care by health and social work organisations. In 2007/8 it was estimated that workplace stress, depression or anxiety in the UK resulted in the loss of 13.5 million working days (Health and Safety Executive, 2009). The aim of the project was to develop a bespoke mental well-being strategy in each of these workplaces, based on the concerns and ideas of the organisations' employees and senior managers. The research question was typically developmental in nature, and for both organisations was 'How do we best address staff stress in our organisation?'

The methodological approach

The project was based on a participatory action research (PAR) approach, since it involved a change or development during the research process and actively engaged stakeholders in the development of the project and in generating shared solutions to shared problems. The collaboration was two-fold within the project. The university project team (n=10) was multidisciplinary and included staff from various backgrounds including social work, mental health, health psychology, social policy and business, and ranged from senior lecturers to professors. As a team we worked as

facilitators with frontline practitioners and middle and senior managers in the two organisations, both of which were undergoing structural change (see Ramon and Hart, 2003).

Because of the hierarchical nature of the organisations, the lead researcher first had to negotiate access to staff members as well as agreeing on the overall purpose and format of the research. Ethics approval was gained via the university approval process. Once this stage was complete, in both organisations we recruited staff who had showed an interest in the project and would be prepared to actively contribute to five participatory workshops at fortnightly intervals, each lasting two and a half hours. These workshops were structured around some key exercises covering different aspects of stress; the methods included the use of small-group exercises and discussions related to presentations (by the university team plus invited speakers), vignettes and role play. The 'data' were the issues and discussion points that derived from these methods. At each workshop notes and flipcharts of the core issues were recorded, and the contents were written up as 'themes' and disseminated to group members before the next meeting. The subsequent workshop would begin with participants' observations or queries arising from the last session. On occasion participants were sometimes requested to do some work between sessions related to the issues being raised, for example writing examples from their work which highlighted relevant issues and strategies. Although each session had a pre-defined format and content, the university team responded to issues raised by participants during the workshop sessions and adjusted future sessions accordingly.

Alongside these workshops which yielded qualitative data, we undertook in both organisations an anonymous quantitative survey of all staff based on the Maslach Burnout Inventory (Maslach and Jackson, 1986) to ascertain the wider staff groups' views on stress at work.

As we saw earlier, it is the sequence of several phases of critical reflection within an AR project that carries forward its development (Winter and Munn-Giddings, 2001: 235) – that is, each stage of data analysis helps in the next practical step of the project. The data analysis techniques were similar to those used in some other types of projects. The qualitative data were analysed thematically (Aronson and Calsmith, 1990) to draw out the key issues. However, in contrast to some other methodologies in this project, the six workshops were used as building blocks and the analysis that was done after each workshop informed the debate in the subsequent workshop. Thus each session built towards finalising the data and suggestions that formed the final strategy document presented to senior managers. The results of the survey were analysed in the IBM® SPSS Statistics software (SPSS®) statistical package,[1] for both descriptive and inferential statistics, and these data were also included in the final well-being strategy document.

In AR, data analysis is a collaborative process of negotiation. In this example study, participants were agreeing the core themes on flipcharts at the end of each session. One of the university team took these interpretations, revisited the data collected in each session, and wrote these up for all involved. As above, these were revisited at the start of each session. At the end of the project the university team were involved in looking across the data from all six workshops and giving their overall interpretations, as well as making suggestions about the practical implications from the data. These were then taken back to be firmed up with the participants. In some action research studies participants in the situation are much more actively involved in that process. Ours was a pragmatic solution to working with organisations where staff time was limited.

The primary outcome of the study was an organisationally bespoke strategy document which contained staff perspectives on the core issues causing or aggravating mental distress at work and suggestions for short-/medium- and long-term actions to be carried out. These action areas also identified a process by which issues could be resolved and by whom. A secondary and unanticipated outcome emerged from the process which was to use the data to inform a returning-to-work support group together with a self-management pack primarily informed by the data collated during the project (see Backwith and Munn-Giddings, 2003).

For a reflective and more detailed account of the content, process and outcomes see Munn-Giddings et al. (2005).

Conclusion

AR is an ideal methodology for critical educationalists since its starting point is the core concerns of a community (geographical or professional) who seek to make positive changes based on the ideas, perspectives and solutions of the people whose lives will be most directly affected by the change. It is educational in the broadest terms as the research process integrally involves raising awareness about the issue in hand, and that knowledge is gained, developed and distilled not by an 'outsider' researcher but by the research team who will continue to work in the practice situation or community in the years to come. The history and practice of AR challenges assumptions about who can do research, how it might be undertaken and who decides its worth.

Whilst AR does not escape broader power dynamics both within research teams and in broader structures, it offers us a process that renders power differentials more transparent. Whilst being context specific, in keeping with broader qualitative traditions, it also offers the potential for other researchers to learn from the processes that are adopted as well as from the core findings and their applicability (or otherwise) in their own setting.

Questions for further investigation

1. One of the key advantages of action research is that the practitioner brings their practice knowledge to the research process – but how can we

(Continued)

(Continued)

ensure we challenge our own assumptions and genuinely hear the other 'voices' in our research?

2. If taking part in an AR study is a 'journey' and 'evolves', how can informed consent be meaningful and how often do we need to address it?

3. Can we really make meaningful 'changes' without addressing the structural issues that create and reinforce substantive inequalities?

4. In what way(s) can we hope to sustain change once an AR project is 'completed'?

Note

1. SPSS, Inc. was acquired by IBM in October 2009.

Suggested further reading

The project description I have provided above is illustrative of some key features of the action research approach. However, to get a feel for the range of approaches it is important to look at different examples of AR projects and design. A good starting point would be the specialist journals in the area such as *Educational Action Research, Action Research and Systemic Practice* and *Action Research*. It is also worth getting a feel of projects that involve singular or small groups of practitioners examining their practice (see for example Bana, 2010) and comparing this with projects that involve collaborations between different groups (see Bland and Atweh's [2007] account of students, teachers and university researchers working together). It is also useful to look at articles where collaborators work in different organisational settings – a particularly interesting and innovative example of a project sustained over many years that began as an educational curriculum project and developed into an action-based group in a hospital can be found in Jayne Crow et al.'s account

(2005, 2009). How to engage people in AR projects is an ongoing issue. Cotterell (2008) provides an interesting account of involving people with life-limiting conditions as co-researchers throughout the research process, focusing on the data analysis stage of the project. As mentioned earlier, some writers use the creative arts as part of their methodology; for students interested in this area see, for example, Burchell (2010), who uses poetic expression and form as part of her methodology. Finally, many of the AR textbooks provide very useful 'how-to' guides for those new to AR (as well as reminders for more experienced researchers!) – see Winter and Munn-Giddings (2001) in relation to projects in health and social care; Stringer (1996, 2014) in relation to community development; and McNiff (2010), Townsend (2012) and McAteer (2013) in relation to undertaking AR in educational settings.

References

Aronson, E. and Calsmith, J. (1990) *Methods of Research in Social Psychology*. New York: McGraw-Hill Education.

Backwith, D. and Munn-Giddings, C. (2003) 'Self-help/mutual aid in promoting mental health at work', *Journal of Mental Health Promotion*, 2(4): 14–25.

Bambino, D. (2002) 'Critical friends', *Redesigning Professional Development*, 59(6): 25–7.

Bana, Z. (2010) '"Great Conversation" for school improvement in disadvantageous rural contexts: a participatory case study', *Educational Action Research*, 18(2): 213–17.

Bland, D. and Atweh, B. (2007) 'Students as researchers: engaging student voices in PAR', *Educational Action Research*, 15(3): 337–49.

Burchell, H. (2010) 'Poetic expression and poetic form in practitioner research', *Educational Action Research*, 18(3): 389–400.

Cook, T. (2009) 'The importance of mess in action research', *Educational Action Research*, 17(2): 277–91.

Cotterell, P. (2008) 'Exploring the value of service user involvement in data analysis', *Educational Action Research*, 16(1): 5–17.

Crow, J., Smith, L. and Keenan, I. (2005) 'Journeying between the Education and Hospital Zones in a collaborative action research project', *Educational Action Research*, 14(2): 287–306.

Crow, J., Smith, L. and Keenan, I. (2009) 'Sustainability in an action research project: 5 years of a Dignity and Respect action group in a hospital setting', *Educational Action Research,* 15(1): 55–68.

Elliott, J. (1991) *Action Research for Educational Change.* Buckingham: Open University Press.

Ernest, P. (1994) *An Introduction to Research Methodology and Paradigms.* Educational Research Monograph Series. Exeter: University of Exeter.

Gelling, L. and Munn-Giddings, C. (2011) 'Ethical review of Action Research: the challenges for researchers and research ethics committees', *Research Ethics,* 7(3): 103–9.

Hart, E. and Bond, M. (1995) *Action Research for Health and Social Care.* Milton Keynes: Open University Press.

Health and Safety Executive (2009) *Health and Safety Statistics 2007/8 Labour Force Survey* [online]. Available at www.hse.gov.uk/statistics/overall/hssh0708.pdf (accessed 26 September 2016).

Heron, J. and Reason, P. (1997) 'A participative inquiry paradigm', *Qualitative Inquiry,* 3(3): 274–94.

Kember, D., Ha, T-S., Lam, B-H., Lee, A., Ng, S., Yan, L. and Yum, J.C.K. (1997) 'The diverse role of the critical friend in supporting educational action research projects', *Educational Action Research,* 5(3): 463–81.

Lewin, K. (1946) 'Action research and minority problems', *Journal of Social Issues,* 2(4): 34–46.

McAteer, M. (2013) *Action Research in Education.* London: Sage.

McNiff, J. (2010) *Action Research for Professional Development.* Dorset: September Books.

Maslach, C. and Jackson, S. (1986) *The Maslach Burnout Inventory.* Palo Alto, CA: Consulting Psychologists Press.

Munn-Giddings, C., Hart, C. and Ramon, S. (2005) 'A participatory approach to the promotion of wellbeing in the workplace: lessons from an empirical research', *International Review of Psychiatry,* 17(5): 409–17.

Ramon, S. and Hart, C. (2003) 'Promoting mental wellbeing in the workplace: a British case study', *International Journal of Mental Health Promotion,* 5: 37–44.

Roche, M. (2011) 'Creating a dialogical and critical classroom: reflection and action to improve practice', *Educational Action Research,* 19(3): 327–43.

Schon, D.A. (1991) *The Reflective Practitioner.* Aldershot: Ashgate.

Stringer, E.T. (1996) *Action Research: A Handbook for Practitioners.* Thousand Oaks, CA: Sage.

Stringer, E.T. (2014) *Action Research,* 4th edn. Thousand Oaks, CA: Sage.

Townsend, A. (2012) *Action Research: The Challenges of Understanding and Changing Practice.* Maidenhead: Open University Press/McGraw-Hill Education.

Winter, R. and Munn-Giddings, C. (2001) *A Handbook for Action Research in Health and Social Care.* London: Routledge.

Zuber-Skerritt, O. (1992) *Action Research in Higher Education: Examples and Reflections.* London: Kogan Page.

Naturalistic research

Rob Walker

9

Naturalistic enquiry

The immediate appeal of naturalistic methods to many is that they appear to be non-technical and even just an extension of the research practices of everyday life. Unlike many other approaches, naturalistic research (by its very name) seems readily accessible and available without special equipment or facilities. Anyone can do it, anywhere and at any-time. Primarily based on participant observation and informal interviewing, naturalistic methods extend practices that appear to require little training and no specialised resources. The forms of writing and analysis used (descriptive, narrative, interpretive) are familiar and much like those we encounter day to day in other aspects of our lives. Naturalistic methods appear based on common sense and report their explorations of the social world in forms that avoid esoteric concepts, speaking directly to those who Jean Lave, with an ironic sideways glance at conventional social science, calls jpfs ('just plain folks') (Lave, 1988).

But all is not what it seems. Observation of social settings turns out to be a conceptually complex process; interviewing is not quite the same as conversation (and conversation itself is more problematic and less transparent than we might think). And description too is more problematic than first impressions might suggest. What we take to be 'natural' when we start out, quickly trips us up once we begin using its methods for research. And these effects are amplified by the kinds of recording technology we now have to hand, the smartphones we now have constantly within reach and switched on ready to go, near instant access to a wide array of digital publishing software, audiences that include our peers but also extend well beyond academic circles. Small wonder that a disproportionate amount of the research literature is devoted to problematic issues of methodology, problematic social relationships within organisations and research ethics.

A brief history

Naturalistic methods have a long history and can be said to have their social science origins in the classic Victorian studies of urban London, Manchester and Middlesborough (Booth, Mayhew, Engels, Bell). In their modern form they derive primarily from the work of the Chicago School (Adelman, 2010; Norris and Walker, 2005). The Chicago School was a collection of social scientists, including criminologists, geographers, city planners and journalists, who combined their efforts to study the rapidly growing city in the 1920s, work that has continued up until the present. From a university campus based within the city, the Chicago School social scientists sought to understand the dramatic social changes they saw around them in the urban environment: changes in land use, in populations, in urban culture, and in the emergence of new occupations, economies and professions. The geographers introduced to social science ideas from ecology, and in particular they adapted the idea of 'succession' (in plant communities) to changes in land use, population dynamics, and occupation – an idea that is current today, as patterns of urban land use and occupation continue to change at great speed in cities around the world (see, for example, the remarkable resources *Growing Up in Cities* and *Gapminder*).

The Chicago sociologists and criminologists also focused on studying occupations and careers, both formal and informal, as these could be traced through changing social landscapes – studies of white-collar crime, of street life and the emergence of gangs. In doing this work they were not restricted to desk research but took to the field. 'Fieldwork' became central to their methods, and in reporting it they were drawn to the methods of journalism and documentary reporting, and – though less often acknowledged – photography, oral history, soundscapes and film.

In education, key works of the School include an evocative study of public school teaching (Waller, 1932), which remains a classic in the field of research on teaching. In the 1950s Howard Becker introduced the idea of 'horizontal mobility' in the careers of teachers (Becker, 1952), identifying the ways in which teachers would move 'sideways' in the career structure to take jobs in better schools. He also studied the occupations and 'careers' of university students, particularly medical students (Becker et al., 1961), and of jazz musicians (Becker and Faulkner, 2009). In the 1960s, Philip Jackson, a Chicago psychologist, made an influential 'naturalistic' study of school classrooms (Jackson, 1968). Interested by the emerging field of ethology, and the work of field biologists who devoted long hours (and days, months and years) to observing primates in the wild, Jackson began observing in elementary classrooms, watching and waiting for events to occur. His research was based on long periods of immersion in elementary school classrooms, in which he reflected on the occupations, actions and behaviour of both teachers and students.

Aside from the detailed attention they paid to the observation of behaviour in a particular social environment, a key aspect of the methods used in these studies is that the personal experiences and life stories of the researcher become incorporated into the studies. In naturalistic research, the researcher does not stand apart from data collection but is intimately involved in it, and in many cases the questions they choose to pursue derive from personal experience. Objectivity is hard won rather than embedded in procedures. Willard Waller drew heavily on his family experiences (his father was a teacher and school superintendent), Howard Becker's studies of jazz musicians are strongly connected to his own practice as a musician, and Philip Jackson later became Director of the University of Chicago Laboratory School, founded by John Dewey.

The work of the Chicago School inspired a move among educational researchers to extend the use of qualitative methods in educational research, a field traditionally limited to measurement. From the 1960s researchers became seriously interested in the long-term participant observation of schools, classrooms and other educational settings. In the UK, the pioneering studies of Lacey (1970) and Hargreaves (1967) were followed by a succession of PhD studies (notably Stephen Ball at Sussex, David Hamilton, Sara Delamont, Paul Atkinson and Michael Stubbs at Edinburgh, and Martyn Hammersley at Leeds). From a starting point in sociology, and using methods partially derived from ethnography, influences from elsewhere were adapted – from sociolinguistics, from ethnomethodology, and from history. In turn this was succeeded by more strongly critical influences from participatory action research (Carr and Kemmis, 1986) and feminist theory (Davies, 1993; Kenway and Bullen, 2001).

In the USA the pioneering work of Roger Barker at the University of Kansas, in which he set out to study the ecology of children's lives in the rural town of 'Midwest', influenced a generation of classroom research (Jacob Kounin, Bruce Biddle, Paul Gump and Louis Smith, among others). This led into a different strand of work, some still avowedly ethnographic (the Spindlers and their many students and collaborators), some influenced by a strong interest from educational evaluators (in particular Robert Stake), others moving more to measurement and the use of emerging video technologies, though it was some time before video became mobile and flexible enough for it to become 'naturalistic' (for example in the work of Ricki Goldman)

The consequence of these developments for naturalistic enquiry as a social science research approach is that it can no longer be reduced to a simple collection of readily available methods, but needs to engage with social theory; otherwise it becomes vulnerable to the critique of empiricism, the very point from which it first developed.

Issues in naturalistic enquiry

Participatory research

Naturalistic enquiry is often the design of choice for those working in participatory projects. Because the methods are immediately available this means that 'plain folks' can quickly engage with research – collecting data, analysing these, and incorporating them into their projects. They can also bring to bear specialised skills and knowledge that may be beyond the researcher. There are however some dangers in this, since commitments and bias are never far from the stage. Using naturalistic methods requires paying constant attention to self-reflection, self-critique and concurrent active reading to keep the study intellectually mobile and sharp. The location of the research process within groups can be invaluable in keeping the research honest.

Training

Getting started with naturalistic enquiry requires no specialised training, but doing it well requires a level of awareness, a capacity for self-reflection, a range of experience, and a facility with the written word. Frequent problems involve issues of fieldwork ethics, conducting effective interviews, accumulating excessive data and rushing to closure. The problems are less technical than ethical and interpretive, and require critical reflection on

experience rather than skill training. But beyond the technical, naturalistic methods draw on more of the person, and so the background experience of the researcher becomes an important, if not always visible, resource. To give a recent example, Sherry Turkle's recent book on the ways in which digital technologies have changed people's lives might seem descriptive, even at times journalistic, but this is misleading. Her interviews, editing, interpretation and writing are deeply informed at every point by her many years studying the subject, her work as an academic at MIT, and her training in psycho-analysis.

Design

Naturalistic methods do not fit well with rational design. Critical variables are discovered rather than preordinately determined. Interpretation is emergent rather than driven by extant substantive theory. What they do well is identify unforeseen outcomes in specified contexts and uncover hidden influences in particular settings. They resist generalisation and reduction to simple causes and effects. Somewhat perversely in the eyes of some, their value is that they tend to make interpretation more complicated and decision making more difficult.

Ethics

Naturalistic studies often run into difficulties negotiating their way through institutional ethics procedures. The field relationships that are central to the approach, the lack of specificity of outcome measures, the demands on participants in terms of time, all invite scepticism at best, and more often rejection. In some settings, for example in health research and in work with children, many previous studies are no longer replicable. On the other hand, new areas of study have opened up, in studying new areas of social change and new cultural forms, for instance in the new media and digital cultures, in areas of crisis (of which they are many) and in areas of social life where new forms seem to be emerging, in families, in the workplace, in youth cultures and in the media. It is perhaps characteristic of naturalistic research that it is to be found early in the life of new social phenomena where there is a press to understand rather than measure.

Case studies

The predominant form of reporting naturalistic studies is that of the case study, though this is not always the case. Philip Jackson's studies of classrooms are, for instance, reported in a style more like that of the ethnographic monograph, predominantly analytic but well illustrated with telling examples. Meanwhile, 'Case study' has developed new forms, and a discipline and a literature of its own, in particular in the work of Robert Stake. For Stake the case is not illustrative but exemplary. It provides ground for the reader to engage in 'vicarious experience' and in developing their capacity for understanding ('vehrstehen' in the classical sense). It is less about being told than about developing the sympathetic understanding and critical capabilities of the reader.

Methods of naturalistic enquiry

In terms of methods, naturalistic enquiry can be seen as a subset of qualitative research. It differs from other qualitative methods in that it relies more heavily on the social and interpretive skills of the human observer and on vernacular methods of enquiry. These include the analysis of found documents, reported conversations, descriptions of events, locations and the actions of individuals, all often linked by narrative. In this it is less empiricist than some other qualitative methods (for example, the use of Computer-Assisted Qualitative Data Analysis (CAQDAS) in analysing transcripts), more reliant on the interpretive work of the researcher, and at least at first sight, less driven by theory.

There is however another aspect (and another significant source of appeal) in naturalistic research, which is that it invites the researcher to engage in personal expression. Fieldwork especially requires

the researcher to immerse themself in the lives and cultures of others. It is not just external, but also internal in its reach and in its discipline. It is this aspect that creates nervousness among many other researchers, for it invites accusations of bias, of self-indulgence, of self-delusion, and of 'going native'. There is clearly truth in this, and while there are techniques for maintaining distance, for remaining critical and for seeing multiple perspectives, the risk remains. Most of us, at one time or another, have found ourselves straying over the line. But despite the risks, we also recognise that this is a form of research which gives access to ways of thinking about social life that cannot be gained in other ways.

Classic and exemplary cases

Naturalistic studies are not bound by disciplines, topics or fields of study. At one edge they shade into documentary (in film, radio and television), at another into journalism and literature. Each reader will have a list of favourite studies. My own list would include Robert Coles' books about the migrant experience in the United States, beginning with *The South Goes North*, which chronicles the lives of African-Americans moving to northern cities in the 1950s and 1960s; Thomas and Znaniecki's earlier account of migration recorded in the letters written home by Polish migrants to Chicago; the close documentation of the Sanchez family in Mexico recorded by Oscar Lewis; John Dollard's *Caste and Class in a Southern Town*; and the wider tradition of community studies which described life in towns and villages in the USA and UK. (Ronald Frankenberg's book *Communities in Britain* provides a useful introduction to the UK studies.)

Many of these projects were lifetime obsessions for their authors, and for some their families and colleagues too. The Lynds' *Middletown* books, Roger and Louise Barker's long-time immersion in life in the small town of Midwest in Kansas, and also their time in Leyburn in North Yorkshire, the thousands of hours Philip Jackson sat in elementary school classrooms, the photo archives of Milton Rogovin in which David Isay worked with him to photograph 20 families over four decades, the 7000 tapes in the audio libraries of Studs Terkel, the street cries recorded by Mayhew in Victorian London. The list could go on (and does).

Is there a future for naturalistic research?

Naturalistic approaches may seem to have run their course. The methods of observation, conversation and descriptive reporting remain, but we live in new worlds where the boundaries between the real and the surreal, objectivity and subjectivity, the present and the future, action and reflection, analysis and synthesis, writers and readers, landscapes and screenscapes are all unclear and constantly changing. The conceptual separations between self and society – events, actions and contexts that made naturalistic research possible – are (or seem) more fluid than we once imagined.

Exemplary cases remain and can be found across disciplines and diverse fields of study. What has stayed mostly unexplored is the potential of digital technologies in relation to naturalistic methods. I have made attempts to create digital archives which are based around case studies of schools (Walker and Lewis, 1998). These are based on the premise that the (creative and interpretive) act of writing a case study can be separated from the intensive act of data collection. By assembling multimedia resources that are large collections of information, the audience can then be placed in an environment where they can produce their own case studies. This was an idea first proposed by Lawrence Stenhouse before digital methods became available but now can be explored in new ways (Stenhouse, 1978; Walker, 2002). The promise of these approaches is that they can provide a way of synthesising classical naturalistic methods with statistical data (especially local area census data) and with document collections and archives. The approach is demanding on the reader (who must become less a passive recipient and more an active reader–researcher–writer), but does provide a way to reconceptualise naturalistic research in response to its critics.

Questions for further investigation

1. There is no better way to start than by keeping a journal, and a good way to start that journal is by taking one object, incident or event each day and taking 30 minutes to write about it. Over a period of time the journal becomes less a way to write and more a source to read, and it is in this reflective space that enquiry begins.
2. Try describing from memory a setting you know well. Part of the route home from work, your workplace, the notes and messages on the fridge door at home. Observe the site and return to your notes, amending these where you can. Repeat the process. See how your memory and perception change with repetition.
3. Recall a recent conversation. Write down as much of it as you can remember. Show your account to the person or people involved. See if their recall is the same as yours and note where it is different. Try and recall not just what was said, but also intonation and phrasing, emphasis and gestures.

Suggested further reading

Cambridge Evaluation Conferences (n.d.) Available at http://groups.tlrp.org/access/content/group/e0 462675-d837-46dd-00b5-403deb2957b7/EdEval_2.0/edeval_2.0.html. This series of conferences brought together educational researchers, evaluators and policy people from the USA and UK over a thirty-year period from the early 1970s. Robert Stake, mentioned above, was a key contributor. As part of an ESRC TEL Project, this recently developed online resource has archived some of the key naturalistic case studies associated with the conference group, many of which are unpublished or difficult to obtain through libraries.

Greene, J.C. (2004) 'Memories of a novice, learning from a master', *American Journal of Evaluation,* 29: 322. (The online version of this article can be found at http://aje.sagepub.com/content/29/3/322.citation.) By way of an obituary for Egon Guba, one of the leading advocates of naturalistic enquiry in evaluation, this short personal account describes the development of qualitative methods in educational evaluation in the USA.

Stake, R. (n.d.) *University of Illinois, Course EDPSY 490E Case Study Methods.* Available at www.ed.uiuc.edu/circe/ EDPSY490E/Index.html. Robert Stake is perhaps the single most significant figure in naturalistic methods in educational research, especially in his advocacy of 'case study'. His book, *The Art of Case Study* (Sage, 1995) is a key text. This outline of his course (which he has taught for many years at the University of Illinois) reveals something of his intellectual style – concise, principled, yet (somewhat paradoxically) terse to the point of enigmatic. There is a useful reading list, a description of the tasks set for students, and an insistence on studying the particular and individual case rather than attempting to generalise from observations.

Bibliography

Adelman, C. (2010) 'The Chicago School', in A.J. Mills (eds), *Encyclopedia of Case Study,* Vol. I. Thousand Oaks, CA: Sage, pp. 140–4.

Barker, R.G. (1968) *Ecological Psychology: Concepts and Methods for Studying the Environment of Human Behaviour.* Stanford, CA: Stanford University Press.

Becker, H.S. (1952) 'The career of the Chicago public schoolteacher', *American Journal of Sociology,* 57 (5): 470–7.

Becker, H.S. and Faulkner, R.R. (2009) *Do You Know …? The Jazz Repertoire in Action.* Chicago: University of Chicago Press.

Becker, H.S., with Geer, B., Hughes, E.C. and Strauss, A. (1961) *Boys in White: Student Culture in Medical School.* Chicago: University of Chicago Press.

Bell, Lady (1907) *At the Works: A Study of a Manufacturing Town.* London: Edward Arnold. See also https://archive.org/details/atworksstudyofma 00belluoft

Biddle, B.J. (1979) *Role Theory: Expectations, Identities and Behaviours.* New York: Academic Press.

Booth, C. (undated) http://booth.lse.ac.uk/static/a/7.html (last accessed 20 July 2016).

Carr, W. and Kemmis, S. (1986) *Becoming Critical: Education, Knowledge and Action Research.* Geelong: Deakin University Press.

Coles, R. (1973) *The South Goes North (Children of Crisis).* New York: Little Brown & Co.

Davies, B. (1993) *Shards of Glass.* New York: Hampton.

Dollard, J. (1937) *Caste and Class in a Southern Town.* New Haven: Yale University Press.

Engels, F. (1845) *The Condition of the Working Class in England.* Leipzig: Otto Wiegand.

Frankenberg, R. (1969) *Communities in Britain: Social Life in Town and Country.* Harmondsworth: Pelican.

Gapminder (n.d.) www.gapminder.org (last accessed 20 July 2016).

Goldman, R. et al. (2007) *Video Research in the Learning Sciences.* Mahwah, NJ: Lawrence Erlbaum.

Growing Up in Cities (n.d.) www.unesco.org/most/guic/guicmain.htm (last accessed 20 July 2016).

Gump, P. (1967) *The Classroom Behaviour Setting, its Nature, and Relation to Student Behaviour.* Oskaloosa, Kansas: Research Report from the Midwest Field Station.

Hargreaves, D. (1967) *Social Relations in a Secondary School.* London: Routledge & Kegan Paul.

Jackson, P.W. (1968) *Life in Classrooms.* New York: Holt, Rinehart & Winston.

Kenway, J. and Bullen, E. (2001) *Consuming Children: Entertainment, Advertising and Education.* Milton Keynes: Open University Press.

Kounin, J. (1970) *Discipline and Group Management in Classrooms.* New York: Holt, Rinehart & Winston.

Lacey, C. (1970) *Hightown Grammar.* Manchester: Manchester University Press.

Lave, J. (1988) *Cognition in Practice.* Cambridge: Cambridge University Press.

Lewis, O. (1961) *The Children of Sanchez: Autobiography of a Mexican Family.* New York: Vintage.

Lynd, R.S. and Lynd, H.M. (n.d) The Ball State University, Centre for Middletown Studies. http://cms.bsu.edu/academics/centersandinstitutes/middletown/ (last accessed 20 July 2016).

Norris, N. and Walker, R. (2005) 'Naturalistic enquiry', in B. Somekh and C. Lewin (eds), *Research Methods in the Social Sciences.* London: Sage, pp. 131–7.

Plowden, B. (1967) *Children and their Primary Schools* (The Plowden Report). London: HMSO.

Rogovin, M. (1972–2002) *Photo Series: Lower West Side Quartets*, available at www.miltonrogovin.com.

Smith, L.M. (1968) *Complexities of an Urban Classroom*. New York: Holt, Rinehart & Winston.

Spindler, G. (2006) *Innovations in Educational Ethnography: Theory, Methods and Results*. Mahwah, NJ: Lawrence Erlbaum.

Stenhouse, L.S. (1978) 'Case study and case records: towards a contemporary history of education', *British Educational Research Journal,* 4(2): 21–39.

Terkel, S. (n.d.) [Terkel donated his extensive audio collection to the Chicago History Museum.] www.lib guides.chicagohistory.org (last accessed 19 July 2016).

Terkle, S. (2013) *Alone Together: Why We Expect More From Technology and Less From Each Other*. New York: Basic.

Terkle, S. (2015) *Reclaiming Conversation: The Power of Talk in the Digital Age*. New York: Penguin.

Thomas, W.I. and Znaniecki. F. (1958) *The Polish Peasant in Europe and America,* 2 vols. Mineola, NY: Dover.

Walker, R. (2002) 'Case study, case records and multimedia', *Cambridge Journal of Education,* 32(1): 109–27.

Walker, R. and Lewis, R. (1998) 'Media Convergence and Social Research: The Hathaway Project', in J. Prosser (ed.), *Image-based Research*. London: Falmer.

Waller, W. (1932) *Sociology of Teaching*. New York: Wiley.

Ethnographic research

Ghazala Bhatti

10

Definition and brief history

Ethnography has a long history which can be traced back to the late nineteenth and early twentieth century. It has its roots in anthropology, which involved travelling to distant places to collect insiders' accounts of what were then colonial outposts (Gobo, 2011). From the 1930s onwards, sociologists at the University of Chicago employed methodologies which were exploratory both conceptually and empirically, leading to innovative ways of representing the realities of people living in communities which were not located in faraway and distant places. Instead, these could be found much closer to home and sometimes round the corner (Whyte, 1993). The work of the Chicago School captures aspects of society which were both vaguely familiar and yet unfamiliar in the society where they were embedded. These lived realities, represented from the point of view of the research participants, provided a description of what was happening at the time, while implicitly or explicitly also highlighting the existence of inequality and marginality in society. Both social anthropologists and sociologists have used ethnography to advance a deeper understanding of social norms. These disciplines have influenced the choice of theory and analytical frameworks used by researchers. The content and conduct of ethnographic research are contested. Epistemological questions have been raised about the relationship between discourse analysis and ethnography, and whether ethnography should have a political and practical intent (see Hammersley, 2006). Ethnography has been used by researchers with an interest in history (Skinner, 2012), geography (Raaflaub and Talbert, 2012), politics (Schatz, 2009), science (Barton, 2001) and other subjects to study a broad spectrum of subjectivities, structures, spaces and places. Ethnographers have studied organisations such as the police (Katz, 2003), medical matters (e.g. nursing, Cruz and Higginbottom, 2013), cancer management (LeBaron et al., 2014), total institutions (Fine and Martin, 1995), and of course education (Mills and Morton, 2013). There are many 'ethnographic turns', such as critical ethnography (Foley, 2002; Heller, 2011), autoethnography (Muncey, 2010), online ethnography (Gatson, 2011), and performance ethnography (Hamera, 2011). This chapter is a brief introduction to some ideas about using ethnography as a tool and as a methodology for researching everyday reality.

Ethnography has made a significant contribution to our understanding of participants' worlds, their cultures and sub-cultures, by offering in-depth insider accounts which cannot be gathered hurriedly. Ethnography demands a sustained investment of interest and commitment over time. It has gained in popularity among researchers who have studied naturally occurring phenomena in naturalistic settings. Ethnography cannot happen in an artificial and contrived environment, nor will it work as an experiment specially set up to investigate a hypothetical situation. The very process of an ethnographic enquiry can uncover artifice and name it for what it is by describing what the 'norm' is in a given setting. This is because ethnographic research is created through a researcher's immersion in the field, which is dependent on building and maintaining trusting relationships with research participants. The ethnographic gaze seeks to capture the reality as experienced by the participants.

Ethnographic research has enriched our understanding of how individuals and groups behave in different settings; how they make sense of their lives, what choices they make, and how they present themselves. An ethnographer is an observer of people and events as they unfold. What might have seemed simplistic, hazy or inexplicable at first sight, becomes complex and multi-layered during detailed observations, interviews and data analysis. A slice of everyday life is imbued with a multitude of meanings. An accurate representation of this complex and messy reality can become quite challenging. The ethnographer must seek out significant strands which are enmeshed in the data and can be teased out to represent this unfolding reality. The researcher's encounter with finer details which field notes and other forms of recording capture must be analysed so they might be shared more widely. Ethnographers have to work creatively with reflexivity. Some ethnographers have used symbolic interactionism which means trying to access how people define and understand the situation they are in and how they behave in those situations (Woods, 1992). Ethnography relies heavily on the researcher's interaction with and commitment to the field of enquiry, so that the researcher becomes, as far as possible, a part of the world they are trying to study. Ethnography seeks to represent the realities of participants in a way that the participants would recognise to be true. However, the analysis which the ethnographer presents may not echo the subjective realities of each individual participant, but instead create a composite picture of the whole scene in which individual participants play a part. The final text is a combination of many perspectives. Ethnographic research is built on a systematic enquiry which captures high and low

moments, harmony as well as discord, and contradictions revealed in the tales from the field (Van Maanen, 1988). A criticism that has been levelled against ethnography is that of researcher bias (Hammersley, 1992). Can we trust a lone researcher? Ethnographers address this by describing in detail how the data were collected and analysed, and what role they adopted in the field, how they presented themselves, and how they think others perceived them. They may be assigned a role or they may adopt one which is convenient and acceptable to those around them. This in turn is connected to the power they may or may not have. The data can be affected by many factors, including who introduced them to the research setting. In the case of a school, for example, was it the head teacher or a newly qualified teacher on a temporary contract? The quality of interactions with those in different hierarchical positions will affect the data, as will a combination of the researcher's personal attributes and overall reach and capacity for data capture. It is impossible to predict in advance exactly what an ethnographer will discover.

Methodologically, ethnographic research can take different turns. It does not have a fixed and inflexible parameter. Those new to ethnography might like to consider some basic questions, such as:

1. *Is the ethnography meant to be an exploration?* For example, what is it like to be an orphaned 10-year-old and in care? What do these children feel? What do their carers think? What if the child is a refugee? What do social workers who organise placements think about this? What happens when things go wrong? Whose responsibility are these children – social services, teachers or the children's relatives?

2. *Is it a piece of research about a situation/ phenomenon?* For example, how does an organisation make senior staff redundant? What processes are put in place? How do people positioned at different levels of seniority act? Is the union effective in overturning decisions and negotiations? Does it matter if this happens in a car factory, hospital, bank or a university? How does the organisation protect its reputation?

3. *Is the ethnography about investigating the impact of policy on practice?* For example, will more young people from poor backgrounds in England apply to study in a particular university if the current annual fee is doubled in 2021? How will young people feel and act? What do their parents think? Who will lose out and who will win? Does it matter if higher education is 'rationed' – to borrow a term from Gillborn and Youdell (2000)?

The research design adopted in any of the above cases would be directly connected to the research focus, as well as the time, funding and resources available for that research. If the same ethnographer were to conduct all of the above studies one after another – for they cannot all be conducted simultaneously – they are bound to write a different kind of ethnography each time, depending on what actually happens in the field. The outcome of ethnographic research is a combination of what is accessible, what is discovered, and how the researcher presents the findings. Ethnography must be composed of 'thick descriptions' (Geertz, 1973) contextualising both behaviour and the values implicit in the behaviour. If something does not seem to make sense ethnographers will quite often check their understanding or misunderstanding of a situation with participants. The values a researcher brings to the field will influence the final text and how it is documented. Sometimes these values are implicit in the text and at others researchers will openly declare their standpoint.

Research question and paradigmatic location

Ethnographers will usually begin with an open-ended question and try to explore what is happening in the field. It is not uncommon for researchers to start with one set of questions but to then end up describing a different set of findings which have a tenuous connection with the researchers' original starting point. Ethnography is unpredictable. An example here is Burgess's (1987) story of a casual meeting with a headmaster that led to fifteen years

of productive research. What actually happens in the field influences the final focus of the research and the way in which it is written and presented.

One of the guiding principles for researching and writing ethnography is to make the 'familiar strange'. This is not as easy as it sounds. If a researcher takes everything at face value or for granted then many novel insights will be lost. Researching a familiar situation in an unfamiliar place poses its own challenges. Parman summarised Spindler's assertion as:

> Each setting imposes its own anthropological dilemma: first how to observe situations so familiar that it is almost impossible to extract oneself from one's own cultural assumptions and be objective; the second, how to observe situations so different from what one is used to that one responds only to differentness. (cited in Delamont, 2012: 7–8)

This 'familiarity problem' (Delamont, 2012: 8) is something all ethnographers must learn to manage. This view has been expressed by many ethnographers in reflexive accounts of their research journeys.

For researchers who are interested in conducting ethnographic research, some questions worth considering might include:

1. What am I going to study?
2. How strongly should I define a clear focus from the outset?
3. How will I choose a site for my study?
4. Who will help me gain access to people/places/documentary evidence?
5. Why am I studying these people/places/phenomena at this particular moment?
6. Will I be able to choose a sample of participants?
7. What are my main ethical concerns?
8. How will I ensure that I do justice to different/conflicting points of views?
9. How will I manage role conflicts and different expectations during and after the research?
10. Whose side am I on and does it matter? (Becker, 1967)
11. How and when will I leave the field?

Becoming an ethnographer

At the outset research can be an unsettling experience. A researcher may not be in a position of control and must be prepared to work with whatever is open to negotiation. What a new researcher or their more experienced supervisor/tutor may encounter in the same organisation might be qualitatively different, though equally valid, provided due care is taken in ethical and methodological terms. Access is the principal key to good ethnography, and yet all ethnographers will admit that it can be problematic. For example, access may be gained to a particular institution but not to everyone or everything within that institution. Access may be granted on conditions that are not explained clearly to the researcher at the start but are patently obvious to everyone else. For example, staff meetings or governing body meetings at a school might not encourage a researcher's presence, whereas another school might expect and welcome the same researcher at such events. In either case, investigating *why* is bound to produce unexpected answers about the hidden curriculum. Exploring w*hy* and *how* events unfold the way they normally do can shed light on where power and privileged knowledge are situated. Ethnographers can locate and some have lucidly described the presence or absence of transparency, democratic processes and accountability at work. In the field things are seldom as they appear. An ethnographer can be relied upon to step back stage, work unobtrusively and sensitively, and decode what is happening, describe competing interests, and offer as even-handed and fair an interpretation as possible under the given circumstances. The findings are mostly described within the context of the limitations encountered.

Role conflict and ethical dilemmas

Most importantly, the main tool or instrument of data collection is the researcher's own self (Eisner, 1991). A successful ethnographer is one who is self-aware and reflexive, someone who has the capacity for both empathy and distance, honesty and discretion. The need to nurture these

simultaneously brings its own set of contradictions and conflicts which may be written up in field notes, but which the ethnographer is not able to share with the researched at the time. Unguarded comments can mean expulsion from the research site – so what should one do? Field notes and field diaries become very important and act as safety valves at difficult times. Ethnographers have acknowledged the inevitable tension entailed in being insiders and outsiders simultaneously (Hammersley and Atkinson, 1983). They have to learn to hold these contradictions together for the duration of the research. Ethnographers need to cultivate the ability to live with uncertainty and self-doubt, as well as the ability to collect evidence which can convince their readers, who never having stepped into the field with the ethnographer, should nevertheless get a feel for the place, events and people. An ethnographer can only succeed if they can communicate the findings accurately and with conviction. Conviction and authenticity are achieved only when the data have been collected rigorously and systematically, and have been lived with and analysed carefully with due attention given to detail.

Methods, data collection and analysis

The research question which is under consideration will define exactly how a researcher may go about collecting the data. For example, if a piece of research is about how English is taught in a secondary school over a year, it would be important for the researcher to be familiar with the demands on teachers at different stages and ages – from the beginning of the year to the end. The researcher will need to know about any changes in the laws governing the acquisition of English, both on a national and local school level. Syllabi, curriculum content, the choice of books and other materials, the school budget in general and with reference to English in particular, the relative experiences of different teachers – all of these factors will define what the researcher must rehearse before entering the field. What if there are children for whom English is an additional language? Is there a helpful national or local policy? Do all mainstream class teachers have equal access to relevant resources or are they expected to send all bilingual children to Special Needs classes where children with autism, ADHD and dyslexia might be receiving assistance? These are difficult questions. What kinds of questions should be asked, how frequently, and of whom must be considered carefully. Are some children struggling with basic literacy while others are fluent readers? What sort of help is available or affordable? Who decides which student will get extra hours of individual teaching? The researcher would need to find out about teacher autonomy. Where do teachers site control of the subject (English) – within the school, the classroom, or in government departments? This might depend on the 'status' of the subject in the school in relation to other subjects. Are these questions relevant for all classes in the school? Even before drawing up a list of teachers to approach and students to observe, a lot of groundwork must be done. Data can be collected through participant and non-participant observation, interviews and documentary analysis. Grounded theory is quite useful for ethnography where the theory emerges from the data and is not imposed on the data from the outset, thus giving the researcher some space to react and think again (Charmaz, 2014). The choice of theory will depend on the researcher and the focus of the research.

Conclusion

There are many ethnographies of educational institutions. Each deals with a different aspect of education. From Colin Lacey, David Hargreaves and Stephen Ball, who studied how schools affect the kinds of experiences children have, to more recent studies, it is possible to see a whole range of topics. Ethnographic research can be about labelling and bullying, racism, gender, sexuality, religious education, special education and other areas. Benjamin (2002) has looked at the experiences of young women who struggle at school because of their learning difficulties. Race has been studied by researchers such Gillborn (1990) and Wright (1992). Skelton (2001) focused on the schooling of boys. If we extend 'education' to include out-of-school or vocational activities then there are many sites where participants such as dancers (Delamont, 2006) and musicians (Buscatto, 2007) acquire knowledge and skills.

Ethnographies are informative, meaningful and interesting to read. The close engagement and immersion in the field and the immediacy of the world they describe are what draw researchers to ethnography. According to Walford (2002):

> … doing ethnographic fieldwork, analysing the data and writing the full account [require] personal commitment of a very high order and a vast amount of sheer hard work.

It may be very hard work but it takes the ethnographer on an unforgettable, transformative journey!

Questions for further investigation

1. Think of a topic that you are interested in studying in depth. What is it about this topic which inspires you or makes you curious enough to commit time to investigating it? Can you identify a naturally occurring setting where you can conduct this ethnographic enquiry?

2. What personal and professional qualities will you take to the field as a researcher? Can you take a back seat and become unobtrusive, or do you want to become a participant observer? What are your strengths,

(Continued)

(Continued)

and where do you think you need some more practice before you collect data? (e.g. Are you a good listener? Can you sit quietly at the back of the classroom day after day for long periods of time without intruding, if you are not invited to join in?)

3. How will you deal with your own bias during fieldwork? You will face ethical dilemmas on a regular basis. What will you do in uncomfortable situations? If you are studying behaviour management in classrooms for example, and you see a child bullying another child and this is happening far away from the teacher's gaze, what will you do?

4. There are many kinds of ethnographies (critical ethnography, autoethnography, performance ethnography, feminist ethnography). Which is your preference and why?

Suggested further reading

Cohen, L., Manion, L. and Morrison, K. (2011) 'Naturalistic, Qualitative and Ethnographic Research', in *Research Methods in Education*, 7th edn. London: RoutledgeFalmer, pp. 217–47. This chapter provides a good overview of ethnography and qualitative research, together with a discussion of the problems which ethnography can pose such as the Hawthorne effect when the presence of the researcher can alter the research situation. It also raises important questions which often trouble ethnographers, such as how to write up multiple realities and who owns the data.

Creswell, J.W. (2014) ' Ethnographic Designs', in *Educational Research: Planning, Conducting and Evaluating Quantitative and Qualitative Research*, 4th edn. Harlow: Pearson, pp. 489–528. This chapter is a useful starting point for those who are new

to ethnography. Different types of ethnographic designs are described, such as realist ethnography, case study and critical ethnography. The discussion of key characteristics of ethnographic design includes culture, fieldwork, context and researcher reflexivity. An extract from an ethnographic study is used as an illustration of what an ethnography looks like and what it might contain.

Delamont, S. (2012) '"Traditional" Ethnography: Peopled Ethnography for Luminous Description', in S. Delamont (ed.), *Handbook of Qualitative Research in Education*. Cheltenham: Edward Elgar, pp. 342–53. This chapter highlights the complexity and challenges posed by a sociological and anthropological ethnography of education. It defines how observation works and how data can be recorded and analysed. More interestingly, it describes *what* researchers do: 'Researchers discover what "their" people believe; what they do at work and in their leisure time; what makes them laugh, cry and rage; who they love, hate and fear; and how they choose their friends and endure their relations' (p. 343).

References

Barton, A.C. (2001) 'Science education in urban settings: seeking new ways of praxis through critical ethnography', *Journal of Research in Science Teaching*, 38(8): 899–917.

Becker, H.S. (1967) 'Whose side are we on?', *Social Problems*, 14(3): 239–47.

Benjamin, S. (2002) *The Micropolitics of Inclusive Education*. Buckingham: Open University Press.

Burgess, R.G. (1987) 'Studying and Restudying Bishop McGregor School', in G. Walford (ed.), *Doing Sociology of Education*. London: Falmer.

Buscatto, M. (2007) 'Contributions of ethnography to gendered sociology: the French jazz world', *Qualitative Sociology Review*, 3(3): 46–58.

Charmaz, K. (2014) *Constructing Grounded Theory*, 2nd edn. London: Sage.

Cruz, E.V. and Higginbottom, G. (2013) 'The use of focused ethnography in nursing research', *Nurse Researcher*, 20(4): 36–43.

Delamont, S. (2006) 'The smell of sweat and rum: teacher authority in *capoeira* classes', *Ethnography and Education*, 1(3): 161–75.

Delamont, S. (2012) *Handbook of Qualitative Research in Education*. Cheltenham: Edward Elgar.

Eisner, E. (1991) *The Enlightened Eye: Qualitative Inquiry and the Enhancement of Educational Practice*. New York: Macmillan.

Fine, G.A. and Martin, D.D. (1995) 'Humour in Ethnographic Writing: Sarcasm, satire and irony as voices in Erving Goffman's *Asylums'*, in J. Van Maanen (ed.), *Representation in Ethnography*. London: Sage, pp. 185–-97.

Foley, D.E. (2002) 'Critical Ethnography: the reflexive turn', *International Journal of Qualitative Studies in Education*, 15(4): 469–90.

Gatson, S.N. (2011) 'The Methods, Politics and Ethics of Representation in Online Ethnography', in N.K. Denzin and Y.S. Lincoln (eds), *The SAGE Handbook of Qualitative Research*. Thousand Oaks, CA: Sage, pp. 513–28.

Geertz, C. (1973) 'Thick Description: Towards an interpretive theory of cultures', in C. Geertz (ed.), *The Interpretation of Cultures*. New York: Basic.

Gillborn, D. (1990) *'Race', Ethnicity and Education*. London: Unwin Hyman.

Gillborn, D. and Youdell, B. (2000) *Rationing Education*. Buckingham: Open University Press.

Gobo, G. (2011) 'Ethnography', in D. Silverman (ed.), *Qualitative Research*. London: Sage.

Hamera, J. (2011) 'Performance Ethnography', in N.K. Denzin and Y.S. Lincoln (eds) *The SAGE Handbook of Qualitative Research*. Thousand Oaks, CA: Sage, pp. 317–30.

Hammersley, M. (1992) *What's Wrong with Ethnography?* London: Routledge.

Hammersley, M. and Atkinson, P. (1983) *Ethnography: Principles in Practice*. London: Tavistock.

Hammersley, M. (2006) 'Ethnography: problems and prospects', *Ethnography and Education,* 1(1): 3–14.

Heller, M. (2011) *Paths to Post-Nationalism: A Critical Ethnography of Language and Identity*. Oxford: Oxford University Press.

Katz, C.M. (2003) 'Issues in the production and dissemination of gang statistics: an ethnographic study of a large Midwestern police gang unit', *Crime and Delinquency,* 3(3): 485–516.

LeBaron, V., Beck, S.L., Maurer, M. et al. (2014) 'An ethnographic study of barriers to cancer pain management and opioid availability in India', *The Oncologist,* 19(5): 515–22.

Mills, D. and Morton, M. (2013) *Ethnography in Education*. London: Sage.

Muncey, T. (2010) *Creating Autoethnographies*. Thousand Oaks, CA: Sage.

Raaflaub, K.A. and Talbert, J.A. (eds) (2012) *Geography and Ethnography: Perceptions of the World in Pre-Modern Society*. Oxford: Wiley Blackwell.

Schatz, E. (ed.) (2009) *Political Ethnography: What Immersion Contributes to the Study of Power*. Chicago: University of Chicago Press.

Skelton, C. (2001) *Schooling the Boys*. Buckingham: Open University Press.

Skinner, J.E. (2012) *The Invention of Greek Ethnography: From Homer to Herodotus,* Oxford: Oxford University Press.

Van Maanen, J. (1988) *Tales of the Field: On Writing Ethnography*. Chicago: University of Chicago Press.

Walford, G. (2002) 'Introduction', in *Doing a Doctorate in Educational Ethnography*. Oxford: Elsevier.

Whyte, W.F. (1993) *Street Corner Society: The Social Structure of an Italian Slum*, 4th edn. Chicago: University of Chicago Press.

Woods, P.H. (1992) 'Symbolic Interactionism: Theory and method', in Le Compte, Milroy and Preissle (eds), *Handbook of Qualitative Research in Education*. San Diego CA: Academic Press, pp. 337–404.

Wright, C. (1992) 'Early Education: Multiracial primary school classrooms', in G. Dawn, B. Mayor and M. Blair (eds), *Racism and Education*. London: Sage.

Visual methodologies

Claudia Mitchell

11

Introduction

'Draw a scientist'. 'Take pictures of where you feel safe and not so safe'. 'Produce a video narrative or documentary on an issue "in your life"'. 'Find and work with seven or eight pictures from your family photographs that you can construct into a narrative about gender and identity'. Each of these prompts speaks to the range of tools that might be used to engage participants (learners, teachers, parents, pre-service teachers) in visual research (a drawing, digital cameras, camcorders, cellphones, video cameras, family photographs) and suggests some of the types of emerging visual data: the drawing, the photographic images and captions produced in the photovoice project, the video texts produced in a community video project, and the newly created album or visual text produced by the participants in an album project.

In each case there is the immediate visual text (or primary text as John Fiske [1989] terms it), the drawing, photo image, collage, photo-story, video narrative or album, which can include captions and more extensive curatorial statements or interpretive writings that reflect what the participants have to say about the visual texts. In essence, their participation does not have to be limited to 'take a picture' or 'draw a picture', though the level of participation will rest on time, the age and ability of the participants and even their willingness to be involved, and a set of drawings or photos produced in isolation from their full participatory context (or follow-up) does not mean that they should therefore be discarded, particularly in large-scale collections (Mitchell et al., 2005a; Mitchell et al., 2016).

Each of these examples can also include what Fiske (1989) terms 'production texts' – or *how* participants engaged in the process describes the project, regardless of whether they are producing drawings, photographic images or video narratives, or 'reconstructing' a set of photographs into a new text, and indeed what they make of the texts. These production texts are often elicited during follow-up interviews. The production texts can also include secondary visual data based on the researcher taking pictures during the process and can show levels of engagement, something Pithouse and Mitchell (2007) in an article called 'Looking at looking' describe as a result of the visual representations of the engagement of children looking at their own photographs. Each of the visual practices noted above and described in more detail below brings with it, of course, its own methods, traditions and procedures. Taken as a whole these approaches all fall under the umbrella term 'visual methodologies'. Clearly, as noted above, such approaches can range from those which are relatively 'low-tech' and which can be easily carried out without a lot of expensive equipment through to those which require more expensive cameras, from those that are camera-based to those that provide for a focus on things and objects (including archival photographs), from those where participants are respondents to the visual (in the case of photo elicitation) to those which fully engage participants as producers. The constant is some aspect of the visual.

Mapping the terrain of visual methodologies

There is a variety of visual methodologies, each with its own advantages, challenges and limitations. This section offers a map of the range of approaches, followed by a section on interpretive possibilities and another on challenges and limitations.

Visual approaches

Drawings

The use of drawings to study emotional and cognitive development, trauma and fears, and more recently issues of identity, has a rich history, and using drawings in participatory research with children and young people along with adult groups, such as beginning teachers, is a well-established 'low-tech' methodology. As a recent Population Council study points out, drawings offer children an opportunity to express themselves regardless of linguistic ability (Chong et al., 2005). They also point out that work with drawings within visual methodologies is economical as all it requires is paper and a writing instrument. Drawings have been used with pre-service teachers in South Africa to study their metaphors on teaching mathematics in the context of HIV and AIDS (Van Laren, 2007), with children and pre-service teachers to study images of teachers, and with children to study their perceptions of illness, of living on the street and of violence in refugee situations, and on the perceptions of girls and young women in Rwanda on gender violence (Mitchell and Umurungi, 2007; Theron et al., 2011).

Photovoice

Made popular by the award-winning documentary *Born into Brothels,* photovoice, as Caroline Wang

(1999) terms the use of simple point-and-shoot cameras in community photography projects, has increasingly become a useful tool in educational research in South Africa. Building on Wang's work, which looks at women and health issues in rural China, Mary Brinton Lykes's (2001) work with women in post-conflict settings in Guatemala, Wendy Ewald's (2000) photography work with children in a variety of settings, including Nepal, the Appalachian region of the USA and Soweto, and James Hubbard's (1994) work with children on reservations in the USA, researchers in South Africa have worked with rural teachers and community healthcare workers to examine the challenges and solutions in looking at HIV and AIDS (Mitchell et al., 2005a; De Lange et al., 2007), with teachers exploring gender, with learners in a variety of contexts, including exploring stigma and HIV and AIDS (Moletsane et al., 2007), with rural learners, and with teachers addressing poverty and safe and unsafe spaces in schools (Mitchell et al., 2005b), to name only some of the school-based research using photovoice.

Family photographs

Clearly much has been done already on family albums, particularly in the area of the visual arts and art history. These studies range from work on one's own family album(s) (Spence, 1988) to the work of Hirsch (1997) and Langford (2001), to name only a few of the scholars who examine 'other people's albums'. These various album projects have highlighted the personal aspect in looking at or working with one's own photographs, but there is also, as in the case of Langford, the idea of explicitly looking at 'other people's photo albums' through a socio-cultural lens. The issues that they have explored range from questions of cultural identity and memory, through to what Spence (1988) has described as 'reconfiguring' the family album. Research on family albums in South Africa points to the rich possibilities for this work in exploring apartheid and post-apartheid realities. Mitchell and Allnutt (2007) have applied this work on family albums to participatory work with teachers in Canada and South Africa.

Participatory video

The use of participatory video in educational research (beyond the use of videotaping classrooms and other settings or videotaping interviews) may be framed as collaborative video, participatory video, indigenous video, community video, and as we see with the ubiquity of mobile technology, cellphilms or videos made with a cellphone (Mitchell and De Lange, 2013). Sarah Pink (2013) argues that video within ethnographic research can break down the traditional hierarchies between visual and textual data. She maintains that these hierarchies are irrelevant to a reflexive approach to research that acknowledges the details, subjectivities and power dynamics at play in any ethnographic project. What runs across this work is the idea of participants engaged in producing their own videos across a variety of genres, ranging from video documentaries to video narratives (melodramas or other stories) or public service narratives. As with the work with photovoice, both the processes and the products lend themselves to data analysis within visual studies.

In terms of process and video-making in Southern African schools, Mitchell et al. (2007) and Moletsane et al. (2009) write about the ways in which young people might participate in this work, noting its particular relevance to addressing gender violence and HIV and AIDS. Equally, though, the work with adults, teachers, parents and community healthcare workers is also critical, as can be seen in research by Moletsane et al. (2009). Building on the work of Jay Ruby (2000) and others in relation to the idea of the ethnographic video as text, researchers have reflected on what might be described as a meta-narrative on working with community-based video through the researcher-generated production of a composite video of each project. The production of these composite videos is an interpretive part of the process (in relation to the research team). These composite videos become tools of dissemination, but also serve to become new tools of enquiry when community participants view them.

Material culture

How objects, things and spaces can be used within visual research in education draws on work in socio-semiotics, art history and consumer research. Stephen Riggins' (1994) generative and groundbreaking essay on studying his parents' living room offers a systematic approach to engaging in a denotative and connotative reading of the objects and things in one physical space. This work can be applied to a variety of texts, ranging from clothing and identity, bedrooms, documents and letters, and even desks and bulletin boards as material culture. However, some of the 'photo subjects' are objects: a school bus, empty chairs and hairdryers in a beauty salon, or a shrivelled tree. Weber and Mitchell (2004), in the edited book *Not Just Any Dress: Narratives of Memory, Body and Identity*, offer a series of essays on the connotative meanings of various items of clothing. The collection of dress stories – divided into 'growing up with dresses', 'dress and schooling', 'dress rituals and mothers', 'of dresses and weddings', 'dressing identity' and 'bodies, dress and mortality' – offers a reading on a wide range of issues of identity (mostly women's) across the lifespan.

Interpretive processes and visual research

There is no quick and easy way to map out the interpretive processes involved in working with visual research any more than there is a quick and easy way to map out the interpretive processes for working with any type of research data, though Prosser (1998), Banks and Zeitlyn (2015), Rose (2012) and Pink (2013), among other researchers working in the area, offer useful suggestions and guidelines. Some considerations include the following:

1. Reflexivity is at the heart of the visual research process. Situating oneself in the research texts is critical to engaging in the interpretive process.

2. Close reading strategies (drawn from literary studies, film studies and socio-semiotics, for example) are particularly critical to working with visual images. These strategies can be applied to working with a single photograph, a video documentary text or a cinematic text (Mitchell and Weber, 1999).

3. Visual images are particularly appropriate to drawing in the participants themselves as central to the interpretive process. In work with photovoice, for example, participants can be engaged in their own analytic procedures with the photos: which ones are the most compelling? How are your photos the same or different from others in your group? What narrative do your photos evoke? Similarly with video documentaries produced as part of community video, participants can be engaged in a reflective process, which also becomes an analytic process: What did you like best about the video? What would you change if you could? Who should see this video? The interpretive process does not have to be limited to the participants and the researcher. Communities themselves may also decide what a text means.

4. The process of interpreting visual data can benefit from drawing on new technologies, particularly in relation to the idea of the digital archive (Mitchell, 2011).

5. Photos (both public and private) bring their own materiality with them and may be read as objects or things. Where are they stored? Who looks after them? How do we look at audiences? (See also Rose, 2012; Mitchell, 2015.)

6. Visual data (especially photos produced by participants), because they are so accessible, are often subjected to more rigorous scrutiny by ethics boards than most other data. There are many different ways of working with the visual and the choice of which type of visual approach should be guided by, among other things, the research questions, the feasibility of the study, the experience of the researcher, and the acceptability to the community under study. (See also Akesson et al., 2014.)

On the limitations and challenges in working with the visual

Lister and Wells (2001) stress the unprecedented importance of imaging and visual technologies in contemporary society and urge researchers to take account of those images in conducting their investigations. Over the last three decades, an increasing number of qualitative researchers have indeed taken up and refined visual approaches to enhance their understanding of the human condition. These uses encompass a wide range of visual forms, including films, videos, photographs, digital stories, cellphilms drawings, cartoons, graffiti, maps, diagrams, cyber graphics, signs and symbols.

Although many of these scholars normally work in visual sociology and anthropology, cultural studies, and film and photography, a growing body of interdisciplinary scholarship is incorporating certain image-based techniques into its research methodology. Research designs which use the visual raise many new questions and suggest new blurrings of boundaries: Is it research or is it art? Is it truth? Does the camera lie? Is it just a 'quick fix' on doing research? How do you overcome the subjective stance? The emergence of visual and arts-based research as a viable approach is putting pressure on the traditional structures and expectations of the academy. Space, time and equipment requirements, for example, often make it difficult for researchers to present their work in the conventional venues and formats of research conferences.

Applying the methods: the Friday Absenteeism Project

In this project children from an informal settlement in rural South Africa became involved in a photovoice project which led to several policy changes in relation to food security and gender violence – both critically linked to HIV and AIDS (see also Mitchell 2011; Mitchell et al., 2005b; Mitchell et al., 2006; Moletsane and Mitchell, 2007; Moletsane et al., 2007). A key issue in the school was the fact that many of the children in the senior primary school missed school on Fridays. This was perhaps understandable in a community where problems of poverty, unemployment and high rates of HIV infection and illness abound, and where, as the principal and staff noted, children missed school on Friday – market day – when many of them were often called on to work in the market to earn money to provide for at least the basic nutritional needs of the families over the weekend. This is an important point since although there was a school feeding-scheme from Monday to Friday, no provision existed for help with food over the weekends. The principal was concerned because the learners could not afford to miss a day a week of school, and because this behaviour also sent a message to other learners that school wasn't important. From this understanding of the issues, the principal saw the potential for the children to use photography not only to document the problems they faced, but also to identify and/or influence the development of strategies within the school and the community, as well as in the government departments responsible for their well-being. So, through a photovoice project, the children worked in small groups with disposable cameras to document their community. Once they had taken the photographs they were involved in analysing their own photos according to the problems and possible solutions affecting the community, and writing captions. Each group produced a poster where they analysed the issues.

The children's narratives in the photographs, posters and writing revealed a variety of issues. These included alcoholism among adults in the community and this is captured in a caption to a photograph: 'If we look at these people who are living in this shack, they are drinking alcohol. They are not working. The schoolchild cannot survive in this condition'. Other issues they identified included high levels of unemployment, the need for housing, the lack of clean water and sanitation, the danger to children of even coming to school because they have to cross a wide highway that has no bridge over it. Most importantly, the photographs draw attention to the effects of poverty, and they provide visual evidence of why children as young as 11 or 12 must supplement the family income. Poverty also led to some of them

having to miss school to take care of younger siblings. In a caption to one of the photographs, the students note: 'This photo shows us the rate of children who are absent from schools. These children are absent because they have to look after their baby sister or brother while their parents are working'. The photographs taken in the market not only showed images of the adults who run the market trying to make a living, but also showed the children's peers at work, and so very obviously not at school. The children also took pictures of learners from nearby schools, demonstrating that Friday absenteeism was a widespread problem in the district. One particular photograph was of a boy who was working in the market to raise money for a school trip to Durban, which he could not otherwise afford: 'He absented himself from school because they had a trip to Durban. He decided to look for a part-time job because he needs the money. He has no parents'. The photographs and captions also reflected upon the conditions of the school itself. For example, one of the girls who was working in the market spoke about issues of safety and security in her classroom. Her teacher, she indicated, had been making sexual advances towards her. Being away from school on Fridays was an escape from this unwanted attention. The rich insider data produced by the children in the photovoice project had major implications for policy development at the school and community level. For example, from the data, the principal instituted disciplinary action against the teacher who allegedly was sexually harassing a female learner. He also raised the issue of absenteeism with other principals in the district, and planned for a community-based stakeholders' forum where the children were to present their posters. From this work he was able to approach donors and corporate funders with the children's images and captions, and attract financial support for a feeding scheme at the weekends as well as during the week.

Conclusion

The overview of visual methodologies has focused largely on the use of such methods in the service of social change and where the visual can serve as a mode of enquiry as well as a mode of dissemination. Many would also argue that much of the work, whether it is with drawings or cameras, also has the potential to serve as transformative for the participants who are, in a sense, the principal actors in the process. More than anything, the use of the visual also means that participants can be engaged in the process of interpretation: 'This is why I took the photograph'. For researchers seeking approaches that have the potential to bring about change in the process of doing, visual methodologies are ideal.

Questions for further investigation

1. Do we as researchers conduct ourselves differently when the participants of our studies are 'right there', particularly in relation to the photos or videos they have produced?

2. How can visual interventions be used to educate community groups and point to ways to empower and reform institutional practices?

3. What ethical issues come to the fore in these action-oriented studies? How do we work with such concepts as 'confidentiality' and 'anonymity' within visual work?

4. How can we begin to study this work in the context of community dialogue and policy change?

Suggested further reading

D'Amico, M., Denov, M., Linds, W. and Akesson, B. (2016) 'Research as intervention? Exploring the health and well-being of children and youth facing global adversity through participatory visual methods', *Global Public Health:* 1–18. doi: 10.1080/17441692.2016.1165719. This article is an important one for linking the idea of intervention research and social change.

De Lange, N., Mitchell, C. and Stuart, J. (eds) (2007) *Putting People in the Picture: Visual Methodologies for Social Change.* Amsterdam: Sense. This collection, while focused primarily on South Africa, offers an overview of many different methodologies and critical issues, using case studies. It has a strong education focus.

Ewald, W. (2000) *Secret Games: Collaborative Works with Children, 1969–99.* Berlin and New York: Scalo. For anyone working with children as photographers, this book is key. We get to appreciate the photographers as artists and not just as social documentarians.

Gubrium, A., Harper, K. and Otenez, M. (eds) (2015) *Participatory Visual and Digital Research in Action.* Walnut Creek, CA: Left Coast. This book offers a comprehensive view of a variety of visual methodologies, including digital storytelling. The idea of 'research in action' links nicely with social change.

Knowles, G. and Cole, A. (eds) (2007) *The SAGE Handbook of the Arts in Qualitative Research: Perspectives, Methodologies, Examples and Issues.* London: Sage. This is one of the most comprehensive books on arts-based methodologies, including many visual approaches.

Mitchell, C. (2011) *Doing Visual Research.* London: Sage. This book provides a practical look at participatory visual methodologies.

Rose, G. (2012) *Visual Methodologies: An Introduction to Researching with Visual Materials,* 3rd edn. London: Sage. This book has a strong theory base. For anyone who is interested in applying discourse anlaysis to working with visual images, this book is key. It is a particularly useful reference on audiencing.

Sontag, S. (1977) *On Photography.* New York: Doubleday. Sontag's work is a classic in doing visual studies. It provides an excellent theoretical base for any visual work.

Wang, C. (1999) 'Photovoice: a participatory action research strategy applied to women's health', *Journal of Women's Health,* 8(2): 85–192. Caroline Wang coined the term 'photovoice' and as such her work is basic in the whole area of photography and photo elictation.

References

Akesson, B., D'Amico, M. et al. (2014) '"Stepping back" as researchers: addressing ethics in arts-based approaches to working with war-affected children in school and community settings', *Educational Research for Social Change (ERSC)*, 3(1): 75–89.

Banks, M. and Zeitlyn, D. (2015) *Visual Methods in Social Research*, 2nd edn. London: Sage.

Chong, E., Hallman, K. and Brady, M. (2005) *Generating the Evidence Base for HIV/AIDS Policies and Programs*. New York: Population Council.

De Lange, N., Mitchell, C., Moletsane, R., Stuart, J. and Buthelezi, T. (2006) 'Seeing through the body: educators' representations of HIV and AIDS', *Journal of Education*, 38: 45–66.

De Lange, N., Mitchell, C. and Stuart, J. (eds) (2007) *Putting People in the Picture: Visual Methodologies for Social Change*. Amsterdam: Sense.

Emmison, M. and Smith, P. (2000) *Researching the Visual: Images, Objects, Contexts and Interactions in Social and Cultural Inquiry*. London: Sage.

Ewald, W. (2000) *Secret Games: Collaborative Works with Children, 1969–99*. Berlin and New York: Scalo.

Fiske, J. (1989) *Understanding Popular Culture*. Boston, MA: Unwin.

Hirsch, M. (1997) *Family Frames: Photography, Narrative and Postmemory*. Cambridge, MA: Harvard University Press.

Hubbard, J. (1994) *Shooting Back from the Reservation*. New York: New Press.

Langford, M. (2001) *Suspended Conversations: The Afterlife of Memory in Photographic Albums*. Montreal: McGill-Queen's Press.

Lister, M. and Wells, L. (2001) 'Seeing Beyond Belief: Cultural studies as an approach to analysing the visual', in T. van Leeuwen and C. Jewitt (eds), *The SAGE Handbook of Visual Analysis*. London: Sage, pp. 61–91.

Lykes, M.B. (2001) 'Creative Arts and Photography in Participatory Action Research in Guatemala', in P. Reason and H. Bradbury (eds), *The SAGE Handbook of Action Research: Participative Inquiry and Practice*. Thousand Oaks, CA: Sage, pp. 363–71.

Mitchell, C. (2011) 'What's participation got to do with it? Visual methodologies in "girl-method" to address gender based violence in the time of AIDS', *Global Studies of Childhood*, 1(1): 51–59.

Mitchell, C. (2015) 'Looking at showing: on the politics and pedagogy of exhibiting in community based research and work with policy makers', *Educational Research for Social Change*, 4(2): 48–60.

Mitchell, C. and Allnutt, S. (2007) 'Working with Photographs as Objects and Things: Social documentary as a new materialism', in G. Knowles and A. Cole (eds), *The SAGE Handbook of the Arts in Qualitative Research: Perspectives, Methodologies, Examples and Issues*. London: Sage, pp. 251–63.

Mitchell, C. and De Lange, N. (2013) 'What can a teacher do with a cellphone? Using participatory visual research to speak back in addressing HIV & AIDS', *South African Journal of Education*, 33(4): 1–13.

Mitchell, C. and Umurungi, J.P. (2007) 'What happens to girls who are raped in Rwanda?', *Children First*, pp. 13–18.

Mitchell, C. and Weber, S. (1999) *Reinventing Ourselves as Teachers: Beyond Nostalgia*. London: Falmer Press.

Mitchell, C., De Lange, N., Moletsane, R., Stuart, J. and Buthelezi, T. (2005a) 'The face of HIV and AIDS in rural South Africa: a case for photo-voice', *Qualitative Research in Psychology*, 3(2): 257–70.

Mitchell, C., De Lange, N., Moletsane, R., Stuart, J. and Buthelezi, T. (2005b) 'Taking pictures/taking action! Using photo-voice techniques with children', *ChildrenFIRST*, 9(60): 27–31.

Mitchell, C., De Lange, N. and Nguyen, X.T. (2016) 'Visual Ethics With and Through the Body: The participation of girls with disabilities in Vietnam in a photovoice project', in H. Cahill, J. Coffey and S. Budgeon (eds), *Learning Bodies: The Body in Youth and Childhood Studies*. Dubai, UAE: Springer-Verlag Singapore, pp. 241–57.

Mitchell, C., Moletsane, R. and Stuart, J. (2006) 'Why we don't go to school on Fridays? Youth participation and HIV and AIDS', *McGill Journal of Education*, 41(3): 267–82.

Mitchell, C., Walsh, S. and Weber, S. (2007) 'Behind the Lens: Reflexivity and video documentary', in G. Knowles and A. Cole (eds), *The Art of Visual Inquiry*. Halifax: Backalong Press, pp. 281–94.

Mitchell, C., Weber, S. and Pithouse, K. (2009) 'Facing the Public: Using photography for self-study and social action', in D. Tidwell, M. Heston and L. Fitzgerald (eds), *Research Methods for the Self-Study of Practice*. New York: Springer, pp. 119–34.

Moletsane, R. and Mitchell, C. (2007) 'On Working with a Single Photograph', in N. De Lange,

C. Mitchell and J. Stuart (eds), *Putting People in the Picture: Visual Methodologies for Social Change*. Amsterdam: Sense, pp. 131–40.

Moletsane, R., De Lange, N., Mitchell, C., Stuart, J., Buthelezi, T. and Taylor, M. (2007) 'Photo-voice as a tool for analysis and activism in response to HIV and AIDS stigmatization in a rural KwaZulu-Natal school', *Journal of Child and Adolescent Mental Health*, 19(1): 19–28.

Moletsane, R., Mitchell, C., De Lange, N., Stuart, J., Buthelezi, T. and Taylor, M. (2009) 'What can a woman do with a camera? Turning the female gaze on poverty and HIV/AIDS in rural South Africa', *International Journal of Qualitative Studies in Education*, 22(3): 315–31.

Pink, S. (2013) *Doing Visual Ethnography*, 3rd edn. Thousand Oaks, CA: Sage.

Pithouse, K. and Mitchell, C. (2007) 'Looking into Change: Studying participant engagement in photo-voice projects', in N. De Lange, C. Mitchell and J. Stuart (eds), *Putting People in the Picture: Visual Methodologies for Social Change*. Amsterdam: Sense, pp. 141–51.

Prosser, J. (ed.) (1998) *Image-Based Research: A Sourcebook for Qualitative Research*. London: Falmer.

Riggins, S. (1994) 'Fieldwork in the living room: An autoethnographic essay', in *The Socialness of Things: Essays on the Socio-semiotics of Objects*. Berlin: Mouton de Gruyter, pp. 101–47.

Rose, G. (2012) *Visual Methodologies: An Introduction to Researching with Visual Materials*, 3rd edn. London: Sage.

Ruby, J. (2000) *Picturing Culture: Explorations of Film and Anthropology*. Chicago: University of Chicago Press.

Schratz, M. and Walker, R. (1995) *Research as Social Change: New Opportunities for Qualitative Research*. London: Routledge.

Spence, J. (1988) *Putting Myself in the Picture: A Political, Personal and Photographic Autobiography*. Seattle: Real Comet.

Theron, L., Mitchell, C., Smith, A. and Stuart, J. (eds) (2011) *Picturing Research: Drawings as Visual Methodology*. Rotterdam: Sense.

Van Laren, L. (2007) 'Using metaphors for integrating HIV and AIDS education in mathematics curriculum in pre-service teacher education: an exploratory classroom study', *International Journal of Inclusive Education*, 11(4): 461–79.

Wang, C. (1999) 'Photovoice: a participatory action research strategy applied to women's health', *Journal of Women's Health*, 8(2): 85–192.

Wang, C.C. and Redwood-Jones, Y.A. (2001) 'Photovoice ethics: perspectives from Flint photovoice', *Health Education and Behaviour*, 28(5): 560–72.

Weber, S. and Mitchell, C. (eds) (2004) *Not Just Any Dress: Narratives of Memory, Body and Identity*. New York: Peter Lang.

Grounded theory

Michael Waring

12

Introduction

Grounded theory continues to be an extremely influential and highly regarded method of social analysis, and a popular methodology predominantly but not exclusively used as part of qualitative enquiry in educational research (Douglas, 2003; Thomas and James, 2006). However, there remains a degree of confusion and uncertainty about the interpretation and implementation of grounded theory (Babchuk, 2009; Buckley and Waring, 2009). This chapter will explore issues associated with the evolving (re)interpretation of grounded theory which is currently taking place. It will identify the philosophical location of the grounded theory researcher, the (mis) use of terminology in defining grounded theory, and the identification of essential elements that make up a grounded theory methodology. In addition, it will provide a pragmatic overview of the 'grounded theory process of analysis' using a model which is particularly helpful to the novice grounded theory researcher, offer advice on writing a grounded theory, and supply an outline of key criticisms of grounded theory.

(Re)interpretations of grounded theory

Almost every chapter or article on grounded theory starts with a historical overview of its development. This may be repetitive, but it is important for at least two reasons. Firstly, it acknowledges the context and how the development of the seminal text on grounded theory – *The Discovery of Grounded Theory: An Approach to Qualitative Research* (Glaser and Strauss, 1967) – was presented at the time to articulate a credible alternative to the considerable dominance of positivistic paradigms and their associated assumptions of the time. Glaser and Strauss attempted to articulate a merger of different epistemologies involving their pragmatist (Strauss) and positivistic (Glaser) backgrounds via a set of systematic procedures to generate theory from empirical data, and in so doing enhance the status of interpretive research (e.g. Thomas and James, 2006). They did not, however, articulate their ontological or epistemological assumptions at that time.

Secondly, it highlights the inherent ethos of grounded theory to be flexible, creative and evolutionary in its approach. As Morse (2009) notes, the demands of a particular context, researcher, participants and research focus will require certain adaptations in the use of grounded theory. Therefore any (re)articulation of grounded theory should not be seen as a negative thing, but as a positive and constructive dimension of its development. Also any researcher employing grounded theory has to be informed of, and able to locate themselves and their research within, the contested and complicated landscape of grounded theory methodology and methods (Morse et al., 2009).

Grounded theory should therefore not only be seen as a methodology to study process but also as a methodology *in* process (Charmaz, 2009). Bryant and Charmaz (2007: 11) reinforce the challenge facing the researcher considering the use of grounded theory when they note that 'anyone who is contemplating the grounded theory method (GTM) landscape must grasp the inherent complexity of what might be termed the "family of methods claiming the GTM mantle"'. So grounded theory is in transition, with many researchers developing their interpretations of grounded theory as part of an ongoing shift and articulation about the assumptions and methods that underpin it. Babchuk (2009) also refers to grounded theory as a 'family of methods' as he succinctly and effectively identifies the historical progression and evolution of grounded theory. Morse (2009: 17) also offers a very helpful illustration of the 'genealogy' of grounded theory which sets out major milestones. In it she clearly and succinctly identifies how in the form of subsequent publications from *The Discovery of Grounded Theory*, Glaser and Strauss and other authors (many of whom were students of Glaser and Strauss) have (re)interpreted grounded theory to reveal a landscape of 'different' grounded theories: Straussian (Strauss, 1987; Strauss and Corbin, 1990, 1994, 1997, 1998; Corbin and Strauss, 2008); Glasarian (also referred to as 'classic' GT by its advocates) (Glaser, 1978, 1992, 2004, 2005, 2008); constructivist (Bryant and Charmaz, 2007; Charmaz, 2009); situational analysis (Clarke, 2007).

Locating yourself as a grounded theorist

As we know, a rudimentary prerequisite for any researcher is a depth of understanding of the configuration of the methodology and associated methods they adopt. Therefore, in order to achieve this, a researcher must be able to articulate their ontological and epistemological positions as these will inform their methodological preferences.

If one looks at the language in *The Discovery of Grounded Theory* (even though Glaser and Strauss did not articulate it at the time), the ontological assumptions being made are realist in nature – they assume that there is a single objective reality that exists independent of individuals' perceptions of it.

The epistemological assumptions are positivistic in nature (i.e. the investigator and the investigated are considered to be independent entities and enquiry takes place as if in a one-way mirror). Strauss and Corbin on the other hand would say that they are firmly located within an interpretive epistemology because they acknowledge and include the perspectives and voices of the individuals that they study. However, it has also been pointed out by Annells (1997) and Charmaz (2000) that the language which is used by these authors, such as 'recognising bias', is very much realist in nature. So Strauss and Corbin (e.g. 1998) (and other Straussian grounded theorists) have adopted the somewhat contradictory epistemology known as post-positivism (i.e. they make interpretive assumptions in that not all aspects of the social world can be measured), as well as contradicting this by attempting to maintain an approach which is objective and free from bias (i.e. where the data are real and represent objective facts, and the researcher is an impartial observer who maintains a distance from those being researched and their realities: the data are uncovered and a theory is developed from them) (Charmaz, 2006; Hildenbrand, 2007). Glaser (1992) is a realist and positivist. Other grounded theorists such as Charmaz and Bryant propose constructivist grounded theory, an interpretation of grounded theory that offers a moderate constructivist ontology and interpretivist epistemology. This means that both data and analyses are seen as social constructions reflecting their process of production, and each analysis is specific to the time, space, culture and situation.

What is grounded theory?

As the originators of grounded theory, Glaser and Strauss (1967) distinguished their methodology from that of others by highlighting the evolutionary nature of the research process through the identification of a set of 'interpreted' procedural steps, rather than the verification of a preconceived theory. One does not begin with preconceived ideas or extant theory and then force them on data for the purpose of verifying them or rearranging them into a corrected grounded theory (Glaser, 1992: 15). Their claim is that data shape the research process and its product in an innovative way. This allows data that are grounded to be identified, discarded, clarified and elaborated upon (relative to that situation) through simultaneous data collection and analysis. As a result, it differs from those theoretical frameworks which are developed deductively, evolved prior to or in isolation from engagement in the field. From the accumulation of data the researcher develops or 'discovers' the grounded theory (Martin and Turner, 1986: 143). One starts with an area of investigation and begins to evolve an appropriate theory from the relevant data specific to the situation under investigation. Thus a grounded theory is:

> … discovered, developed, and provisionally verified through systematic data collection and analysis of data pertaining to that phenomenon. Therefore, data collection, analysis, and theory stand in reciprocal relationship with each other. One does not begin with a theory, and then prove it. Rather one begins with an area of study and what is relevant to that area is allowed to emerge. (Strauss and Corbin, 1990: 23)

Remember, the data are collected in the same ways, using the same techniques as with other research methodologies. Data may be qualitative or quantitative or combinations of both types.

Grounded theory is often said to be rooted in a symbolic interactionist perspective (Clarke and Friese, 2007; Parker and Myrick, 2011). This is a contentious issue and many would disagree with it (e.g. Bryant and Charmaz, 2007; Glaser, 2005). However, grounded theory and symbolic interactionism are very similarly positioned and highly compatible in many respects. They both signify the importance of asking what is happening and why it is happening, assume the capacity of agents to act in a world and be producers as well as products of social systems, the exploration of process, the building of theory

from empirical observations, and the development of conditional theories that address specific realities (Bryant and Charmaz, 2007: 21).

Grounded theory has been described as a method comprising a systematic, inductive and comparative approach for conducting enquiry for the purpose of constructing theory (Bryant and Charmaz, 2007; Charmaz and Henwood, 2008). Glaser and Strauss (1967: vii) note that a central feature of this analytic approach is a 'general method of [constant] comparative analysis'. It has also been described as a simultaneous set of assumptions about the production of knowledge and a set of guidelines for empirical research work (Tesch, 1990: 58), a general methodology for developing theory that is grounded in data systematically gathered and analysed (Glaser, 1992; Strauss and Corbin 1994), and a set of relationships among data and categories that proposes a plausible and reasonable explanation of the phenomenon under study (Moghaddam, 2006). Grounded theory is said to be a general methodology for developing theory that is grounded in data that have been systematically gathered and analysed. The theory that evolves during actual research does so through a continuous interplay between analysis and data collection (Strauss and Corbin, 1998).

Use of the terms 'method' and 'methodology' has often occurred interchangeably and inappropriately so in the literature on grounded theory. In the scheme of things the ontological assumptions (the nature of the social world) inform the epistemological assumptions (how knowledge of the social world is possible), which in turn inform the methodology (which procedures and logic to follow), which informs the methods (the specific techniques used to collect data). There is clearly confusion as to whether grounded theory is a methodology or a set of methods. The short answer is that it is a methodology. However Weed (2009) develops this further, noting that a better term for what is an integrated research strategy that assumes the principles of grounded theory have been followed from the start would be a 'total methodology' that provides a set of principles for the entire research process and not, as he puts it, 'a pick and mix' box.

Having acknowledged the differences between some of the various interpretations of grounded theory, there are also similarities between these: an iterative process (concurrent data generation or collection and analysis); theoretical sampling; theoretical sensitivity; coding and categorisation of data, writing memos and concepts; constant comparative analysis using inductive and deductive logic (abduction); theoretical saturation; fit, work, relevance and modifiability; substantive theory (Birks and Mills, 2015; Bryant and Charmaz, 2007; Weed, 2009, 2013). These can be considered to be the essential elements which together are considered conditions for grounded theory research and are core parts of grounded theory methodology. Therefore, when reading or constructing a grounded theory, you should use these to critique the 'grounded theory'.

The helix model: a framework for enquiry

The novelty of grounded theory exists not in the mode of the investigation associated with it, but as Turner (1983) points out, in the manner in which the information is collected and analysed. This theme has been developed further by Martin and Turner (1986) when they use, quite appropriately, the phrase 'grounded theory *craft*'. The framework of data collection and analysis you are about to be presented with is systematic, however within it there is flexibility which increases proportionally to the researcher's understanding of and familiarity with the methodology, methods and the research setting.

The helix model (see Figure 12.1) draws heavily on the work of Strauss and Corbin (1990) to illustrate the systematic and flexible nature of grounded theory analysis. There can and should be movement backwards and forwards within the helix to suit the research situation and expertise of the researcher. The adoption of a spiral emphasises the notion of continually revisiting aspects of the theory, while maintaining progression towards a substantive theory. However, as has already been pointed out,

theory is a process – an 'ever developing entity, not a perfected product' (Glaser and Strauss, 1967).

Theoretical sensitivity

The term 'theoretical sensitivity' is one which is closely associated with grounded theory (e.g. Glaser, 1978; Glaser and Strauss, 1967; Strauss, 1987). Everyone not only brings to (due to the accumulation of their past experiences and attitudes) but also generates within each research context (as a result of an increased awareness of relevant aspects) theoretical sensitivity. This is something that cannot and should not be ignored.

Theoretical sensitivity is defined as 'sensitive thinking about data in theoretical terms' (Strauss, 1987) or 'the personal quality of the researcher' (Strauss and Corbin, 1990). Due to the accumulation of past experiences people bring theoretical sensitivity to each context, which can increase with their exposure to the research setting. Interpersonal interaction is an essential feature of these experiences, therefore the researcher must not only observe the behaviour of their subjects, but also reflect critically on themselves. This necessitates awareness of one's own preconceptions, which Hutchinson (1988) refers to as 'bracketing'. It would be unrealistic to expect these preconceptions, regardless of how careful the researcher was, to be completely abandoned when entering a research project.

The heart of the matter – coding

If we assume that the experiences which construct each person's reality have patterns, grounded theory makes sense of them. Data analysis is the process of bringing order, structure and meaning to the mass of collected data (Marshall and Rossman, 1989: 112). You should consider carefully the data that you will gather. The nature of the data can be qualitative or quantitative and extremely varied in terms of the means – for example, from interviews, images from video, stills, hand drawings, policy

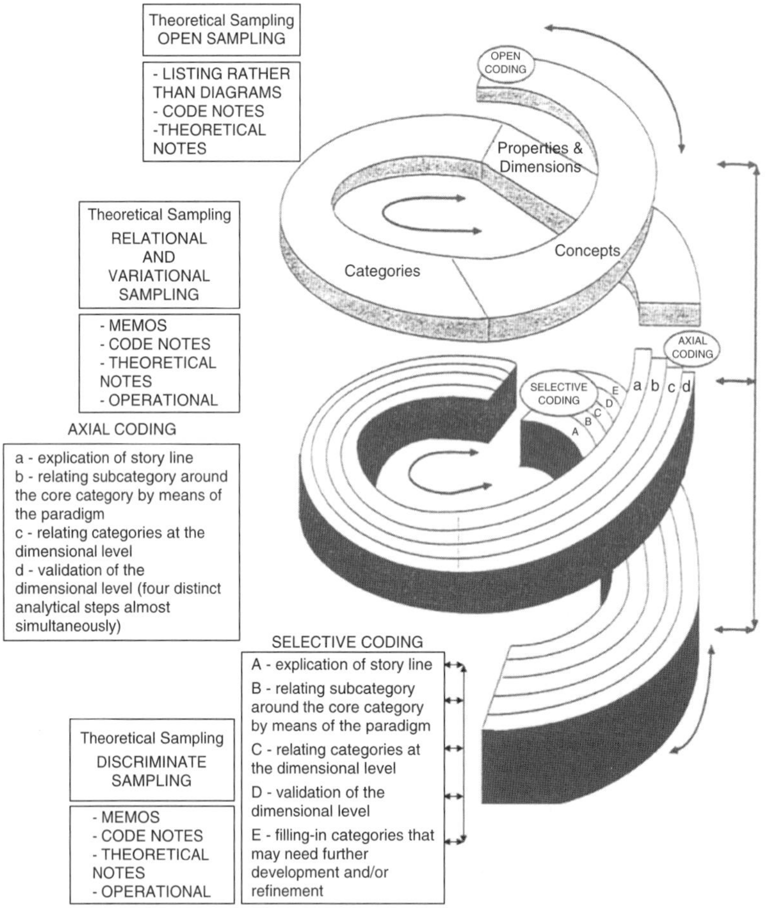

Theoretical Sampling
OPEN SAMPLING
- LISTING RATHER THAN DIAGRAMS
- CODE NOTES
-THEORETICAL NOTES
OPEN CODING
Properties & Dimensions
Concepts
Categories
Theoretical Sampling
RELATIONAL AND VARIATIONAL SAMPLING
- MEMOS
- CODE NOTES
- THEORETICAL NOTES
- OPERATIONAL
AXIAL CODING
a - explication of story line
b - relating subcategory around the core category by means of the paradigm
c - relating categories at the dimensional level
d - validation of the dimensional level (four distinct analytical steps almost simultaneously)
AXIAL CODING
SELECTIVE CODING
E D C B A
a b c d
SELECTIVE CODING
A - explication of story line
B - relating subcategory around the core category by means of the paradigm
C - relating categories at the dimensional level
D - validation of the dimensional level
E - filling-in categories that may need further development and/or refinement
Theoretical Sampling
DISCRIMINATE SAMPLING
- MEMOS
- CODE NOTES
- THEORETICAL NOTES
- OPERATIONAL

Figure 12.1 The helix model

Source: Waring (1995)

documents, observations, field notes, academic literature, informal discussions, etc. However, regardless of how they are gathered, the data need to be fit for purpose. That means the data that are gathered should allow for the researcher to capture relevant, substantial and rich data which involve varied contexts and the detailed views and actions of the participants so as to allow the researcher to fully engage in the process of analysis. The analysis portion of grounded theory is referred to as 'coding'. The focus of analysis is *not* merely on the collecting or ordering of '... a mass of data, but on *organising many ideas*, which have emerged from analysis of data' (Strauss, 1978: 23). This represents the complex operation by which data are broken down, conceptualised and put back together in new ways (Strauss and Corbin, 1990: 57). This is developed by Charmaz (1983: 112) when she comments on the way in which codes provide the pivotal link between the data collection and its conceptual rendering. Thus coding becomes the fundamental means of developing the analysis.

Open coding

Once the researcher has collected their initial set of data, they will embark on open coding which is the initial coding that takes place in the research project. During this process Strauss suggests that 'the point is not so much in the document as in the relationship between it, the inquiring mind and the training of the researcher who vigorously and imaginatively engages in the open coding' (Strauss, 1987). The data that have already been gathered are then broken down, examined, compared, conceptualised and categorised. Glaser (1978) classifies open coding under the heading 'substantive coding', describing the process as 'running the data open'. He defines this as coding the data in every way possible in order to work towards the generation of an emerging set of categories and their properties. Breaking down the data in order to conceptualise them refers to the process of taking an observation, a sentence or a paragraph and giving each of the individual events, ideas and incidents that exist in it a name that represents that phenomenon. Every incident is compared and contrasted with others as the conceptualising process develops. This allows the researcher to take similar phenomena and give them the same conceptual names. When 'labelling the phenomena' in this way, the researcher must endeavour to conceptualise the data (Strauss and Corbin, 1990). This is more than using the remnants of sentences that are being analysed, it requires conceptualisation. Strauss and Corbin (1990) refer to this grouping of concepts around particular phenomena as 'categorising'. The degree of abstraction associated with the concepts is less than with the categories in which they are grouped.

Having begun to identify concepts and then create categories in this open-coding portion of the helix model, the next section of it deals with the properties and dimensions of the categories. Relationships between categories need to be discovered so that the researcher can move towards a single category. The basis on which this is done is the systematic development of their properties and dimensions. The process of open coding stimulates the discovery not only of categories but also of their properties and dimensions. General properties pertain to a category regardless of the situation in which the category is found (Strauss and Corbin, 1990: 70). Each of these general properties exists

along a continuum (dimensional continua). Having identified the dimensional continua, many specific instances identified within a general property can exist at different points along it. This gives rise to the notion of a 'dimensional profile'. As Strauss and Corbin (1990: 70) point out, several of these profiles can be grouped to give you a *pattern*. The dimensional profile represents the specific properties of a phenomenon under a given set of conditions. Open coding is conducted alongside open sampling.

Open sampling

Open sampling is part of the notion of theoretical sampling (i.e. sampling on the basis of concepts that have a proven theoretical relevance to the evolving theory). Proven theoretical relevance indicates that concepts are deemed to be significant because they are repeatedly present or notably absent when comparing incident after incident, and are of sufficient importance to be given the status of categories (Strauss and Corbin, 1990: 176). Open sampling maintains a high degree of flexibility while attempting to uncover as many potentially relevant categories (and their related properties and dimensions) as possible. The researcher must remain open to all possibilities at this stage because all the sources (places, people, circumstances) which yield the necessary evidence for concepts will not be fully appreciated.

Memos and diagrams (the product of analysis) in open coding

The written forms of abstract thinking about data are known as memos. There can be virtually no limit to the kind of memos written in open coding. They can be as uncertain as the researcher likes (i.e. the noting of first impressions and any other thoughts they have had). These should not be considered as 'the' answer, for if they were there would be no need to do the research in the first place. Three 'types' of memo can be defined: *code notes* – memos containing the actual products of the three types of coding, such as conceptual labels, paradigm features and indications of process; *theoretical notes* – theoretically sensitising and summarising memos that contain the products of inductive or deductive thinking about relevant categories, their properties, dimensions, relationships, variations, processes and conditional matrix; *operational notes* – memos containing directions to the researcher (or research team) regarding sampling, questions, possible comparisons, leads to follow up on, and so forth (Strauss and Corbin, 1990: 197). All of these can appear within the same memo, however such a situation would diminish the potential value of each of these because of the ambiguity it would create.

Diagrams are the visual representation of relationships between concepts. Two kinds of diagrams are employed in open coding: *logic diagrams* and *integrative diagrams*. These visually identify relationships between categories and the analytical thinking with conceptual linkages respectively. A list of the categories, their properties and dimensions is drawn to create the foundation for the logic diagrams that will be developed in axial coding.

Theoretical notes extend code notes. Even though they are provisional and in need of verification, these notes can increase the theoretical sensitivity of the researcher. They do this by making them ask more questions about the categories (their properties and dimensions) generated in the interview and/or observational data. Literary sources such as articles can be used to achieve the same results. Importantly, from theoretical notes the researcher can manoeuvre and direct further sampling. For example, having pursued certain questions in one interview the researcher can identify that which appears to be relevant to their work and worth further investigation. Operational notes direct questions and avenues of enquiry in future interviews, representing the point where theoretical notes lead to sampling notes. The process of open coding and sampling could be perpetuated indefinitely, however once the categories and sub-categories have been sufficiently reinforced by subsequent data the researcher will move into the axial-coding phase.

Axial coding

The helix model illustrates the four distinct analytical phases of axial coding that are conducted almost simultaneously: (a) using the paradigm model relating sub-categories to categories; (b) verification of hypotheses against actual data; (c) continued search for the properties of categories and sub-categories and dimensional locations of data; (d) the beginning of the exploration of variation in phenomena. The procedures of axial coding enable the data to be 'put back together' in new ways after open coding and consist of four distinct analytical stages applied almost simultaneously. Once again this is conducted at the same time as sampling procedures (relational and variational sampling) and the development of memos and diagrams.

The paradigm model

The paradigm model (Strauss and Corbin, 1990) enables systematic thinking about the data, which generates more complex relationships between the sub-categories and categories. The model involves the following: the identification of the causal conditions associated with the occurrence or development of a phenomenon; the specification of a category for the phenomenon; the specific set of properties that pertain to a phenomenon; the structural conditions bearing on action/interactional strategies that pertain to the phenomenon; action/interactional strategies devised to manage/respond to a phenomenon under certain circumstances; and the consequences of action and interaction. By asking questions and making comparisons (i.e. those basic analytic procedures mentioned in open coding) links between categories and their development take place. Within axial coding this process becomes much more complicated because there are four quite separate analytical steps conducted almost simultaneously. The whole process of relating sub-categories to categories in axial coding is one which requires complex inductive and deductive thinking, facilitated by asking questions and making comparisons.

Relational and variational sampling

Relational and variational sampling is the theoretical sampling that takes place during the second phase of the helix model. Relational and variational sampling maximises differences at the dimensional level. The researcher has a choice of two approaches to achieve this aim as they sample on the basis of theoretically relevant concepts. Firstly, because of the limitations of time, access and availability, a highly systematic approach can be employed. This would involve a predetermined list of situations/people/documents to be visited. Secondly, the opposite situation may arise where no such preconceived restrictions exist. This allows for a deliberate selection from a variety of sites, documents and/or people which are believed to be the most appropriate as the research continues.

Memos and diagrams in axial coding

The verification of relationships between a category and its sub-categories promoted in axial coding is mirrored in the kind of memos used. They identify all the attempts made to associate each different aspect to the paradigm model. The sophistication of the code notes and theoretical notes increases as the theoretical sensitivity of the researcher develops. The subsequent directness and ability to focus on the most relevant context, people and places highlight this. Operational notes develop in much the same manner, suggesting particular categories to focus upon when conducting further sampling, or to investigate those hypotheses generated and in need of verification in future interviews. As with the memos, the diagrams used in axial coding start by being simplistic in nature (i.e. in the form of a table of rows and columns of certain aspects) but they become much more complex over time.

Selective coding

In the helix model selective coding follows axial coding, but these only really differ in terms of their more abstract level of analysis – axial coding is the foundation on which selective coding takes place. Selective coding involves the selection of a core category and systematically relating it to other categories. Figure 12.1 illustrates how this involves the simultaneous use of five stages, together with discriminative sampling and associated memos and diagrams.

Integrating categories

Strauss and Corbin (1990) suggest there are systematic guidelines that can be used to achieve what is a difficult and complex part of the research, namely 'the final leap between creating a list of concepts and producing a theory'. The steps suggested (which occur at the same time, with movement back and forth between them) are as follow:

1. *Explication of a storyline.* Write thoughts down on paper; use an existing category or create a new category which is abstract enough to consume all that which has been described in the story (this category is the core category that is the central phenomenon around which all the other categories are integrated; Strauss and Corbin, 1990: 116). Once the properties of the core category are identified, the next step is to relate the other categories to it, thereby making them *subsidiary categories*.
2. *Relating the subsidiary categories around the core category by means of the paradigm.* The existing categories are matched to relevant portion(s) of the paradigm (i.e. either to conditions, context, strategies or consequences). This may appear straightforward, however those conditions which influence the action/interactional strategies ('intervening conditions') make it complicated.
3. *Relating categories at the dimensional level.* During selective coding, the categories that were integrated in axial coding by identifying the matrix of conceptual relationships existing between them are refined further through the juxtapositioning between asking questions,

generating hypotheses, and making comparisons as a result of the inductive and deductive thinking going on. This refinement is necessary to enable the theory to cover what will occur in given instances within the research setting. Strauss and Corbin (1990: 131) emphasise that it is very important to identify these patterns and to group the data accordingly, because this is what gives the theory its specificity.

4. *Validating the relationships against the data*. The grounding of the theory is completed once it is validated against the data. This is achieved by drawing or writing memos which represent the theory, then writing statements about the relationships between categories in a variety of contexts which are validated against the data.

5. *Filling in categories that may need further development and/or refinement*. This is necessary in order to achieve *conceptual density* in the theory and to promote *conceptual specificity*.

The sampling that occurs in selective coding is known as discriminative sampling and it is used for verificational purposes. In discriminative sampling, a researcher chooses the sites, persons, and documents that will maximise opportunities for verifying the storyline, the relationships between categories, and for filling in poorly developed categories (Strauss and Corbin, 1990: 187). Something may be discovered which does not fit the storyline and those relationships that have frequently been found. If this situation occurs those factors leading to the occurrence of such an instance must be uncovered to determine whether or not it is due to incorrect thinking or an instance of a variation. Categories are considered theoretically saturated and so make the theory conceptually adequate when: there is no more new or relevant data emerging regarding a category; each category has been linked with the paradigm model and each of its elements are catered for, including the variation and process; relationships between categories are well established and validated. Sampling continues until the researcher can theoretically saturate each category.

Memos at this stage of the analysis are complex, illustrating the depth of thought that mirrors the evolving theory. Code notes in the context of selective coding relate mainly to the filling-in role (i.e. filling in those categories which are not sufficiently saturated). Theoretical notes on the other hand are much more extensive during this period of the analysis: 'It is in the form of theoretical memos that we write the first descriptive rendition of what the research is all about' (Strauss and Corbin, 1990). These memos enable the researcher to identify the core category and its host of sub-categories, as well as elaborate these relationships as hypotheses. The operational notes during this phase are very much more succinct. The exploration phase is now over, and it is a matter of validating and refining the theory.

Diagrams also reflect complexity at this stage. The transference of this complexity from writing to an accurate, but concise, graphic format (a diagram) is difficult. However, the process of doing this aids the classification of many of the relationships between the core category and other categories. Hence this diagram will not only clarify the theory to other people, it will also act as a guide to enable the researcher to keep the nature of the relationships clear when writing the theory. General reading of the memos leads to the writing of a descriptive story which is translated into an analytical one using the categories.

Writing a grounded theory

Writing a 'correct' grounded theory is, on the face of it, even more complicated than writing up the more usual types of qualitative research (Strauss and Corbin, 1990: 233). Writing in grounded theory is a continual process throughout the analysis (i.e. coding, memos, field notes). However, there comes a point when analytical writings need to be translated into a written form that can be digested and understood by its designated audience. Charmaz (1990) develops this further when she comments '… writing and rewriting actually become crucial phases of the analytic process'.

Therefore analysis never really stops, and it would be wrong to suggest that it did when one comes to write the final document.

Numerous questions will arise during the writing-up phase, such as 'What is to be communicated?', 'What order should it take?' and 'Who is to be its audience?' Strauss and Corbin (1990) suggest four things which writing a grounded theory text requires: (1) a clear analytic story; (2) writing on a conceptual level, with description kept secondary; (3) a clear specification of relationships among categories, with levels of conceptualisation also kept clear; (4) the specification of variations and their relevant conditions, consequences and so forth, including the broader ones. May (1986: 150) proposes the following structure for writing up a grounded theory study: (1) a clear statement of the major research question and key terms defined; (2) a literature review section (presents the pertinent literature in the area); (3) a methodology section (the process of grounded theory); (4) a findings section (includes the presentation of the theoretical scheme). There is not usually a separate 'discussion section' as there is with most hypothetico-deductive studies, because in the course of presenting the theoretical scheme the findings are usually presented in sufficient detail.

The audience to which the theory is being presented is also very important, because this will help to determine its format. For example, when writing a 'thesis' something of a standardised format is usually expected (i.e. an introduction, review of the literature, methodology, analysis, discussion, conclusion/implications). This would make the third of the procedures suggested by Strauss and Corbin (1990) (a clear specification of relationships among categories, with levels of conceptualisation also kept clear) much more difficult when writing up a grounded theory investigation. The language employed in the theory will be loaded with certain meanings and interpretations. It is, therefore, the unenviable task of the grounded theory writer to not only accommodate the contextual meaning in the form of terms (categories/concepts) for the researched audience, but also to do so in a way that others outside of the context can appreciate their meanings, interpreting these in the way they were intended. There is a very delicately drawn line between 'coining a term and inventing jargon' (May, 1986).

Criticisms of grounded theory

Many criticisms of grounded theory turn on misunderstandings or misuse of the methodology. The major problems with the grounded theory method lie in the limited explication of its epistemological assumptions and in minimising its relation to extant sociological theory (Bryant and Charmaz, 2007; Charmaz, 1990).

Charmaz (1990) has emphasised that a number of criticisms of grounded theory stem from an incomplete understanding of the logic and strategies of the methodology. For example, most authors discussing grounded theory have drawn attention to the *tabula rasa* (blank slate) view of enquiry which grounded theory espouses (e.g. Bulmer, 1979; Charmaz, 1990; Hammersley, 1992). Glaser and Strauss (1967: 33) advocated that a researcher should go into the research setting 'without any preconceived theory, that dictates prior to the research "relevancies" in concepts and hypotheses'. Grounded theory is not pure induction, but a matter of 'maintaining the balance between the two logics *(inductive and deductive)*' (Glaser, 1978: 90), even though it is inductive as a theory emerges after the data collection has started. However, deductive work guides theoretical sampling. Sparkes (1987: 138) notes that inductive theory formation is open to criticism centring on the notion of 'underdetermination', and that no process is ever completely reliant upon either induction or deduction.

Grounded theory's apparent affinity with positivism, or viewing it as a form of 'inductivist positivism' (Stanley and Wise, 1983: 152), creates problems for theorists (see Roman and Apple, 1990; Henwood and Pidgeon, 1993; Woods, 1992). Glaser and Strauss (1967: 3) acknowledge in a footnote the use of existing knowledge, as long as it is well grounded.

However, Charmaz (1990: 1163) emphasises a delay and not the complete removal of the literature review from the whole process.

Sanger (1994: 179) notes, 'their [Strauss and Corbin's] view conflates creativity with "theoretical sensitivity"'. Strauss and Corbin (1990) facilitate creativity within a systematic analysis by suggesting that the manipulation of categorised data is a creative enterprise. This creativity involves an open-minded, generative approach, which not only entertains alternative notions, but is also able to cope with these in its framework relative to the perspective of the researcher and their interpretive skills. Catering for this creativity is a compromise not only for Strauss and Corbin (1990) but also for any researcher between a systematic structure and freedom. To systematise this creativity, however, runs the risk of the criticism that one might as well adopt a computer program that categorises key words and phrases.

Another criticism levelled at grounded theory is the lack of rigour associated with it (e.g. Hammersley, 1989). There is no rigid divorce between discovery and verification. Yes, Glaser and Strauss (1967) did contrast the discovery and verification approaches, but this was to emphasise the desire and need to develop new avenues of theoretical development. Grounded theory specifically, and qualitative research generally, do not employ the hypothetico-deductive verification model. It emphasises inductive, open-ended, intuitive approaches to data gathering. Grounded theory does provide a rigorous method, however this must be assessed from the internal logic of its own method (Charmaz, 1983) and not by criteria found in and appropriate to other methods.

Conclusion

The (re)interpretation and evolution of grounded theory methodology is a positive and constructive dimension of its development. However, any researcher employing grounded theory has to fully understand and articulate their ontological, epistemological and methodological location within that changing landscape. Writing a grounded theory is challenging and complicated in that it is part of a continual process throughout the analysis and actually forms part of that analysis. The form of the final report or dissertation will be determined very much by the particular audience and the substantive theory. It therefore does not usually adhere to the standard modes of presentation. Those criticisms of grounded theory methodology mainly stem from a lack of articulation or thought about the assumptions which underpin the methodology. The misinterpretations which form many of the criticisms are being eroded by researchers' (re)interpretation and greater clarification of grounded theory methodology.

Questions for further investigation

1. Why have you selected/considered grounded theory methodology? What is it about this methodology that is attractive to you in terms of addressing the particular area of research, as well as yourself as a researcher?
2. What are the ontological and epistemological differences between the main (re)interpretations of grounded theory (constructivist, Glasarian, Straussian)? Where would you locate yourself and why?
3. What is theoretical sensitivity and how will your ontological and epistemological assumptions influence your interpretation of it?
4. Relative to an area of investigation of your choice, consider how and what different kinds of data you would need to gather to ensure that it was relevant, had depth, and provided a detailed viewpoint of the participants.

Suggested further reading

Birks, M. and Mills, J. (2015) *Grounded Theory: A Practical Guide* (2nd edn. London: Sage. A good starting point for researchers unfamiliar with grounded theory. This text offers an accessible, logical and succinct practical guide addressing those questions and aspects of grounded theory that a researcher familiarising themself with it would ask.

Bryant, A. and Charmaz, K. (eds) (2007) *The SAGE Handbook of Grounded Theory.* London: Sage. An excellent text which draws together chapters from leading researchers and practitioners in grounded theory, providing a comprehensive overview of the major perspectives on grounded theory from across the world.

Clarke, A. and Charmaz, K. (eds) (2014) *Grounded Theory and Situational Analysis.* Thousand Oaks, CA: Sage. This is a four-volume publication which offers a comprehensive historical background and overview of key debates in grounded theory. A key feature is the way in which it presents a range of issues and examples of grounded theory from a variety of discipline perspectives. The final volume is devoted to situational analysis methodology, the first part of which is devoted to its relationship with grounded theory.

Morse, J.M., Stern, P.N., Corbin, J., Bowers, B., Charmaz, K. and Clarke, A.E. (2009) *Developing Grounded Theory: The Second Generation.* New York: Left Coast Press. This text is a result of a meeting of the 'second generation' of grounded theory methodologists (many students of Glaser and Strauss) in 2007. It is very helpful in that it shares the experiences, thoughts and insights of key protagonists involved in the evolution of grounded theory.

Strauss, A. and Corbin, J. (1990) *Basics of Qualitative Research: Procedures and Techniques.* Thousand Oaks, CA: Sage. Strauss, A. and Corbin, J. (1998) *Basics of Qualitative Research: Techniques and Procedures for Developing Grounded Theory,* 2nd edn. Thousand Oaks, CA: Sage. Corbin, J. and Strauss, A. (2008) *Basics of Qualitative Research: Procedures and Techniques,* 3rd edn. Thousand Oaks, CA: Sage. These three texts illustrate the progression of an interpretation of grounded theory which has strongly influenced the organisation and formulation of the helix model presented here to illustrate grounded theory analysis and substantive theory generation.

References

Annells, M. (1997) 'Grounded theory methods, part 1: within the five moments of qualitative research', *Nursing Inquiry,* 4(2): 120–9.

Babchuk, W.A. (2009) 'Grounded Theory for Practice-Based Application: Closing the Embarrassing Gap Between Theory and Empirical Research'. Paper presented at the Midwest Research-to-Practice Conference in Adult, Continuing, Community and Extension Education, Northeastern Illinois University, Chicago, 21–23 October.

Birks, M. and Mills, J. (2015) *Grounded Theory: A Practical Guide,* 2nd edn. London: Sage.

Bryant, A. and Charmaz, K. (eds) (2007) *The SAGE Handbook of Grounded Theory.* London: Sage.

Buckley, C. and Waring, M. (2009) 'The evolving nature of grounded theory: experiential reflections on the potential of the method for analysing children's attitudes towards physical activity', *International Journal of Social Research Methodology,* 12(4): 317–34.

Bulmer, M. (1979) 'Concepts in the analysis of qualitative data', *Sociological Review,* 27: 651–77.

Charmaz, K. (1983) 'The Grounded Theory Method: An explication and interpretation', in R.M Emerson (ed.), *Contemporary Field Research: A Collection of Readings.* Boston: Little Brown.

Charmaz, K. (1990) '"Discovering" chronic illness: using grounded theory', *Social Science and Medicine,* 30(11): 1161–72.

Charmaz, K. (2000) 'Grounded Theory: Objectivist and constructivist methods', in N.K. Denzin and Y.S. Lincoln (eds), *Handbook of Qualitative Research,* 2nd edn. Thousand Oaks, CA: Sage.

Charmaz, K. (2006) *Constructing Grounded Theory: A Practical Guide Through Qualitative Analysis.* London: Sage.

Charmaz, K. (2009) 'Shifting Grounds: Constructivist grounded theory methods', in J.M. Morse et al. (eds), *Developing Grounded Theory: The Second Generation.* New York: Left Coast Press, pp. 127–54.

Charmaz, K. and Henwood, K. (2008) 'Grounded Theory', in C. Willig and W. Stainton-Rogers (eds), *The SAGE Handbook of Qualitative Research in Psychology.* London: Sage.

Clarke, A. (2007) 'Grounded Theory: Critiques, debates and situational analysis', in W. Outhwaite and S.P. Turner (eds), The SAGE *Handbook of Social Science Methodology.* London: Sage, pp. 423–42.

Clarke, A. and Friese, C. (2007) 'Grounded Theorizing Using Grounded Theory', in A. Bryant and K. Charmaz (eds),*The SAGE Handbook of Grounded Theory*. London: Sage, pp. 363–97.

Corbin, J. and Strauss, A. (2008) *Basics of Qualitative Research: Techniques and Procedures for Developing Grounded Theory*, 3rd edn. Thousand Oaks, CA: Sage.

Douglas, D. (2003) 'Reflections on research supervision: a grounded theory case of reflective practice', *Research in Post-Compulsory Education,* 8(2): 213–29.

Glaser, B.G. (1978) *Theoretical Sensitivity: Advances in the Methodology of Grounded Theory*. Mill Valley, CA: Sociology Press.

Glaser, B.G. (1992) *Basics of Grounded Theory Analysis*. Mill Valley, CA: Sociology Press.

Glaser, B.G. (2004) 'Remodelling grounded theory', *Forum: Qualitative Sozialforschung/Orum: Qualitiative Social Research,* 3(3).

Glaser, B.G. (2005) *The Grounded Theory Perspective III: Theoretical Coding*. Mill Valley, CA: Sociology Press.

Glaser, B.G. (2008) *Doing Quantitative Grounded Theory*. Mill Valley, CA: Sociology Press.

Glaser, B.G. and Strauss, A.L. (1967) *The Discovery of Grounded Theory: An Approach to Qualitative Research*. New York: Aldine.

Hammersley, M. (1989) *The Dilemma of Qualitative Method: Herbert Blumer and the Chicago Tradition*. London: Routledge.

Hammersley, M. (1992) *What's Wrong With Ethnography?* London: Routledge.

Henwood, K.L. and Pidgeon, N.F. (1993) 'Qualitative Research and Psychological Theorizing', in M. Hammersley (eds), *Social Research: Philosophy, Politics and Practice*. London: Sage, pp. 14–32.

Hildenbrand, B. (2007) 'Mediating Structure and Interaction in Grounded Theory', in A. Bryant and K. Charmaz (eds), *The SAGE Handbook of Grounded Theory*. London: Sage, pp. 539–64.

Hutchinson, S.A. (1988) 'Education and Grounded Theory', in R.R. Sherman and R.B. Webb (eds), *Qualitative Research in Education: Focus and Methods*. London: Falmer.

Marshall, C. and Rossman, G.B. (1989) *Designing Qualitative Research*. Newbury Park, CA: Sage.

Martin, P.Y. and Turner, B.A. (1986) 'Grounded theory and organisational research', *Journal of Applied Behavioural Science,* 22(2): 141–57.

May, K.A. (1986) 'Writing and Evaluating the Grounded Theory Research Report', in C.W. Chentiz and J.M. Swanson (eds), *From Practice to Grounded Theory: Qualitative Research in Nursing*. Menlo Park, CA: Addison-Wesley, pp. 146–54.

Moghaddam, A. (2006) 'Coding issues in grounded theory', *Issues in Educational Research,* 16(1): 52.

Morse, J.M. (2009) 'Tussles, Tensions and Resolutions', in J.M. Morse et al. (eds), *Developing Grounded Theory: The Second Generation*. New York: Left Coast Press, pp. 13–19.

Morse, J.M., Stern, P.N. et al. (2009) *Developing Grounded Theory: The Second Generation*. New York: Left Coast Press.

Parker, B. and Myrick, F. (2011) 'The grounded theory method: deconstruction and reconstruction in a human patient simulation context', *International Journal of Qualitative Methods,* 10(1): 73–85.

Roman, L.G. and Apple, M.W. (1990) 'Is Naturalism a Move Away from Positivism? Materialist and feminist approaches to subjectivity in ethnographic research', in E.W. Eisner and A. Peshkin (eds), *Qualitative Inquiry in Education: The Continuing Debate*. New York: Teachers College Press, pp. 38–73.

Sanger, J. (1994) 'Seven types of creativity: looking for insights in data analysis', *British Educational Research Journal,* 20(2): 175–85.

Sparkes, A.C. (1987) 'The Genesis of An Innovation: A Case of Emergent Concerns and Micropolitical Solutions'. PhD thesis, Loughborough University.

Stanley, L. and Wise, S. (1983) *Breaking Out: Feminist Consciousness and Feminist Research*. London: Routledge & Kegan Paul.

Strauss, A.L. (1987) *Qualitative Analysis for Social Scientists*. New York: Cambridge University Press.

Strauss, A. and Corbin, J. (1990) *Basics of Qualitative Research: Procedures and Techniques*. Thousand Oaks, CA: Sage.

Strauss, A. and Corbin, J. (1994) 'Grounded Theory Methodology', in N.K. Denzin, and Y.S. Lincoln (eds), *Handbook of Qualitative Research*. Thousand Oaks, CA: Sage, pp. 273–85.

Strauss, A. and Corbin, J. (eds) (1997) *Grounded Theory in Practice*. Thousand Oaks, CA: Sage.

Strauss, A. and Corbin, J. (1998) *Basics of Qualitative Research: Techniques and Procedures for Developing Grounded Theory*, 2nd edn. Thousand Oaks, CA: Sage.

Tesch, R. (1990) *Qualitative Research: Analysis Types and Software Tools.* London: Falmer.

Thomas, G. and James, D. (2006) 'Reinventing grounded theory: some questions about theory, ground and discovery', *British Educational Research Journal,* 32(6): 767–95.

Turner, B.A. (1983) 'The use of grounded theory for the qualitative analysis of organisational behaviour', *Journal of Management Studies,* 20(3): 333–48.

Waring, M. (1995) 'Gatekeeping Processes: Grounded Theory, Young People and Physical Activity'. Unpublished PhD thesis, Loughborough University.

Weed, M. (2009) 'Research quality considerations for grounded theory research in sport and exercise psychology', *Psychology of Sport and Exercise,* 10: 509–10.

Weed, M. (2013) 'Research Quality Considerations for Grounded Theory Research in Sport and Exercise Psychology', in A.E. Clarke and K. Charmaz (eds), *Grounded Theory and Situational Analysis.* Thousand Oaks, CA: Sage, Volume 2.

Woods, P. (1992) 'Symbolic Interactionism: Theory and method', in M. LeCompte, W.L. Millroy and J. Preissle (eds), *The Handbook of Qualitative Research in Education.* San Diego, CA: Academic Press, pp. 337–404.

Case study research

Laura Day Ashley

13

What is case study research?

The case study is a popular research approach in the social sciences. It has been referred to as a research 'strategy' (Robson, 2011), a 'design frame' (Thomas, 2013a), and a research 'genre' (Hamilton and Corbett-Whittier, 2013). It has also been argued that 'case study is not the name of a method', rather it is open to many different types of method (Golby, 1994: 11). Robson (2011: 136) describes the case study as:

> … a strategy for doing research which involves an empirical investigation of a particular contemporary phenomenon within its real life context using multiple sources of evidence.

What constitutes a 'case' for empirical research is wide ranging and without obvious limitation (Golby, 1994): it may be an individual, such as a teacher or student; an institution, such as a school; an event, project or programme within an institution; it may be a policy, or other types of system. The strength of case study research lies in its ability to enable the researcher to intensively investigate the case in depth, to probe, drill down and get at its complexity, often through immersion in, repeated visits to, or encounters with, the case. A case may be described as 'a bounded system' (Smith, cited in Stake, 1995: 2) whereby its 'parameters of particularity are set by spatial, temporal, personal, organizational or other factors' (Thomas,

2011a: 512). The contextual conditions within which the case is situated – and with which it interacts – also tend to be analysed in relation to the case (Yin, 2014). Such contexts may be local, national or international, or personal or professional communities (Hamilton and Corbett-Whittier, 2013). However, the boundaries between the case and the context are often blurred (Yin, 2014).

The purpose of case study research might be to *explore* a phenomenon about which not much is known, or to *describe* something in detail, or to *explain* what is happening. Yin (2014) argues that case studies have a particular ability to answer *why* and *how* research questions rather than simply *what*, and therefore they also have the potential to *evaluate* or *explain*, for example, why a particular programme did or did not work. Yin (2014) also proposes that case study research is most appropriate to answer (a) *how* and *why* research questions that (b) focus on *contemporary phenomena within real-life contexts* and (c) over which the researcher has *little control*.

Types of case study and selection of cases

Two main forms of case study are identified by Yin (2014): firstly, a 'holistic' case study which focuses on the case (e.g. a school) as the unit of analysis in its entirety; and secondly, an 'embedded' case study which focuses on one or more aspect(s) or sub-units of the case (e.g. one or more project(s) being carried out within a school). Both types of case study present their own challenges. By focusing on the case as a whole within its context, the holistic case study inevitably entails a trade-off of breadth over depth, however a key concern in the embedded case study is to ensure that it does not focus solely on the sub-units of analysis but also pays attention to the unit of analysis – the case. Single case studies may also be conducted in more than one context, or as Golby (1994) describes, in 'multiple sites'; an example from my own research is the case of a Forum theatre workshop (case) created by a UK-based theatre company and delivered in a number of secondary schools (sites) in London (Day, 2002).

Another area of differentiation between types of case study is between the single case study and the multiple case study. The multiple case study involves the study of a small number of cases of a phenomenon, each of which is situated within its own specific context. Both single and multiple case studies might follow either the holistic design or the embedded design. However the rationales for the selection of single cases and multiple cases differ. Yin (2014: 51–3) sets out five key rationales for selecting a single case:

1. The 'critical' case that seeks to test theory.
2. The 'extreme' or 'unusual' case.
3. The 'common' case.
4. The 'revelatory' case that is important because it may not have been previously investigated.
5. The 'longitudinal' case which is studied at different moments in time with a focus on change.

That a case might be 'representative' is questioned by Thomas (2011b: 31), who emphasises that the case study is limited to 'a particular representation given in context and understood in that context'. Generalisation to larger populations is not a strength or even a key intention of case study research. Yin (2014) explains that multiple case studies do not follow a 'sampling logic' on which the statistical generalisation to populations is based, but a 'replication logic' which is not dissimilar to the logic used in multiple experiments.

According to Yin (2014), the rationale for the selection of multiple cases, therefore, is either that (a) they are expected to lead to similar findings, or because (b) they are expected to lead to different findings for specific reasons. Multiple case studies may have the potential to be stronger than single case designs but they also may entail more time and resources (Yin, 2014). Later in this chapter I discuss an example from my own research of a multiple case study design.

Further types of case study are described by Hamilton and Corbett-Whittier (2013). These include the *reflective case study* in which the researcher is the focus of the study, with data collection methods including reflective journals and audio- and video-recording to encourage self-reflection, and the *longitudinal case study* which involves immersion in the case for an extended period of time (rather than an intensive and short period of time), and where the focus is to investigate processes and the dynamics of change over time. Hamilton and Corbett-Whittier (2013) also identify three overlapping models for generating a number of case studies related to a theme. These are *cumulative case studies* which seek to build on or replicate existing case studies, *collective case studies* whereby researchers work separately on case studies on a theme with a shared purpose but may vary in their approach to data generation, and *collaborative case studies* whereby colleagues conduct case studies in different contexts but with a shared purpose and approach to data generation.

Case study research and validity

We have established that statistical generalisation to larger populations from a single case or small number of cases is not the aim of case study research. However, this does not mean that the findings from case study research are restricted to understanding the particularity of a case. A key question to ask in case study design is 'what is this case *a case of*?' – the very selection of a case indicates that the researcher is connecting it to a broader phenomenon or group of cases of its kind and to a collective understanding of that phenomenon. Yin (2014) argues that case study findings may also be considered in relation to a wider set of theoretical ideas potentially leading to 'analytic generalisation', and it is this type of generalisation by which the *external validity* of case study research might be assessed.

In terms of *internal validity*, a strength of case study research lies in its potential to make inference about causal *mechanisms* and *pathways* (e.g. how and why are x and y connected?). This is arguably more possible in case studies (Gerring, 2007) that focus on 'the complex interaction of many factors in few cases' (Thomas, 2011a: 512) than it is in '"variable-led" research' (Thomas, 2011a, citing Ragin) that focuses on 'few variables in a large number of cases' (2011a: 512). To strengthen confidence in the causal inference made from case study research, Yin (2014: 142–68) identifies five analytic tactics that might be employed: pattern matching, explanation building, time-series analysis, logic models, and cross-case synthesis.

To generate rich data rigorously and in a way that reduces subjectivity and increases *construct validity*, case study research tends to rely on multiple methods and sources of data collection. Thus an in-depth understanding of cases is achieved through the triangulation of methods and sources to confirm emerging findings and point to contradictions and tensions – an 'awareness of anomaly' (Kuhn, cited in Thomas, 2010: 580) that may highlight areas for analysis and help draw insights and interpretations. Case study research allows for a certain degree of methodological eclecticism which typically includes asking people questions, observing what happens, and analysing documents (Bassey, 1999). These methods of data collection may be qualitative or quantitative, or a combination of both (Gerring, 2007). A particular data collection and analysis concern for multiple case studies is how to preserve in-depth understandings of the uniqueness of individual cases – their 'meaning in context' (Mishler, 1979, cited in Noblitt and Hare, 1988: 17) – and at the same time ensure a consistency of approach across the cases

to enable cross-case comparison. In the following section I will discuss how I addressed this and other design issues mentioned above in a multiple case study research project of my own.

Example: Multiple case study of private school outreach in India

This doctoral research (conducted in 2000–2003) focused on a phenomenon in the Indian context that I have termed 'private school outreach' (Day Ashley, 2005, 2006, 2010, 2013) and defined as follows:

> Private schools that extend their activities beyond the usual remit of providing middle-class children with fee-charging education and additionally provide education free of charge (or for a nominal fee) to socio-economically disadvantaged children who would otherwise be out of school.

Despite its apparent increasing incidence, the phenomenon of private school outreach had barely been researched at the time – only a couple of short descriptions about this type of activity existed within other works (Jessop, 1998; Tooley, 2001). Therefore, I decided upon a case study strategy to explore this phenomenon and gain an in-depth understanding of its complexities, and in particular the dynamics of the attempt to educate children from very different socio-economic backgrounds by the *same institution*. In this respect, private school outreach presented an unusual case in the Indian context, where the education system has been described as the grouping of children into 'different types of institutions according to their socio-economic background' (Kumar, 1987: 38) – a situation that was exacerbated with the mushrooming of low-fee private schools (De et al., 2000) at the time of research, thereby adding another layer of institution catering for a specific socio-economic group. However, in private school outreach, although educated by the same institution, private school students and out-of-school children were not usually educated together in the *same classrooms* but separately, with the former receiving a formal English-medium private education and the latter being given a non-formal education in their local languages in what I refer to as 'outreach programmes'. This anomaly of the same institution educating diverse children (but separately) led to the development of the overarching research question:

Does private school outreach in the Indian context contribute to bridging educational and social divides, or does it serve to maintain and reinforce them?

I decided to carry out a multiple case study rather than a single case study because I was interested to make some broad comment about what characterises private school outreach; in a single case study it would be difficult to separate private

school outreach as a phenomenon from what was idiosyncratic about that particular case. A multiple case study then would transcend 'the radical particularism' (Firestone and Herriott, 1983) of the single case and ask the question 'Do these findings make sense beyond a specific case?' (Miles and Huberman, 1994: 173).

Since private school outreach was relatively new research terrain, the strategy of 'maximum variation' (Patton, 2015) was adopted for case selection. This allowed for common patterns across the diverse cases to be traced, leading to the identification of key characteristics of private school outreach. It also enabled an exploration of variation – to investigate the different conditions in which variation between cases occurred (Becker, 1990), as well as its meaning and effects. Of the ten examples of private school outreach identified during a pre-study visit, three of these were selected for the multiple case studies. This

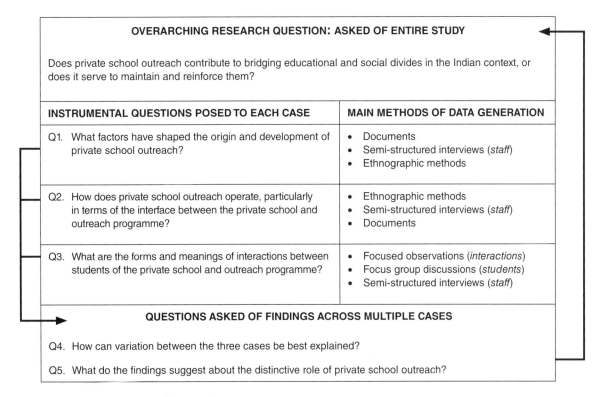

Figure 13.1 Set of research questions

was considered a sensible number of cases given the size of the project and time available to balance an in-depth understanding of each case with the breadth of understanding gained by investigating multiple cases (Schofield, 1990). The first criterion was that the three cases were not directly influencing each other and so cases were selected that were not part of the same network. Other criteria included: variation in the philosophical foundations of the schools; variation in the length of time since the schools had been founded; variation in the physical set-up of the outreach programmes in relation to the private schools; variation in the student clientele of both the private school and outreach programme; and variation in their geographical location (i.e. to include both urban and rural cases).

A set of research questions served as a guiding framework for the data collection and analysis (see Figure 13.1). In order to answer the overarching research question, instrumental research questions were used to guide the empirical data collection in each case. The types of methods of data collection used to address each instrumental research question are indicated in the right-hand column, with data sources in brackets. These data were drawn on to answer the research question asked of findings across the multiple cases, which in turn served as a vehicle for answering the overarching question asked of the entire study.

A data collection procedure based loosely on Yin's (2014) concept of 'case study protocol' was devised which served as a practical guide to the collection of data in all three cases and was piloted and subsequently refined during a visit to the field in a private school outreach setting separate from the three actual cases for the study. This procedure (see Figure 13.2) involved a progressive structuring of the research process, inspired by Firestone and Herriott's (1983) formalisation of qualitative research processes. In each case it comprised two phases of research over a six-week to two-month period: an exploratory phase, followed by (and overlapping with) a semi-structured phase, with each phase lasting approximately 3–4 weeks. The exploratory phase involved a period of looser, more unstructured methods of data collection, which included sourcing, reading and analysing documents relating to the schools and their outreach work, and ethnographic methods. The process, which I describe as 'outwards mapping' (inspired by the 'backward mapping' used by Dyer [2000, citing Elmore, 1980] to research policy by starting at the grassroots level) was used as a technique to explore the possible vantage points from which the researcher could be positioned during the semi-structured phase. Taking the outreach programme in each case as a starting point and working outwards, it involved a strategic identification of the people, places and practices associated with it.

As well as being a source of richly contextual data about each case, in many ways the exploratory phase provided the groundwork for the

EXPLORATORY PHASE		
Documentary analysis	Ethnographic methods	'Outwards mapping'
SECOND SEMI-STRUCTURED PHASE		
Semi-structured interviews	Focus group discussions	Focused observations

Figure 13.2 Progressive structuring of the research process

semi-structured phase, in terms of establishing a rapport with key informants, identifying participants and settings for selection, and generally understanding how the cases worked. This informed the questions posed during the semi-structured interviews, focus group discussions and focused observations of interactions, which could be more deeply probing and strategic in their nature. Understandings derived from the exploratory phase also informed how the data collection methods in the semi-structured phase might be tailored in ways that were more suited and sensitive to specific cases. Equally, this data collection procedure ensured that during the semi-structured phase the same types of questions were asked of all three cases in broadly similar ways, and provided a 'coherent system ... for collecting information from a range of informants, across a potential range of sites, in a roughly comparable format' (Huberman and Miles, 1994: 430).

Initial data analysis of individual cases began in the field; this enabled me to return to each case to check emerging findings and explore issues that had been drawn to my attention in one case but not in the other two. This strengthened the more intense within- and cross-case analysis that followed on my return from the field. At this stage the data had been organised into various forms: individual case study reports, the semi-structured data (both those acquired through semi-structured research methods and the transformed unstructured data), and the original unstructured data. Initially, a re-reading of the entire data set was conducted to bring the researcher close to the data to discover areas which may not have been dominant in the emerging analyses whilst in the field. During this re-reading a 'cross-sectional indexing system' (Mason, 2002) was developed which was applicable to the whole data set. Thus, the data set was reduced to a system of categories which revealed broad conceptual patterns across the three cases as well as areas of variation. This was followed by in-depth within-case analyses to view the categories in the context of the complexities and dynamics pertaining to each case, and relate these back to the original field notes, interview transcriptions and

documentary sources (Coffey and Atkinson, 1996). Connections between the categories were investigated and during this process displays were used in order to see more clearly the associations and configurations (Miles and Huberman, 1994). Finally, the displayed data from each of the cases were compared. This phase involved the researcher in the process of interpretation: 'drawing meaning from the displayed data' (Huberman and Miles, 1994: 429). In this way an explanatory picture for the variation between the three cases was built and the findings that emerged were verified through processes of triangulation.

Other examples of case study research

This description of my own case study research is intended to provide the reader with an example of how a multiple case study might be done; however, it is important to note that this is just one specific case study design tailored to a particular research focus, and there are many other types of design possibilities. Some recent examples of multiple case studies include research by Coronel et al. (2010) on the leadership roles of eight female school principals in Spain, and Meirink et al.'s (2010) study of five teacher learning and collaboration teams in Dutch secondary schools; the latter study involved a combination of qualitative and quantitative methods. In terms of single case studies, some recent examples include ethnographic case studies such as that by Theodorou and Nind (2010) of a young child with autism in England, and by McKinney (2010) of a desegregated girls' school in South Africa. The last example given is Nilholm and Alm's (2010) case study of an inclusive classroom in Sweden, which explicitly attempts to develop a methodology to study inclusiveness transparently to include pupil experience, and creatively makes use of a range of data collection methods including sociograms and children's poetry. As a final note, I would suggest (following Mason, 2002) that this type of creative thinking, as well as strategic thinking, is key to research design (not only case study research) since it can help researchers formulate the best available research design for the specific research project. For other practical examples of case study research, see Yin (2012) for case study applications in social science research, and Thomas (2013b) for a collection of examples of case study research in education.

Questions for further investigation

1. Consider if case study research is appropriate for your intended research project by following Yin's (2014) key criteria: i.e. does it ask (a) *how* and *why* research questions that (b) focus on *contemporary phenomena within contexts in the 'real world'* and (c) over which the researcher has *little control*?

2. Try to diagrammatically represent your case(s) within their context(s). Explain the rationale for the type of case study you have selected: is it embedded or holistic? Is it a multiple or single case study? Does it follow any of the following models, e.g. reflective, longitudinal, collaborative, cumulative, collective? What rationale can you give for the selection of your individual case(s)? What is your case *a case of*?

3. What methods of data collection and sources do you intend to use to address your research question(s) and why? How do you intend to compare and contrast data across data collection methods and sources? How do you intend to relate your case study to theory; do you intend to make analytic generalisations or causal inferences?

Suggested further reading

Stake, R. (1995) *The Art of Case Study Research*. Thousand Oaks, CA: Sage. This book presents a disciplined, qualitative exploration of case study methods by drawing from naturalistic, holistic, ethnographic, phenomenological and biographic research methods.

Thomas, G. (2016) *How to Do Your Case Study: A Guide for Students and Researchers*, 2nd edn. London: Sage. A well-written and easy to read introduction to case study research.

Yin, R.K. (2014) *Case Study Research: Design and Methods*, 5th edn. Thousand Oaks, CA: Sage. A comprehensive text covering a wide range of issues relating to designing and conducting case studies in social science research.

References

Bassey, M. (1999) *Case Study Research in Educational Settings*. Buckingham: Open University Press.

Becker, H.S. (1990) 'Generalizing from Case Studies', in E.W. Eisner and A. Peshkin (eds), *Qualitative Inquiry in Education: The Continuing Debate*. New York: Teachers College Press.

Coffey, A. and Atkinson, P. (1996) *Making Sense of Qualitative Data: Complementary Research Strategies*. Thousand Oaks, CA: Sage.

Coronel, J.M., Moreno, E. and Carrasco, M.J. (2010) 'Beyond obstacles and problems: women principals in Spain leading change in their schools', *International Journal of Leadership in Education*, 13(2): 141–62.

Day, L. (2002) '"Putting yourself in other people's shoes": the use of Forum theatre to explore refugee and homeless issues in schools', *Journal of Moral Education*, 31(1): 21–34.

Day Ashley, L. (2005) 'From margins to mainstream: private school outreach inclusion processes for out-of-school children in India', *International Journal of Educational Development*, 25(2): 133–44.

Day Ashley, L. (2006) 'Inter-school working involving private school outreach initiatives and government schools in India', *Compare*, 36(4): 481–96.

Day Ashley, L. (2010) 'The use of structuration theory to conceptualize alternative practice in education: the case of private school outreach in India', *British Journal of Sociology of Education*, 31(3): 337–51.

Day Ashley, L. (2013) 'The shifting politics of the private in education: debates and developments in researching private school outreach in India', *Comparative Education*, 49(2): 206–25.

De, A., Majumdar, M., Samson, M. and Noronha, C. (2000) *Role of Private Schools in Basic Education*. New Delhi: NIEPA (National Institute for Educational Planning and Administration) and Indian National Commission for Cooperation with UNESCO, Ministry of Human Resource Development, Government of India.

Dyer, C. (2000) *Operation Blackboard: Policy Implementation in Indian Elementary Education*. Oxford: Symposium Books.

Firestone, W.A. and Herriott, R.E. (1983) 'The formalization of qualitative research: an adaptation of "soft" science to the policy world', *Evaluation Review*, 7(4): 437–66.

Gerring, J. (2007) *Case Study Research: Principles and Practice*. New York: Cambridge University Press.

Golby, M. (1994) *Case Study as Educational Research*. Educational Research Monograph Series. Exeter: School of Education, Research Support Unit, University of Exeter.

Hamilton, L. and Corbett-Whittier, C. (2013) *Using Case Study in Education Research*. London: Sage.

Huberman, A.M. and Miles, M.B. (1994) 'Data Management and Analysis Methods', in N.K. Denzin and Y.S. Lincoln (eds), *The SAGE Handbook of Qualitative Research*. Thousand Oaks, CA: Sage.

Jessop, T. (1998) *A Model of Best Practice at Loreto Day School, Sealdah, Calcutta*. Occasional Paper No.1, Education Sector Group, Department for International Development, India.

Kumar, K. (1987) 'Reproduction or Change? Education and elites in India', in R. Ghosh and M. Zachariah (eds), *Education and the Process of Change*. New Delhi: Sage.

Mason, J. (2002) *Qualitative Researching*, 2nd edn. London: Sage.

McKinney, C. (2010) 'Schooling in black and white: assimilationist discourses and subversive identity performances in a desegregated South African girls' school', *Race Ethnicity and Education*, 13(2): 191–207.

Meirink, J.A., Imants, J., Meijer, P.C. and Verloop, N. (2010) 'Teacher learning and collaboration in innovative teams', *Cambridge Journal of Education*, 40(2): 161–81.

Miles, M.B. and Huberman, A.M. (1994) *Qualitative Data Analysis: An Expanded Sourcebook*. London: Sage.

Nilholm, C. and Alm, B. (2010) 'An inclusive classroom? A case study of inclusiveness, teacher strategies, and children's experiences', *European Journal of Special Needs Education*, 25(3): 239–52.

Noblitt, G.W. and Hare, R.D. (1988) *Meta-Ethnography: Synthesising Qualitative Studies*. Newbury Park, CA: Sage.

Patton, M.Q. (2015) *Qualitative Research and Evaluation Methods*, 4th edn. Thousand Oaks, CA: Sage.

Robson, C. (2011) *Real World Research: A Resource for Users of Social Research Methods in Applied Settings*, 3rd edn. Chichester: Wiley.

Schofield, J.W. (1990) 'Increasing the Generalizability of Qualitative Research', in E.W. Eisner and A. Peshkin (eds), *Qualitative Inquiry in Education: The Continuing Debate*. New York: Teachers College Press.

Stake, R. (1995) *The Art of Case Study Research*. Thousand Oaks, CA: Sage.

Theodorou, F. and Nind, M. (2010) 'Inclusion in play: a case study of a child with autism in an inclusive nursery', *Journal of Research in Special Educational Needs*, 10(2): 99–106.

Thomas, G. (2010) 'Doing case study: abduction not induction, phronesis not theory', *Qualitative Inquiry*, 16(7): 575–82.

Thomas, G. (2011a) 'A typology for the case study in social science following a review of definition, discourse and structure', *Qualitative Inquiry*, 17(6): 511–21.

Thomas, G. (2011b) 'The case: generalisation, theory and phronesis in case study', *Oxford Review of Education*, 37(1): 21–35.

Thomas, G. (2013a) *How to Do Your Research Project: A Guide for Students in Education and Applied Social Sciences*, 2nd edn. London: Sage.

Thomas, G. (ed.) (2013b) *Case Study Methods in Education. Volume Four: Examples of Case Studies in Education*. London: Sage.

Tooley, J. (2001) *The Global Education Industry: Lessons from Private Education in Developing Countries*. London: The Institute of Economic Affairs.

Yin, R.K. (2012) *Applications of Case Study Research*, 3rd edn. Thousand Oaks, CA: Sage.

Yin, R.K. (2014) *Case Study Research: Design and Methods*, 5th edn. Thousand Oaks, CA: Sage.

Secondary data

Emma Smith

14

Introduction

This chapter provides a brief introduction to using secondary data in education research. Secondary data analysis is a relatively under-used research technique in the field of education yet the potential for its use, among novice researchers in particular, is huge. From a nation's population census to public opinion polls about the outcome of TV talent show competitions, there are not many aspects of the social world that have not been covered by some type of survey or opinion poll. Indeed, it is very likely that whatever your research topic, the answers to at least some of your research questions can be found by analysing secondary data.

What is secondary data analysis?

Secondary data analysis can be defined as 'an empirical exercise carried out on data that has already been gathered or compiled in some way' (Dale et al., 1988: 3). In other words, it is an approach where the researcher analyses data which have already been collected, usually by someone else. This analysis may involve using the original, or novel, research questions, statistical approaches and theoretical frameworks. Secondary data come in many forms. These can include the data generated from systematic reviews or from documentary analysis, as well as from the results from large-scale surveys such as the National Census or the Programme for International Student Assessment (PISA). Secondary data can be numeric or non-numeric. Non-numeric, or qualitative secondary data, can include data retrieved second-hand from interviews, ethnographic accounts, documents, photographs or conversations. In the UK, for example, an excellent source of archived qualitative data is provided by the UK Data Service. Data include in-depth interviews, field notes and observations, as well as personal documents. The service provides support and training, as well as access to classic postwar studies of British society, including the research papers and data for Jackson and Marsden's classic (1962) study, *Education and the Working Class*.

However, our interest in this chapter lies with numeric secondary data. This focus on numeric (or quantitative) data is important. Being able to engage confidently with numbers is a great advantage when doing research in education, or in any social field. It enables the researcher, whether an undergraduate or a professor, to use a wide range of research tools – from surveys to experiments, from digital media to archives of open data. And, crucially, it will also allow the researcher to engage with other people's numeric research. We are often told that we live in a 'data age' and the ubiquity of statistics makes it essential that citizens are able to engage fluently and confidently with numbers. A numerate society is important for many reasons: consumers need to be able to make decisions about mortgage or lending rates; voters need to be able to assess competing political claims about rising or falling levels of immigration; newspaper readers need to use basic arithmetic to be able to judge the trustworthiness of competing views on the economy and so on. So being able to engage with numbers is vital for our role as citizens as well as researchers. However, we are often told that in the UK, possibly more than in any other similar nation, we have a numerical skills deficit. Indeed according to a recent report by the British Academy, 'the case to raise the UK's game on quantitative skills is urgent. The country is facing a crisis in levels of numeracy' (2015: 3). This deficit, we are told, is especially pronounced in the social sciences, and in the field of education research in particular.

Using secondary data offers us a partial solution to both the dearth of numeric research in education and the relative lack of numeric skills among both students and the academics who work and teach within this field. As we shall see in this chapter, secondary data analysis offers opportunities for novice, as well as more experienced, researchers to engage with numeric data in the field of education. Indeed, one of the key attractions of this approach is that you do not have to be a statistician or possess high levels of numeric skills to access and engage with this type of secondary data. Some of the most powerful and useful analyses can be done by using relatively straightforward arithmetic techniques which are well within the capabilities of even the most stats-phobic education researcher. In the next section we will briefly consider some of the advantages of the technique before providing some illustrations of how secondary data might be used in education research.

The promises of secondary data analysis

The promises of secondary data analysis are many. It can allow researchers to access data on a scale that they could not hope to replicate firsthand, and the technical expertise involved in developing good surveys and good datasets has produced data that can be of the highest quality. Secondary data can be analysed from different empirical or theoretical perspectives, and in this way can provide opportunities for the discovery of relationships not considered in the primary research (Smith, 2008). In addition, secondary analysis is a very democratic research method. The availability of low-cost, high-quality datasets means that secondary analysis can ensure that 'all researchers have the opportunity for empirical research that has tended to be the privilege of the few' (Hakim, 1982: 4). As 'it is the costs of data collection that are beyond the scope of the independent researcher, not the costs of data analysis' (Glaser, 1963: 12), the very accessibility of the data enables novice and other researchers to retain and develop a degree of independence. Often when researchers are employed on busy projects (or undertaking undergraduate, Master's or doctoral level study) there is limited time and resources to apply for grants or other funding, and if successful there are likely to be difficulties in securing opportunities for fieldwork. By circumventing the data collection process, secondary analysis can enable novice researchers – including students – to gain valuable experience in undertaking independent research in an area of their own interest, as well as presenting opportunities to publish and present their findings as independent researchers. In this sense secondary data analysis has a valuable role in the capacity building of research skills, as well as in developing an early career researcher's theoretical and substantive interests (for examples from my own early, unfunded, research see Smith, 2005a, 2005b). In the following section I will briefly introduce the range of different sources of secondary data.

Sources of secondary data

We are fortunate in the United Kingdom to have access to a huge source of digital data on everything from voting habits to food preferences. If you are based in a university or college these data are often free to access. It is impossible to list all possible sources of secondary data in a short chapter like this, and so instead I have organised the description into six different categories. For a more complete list of international and UK-based data sources, please go to https://secondarydata analysis.wordpress.com/

- *Census data* These include the huge decennial national population census and the first example below shows how researchers can easily produce basic research using these data. Within the field of education, perhaps the most useful census would be the annual school and pupil census that forms part of the National Pupil Database (or NPD). The data available cover pupil and school characteristics, as well as examination outcomes. The NPD covers England only, data are available back to 2002, and while these data are free to access, there is an application process.
- *UK Government surveys* In the UK we are fortunate to have a vast range of 'official' survey data, such as the Labour Force Survey, the British Social Attitudes Survey, the Annual Population Survey, and the ONS Opinions Survey. While these surveys are not explicitly about education they still gather data on topics such as education background, child development, basic skills, education spending, and attitudes to learning.
- *Longitudinal studies* Studies such as the Millennium Cohort Study, the Longitudinal Study of Young People in England and the 1970 British Cohort Study provide a fascinating snapshot of how British society has changed over time. Many of these longitudinal studies have an explicit focus on educational issues and topics such as child development and education participation, as well as attitudes towards and experiences of schooling.
- *Administrative data* While these data might have been collected for administrative rather than research purposes, they are a rich source of secondary data, especially for those interested in monitoring trends over time. Such data often come in aggregate form and analysis can be relatively straightforward. Administrative data might include applications to UK higher education courses, or school performance data gathered by government organisations such as

the Department for Education and the Higher Education Statistics Agency.

- *International surveys* While the above sources have an explicit UK (often England) focus, it is worth remembering the vast source of international comparative data. In the field of education, this might include data from international comparative tests such as the Programme for International Student Assessment (PISA), the Progress in International Reading Literacy Study (PIRLS) and the Trends in International Maths and Science Study (TIMSS). These data, and the tools used to gather them, are available free of charge and are well supported with documentation and copies of the survey material.
- *Open data sources* The explosion in the availability of open data sources is one important recent development in the field. Open data, as the name suggests, are data that are freely and openly available to the user. They may contain features of the government data described above but in addition may be applied to scientific data more widely. Examples of international open data sources include data.gov.uk; data.gov (for the USA); and data.europa.eu (for the European Union).

The above list is not exhaustive and suggestions for ways to access this sort of data are provided at the end of the chapter.

The role of big data in education research

A more recent, and arguably less well explored, source of secondary data within the field of education research is 'big data'. The term 'big data' has many contrasting meanings, but it tends to refer to large volumes of structured and unstructured data – one obvious application for such data in the social sciences is in researching social media interactions. However, as education is increasingly occurring online or through educational software this has resulted in a proliferation of the data that can be used to improve educational effectiveness and support research on learning. This is opening up a new field of education data mining and learning analytics which can collect and model data on students' engagement levels, behaviour, use of classroom resources, social habits, language and vocabulary use, attention span, academic performance and so on (see, for example, Cope and Kalantzis, 2015; Selwyn et al., 2016). One example of this innovative approach to using 'big data' in education is the private AltSchools in California which use technology to provide highly personalised educational experiences for their pupils (Herold, 2016). Applications of 'big data' are not confined to compulsory schooling – within higher and further education data are available on course selection and registration, financial and work arrangements, class participation and engagement, online and library resource usage, textbook purchases and so on (Educause, 2013).

The use of 'big data' in education research and practice will present challenges. The role of computers in enhancing learning is still largely unproven and the data that are generated can be messy, partial and inconsistent. However, using 'big data' to support education research may provide opportunities for improving learning, teacher feedback, institutional accountability, educational software design, resource development and, of course, for education research (Cope and Kalantzis, 2015). While this is a somewhat different application from the more traditional forms of secondary analysis that are described in this chapter, it seems likely that 'big data' will have some role in helping shape the (virtual) classroom or lecture hall of the future.

Using secondary data to provide a context for small-scale research

One excellent application of secondary data analysis is to provide a context for a more in-depth study. An example of this might be to use data from the UK National Census to characterise the population of the area in which a small-scale piece of work will take place; another might be to use secondary data to draw a sample from a larger population for more in-depth research.

The following illustrates the use of census data to characterise the local population of an area which is the focus of a small-scale case study. This study is concerned with examining the interactions between users and providers who are involved in one children's centre in a suburb of one English city. The study that is being introduced here involves a small-scale longitudinal examination of the experiences of the practitioners and users at the children's centre. In order to situate the study in the wider context of who might access the service in terms of their social and economic characteristics, a useful place to start is with the UK National Census data. Using a tool called InFuse it is possible to access aggregate data from the 2011 census (the most recent at the time of writing, but for access to earlier census data see the CASWEB database which works in a similar way to InFuse). Although a large range of data is available through InFuse, in this example we only consider the ethnic composition of the suburb in which the children's centre is located. InFuse is relatively straightforward to use but I would suggest you follow the tutorials which offer step-by-step instructions that will lead you through each stage in retrieving your data. The InFuse homepage can be accessed from http://infuse.ukdataservice.ac.uk/

The data presented in Table 14.1 were retrieved from InFuse and can provide us with some basic contextual information about the suburb in which the children's centre is located and then compare this with data for the whole city. The data show that the largest ethnic group in this neighbourhood is Asian/Asian British Indian (65%), compared with the whole city where the largest ethnic group is white (50%). The ethnic profile of the other residents in this neighbourhood suggests a predominately Asian population, with just 16% identifying as white in Census2011.

In addition to demographic data, like ethnicity, INFUSE will also provide data on the health, housing and occupational characteristics of a local population. So, for example, it is possible to examine the composition of households in the children's centre location in terms of how many families have children and the employment status of all adults. This relatively straightforward analysis

Table 14.1 Ethnic group composition of children's centre location and city

	Children's centre location (%)	City (%)
White	16	50
Mixed/multiple	2	4
Asian/Asian British Indian	65	28
Asian/Asian British Pakistani	2	2
Asian/Asian British Bangladeshi	1	1
Asian/Asian British Chinese	0.5	1
Asian/Asian British Other Asian	9	4
Black/African/Caribbean/ Black British	3	6
Other ethnic group	2	3
Total (N)	11,558	329,839

Source: UK National Census, 2011

will therefore enable the researcher to provide an indication of the types of households that might be using the children's centre, and the extent to which these are representative of both the local area and the wider city.

Data of this type could be very useful for providing a context to the more in-depth information that would be collected from more detailed accounts of life at the children's centre. This sort of secondary data is also useful for providing a framework for drawing the sample for a study. For example, in the scenario just examined, if researchers wished to interview a sample of users or potential users of the children's centres, they might wish to ensure that their sample is representative of the local population. One way of doing this would be to ensure that a representative proportion of people of Indian origin were identified for inclusion in the study.

Using secondary data to monitor trends over time

The second example comes from my own recent research into the career destinations of science and

engineering graduates (Smith and White, 2016). For many decades claims have been made, by both industry and governmental bodies, that the supply of science and engineering graduates is crucial to the current and future economic prosperity of the nation, but that employers are currently unable to recruit a sufficient number of workers with the right skills.

We can consider this purported skills deficit by examining secondary data on graduate career destinations. Using these data it is possible to examine trends in the proportions of graduates who enter different types of occupations, remain in further study, or struggle to find work soon after graduation. Here we look at occupational data between 1994 and 2011. Although we have data that are more recent than 2011, the categories that were used to group these data have now changed, and so we cannot really use them to compare trends with data earlier than 2011 – one of the frustrations of using secondary data to measure changes over time! Despite this, data from 1994 to 2011 can tell us a great deal about the demand for science and engineering graduates in the labour market and help in our understanding about the extent, if any, of a skills shortage. The data needed to undertake this analysis were accessed from the Higher Education Statistical Agency (HESA).

The graph in Figure 14.1 shows the destinations of engineering science graduates six months after leaving university. It indicates that well over half of all engineering graduates went into some form of employment. The slight dip in the proportion entering employment between 2007/08 and 2008/09 may be a consequence of the UK economy being in recession. Trends for those entering further study or being unemployed were very similar and changed little over the seventeen years we consider here. It is worth noting that, over the period as a whole, around 10% of all engineering graduates were unemployed six months after graduation (this is very close to the average for all graduates). What is also evident from these data is the relative stability of graduate destinations over a decade and a half, despite

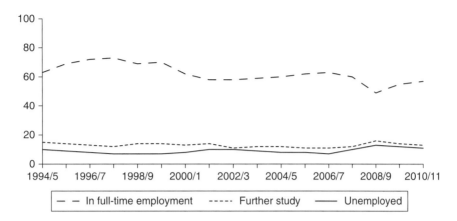

Figure 14.1   First destinations of engineering science graduates, 1994/5–2010/11

considerable changes in both the higher education sector and the UK economy.

We can also use these data to examine the types of jobs that science and engineering graduates actually do and look at the extent to which those jobs differ from those held by graduates from other subject areas. Figure 14.2 shows the proportion of graduates from selected subject areas who entered 'graduate-level' employment (as defined by Elias and Purcell, 2004). The graph shows data from a selection of science and non-science subjects, chosen to best illustrate the variation between subject groups.

Of those who enter employment, between two-thirds and three-quarters of engineering science graduates enter 'graduate-level' jobs. As can be seen in Figure 14.2, this figure is noticeably higher than the rates for the physical and biological sciences, languages and social studies, which have much more similar levels for graduate-level

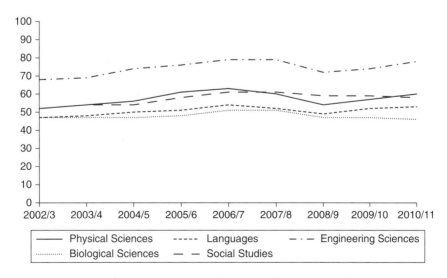

Figure 14.2   Percentage of students entering employment who gain 'graduate'-type jobs, selected subject areas, 2002–2010/11

employment. Over the period considered, similar proportions of physical science and social studies graduates entered 'graduate' jobs, with biological sciences graduates having slightly lower entry rates. With the exception of engineering graduates there appear to be no major differences between the proportion of students entering 'graduate'-type jobs from among the 'science' and 'non-science' subject areas examined here.

These data show that it is not only the case that, as a group, science and engineering graduates do not have a substantially higher level of employment than graduates from other disciplines, neither do they have much greater chances of obtaining a graduate-level job. This relatively straightforward secondary analysis of data on early graduates' career destinations tells us several interesting things about the apparent science and engineering skills crisis. Firstly, it tells us career patterns are very stable, and while affected by the 2007/8 economic slowdown do not appear to vary much in light of the mass expansion of higher education and other changes in the global demand for scientific and technological goods that have occurred since the mid-1990s. Secondly, it tells us that many science graduates are less likely than arts and humanities graduates to secure graduate employment six months after graduation. This is an interesting result in the context of longstanding concerns over shortages of science and engineering graduates – as is the finding that around 10% of engineering graduates are unemployed six months after leaving university.

Conclusion

This chapter has introduced some of the key advantages of undertaking secondary data analysis in educational research. Of course there are many more complex applications of the technique, but the aim here has been to demonstrate the potential of secondary data analysis in small-scale mixed-method research as well as a primary method in its own right.

Questions for further investigation

1. Think about your own research questions. Can they be answered, at least in part, by data that are taken from secondary sources?
2. If you think that you can use secondary data in your research, can you locate suitable data? If not you might want to look at some of the suggestions below and the links at https://secondarydata analysis.wordpress.com/
3. Once you have found your data, how will you analyse these? What further training might you need? The other chapters in this book will help with this, or you might also look at some of the training resources listed at https://secondarydataanalysis.word press.com/

Suggested further reading and resources

UK Data Service The UK Data Service provides an access and support gateway to a wide range of economic and social data. Access to the datasets requires registration but is free to academic users. The Nesstar analysis tool is also worth looking at – this enables researchers to analyse data without needing to download whole datasets. Data accessible through the UK Data Service include:

- British Social Attitudes Survey;
- Labour Force Survey;
- ONS Opinions Survey;
- Millennium Cohort Study;
- Youth Cohort Study;
- Longitudinal Study of Young People in England.

Organisation for Economic Cooperation and Development The Organisation for Economic Cooperation and Development (OECD) is well known for its publications and statistics covering economic and social issues, including trade, health and education. There is a huge amount of data available through the OECD website (www.oecd.org), including e-books, annual compendia of data, etc. Selected original datasets can also be downloaded, including those linked to the Programme for International Student Assessment (PISA). A good place to start is with the *Education at a Glance* publication, which is a useful comparative resource on areas such as financial and human investment in education, access to education, learning conditions and educational outcomes.

Smith E. (2008) *Using Secondary Data in Educational and Social Research*. Buckingham: Open University Press. This book provides an introduction to using secondary data in social and educational research. It assumes no prior mathematical expertise and is intended as a practical resource for researchers who are new to the field of secondary data analysis. It provides an overview of the field, lists resources, and provides step-by-step instruction on accessing and preparing secondary datasets for analysis.

https://secondarydataanalysis.wordpress.com/ This website provides links to a large range of national and international sources of secondary data in the field of education.

SPSS tutorials The data you will be using for secondary analysis will often need to be analysed in an SPSS format. Although sometimes daunting to learn to use at first, SPSS is a very useful and easily accessible tool for data analysis. Dr Patrick White's series of SPSS videos assume no prior knowledge and are highly recommended. Find them at www.youtube.com/user/patrickkwhite

References

British Academy (2015) *Count Us In: Quantitative Skills for a New Generation*. London: The British Academy.

Cope, B. and Kalantzis, M. (2015) 'Sources of evidence-of-learning: learning and assessment in the era of big data', *Open Review of Educational Research*, 2(1): 194–217.

Dale, A., Arber, S. and Procter, M. (1988) *Doing Secondary Analysis*. London: Unwin Hyman.

Educause (2013) 'The Rise of Big Data in Higher Education'. Educause Briefing Paper, accessed from https://net.educause.edu/ir/library/pdf/LIVE1208s.pdf

Elias, P. and Purcell, K. (2004) *Researching Graduate Careers Seven Years On*, SOC (HE): A classification of occupations for studying the graduate labour market, Research paper No. 6, Warwick Institute for Employment Research, accessed from www2.warwick.ac.uk/fac/soc/ier/research/completed/7yrs2/rp6.pdf

Glaser, B.G. (1963) 'Retreading research materials: the use of secondary analysis by the independent researcher', *American Behavioral Scientist*, 6(10): 11–14.

Hakim, C. (1982) *Secondary Analysis in Social Research: A Guide to Data Sources and Methods with Examples*. London: Allen & Unwin.

Herold, B. (2016) 'The Future of Big Data and Analytics in K-12 Education', *Education Week*, 13 January, accessed from www.edweek.org/ew/articles/2016/01/13/the-future-of-big-data-and-analytics.html

Jackson, B. and Marsden, D. (1962) *Education and the Working Class*. London: Routledge.

Selwyn, N., Henderson, M. and Chao, S.H. (2016) 'The possibilities and limitations of applying "open data" principles in schools', *Cambridge Journal of Education*, doi: 10.1080/0305764X.2016.1143449

Smith, E. (2005a) *Analysing Underachievement in Schools*. London: Continuum.

Smith, E. (2005b) 'Raising standards in American schools: the case of No Child Left Behind', *Journal of Educational Policy*, 20(4): 507–24.

Smith, E. (2008) *Using Secondary Data in Educational and Social Research*. Buckingham: Open University Press.

Smith, E. and White, P. (2016) 'A "great way to get on"? The early career destinations of science, technology, engineering and mathematics graduates', *Research Papers in Education*, doi: 10.1080/0267 1522.2016.1167236

Longitudinal research

Anna Vignoles

15

Longitudinal data and research designs

There are various types of data a researcher can use. Cross-section data are the most common type, which are data collected at one point in time. Examples of cross-section data include the Labour Force Survey,[1] which tells us about people currently in the UK labour market, or opinion polls, which tell us about people's opinions at a given point in time. Another type of data that is collected over several points in time, such as throughout a person's life, is called longitudinal data. Longitudinal data are extremely useful for research purposes because they help researchers to better address issues of causality.

To take a specific example, imagine you want to determine whether unemployment causes poor health. If you use cross-section data, you will be able to determine whether people who are currently unemployed also have poor health. You will not, however, be able to tell whether unemployment actually leads to poor health. Longitudinal data by contrast can tell you whether the health problem occurred before the period of unemployment rather than the other way around. Of course cross-section surveys can always ask respondents about the past. In this example, one could ask the respondent whether the spell of unemployment came about after the health problem started. However, retrospectively asking people about things that happened a long time ago is often unreliable.

Longitudinal data can also enable the researcher to model the impact of an event at one point in time on outcomes that happen later in an attempt to determine cause and effect. A longitudinal research design can be used with either qualitative or quantitative survey data and a discussion of both types of data can be found in Creswell (2003): for more on carrying out mixed-methods research see Chapter 19. With quantitative data, there are numerous complex statistical and econometric models that can be utilised to improve the researcher's ability to establish causality using longitudinal data (see for example Baltagi, 2001, or for an easier introduction to some basic longitudinal models see Gujarati, 2003).

Data

There are different types of longitudinal data and the terminology can be confusing. One important type of longitudinal data is cohort data, which are data collected over time about a group of individuals of the same age. These data are powerful when analysing factors that impact over the life course (e.g. the impact of education on later earnings). They have been used to study a range of different social and medical issues, and many cohort data sets were originally set up to study issues relating to child health. There is a range of resources available to help guide the researcher on the cohort data that are available, both internationally and in the UK context (an in-depth discussion of secondary data can be found in Chapter 14 of this book). Most cohort data sets are large studies that are supported by a team of individuals and hence are very well documented. For example, journals often publish information on what is contained in these data sets (see, for example, Steptoe et al. [2013] on The English Longitudinal Study of Ageing, or Fraser et al. [2013] on The Avon Longitudinal Study of Parents and Children). In the UK context, the Economic and Social Research Council has also invested in infrastructure that is designed to guide researchers in the use of cohort and longitudinal data and facilitate access to such data. For example, CLOSER (Cohort & Longitudinal Studies Enhancement Resources) is a centre that was set up to help researchers access and use a range of UK longitudinal data sets (www.closer.ac.uk/).

Cohort data only provide information on one cohort however, and cannot be used to study events that may affect different cohorts differently (e.g. economic recessions). Panel data are collected over time about a group of individuals of mixed ages, and enable us to determine both time and cohort effects, such as the impact of a recession on different age groups. Panel data sets offer some advantages over cohort data sets for particular research designs. For instance, the sample size in panel data sets is often larger and the frequency of surveying respondents can often be more frequent (annually for example as distinct from every 3–5 years or so, which is more common with cohort data sets). An example of a high-quality longitudinal panel data set is Understanding Society, formerly known as The British Household Panel Survey (www.understandingsociety.ac.uk), which has been used to address a range of issues, including changes in income inequality over time and inequality across different households.

Longitudinal data do suffer from some difficulties. When surveying individuals throughout their lives with long gaps between surveys, longitudinal surveys may still require individuals to remember events that happened in the past. This is problematic as there may be recall bias, such as when individuals do not recall an event a long time in the past accurately. Cross-section data always suffer

from this potential problem. Longitudinal data are also extremely costly to collect as one has to follow the same individuals or families or schools over a long period of time. Remaining in touch with these subjects over time is problematic and this is particularly the case for cohort data sets which may span many decades. This means that some people will drop out of a study, causing longitudinal studies to suffer from what is known as attrition (see Olsen [2005] for a full discussion). A major issue here is that those who drop out from longitudinal studies (whether cohort studies or panel data studies) are often different from those who remain in such studies. For example, individuals who work longer hours or those who have had a family break-up recently are more likely to drop out or 'attrit'. This means that those who remain in a study over a long period of time, and in the case of cohort studies up to sixty years or more, are not necessarily representative of the original population from which they were selected. Researchers then have to use various statistical methods to address the biases in the data that arise from a lack of representativeness and the differential attrition of different types of individuals.

Despite these limitations, longitudinal survey data remain a powerful tool for addressing some types of research questions (see Chapter 4 for more on research design and formulating research questions), as illustrated by the research designs and applications discussed in the next sections.

Longitudinal research designs

A key advantage of longitudinal data is that they enable the researcher to assess and measure change within the unit of observation over time, for example the change for the same individual over time. Cohort designs are particularly good for this and the UK has some world-leading cohort studies as exemplars. The basic cohort sequential design for a selection of UK cohort studies is shown in Figure 15.1. The examples given are the 1958 National Child Development Study cohort, the British Cohort Study which follows a cohort born in 1970, the Next Steps cohort (also known as the Longitudinal Study of Young People in England), and the Millennium Cohort Study which follows a cohort born in 2000. These data sets are managed by the Centre for Longitudinal Studies (www.cls.ioe.ac.uk) which provides excellent guidance in their potential uses. Figure 15.1 illustrates the fact that these cohorts are studied for very long periods of time and in many cases from birth. For example, the National Child Development Study, the British Cohort Study and the Millennium Cohort Study all follow individuals from birth. Individuals, or rather their parents, were surveyed at birth and then repeatedly throughout their childhood, into their teens and beyond as they progressed into adulthood and then middle age. The figure also illustrates the potential of making comparisons across these cohorts. Such comparisons would enable the researcher to consider the changing environment over a particular period of time and its implications for individuals of different ages. For example, one could examine the socio-economic circumstances of individuals through the Great Recession in 2008, considering the experiences of those who were born in 1958 and hence who were experiencing this in their fifties, compared to those who were born in 1970 and who were experiencing this in their forties. This is a potentially powerful comparative longitudinal research design which would separate out the effects of time and age.

The data sets shown in Figure 15.1 contain a range of different information. To take one example, the Millennium Cohort Study collected data on mothers, fathers and the newborn baby in 2000. These data included information on the health of the mother, her education, her attitude to her baby, the birth weight of the child, the occupation of the father, and much much more. Then, as the child aged, further information was collected, including information on their pre-school experiences, whether they attended nursery school and if so what type, and again whether they had any health issues during this early childhood period. Even at this early stage the data provided an opportunity

to explore the relationships between family background and early child development and health, as well as the importance of early parenting. Later, as the child entered primary school, administrative data were obtained from the school system and linked to these cohort data, enabling the researcher to know a lot about which school the child attended and indeed their achievement in school. These data enabled researchers to examine issues such as unequal access to high quality schooling and the preparedness of children from different backgrounds for school. These children continue to be followed as they pass through their adolescence, and the study has asked them about a range of issues, from teen sexuality through to incidences of bullying, from issues relating to their engagement with school through to whether they have had tutoring. All these data have provided researchers with an opportunity to undertake longitudinal research on the origins of teens' attitudes and outcomes, for example enabling them to better understand the challenges that children from different socio-economic backgrounds face in their teens. In summary, these data sets are incredibly rich in the information they contain and hence provide myriad opportunities to research a range of different questions about the lives and experiences of these individuals.

As has been said, the key feature of longitudinal studies is that they enable the researcher to measure change within an individual over time or perhaps within an institution, such as a company or a school. This is why these are such powerful data to use to study issues that are inherently related to change, such as child development or ageing, to name but two examples. One illustration of both the challenges and advantages of using longitudinal data in assessing changes in children's cognitive skill as they age can be found in Jerrim and Vignoles (2013). This research built on the cohort designs described above, and used the 1970 British Cohort Study data to measure the gap in cognitive skill between richer and poorer children from an early age and over time. In particular, the work challenged previous evidence which had suggested that high-achieving children from disadvantaged

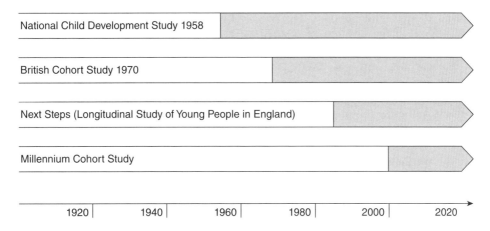

Figure 15.1 Selected UK cohort studies

Source: Centre for Longitudinal Studies

homes were overtaken by their richer but less high-achieving peers during primary school. Jerrim and Vignoles' work addressed the methodological issues and complexities in measuring change over time, including the problem of regression to the mean, and concluded that there was not convincing evidence that initially high-achieving disadvantaged pupils had fallen behind their more advantaged counterparts, at least not early in primary school. Later work, again using longitudinal data but this time from administrative data sources, has found substantial widening of the socio-economic gap in achievement during secondary school (Crawford et al., 2016). The key point however is that in order to understand the different trajectories taken by students from different backgrounds the researcher needs data that follow the individual child through these formative years, and specifically this kind of research design requires consistent information collected repeatedly over time.

Longitudinal research designs are also often used in policy research (i.e. when the government has introduced a particular policy and wants to determine whether it has had a positive effect). If one simply uses cross-section data to undertake policy evaluation, it is often not clear whether the policy is actually causing a positive effect as both the implementation of the policy and the outcome are observed simultaneously. Ideally one might use an experiment to measure the impact of a particular policy (see Chapters 17 and 18). So if, for instance, the government wants to introduce a parenting support programme, one might randomly allocate mothers to the programme or a control group (a group that does not get the programme). One could then compare the outcomes for children whose mothers went through the programme with the outcomes for children whose mothers did not. Since the mothers are allocated randomly to the programme one can say with some certainty that if their children do better than those whose mothers did not go through the programme, the policy is having a positive impact. If mothers were not allocated randomly to the programme but instead *chose* to participate, there would be concern that better mothers are more likely to choose to take the programme, and hence their children will do better not because to the programme, but because their mothers are inherently better at parenting. However, a purely experimental approach is often not feasible in real-world policy making. For instance, in our example it would not necessarily be seen as fair to randomly allocate some mothers to receive help while others lose out. If an experiment is not possible, one might instead adopt a longitudinal research design. In this instance one would survey the mothers and their children prior to the programme and then see if the children of mothers who took the programme *make more progress* than children of mothers who did not. Even if the behaviour of children whose mothers participated in the programme is better to start with, the longitudinal approach will take this into account by measuring differences in the progress made by children in the programme and those who did not participate (this modelling approach is called 'difference in difference').

These are just a few examples of potential longitudinal research designs, and some further practical illustrations are given below.

Applications of longitudinal research

One practical application of a longitudinal research design is some recent work undertaken by Chowdry et al. (2013) to identify the determinants of higher education (HE) participation. The research was asking why poorer children were less likely to enrol in HE. This work made use of a series of linked English administrative data sets to construct a longitudinal record of each pupil's schooling. The study used longitudinal data on two cohorts of students (each cohort had around half a million pupils each), with information on their schooling dating back to primary school. A longitudinal research design was crucial since there is clear evidence from other studies that socio-economic gaps in education achievement emerge early in children's lives (Cunha and Heckman, 2007). Hence it was essential that the research made use of data on children's early childhood achievement in order to understand why they did not go to university.

The research followed two cohorts of students in England – those who took GCSEs in 2001–2 and 2002–3 – from age 11 to age 20. The findings from

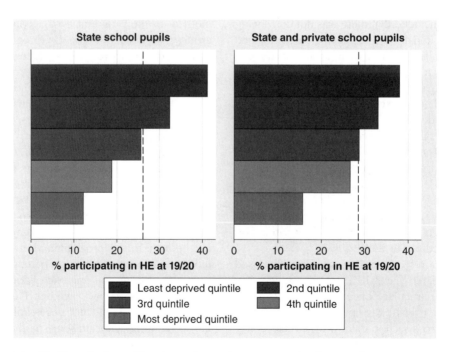

Figure 15.2 The likelihood of enrolling in HE by socio-economic background

Source: See Chowdry et al. (2013) for details of how deprivation was measured in this study

this research indicated that there were extremely large differences in the likelihood of going to university for students with different socio-economic backgrounds. As illustrated in Figure 15.2, the likelihood of a young person going to university is considerably higher if they come from a less deprived family background.

However, the research also indicated that the large gaps in HE participation between rich and poor students substantially reduced once an allowance was made (in a longitudinal model) for pupils' prior attainment in both primary and secondary school. Figure 15.3 shows that the likelihood of going to university for poor and rich students is quite similar for a given A-level point score. Hence if a poor student achieves well in primary and secondary school, ending up with a good set of A-levels, they have a similar chance of going to university as compared to a richer student. This suggests that poor attainment in primary and secondary schools is more important in explaining lower HE participation rates among students from disadvantaged backgrounds than barriers arising at the point of entry into HE. These findings highlight the need for an earlier policy intervention to raise HE participation rates among disadvantaged youth.

The above example is one of many studies that have made use of longitudinal research designs in the field of education. Another example is work investigating the impact of education on individuals' earnings. This work aims to measure the genuinely causal impact of education on earnings. This is difficult to do as individuals who are socially advantaged and more able also tend to experience more education. Such advantaged people would earn more in the labour market with or without this education, and hence getting at the causal impact of education on earnings is problematic. One approach to overcome this methodological challenge is to have longitudinal data on individuals' family background and early IQ/ ability, and then to use this to identify the additional impact of education on earnings for a given level of ability. A key study that used this approach with British cohort data (the 1958 National Child Development Study) was undertaken by Blundell et al. (2005). They showed that education has a genuinely causal impact on individuals' wages, over and above any impact from ability and family background.

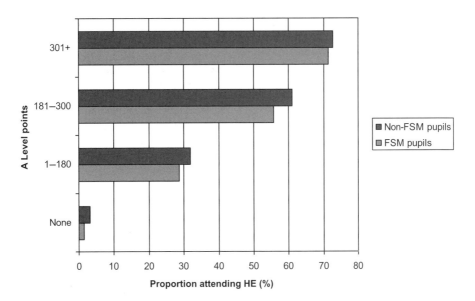

Figure 15.3 The likelihood of going to university for FSM (free school meals) and non-FSM pupils

Longitudinal research designs have also been used in child development research, as has already been mentioned. A number of studies have examined the impact of different childcare settings on children's cognitive and non-cognitive achievement. In the USA, Currie and Thomas (1995) looked at the impact of a parenting programme called HeadStart on children's cognitive achievement. Sylva et al. (2004) did the same for the UK's SureStart programme. Both these studies required not just information on the child's involvement in the programme but also details of their family background and early ability, to allow for other differences between children that might explain the differences in outcomes. Both studies found positive effects from these programmes.

Longitudinal research designs have also been used in school effectiveness research. The difficulty of establishing the impact of schools on pupil performance using a cross-section design has long been recognised. In a cross-section data set, the researcher simply observes that some schools have high-performing pupils and others low-performing pupils. Yet some schools enrol more socially advantaged pupils than others, and these students are likely to show higher achievement anyway. One needs longitudinal data to measure the progress made by pupils in different schools before one can deduce that some schools are more effective than others (Goldstein and Blatchford, 1998).

Conclusion

The examples discussed above illustrate the powerful way in which a longitudinal research design, along with quantitative or qualitative longitudinal data, can help researchers identify the causal impact of government policy. While longitudinal data have their own methodological challenges such as attrition, there is no doubt that rich longitudinal data and longitudinal methods of analysis often enable researchers to get much closer to establishing causal relationships.

Questions for further investigation

1. What existing secondary data are available for you to use? Which secondary data set is suitable to address your research questions?
2. What statistical techniques, such as multiple imputation, can you learn about to address the problems of attrition and non-response that are a major issue with longitudinal data sets?
3. Which panel data methods of analysis will enable you to take full advantage of the fact that longitudinal data records change over time within a unit of observation, such as an individual, and how can this enhance your research design?

Note

1. Although this survey also has a longitudinal element over five quarters.

Suggested further reading

Dale, A. and Davies, R.B. (1994) *Analyzing Social and Political Change*. Online at: http://srmo.sagepub.com/view/analyzing-social-and-political-change/n2.xml?rskey=kWinQS. This book includes a number of excellent chapters which provide empirical applications of longitudinal research methods and tell the reader how one goes about analysing socio-economic and political change.

Kalaian, S.A. and Kasim, R.M. (2008) 'Longitudinal Studies', in P. Lavrakas (ed.), *Encyclopedia of Survey Research Methods*. Online at: http://srmo.sagepub.com/view/encyclopedia-of-survey-research-methods/n280.xml?rskey=UYmFQo. This online encyclopaedia provides a number of concise entries on the major research methods. Of particular relevance is this entry on longitudinal studies by Kalaian and Kasim.

Mason, W.M. and Fienberg, S. (eds) (2012) *Cohort Analysis in Social Research: Beyond the Identification Problem*. Berlin: Springer Science & Business Media. This book provides a practical and thoughtful guide to the application of longitudinal data, and specifically cohort data, in social science research. It is particularly good for those considering issues around causality.

Ployhart, R. and Vandenberg, R.J. (2010) 'Longitudinal research: the theory, design, and analysis of change', *Journal of Management,* 36(1): 94–120. An article covering not just a description of how one might use longitudinal data in research, but also, more specifically, effective longitudinal research design.

References

Baltagi, B. (2001) *Econometric Analysis of Panel Data*. Chichester: Wiley.

Blundell, R., Dearden, L. and Sianesi, B. (2005) 'Evaluating the impact of education on earnings in the UK: models, methods and results', *Journal of the Royal Statistical Society, Series A,* 168(3): 473–512.

Bound, J., Brown, C. and Mathiowetz, N. (2001) *Measurement Error in Survey Data*, PSC Research Report No. 00-450. Ann Arbor, MI: Population Studies Center at the Institute for Social Research, University of Michigan.

Chowdry, H., Crawford, C., Dearden, L., Goodman, A. and Vignoles, A. (2013) 'Widening participation in higher education: analysis using linked administrative data', *Journal of the Royal Statistical Society: Series A (Statistics in Society)*, 176(2): 431–57.

Crawford, C., Macmillan, L. and Vignoles, A. (2016) 'When and why do initially high attaining poor children fall behind?', *Oxford Review of Education*. DOI: 10.1080/03054985.2016.1240672

Creswell, J.W. (2003) *Research Design: Qualitative, Quantitative, and Mixed Methods Approaches*. Thousand Oaks, CA: Sage.

Cunha, F. and Heckman, J. (2007) 'The technology of skill formation', *American Economic Review,* 92: 31–47.

Currie, J. and Thomas, D. (1995) 'Does Head Start make a difference?', *American Economic Review,* 85(3): 341–64.

Fraser, A., Macdonald-Wallis, C., Tilling, K., Boyd, A., Golding, J., Smith, G.D., Henderson, J., Macleod, J., Molloy, L., Ness, A. and Ring, S. (2013) 'Cohort profile: the Avon Longitudinal Study of Parents and Children: ALSPAC mothers cohort', *International Journal of Epidemiology*, 42(1): 97–110.

Goldstein, H. and Blatchford, P. (1998) 'Class size and educational achievement: a review of methodology with particular reference to study design', *British Educational Research Journal,* 24(3): 255–67.

Gujarati, D.N. (2003) *Basic Econometrics*. New York: McGraw-Hill.

Jerrim, J. and Vignoles, A. (2013) 'Social mobility, regression to the mean and the cognitive development of high ability children from disadvantaged homes', *Journal of the Royal Statistical Society: Series A (Statistics in Society)*, 176(4): 887–906.

Olsen, R.J. (2005) 'The problem of respondent attrition: survey methodology is key', *Monthly Labor Review,* February.

Ruspini, E. (2002) *Introduction to Longitudinal Research*. London: Routledge.

Steptoe, A., Breeze, E., Banks, J. and Nazroo, J. (2013) 'Cohort profile: the English longitudinal study of ageing', *International Journal of Epidemiology*, 42(6): 1640–8.

Sylva, K., Melhuish, E., Sammons, P., Siraj-Blatchford, I. and Taggart, B. (2004) *The Effective Provision of Pre-School Education (EPPE) Project: Final Report. A Longitudinal Study Funded by the DfES 1997–2004*. London: Department for Education and Skills.

Statistical and correlational techniques

Stephen Gorard

16

Introduction

This chapter presents a simple introduction to some of the uses of numbers in education research, illustrating a few of the many and varied research questions that can be addressed with numeric evidence. It is important to realise that using numbers involves no kind of paradigmatic or epistemological assumptions – the supposed 'paradigms' of quantitative and qualitiative research are just red herrings. The chapter outlines some common sources of data and methods of analysis, before a relatively simple real-life example is presented. The bulk of the analysis was completed in less than two months and quickly led to several articles in high-prestige journals. Shorn of the schismic and other barriers that some commentators write about, apparently instead of doing research itself, doing research is really rather easy. And this is true even of work involving large-scale numeric datasets. The chapter ends by suggesting a few further examples of similar simple techniques.

Statistical and correlational research

It is not possible to do justice to all of the approaches that might come under the heading of statistical and correlational research in a chapter of this brevity, especially as the main focus is on a real-life case study of research. There *is* a subset of statistical work that is based on random sampling theory and that is intended to help analysts estimate whether a result they have for a random sample is also true for the population from which that sample was drawn. It involves p-values, significance tests, confidence intervals and similar hard to comprehend ideas. That kind of work, while widespread, is not covered here for a number of reasons. The whole approach is unrealistic since true random samples are so rare, and because it relies on a number of prior assumptions about measurement accuracy and a complete response rate that are even rarer in practice. The approach is also based on a fundamental error of confusing the probability of the data observed given a pre-specified hypothesis with the probability of that hypothesis being true given the data observed. The two values are very different, and one cannot be converted into the others without a third and unknown value (Gorard, 2010a). Finally, the approach is very limited in only being concerned with generalisability to a population. It does not help analysts decide the really important point, which is whether the result is substantively important (and this is what they have to do subsequently, whether they want to generalise that conclusion or not). In general, researchers working with numbers and reading the work of others can safely ignore p-values however portrayed – focusing instead on the number of cases, the problems caused by missing data, the quality of any measurements, and the fit between the research design and the research questions (Gorard, 2013).

This chapter looks at the far more important second issue (about the substantive importance of results), one which is common to, and faced by, *all* analysts at some stage. The same kind of judgement about the importance and robustness of a numeric result is made when considering a non-numeric result (Gorard, 2010b). This logic of analysis is universal, and there are no paradigmatic differences in education research, any more than there are in real life. Take something everyday like the use-by date on food products in the UK. This is numeric information that requires no epistemological commitment or paradigmatic beliefs. Stores can use it to ensure produce is fresh and customers can use it to help decide whether to buy the product. Everyone will realise, if they think about it, that the date could be in error (mislabelled in printing for example), that nothing dramatic happens on that date (it is a limit stamped onto a continuous process of food becoming less fresh over time), that due to circumstances (like poor storage) the food may be beyond use before that date, and otherwise that much foodstuff is still safely edible the day after the use-by date. A customer using the date information to decide whether to buy or eat the product makes a subjective judgement. This, in summary, is what numeric analysis in social science also involves, and very similar steps can be used to describe textual and all other analyses. For example, a textual analyst knows that what they read could be a misprint, it could represent exactly what the writer intended to convey, or it could be an attempt to mislead. In coding, they must make a subjective judgement about what the text portrays and hope that this does not mislead their own readers, and so on.

However, some different techniques of analysis *are* differentially suitable for certain kinds of research questions. Generally, researchers using numeric data want to know how strong their finding is, where that finding could be expressed as a difference, trend, or pattern. This estimate of the strength of a finding is usually computed as an 'effect' size. When considering a difference between two sets of measurements, a common approach would be to find the difference between the means

of the two groups, and divide the result by the standard deviation of both groups combined. This 'effect' size is a standardised difference between means, and could be used to portray how much one group of learners was out-performing another group, or by how much one group of learners had improved over time, for example.

Correlational research, on the other hand, addresses questions about the relationship between two or more variables, and the extent to which they co-vary. The most commonly used technique for correlation/regression is based on the Pearson's R correlation coefficient. An R score of 1 means a perfect correlation or even identity, an R of –1 means a perfect inverse, and an R of 0 means no correlation at all between the two variables. Usually you will uncover R values between these extremes. Squaring the R value, to give R-squared, yields a different kind of 'effect' size to that above. Here, the R-squared represents how much of the variation in one score is common to the variation in the other score. (See Chapter 35 on 'Multiple Linear Regression' in this book, or Gorard [2001] for a further explanation of correlation coefficients and examples of using Pearson's R.)

Correlation is the basis of many more advanced techniques for analysis, such as factor analysis, regression and structural equation modelling. In the example below, it is used to help see the possible common patterns in 12 trends over time.

An example: Correlational research

Previous international work has shown that clustering pupils with similar characteristics in particular schools yields no clear academic benefit and can be disadvantageous to pupils both socially and personally (Gorard and Smith, 2010). It needlessly increases divisions between rich and poor in education and outcomes (Goldhaber et al., 2015; Yeung and Nguyen-Hoang, 2016). Understanding how and why this clustering happens, and how it may be reduced, is therefore important for policy. Yet previous work has tended to focus on only one kind of clustering at a time. In the USA, for example, black–white segregation of pupils has been the key issue. In the UK, and across Europe, the focus has been on social background, especially on the clustering or segregation in specific schools of pupils living in poverty. In the UK, segregation between schools by poverty has been considered an outcome of the regional stratification of economic activity, housing prices and social housing policies, increased diversity of schools and the process of school place allocation (Gorard et al., 2003). There is also evidence that changes in the overall number of schools, and changes in the prevalence of poverty, are related to the precise level of local between-school segregation. In the limited sense that segregation other than by poverty (such as by ethnicity) has been considered in the UK, it has been assumed that the same kinds of reasons apply for all measures. So the assumption has been that segregation by ethnicity and segregation by poverty have the same determinants. But is this true? Is there one process, perhaps involving a

number of indicators of disadvantage, that clusters similar pupils together in schools however their similarity is measured? Or do these factors operate differently, or perhaps not operate at all, in separate processes of segregation depending on which pupil characteristics are considered?

The analysis presented here is based on figures from the Annual Schools Census (ASC) for all state-funded secondary schools in England (Gorard and See, 2013). It used official school-level figures for the number of full-time equivalent pupils on roll in each school for January of each year, the number eligible for and taking free school meals (FSM), which is a measure of family poverty, and those with a declared additional or special educational need with or without a statement (SEN), in each minority ethnic group, and those speaking a first language other than English. These are all indicators of possible educational disadvantage. For each indicator, there are two estimates of how clustered each pupil characteristic is. These estimates are the Gorard segregation index (GS) and the dissimilarity

Table 16.1 Segregation 1996–2009, all indicators, secondary schools in England

	1996	1997	1998	1999	2000	2001	2002	2003	2004	2005	2006	2007	2008	2009
FSM takeup D	0.35	0.34	0.35	0.36	0.37	0.37	0.39	0.38	0.38	0.38	0.39	0.39	0.38	0.38
FSM takeup GS	0.30	0.30	0.31	0.32	0.33	0.33	0.34	0.34	0.34	0.34	0.35	0.35	0.35	0.34
FSM eligible D	0.38	0.38	0.38	0.39	0.39	0.39	0.39	0.39	0.39	0.40	0.39	0.39	0.39	0.39
FSM eligible GS	0.31	0.31	0.32	0.32	0.33	0.33	0.33	0.34	0.34	0.34	0.34	0.34	0.34	0.33
SEN statement D	0.30	–	0.28	0.28	0.27	0.27	0.27	0.26	0.25	0.25	0.24	0.24	0.25	0.25
SEN statement GS	0.29	–	0.28	0.27	0.27	0.26	0.26	0.25	0.25	0.24	0.24	0.24	0.24	0.24
SEN no statement D	0.32	–	0.28	0.26	0.25	0.25	0.27	0.28	0.27	0.26	0.26	0.26	0.26	0.26
SEN no statement GS	0.27	–	0.24	0.22	0.21	0.21	0.22	0.24	0.24	0.23	0.22	0.22	0.22	0.21
Non-white D	–	0.68	0.67	0.65	0.65	0.64	0.65	0.59	0.57	0.55	0.54	0.54	0.54	0.55
Non-white GS	–	0.60	0.60	0.56	0.56	0.55	0.54	0.48	0.46	0.45	0.44	0.43	0.43	0.43
ESL D	–	–	–	–	0.70	0.70	–	0.66	0.66	0.66	0.64	0.63	0.63	0.63
ESL GS	–	–	–	–	0.65	0.64	–	0.61	0.60	0.60	0.59	0.56	0.56	0.55

Notes: Figures are presented to only two decimal places for ease of reading. The DfE (Department for Education) figures for SEN in 1997 are only half those of 1996 and 1998, yielding much higher levels of segregation. They cannot be correct, and so we exclude them from our analysis. DfE can provide no figures for first language in 2002. Ethnicity was collected from 1997 onwards, and language from 2000 onwards.

index (D). The two indices are very similar, with a higher value (nearer one) representing a very segregated system, while both would be zero if all schools have their proportionate share of potentially disadvantaged pupils. There is no space here to explain the calculation of these indices in more detail (but see Gorard et al., 2003; or Cheng and Gorard, 2010). The six indicators of disadvantage each summarised with these two indices yield 12 distinct measures of pupil segregation between schools which have been tracked for fourteen years from 1996 to 2009.

The trends in between-school segregation, in terms of pupil backgrounds from 1996 to 2009,

show several different characteristics (Table 16.1). Both indices (GS and D) tend to give very similar results for each indicator. However, the levels of clustering between schools in terms of different indicators are very different. Segregation by poverty is about 0.3, meaning that around a third of pupils with free school meals would have to exchange schools for poverty to be distributed between schools in proportion to their size. Segregation by pupil special need is a little less than this but is of the same order of magnitude (around 0.28). Segregation by minority ethnic group (non-white) and for those not speaking English as a first language is around twice these

Table 16.2 Correlations between trends in all 12 measures of segregation, secondary schools in England

	FSM takeup D	FSM takeup GS	FSM eligible D	FSM eligible GS	SEN statement D	SEN statement GS	SEN no statement D	SEN no statement GS	Non-white D	Non-white GS	ESL D	ESL GS
FSM takeup D	1	1	0.79	0.96	−0.93	−0.93	−0.54	−0.47	−0.82	−0.87	−0.83	−0.79
FSM takeup GS	1	1	0.79	0.97	−0.95	−0.95	−0.58	−0.51	−0.86	−0.89	−0.86	−0.82
FSM eligible D	0.79	0.79	1	0.89	−0.7	−0.72	−0.62	−0.47	−0.54	−0.54	0.29	0.36
FSM eligible GS	0.96	0.97	0.89	1	−0.96	−0.97	−0.65	−0.55	−0.87	−0.89	−0.66	−0.61
SEN statement D	−0.93	−0.95	−0.7	−0.96	1	1	0.59	0.53	0.97	0.98	0.88	0.84
SEN statement GS	−0.93	−0.95	−0.72	−0.97	1	1	0.6	0.54	0.96	0.97	0.86	0.82
SEN no statement D	−0.54	−0.58	−0.62	−0.65	0.59	0.6	1	0.98	0.07	0.05	−0.2	−0.16
SEN no statement GS	−0.47	−0.51	−0.47	−0.55	0.53	0.54	0.98	1	0.03	0.01	−0.02	0.03
Non-white D	−0.82	−0.86	−0.54	−0.87	0.97	0.96	0.07	0.03	1	0.99	0.92	0.89
Non-white GS	−0.87	−0.89	−0.54	−0.89	0.98	0.97	0.05	0.01	0.99	1	0.94	0.92
ESL D	−0.83	−0.86	0.29	−0.66	0.88	0.86	−0.2	−0.02	0.92	0.94	1	0.99
ESL GS	−0.79	−0.82	0.36	−0.61	0.84	0.82	−0.16	0.03	0.89	0.92	0.99	1

values however (0.6 or more). Another difference is that segregation by FSM increased from 1996 to 2005/6 and subsequently dropped a little. All other indicators, on the other hand, have shown an annual decline in segregation.

So, perhaps there are three kinds of segregation going on here. The first is for FSM, which shows a different level from ethnicity and language and a different trajectory of change over time from SEN. The second is SEN, which shows a very different level of segregation to the third group of ethnicity and language but a similar trajectory over time. Why has segregation by poverty risen while segregation by ethnicity and language has fallen? Many of the kinds of factors that might affect segregation by poverty, including increased diversity in types of school or school closures, would surely also influence segregation in terms of other pupil characteristics. So are there genuinely different patterns of clustering in schools depending upon the kinds of pupil background measures used, with different determinants? One way of investigating this further is to calculate the *correlation* between the changes over time in each measure.

Table 16.2 shows the correlation coefficients for all 12 national measures of segregation over time (as in Table 16.1). A correlation of 1 means that the two variables are, in effect, measuring the same thing (like Centigrade and Fahrenheit for temperature). Of course, each variable has a correlation of 1 with itself (the diagonal). We also learn from Table 16.2 that, for most practical purposes, the two indices of D and GS serve the same purpose. Whatever their theoretical differences, their values for each of the

six indicators correlate very highly. Indeed, the correlation between D for segregation by free school meal take-up and GS for the same indicator is 1 (top left of table). The correlation between D for segregation by English as a second language and GS for the same indicator is + 0.99 (bottom right of table).

For ease of analysis, therefore, Table 16.3 shows the same values as Table 16.2 but with the duplication of indices eliminated (only GS is retained). (For a fuller analysis, see Gorard and Cheng, 2011). What becomes clearer in this simplified table is that the values of GS for free school meal take-up and eligibility are very strongly related (see top left of table). Whichever way we measure free school meals, the results and their correlations with the other four indicators are similar. So in using correlation, making some justifiable assumptions about correlations near 1 and ignoring FSM eligibility, we have 'reduced' 12 measures to five only. This kind of data reduction can make seeing the patterns in the data much easier.

A fairer estimate of the strength of the relationship between any two variables is the effect size found by squaring the R correlation coefficient. R-squared shows how much of the variance in one variable is common to the other. Table 16.4 shows the R-squared values from Table 16.3, but ignoring the second measure of free school meals. Many of these values are very small. For example, the R-squared between special needs with no statement and non-white ethnic origin is 0.0001. All such values less than 0.5 have been ignored for ease of analysis. What Table 16.4 now makes clear is that measures of segregation by special needs

Table 16.3 Correlations between trends in all six indicators, using GS index of segregation, secondary schools in England

	FSM takeup	FSM eligible	SEN statement	SEN no statement	Non-white	ESL
FSM takeup	1	0.97	−0.95	−0.51	−0.89	−0.82
FSM eligible	0.97	1	−0.97	−0.55	−0.89	−0.61
SEN statement	−0.95	−0.97	1	0.54	0.97	0.82
SEN no statement	−0.51	−0.55	0.54	1	0.01	0.03
Non-white	−0.89	−0.89	0.97	0.01	1	0.92
ESL	−0.82	−0.61	0.82	0.03	0.92	1

Table 16.4   R-squared between trends in five indicators, using GS index of segregation, secondary schools in England

	FSM takeup	SEN statement	SEN no statement	Non-white	ESL
FSM takeup	1	0.90	–	0.79	0.67
SEN statement	0.90	1	–	0.94	0.67
SEN no statement	–	–	1	–	–
Non-white	0.79	0.94	–	1	0.84
ESL	0.67	0.67	–	0.84	1

Note: Values less than 0.5 have been suppressed.

with no statement are unrelated to any other measure used here. This is a somewhat different and more sophisticated analytical conclusion than that suggested by Table 16.1 which initially led to both indicators of SEN being treated together (see above). This finding could be important, because it suggests that whatever causes changes in segregation by SEN without statements is not the same thing that causes segregation by poverty, language and ethnicity, or by SEN with statements.

The other four indicators have substantial variation in common over time (reasonably high values of R), and so it may be that whatever causes change in these values has some similarity for all of them. The values for free school meal segregation and the other three measures are negatively related (see Table 16.3), which means that whatever drives changes does so in opposite directions for these two groups of indicators. It is reasonable to assume, for simplicity at present, that whatever causes segregation by ethnic origin is also related to what causes segregation by language in England. Segregation of pupils from families living in poverty (FSM) is to some extent a separate process from segregation by language/ethnicity, having a very different scale and a near opposite trend over time, and to some extent it is an inverse. So, their determinants might be related but in an opposite direction, although this seems an unlikely situation. For example, if selection by aptitude (known as 'tracking' in some countries) is a process likely to segregate pupils by poverty, it seems unlikely that it would also *desegregate* them by language/ethnicity (since origin and socio-economic status [SES] are often strongly related).

Although simple, this is a valuable analysis which will assist in the search for the causes of, and so the solutions to, segregation by disadvantage in schools. This is because it shows that the clustering of pupils with similar characteristics in schools is not just one process, but at least two. It is important because segregation is important, and because understanding how it occurs is a key part of overcoming its dangers. What these processes are and how they differ cannot be estimated using these same data, so as usual numeric analysis is not the end of an investigation but merely the start of a more detailed study.

Questions for further investigation

1. Find a dataset in your own area of interest that contains a large number of cases and at least two real-number variables. Select two variables, and draw a cross-plot graph of their relationship. Is the relationship anything like a straight line? Calculate the correlation coefficient.

2. Find a data set in your own area of interest that contains a large number of cases and at least one real-number variable. Create a second variable 'group', giving half of the cases the value 1 and half

(Continued)

(Continued)

the value 0. Now find the mean score of the first variable for all cases labelled 1 in the second variable. Then find the mean score for all cases labelled 0. Note the standard deviation for each mean, and find the average of these two standard deviations. Find the difference between the two mean scores, and divide by their average standard deviation. This is a standardised 'effect' size. Why is it not necessarily evidence of a cause–effect relationship here?

3. Find an article in your area of interest that uses correlation or factor analysis. Prepare a critique, noting how well and fully the paper presents the methods, whether the paper includes undigested computer output or whether the tables are made easy to read, whether the paper uses significance incorrectly (with population data or a convenience sample), and whether the paper uses causal words like 'influence' or 'impact' without justification.

Suggested further reading

Department for Education, England, School Performance Tables (2015) – online at: www.education.gov.uk/schools/performance/index.html/. This fantastic UK website provides data relevant to the performance of every school and college in England for as many years as these are available. Try some of the ideas in this chapter, by correlating scores for schools over time, for progress from one formal assessment to another, or examine the results in terms of other useful data provided, such as the level of student absence. Many other countries will have their own versions of this data set.

Gigerenzer, G. (2002) *Reckoning with Risk*. London: Penguin. This is a brilliant book for anyone who wants to think more clearly about numbers and the use of numeric evidence in social science. It shows how experts and advisers frequently present real evidence in ways that are deeply misleading. And it does so in a way that is easy for any reader. Primary school arithmetic only is required.

Gorard, S. (2001) *Quantitative Methods in Educational Research: The Role of Numbers Made Easy,* London: Continuum. This is a popular introduction to reasoning with statistics, including how to calculate and use correlations. The book has become a standard for many courses because it presents everything from the outset so simply and without the clutter of technical language.

References

Cheng, S.C. and Gorard, S. (2010) 'Segregation by poverty in secondary schools in England 2006–2009: a research note', *Journal of Education Policy,* 25(3): 415–18.

Goldhaber, D., Lavery, L. and Theobald, R. (2015) 'Uneven playing field? Assessing the teacher quality gap between advantaged and disadvantaged students', *Educational Researcher,* 44(5): 293–307.

Gorard, S. (2001) *Quantitative Methods in Educational Research: The Role of Numbers Made Easy.* London: Continuum.

Gorard, S. (2010a) 'All evidence is equal: the flaw in statistical reasoning', *Oxford Review of Education,* 36(1): 63–77.

Gorard, S. (2010b) 'Research Design, as Independent of Methods', in C. Teddlie and A. Tashakkori (eds), *The SAGE Handbook of Mixed Methods.* Los Angeles, CA: Sage.

Gorard, S. (2013) *Research Design.* London: Sage.

Gorard, S. and Cheng, S.C. (2011) 'Pupil clustering in English secondary schools: one pattern or several?', *International Journal of Research and Method in Education,* 34(3): 327–39.

Gorard, S. and See, B.H. (2013) *Overcoming Disadvantage in Education.* London: Routledge.

Gorard, S. and Smith, E. (2010) *Equity in Education: An International Comparison of Pupil Perspectives.* London: Palgrave.

Gorard, S., Taylor, C. and Fitz, J. (2003) *Schools, Markets and Choice Policies.* London: RoutledgeFalmer.

Yeung, R. and Phuong Nguyen-Hoang, P. (2016) 'Endogenous peer effects: fact or fiction?', *Journal of Educational Research,* 109(1): 37–49.

Impact evaluation

Steve Higgins

17

Introduction

The aim of this chapter is to present a case study of a large-scale project in the UK where interactive whiteboards (IWB) were introduced into about 250 classrooms of the teachers of 9–11-year-olds in England (Higgins et al., 2005). This case study is set in the context of an overview of impact evaluation in education and the strengths and weaknesses of different designs and approaches. This is to provide a broader critique of the evaluation, the design rationale and findings to help identify some of the key issues in impact evaluation more generally. The tensions inherent in evaluating a high-stakes, government-funded pilot project with as rigorous and informative research data as possible, as well as the practicalities of evaluation in schools, will also be explored through the analysis and reflection presented below.

Impact evaluation in education

Impact evaluation in education usually means assessing the effects of policies and initiatives or other intentional change on the educational outcomes for learners; though it may also include impact on educational systems or the perceptions of those involved. The goal is to identify the impact of the change so as to provide a summative assessment of the effectiveness of the policy. The aims of the initiative will therefore determine

the main questions for the evaluation (Rossi et al., 2003). These are usually causal questions as policy makers, practitioners and researchers want to know whether the initiative has been responsible for improvement (see Chapter 4 for an overview of research designs for causal inference, as well as a discussion of types of validity). Impact evaluation is usually summative rather than formative, in that the aim is to demonstrate the impact of what has happened, rather than improve the effectiveness of a policy or intervention for the future. A key concept in impact evaluation is therefore understanding the nature of any comparison being made, or the 'counterfactual' condition. We would ideally like to know what would have happened to students' learning both with and without the initiative taking place. This is not possible as a single student cannot both experience and not experience an initiative. Different kinds of comparisons provide evidence for a stronger or weaker argument about the robustness of any causal claim in terms of whether an initiative has had an impact or not (see also Chapter 18 for information on randomised designs). The nature of the particular counterfactual or comparison in an impact evaluation affects what is a plausible explanation or a reasonable interpretation of the findings. More specifically it affects the internal validity of the evaluation claims: what is the evidence that it has actually worked? Each of the approaches to impact evaluation in Table 17.1 seeks to understand whether an initiative has achieved its aims or not. The strength of the claim

Table 17.1 Counterfactual comparisons and threats to internal validity in evaluation design

	Design	Counterfactual	Internal validity
Experimental	Randomised controlled trial	Comparison of average outcomes from random allocated groups of students who are equivalent and either do or do not experience the change.	Provides a counterfactual which can infer causation. Controls for selection or allocation bias, regression to the mean effects and temporal effects; controls for both known and unknown characteristics which may influence learning outcomes (the majority of the time with a sufficient-sized sample), except for the play of chance.
			Can control for the effects of innovation or novelty with an appropriate design (e.g. three arm trial with 'business as usual' and 'placebo' comparison).
	Regression discontinuity	Statistical model of average outcomes just above the cutoff in relation to the outcomes from all students.	Controls for selection and maturation effects by modelling the pre-post relationship at the cut-off point. This cut-off point must not be manipulable (i.e. the cut-off is arbitrary on all but the cut-off scale).
			Does not control for effects of innovation or novelty.
			Assumes pre-post relationship can be accurately modelled.
	Quasi-experimental design	Comparison of average outcomes from allocated groups of students who are non-equivalent and either do or do not experience the change.	Provides a limited counterfactual which can infer limited causation. Does not control for selection or allocation bias, regression to the mean effects and temporal effects; does not control for any unknown characteristics which may influence learning outcomes.
			Does not control for effects of innovation (unless more than one intervention condition is included).
Observational	Natural experiments	Outcomes from similar students who do not experience the change.	Does not control for selection or allocation bias that is related to unobserved or unmatched characteristics.
	Matched comparison groups		Groups must be sufficiently similar for analysis.
	Difference in difference		Does not control for effects of innovation.
	Time-series (e.g. single group design)	Outcomes from the same students, a number of times before and after a change (usually a minimum of three occasions).	Does not control for selection or allocation, other external change, or maturation and growth.

weakens as the comparison is less capable of ensuring that the change which is being evaluated is the cause of any improvement. The counterfactual becomes less convincing.

A further goal may be to identify and test a specific causal model or to validate *how* the change has been effective or which students benefited most. Approaches such as theory-based evaluation seek to do this by having a clear conceptualisation or logic model which attempts to explain how the policy or intervention produces the desired effects (Fitz-Gibbon and Morris, 1996). In this approach factors or features of the theoretical model are included in the evaluation design so that any association can be explored. This might include aspects of fidelity (tracking how faithfully those involved adopted the changes in practice) or measures which might indicate changes in participants' behaviours or the processes of the new practices being evaluated.

The 'Embedding ICT' impact evaluation

In this particular case study of an impact evaluation the key objectives were to identify any effects from the use of interactive whiteboards (IWBs) on literacy and mathematics teaching and learning. The initiative was designated as a national pilot project with the key goal of raising levels of attainment in literacy and mathematics, which were at the heart of the UK government's Primary National Strategy. The model of impact involved checking implementation fidelity (teachers' weekly logs of IWB use) and identifying short-term indicators focusing on teaching and learning processes (participants' perceptions and observed changes in patterns of classroom interaction) and then educational outcomes (students' attainment in literacy and mathematics).

A review of the available evidence about interactive whiteboards indicated that perceptions were generally very positive, but that data about the impact on classroom interaction or measures of attainment were scarce and inconclusive (Smith et al., 2005). Other evaluative approaches were discussed with the sponsor (such as cluster randomised trials and regression discontinuity design options) to control for aspects of bias discussed at the beginning of the chapter.

However, none of these options were acceptable for a range of reasons to do with the selection of schools and a perceived need for all of the project schools to adopt nationally approved approaches to teaching in literacy and mathematics. A further challenge was imposed in terms of timescales in that the evaluation evidence was needed to inform policy decisions about a wider roll-out of the technology across England, ideally within 18–24 months of commissioning. Working with schools also had a number of constraints relating to the timing of data collection and permissions for video and audio recording in relation

to the school year. The evaluation design therefore had an implicit rationalist paradigm (Young, 1999), but was influenced by post-positivist approaches such as scientific realism (Pawson and Tilley, 1997), responsive evaluation (Stake, 2004) and theory-based approaches (Fitz-Gibbon and Morris, 1996).

Evaluation design, aims and methods

The initial literature scoping (Smith et al., 2005) was used to identify focal issues at the implementation stage, as well as themes to pursue in the structured classroom observations and interview schedules. Three main strands of data were identified as central to the evaluation (see Table 17.2 below). These were, first, tracking use of the technology, as previous studies of teacher use of technology for instruction suggested that this may be relatively low (e.g. Russell et al., 2003). Second, aspects of the process of using the technology in classrooms were studied using structured observations of classroom interaction (see Smith et al., 2006; Smith et al., 2007; for full details). The sample size had sufficient power to compare literacy and numeracy lessons and examine any interaction effect between the technology (lessons with/without an IWB) and subject area (literacy/mathematics) using ANOVA and independent t-tests (see Chapter 34). Additionally, 15 teachers volunteered to be videoed to ensure other aspects of classroom interaction were not missed (see Smith and Higgins, 2007). Interviews were conducted with teachers, pupils and those responsible for the project at local authority level (Hall and Higgins, 2005; Wall et al., 2005). The interviews with pupils used two approaches: focus groups and pupil views templates (a visual method: see Chapter 11). Finally, outcome data on pupils' attitudes and attainment were collected to identify any quantitative impact of the technology on their learning.

There are limitations in this evaluation design in terms of the inferences which can be drawn from the findings, as discussed above. The lack of control over allocation of the technology and

Table 17.2 Evaluation overview

Evaluation approach	Timing/frequency/sample	Evaluation focus
Weekly record of daily IWB use	2 × 6 weeks blocks 12 months apart	Implementation fidelity
		Changes in patterns of use after one year
Structured classroom observation data	*Year 1:* 30 randomly selected teachers observed four times (with and without IWB for both literacy and mathematics)	Impact on classroom interaction
		IWB/no IWB comparison
		Literacy/mathematics differences
		Gender differences
	Year 2: Same 30 teachers observed with IWB for literacy and mathematics	Changes after one year – embedding effect
		Literacy/mathematics differences
		Gender differences
Lesson videos	15 volunteer teachers videoed twice in second year of the evaluation	Wider aspects of classroom interaction Teacher use of IWB for presentation
Teacher interviews	68 teachers randomly selected, semi-structured telephone interview	Teacher perceptions of IWB impact on classroom interaction, attainment, gender
Pupil interviews	12 focus groups of six pupils; schools randomly selected, but pupils selected by schools	Pupils' perceptions of IWB impact on classroom interaction, attainment, gender
	80 pupils completed mediated interviews using pupil views templates (opportunity sample collected by researchers visiting project schools)	Pupils' reflections on impact of IWB on their learning (meta-cognition)
Pupil attitude data	Quantitative attitudinal data collected from 3,042 pupils in Year 1 and Year 2 of the project (12 months apart)	Impact on pupil attitudes to learning
Attainment data	67 project schools matched with a comparison group using national test data from previous year's data (n = 2,900)	Initial impact on pupils' test performance in literacy, mathematics and science (after six months' use of IWBs)
	Similar analysis one year later (n = 2,800)	Impact on pupils' test performance in literacy, mathematics and science (after 18 months' use)

absence of randomisation were of particular concern in an evaluation which sought to inform a national expansion of the initiative. We were confident that we would identify any differences at the process or classroom level (i.e. those based on within-sample comparisons), and that the random sampling of project teachers for observation and interview would capture a reasonable snapshot of use and perceptions across the project. However, we were also concerned that the attainment data analysis would not provide confidence or warrant for any causal link between IWB use and attainment which could be generalised, though if there were differences associated with IWB adoption the sample size and use of a matched comparator sample would be likely to identify the extent of these. In this study the counterfactual was therefore a sample of similar schools matched on co-variates known to be related to attainment at school level. The design was problematic in terms of the risk of allocation bias (schools performing above average on national tests were selected) and we could only match on factors known to be associated with differences in attainment at school level which were available in the dataset.

Results of the evaluation

The teachers reported using IWBs initially in about two-thirds of lessons, then nearly three-quarters of lessons one year later. Reported software use indicated they were developing or adapting resources more in the second year, suggesting increased confidence in using the technology. The pilot project was therefore successful in embedding use of the technology in the majority of lessons in project schools.

The use of IWBs also seemed to make a difference to aspects of classroom interaction. There were fewer pauses in IWB lessons and by the second year of the project there were more open questions, repeat questions, probes, longer answers from students and more general talk. There was a faster pace in the IWB lessons which were observed with almost twice the amount of evaluative responses from teachers and longer answers from students.

Interpreting these observational findings is challenging. There were clear differences associated with the technology and some of these changes were consistent with more effective teaching (e.g. Nystrand and Gamoran, 1991; Muijs and Reynolds, 2001). In particular, the increase in open questions, length of answers and use of 'probes' or follow-up questions indicated a more interactive style of classroom discourse (Galton et al., 1999: see also Chapter 30). Others may or may not be beneficial. Pace of lessons is an example of this (Muijs and Reynolds, 2001: 9). Inspection reports in the UK often comment favourably that one of the benefits of information and communications technology is enabling a faster pace of lessons and it is certainly the case that IWB lessons had a faster pace (at least as measured by the number of interactions).

Overall, the teachers interviewed were extremely positive about the impact of IWBs on their teaching. The students were also very positive about the use of IWBs, and particularly enjoyed the multimedia potential of the technology, believing that they learned better when an IWB was used in the classroom and suggesting the technology helped them to pay better attention.

Data at individual student level from the national tests in English, mathematics and science for 11-year-olds were obtained from the UK's Department for Education and Skills (DfES) for the year before the project (for identification of a matched comparison group) and for two subsequent years. Use of nationally available data reduced the cost of the evaluation by removing the need for additional pre- and post-testing (Bamberger et al., 2011). These data were then analysed (comparing means, using t-tests, ANOVA and calculating effect sizes) to identify any impact of the use of IWBs in the project schools and to see if there was any difference in impact according to gender or for high- or low-attaining students. The first tests were after about six months of use of IWBs in the project schools. This is a relatively short time for any effect to become apparent, but as shown in Table 17.3, the mean test scores in the IWB schools are slightly higher than in the control schools, with statistically

Table 17.3 Comparison of student attainment data in the first year of the project

Subject	Group	n students	Mean test score	s.d.	t	p	Effect size
English	IWB	2,879	58.69	16.39	1.28	n.s.	0.04
	Controls	2,085	58.09	16.32			
Maths	IWB	2,892	63.93	21.00	3.62	<0.001	0.10
	Controls	2,094	61.75	21.06			
Science	IWB	2,921	59.42	11.94	3.79	<0.001	0.11
	Controls	2,108	58.10	12.30			

National test scores: IWB and controls – student level.

significant margins for mathematics and science. The effect sizes (the extent of the differences) in all cases are very small however (see Chapter 37 for a fuller explanation of effect sizes).

A year later a similar comparison was made after 18 months of technology use (Table 17.4). There were no significant differences between the two groups and the effect sizes are negligible. The small benefit for the IWB schools seen in

mathematics and science test results in the first year was not sustained.

The early improvement seen after the first few months may have been a 'halo' or novelty effect of some kind. It did not lead to further improvement in the following year, which might have been expected on the inference from the observations that classes were taught more actively with an IWB.

Table 17.4 Comparison of student attainment data after 18 months

Subject	Group	n students	Mean test score	s.d.	t	p	Effect size
English	IWB	2,763	55.36	15.08	0.63	n.s.	0.02
	Controls	1,965	55.08	14.89			
Maths	IWB	2,824	66.53	21.41	0.09	n.s.	0.00
	Controls	1,980	66.47	21.20			
Science	IWB	2,850	57.29	12.45	1.16	n.s.	−0.03
	Controls	1,944	57.71	11.99			

National test scores: IWB and controls – student level.

Challenges for interpretation from the evaluation design

One obvious question raised by the evaluation is whether the project was successful. There was evidence that the technology was effectively embedded in teachers' practice and that there were some changes in the patterns of interaction which could be associated with more effective teaching in the wider research literature. Participants, both teachers and students, were confident that IWBs improved teaching and learning in their classrooms. However, the quantitative attainment data did not show any sustained improvement associated with the technology. It may be that the evaluation design was not robust enough to identify differences in test scores as the allocation and matching processes limited the inferences which can reasonably be drawn. It may also be that the teachers and pupils were mistaken in their belief that learning improved, or that

aspects of learning were improved, but were not captured by test scores. We believe that the design was sufficient to identify any quantitative changes associated with the introduction of interactive whiteboards in terms of the project aims. If a substantial difference had been found, we would have had reservations, however, about any strong causal claims or generalisability as the schools selected were above average in terms of their students' attainment. In terms of the politics of the evaluation, the analysis of the final results came after the decision had been made to expand the pilot, which was based on (or bolstered by) the interaction and perception data available earlier in the evaluation.

Conclusion

Many of the challenges in this particular evaluation are well known and there are numerous examples of similar issues in the evaluation of technology in education more widely (see Weston,

2004 for example). Commissioners of evaluations often impose constraints, particularly in terms of the costs of evaluations, though ways to overcome the challenge of 'shoestring' evaluation have been proposed (Bamberger et al., 2011). Good evaluation design attempts to mitigate these challenges to provide as robust an answer to the evaluation research questions as the constraints allow. The nature of the evaluation design and the particular comparison made (or the 'counterfactual') determines the causal inferences which can be drawn. Since this evaluation was completed in the UK, we have seen an important shift towards use of more powerful designs for causal inference in educational evaluation (e.g. Torgerson et al., 2011), highlighting the value of randomisation and the use of independent evaluation teams. This is particularly apparent in the work of organisations like the Education Endowment Foundation. It reflects a wider move internationally to identify impact, explain variation, and develop effective predictive models for educational improvement (see Coryn et al., 2011 for a systematic review of theory-driven evaluation practice from 1990 to 2009). Robust designs are necessary to draw legitimate causal conclusions, but they are not sufficient to understand how and why approaches work, or to understand what has been effective for whom and under what circumstances so that we can use this information to improve educational practice in other contexts.

Questions for further investigation

1. How important is it to be able to make causal claims about educational change? How robust do these claims need to be?
2. What tensions might arise between the commissioner of an evaluation and an independent evaluation team? How might these best be managed?

3. How do the ethical issues differ between the various evaluation designs in Table 17.1? How ethical is it *not* to know what is effective?

Suggested further reading

Bamberger, M., Rugh, J. and Mabry, L. (2011) *RealWorld Evaluation: Working Under Budget, Time, Data, and Political Constraints*, 2nd edn. Thousand Oaks, CA: Sage. This book aims to help evaluators design and conduct evaluation studies, while pragmatically taking into account resource and data constraints. The themes are developed around a seven-step model with vignettes and case studies from practice. The approach explicitly draws on quantitative, qualitative and mixed-method designs.

Khandker, S.R., Koolwal, G.B. and Samad, H.A. (2010) *Handbook on Impact Evaluation: Quantitative Methods and Practices*. Washington, DC: World Bank Publications. Available at https://openknowledge.worldbank.org/handle/10986/2693. This text reviews a range of quantitative methods and models of impact evaluation. It also details some of the challenges in other areas of evaluation, such as monitoring and evaluation, operational evaluation, and mixed-methods approaches. A series of chapters reviews different designs and appropriate analytic methods from a practical perspective, with a review of the strengths and weaknesses of different approaches.

Stufflebeam, D.L. and Coryn, C.L.S. (2014) *Evaluation Theory, Models, and Applications* (Research Methods for the Social Sciences), 2nd edn. London: Jossey Bass. This book contains an overview of the field of evaluation, a discussion of evaluation theory, a review of standards for assessing evaluations, descriptions and analysis of the most widely used evaluation approaches, and a discussion of meta-evaluation and the importance of systematic evaluation.

The Education Endowment Foundation's website (https://educationendowmentfoundation.org.uk) sets out its approach to evaluation, supported with resources for evaluators and links to independently conducted project evaluations of the impact of a range of educational initiatives on students' learning. By 2016 there were over 60 reports available. The evaluation approach includes a rating system for judging the internal validity of the evaluation findings.

References

Bamberger, M., Rugh, J. and Mabry, L. (2011) *RealWorld Evaluation: Working under Budget, Time, Data, and Political Constraints*. Thousand Oaks, CA: Sage.

Coryn, C.L., Noakes, L.A., Westine, C.D. and Schröter, D.C. (2011) 'A systematic review of theory-driven evaluation practice from 1990 to 2009', *American Journal of Evaluation*, 32(2): 199–226.

Fitz-Gibbon, C.T. and Morris, L.L. (1996) 'Theory-based evaluation', *Evaluation Practice*, 17(2): 177–184.

Galton, M., Hargreaves, L., Comber, C., Wall, D. and Pell, A. (1999) *Inside the Primary Classroom: 20 Years On*. London: Routledge.

Hall, I. and Higgins, S. (2005) 'Primary school students' perceptions of IWBs', *Journal of Computer Assisted Learning*, 21: 102–17.

Higgins, S. (2010) 'The impact of IWBs on classroom interaction and learning in primary schools in the UK', in M. Thomas and E. Cutrim-Schmid (eds), *Interactive Whiteboards for Education: Theory, Research and Practice*. Hershey, PA: IGI Global, pp. 86–101.

Higgins, S., Falzon, C., Hall, I., Moseley, D., Smith, F., Smith, H. and Wall, K. (2005) *Embedding ICT in the Literacy and Numeracy Strategies: Final Report*. Newcastle-upon-Tyne: Newcastle University. Available at http://dro.dur.ac.uk/1899/1/1899.pdf (last accessed 26 June 2016).

Khandker, S.R., Koolwal, G.B. and Samad, H.A. (2010) *Handbook on Impact Evaluation: Quantitative Methods and Practices*. Washington, DC: World Bank.

Mroz, M.A., Smith, F. and Hardman, F. (2000) 'The discourse of the literacy hour', *Cambridge Journal of Education*, 30(3): 379–90.

Muijs, D. and Reynolds, D. (2001) *Effective Teaching: Evidence and Practice*. London: Paul Chapman.

Nystrand, M. and Gamoran, A. (1991) 'Student Engagement: When recitation becomes conversation', in H.C. Waxman and H.J. Walberg (eds), *Effective Teaching: Current Research*. Berkley, CA: McCutchan.

Pawson, R. and Tilley, N. (1997) *Realistic Evaluation*. Thousand Oaks, CA: Sage.

Reynolds, D. and Muijs, D. (1999) 'The effective teaching of mathematics: a review of research', *School Leadership and Management*, 19(3): 273–88.

Rossi, P.H., Lipsey, M.W. and Freeman, H.E. (2003) *Evaluation: A Systematic Approach*. Thousand Oaks, CA: Sage.

Russell, M., Bebell, D., O'Dwyer, L. and O'Connor, K. (2003) 'Examining teacher technology use: implications for preservice and inservice teacher preparation', *Journal of Teacher Education*, 54: 297–310.

Smith, H. and Higgins, S. (2007) 'Opening classroom interaction: the importance of feedback', *Cambridge Journal of Education*, 36(4): 485–502.

Smith, F., Hardman, F. and Higgins, S. (2006) 'The impact of IWBs on teacher–pupil interaction in the national literacy and numeracy strategies', *British Educational Research Journal*, 32(3): 443–57.

Smith, F., Hardman, F., Mroz, M. and Wall, K. (2004) 'Interactive whole-class teaching in the national literacy and numeracy strategies', *British Educational Research Journal*, 30(3): 395–411.

Smith, F., Higgins, S. and Hardman, F. (2007) 'Gender inequality in the primary classroom: will IWBs help?', *Gender and Education*, 19(4): 455–69.

Smith, H., Higgins, S., Wall, K. and Miller, J. (2005) 'Interactive whiteboards: boon or bandwagon? A critical review of the literature', *Journal of Computer Assisted Learning*, 21: 91–101.

Stake, R. (2004) *Standards-based and Responsive Evaluation*. Thousand Oaks, CA: Sage.

Torgerson, C.J., Wiggins, A., Torgerson, D.J., Ainsworth, H., Barmby, P., Hewitt, C., Askew, M., Bland, M., Coe, R., Hendry, V., Higgins, S., Hodgen, J., Hulme, C., Jones, K. and Tymms, P. (2011) *Every Child Counts: The Independent Evaluation*. York: Institute for Effective Education, University of York.

Wall, K., Higgins, S. and Smith, H. (2005) '"The visual helps me understand the complicated things": pupil views of teaching and learning with IWBs', *British Journal of Educational Technology*, 36(5): 851–67.

Weston, T. (2004) 'Formative evaluation for implementation: evaluating educational technology applications and lessons', *American Journal of Evaluation*, 25(1): 51–64.

Young, M.D. (1999) 'Multifocal educational policy research: towards a method for enhancing traditional educational policy studies', *American Educational Research Journal*, 36(4): 677–714.

Interventions: experiments   18

Peter Tymms

Introduction

An intervention is a deliberate attempt to change the world in some way with a view to assessing the impact of that intervention. The intervention is arranged (designed) so that the researcher can ascribe cause to the results (see Chapter 4, 'Design of Empirical Research'). At its simplest, this can be done by creating two equal groups by randomly assigning membership of the groups (see, for example, Campbell and Stanley, 1966; Boruch, 1997; Shadish et al., 2002). There are many variations on this theme but from an educational perspective there are two broad levels: one involves individuals and the other involves groups. The assignment of individuals to different treatments (interventions) has the longest history. In medicine interventions are often called clinical trials and one of the first investigations was carried out by James Lind. He showed that the eating of oranges and lemons was a clear winner in comparison with alternative suggestions when it came to treating scurvy on board ships in the eighteenth century (Lind Alliance, 2010). Although he only used one sailor for each treatment it was a major breakthrough. The random assignment of treatments to individuals is very common in, for example, psychological research (Abelson et al., 2014). The second approach involves units made up of individuals such as schools or classrooms. This is known as a clustered randomised control trial and is well suited to assessing the impact for potential policy initiatives.

A note on terminology: Interventions are also known as trials, manipulated treatments or experiments. When one group is randomly assigned to treatment, the design is known as a true experiment or a randomised experiment. If the assignment is not random then it is known as a quasi-experiment. If the design involved repeated measurement over time with an intervention at some time point, or points, then it is known as an interrupted time series.

The kinds of research questions which interventions seek to address

The kinds of research questions which might be tackled using the two levels of intervention include:

Individual random assignment:

- 'What is the impact on pupils' understanding of mathematics when they themselves teach other pupils as opposed to being taught by teachers?'
- 'How much difference does giving homework once a week for six weeks in mathematics make to the knowledge of 11-year-olds, compared to giving no homework at all?'
- 'What is the impact of arresting someone who has been reported for beating their partner as opposed to simply being warned or cautioned by the police?'

Clusters randomly assigned:

- 'Does tough inspection improve the examination results of schools?'
- 'Does the introduction of performance-related pay for teachers improve the motivation of teachers?'

Paradigmatic location

Intervention research presumes that the world can, at least partially, be understood in terms of cause and effect. It seeks to find causal relationships and in doing so it can test hypotheses, help to refine theories, and assist in evaluating potential policy changes. This is not to deny that the world is extremely complex. Indeed, in a complex, hard-to-predict world there is a great need for research using interventions. We need to know how much store we can place on advice, how generalisable our results are, and how well they travel from country to country, age group to age group and so on. Scientists involved in intervention research understand that challenges such as these can be met through interventions and the systematic review of interventions (see Chapter 20, 'Systematic Reviews') is also relevant. It is also worth noting that what might appear to be complex and unpredictable at the individual level can become more tractable at the aggregate level (see Tymms et al., 2008 and discussion in the same volume). A parallel is provided from the physical sciences where the movement of molecules in gases is bewilderingly complex but their behaviour gives rise to the simple gas laws (Feynman et al., 2015).

Why randomisation is important

Educational researchers often want to compare one option with another. They would like to know if one approach to the teaching of mathematics is superior to another or whether a particular policy can be shown to be more effective than another. Although we are interested in the ideas (the theory) behind the different approaches or policies, and

although we will want to know how the new approaches are implemented, we are undoubtedly keen to assess how the new approaches have affected the outcomes.

Let us consider the case of mathematics and imagine that a new approach called NewMaths is entirely individualised and involves the use of software on a computer. The plan is to compare established teaching practices, which we will call StandardMaths, with NewMaths. We might find that some teachers or groups of schools are already using NewMaths, and we could look at the maths scores of the children who were taught in the new way and compare them to the scores of children in other schools using StandardMaths. But we would immediately be faced with a problem – we would not be comparing like with like, as the teachers and students in the NewMaths schools would be systematically different from the teachers and students in the StandardMaths schools. This is a threat to the validity of the interpretation we might make when comparing test scores. The schools that introduced NewMaths were early adopters and may have teachers who were particularly enthusiastic; perhaps the children from NewMaths schools were from more affluent backgrounds, perhaps they were already high maths achievers before the new approach was adopted.

In trying to think the issues through we will keep it simple and consider just one class taught by one teacher. What we want to do is compare similar children who have been taught using StandardMaths or NewMaths. In order to do so, we might assert that we know what the key things are that predict the children's later success and argue that we need to factor those out (a standard statistical technique known as regression analysis will help us to do that; see Chapter 35 on multiple linear regression). And so we might get measures of home background and ensure that we only compare children of similar backgrounds in the two situations. But that will not go far enough, because amongst children from the same backgrounds there is great variation in maths ability. Therefore, we would want to control for a measure of prior maths attainment as well as home background before we do the comparison. But even then, we would not have controlled for everything that might be important about children in their maths progress. This could include for example gender, motivation, non-verbal ability and vocabulary.

The whole thing looks a mess – comparing like with like seems to be an impossible dream. For every variable which we can think of which is important in making fair comparisons there may be another unconsidered variable which is also crucial. But there is a way to cut this Gordian knot. It is called randomisation; it enables us to compare like with like and make fair comparisons.

Let us suppose that we have a set of 30 children and that we arrange them alphabetically and create 15 pairs by taking two from the top of the list to make the first pair and then so on down the list. Then, on the toss of a coin, we put one child from the first pair into the StandardMaths group and the other into the NewMaths group. Again, we continue down the list. There is now no difference between the groups other than the chance differences that arise from random assignment. They will be balanced on home background, maths ability motivation, geographical area, and everything else we can and cannot think of. In other words, what the randomisation does is control for the bias – we have controlled for all the variables through randomisation.

How can randomisation be carried out?

In the example above, randomisation was carried out at the toss of a coin. But there are other ways in which groups can be formed. One simple way would be to throw a dice: to create two groups; the numbers 1, 2 and 3 would indicate one group and the higher numbers the other. An alternative approach would be to select cards from a deck with the black cards indicating assignment to one group and red cards to another. If three or more groups were required slight variations in the procedure would be needed. But these methods would be tedious if the number of cases was large. It would then make sense to use some electronic random number generator.

Imagine that we wanted three groups and we had allocated an identifier for each case. In a column in Excel beside each identifier we could put a random number from 1 to 3 using =RANDBETWEEN(1, 3) in each cell. Of course this may result in three unequal-sized groups, but if this is a problem a slight adjustment to the procedure would ensure the three groups are of equal size.

The final point to note is that the investigator might be tempted to adjust the randomisation to help their case in some way. This would, of course, be quite contrary to scientific investigation. But it could happen! For this reason it is appropriate to enlist an independent, competent person to carry out the randomisation for the investigation.

Further threats to validity

The section above deals with the major threat to validity of the interpretation of the results of an intervention. But there are others that have been considered in some detail in the classic text by Campbell and Stanley (1986) which has been updated and extended by Shadish et al. (2002). They divide a discussion of validity into questions surrounding internal and external validity. The former refers to the extent to which we can conclude that an intervention has had an effect in a specific experiment, whilst the latter refers to the extent to which we can conclude that the findings from an experiment are relevant to other situations.

The most important threats to internal validity are set out in Chapter 4 of this book. The series of experimental designs which deal with the threats are outlined by Shadish et al. (2002). A more statistical approach can be found in Gerber and Green's (2012) work. They deal, for example, with the issue of missing data which arises when outcome information cannot be collected by individuals or groups who were randomly assigned as part of the design.

One additional issue which should be considered when designing an experiment is power, or the extent to which the sample size is sufficiently large to give a reasonable expectation of finding a statistically significant result. No one would suggest a trial involving just one subject per treatment for scurvy as in the historically interesting example mentioned above, but how large should the sample be? This will depend on how large an impact the intervention is expected to have and how much the subjects vary on the outcome of interest. Fortunately, a number of software packages have been developed to help designers deal with the issue of power.

Some careful thought behind the design of experiments has resulted in some useful guidelines under the heading Consolidated Standards of Reporting Trials (CONSORT Statement, 2010). Useful checklists have been provided for individualised and clustered trials.

External validity, also known as generalisability, is perhaps best approached by considering the extent to which the findings from one experiment are reproduced in other experiments. This is the subject of meta-analysis which is discussed in Chapter 38 of this book and by the originator in Glass (2016).

Individual random assignment

As noted above, this has a long history in social science and medical research. It seeks either to establish basic psychological, medical or social relationships or to act as a preliminary investigation designed to be followed by larger-scale work. Within the medical world, the dominant paradigm is that the fundamental features of the human body hold true for people across the world and across time. It is acknowledged that different people may respond differently to differing treatments but it is still thought that this is predictable. Indeed, there is talk of using individual genomes to target treatment. Within psychological studies a similar view is taken, but there is a greater acceptance that contact and culture is important although the ideas are disputed (see, for example, Grigorenko, 2009). In education, the results of experiments appear to be still more dependent on context (Glass, 2016).

Clusters randomly assigned

Clustered trials are designed to investigate the working of systems rather than the individuals within them. Here the artificial world created by humans is being studied (Simon, 1969). There is, in some, a hope that eternal truths will be found and it is acknowledged that it is more likely that solutions to temporal problems will be discovered. But this does not diminish their importance: policy makers need to know what has been shown to be effective while not assuming that what worked in the past will definitely work in the future.

Methods of data collection and analysis

In this kind of design, the focus is typically on an outcome which needs to be measured. This might be one or more of a great many constructs such as knowledge or understanding or motivation or anxiety or behaviour. The collection of data might involve questionnaires, tests or observations. These will quantify the outcome that we are interested in and there may also be an initial assessment – a baseline. Such a baseline can enhance the power of the statistical tests of the impact of the intervention when they are used as controls. Additional data on the background of the participants, such as sex, age, social class and ethnicity, are routinely collected, and for groups, measures of the groups are also common, such as size of group, percentage of free school meal entitlement and other aggregate scores of individuals.

One wants to know very clearly what has happened during the intervention. In a short and straightforward study with a small number of individual cases, a special data collection exercise may not be needed, but in a more complex design over a longer period across many sites, then it would be vital to assess the extent to which the intervention has actually happened – fidelity to treatment. In order to assess this, there have to be ways to collect those data and typically that would be by observation. The amount of data collected would be an important consideration for those designing the experiment because observers can be expensive. Questionnaires for participants can also be used but it is important to doubt their veracity in this situation.

Analysis of the data is typically much simpler than the kinds of modelling that one can expect without intervention. For interventions with individuals, a t-test, or possibly a non-parametric alternative, can be used to establish statistical significance (see Chapter 33, 'Statistical Hypothesis Tests'), and the effect size should also be calculated (Fitz-Gibbon and Morris, 1990; and Chapter 37 in this book).

For clustered trials, multilevel models (see Snijders and Bosker, 1999; and Chapter 36, 'Multilevel Analysis', in this book) are appropriate with dummies used to identify the interventions. Effect sizes should also be calculated (Tymms, 2004).

Example of a clustered randomised control trial

One recent example of a clustered randomised control trial involved peer learning within the Fife authority in Scotland. It was decided that there was enough individual experimental evidence to show that peer tutoring had an impact (see, for example, Cohen et al., 1982). What we were concerned to do was to show how this work could be extrapolated into many schools on an authority-wide basis. To find out what worked best in such an approach we were not sure if cross-age tutoring, which is difficult to organise but often produces better effects, would work more sustainably than same-age tutoring, which is relatively easy for a teacher to organise in class but is not as effective. We also were not sure if running peer tutoring in Maths or in Reading would be most effective, or if indeed the two together would work better, or how often it should be done – lightly (once a week) or intensively (three times a week).

We invited the heads of all 145 Fife schools to join the project on the understanding that they would be randomly assigned to various modes of intervention. We planned to assign schools either to cross-age or same-age, to Maths or Reading or

Maths and Reading, and to light or intensive. One hundred and twenty schools agreed to join the project and on that basis we set up the interventions which were run over two years. The schools were assisted by researchers in preparing material and preparing the tutors. They also carried out observations going into the classrooms and collecting questionnaire data on how the project was working. The outcome measures were collected and analysed separately. The analyses involved multilevel models with pupils nested within schools with dummies to represent for the interventions.

The results indicated that what really worked was cross-age peer tutoring, with an effect size of 0.2. It was better than same-age peer tutoring and it mostly did not matter if the approach was intensive or light (Tymms et al., 2011).

Questions for further investigation

1) Try to rank order the value of each of these possible sources of information for their value for policy making and give reasons: a) a group of esteemed head teachers; b) the latest randomised controlled trial; c) a meta-analysis; d) a study of what the countries that top the PISA league tables do; e) theory.

2) A student cannot see the value of randomisation, stating 'there are just too many variables'. How would you explain the advantage of randomisation which would convince sceptics from a non-scientific background?

3) Take a suitable topic of interest to you and design an experiment on paper to help advance the field. Then look at the CONSORT guidelines and check the extent to which your plans pass muster.

Suggested further reading

There is a burgeoning literature on interventions in the social sciences. For methodological issues two texts are recommended:

Shadish, W.R., Cook, T.D. and Campbell, D.T. (2002) *Experimental and Quasi-experimental Designs for Generalized Causal Inference.* Boston, MA: Houghton, Mifflin and Company.

Schneider, B., Carnoy, M., Kilpatrick, J., Schmidt, W. H. and Shavelson, R.J. (2007) *Estimating Causal Effects Using Experimental and Observational Designs.* Washington, DC: American Educational Research Association.

For a text that looks at impact and at methodology:

Yeager, D.S. and Walton, G.M. (2011) 'Social-psychological interventions in education: they're not magic', *Review of Educational Research*, 81(2): 267–301.

Many different units have been set up to bring the results of educational interventions together and to synthesise the results. These include:

- What Works Clearing House (http://ies.ed.gov/ncee/wwc/);
- Campbell Collaboration (www.campbellcollaboration.org/);
- Best Evidence Encyclopedia (www.bestevidence.org/).

All of these units start by finding high-quality research, and commonly well-designed intervention studies, and then synthesising the results. As part of the systematic reviews meta-analysis is often used to bring together and understand the results as a whole, each of which, alone, might not tell a stable story (see, for example, Hedges and Olkin, 2014).

References

Abelson, R.P., Frey, K.P. and Gregg, A.P. (2014) *Experiments with People: Revelations from Social Psychology.* New York: Psychology Press.

Boruch, R. (1997) *Randomised Experimentation for Planning and Evaluation: A Practical Guide.* Thousand Oaks, CA: Sage.

Campbell, D.T. and Stanley, J.C. (1966) *Experimental and Quasi-Experimental Designs for Research.* Chicago, IL: Rand McNally.

Cohen, P.A., Kulik, J.A. and Kulik, C.C. (1982) 'Educational outcomes of tutoring: a meta-analysis of findings', *American Educational Research Journal*, 19: 237–48.

CONSORT statement (2010) www.consort-statement.org/ (accessed 1/7/16).

Feynman, R.P., Leighton, R.B. and Sands, M. (2015) *The Feynman Lectures on Physics, Vol. I: The New Millennium Edition: Mainly Mechanics, Radiation, and Heat.* Vol. 1. New York: Basic.

Fitz-Gibbon, C.T. and Morris, L.L. (1990) *Program Evaluation Kit: How to Analyze Data.* Newbury Park, CA: Sage.

Gerber, A.S. and Green, D.P. (2012) *Field Experiments: Design, Analysis, and Interpretation.* New York: Norton.

Glass, G.V. (2016) 'One hundred years of research prudent aspirations', *Educational Researcher*, 45(2): 69–72.

Grigorenko, E.L. (ed.) (2009) *Multicultural Psychoeducational Assessment.* New York: Springer.

Hedges, L.V. and Olkin, I. (2014) *Statistical Methods for Meta-analysis.* New York: Academic.

Lind Alliance (2010) Available at www.jla.nihr.ac.uk (accessed 10/4/2016).

Shadish, W.R., Cook, T.D. and Campbell, D.T. (2002) *Experimental and Quasi-experimental Designs for Generalized Causal Inference.* New York: Houghton, Mifflin and Company.

Simon, H.A. (1969) *The Sciences of the Artificial.* Cambridge, MA: MIT Press

Snijders, T. and Bosker, R. (1999) *Multilevel Analysis: An Introduction to Basic and Advanced Multilevel Modeling.* London: Sage.

Tymms, P. (2004) 'Effect Sizes in Multilevel Models', in I. Schagen and K. Elliot (eds), *But What Does It Mean?* Slough: National Foundation for Educational Research, pp. 55–66.

Tymms, P., Merrell, C. and Coe, R. (2008) 'Open dialogue: educational policies and randomized controlled trials', *Psychology of Education Review*, 32(2): 3–7.

Tymms, P., Merrell, C., Thurston, A., Andor, J., Topping, K. and Miler, D. (2011) 'Improving attainment across a whole district: school reform through peer tutoring in a randomized controlled trial', *School Effectiveness and School Improvement*, 22(3): 265–89.

Mixing methods in educational research

Gert Biesta

19

Introduction

Since the 1990s mixed-methods research has become a popular and increasingly influential way to understand and conduct research in the social sciences, including in the field of education (for the latter see, for example, Gorard, 2004, and Johnson and Christensen, 2017). In its most basic form mixed-methods research entails a combination of 'qualitative' and 'quantitative' approaches, with the ambition to generate a more accurate and adequate understanding of social phenomena than would be possible by using only one of these approaches. During the second half of the twentieth century the discussion about social research was characterised by strongly opposing views about what counts as good and worthwhile research – a discussion often referred to as the 'paradigm wars'.

The advance of mixed-methods research has brought about a degree of pacification (see Denzin, 2008), acknowledging that 'qualitative' and 'quantitative' approaches both have their strengths and weaknesses, so that a combination of the two might be a more fruitful option. Proponents of a mixed-methods approach thus advocate a *pragmatic* rather than a *principled* approach, arguing that decisions about design and methods should be driven by the aims, objectives and research questions and not by the a priori choice of a particular research 'paradigm' (see also Biesta, 2015). Johnson and Onwuegbuzie (2004: 17) formulated this as the idea that one should 'choose the combination or mixture of methods and procedures that works

best for answering your research questions', while Tashakkori and Teddlie (1998: 20), in a rather 'strong' formulation, called it the 'dictatorship of the research question' (see, however, below).

The idea of mixed-methods research can be said to have developed from the notion of 'triangulation', which expresses the belief that the convergence of evidence stemming from two or more methods can enhance the strength and validity of research findings. *Triangulation* – seeking the convergence and corroboration of results from different methods and designs studying the same phenomenon – is indeed one of the five major purposes or rationales for a mixed-methods approach as indicated by Greene et al. (1989). The others are *complementarity* (seeking elaboration, enhancement, illustration and clarification of the results from one method with results from the other method); *initiation* (discovering potential paradoxes and contradictions that lead to a re-framing of the research question); *development* (using the findings from one method to help inform the other method); and *expansion* (seeking to expand the breadth and range of research by using different methods for different enquiry components) (see also Johnson and Onwuegbuzie, 2004: 21–2).

There are ongoing discussions about the precise definition of mixed-methods research (for the most comprehensive overview of the field see Tashakkori and Teddlie, 2010; for a detailed discussion of different mixed designs see Creswell and Plano Clark, 2007; and for a comprehensive introduction see Plano Clark and Ivankova, 2015).

Johnson et al. (2007: 123) have suggested defining mixed-methods *research* as 'the type of research in which a researcher or team of researchers combines elements of qualitative and quantitative research approaches (e.g. use of qualitative and quantitative viewpoints, data collection, analysis, inference techniques) for the broad purposes of breadth and depth of understanding and corroboration'. They distinguish this from a mixed-method *study* which involves 'mixing within a single study' and from a mixed-method *programme* which involves 'mixing within a program of research [where] the mixing might occur across a closely related set of studies' (2007: 123).

The nature of mixed-methods research

While it is relatively easy to say that mixed-methods research is about the combination of qualitative and quantitative approaches, it is more difficult to articulate exactly what this means and entails. This has to do with the fact that under the labels 'qualitative' and 'quantitative' a wide range of differing concepts, ideas, values and opinions is clustered together (which is one reason why, in the English-speaking world, authors often speak about two different paradigms of research rather than two different approaches).[1] This not only means that when one claims to be combining 'qualitative' and 'quantitative' approaches it is not immediately and automatically clear what one is actually trying to mix or combine. More importantly, whereas the combination of some aspects of these two approaches is relatively unproblematic, there are also aspects where mixing is far more complicated and perhaps even impossible.

Researchers wanting to use a mixed approach therefore at least need to be aware of the different 'levels' at which one might aim to mix or combine. Elsewhere (Biesta, 2010) I have therefore suggested that we should distinguish between seven levels or dimensions of research at which mixing might take place. At each level one can ask to what extent

mixing is possible and for what reasons it might be desirable. These comprise:

1. *Data* – is it possible to combine text and numbers?
2. *Methods* – is it possible to combine different methods of data collection and/or data analysis?
3. *Designs* – is it possible to combine experimental/interventionist and naturalist/non-interventionist designs?
4. *Epistemologies* – is it possible to combine different views about knowledge?
5. *Ontologies* – is it possible to combine different views about (social) reality?
6. *Research purposes* – is it possible to combine the intention to generate causal explanation with the intention to generate interpretive understanding?
7. *Practical orientations* – can research be orientated towards both the production of solutions, techniques and technologies, and the development of critical understanding and analysis?

While it is relatively uncontroversial to combine different data and different data-collection and data-analysis strategies within the same study (levels 1 and 2), and while it is also relatively uncontroversial to combine different designs within the same programme (level 3), things become more complicated when one reaches questions about what knowledge 'is' and what kind of knowledge research is able to generate, or how we should understand the reality that is the object of our investigation (levels 4 and 5). This, in turn, may have an impact on the extent to which different purposes of research can be combined (level 6) – something which is more feasible within a programme than within a study – not least because one's answer to the question whether it is possible to provide causal explanations of social phenomena (level 6) strongly depends on one's views about social reality (level 5). All this is, finally, also connected with the way in which one articulates the practical orientations of one's research, that is what one hopes the research will achieve and contribute to fields of practice (level 7) – which is, of course, a crucial concern in the domain of education.

Seeing that the question of mixing is more multi-layered and more complicated than what is often assumed, this could not only help researchers in being more precise about the ways in which their work would count as a case of mixed-methods research, but could also perhaps counter a certain 'inflation' of the label that seems to have resulted in a situation where almost all the research in the social and educational sciences is termed 'mixed methods', often only because it makes use of text and numbers.

Different mixed designs

Given the foregoing observations, it will not come as a surprise that there are many ways in which one can combine different elements within a mixed research study or research programme. As a result, authors within the field of mixed methods have developed a range of different typologies in order to characterise different mixed approaches (see particularly the contributions by Greene et al., 1989; Tashakkori and Teddlie, 1998, 2003; and Creswell et al., 2003).

One important distinction is that between *concurrent* and *sequential* designs. In concurrent designs qualitative and quantitative elements occur within the same study. For example, in a case study of a school, quantitative data may be collected about student performance and interviews conducted with teachers and students, with both sources of information being used to build up the case study. Triangulation, where separate studies of the same phenomenon are conducted and the findings of the two studies are brought together after they have been concluded, is another example of concurrent design. In sequential designs qualitative and quantitative elements alternate. For example, statistical information about the relationship between student characteristics and educational achievement may be collected and analysed first and then, once certain patterns have been identified, these are followed up with in-depth interviews in order to gain a deeper understanding of why these patterns might occur.

Alternatively, life-history interviews may be conducted with teachers in order to explore their career development and motivation and then a statistical analysis of population data about teachers' careers could be undertaken in order to expand the insights acquired through the interviews.

In the literature concurrent and sequential approaches are often depicted as 'QUAL + QUAN' and 'QUAL → QUAN' or 'QUAN → QUAL' respectively. When 'QUAL' and 'QUAN' are both written in capitals this is to indicate that equal status is given to both approaches. If, on the other hand, one of the approaches is given a dominant status, only this approach is written in capitals. In that case there are two potential concurrent combinations – QUAL + quan and QUAN + qual – and four potential sequential combinations – QUAL → quan; qual → QUAN; QUAN → qual; quan → QUAL.

The issue of dominance might best be understood in relation to dimension 6 discussed above (i.e. the aspect of the purposes of research). Here one could imagine that a QUAN approach is one that aims to generate causal explanations of social phenomena. If, within such an orientation, qualitative data and analysis are used, it is done to strengthen the explanatory power of the research – and in precisely this regard this approach is different from triangulation. If, for example, one aims to provide an explanation of the factors that cause the underachievement of boys in secondary education one might, to deepen understanding of the causal patterns, conduct interviews with students in order to add a qualitative understanding of one's explanations. In that case the design could be depicted as 'QUAN → qual'. Creswell and Plano Clark (2007) refer to such a design as *explanatory*.

A 'QUAL → quan' design, on the other hand, would be one where the overriding aim is to generate interpretive understanding (i.e. giving an account of why people act as they act), where quantitative information can be added to deepen the interpretation and provide a more robust confirmation of the understandings acquired through the collection of qualitative data. The example mentioned above of a life-history project with additional quantitative information could be constructed in this way. Creswell and Plano Clark (2007) refer to such a design as *exploratory*.

One important lesson that follows on from this is that there are no typical methods for data collection in mixed research. Depending on what one aims to achieve, any method can, in principle, be included. In a sense there are also no typical methods for data analysis, other than that it is of crucial importance that the analysis of the data is congruent with the design of the research and, most importantly, with the overall purpose of the research. This suggests that the conduct of mixed-methods research depends first of all on one's research purpose and, once this has been clarified, on the particular design that best meets this purpose. This also means that, unlike what many authors who write about mixed research maintain, it is not the research question that is the very first step in a mixed process but rather the formulation of the research purpose – something which can only be stated if one has a good grasp of the problems one wishes to address through research.

One could say, therefore, that for mixed research – as for all good research – one should start with identifying a problem. One should then identify to what extent research might make a contribution to addressing the problem – some problems, after all, do not need research to be addressed – after which one can begin to state the overall research purpose and more specific aims and objectives. It is only after this has been done that it becomes possible to formulate research questions, construct a design, and decide about methods for data collection and data analysis. To suggest that research questions just emerge 'out of the blue' is not only naïve given all that needs to be into place before one can begin to formulate questions for research, it also appears to forget that one of the significant contributions research can make is to arrive at better questions for (further) research.

An example: The Learning Lives project

While the inclusion of qualitative and quantitative data in a small-scale research study can in itself

already be an example of a mixed approach, my own experience with mixed-methods research has been in large-scale educational research projects, one on learning cultures in further education (James and Biesta, 2007) and one on the role of learning in the life course: the Learning Lives project (Biesta et al., 2011). The latter project is interesting from a design point of view as it actually combined *three* different approaches: interpretive life-history research and two forms of life-course research, longitudinal interpretive life-course research and longitudinal quantitative survey research. The life-history research sought, through extensive individual interviews, to understand the role of learning in the lives of the participants up until now, whereas the longitudinal interpretive life-course research aimed to track the role of learning in the lives of the participants during the three years the project lasted. The overall aim of the project was to deepen understanding of the complexities of learning in the life course while identifying, implementing and evaluating strategies for sustained positive impact upon learning opportunities, dispositions and practices, and upon the empowerment of adults. For this we were particularly interested in the interrelationships between learning, identity and agency in the life course.

The project was initially set up as a sequential mixed design where the findings from the two QUAL parts of the project (interpretive life-history research and longitudinal interpretive life-course research) would feed into the construction of a survey, the findings of which would feed back into the next cycle of interpretive research and so on – thus following an extended sequential pattern of QUAL → QUAN → QUAL → QUAN and so on. This, however, turned out to be too complicated, partly because the data collection and analysis of the QUAL phase would take so much time that there would be insufficient time left for survey construction, and partly because within the resources available for the project it would be too difficult to generate high-quality longitudinal survey data. Instead, therefore, the QUAN part of the project came to be based on secondary analysis of data from the British

Household Panel Survey, thus turning the project from a sequential into a concurrent mixed design.

Although to a certain extent the QUAL and QUAN parts of the project operated on equal terms, one could argue that the QUAL part was slightly more dominant in that the overall aim of the project was to deepen understanding of the complexity of learning in the life course – a research aim that focuses on understanding rather than causal explanation – albeit that within this wider aim, the project had a clear interest in the relationships between learning, identity and agency, and in factors that might contribute to the improvement of learning through the life course – which thus added questions about relationships and interactions that moved the overall aims of the project in the direction of explanation. Nonetheless, the main approach for identifying such connections was through interpretive modes of research with additional insights from the survey part of the project. It appears, therefore, that the Learning Lives project was more of a QUAL + quan design than a fully blown QUAL + QUAN, at least, that is, if we focus on the overall aims and purposes of the research.

While informed by the same set of questions, concepts and theories, the QUAL and the QUAN part of the project operated relatively independently with regard to data collection and data analysis. It was only once the analysis within the separate strands had been conducted that insights were brought together – and even then at a relatively high level of abstraction. One could therefore argue that the mixing that took place within the Learning Lives project was a form of triangulation, albeit not in the narrow sense of two approaches investigating the same phenomenon, but in the broader sense of different approaches trying to generate answers to the same set of research questions.

The Learning Lives project is therefore of interest, partly because it provides an example of a more complicated mixed design than most of the literature on mixed-methods research assumes, and partly because it reveals that, while in theory mixed designs may be very attractive, in practice they can become quite complicated, particularly if either time or financial resources are limited or if the project is large in scale. This should function as a warning that mixed-methods research poses a number of additional challenges to researchers so that it is even more important to think carefully through the design of one's research if one wishes to make use of the unique opportunities of mixed approaches.

Note

1. It is important to be aware of the fact that the idea of 'research paradigms' is a typical Anglo-American way to engage with questions concerning the methods and methodologies of research. In continental traditions there is a much stronger emphasis on explanation and understanding as two distinctively different orientations in social and behavioural research – a discussion at least going back to the late 1950s (see Frisby, 1972). In this tradition one would often argue that, in addition to an approach focused on explanation and one focused on understanding, there is a third approach focused on emancipation or, in the words of Carr and Kemmis (1986), on 'becoming critical'.

Questions for further investigation

1. Although much discussion in the field of mixed methods focuses on design and on the methods for data-collection and data-analysis, the most important question for all social and educational research is whether the purpose of the research is to generate (causal) explanation or (interpretive) understanding. Explanation and understanding come with different assumptions about the nature of social reality and how processes function or 'work' (on the question of how

(Continued)

(Continued)

education 'works', see Biesta, 2016). Try to describe for yourself what explanation and understanding are as purposes of research, how they differ, and what the different assumptions about the nature of social and educational reality are.

2. Describe the ambition and purpose of your own research and indicate to what extent this requires explanation and/or understanding. If there are elements of both, explore whether this raises any particular challenges for your research.

3. If you are using a mixed approach, explore whether your work is mixed-methods research, a mixed-methods study, or a mixed-methods research programme (Johnson et al., 2007).

Suggested further reading

The idea of mixed methods has become popular in many areas of social research, including the field of education. Whereas many researchers now characterise their work in terms of mixed methods, the wide variety of approaches that can go under this general label implies that in some cases this means hardly more than that different data are used. Only in a very limited number of cases will researchers be using the full potential a mixed approach can offer. This is why it is important – both for those who read research and those who design and conduct research – not to assume that all research that uses the label of mixed methods is of similar design and, more importantly, of similar quality. For those who wish to read more about mixed-methods research, its range of designs and its strengths and weaknesses, Plano Clark and Creswell's *Mixed Methods*

Reader (Sage, 2008) provides a good starting point, while Plano Clark and Ivankova's *Mixed Methods Research: A Guide to the Field* (Sage, 2015) provides a helpful more systematic introduction to the field. Much more detailed discussions about the many varieties of mixed methods research can be found in the second edition of Tashakkori and Teddlie's *Handbook of Mixed Methods in Social and Behavioral Research* (Sage, 2010). The *Journal of Mixed Methods Research* provides many up-to-date examples of mixed-methods approaches from across the social and behavioural sciences. In addition many journals in the field of educational research are increasingly publishing work that uses some form of mixed-methods design.

References

Biesta, G.J.J. (2010) 'Pragmatism and the Philosophical Foundations of Mixed Methods Research', in A. Tashakkori and C. Teddlie (eds), *The SAGE Handbook of Mixed Methods in Social and Behavioral Research*, 2nd edn. Thousand Oaks, CA: Sage, pp. 95–118.

Biesta, G.J.J. (2015) 'No Paradigms, No Fashions, and No Confessions: Why researchers need to be pragmatic', in A.B. Reinertsen and A.M. Otterstad (eds), *Metodefestival og Øyeblikksrealisme*. Bergen: Fagbokforlaget, pp. 133–49.

Biesta, G.J.J. (2016) 'Improving education through research? From effectiveness, causality and technology, to purpose, complexity and culture', *Policy Futures in Education,* 14(2): 194–210.

Biesta, G.J.J., Field, J., Hodkinson, P., Macleod, F.J. and Goodson, I.F. (2011) *Improving Learning Through the Lifecourse: Learning Lives*. London and New York: Routledge.

Carr, W. and Kemmis, S. (1986) *Becoming Critical.* London: Falmer.

Creswell, J.W. and Plano Clark, V.L. (2007) *Designing and Conducting Mixed Methods Research.* Thousand Oaks, CA: Sage.

Creswell, J.W., Plano Clark, V.L., Gutmann, M.L. and Hanson, W.E. (2003) 'Advanced Mixed Method Research Designs', in A. Tashakkori and C. Teddlie (eds), *The SAGE Handbook of Mixed Methods in Social and Behavioral Research*, 2nd edn. Thousand Oaks, CA: Sage.

Denzin, N.K. (2008) 'The new paradigm dialogs and qualitative inquiry', *International Journal of Qualitative Studies in Education,* 21(4): 315–25.

Frisby, D. (1972) 'The Popper-Adorno controversy: the methodological dispute in German sociology', *Philosophy of the Social Sciences,* 2: 105–19.

Gorard, S. with Taylor, C. (2004) *Combining Methods in Educational and Social Research.* Maidenhead: Open University Press.

Greene, G.C., Caracelli, V.J. and Graham, W.F. (1989) 'Toward a conceptual framework for mixed-method evaluation design', *Educational Evaluation and Policy Analysis,* 11(3): 255–74.

James, D. and Biesta, G.J.J. (2007) *Improving Learning Cultures in Further Education.* London: Routledge.

Johnson, R.B. and Christensen, L.B. (2017) *Educational Research: Quantitative, Qualitative and Mixed Approaches,* 6th edn. Thousand Oaks, CA: Sage.

Johnson, R.B. and Onwuegbuzie, A.J. (2004) 'Mixed methods research: a research paradigm whose time has come', *Educational Research,* 33(7): 14–26.

Johnson, R.B., Onwuegbuzie, A.J. and Turner, L.A. (2007) 'Toward a definition of mixed methods research', *Journal of Mixed Methods Research,* 1(2): 112–33.

Plano Clark, V.L. and Creswell, J.W. (2008) *The Mixed Methods Reader.* Thousand Oaks, CA: Sage.

Plano Clark, V.L. and Ivankova, N.V. (2015) *Mixed Methods Research: A Guide to the Field.* Thousand Oaks, CA: Sage.

Tashakkori, A. and Teddlie, C. (1998) *Mixed Methodology: Combining Qualitative and Quantitative Approaches.* Thousand Oaks, CA: Sage.

Tashakkori, A. and Teddlie, C. (2003) 'The Past and Future of Mixed Methods Research: From data triangulation to mixed model design', in A. Tashakkori and C. Teddlie (eds), *The SAGE Handbook of Mixed Methods in Social and Behavioral Research*, 2nd edn. Thousand Oaks, CA: Sage, pp. 671–701.

Tashakkori, A. and Teddlie, C. (eds) (2010) *The SAGE Handbook of Mixed Methods in Social and Behavioral Research*, 2nd edn. Thousand Oaks, CA: Sage.

Systematic reviews

Carole Torgerson, Jill Hall and
Kate Lewis-Light

20

Overview

Systematic reviews are rigorously designed and conducted literature reviews that aim to exhaustively search for, identify, appraise the quality of and synthesise all the high-quality research evidence in order to answer a specific research question. Systematic reviews are designed to limit all potential sources of bias in reviewing a body of literature.

Introduction

Traditional literature reviews

Literature reviews seek to consolidate existing theoretical and empirical knowledge on specific issues. 'Traditional' literature reviews, sometimes termed 'narrative' or 'expert' reviews, are generally based on expert substantive knowledge in a given area. Generally, there is little or no clear rationale for the design and methods of such reviews. Typically, an expert in a substantive topic area gathers together and interprets previous research in the field and draws conclusions about the studies selected. However, the selection of studies for inclusion is usually not explicit, and whether the included studies are a truly representative or a 'biased' sample of the existing literature is often not clear. There are a number of potential problems with traditional literature reviews, including a pre-existing author bias towards a particular hypothesis, which may in turn lead to a biased review.

Systematic reviews

A systematic review has been defined as ' ... the application of strategies that limit bias in the assembly, critical appraisal and synthesis of all relevant studies on a given topic' (Chalmers et al., 2002). The philosophy underpinning systematic review design is based on the scientific principle of replication. Systematic reviews are designed to be explicit, transparent and replicable in order to overcome many of the potential problems associated with the design of traditional reviews. If a review is to be replicable it needs to be explicit about how the various studies included in the review were identified and synthesised. All assumptions and reviewer judgements are made explicit and open to scrutiny and replication. Systematic reviews also seek to search exhaustively for all the relevant studies, whether formally published or listed in the 'grey' literature, and to include the 'totality' of studies in a field. Therefore systematic review design is less likely to suffer from reviewer selection bias. In addition, the exhaustive nature of the review process offers some protection against other forms of potential bias, in particular publication bias (see below).

Systematic reviews have a long history, with some of the first being reported in astronomy more than a hundred years ago (Petticrew, 2001; Chalmers et al., 2002). Glass first invented meta-analysis, a statistical method for combining similar studies, for use in the field of education/psychology in the 1970s (Glass, 1976; Glass et al., 1981), and he pioneered the use of systematic reviews and meta-analysis in the field of education. After a period in which systematic reviews and meta-analyses tended to fall out of use, in the last twenty years or so their use has increased in prominence, first in the field of healthcare research and more recently in education and the social sciences.

Focus of this chapter

Systematic review methodology can be used to inform the design of a number of types of review. Scoping reviews can map out the research in a field while tertiary reviews can locate, critically appraise and synthesise existing systematic reviews in a field. Systematic reviews vary in emphasis in terms of their design and the inclusion of studies selected for specific kinds of research questions. It should be noted that systematic reviews can answer questions of 'why?' or 'how?', where it might be appropriate to identify empirical research using qualitative designs. Much of the information on the design and methods of systematic reviews contained within this chapter can be applied to systematic reviews of this nature. However, this chapter focuses on effectiveness questions and therefore on experimental research, as those studies most likely to be included in systematic reviews address these types of questions. These designs offer the potential of a counterfactual to demonstrate what would have happened to the participants had the intervention not been introduced. Ideally the same school, class or group of individuals would be observed under one condition and then observed again under the alternative condition. However, this is generally not possible (except in the relatively unusual circumstances of a cross-over trial). Consequently it is necessary to assemble two or more groups, with one group receiving the intervention and the other receiving an alternative intervention or 'business as usual'. It is then possible to compare the groups to see if there are any differences and potentially ascribe those differences to the intervention under evaluation.

Systematic review design and methodology

The rationale for systematic reviews focuses on the key principles of objectivity and scientific rigour. Systematic review design enables potentially unmanageable amounts of literature to be managed in a scientifically credible and reliable way, and it enables the consistency and generalisability of research findings to be tested and all potential sources of bias to be minimised (Mulrow, 1994; Chalmers et al., 2002).

Systematic reviews use explicit methods to locate, appraise the quality of and synthesise the results of relevant research. To minimise the risk of bias the methods are pre-defined. This is important because once studies are identified it is critical that the inclusion/exclusion criteria are not changed in order to support a hypothesis that has been developed through exposure to some of the studies identified. There is a consensus regarding the design, methodology and methods of systematic reviews, a generally accepted set of core principles, underpinned by philosophy, methodological work and expert opinion. A considerable amount of work by leading review methodologists has been undertaken in developing guidance in the design and conduct of systematic reviews. Such guidance has been codified to enable researchers to judge whether a given systematic review is likely to be of high or low quality.

Key features of systematic reviews

1. A transparent, comprehensive search strategy.
2. Clear pre-specified inclusion/exclusion criteria.
3. Explicit methods for coding, quality appraising and synthesising included studies.

Quality of systematic reviews

Systematic reviews, like any other form of research, can be of variable quality. To ensure the highest quality in design and methods in undertaking a systematic review methodologists have developed a number of guidance statements.

The Preferred Reporting Items for Systematic Reviews and Meta-Analyses (PRISMA) Statement (Moher et al., 1999; Shea et al., 2001) (which supersedes the QUOROM Statement) is a minimum set of items for reporting systematic reviews and meta-analyses, developed through methodological work. The aim of the PRISMA Statement is to help authors improve the reporting of their systematic reviews and meta-analyses. PRISMA focuses on systematic reviews of randomised controlled trials, but it can also be used as a basis for reporting systematic reviews of other types of research, particularly evaluations of interventions. PRISMA may also be useful for a critical appraisal of published systematic reviews. The PRISMA Statement consists of a 27-item checklist and a four-stage flow diagram. The 27 items are included under seven subsections: title, abstract, introduction, methods, results, discussion, funding. So, for each stage of the systematic review, explicit guidance is given on how it should be reported. Authors of systematic reviews in any field, including education, are recommended to use the PRISMA checklist in the design, conduct and reporting of their reviews. The PRISMA flow diagram depicts the flow of information through the four different phases of a systematic review, including the number of records identified in the searches, the number assessed for eligibility, inclusion and exclusion, and the reasons for the exclusions.

Stages of a systematic review

A systematic review can be seen as having seven main stages which are well established in health care, education and social science research:

1. *Research question.* Development of a well-focused, clear research question which can be addressed by a systematic review; establishing the review team and the parameters of the review.
2. *Protocol.* Development of a protocol or plan of the review, including an *a priori* statement of the design and methods for each stage of the review.

3. *Information retrieval and study selection.* Development of a search strategy, searching and screening to identify/select the studies included in the review.
4. *Coding.* Extraction of data from each of the included studies using a coding form developed for the review.
5. *Quality appraisal.* Assessment of risk of bias in each of the included studies using, for example, a tool developed from the CONSORT Statement (see below).
6. *Synthesis.* Results of all the included studies are combined (this may include a meta-analysis).
7. *Report writing.* The systematic review is disseminated through a report or published article.

Undertaking a systematic review

In the following, detailed guidance on methods for undertaking the seven stages of a systematic review has been applied to an exemplar review in the field of educational research.

Exemplar: Writing review

The title for the exemplar review is: 'A systematic review of the effectiveness of writing interventions on written composition' (hereafter 'writing review'). This is an effectiveness review which means that the primary studies included in the review would be studies using an experimental design.

1. Research question

The research question is the first stage in any systematic review. Once a question is established which is of substantive, methodological or policy importance, a rapid scope (preliminary search of the main electronic databases) can be undertaken to check whether any previous systematic reviews have already been undertaken. If no previous reviews exist or if any previous reviews are out of date, a systematic review is justified and the parameters of that review can be established. The parameters limit the scope of the review, and include such items as the language and publication dates of the studies to be included. All parameters require a justification. The research question can be framed in terms of the participants, interventions, outcomes, study designs (PICOS) categories (Moher et al., 1999 – see below).

Once it has been established that a systematic review is justified, the review team can be set up. A key aspect of the design of a systematic review is that it should be undertaken by a team of researchers rather than by a single researcher. This is because more than one person is required to assure the conduct of the review is of the highest quality. For example, double screening and coding (data extraction) are recommended to make certain that there is minimal error or bias in the review. Both substantive and methodological experts are required to work as a team to develop the research question, develop the search strategy, and interpret the findings of the review; methodological experts are required to quality assure the review, and statistical experts are necessary to undertake any meta-analysis.

Summary

- The research question should be an important substantive, methodological or policy question.
- It establishes the parameters and restricts the scope of the review; it drives all the subsequent stages of the review.
- The research question can be framed in terms of the PICOS categories.

2. Protocol

The protocol or plan for the research describes the design and methods of the systematic review in advance of the identification of the studies included in the review. The design of the review will include such features as the conceptual underpinning of the review, the parameters of the review, and the rationale for the research question being addressed by the studies included in the review. In addition,

the protocol specifies the study characteristics, using the categories participants, interventions, outcomes, study designs (PICOS) (Moher et al., 1999), and these will be used as criteria for eligibility for inclusion in the review. The research question and objectives, the scope of the review, its parameters and strategy for information retrieval, inclusion/exclusion criteria, methods for searching, coding (data extraction) and the development of an assessment of the risk of bias tool for quality appraisal of included studies are all pre-stated in the protocol. This will reduce the possibility of reviewer selection bias and inclusion bias.

The main reason for developing a protocol in advance of undertaking the review is to limit the bias potentially introduced by the reviewers. If the main research question is developed and the methods are specified in advance *before* the literature is identified, this prevents the research question being altered by the data. For example, if it is pre-specified that only randomised controlled trials (RCTs) will be included, but during the search a large quasi-experimental study is found, the results of which support a prior hypothesis, including this study at this stage would require a change to the methods of the review, and this may introduce a potential source of bias. While the review might refer to the quasi-experiment to set the experimental studies in context, the main finding should, in this case, be based on a synthesis of the experimental studies. Reviewers may go on and develop a further review protocol that states quasi-experiments will be included in an update of the review, but they should not be included in the current review as they were not pre-specified.

Although the process of undertaking a systematic review can include an iterative process, any changes after the finalising of the protocol have to be made explicit and justified, and for this reason the protocol is generally sent for peer review and 'published' in a public place (a website or online journal) to increase the rigour and transparency of the review.

The background to the review will include its rationale in the context of what is already known, previous theoretical and empirical research including

Research question: What is the effectiveness of writing interventions on the written compositional skills of children aged 7 to 16 in mainstream school settings?

Objective: The objective of the review is to systematically search for, identify, locate and quantitatively synthesise (meta-analyse) the high-quality evidence of the effectiveness of writing interventions aimed at either improving or reducing or preventing writing difficulties of children and young people aged between 7 and 16 in mainstream school settings.

Rationale for review/background: Confidence and accuracy in written expression should be an attainable outcome for all children in mainstream education. In addition, quality of written expression is related to children's ability to access and achieve in all areas of the curriculum in both the primary and secondary phases of education. A number of interventions have been developed for those target groups which researchers have identified as underachieving at writing. Although there have been a number of systematic reviews and meta-analyses in the topic area of writing, a tertiary review identified no review that synthesised the experimental research on the effectiveness of writing interventions in all writing genres (Torgerson, 2007). There is therefore a need for such a review to be undertaken in order to inform policy and practice.

Conceptual issues: The conceptual issues include the nature of writing development in a variety of genres, theories of the development of writing abilities, writing interventions and outcomes, potential mediators and moderators, and conceptual issues regarding appropriate research designs to address an effectiveness question.

Design and method: The design of the review is a full systematic review; design and methods of the review are informed by the Campbell Collaboration policy briefs (see http://www.campbellcollaboration.org/); 'Systematic reviews: CRD's guidance for undertaking reviews in health care' (see http://www.york.ac.uk/inst/crd); the 'Cochrane Collaboration Handbook' (see http://www.cochrane-handbook.org/); the (1994) *Handbook of Research Synthesis* (eds) Cooper, H., Hedges, L. and Torgerson, C. (2003) *Systematic Reviews.* London: Continuum.

Design of studies included: Studies that can adequately address the research question (which is an effectiveness question) are high-quality evaluations of interventions to improve the quality of expression in pupils' written work using experimental designs: randomised controlled trials and quasi-experiments. This is because, in order to establish causality (i.e. to be able to state that a specific teaching practice *causes* an improvement in written outcomes) study designs which can adequately control for all other known and unknown variables that could affect outcome are required (Cook and Campbell, 1979; Shadish et al., 2002). The review will focus on research evidence from academic journals and other published research and, in order to limit the possibility of publication bias, research from the difficult-to-locate 'grey' literature:

1.   Randomised controlled trials (allocated at either the individual level or cluster level e.g. class/school/district).
2.   Quasi-experimental studies of any design (including regression discontinuity design, interrupted time series design).

Studies in which at least one of the groups received a writing intervention compared to standard practice ('business-as-usual') or an alternative writing intervention will be included. Studies in which the control group did not receive any writing instruction will be excluded. Citation searches will be conducted on any located previous systematic reviews/meta-analyses.

Types of participants in included studies: Studies in which participants have English as a first, second or additional language will be included. Studies evaluating interventions in children or young people aged 7 to 16 years in a full-time mainstream educational setting will be included. Studies evaluating interventions in children of all learner characteristics attending mainstream schools and classes will be included.

Types of interventions (and comparisons) included: Studies evaluating any whole text writing intervention will be included, for example: provision of model writing structures; guided practice; advanced planning strategies (strategies for developing, evaluating and organising ideas); collaborative or cooperative editing and revision; self-regulated strategy development (e.g. goal setting, self-monitoring, self-regulation), strategies for editing and revision, text analysis, writing prompts, strategies for composing, editing and revising different text types, strategies for directing processes for planning and composing. Strategies for improving writing in the following genres will be included: descriptive writing, expository writing, narrative writing, poetry, drama, instructional writing, argumentation, letter writing, discursive writing and persuasive writing.

Types of outcomes included: Studies will be included if they contain at least one of the following kinds of quantified outcomes: holistic writing quality, length of composition, planning and composing times, essay elements, essay coherence, maturity of vocabulary, reader sensitivity, productivity, elements or features of writing in different genres, e.g. quality of argument, quality of persuasiveness, quality of description, quality of narrative writing, text structure.

Proposed codings for assessment of risk of bias in included studies: A modified version of the CONSORT Guidelines will be used in order to develop a tool to assess the risk of bias in the included randomised and quasi-experimental studies. This assessment of methodological quality of the included studies will include reviewer judgement of the following: method to generate allocation to groups and concealment of that allocation; evidence of sample size calculation; eligibility criteria specified; blinding of intervention provider, participants and outcome assessor; presentation of estimate of effect size and its precision; attrition; primary analysis, i.e. intention-to-treat or on-treatment analysis. A subgroup analysis of the higher quality trials will be undertaken, if appropriate.

Methods for coding (extracting data from) included studies: Data from the included studies will be extracted onto a specially designed coding form. Data to be extracted will include: country, setting, aims and objectives, research design, participants, inclusion criteria, interventions and control or comparison conditions, outcomes, results.

Synthesis: A narrative synthesis will be undertaken to combine the results of the included studies and, if appropriate a meta-analysis (statistical synthesis) will be undertaken.

Proposed quality assurance procedures: Independent double screening, data extraction, quality appraisal (assessment of risk of bias) and extraction of quantified outcomes will be undertaken. Procedures to assure the quality of each stage of the review will be set up.

References
Cook, T. D. and Campbell, D. (1979) *Quasi-Experimentation: Design and Analysis Issues for Field Settings.* Boston, MA: Houghton-Mifflin.
Shadish, W. R., Cook, T. D. and Campbell, T. D. (2002) *Experimental and Quasi-experimental Designs for Generalized Causal Inference.* Boston, MA: Houghton-Mifflin.
Torgerson, C. (2007) 'The quality of systematic reviews of effectiveness in literacy learning in English: a "tertiary" review', *Journal of Research in Reading,* 30(2).

Figure 20.1 Exemplar protocol

previous systematic reviews, informed by a 'rapid scope' of the literature and the policy and practice context to the review. The protocol also includes the parameters of the review, the inclusion criteria (with justifications), the categories for coding, and the criteria for assessing the risk of bias in the included studies. The proposed nature of the synthesis is also pre-specified in the protocol. In Figure 20.1 a brief exemplar protocol for the writing review is presented.

The inclusion and exclusion criteria are developed alongside the protocol and are based on the research question and parameters of the review. The inclusion and exclusion criteria are used for checking all studies that could be potentially included in the review in order to determine their eligibility for inclusion. In Figure 20.2 the inclusion and exclusion criteria for the exemplar writing review are presented. The criteria focus on the topic area, the study design, the participants, the interventions, the comparison or control conditions and the outcomes. Each inclusion criterion is mirrored by an exclusion criterion, which enables the process of screening to be operationalised and the reasons for exclusion to be documented.

Summary

- The protocol is a plan of the review, written in advance of study identification or selection in order to limit bias.
- It contains the design and methods of the review, including the research question, search strategy, inclusion/exclusion criteria and proposed methods for synthesis.

Inclusion criteria

(1) **Topic:** Studies about writing in English-speaking countries (English as *first, second or additional language*).

(2) **Study design:** Studies with designs where there is a control or comparison group - randomised controlled trials (individual or cluster); quasi-experiments (case control studies, cohort studies, regression discontinuity studies, interrupted time series).

(3) **Participants:** Studies where the participants are aged between 7 and 16 years (inclusive) and in full-time mainstream education.

(4) **Interventions:** Studies evaluating whole-text writing interventions in the following genres: description, expository writing, narrative writing, poetry, drama, instructional writing, writing argument, letter writing, discursive writing and persuasive writing.

(5) **Intervention and control or comparison treatments:** Studies in which at least one of the groups received a writing intervention compared to standard practice ('business-as-usual'), or an alternative writing intervention.

(6) **Outcome:** Studies in which participants are measured at post-test on a writing outcome, e.g., holistic writing quality, length of composition, planning and composing times, essay elements, essay coherence, maturity of vocabulary, reader sensitivity, productivity, elements or features of writing in different genres, e.g. quality of argument, quality of persuasiveness, quality of description, quality of narrative writing, text structure.

Exclusion criteria

(1) **Topic:** Studies about writing English as a *foreign language.*

(2) **Study design:** Studies with designs where there is no control or comparison group.

(3) **Participants:** Studies in which the participants are below the age of 7 or above the age of 16 or in which the participants do not attend mainstream schools.

(4) **Interventions:** Studies which do not evaluate whole-text interventions in the stated writing genres.

(5) **Intervention and control or comparison treatments:** Studies in which the control group did not receive any writing instruction.

(6) **Outcome:** Studies in which participants are not measured at post-test on a writing outcome.

Figure 20.2   Exemplar inclusion and exclusion criteria

- The protocol can be changed during the course of the review but all changes should be documented and justified.

3. Information retrieval and study selection

Information retrieval and study selection refers to the methods for searching, locating and checking the inclusion eligibility of potentially relevant studies. These methods should be rigorous to ensure that a high proportion of the eligible published and unpublished studies will be located, retrieved and included. Systematic information retrieval is critical to a systematic review as it ensures an unbiased compilation of potentially relevant research by minimising bias and maximising coverage. The main thrust of the search is likely to use the electronic sources, although other methods of retrieval can supplement the electronic searches. For the electronic searches, an exhaustive search strategy is important. High sensitivity (i.e. identifying as many relevant papers as possible), may result in low precision (i.e. most papers identified are not relevant to the review), so a judicious balance between the two is recommended. Ideally, an experienced information scientist should be consulted for this aspect of the review.

The strategy used to search the electronic databases is usually based on one or more of the PICOS elements used to produce the inclusion and exclusion criteria (see above). The information contained in database abstracts is limited and rarely reports all of the inclusion criteria required by the review. For this reason it is advisable to use as few PICOS elements as possible, to avoid missing relevant material. The search strategy constructed for the exemplar writing review used only two facets, intervention (writing interventions) and outcome (writing composition). Each facet should contain a variety of terms to capture that element of the review question. Terminology will differ from article to article, even when the same topic is being addressed, so it is important to use synonyms to capture as many relevant papers as possible. The use of indexing terms can help with this, so where these are available they should be used alongside free text (or natural language) terms.

The creation of the search strategy is an iterative process and the strategy may go through a number of versions in response to feedback on the material retrieved. Ideally, the search strategy should be peer-reviewed, and it may evolve still further in light of this process. Copies of all search strategies should be kept, along with information about which databases were searched and when the searching was undertaken. This will assist with the writing of the final report and enable a critical appraisal of the search element of the review. Once the basic search strategy for the electronic databases has been finalised, the searches can be undertaken.

As mentioned above, the main thrust of identifying research studies is likely to be on the electronic searches, but these can be supplemented through the hand searching of key journals. This may be of particular benefit if the area is a 'niche' subject with a few specialist journals publishing relevant material or if the subject is difficult in

terms of the key words that can be used to identify relevant material. Furthermore, older publications, in particular, may not specify their design particularly well, making some relevant studies difficult or impossible to locate using electronic means. Relevant studies can also be identified through citation searching and checking the bibliographies of previous systematic reviews and seminal studies. Also, reviewers may contact authors of relevant publications to ask them if they are aware of any other relevant studies, including their own, and particularly unpublished studies. Nevertheless, however rigorous the method of searching, a number of potential sources of bias can be introduced through the search. These include a publication bias, language bias, time lag bias and database bias, all of which have the potential to introduce a source of bias into the review.

Publication bias is the phenomenon whereby studies with 'positive' findings are more likely to be reported in the peer-reviewed literature than studies with null or negative effects. If primary research studies remain unpublished and if there is a relationship between non-publication and their outcomes this can, in turn, affect the findings of systematic reviews. In systematic reviews potential sources of publication bias are not searching the grey literature for unpublished (but in the public domain) reports and studies not having been published (and therefore are not able to be included in the review). Publication bias has been described as the Achilles' heel of any literature review (Torgerson, 2006). If non-publication was a random event this would only matter in our level of uncertainty. A meta-analysis that indicates a non-statistically significant benefit of an intervention may, in fact, be recording a Type II error (i.e. concluding erroneously there is no statistically significant difference), when in fact, if all of the studies ever undertaken had been assembled, then the difference would have been statistically significant. However, this is the lesser of the two problems: the second problem of bias is more serious. Usually there is a reason why studies are not published and this often relates to the study's findings. A study that finds either no effect or a difference going in the opposite direction to that hypothesised has a lower possibility of being published. Authors of such studies may feel journals are less likely to accept these (a self-fulfilling prophecy) and not submit them, while editors and reviewers may be more likely to reject them. Even when negative studies are published the process often takes longer than for positive studies. In contrast, studies that have a positive result, especially a statistically significant one, are often fast-tracked by the authors for submission and are more likely to be accepted by referees and editors than negative studies. Consequently, at any one time the published literature is more likely to be over-representative of positive results than negative findings.

The other biases that can affect systematic reviews include a language bias, time lag bias and database bias. It may be the case that important papers are not published in English and are excluded from the review because of the cost of requiring necessary translations. Time lag bias is a form of publication bias described above whereby

Search strategy for ERIC (EBSCO):
S1. DE "Writing (Composition)".
S2. DE "Writing Processes"
S4. TI ((descriptive N5 (write or writing or written or essay or essays or composition or paper or papers or text or texts or assignment or assignments or document or documents or prose))) OR AB ((descriptive N5 (write or writing or written or essay or essays or composition or paper or papers or text or texts or assignment or assignments or document or documents or prose)))
S4. TI ((discursiv* N5 (write or writing or written or essay or essays or composition or paper or papers or text or texts or assignment or document or documents or prose))) OR AB ((discursiv* N5 (write or writing or written or essay or essays or composition or paper or papers or text or texts or assignment or document or documents or prose)))
S5. TI "written expression" OR AB "written expression"
S6. S1 OR S2 OR S3 OR S4 OR S5 **[brings together all the terms for writing composition]**
S7. TI ((model* N5 (write or writing or written) N5 structure*)) OR AB ((model* N5 (write or writing or written) N5 structure*))
S8. TI (collaborat* N5 (edit or editing or revision*)) OR AB (collaborat* N5 (edit or editing or revision*))
S9. TI (((strategy or strategies) N5 (edit or editing or edits or compose or composition or revise or revision or write or written or writing))) OR AB (((strategy or strategies) N5 (edit or editing or edits or compose or composition or revise or revision or write or written or writing)))
S10. S7 OR S8 OR S9 **[brings together all the terms for writing interventions]**
S11. (S6 AND S10) **[retrieves papers that include terms for both a writing intervention and a writing outcome]**

Figure 20.3 Exemplar search strategy

Key:

DE = restrict search to exact index term

TI = restricts search to title

AB = restricts search to abstract

* = truncate term

Use of quotation marks - " " = finds terms next to each other

N5 = finds terms within five words of each other

'negative' studies take longer to publish than positive studies. Database bias may occur if the choice of databases means that a significant proportion of unpublished (or 'grey' literature) studies are excluded because they are not present in the narrow choice of databases used for the search.

Details about how the search strategy was developed and which databases and journals will be searched should be clearly described in order to permit scrutiny and replication. To ensure that any search is replicable the PRISMA Statement recommends that all information sources are described in detail, including the date the searches were undertaken. It also recommends that at least one full electronic search strategy is presented in the report, together with any limits in order that it could, in theory, be replicated. A simplified version of a search strategy for the exemplar writing review is reproduced in Figure 20.3. (This is for illustrative purposes only – the original contained many more search terms.)

During screening the inclusion criteria are applied to the results of the searches in a three-step process which should be pre-specified in the protocol: prescreening (to filter out studies that are immediately and easily identified as being irrelevant to the review), first-stage screening (of titles and abstracts) and second-stage screening (of full papers). The identified articles are checked against the predetermined criteria for eligibility and relevance. This process should be undertaken rigorously and quality assured in order to minimise bias. It is recommended that two reviewers screen at each stage independently and then compare their decisions. If this is not possible due to resource constraints the database of potentially relevant studies can be screened by one reviewer, with a random sample of studies screened by a second reviewer at each stage. If this process is adopted the inter-rate reliability of the screening of the two reviewers should be checked through (e.g. the calculation of a Cohen's Kappa statistic), and if agreement is low (as demonstrated by a low Cohen's Kappa statistic), then the entire dataset will need to be screened by two reviewers (independent double screening).

Summary

- The research question determines the limits of the search which should be comprehensive, explicit and replicable.
- The main focus of the search strategy is likely to be on the electronic searches, but these should be supplemented by other means, such as hand searching of key journals or citation searching.
- Studies should be screened for selection into the review using pre-specified inclusion and exclusion criteria.

4. Coding

Once the screening has been completed the included studies should be coded. Coding, or data extraction, is the process by which the included studies are described and classified. A paper-based or electronic coding instrument should list all the items for which data will be sought. This will include, as a minimum, data extraction of information about the bibliographic details of the study and its aims and objectives, and key items using the PICOS categories (see above): participants, intervention, control or comparison conditions, outcomes and study designs. It will also state the quantified outcomes which will be extracted (e.g. the means and standard deviations of all pre- and post-tests for all groups).

In addition, the items which will be used to appraise the quality of the included studies (see below) should be coded, and the quality assurance procedures for ensuring the reliability of the coding should be recorded. Ideally this should involve independent double coding, with a plan for comparing information on the coding form and procedures to follow when two reviewers disagree. The coding instrument should ideally be piloted using draft versions to extract data from a dozen or so papers to test the efficacy of the instrument with a relatively small sample of studies: it can then be amended if necessary. If possible, the coding should be undertaken 'blind' to authors of the included studies, although to do this may be costly and time-consuming.

5. Quality appraisal

In order to limit the potential for introducing bias into a systematic review because of design bias it is necessary to critically appraise the included studies in order to assess the potential for risk of bias. In the case of randomised controlled trials, which vary in quality, pooling the results of a number of RCTs with risk of bias due to methodological shortcomings in their design needs to be explored in the review. Methodological work, mainly in the field of healthcare research, has led to the development of a number of tools designed to quality appraise RCTs. The Consolidated Standards of Reporting Trials (CONSORT) Statement (Schultz et al., 2010) is not a quality assessment tool, but a minimum set of recommendations for reporting RCTs in a standardised way in order to increase transparency and help with the critical appraisal of trials. A form of the CONSORT Statement, adapted to make it relevant to educational research, can be used to develop a quality appraisal (or assessment of risk of bias) tool. The CONSORT Statement comprises a 25-item checklist and a four-stage flow diagram. The tool should focus on the most important reporting issues such as trial design and analysis, for example whether the allocation was independent and concealed, whether a sample size calculation was undertaken, whether the unit of analysis matched the unit of allocation, and whether there was high or differential attrition between the arms of the trial. The four-stage flow diagram depicts the flow of participants through the key stages of the trial: enrolment, allocation, follow-up and analysis.

Quality appraisal of studies should include whether or not a CONSORT-type flow diagram was included in the report. This is important as a significant source of bias can be introduced through high attrition and the flow diagram is a visual way of presenting these data. The potential impact of the quality of the included studies should be considered in the synthesis.

Summary

- Coding involves the extraction of information from the included studies to describe and classify the studies.
- The kind of data extracted will depend on the research question and the type of synthesis that will be undertaken.
- The categories for coding should be pre-specified, piloted on a sample of studies, and based on the PICOS categories.
- Quality appraisal involves assessing the included studies for key sources of risk of bias and methodological rigour.
- It can be undertaken using a tool developed from the CONSORT Statement.
- Methods for quality assuring the coding and quality appraisal should be predetermined, and rigorously undertaken and reported.

6. Synthesis

The synthesis involves combining the results of the individual studies using a framework or structure.

Study characteristics (e.g. publication year)
Methodological characteristics (e.g. method of assignment to condition, study design)
Participant characteristics (e.g. gender, SES, baseline writing)
Intervention characteristics and implementation fidelity
Control/comparison characteristics and implementation fidelity
Outcome measures

Figure 20.4 Exemplar coding book

This can be done in a number of different ways. For example, a 'qualitative' or 'narrative' synthesis may be undertaken, or a quantitative or statistical 'meta-analysis' may be used to combine the results of homogeneous studies and increase the power and precision in the measurement of effect sizes.

In a 'narrative' synthesis the included studies are grouped thematically in terms of their characteristics; for example, different varieties of the intervention being evaluated and different learner characteristics, and then commonalities between studies (whether of all the studies or a sub-group of them) can be described. However, systematic reviews of randomised controlled trials and quasi-experiments often, but not always, use statistical techniques (meta-analysis) to combine quantitatively the results of the eligible studies. Whether a narrative or a statistical synthesis is undertaken, the strengths and limitations of each of the included studies (based on the quality appraisal undertaken in step 5 – see above) should be taken into account in drawing conclusions based on the results of the synthesis.

Meta-analysis

Probably the most frequently used method of synthesising quantified data is meta-analysis. Simply put, a meta-analysis combines all the studies to give an overall or summary estimate of effect. Generally, meta-analyses use a process of giving greater weighting to larger studies as these are usually likely to be the most reliable studies in the review. Authors of the systematic review should consider, first, whether a meta-analysis is appropriate, given that in any systematic review the included studies may not be homogeneous in terms of participants, interventions and outcomes, etc. If a meta-analysis is deemed to be appropriate, authors should include, as a minimum, the following: a pooled effect size of all studies eligible to be included in the meta-analysis, with confidence intervals; an indication of how heterogeneity between the studies was explored; whether a fixed-effect model or a random-effects model was used for the meta-analysis; and the pre-specified sub-group and sensitivity analyses that were undertaken. An indication of whether and how the potential for publication bias has affected the results of the meta-analysis should be included, for example through the use of a 'funnel plot'. Given sufficient numbers of studies, a meta-regression analysis can be undertaken to explain some of the heterogeneity observed within the component studies. For example, in the writing review whether or not age of pupil affects outcomes or whether underlying ability interacts with the intervention could be explored through a meta-regression. Furthermore, it is possible to see if the results are affected by the underlying quality of the component studies. Do methodologically weak studies, for example, generate larger effect sizes? The advantage of a meta-regression is that it may help to explain the heterogeneity of the findings. However, there does need to be caution when interpreting any findings from a meta-regression. First, the statistical power of any meta-regression is relatively small; consequently there may be relatively important interactions that the analysis does not uncover. Second, some false positive interactions may be observed. Despite there being a statistically significant interaction with, say, gender, in truth no such relationship may exist. Therefore such findings should be used to generate hypotheses and be confirmed, ideally, in a large, robustly designed RCT.

There are a number of different techniques that can be used to undertake a meta-analysis, a detailed description of which is beyond the scope of this chapter (see Chapter 38 in this book for detailed guidance on the use of meta-analytical techniques; see also Lipsey and Wilson, 2001 for a detailed text on meta-analysis, and Borenstein et al., 2011 for a practical introduction).

Summary

- The synthesis involves the combining of the results of the review.
- Where possible, the nature of the synthesis should be proposed in advance.
- It can take a variety of forms, including a 'narrative' synthesis or a meta-analysis.

- The quality appraisal judgements for each included study should be taken into consideration in the synthesis.
- Meta-analyses are sometimes appropriate in systematic reviews of experimental research in order to provide a pooled effect size of a group of homogeneous studies.
- If a meta-analysis is undertaken, the possible presence of publication bias should be investigated.

7. Report writing

Like all primary research, systematic reviews should be written up and published as soon as possible after their completion. Indeed, there is, arguably, a stronger imperative for publishing reviews as swiftly as possible as they will tend to become outdated more quickly than primary research as the search strategy for the systematic review is time-limited. The process of writing up the final report ought to be guided by the PRISMA Statement to ensure its results are deemed to be of high quality. The report should refer to the existing protocol and be written so that it is as accessible as possible to the widest audience, including policy makers and practitioners.

Summary

- The design, methodology and methods of a systematic review should be written up in a report and published and disseminated widely in a timely manner, as reviews soon become outdated.
- The process of writing the report can be guided by the PRISMA Statement which will increase the rigour of its reporting.
- The report should be accessible to the widest possible audience, including policy makers, practitioners and researchers.

Conclusion

With the explosion of research endeavour across the world it is difficult or impossible for researchers, practitioners and policy makers to keep abreast of new research findings by reading all of the primary research. Systematic reviews enable researchers and others to access the literature in a comprehensive and unbiased manner. In this chapter the basic design and methods underpinning a systematic review have been described. Systematic reviews are an essential precursor to sophisticated synthesis methods such as meta-analysis. A meta-analysis is only as good as its component studies. Should these be from a biased sample of studies then even the most sophisticated statistical techniques cannot rescue the results. Consequently meta-analysts should pay careful attention to how the studies they are including in their statistical synthesis were identified.

In summary, systematic reviews are scientific reviews which have explicit, transparent and theoretically replicable designs and methods. The key features of their design limit any potential biases. They can increase evidence-based education by synthesising a body of literature in a topic area to address a specific research question. They can also identify 'gaps' in the literature, and inform the design of a randomised controlled trial or a future research agenda. However, systematic reviews, like all forms of research, can vary in terms of their quality. Therefore any users of systematic reviews should pay critical attention to the quality of their design, conduct and reporting.

Questions for further investigation

1. Find a systematic review in your area of interest. Prepare a critique of the review in terms of transparency, explicitness and replicability. Make an assessment of the reliability of the findings of the review.

2. Write a research question for a systematic review in a topic area of interest together with a compelling rationale for its significance. Develop the following: parameters for the

review: inclusion and exclusion criteria; methods for searching, screening,
coding and synthesis. Note any challenges to designing this review.

Suggested further reading

Campbell Collaboration at: www.campbellcollabora
tion.org The Campbell Collaboration prepares,
maintains and disseminates systematic reviews in
education, crime and justice, and social welfare.

Cochrane Collaboration at: www.cochrane-handbook.
org The Cochrane Collaboration prepares, updates
and promotes systematic reviews in health care. See
also: Higgins, J.P.T. and Green, S. (eds), *Cochrane
Handbook for Systematic Reviews of Interventions*,
Version 5.0.2 (updated September 2009); Chandler, J.,
Churchill, R., Higgins, J., Lasseron, T. and Tovey, D.
(2013) *Methodological Standards for the Conduct of
New Cochrane Intervention Reviews.*

Gough, D. and Thomas, J. (2016) 'Systematic reviews
of research in education: aims, myths and multiple
methods', *Review of Education*, 4 (1); 88–102.
Theoretical perspectives, methodologies and purposes of systematic reviews.

James Lind Library (2015) at: www.jameslindlibrary.
org/ The James Lind Library prepares and maintains
systematic reviews.

Meta-analysis in Education Research at: www.dur.ac.
uk/education/meta-ed/ The Economic and Social
Research Council (ESRC) Researcher Development
Initiative (RDI): Training in Quantitative Synthesis
(Meta-analysis) aims to develop understanding of the
design, methodology and methods of meta-analysis.

Preferred Reporting Items for Systematic Reviews and
Meta-Analyses (PRISMA statement) at: http://
prisma-statement.org/ PRISMA is an evidence-
based minimum set of items for reporting systematic reviews and meta-analyses.

Moher, D., Liberati, A., Tetzlaff, J., Altman, D.G.,
PRISMA Group (2009) 'Preferred Reporting Items
for Systematic Reviews and Meta-Analyses: The
PRISMA statement', *BMJ*, 339.

References

Borenstein, M., Hedges, L.V., Higgins, J.P. and
Rothstein, H.R. (2011) *Introduction to Meta-
analysis*. Chichester: Wiley.

Chalmers, I., Hedges, L.V. and Cooper, H. (2002) 'A
brief history of research synthesis', *Evaluation and
the Health Professions*, 25: 12–37.

Cooper, H. and Hedges, L.V. (eds) (1994) *The
Handbook of Research Synthesis*. New York: Russell
Sage Foundation.

Glass, G.V. (1976) 'Primary, secondary and meta-
analysis', *Educational Researcher*, 5: 3–8.

Glass, G.V., McGaw, B. and Smith, M.L. (1981) *Meta-
analysis in Social Research*. Beverly Hills, CA: Sage.

Lipsey, M.W. and Wilson, D.B. (2001) *Practical Meta-
analysis*, Applied Social Research Methods Series
49. Thousand Oaks, CA: Sage.

Moher, D., Cool, D.J., Eastwood, S., Olkin, I.,
Rennie, D. and Stroup, D.F. (1999) 'Improving the
quality of reports of metaanalyses of randomized
controlled trials: the QUOROM Statement', *Lancet*,
354: 1896–900.

Mulrow, C. (1994) 'Rationale for systematic reviews',
BMJ, 309: 597.

Petticrew, M. (2001) 'Systematic reviews from astronomy to zoology: myths and misconceptions', *BMJ*,
322: 98.

Schultz, K.F. et al. (2010) CONSORT Statement
(online). www.consort-statement.org/ (accessed
20 September 2011).

Shea, B., Dube, C. and Moher, D. (2001) 'Assessing
the Quality of Reports of Systematic Reviews: The
QUOROM statement compared to other tools', in
M. Egger, G. Davey-Smith and D. Altman (eds),
*Systematic Reviews in Healthcare: Metaanalysis
in Context*, 2nd edn. London: BMJ Publishing
Group.

Torgerson, C. (2003) *Systematic Reviews*. London:
Continuum.

Torgerson, C. (2006) 'Publication bias: the Achilles'
heel of systematic reviews?', *British Journal of
Educational Studies*, 54(1).

Torgerson, D. and Torgerson, C. (2008) *Designing
Randomised Trials in Health, Education and the
Social Sciences*. London: Palgrave Macmillan.

Part IV

Data collection tools

In-depth interviews

Carolyn L. Mears

21

Introduction

Educational researchers study the world of teaching and learning in order to understand, inform and improve practice. They often attempt to explain a phenomenon, describe a culture, disclose life experience, predict outcomes or assess variables and impacts. Researchers determine the method for their study by clarifying the questions they want answered and their purpose for asking. Some researchers conduct quantitative studies to reveal broad patterns or trends across populations. Others prefer qualitative study of individuals or small groups to produce a deeper understanding and appreciation for the circumstances of people's lives.

If you are entering into the world of educational research, one of your first steps will be to consider what you want to learn from your investigation. Are you looking for broad trends or deep insights, cause and effect or interpretations of meaning, variables or personal stories, or perhaps some combination of pursuits? If you want to learn from the qualities of experience and the significance of events or situations, your methodology will probably involve interviewing. While serving as a primary tool for data collection, in-depth interviewing can also function to clarify or triangulate data obtained through other means.

This chapter introduces you to the practice of interviewing for research, with particular attention given to semi-structured, in-depth interviews that are intended to go beyond what can be learned through focus groups or tightly scripted protocols. It provides an overview of a process for using open-ended questions to explore participants' experiences and understandings, and it considers the challenges to be faced and standards to be met.

Interviewing: It's more than questions and answers

In-depth interviews are purposeful interactions in which an investigator attempts to learn what another person knows about a topic, to discover and record what that person has experienced, what he or she thinks and feels about it, and what significance or meaning it might have. This process appears to be innately simple and intuitive. After all, we are accustomed to having routine conversations in which information is easily exchanged. Someone asks a question; someone responds; experiences, opinions and perceptions are shared. Graduate students I've worked with often consider an interview-based approach for their research under the mistaken assumption that interviewing is 'easy'. But don't be fooled! Interviewing for research is quite different from common conversation and requires a well-envisioned design, a great deal of preparation, purposeful conduct and attentive listening. You are not just passing the afternoon. You are collecting data that can allow insightful analysis and produce defensible findings.

Several years ago when I studied the aftermath of the Columbine shootings, I discovered a term that has shaped my understanding of research. In preparing for the work, I spent considerable time learning about the impact of trauma. In the process, I found that individuals who survive a traumatic event commonly feel distanced from others because of their own life experience. As a result, victims commonly withdraw behind what psychologists call a *trauma membrane* to avoid further victimisation or misunderstanding (Lindy et al., 1981).

I find this concept of separation serves as a powerful metaphor to describe the challenge of researching *any* lived experience, whether traumatic or mundane. Each of us has a unique awareness and response to life events. What we do, see, think, believe and hope for is distinctive to us, and until we share that perspective with others it remains within our own personal membrane of knowing. An in-depth interview provides a way for a researcher to cross this boundary, to journey into another's perspective about a circumstance or event, so meaning can be learned and significance shared. In this way, in-depth interviews offer a path to discovery and greater understanding.

Before considering the mechanics of interviewing, it is important to address its use in research. If you're about to begin a thesis or dissertation, your first job is not to identify a method but to clarify the question you want your research to answer and the purpose you want it to serve. When you know what you want to learn and why, you can determine your method.

'At the root of in-depth interviewing is an interest in understanding the experience of other people and the meaning they make of that experience' (Seidman, 2012: 9). Research questions that can be answered through interviewing commonly address matters of *what* or *how* related to lived experience, for example:

- *What are the long-term consequences of … ?*
- *What is the experience of … ?*
- *What characteristics emerge when … ?*
- *How does participation in … ?*
- *How do changes influence … ?*
- *How do students perceive … ?*

In the pursuit of a depth of understanding that cannot be accessed through brief interaction, questions like these would require you to decide who holds the needed information, what to ask, how many interviews will be optimal, and how to manage and analyse the data. Your research question guides your design.

For example, if you want to understand situations influencing teacher retention, you would, of course, want to interview teachers and possibly former teachers, but which ones? Because the goal is depth not breadth, you will spend considerable time with a small number of participants. As a result, you should select 'information-rich cases … those from which one can learn a great deal about issues of central importance to the purpose of the research' (Patton, 2015: 230). While not seeking randomness, you need to be intentional in making your selection and that requires preparation. Your research purpose and awareness of context will drive your strategies for sampling; for example, you might want to study extreme cases at the far ranges of experience, a convenience sample of those easily accessed, or a snowball sample in which participants lead you to other informants (see Patton, 2015).

Determining the number of participants for your study is a little trickier, since there is no universal standard for this but is instead relative to the data you collect. Essentially, you are required to collect sufficient data to represent the experience you are investigating, and you may stop when you reach saturation (i.e. no longer hear anything new). The proposed number to interview is often expressed as a range (e.g. 6–8 participants). You will negotiate this matter with your research advisor and learn by doing.

Achieving a level of in-depth reflection usually requires multiple interviews with each participant. The first responses you hear undoubtedly will be the oft-told tale, the frequently shared story of events, or happenings without much depth, detail or reflection. You want to get beyond these simple facts, which provide context but are unlikely to bring you to an enriched understanding or fresh insight. A series of two or three, 90-minute interviews spaced about a week or two apart, for example, will provide a greater opportunity to build a rapport and achieve deeper reflection. Also, when you ask participants a question, related information may rise in their memory later, and multiple sessions will give you the chance to access this.

Conducting the interview

A research interview is a collaborative activity, a two-way exchange is most productive when a researcher accounts for any power differential, thereby increasing the potential for building rapport, candour and openness. Whether you are interviewing an unemployed single mother, or an undocumented alien, or perhaps an empowered policy maker or corporate executive, you will do well to address the distinctions in status that separate their world from yours. Educate yourself about the culture within which you will be working so you can prepare for and conduct each interview with that in mind. This preparation includes everything from the way you frame your questions to how you understand their answers and even how you dress for the interview.

Effective interviewing depends on a well-planned interview guide to ensure that you cover the topics you want your participants to address. For standardised or focused interviews, a structured guide specifies each question to be asked so the exact wording can be used with each participant. A question is read, the respondent's answer is recorded, then the next question is read, and so on.

For in-depth interviews, however, a more open format is employed. Instead of scripted questions, your guide will list primary areas of exploration for each session. You will let your study participants know what interests you and invite them to tell you more. For example, to study the effects of participation in an adult literacy programme, you might begin with the following plan:

First session: Ask about experiences while in the programme; motivation to enrol; effects; challenges; relationships; employment.

Second session: Clarify the points from Session One. Ask about their perspective after graduation; overall feelings about how the programme affected their life, goals, identity; how they would describe it to someone considering enrolment.

These general focal points will help you generate the questions to begin your interview, but remember that your research questions are not your interview questions. While you want to answer an overarching research question, it is not your participant's job to answer it for you! You will ask participants about related matters and to tell their experiences, share their feelings or thoughts, and reflect on decisions and events. From their narratives, you will be able to analyse the information and answer your research question. For example, if your research question is 'What is the effect of completion of an adult literacy programme on life satisfaction?', you can't really expect someone in your study to know the answer to this. However, graduates of such a programme can tell about *their* experience and that will help *you* find the answer. By compiling and analysing all your participants' stories, you will see patterns or themes related to their overall life experience, satisfaction, attitudes, challenges and such.

At the first session, you start by introducing your study: explain its intent, the risks, the potential benefits; answer any questions; and ask the participant to sign an *informed consent* to be in the study. Your candour, interest and respect throughout the process helps to establish the trust and rapport that can create an environment for sharing. Remember, if your study includes participants from marginalised or underrepresented groups, pay particular attention to perceived differences in status, power or background. Although you cannot make differences disappear, you can consider how participants might respond to you and attend to perceptions that could negatively affect your research.

In the interview, your job is to invite participants to tell you about matters that interest you and to listen carefully to their response. Your interview guide frames the area to be investigated, but with open-ended or semi-structured questions you can't be certain exactly where the answer will lead. The first response you hear may be a general description, but buried in that response, you will find the markers that point to other areas to explore. Noticing these signs requires that you stay aware and that you confirm you understand what you think you are hearing. If something seems contradictory or unclear, express your confusion, or rephrase the question and ask again. Monitor your assumptions and don't take for granted that you understand everything you hear. Words have different meanings in different contexts, so take time to build comprehension. Listen for expressions that challenge what you were thinking, then explore a little further.

To get the most from interviews, it helps to ask questions in a way that first sets a context and then opens avenues for a response (Morrissey, 1987). A closed or tightly scripted question such as 'How long did it take you to complete the literacy programme?' doesn't leave much room for exploration. However, you could learn much more if you phrase your question as 'I am interested in learning about adult literacy programmes. Please tell me about your experience in such a programme.' This defines the area of interest, and instead of limiting the response lets the participant decide what seems most important and worthy of sharing. From this discussion, you will have many paths to pursue. At the end of each interview, be sure to express your sincere gratitude for the participant's contribution to your study.

Be sure also to transcribe each interview before conducting the next one. Review your notes and the transcript carefully in preparation for the next interview. Highlight areas of discussion that may have been approached but left incomplete; note any topics yet to be covered; identify salient lines of investigation to pursue. Be sure to ask your participant to help you know what you may have overlooked, what questions they expected you to ask, and what seems most important to be included in your report.

In some cases, you may need to conduct your interviews over the telephone. The considerations that apply to face-to-face interviewing also apply to telephone interviews: the importance of careful preparation, purposeful questioning, attentive listening, a perceptive follow-up, and appreciation for the participant's contribution to your study. The primary difference is that telephones don't provide the visual cues of body language or facial expression. This means that you must attend to the voice even more carefully, noting pauses, emphasis, silences and sighs. Technologies such as Skype and Facetime offer promise in allowing the use of computers to provide a video as well as an audio connection. However, for some, the technology may be distracting, and you want the attention to be on the dialogue, not on the uniqueness of the experience.

Conducting interviews is merely one phase of interview-based research. Before you can begin the analysis phase, you need to ensure that your data are correct. To do this, you can conduct a member check to confirm the accuracy and completeness of the transcripts (Lincoln and Guba, 1985), or perhaps a narrator check in which you meet with each participant for another interview to review and reflect on your interpretation of their meaning (Mears, 2015).

There are many models for data analysis. Some researchers employ qualitative software while some prefer a more hands-on approach for coding and theme-finding. Rather than guiding you through a variety of approaches here, I recommend that you check the resources included in the Suggested Further Reading section at the end of this chapter.

Challenges and dispositions

No discussion of in-depth interviewing would be complete without acknowledging the challenges it poses, namely that it requires patience, demands considerable time and energy, and involves coordinating your schedule with the busy calendars of others. In addition, the 'lack of rules, vast amounts of data to process, the tasks of writing are baffling to some' (Lichtman, 2012: 27). Instead of a simple set of clearly defined steps, interview research is characterised by an emerging design, with data collection blurring into data analysis, countless hours devoted to transcription, and no iron-clad rules of what constitutes sufficient data.

In interview research, you cross borders of experience in order to learn from others, and since interviews are interactions with people, there's always an element of unpredictability. 'Research – like life – is a contradictory, messy affair' (Plummer, 2011: 195), yet in this messiness lies the opportunity for discovery and enriched understanding. Interviews may not go as planned; a participant may not have the desired information; someone may cancel or drop out altogether. However, your dedication to learning from others will help you to collect data that inform your topic, to analyse that data to discover meaning, and to share that meaning with others.

Before proceeding, it might be wise for you to take a moment to self-reflect and consider your readiness for this type of research. Do you ask the kind of questions that can only be answered by learning from another's perspective? Do you enjoy interacting with people, take a certain pleasure in exploring the unique ways people experience their world, feel comfortable finding your own path on a complex, unmarked journey? In short, do you think you could complete a study that requires you to:

- enter into the complexity of people's lives?
- establish a rapport that encourages communication?
- ask challenging questions and pose a meaningful follow-up?
- attend to nuances of expression, silences and non-verbal cues?
- hear meaning from another's perspective?
- refrain from judgement and argument?
- organise, manage and analyse an abundance of verbal data?
- synthesise information from a variety of sources?
- accurately report what others express?
- maintain healthy boundaries?
- engage in self-reflection?
- write and communicate effectively?

Certain skills and dispositions can help you meet the challenges. Some of these traits you may already have. Others will require practice. It is important that you appreciate what is involved before you begin.

Standards

When you set out to learn from others, it is important to consider how your work will affect them. The imperative of *first, do no harm* should drive every action and decision. Respecting participants in your study, ensuring genuine informed consent, maximising benefits, minimising risks, and assuring fairness and equity in selecting participants are mandates of the human-subjects review boards governing research. However, an ethics of accuracy and principled conduct is also required, as is ensuring that your research practices account for and adjust to differences in social status, gender, age, race, culture, education, and other factors of rank or position. As a visitor in your study participants' world, you are responsible for communicating honestly, treating them fairly, accurately representing their meaning, and using their interviews only as promised.

Beyond the issues of ethics, you also need to achieve rigorous standards for quality. Standards traditionally applied to quantitative research, however, mean something different to qualitative researchers.

The validity of interview research is related to its appropriateness for studying what it claims to inform and its veracity in reporting. However much we are committed to achieving this standard, an assessment of qualitative research in terms of validity 'does not lead to a dichotomous outcome (i.e. valid vs. invalid), but represents an issue of level or degree' (Onwuegbuzie and Leech, 2007: 239). Lummis (2006) observes that 'the validation of oral evidence can be divided into two main areas: the degree to which any individual interview yields reliable information on the experience, and the degree to which that individual experience is typical of its time and place' (2006: 273). These are matters for you to consider as you design your study and select your participants.

Reliability, which 'refers to the trustworthiness of observations or data' (Stiles, 1993: 601), can be measured by how accurately the study reflects the participants' meaning and their authority to comment on the matters being studied. Member check and/or narrator check are essential for establishing reliability.

Achieving replicability does not mean that a qualitative study can be exactly duplicated in another setting; instead, it relates to the transparency of the work. By providing a thorough account of your procedures (e.g. participant selection, interviewing, data confirmation, analysis) along with a clear rationale for your decisions at each step of the way, you can provide an audit trail for others to follow and continue or extend your study – a mark of replicability.

For interview-based investigations, rather than questing for objectivity, it is more productive to evaluate the extent to which any preformed opinions may have tarnished the legitimacy of the research. While neutrality may seem a desired stance, subjectivity has its virtues (Peshkin, 1988), and skilled investigators use their prior knowledge and experience to good advantage. Thus 'the real aim [for a researcher] … should be to reveal sources of bias, rather than to pretend they can be nullified … by a distanced researcher without feelings' (Thompson, 2000: 137). In writing up your research, disclose anything that might have subjectively affected your work and explain what you did to limit its negative impacts.

While interview studies do not aspire to generalisability, their findings can have implications for other settings. Semi-structured or open-ended interviews invite participants to share their experience and understanding, thereby revealing the 'possibilities and limits of what people may do in similar circumstances, even when we cannot predict what they will do. By indicating what might happen, stories enable us to prepare for a range of eventualities' (Stiles, 1993: 601). As you generate your findings, you will point out the potential significance for other settings and situations.

Conclusion

In-depth interviewing can help us learn about the world in terms of human experience. Skilled and insightful interviews have contributed to discoveries of how we think and what we believe. For example, the ground-breaking work on attitudes about end-of-life experience, *On Death and Dying* (1969), was the product of Elisabeth Kubler-Ross's extensive interviews of terminally ill patients. *Women's Ways of Knowing* by Mary Belenky and colleagues (1997) is another masterful example of the power of interviews, in this case deepening understanding of how women experience and express knowledge. The product of interview research, clearly, is not limited to scholarly tomes lining library shelves but may be easily shaped for a wide audience. By collecting stories, analysing their contents, finding patterns and sharing what is learned, researchers can help us better understand our world and what it means to be human.

I would encourage you to consider an interviewer's path in pursuit of learning from the experiences of others. Ask the questions that interest you, and share the answers you hear in ways that illuminate and deepen our understanding.

Questions for further investigation

1. Develop ten research questions that could be answered through in-depth interviewing. List appropriate types of interviewees for each.
2. Write five interview questions to use in researching one of the research questions from 1 above. Meet with another student and take turns interviewing each other for 15 minutes each, taking notes on responses. After completing both interviews, share what you heard each other say. Discuss the process. How did your questions shape

the response? What do you feel went well? What changes would you make?

3. With your class, discuss any ethical considerations that would require you to terminate an interview.

Suggested further reading

Glesne, C. (2015) *Becoming Qualitative Researchers: An Introduction*, 5th edn. Boston, MA: Allyn & Bacon. An informative introduction to qualitative research practices.

Mears, C.L. (2015) *Interviewing for Education and Social Science Research: The Gateway Approach*. New York: Palgrave Macmillan. A handy guide to in-depth interviewing to create a gateway to deeper understanding.

Miles, M.B., Huberman, A.M. and Saldaña, J. (2013) *Qualitative Data Analysis: A Methods Sourcebook*, 2nd edn. Thousand Oaks, CA: Sage. A manual on the fundamentals of research design and data management.

Mishler, E.G. (1991) *Research Interviewing: Context and Narrative*. Boston, MA: Harvard University Press. Examination of the process of interviewing for narrative research.

Patton, M.Q. (2012) *Qualitative Research and Evaluation Methods*, 4th edn. Thousand Oaks, CA: Sage. A comprehensive guide to qualitative practice, with sound advice on interview research.

Rubin, H. and Rubin, I. (2011) *Qualitative Interviewing: The Art of Hearing Data*, 3rd edn. Thousand Oaks, CA: Sage. A practical resource on interview research.

Saldaña, J. (2015) *The Coding Manual for Qualitative Researchers*, 3rd edn. Thousand Oaks, CA: Sage. A helpful guide to multiple strategies for coding qualitative data.

Seidman, I. (2012) *Interviewing as Qualitative Research: A Guide for Researchers in Education and the Social Sciences*, 3rd edn. New York: Teachers College Press. Classic resource on interviewing for phenomenology and other applications.

Weiss, R. (1994) *Learning From Strangers: The Art and Method of Qualitative Interview Studies*. New York: Free Press. Handbook offering insights into effective interviewing, its risks and opportunities.

References

Belenky, M., Clinchy, B., Goldberger, N. and Tarule, J. (1997) *Women's Ways of Knowing*. New York: Basic.

Kubler-Ross, E. (1969) *On Death and Dying*. New York: Scribner.

Lichtman, M. (2012) *Qualitative Research in Education: A User's Guide*, 3rd edn. Thousand Oaks, CA: Sage.

Lincoln, Y.S. and Guba, E.G. (1985) *Narrative Inquiry*. Newbury Park, CA: Sage.

Lindy, J.D., Grace, M. and Green, B. (1981) 'Survivors: outreach to a reluctant population', *American Journal of Orthopsychiatry*, 51: 468–78.

Lummis, T. (2006) 'Structure and Validity in Oral Evidence', in R. Perks and A. Thomson (eds), *The Oral History Reader*, 2nd edn. London: Routledge, pp. 255–60.

Mears, C.L. (2015) *Interviewing for Education and Social Science Research: The Gateway Approach*. New York: Palgrave Macmillan.

Morrissey, C. (1987) 'The two-sentence format as an interviewing technique in oral history fieldwork', *Oral History Review*, 15: 43–53.

Onwuegbuzie, A.J. and Leech, N.L. (2007) 'Validity and qualitative research: an oxymoron?', *Quality & Quantity*, 41: 233–49.

Patton, M.Q. (2015) *Qualitative Research and Evaluation Methods*, 4th edn. Thousand Oaks, CA: Sage.

Peshkin, A. (1988) 'Virtuous Subjectivity: In the participant-observer's I's', in D.N. Berg and K.K. Smith (eds), *The Self in Social Inquiry: Researching Methods*. Newbury Park, CA: Sage, pp. 267–81.

Plummer, K. (2011) 'Critical Humanism and Queer Theory: Living with tensions', in N.K. Denzin and Y.S. Lincoln (eds), *The SAGE Handbook of Qualitative Research*, 4th edn. Thousand Oaks, CA: Sage pp. 208–12.

Seidman, I. (2012) *Interviewing as Qualitative Research: A Guide for Researchers in Education and the Social Sciences*, 4th edn. New York: Teachers College Press.

Stiles, W.B. (1993) 'Quality control in qualitative research', *Clinical Psychology Review*, 13(3): 593–618.

Thompson, P. (2000) *The Voice of the Past: Oral History*. Oxford: Oxford University Press.

Focus groups and group interviews

Anita Gibbs

22

Introduction

Focus groups and group interviews are methods often used synonymously to mean an organised discussion with a selected group of individuals to gain collective views about a research topic. Group interviews are a way to gather many opinions from individuals within a group setting but are largely didactic between an interviewer and each individual in the group. The distinguisher of focus groups is that they are *interactive*, the group opinion is at least as important as the individual opinion, and the group itself may take on a life of its own not anticipated or initiated by the researcher. In this chapter I will be primarily referring to focus groups as the more widely used technique in educational-based research and because this term has come to be accepted as the term for research utilising a group method. In educational research focus groups can be used for a multitude of purposes, for example co-constructing new knowledge, gauging opinion, evaluating services, generating theory, learning from experiences, understanding the everyday use of language, interpreting cultures, reshaping people's views, political action and empowerment of marginalised groups (Cousin, 2009; Halcomb et al., 2007; Hopkins, 2007). Perhaps less suitable for focus group study would be: the confirmation or disconfirmation of hypotheses; pre- and post- group assessment of interventions; any study where generalisations to whole populations might be required; or studies that are predictive in nature (Vaughn et al., 1996).

Focus groups can be used as a method in their own right but are often utilised to complement other methods, for example to develop or refine survey questions. Reasons to choose focus groups over other methods might include the need to gather reasonable numbers of people together for a group view on a topic, the need to gauge multiple perspectives about a topic in the emotive and interactive way that only a focus group can achieve, and as a cheaper or speedier way of doing interviews where easily accessible groups of participants can be readily assembled instead of interviewing many individuals, especially when assembled online.

The rest of this chapter considers the strengths and weaknesses of focus groups, how to set up and run focus groups, the ethical dilemmas and cultural challenges to consider when undertaking focus group studies, and the use of 'online' focus groups. The chapter also provides two exemplars of educational-based research focus groups and advice on further reading, as well as some questions for discussion.

Strengths and weaknesses of focus groups

Halcomb et al. (2007: 1008), and Stewart and Shamdasani (2014), discuss the strengths and weaknesses of focus groups. Benefits include: discovering the collective perspective; the 'synthesis and validation of ideas and concepts'; the involvement of diverse groups of people; and access to potentially a large number of participants. On the downside, Halcomb et al. (2007: 1008) consider that focus groups have potential for problems with confidentiality (see also Tolich, 2009), can produce conflicts resulting in problems in managing group interaction, can be poorly run if moderators are not highly skilled, and can sometimes produce complex verbal and non-verbal responses from participants, thereby making analysis and interpretation a challenging task. Others have argued that focus groups can also produce shallow or poor quality data, thus reducing the quality of insight overall (Hopkins, 2007).

Yet the benefits to focus group participants themselves should not be underestimated. People may feel strongly about a topic and may enjoy discussing it with others who share some of their concerns; they may also enjoy group debate on a topic in such a way that they feel empowered by the group dynamic. Participants in focus groups may feel able to talk about sensitive topics in a way in which they would not do in an individual interview, and they may gain strength from the energy of a group setting. Of course, the researcher may not be able to predict or control whether focus group participants do have such experiences, and ultimately has to decide if their research questions are best answered by this method. For researchers, a clear strength of focus groups is that they allow information to be collected on *why* an issue is salient, as well *how* it may be salient or in *what* ways it may be salient – all at the same time. Hence the gap between what people say and what they do can be better understood.

Another advantage of focus groups is their potential for change, whether during a group session or post sessions. This could of course be perceived as a disadvantage if change occurs in the negative. Potentially though, changes in education to policy, practice or theory may occur through focus group research because new ideas have emerged during the dialogues between participants who may themselves be capable of initiating change. Researchers can also initiate change in the way they choose to present the analysis from focus group studies.

The context in which a focus group occurs and its influence is particularly pertinent to consider, as potentially the contributions made by participants will be swayed by such factors as location, culture, age and gender balance, status, capabilities, physical abilities and so on. Each focus group meeting needs to be understood in its contextual setting in an entirely different way from that of an individual interview. The timing of a group is also an important contextual consideration: trying to get parents of school-aged children to focus groups during school holidays is a non-starter for example.

On a practical note, focus groups can be difficult to assemble (see next section). It may not be easy to get the sample that is able to answer your research questions, and focus groups may discourage certain people from participating, for example those who are not very articulate or confident, and those who have communication challenges or special needs. People more likely to participate in group-based research will be confident and articulate, although it may be possible to gain more vulnerable or marginalised perspectives if participants are part of a pre-existing group. If the researcher is also part of the marginalised group, perhaps as a service user or as an invited guest, then again it may be possible to obtain the perspectives of less confident participants.

How to set up and run a focus group

Focus groups are particularly suited to qualitative research but that does not mean they cannot complement a quantitative and positivist-oriented study (i.e. survey plus group interviews). Mixed methods are fine but also a stand-alone focus group study can be undertaken. Once a decision has been made that focus groups might best answer a particular research objective or question then the initial planning can begin. Selecting the groups of participants is a crucial stage. A focus group researcher will need to decide how many groups, of what size, of what composition and so on. Most texts advise groups composed of between 4 and 12 people but there have been studies outside of these guidelines (Cousin, 2009; Hopkins, 2007; Stewart and Shamdasani, 2014). Toner (2009), for example, who used as few as two participants for focus group studies about women who had abused illegal substances, argues that small groups still follow typical group development and can be analysed in the same way as larger focus groups. Toner (2009) believes that feminist research principles of collaboration and emancipation enable an acceptance of the validity of very small focus groups (VSFGs as they are known), especially with hard to reach groups. As to how many groups, again that depends somewhat on the research questions, but from a grounded theory perspective 'how many?' may need to be decided after the data collection has begun. Often people conduct one-off groups with three or more different focus groups, but also many meetings of the same group of participants can be undertaken. The researcher will need to decide when they have gathered enough data to achieve their research goals and when they have analysed enough groups to reach saturation and meaning, and are able to justify clear themes and add new concepts.

In order to undertake a focus group study in education the researcher will have prepared information sheets, consent forms, and obtained ethics approval. Accessing participants may require the use of key informants or go-betweens who can contact likely participants and recruit them. These recruiters undertake a pivotal role, and will need to be acknowledged and thanked, perhaps through a gift or financial payment. The participants themselves may need to be offered a small incentive for taking part, or offered food or refreshments during attendance at focus group meetings. The researcher will need to determine the time, place and format of meetings. The selection of participants will need to reflect whether the research question can best be answered with diversity of groups or homogeneity. In the past, focus group researchers were advised to make up the groups with similar kinds of people (e.g. single-sex, same ages, same ethnicities), but nowadays focus groups are full of a greater range of mixed characteristics. Diversity is

welcomed but a researcher must always be mindful of the impact of status and power on group dynamics and getting it wrong can result in poor quality interaction and data. Too many power differentials can mean some people will not speak and may even be upset by comments from powerful others. Can the group mix best answer your research questions and will the focus group experience be safe for participants? These two questions should guide selection. It is always best to over-recruit by as much as 30%, as not everyone will make it. It is quite common to do additional individual interviews with people who agreed to participate in the study but then failed to turn up to the actual group meeting. For an online guide and handy checklists for running focus groups the following website has useful information: http://videos.med.wisc.edu/videos/10479

The moderator, researcher or group facilitator plays a critical role in determining the outcomes and experiences of the focus group. Nearly every text suggests that they need to be knowledgeable of group processes and skilled in group facilitation (Halcomb et al., 2007; Toner, 2009). Key characteristics of moderators are good interpersonal skills and the ability to handle conflict as well as to nurture contributions, thus enabling interaction between participants while being reflective and non-judgemental. Ultimately, the quality of data produced is dependent on the ability of the moderator to get people talking to each other, in-depth, about the topic in hand. When running the actual focus group the moderator will undertake introductions, the setting of groundrules and the facilitation of discussion. In some cases they will be assisted by an observer who might take notes, help with other recording equipment, or ask the occasional question of the group. An observer can be very helpful after a group has finished discussing key themes arising from group interaction. The moderator is likely to have prepared an interview guide but must be fully prepared not to have all their questions covered, so the fewer the questions the better. Focus groups are likely to cover areas of discussion not anticipated by the researcher but a skilled moderator can make the most of these 'new' areas as well as bring the discussion back to the main points. At the end of a group, which usually lasts between 45 minutes and two hours (although there have been examples of less than 30 minutes for children, and four hours for Maori – see the Suggested Further Reading and References sections at the end of the chapter), the moderator will thank participants and sum up. It is likely that transcripts of sessions will be prepared and sent to participants for checking and/or further comment.

For analysis (see Stewart and Shamdasani, 2014; Wilkinson, 2011 in the Suggested Further Reading), the focus group researcher needs to bear in mind that the unit of analysis is the collective perspective. Too often in the reporting of focus groups the analysis is presented as if there had been only a conversation between the researcher and each individual participant whereas there has mostly been group dialogue. The reporting of findings needs to show the interaction between and influence of participants upon each other to fully represent what has occurred in the focus group. The analysis of focus group data will include deductive reasoning from the original research questions and inductive reasoning to allow new concepts, themes and ideas to emerge. Consensus of views as well as divergence of opinion will all be captured and reported upon in final reports. The validity and reliability of focus group data can include triangulation, audit trails, and respondent and inter-rater checking (Toner, 2009).

Ethical dilemmas

Tolich (2009) and Halcomb et al. (2007) identify many ethical dilemmas peculiar to focus groups. These include issues to do with confidentiality and fully informed consent, arguing that focus groups present extra dilemmas and risks because of their group nature. They argue that it is not possible to ensure confidentiality because all participants hear the discussion in a group even if they do not share it beyond the group. Likewise, the nature of the research questions and actual discussion taking place in a focus group may differ somewhat from

the schedule suggested in the information sheets. This is because in a group the interaction levels can change the flow of the topic and the researcher inevitably has less control even if they are highly skilled in group research. Tolich (2009) argues that some of the ethical issues can be overcome by more detailed information sheets which clearly lay out the risks of participation, as well as researchers reiterating at the start of focus group meetings that people should be wary of sharing too much personal information and that the researcher may be limited in their abilities to minimise harm. Tolich also wisely reminds us that viewing focus groups as a kind of *public meeting* rather than a private meeting is more helpful to participants in enabling them to decide what to say. In any good ethical research participants should be offered the chance to debrief, and/or, contact the researcher to follow up concerns. In very sensitive research additional services should be offered, for example a counsellor or other professional service, for participants who feel they have experienced distress from participating in a focus group. In VSFGs extreme care should be taken to protect the identity of participants through the anonymisation of their characteristics.

Cultural challenges

Much has been written about the need to ensure an appropriate mix of focus group participants in a way in which is not discriminatory or offensive to different cultural groups, and which also takes account of different cultural practices (Halcomb et al., 2007). Issues of sample size, status, gender, age, location, recruitment and question procedures all need to be reflected upon in culturally appropriate terms. Sometimes, even when appropriate cultural protocols have been followed and participants have felt comfortable to participate in a focus group, unintended consequences will occur. Pere and Barnes (2009) provide an example of a focus group study with Maori where one focus group proceeded well and another one resulted in causing offence to some people, even though the same culturally sensitive practices had been in place prior to the group meeting. Pere and Barnes (2009) conducted a study to ascertain the views of mental health service users on the concept of self-stigma. Pere was Maori and Barnes non-Maori but could speak Maori. The researchers consulted appropriately with, and enlisted the help of, respected Maori leaders to run the focus groups. In one of the focus groups the Maori leader was critical of research procedures which failed to understand the complexities of Kaupapa Maori (i.e. Maori ways of doing and self-determination). The focus group facilitated by this Maori leader was conducted very differently from other groups, but in a way in which participants felt that Maori protocol had been adhered to and useful data were still collected. Pere and Barnes concluded that it is vital to allow Maori to define their own ways of doing research even if it contrasts with the assumed 'normal' Western ways of doing it. Other cultures may favour alternative ways of conducting focus group research, and it is therefore important for people planning focus group studies to allow extra time for working in culturally appropriate ways.

Online focus groups

While this chapter concentrates on 'traditional' face-to-face group interviewing, future focus group research will increasingly be done online, via email or the Internet, or by using remote audio and video technology (Stewart and Shamdasani, 2014). The issues to consider when using distance methods for focus groups will be similar to those for traditional focus groups but will also involve new challenges for researchers: for example, in recruitment, getting people together at exactly the same time or at different times but in different locations, operating the equipment and dealing with technology hiccups, and in the recording and management of data. Online focus groups have the potential of convenience for participants and researchers, reduced costs, ongoing dialogue, inclusiveness and greater anonymity. An excellent example of an online discussion board-style focus group is provided by Yick et al. (2005), who organised an asynchronous focus group for 28 academics to explore their experiences of distance education and online teaching. The online discussion board ran for three weeks and three researchers posted new discussion questions each week. All the participants were encouraged to respond and also to engage in dialogue with each other (*interaction* in other words). The researchers moderated the discussions and participants were encouraged to revisit any previous discussions and continue current conversations. All discussion postings were downloaded (the data) and analysed using a content analysis to develop key themes. The article by Yick et al. was, not surprisingly, published in an online journal (see References below).

Exemplars

Jankie et al. (2011) conducted a focus group study with students at high schools in Botswana on the sensitive topics of sex, sexuality, HIV and AIDS. Researchers competed 11 single and mixed sex semi-structured focus groups in four high schools, with each group having 10–12 students aged from 14 to 17 years in it. The study enabled young people to share diverse knowledge, experiences and perspectives on a range of highly sensitive topics. Particular attention was paid to culturally sensitive practice, especially through allowing participants to use both languages they would have been familiar with – Setswana and English. The group dialogue was recorded and transcribed, and analysed thematically as well as using content analysis. The findings reported the keenness of young people to participate in focus groups; the ease with which they participated; and the need to allow enough time for students to discusss deeply sensitive topics in the group setting.

In a different focus group study, considering discourses and explanations, Tett and Riddell (2009) sought educators' views of gender issues in the teaching profession. Tett and Riddell conducted six focus groups with primary and secondary school teachers (n = 38) and 16 individual interviews with key informants involved in education. They gathered data on educators' opinions about the gender balance in teaching, and their views about why men choose teaching and how more men can be encouraged into teaching. Each focus group lasted about 45 minutes and was transcribed and analysed thematically. The main strength of this paper is that it shows how focus groups alongside individual interviews can assist in the furthering of theoretical ideas about a topic. The findings themselves were presented to answer 'why' rather than 'what' questions, and this piece adds nicely to what we know about gender imbalances in the teaching profession.

Conclusion

Focus groups are highly suited to many kinds of educational research. When undertaken well they can be rewarding for participants, present exciting challenges for researchers, and produce quality in-depth interactional data of a kind not possible through other methods.

Questions for further investigation

1. What kinds of educational research might be suited to focus-group research?
2. What are the main ethical issues a novice researcher might face when undertaking an education-based focus group study?
3. How would you prepare and plan for an email, Internet-based or online group-based research meeting?
4. What cultural assumptions do you bring as a researcher to group-interviewing research?

Suggested further reading

Bagnoli, A. and Clark, A. (2009) 'Focus groups with young people: a participatory approach to research planning', *Journal of Youth Studies*, 13(1): 101–19. An excellent report on research undertaken with 12- and 13-year-olds, demonstrating the empowering and participatory nature of focus groups as well as the *basics* of using focus groups for recruitment and research with young people. Bagnoli and Clark used video excerpts as part of their research and gauged feedback on the usefulness of this, as well as young people's views of being involved in focus groups as research participants.

Krueger, R. and Casey, M. (2014) *Focus Groups: A Practical Guide for Applied Research*, 5th edn. Thousand Oaks, CA: Sage. The 'nuts and bolts' guide to organising focus groups, with detailed advice on how to think about and run focus groups. The book also contains material on styles of focus groups, cross-cultural focus group research, telephone and Internet focus groups.

Stewart, D. and Shamdasani, Prem N. (2014) *Focus Groups: Theory and Practice*, 3rd edn. Thousand Oaks, CA: Sage. This easy to read book contains theoretical and practical material to help readers grasp the knowledge and skills required to run focus groups. It has chapters on the history and theory of focus group research, and the basics of setting up, recruiting, designing, and running focus groups. The role of moderator and analysis of focus group research are also covered, and helpfully a chapter on virtual focus groups is included. The book is packed with examples, review questions and exercises.

Wilkinson, S. (1999) 'Focus groups: a feminist method', *Psychology of Women Quarterly*, 23(2): 221–44.

Wilkinson, S. (2004) 'Focus group research', in D. Silverman (ed.), *Qualitative Research*, 2nd edn. London: Sage.

Wilkinson, S. (2011) 'Analysing Focus Group Data', in D. Silverman (ed.), *Qualitative Research*, 3rd edn. London: Sage.

In these three readings Wilkinson covers the groundwork of the pros and cons of focus groups. She provides excellent examples from health and social sciences, and gives detailed reported findings from her own studies as well as details on the analysis of focus group data.

She also explores focus groups as a feminist method and discusses the power issues involved. She is one of the few authors who also details the interactive nature of focus groups and demonstrates this through evidence and quotes from her own research.

References

Cousin, G. (2009) *Researching Learning in Higher Education*. London: Routledge.

Halcomb, E., Gholizadeh, L., DiGiacomo, M., Phillips, J. and Davidson, P. (2007) 'Literature review: considerations in undertaking focus group research with culturally and linguistically diverse groups', *Journal of Clinical Nursing*, 16(6): 1000–11.

Hopkins, P. (2007) 'Thinking critically and creatively about focus groups', *Area*, 39(4): 528–35.

Jankie, D., Garegae, K.G. and Tsheko, G.N. (2011) 'Using focus group interviews to research adolescents' beliefs and perceptions of sex, sexuality, HIV and AIDS in educational settings: methodological successes and challenges', *International Journal of Scientific Research in Education*, 4(2): 131–41.

Pere, L. and Barnes, A. (2009) 'New learnings from old understandings: conducting qualitative research with Maori', *Qualitative Social Work*, 8(4): 449–67.

Stewart, D. and Shamdasani, Prem N. (2014) *Focus Groups: Theory and Practice*, 3rd edn. Thousand Oaks, CA: Sage.

Tett, L. and Riddell, S. (2009) 'Educators' responses to policy concerns about the gender balance of the teaching profession in Scotland', *Journal of Education Policy*, 24(4): 477–93.

Tolich, M. (2009) 'The principle of caveat emptor: confidentiality and informed consent as endemic ethical dilemmas in focus groups research', *Journal of Bioethical Inquiry*, 6(1): 99–108.

Toner, J. (2009) 'Small is not too small: reflections concerning the validity of very small focus groups (VSFGs)', *Qualitative Social Work*, 8(2): 179–92.

Vaughn, S., Schumm, J. and Sinagub, J. (1996) *Focus Group Interviews in Education and Psychology*. London: Sage.

Yick, A., Patrick, P. and Costin, A. (2005) 'Navigating distance and traditional higher education: online faculty experiences', *International Review of Research in Open and Distance Learning*, 6: 2.4. Available at: www.irrodl.org/index.php/irrodl/article/view/235/320 (accessed February 2016).

Internet-based methods

Rhona Sharpe and Greg Benfield

23

Introduction

A single chapter cannot hope to encompass the breadth, depth or complexity of 'Internet research methods' and the research design, data-gathering and ethics issues related to them. This chapter examines one aspect of Internet research in education using the example of a national UK project to explore students' experiences of technology-mediated learning. It examines methods from investigations of learners' experiences of learning in a digital age, and the role that the Internet and other digital technology have played in the development of this field. Much of our perspective originated from our role in the JISC Learner Experiences of E-learning programme,[1] working alongside nine research projects over four years as they collected their data and analysed the findings. We also draw on our leadership of ELESIG[2] – a special interest group of learner experience researchers and practitioners. The approaches described in this chapter continue to be used to uncover the lived experience of learners as their technology-mediated learning environments continue to change rapidly, and the findings are contributing to our understanding of how digital literacies develop within course and institutional contexts.

In this chapter, we show that the Internet has precipitated a change in both research questions and data collection methods. We argue that the pervasive, integrative use of social and personal technology by learners means that the study of educational uses of technology needs to be seen within a wider, holistic context. This chapter explains how such research is being conducted and provides examples of some of the research methods.

The chapter title, 'Internet-based Methods', harbours a duality that is central to our discussion: the Internet is both a repository of research tools and an object of research in its own right. Our examples of research methods for investigating learner experiences encompass both aspects of this duality. Thus we explore some of the online tools and techniques that are being used for gathering data and the methodological issues around their use. We also outline the significance and role of digital technologies in the experiences of today's learners and explore how researchers can take account of this.

We use the example of learner experience research to illustrate how Internet technologies may be used to support three key methodological aims in naturalistic research. The first aim is gaining *sustained engagement* (Lincoln and Guba, 1985) with research participants. We show how online methods can facilitate multiple engagements with participants over extended time periods, allowing the researcher to obtain a more complex picture of dynamic behaviours, perceptions and beliefs than is possible with a single interview or questionnaire. Second, we explore how online methods may be used to improve research validity or *trustworthiness*. This includes the notion of triangulation, that is using a variety of different data types and sources and comparing these for consistency, confirming and crosschecking accounts and observations. This is a cornerstone of naturalistic research and an important way of increasing the trustworthiness of interview data (Cohen et al., 2000; Robson, 2002). Finally, we put forward a position of *participatory*, inclusive evaluation and research as the appropriate standpoint for conducting human research in a digital age.

The impact of the Internet on social science research

It is almost trivial to observe that the Internet is having a major impact on social science research. There are several dimensions to this impact. New topics for investigation continually emerge. For example, learners' experiences in Massive Open Online Courses (Veletsianos et al., 2015) or tablet computers (Rossing et al., 2012) are topics that were unheard of ten years ago. Also, the rapid pace of technological innovation spawns new tools and environments for gathering research data. Ubiquitous mobile phones and a familiarity with photo-sharing have allowed for easier use of visual methodologies (Gourlay and Oliver, 2013), and our ability to mine and process data from digital footprints has given rise to the field of learning analytics (Ferguson, 2012).

What has been learnt from early explorations into Internet-based research is worth revisiting. The commonplace Internet communication tools in the world Mann and Stewart (2000) wrote about in their classic text were email, asynchronous text-based conferencing like the discussion boards found in modern university virtual learning environments (VLEs), and synchronous text-based chat. Ubiquitous social networking, image, video and application sharing, and web-enabled mobile devices were not in existence at that time. As a result, new research tools such as video interviewing and video diaries both remove some of the problems of text-based environments, like establishing participant identity in focus groups, and introduce new issues, such as interpreting data involving significant levels of performance.

The impact of the Internet on researching learners' experiences of e-learning

Learner experience research has prompted a reconsideration of the place and role of technology in students' lives. Previous e-learning research was primarily evaluative, asking questions about the impact of tutor behaviour (e.g. e-moderating; see Salmon, 2004) or presence (see Garrison et al., 2001; Garrison, 2003); pedagogy (e.g. constructivist, see Hughes and Daykin, 2002; Allen, 2005; Gulati, 2008; or collaborative, see Hiltz et al., 2000; McConnell, 2000; Macdonald, 2003; Schweizer et al., 2003; Goodyear and Zenios, 2007); and environment (i.e. technology; see Freeman, 1998; Lockyer et al., 2001; Crook, 2002; Ellis and Calvo, 2004; Kear, 2004) on student learning and satisfaction within a specific educational context. As we noted at the time:

> There is in general a dearth of studies of the learner experience. In particular there is a scarcity of studies that can be characterised as expressing a 'learner voice', i.e. in which the learners' own expressions of their experiences are central to the study. (Sharpe et al., 2005: 3)

Learner experience research takes a different tack, encouraging us to view the experience of being a student from the learner's perspective. Using technology that learners are already familiar with to elicit and record their experiences (see Table 23.2), we are prompted to see the role of technology more holistically. We find that learners use technology primarily not to 'learn' but in pragmatic and conservative ways, such as a source of information, to engage with their social networks, and to improve the presentation of their work (Davies et al., 2008; Gosper et al., 2013). Indeed they may find technology a distraction from learning (Beetham, 2014). We find that technology takes on different roles for various groups of students – having particular significance for disabled and international learners where they have a real need for it (Seale et al., 2010). We find also a vast range of individual differences in how learners use technology, from no use at all to extensive, individual choice in creatively appropriating a range of technologies for learning (Sharpe, 2014).

This change in the way evaluations of technology enhanced learning are conducted is impacting on their research aims and questions. We note a shift from a concern with the actions of course designers and tutors to a focus on the ways in which learners manage their engagement with digital technology (e.g. Andrews and Tynan, 2012; Gourlay and Oliver, 2013). Eliciting learners' experiences is helping us to understand how learners develop skills, practices and make choices, and then to design environments and provide tutoring in ways that will support them at critical moments.

Using online research methods to investigate learners' experiences

For these reasons learner experience research is avowedly naturalistic in approach. It should, in so far as is possible, occur in a natural setting and use methods such as 'interviews, observations, document analysis, unobtrusive clues, and the like' (Lincoln and Guba, 1985: 187). In the JISC Learner Experiences of E-learning programme, this approach was a consequence of both the research questions and our understanding of the role technology plays in the lives of modern students. Our aim was to privilege learners' voices and consider their technology use holistically. This section uses examples from the learner experience field to illustrate the use of naturalistic methods to develop an understanding of the learner in context.

Sustained engagement

Technology has been used in imaginative ways to engage learners in data-gathering over a sustained period of time. Dujardin (2009), in her

'conversations with an e-learner', describes a series of interviews conducted via instant messaging over a five-month period. Masterman (2010) conducted a careful review of the literature on email interviewing in other fields such as health (e.g. Hunt and McHale, 2007) and adapted this for their own project, engaging 23 students in three 'rounds' of questioning over a period of eight to nine months in what they termed the 'pen-pal' method:

> 'Pen-pal' was the name given to the method we devised to meet the challenge of eliciting data from busy students over an extended period with minimal intrusion, and using a simple and robust technology (i.e. email). Each researcher established individual relationships with 6–10 students and conducted an extended email correspondence culminating, as pen-pal relationships can do, in a face-to-face encounter (a semi-structured interview). (Masterman, 2010: 29)

Here questions were derived from the research questions of the study, knowledge of the students' course context and their previous data responses (e.g. 'I note from your survey response that …'). The email correspondence aimed to provide background information to personalise the subsequent interviews and record experiences that might not be remembered in interview.

Sustained engagement has also been achieved through the keeping of diaries or logs. Variants include audio logs (Conole et al., 2007) where students phoned a voicemail service to leave a log entry, and projects where students were given the choice of recording diary entries on a camcorder, webcam or digital voice recorder (Hardy et al., 2008; Jefferies and Hyde, 2009). In the STROLL project at the University of Hertfordshire, students provided diary entries every day for a week, during four weeks spread over 18 months (Jefferies and Hyde, 2009). The videos provided a vivid insight into the worlds, and study bedrooms, of the learners (see Figure 23.1).

Figure 23.1   Screenshot from STROLL video diaries

Trustworthiness

Internet research presents a range of issues around validity or, in naturalistic terminology, the *trustworthiness* of our interpretations of qualitative data. There are different ways of achieving this, which include member checks, debriefings by peers, triangulation, prolonged engagement and persistent observation, the use of reflexive journals and independent audit.

A fundamental principle of learner experience research is that it is holistic. In order to understand how learners experience learning in our technology-rich age, we must ask the participants themselves to define what is talked about. We must go in without preconceptions and ask about all aspects of life. Creanor and her colleagues, in one of the first learner experience studies, interviewed learners using an open set of questions, and improved trustworthiness by engaging three researchers to analyse the resulting transcripts using Interpretive Phenomenological Analysis (see Mayes, 2006; Smith et al., 2009).

Traditionally, validity is improved through the use of mixed-methods designs. In learner experience

research, this approach is exemplified by the Thema project at Oxford University, through their mix of survey and email interviewing as shown in Table 23.1. The 'pen-pal' correspondence culminated in a face-to-face interview, further improving the trustworthiness of the data.

One of the methods in a mixed-method design is often an interview. In conducting interviews – whether online or face to face – the researcher faces the problem of eliciting complete and accurate information where the artificiality of the interview situation may conspire against this aim. Eliciting tacit understandings is notoriously problematic for researchers and in learner experience research we have found that learners may not associate certain activities or technologies with 'learning'.

To help address these problems, the Learner Experiences of E-learning programme adopted an approach called *interview plus* (Sharpe et al., 2005; Creanor et al., 2006; Mayes, 2006). The idea is similar to the 'think aloud' observation technique that is used in cognitive psychology (Ericsson and Simon, 1993), where the 'plus' represents some artefact that is chosen to guide recall during the

Table 23.1   Example of mixed-methods strategy

Study	Technique	Students involved
Preliminary	Online survey	Undergraduate, taught Master's and graduate research students
Main	Online survey	Case study contributors plus other students from the courses involved in the main study
	Email 'pen-pal' correspondence	Case study contributors only
	Online survey	Case study contributors plus other students from the courses involved in the main study
	Face-to-face interview	Case study contributors only

Adapted from Masterman, 2010

interview. This might be a website, blog, wiki, social networking environment, diary, learner progress files or student work. The researcher is taken on a 'guided tour' of the artefact by its creator. In doing so, they hear the participant's explanations while simultaneously comparing these accounts with their behaviours at the computer and onscreen evidence. Interview plus is an important tool in revealing hidden practices and a variant is being used in a large study of academic literacy where multiple data are being collected during interviews, including documents, screen dumps, photos and students' own work as well as interview transcripts (Lea and Jones, 2011).

As part of mixed-method designs, some studies are adding contemporaneous experience probes to interviews and diaries. This is made easier by the ubiquity of mobile phones. For example, in a study of the Net Generation students' use of technology, Jones and Healing (2010) adapted Riddle and Arnold's (2007) day experience method, sending students text messages throughout the day asking them to respond to prompts such as 'What time is it?', 'What are you doing?', 'Where are you?', 'Who are you with?' and 'Are you using any technology and, if so, what is it?'

Participatory approaches

The final methodological aim of naturalistic research into learners' experiences is a participatory approach where learners are involved at all stages of the research. Seale and colleagues, in a

two-year study of disabled learners in higher education, describe such an approach as:

> … involving disabled learners as consultants and partners not just as research subjects. Where disabled learners help to identify and (re)frame the research questions, work with the researchers to achieve a collective analysis of the research issues and bring the results to the attention of each of the constituencies that they represent. (Seale et al., 2008: 11)

The challenge for trustworthiness is to not over-interpret the learner's voice, while balancing that with answering the research questions we have in mind. Participatory approaches allow us to check back with the research participants that the data collected are accurate and that we have consent to use these, and also to check our understanding and interpretation of the data. The researcher's personalised requests for information, conversational style and prompt replies are important in eliciting the data needed and improving validity. Some are extending this approach to using students as researchers (e.g. Veletsianos, 2013).

There are examples of where holistic, participatory methodologies which have engaged learners over extended periods of time have produced unexpected results. The Thema project planned to investigate the use of technology by Master's students, however their final report also tackles issues like adapting to autonomous learning and joining a research community (Masterman and

Shuyska, 2012). Other projects have benefited from having a contextualised understanding of use of technology within the wider choices learners make, such as the notion of the 'digital agility' demonstrated by learners with disabilities (Seale et al., 2010). Despite their benefits, these methodologies are not without their challenges.

Challenges in learner experience research

One of the challenges of the research approaches described in this chapter is that participants who are articulate, reflective and often skilled learners produce the most detailed and useful data. Dujardin (2009), for example, recognises this and talks about the need to have a 'key informant'

willing to engage in reflective conversations with tutors. Other studies purposively sampled learners who were acknowledged as being effective in technology-based learning (e.g. Creanor et al., 2006). Internet-based research methods need to be clear about the extent to which their results can be representative. Those who have used email interviewing, for example, have noted their success in eliciting data from IT literate individuals who have a preference for the written word (Hunt and McHale, 2007).

We have also found that captured learners' voices – whether text, audio or video – can represent their perspectives in powerful and emotive ways. The challenge for researchers is to avoid the temptation to over-emphasise selected verbatim quotes at the expense of the analysis and synthesis of the data.

Table 23.2 Summary of methods used in learner experience research

Method	Description	Strengths	Weaknesses
'Pen-pal' variant of email interviewing (Masterman and Shuyska, 2012)	Researchers enter into a personal dialogue with learners by email. Collects reflective, written contributions over a period of time.	• Can record experiences that learners might subsequently forget. • Can build up a picture of the process of studying as it happens. • Allows researcher to personalise questions. • Minimal intrusion into learners' time. • Maximises sustained participation through establishing a personal dialogue between researcher and learner.	• Time-intensive for researcher to craft individual questions and follow up responses. • Inconsistency in timing and content of questions across students and courses. • Researchers and learner both subjectively involved in interpretation. Requires careful checking for validity against other sources of data (triangulation).
Audio logs (Conole et al., 2007)	Providing facilities for learners to audio record their daily experiences, e.g. a phone-in voicemail number.	• Can provide rich data about day-to-day events. • Less time-intensive for learner than keeping written logs. • Captured voices give insight into the emotion of the experience. • Can provide artefacts for later interviews. • Audio clips can be used in dissemination.	• Instructions need to be clear as researcher is not present to explain. • Participants need to be motivated to stay involved without contact with researcher. • Equipment needs to be easy to use. • Learners need to give informed consent for all possible uses of their voices. • Time-consuming to code data. • Poor recording practice can result in data loss.

Method	Description	Strengths	Weaknesses
Interview 'plus', variant of semi-structured interview (Seale et al., 2010)	Interview which uses an artefact, selected by the participant, to support guided recall, e.g. a blog, email or laptop.	• Prompts discussion of actual learner behaviours, feelings and beliefs. • Allows learners to set the agenda. • Supports recall of actual incidents. • Less time-consuming for researchers than observation. • Allows learner opportunities for reflection.	• Requires skilled interviewer to tease out beliefs, practices and feelings. • Can take more time than other interview techniques. • Some artefacts may be products of group work or held in group spaces, which present ethical difficulties for use as data.
Video diaries (Jefferies and Hyde, 2009; Hardy et al., 2008; Brown et al., 2013)	Participants provided with a set of questions and key dates and record diary entries with a webcam, either at their own location or in the study's 'diary room'.	• Recordings can be made at time and place of student's choosing. • Elicits detailed information and captures thoughts, feelings and opinions at the time. • Prompts can be given for entries around trigger points and significant events. • Resulting videos are compelling viewing. • Videos can be analysed directly without needing to be transcribed.	• Resulting data files may be too large to upload. • Learners need to give informed consent for all possible uses of their images and understand that they cannot be anonymised. This may involve going back to learners at the end of the study to reconfirm their permission to use selected clips.
Synchronous online interviewing (Dujardin, 2009)	One-to-one interviewing using text-based instant messaging software.	• Almost real-time interactions allow for some of the immediacy of face-to-face interactions. • Typing delay gives a few seconds for reflection before answering. • Transcript created in real time and can be returned to during the interview.	• Participant may manage their presentation of self in the explicit record.
Day experience prompts (Jones and Healing, 2010; Andrews and Tynan, 2012)	Participants sent prompts via text message to their mobile phones. Responses to the prompts can be recorded in a voice recorder, video camera or notebook.	• Multiple prompts can be used to capture a day's experience.	• Cost of voice recorders or video cameras in large cohorts. • Produces large volumes of data.

Adapted from the 'Recipe Cards' produced for the JISC Learner Experiences of E-Learning programme at http://wiki.brookes.ac.uk/display/JISCLE2

Video extracts need to illustrate a story which has been derived from an established methodology. Extracts can, however, produce easily digestible and readable findings from large amounts of data (e.g. such as personalised, vivid case studies of individual learners; see, for example, those produced by the PB-LXP project in Thorpe, 2009).

Finally, there are clearly ethical issues in obtaining informed consent for video diary extracts which might be disseminated widely. We also found that holistic, participatory methods encourage participants to reveal information which the researcher will then have to decide is sufficiently important to pass on, such as students revealing difficulties with their course and being in need of support. We recognise the need to develop better guidelines for the ethical use of the digital data provided by research participants.

Conclusion

We hope that this chapter has demonstrated the benefits of adopting a naturalistic stance in Internet-based research and that readers can see parallels between how such approaches have influenced studies of learner experiences of e-learning and their own areas of interest. As these approaches evolve, we are aware of the need to develop methods which draw together data from multiple qualitative projects, perhaps such as meta-ethnography (Lam et al., 2008; Noblit and Hare, 1988; Sharpe, 2014). What is needed is a synthesis and conceptualisation of findings that will take us beyond the stories of individual learners to recommendations which can transform learners' experiences in the future. See Table 23.2 for a summary of the methods used in learner experience research.

Questions for further investigation

1. How effectively are digital tools used on your course? How suitable are they for your area of research interest(s)?
2. List and discuss the many potential pitfalls that surround Internet-based research.

Notes

1. JISC Learner Experiences programme at https://wiki.brookes.ac.uk/display/JISCLE2
2. ELESIG is an international special interest group for those conducting investigations of learners' experiences of e-learning. See http://elesig.net

Suggested further reading

There are some good books and online resources that the Internet researcher can consult. We recommend in particular:

Fielding, N., Lee, R.M. and Blank, G. (eds) (2008) *The SAGE Handbook of Online Research Methods.* London: Sage. This handbook includes practical guidance on online survey design as well as throught-provoking chapters on ethical and legal issues.

Mann, C. and Stewart, F. (2000) *Internet Communication and Qualitative Research: A Handbook for Researching.* London: Sage. Mann and Stewart's early methodological work on computer-mediated communication (CMC) as a research tool has stood the test of time, maintaining its relevance as a manual for researchers on using CMC for interviewing, participant observation, collecting documents, and linguistic analysis.

Savin-Baden, M. and Howell Major, C. (2010) *New Approaches to Qualitative Research: Wisdom and Uncertainty.* Oxford and New York: Routledge. This collection encourages the Internet researcher to consider their position on stance, space and method, with chapters which discuss the complexities of conducting interpretive research. Gourlay's chapter on visual methodologies is recommended reading.

The UK Economic & Social Research Council (ESRC)-funded Research Methods Programme (running from 2002 to 2007, see www.ccsr.ac.uk/methods/), especially the websites Exploring Online Research Methods at www.restore.ac.uk/orm/site/home.htm and Ethnography for the Digital Age at www.cf.ac.uk/socsi/hyper/p02/ index.html.

References

Allen, K. (2005) 'Online learning: constructivism and conversation as an approach to learning', *Innovations in Education and Teaching International,* 42(3): 247–56.

Andrews, T. and Tynan, B. (2012) 'Distance learner: connected, mobile and resourceful individuals', *Australian Journal of Educational Technology,* 28(4): 565–79.

Beetham, H. (2014) 'Editorial: Special issue Digital Technologies in Learning Development', *Journal of Learning Development in Higher Education,* 7.

Brown, M., Hughes, H., Keppell, M., Hard, N. and Smith, L. (2013) 'Exploring the disconnections: student interaction with support services upon commencement of distance education', *FYHE International Journal,* 4(2): 63–74.

Cohen, L., Manion, L. and Morrison, K. (2000) *Research Methods in Education.* London: RoutledgeFalmer.

Conole, G., de Laat, M., Dillon, T. and Darby, J. (2007) '"Disruptive technologies", "pedagogical innovation": what's new? Findings from an in-depth study of students' use and perception of technology', *Computers and Education,* 50(2): 511–24.

Creanor, L., Trinder, K., Gowan, D. and Howells C. (2006) *LEX: The Learner Experience of E-learning, Final report.* Glasgow: Caledonian University.

Crook, C. (2002) 'The Campus Experience of Networked Learning', in C. Steeples and C. Jones (eds), *Networked Learning: Perspectives and Issues.* London: Springer Verlag, pp. 293–308.

Davies, C., Carter, A., Cranmer, S., Eynon, R. et al. (2008) 'The Learner and Their Context – Interim Report: Benefits of ICT Use Outside Formal Education'. Interim report for Becta-funded project 'The Learner and Their Context'.

Dujardin, A.-F. (2009) 'Conversations with an e-learner', *Brookes eJournal of Learning and Teaching,* 2(4). Available at: http://bejlt.brookes.ac.uk/paper/conversations_with_an_e_learner-2/ (accessed 1 December 2016).

Ellis, R. A. and Calvo, R. A. (2004) 'Learning through discussions in blended environments', *Educational Media International,* 41(3): 263–74.

Ericsson, K.A. and Simon, H.A. (1993) *Protocol Analysis: Verbal Reports as Data.* Cambridge, MA: MIT Press.

Ferguson, R. (2012) 'Learning analytics: drivers, developments and challenges', *International Journal of Technology Enhanced Learning,* 4 (5–6). DOI: 10.1504/IJTEL.2012.051816

Freeman, M. (1998) 'Video conferencing: a solution to the multi-campus large classes problem?', *British Journal of Educational Technology,* 29(3): 197–210.

Garrison, D.R. (2003) 'Cognitive Presence for Effective Asynchronous Online Learning: The role of reflective inquiry, self-direction and metacognition', in J. Bourne and J.C. Moore (eds), *Elements of Quality Online Education: Practice and Direction.* Newburyport: Sloan-C, Olin College, pp. 47–58.

Garrison, D.R., Anderson, T. and Archer, W. (2001) 'Critical thinking, cognitive presence, and computer conferencing in distance education', *American Journal of Distance Education,* 15(1): 7–23.

Goodyear, P. and Zenios, M. (2007) 'Discussion, collaborative knowledge work and epistemic fluency', *British Journal of Educational Studies,* 55(4): 351–68.

Gosper, M., Malfroy, J. and McKenzie, J. (2013) 'Students' experiences and expectations of technology: an Australian study designed to inform planning and development decisions', *Australian Journal of Educational Technology,* 29(2): 268–82.

Gourlay, L. (2010) 'Multimodality, Visual Methodologies and Higher Education', in M. Savin-Baden and C. Howell Major (eds), *New Approaches to Qualitative Research: Wisdom and Uncertainty.* Oxford and New York: Routledge, pp. 80–88.

Gourlay, L. and Oliver, M. (2013) 'Beyond "The Social": Digital literacies as sociomaterial practice', in R. Goodfellow and M. Lea (eds), *Literacy in the Digital University: Critical Perspectives on Learning, Scholarship and Technology.* Oxford and New York: Routledge, pp.79–94.

Gulati, S. (2008) 'Compulsory participation in online discussions: is this constructivism or normalisation of learning?', *Innovations in Education and Teaching International,* 45(2): 183–92.

Hardy, J., Haywood, D., Haywood, J., Bates, S. et al. (2008) *Techniques for Gathering Student Views of their Experiences at University.* Edinburgh: University of Edinburgh. Available at: http://www2.epcc.ed.ac.uk/~lead/documents/Methodology_LEaD_Report_final.pdf (accessed 1 December 2016).

Hiltz, S.R., Coppola, N., Rotter, N. and Turoff, M. (2000) 'Measuring the importance of collaborative learning for the effectiveness of ALN: a multi-measure, multi-method approach', *Journal of Asynchronous Learning Networks,* 4(2): 103–25.

Hughes, M. and Daykin, N. (2002) 'Towards constructivism: investigating students' perceptions and learning as a result of using an online environment', *Innovations in Education and Teaching International,* 39(3): 217–24.

Hunt, N. and McHale, S. (2007) 'A practical guide to the email interview', *Qualitative Health Research,* 17(10): 1415–21.

Jefferies, A. and Hyde, R. (2009) 'Listening to the learners' voices in HE: how do students reflect on their use of technology for learning?', *Electronic Journal of e-Learning,* 7(2): 119–26.

Jones, C. and Healing, G. (2010) 'Learning Nests and Local Habitations: Locations for networked learning', in Dirckinck-Holmfeld et al. (eds), *Proceedings of the 7th International Conference on Networked Learning 2010,* pp. 635–42.

Kear, K. (2004) 'Peer learning using asynchronous discussion systems in distance education', *Open Learning,* 19(2): 151–64.

Lam, P., McNaught, C. and Cheng, K. (2008) 'Pragmatic meta-analytical studies: learning the lessons from naturalistic evaluations of multiple cases', *ALT-J,* 16(2): 61–80.

Lea, M.R. and Jones, S. (2011) 'Digital literacies in higher education: exploring textual and technological practice', *Studies in Higher Education,* 36(4): 377–93.

Lincoln, Y.S. and Guba, E.G. (1985) *Naturalistic Inquiry.* Newbury Park, CA: Sage.

Lockyer, L., Patterson, J. and Harper, B. (2001) 'ICT in higher education: evaluating outcomes for health education', *Journal of Computer Assisted Learning,* 17(3): 275–83.

McConnell, D. (2000) *Implementing Computer Supported Cooperative Learning.* London: Kogan Page.

Macdonald, J. (2003) 'Assessing online collaborative learning: process and product', *Computers and Education,* 40(4): 377–91.

Mann, C. and Stewart, F. (2000) *Internet Communication and Qualitative Research: A Handbook for Researching.* London: Sage.

Masterman, L. (2010) *Thema: Exploring the Experiences of Master's Students in a Digital Age: Methodology Report.* JISC Learner Experiences of E-learning programme, University of Oxford.

Masterman, E. and Shuyska, J.A. (2012) 'Digitally mastered? Technology and transition in the experience of taught postgraduate students', *Learning, Media & Technology,* 37(4): 335–54.

Mayes, T. (2006) *LEX – Methodology Report September 2006.* Available at: http://www.jisc.ac.uk/media/documents/programmes/elearningpedagogy/lex_method_final.pdf (accessed 31 March 2011).

Noblit, G.W. and Hare, R.D. (1988) *Meta-ethnography: Synthesizing Qualitative Studies.* Newbury Park, CA: Sage.

Riddle, M.D. and Arnold, M.V. (2007) *The Day Experience Method: A Resource Kit.* Available at: https://minerva-access.unimelb.edu.au/handle/11343/34845 (accessed 1 December 2016).

Robson, C. (2002) *Real World Research,* 2nd edn. Oxford: Blackwell.

Rossing, J.P., Miller, W.M., Cecil, A.K. and Stamper, S.E. (2012) 'iLearning: The future of higher education? Student perceptions on learning with mobile tablets', *Journal of the Scholarship of Teaching and Learning,* 12(2): 1–26.

Salmon, G. (2004) *E-moderating: The Key to Teaching and Learning Online,* 2nd edn. London: RoutledgeFalmer.

Schweizer, K., Paechter, M. and Weidenmann, B. (2003) 'Blended learning as a strategy to improve collaborative task performance', *Journal of Educational Media,* 28(2–3).

Seale, J., Draffan, E.A. and Wald, M. (2008) 'Exploring disabled learners' experiences of e-learning', *LexDis Project Report.* Southampton: LexDis.

Seale, J., Draffan, E.A. and Wald, M. (2010) 'Digital agility and digital decision-making: conceptualising digital inclusion in the context of disabled learners in higher education', *Studies in Higher Education,* 35(4): 445–61.

Sharpe, R. (2014) 'What Does It Take To Learn In Next Generation Learning Spaces?', in K. Fraser (ed.), *The Future of Learning and Teaching in Next Generation Learning Spaces (International Perspectives on Higher Education Research, Volume 12).* Bingley: Emerald, pp.123–46.

Sharpe, R., Benfield, G., Lessner, E. and DeCicco, E. (2005) *Final Report: Scoping Study for the Pedagogy Strand of the JISC E-learning Programme.* Oxford: Oxford Brookes University. Available at: www.jisc.org.uk/uploaded_documents/scoping%20study%20final%20report%20v4.1.doc (accessed 28 September 2016).

Smith, J.A., Flowers, P. and Larkin, M. (2009) *Interpretative Phenomenological Analysis: Theory, Method and Research.* London: Sage.

Thorpe, M. (2009) *JISC Learner Experience Phase 2: PB_LXP: Learners' experience of elearning in practice courses: student case studies.* OU Knowledge Network.

Veletsianos, G. (2013) *Learner Experiences with Open Online Learning and MOOCs e-book* (online).

Veletsianos, G., Collier, A. and Schneider, E. (2015) 'Digging deeper into learners' experiences in MOOCs: Participation in social networks outside of MOOCs, notetaking and contexts surrounding content consumption', *British Journal of Educational Technology,* 46(3): 570–87.

Doing social media research   24
Eve Stirling

Introduction

Social media are now pervasive in the lives of many learners, educators and within many classrooms, across many devices. Social media language such as *to like*, *Instagram it* and *take a selfie* has become mainstream (Oxford Dictionaries, 2013). The social media referred to in this chapter, at the time of writing in 2016, include websites such as *Pinterest*, *Twitter*, *Instagram* and *YouTube* which are also used as apps on smartphones. Other apps such as *WhatsApp* and *Snapchat* are only available on a smartphone. Since the original edition of this book, blogs still feature in the media landscape and of course we cannot escape Facebook. It is still the predominant 'social' site for people to visit, with 1.04 billion daily active users in December 2015 (Facebook, 2016). The language used to describe these sites, which allow users to author and curate content through posting, liking, commenting and sharing, has developed since 2012. In 2009 the special issues of *Learning, Media and Technology* described these sites as 'social software' and these sat within the world of Web 2.0 (Selwyn and Grant, 2009). A seminal overview and definition of social network sites (as they were also called) can be found in boyd and Ellison (2007), which they updated recently (Ellison and boyd, 2013) to acknowledge changes in the architecture of social media. More recently Daniel Miller has led a longitudinal study of social media across the world (Miller et al., 2016) which suggested that the focus of social media is not about the platforms but the *contents* of these sites.

Social media do not appear to be a passing fad (Selwyn and Stirling, 2015). Social media and learning have come into keen focus for educational researchers over the last ten years, and much has changed within the field of learning and the influence of the 'social'. The notion that social media can be a 'data collection tool' is somewhat problematic as that would separate the 'human' and 'social' nature of social media platforms and their use. That said, this chapter will discuss some of the data that are created by social media use, and how an educational researcher might collect those data through using social media and some of the complications relating to this. To do this, a project that used Facebook as the site for the research is taken as an example to discuss some of these complexities. The chapter begins with a discussion of data available via social media – a short review of 'big data versus deep data' – and then looks in more detail at social media 'spaces' and 'places' and how learners might use these. It then goes on to note some ethical concerns that collecting data using social media sites may throw up. The chapter ends with the Facebook study example, highlighting some key methods and reflections on using this (one of the challenges of writing this chapter has been the fast pace of change of social media platforms and their use). Digital technologies, devices, apps and programs update and the tools and opportunities available to a researcher grow – in response to this, the section ends with a note on the availability of data capture that was not around at the time of the study.

Big data and deep data: social media methods

Much of the data shared and created on social media are visual in nature – photos and images of the mundane things of everyday life (Thelwall et al., 2015). Status updates and tweets are text-based and these are often posted alongside the images. Publicly available data on social media sites fall under the term 'big data'. We have been living in the 'big data era' (boyd and Crawford, 2012) for some time now and the huge mass of data on people and things that is available to researchers is overwhelming, even for computational methods (Brooker et al., 2015), let alone humans. Much of our browsing history is tracked and our social media are algorithmically presented back to us, creating challenges to educational researchers. Large amounts of secondary data from social media sites are available and accessed direct from the corporations who own the social media sites. They offer many opportunities and possibilities for data collection and analysis. For example, Twitter data from the Twitter Firehose, which downloads tweets sorted by search term or #, are available for researchers to purchase. Data from other sites can be data-mined (downloaded using web crawler software). Alongside the data you can access there are also advancements in analysis of data, for example sentiment analysis of tweets on Twitter (Thelwall and Buckley, 2013), MobileMiner, an app created to access your own data on your smart phone (Pybus et al., 2015): these tools support our understanding of the social practices which create these big data.

The use of big data may be alluring, the possibilities are great and the data far-reaching, but this may not be appropriate for educational research because you cannot easily find out information on population demographics. It might be more appropriate to support your contextual understanding of a topic. If big data can offer you a contextual understanding of a topic or user group, then deep or 'thick' data (to reference Clifford Geertz's [1973] 'thick' ethnographic description) offer accounts of individual use of social media. Deep data can be more time-consuming to collect as they are often gleaned as a result of a longitudinal study, and an example of this is discussed later in the chapter (writing thick descriptions of how students were using Facebook).

Social media places: a social media site as a space and a place

Research into social media sites sees terms such as 'virtual', 'online' and 'offline' used, very often interchangeably. These can be unhelpful however when researching digital spaces, and particularly when drawing attention to the real and lived experiences of users within the space. Spaces and place are both 'concrete, grounded, real, lived' (Massey, 2005: 185). The digital spaces of the social media sites are not 'out there' and unreal, but geographically grounded in our real lived experiences, and attention should be paid to them as such (Stirling, 2014). The spaces are bounded and yet free-flow; data can move between them. Massey (2005: 184) describes spatialised social practices, which are both open and closed, as the 'sum of our relations and interconnections'. Interactions on a social media make places for users.

Learners' use of social media spaces

The use of social media sites now permeates both formal and informal learning environments and often bridges the two. Social media sites are used for making friends, organising social and academic engagements, managing ongoing relationships between friends, to support academic study through peer support, to play, and as a liminal space in between all of these activities (Stirling, 2014). That said, social media use by young people can be complex, as danah boyd (2014) titled her book on the topic, *It's Complicated*. Young people no longer use one social media site on its own. Research into these complexities has begun to unpick the 'hyper-layered' nature of social media use (see for example Berriman and Thomson, 2015; Hodkinson, 2015) and understand the way social media sites are used concurrently and alongside each other.

Social media, young people and ethical research

Not all learners are young people but there is a significant need to draw attention to the use of social media sites by those aged under 18. Many social media sites have age restrictions on them – you must be 13 or over to have a Facebook account for example – but these are not always followed by the young people who use the sites, often encouraged by their carers (Hargittai et al., 2011). Dawson (2014) draws attention to the need to understand that we cannot always make data that have been created and posted on social media anonymous and so the reach of those data must also be considered – are the data perceived as private data, shared data or public data (Ess, 2015)? The guidelines by Markham and Buchanan (2012) offer an excellent starting point for the reflexive researcher to plan their research design and create an appropriate application for institutional ethical review. What questions can you ask of the data – who produced these? How did you gain access to them? And who was the intended audience?

The next section presents a study which followed six Facebook users for one academic year. This study illustrates some of the methods available when using Facebook as a research site and a research tool (see also Baker, 2013, for a more detailed discussion of Facebook as a tool, data and context) and reflects on the opportunities and tensions surrounding these.

Using Facebook to research first-year transition at a UK university

This section details and explores the methods I used when studying how first-year undergraduate students in the UK use Facebook in their transition to university. It draws on data from a study of undergraduate students at a university in the UK, which explored the cultural practices of the students' use of the social media site Facebook in the context of their university experience (Stirling, 2015 a, b). Facebook is ubiquitous in a great many of the lives of young (18–21 year old) undergraduate students in the UK, and research in this area showed that Facebook is a key tool used for social support and supporting academic study (Selwyn, 2009; Ofcom, 2010).

The focus of the study was to look in detail at the individual students, their Facebook profiles, and how they used these in everyday life. I focused on the role Facebook plays broadly in the student experience of university. I was interested in the changes that go on when a student joins university, the challenges they face in becoming an undergraduate student, and the part Facebook plays in this transition. The participants could be described as heavy Facebook users. Facebook may not be central to a young student's life when they start university, but it more often than not becomes essential to them in order to be able to function socially and academically.

Data gathering on social media in a connective ethnography

A connective ethnography (Hine, 2007) is one that places equal importance on the digital space/site being researched alongside, and equal to, the physical space. It understands that the online and the offline are often simultaneous. This approach allowed for observation, both on Facebook and face-to-face, to explore the complex relationship of the embedded and ubiquitous nature of Facebook in a sample of six undergraduates' lives.

The methods for data collection within the study were both digital and face-to-face (see Table 24.1) and the practicalities and key issues are discussed below.

Gaining access to the field

A digital questionnaire was used to get volunteers for the ethnography. There were n=720 responses with n=32 volunteers. Of these n=6 met with me in person – this was the sample for the ethnography. These participants, my Facebook Friends (FbF), were the focus of the study from 19 August 2010 to 10 June 2011. The participants added me as a friend on Facebook: they did this by searching my name and 'add friend'. This was to give agency to the participants – they did not have to add me and they could delete me from their friend list whenever they wished, I did not control access to their profile.

Methods

- Screenshots of the participants' Facebook profile, status, wall and photos, looked at once a week, and field-notes written to look at patterns of use.
- Each FbF profile was downloaded as a PDF at the end of each semester.

- Semi-structured interviews using Facebook messages and Facebook chat to discuss Facebook usage.
- Face-to-face, semi-structured interviews and focus groups to discuss Facebook usage.

Practicalities

- I met the group of six participants as a focus group in November 2010, to introduce the study and discuss the schedule for the research, the ethical implications of taking part, and the consent forms.
- The consent forms were left with the participants and they posted these back to me.
- The students added me as a friend on Facebook to accept the invitation to take part in the study.
- We met three times over the year for face-to-face interviews in November, January and June.
- Field notes were taken once a week of the Facebook profiles. These included screenshots and handwritten notes.

Ethical decisions

As a researcher of Facebook, decisions have to be made regarding the use of your own Facebook profile and whether or not to set up a different 'researcher' profile. In this study my own profile

Table 24.1 An overview of the data collected

Quantitative	Qualitative
720 digital questionnaire responses.	Downloads of FbF profiles saved as a PDF.
6 FbF profile data	Field notes from Facebook participant observations.
– Number of status updates. – Number of photos. – Number of friends.	Field notes from university campus observations: halls of residence, library, student union, university quad (outside area).
	Focus group and interviews (x2) (Nov).
	Interviews 6 no. (January).
	Interviews 5 no. (June).
	Flat focus group (May).
	Facebook Profile of participants: wall, info, any messages sent, any chat.
	Facebook groups: wall.

was used as I wanted a level of equity between myself and my FbFs. Ethnographic practice is about being embedded in the practices of the cultural group being studied, not merely observing from afar, in order for me to experience the culture alongside my FbF. Using my full profile influenced my understanding of my participants' Facebook practices. Ethically I was mindful of the types of data my participants had access to through my Facebook profile. I made changes to the privacy settings of my profile, particularly with reference to the photographs that my participants can see. For example, I changed the privacy settings so that my participants cannot see photos of my friends' children. Decisions relating to the use or not of a researcher's own profile would be influenced by the presentation of self within the digital environment by the researcher, and should be linked to the research question and the reason for the researcher to use Facebook as a research site. My researcher's view is different to that of my daily use. When undertaking the key data collection time period, I was using Facebook on an hourly basis. Now I check Facebook approximately three times a day.

Analysis and data presentation

The analytical approach was one of interpretation and iteration. Content analysis was used based on themes from my literature review. These were notions of temporality, spatiality and social support. Time was the main analytical framework, whereby I examined the elements of time within the Facebook posts and the interview data.

- Field notes were open coded.
- Facebook profile PDFs were printed and open-coded using highlighter pens.
- Interviews were transcribed and open-coded.

The open-coded datasets were iteratively explored using the constant comparison method, whereby data were compared until key repeating themes were identified. These were then cross-analysed between the Facebook and face-to-face data.

These analyses were then crafted into six ethnographic stories, which represented my FbFs and six different key moments in time within the academic year. The ethnographic stories of my Facebook friends were written using direct quotes from the interview data and the Facebook postings. Some of the key themes, which are presented as ethnographic stories, were 'meeting in the digital before starting university' and 'the use of a Facebook group for academic support'. These stories are the deep data and thick description of ethnographic work to describe the actualities of six students' Facebook use.

Acknowledging and recording the temporal nature of social media

Facebook today is a different site from what it was in 2010 when the data collection for this study was complete: the architecture is different, the interface is different, and the ways in which users interact have changed. The language used to describe use has also changed. We no longer throw sheep at each other and rarely get a 'poke' (which were social interactions in 2010). We are more likely to be tagged in a status update and check-in to a place we are visiting. The interface in 2010 was predominantly text-based, with photos a secondary element accessed from the photos tab. In 2016 photos are larger and feature on multiple layers of the profile page. With this in mind it is pertinent to draw attention to the need for researchers of Facebook (and indeed all social media) to make explicitly clear which version of Facebook they are talking about, and to acknowledge the influences current Facebook architecture and our current Facebook practices have on our frames of analysis.

A note on copyright

When working with screenshots of social media it is important to address the issue of copyright. The AoIR (Markham and Buchanan, 2012) ask researchers to consider whether research materials are subject to copyright:

Many countries have strong restrictions on using screenshots or images taken from the web without permission and certain sites have restrictions in their terms of service. (Markham and Buchanan, 2012)

Widrick (2011) suggests that 'screenshots with personally identifiable information (including photos, names, etc. of actual users) require written consent from the individual(s) before they can be published'. This is in line with the usual institutional ethics regulations, but as discussed previously it can be difficult to ensure full anonymity due to the searchable nature of web data. Facebook has 'asset and logo' guidelines with regard to using Facebook assets for publication purposes, but the information is aimed at business use. Within the outputs of this study, the use of screenshots has been limited to my own Facebook profile. The Facebook assets and logo guidelines give a written definition of each of the sections of a Facebook profile – timeline, messages, news feed – and suggest that 'the Facebook brand includes the words, phrases, symbols and designs that are associated with Facebook and the services Facebook provides' (Facebook, 2016). They also require that the term 'Facebook' is not used as a verb. These regulations (and those of other social media) warrant scrutiny within the research design stage of any project.

Developments in data capture: NCapture

The study presented here was undertaken in 2010 and since then there have been software tool developments that have changed the way data can be downloaded from websites. NCapture is a web browser plugin produced by the manufacturers of NVivo (QSR). It allows you to capture web data, such as Facebook wall posts and tweets from Twitter, and then to import these into NVivo as a data set for sorting, coding and analysis. Downloading carried out using NCapture is in two formats – as a PDF file or as a spreadsheet – and both can be analysed with NVivo. There are challenges when using third-party software such as

NCapture which need to be addressed. It is worth noting that inconsistencies between the PDF download and the NVivo dataset (.nvcx) downloads have been found and this can make analysis somewhat problematic. Social media companies may limit access to their web service (API) and not all data may be downloaded for access in NVivo. The PDF format is most reliable to ensure all data and images are downloaded, but this may require extended researcher input before the PDF is downloaded, such as clicking on all the 'comment' links on a Facebook wall to ensure they are all visible. It is also worth checking compatibility with the software you are currently using. Current advice from QSR is that you can only import social media data from Twitter and Facebook as dataset sources if you are using NVivo for Mac, NVivo 11 Pro for Windows, or NVivo 11 Plus for Windows (QSR, 2016).

Conclusion

Social media are central to many learners' lives and this chapter has aimed to give insight into using it for deep data collection within a connective ethnographic study. Using social media sites and apps as data collection tools means understanding the social nature of media use within the interactions between users and the social media space. The nascent nature of social media and digital methods is passing and they are becoming more mainstream (Snee et al., 2015) but with that researchers should be aware and wary of the fast-paced development of social media platforms by the companies who own them. Social media use is complex, complicated, and layered over our non-mediated interactions.

Questions for further investigation

1. Why is it important to decide the boundary of your study? And why might this be problematic when using social media sites for data collection?

2. What are the opportunities and tensions when using publicly available social media posts versus private posts, and what are the research ethics of analysing and representing these?

Suggested further reading

Markham, A. and Buchanan, E. (2012) *Ethical Decision-Making and Internet research 2.0.* [online]. Available from: www.aoir.org/reports/ethics2.pdf

Snee, H., Hine, C., Morey, Y., Roberts, S. and Watson, H. (eds) (2015) *Digital Methods for Social Science: An Interdisciplinary Guide to Research Innovation.* London: Palgrave Macmillan.

Vis, F. and Thelwall, M. (2013) *Researching Social Media.* London: Sage.

References

Baker, S. (2013) 'Conceptualising the use of Facebook in ethnographic research: as tool, as data and as context', *Ethnography and Education*, 8(2):131–45.

Berriman, L. and Thomson, R. (2015) 'Spectacles of intimacy? Mapping the moral landscape of teenage social media', *Journal of Youth Studies*, 18(5): 583–97.

boyd, d. (2014) *It's Complicated: The Social Lives of Networked Teens.* New Haven, CT: Yale University Press.

boyd, d. and Crawford, K. (2012) 'Critical questions for big data: provocations for a cultural, technological, and scholarly phenomenon', *Information, Communication & Society*, 15(5): 662–79.

boyd, d. and Ellison, N. (2007) 'Social network sites: definition, history, and scholarship', *Journal of Computer-Mediated Communication*, 13: 210–30.

Brooker, P., Barnett, J., Cribbin, T. and Sharma, S. (2015) 'Have we even solved the first 'Big Data Challenge?': Practical issues concerning data collection and visual representation for social media analytics', *Digital Methods for Social Science: An Interdisciplinary Guide to Research Innovation*, p. 34.

Dawson, P. (2014) 'Our anonymous online research participants are not always anonymous: is this a problem?', *British Journal of Educational Technology*, 45(3): 428–37.

Donath, J.S. (1999) 'Identity and deception in the virtual community', *Communities in cyberspace, 1996*, 29–59.

Ellison, N.B. and boyd, D. (2013) 'Sociality through social network sites', *The Oxford Handbook of Internet Studies*, pp. 151–72.

Ess, C. (2015) 'New selves, new research ethics?', *Internet Research Ethics*. Oslo: Cappelen Damm Akademisk.

Facebook (2016) Facebook Stats [online]. Available at: http://newsroom.fb.com/company-info/

Geertz, C. (1973) *The Interpretation of Cultures: Selected Essays*. New York: Basic.

Hargittai, E., Schultz, J. and Palfrey, J. (2011) 'Why parents help their children lie to Facebook about age: unintended consequences of the "Children's Online Privacy Protection Act"', *First Monday*, 16(11).

Hine, C. (2007) 'Connective ethnography for the exploration of e-Science', *Journal of Computer-Mediated Communication*, 12(2): 618–34.

Hodkinson, P. (2015) 'Bedrooms and beyond: youth, identity and privacy on social network sites', *New Media & Society*, DOI: 10.1177/1461444815605454.

Markham, A. and Buchanan, E., with the AoIR Ethics Working Committee (2012) *Ethical Decision-making and Internet Research: Version 2.0*. Association of Internet Researchers. Available from: https://aoir.org/reports/ethics2.pdf (accessed 1 December 2016).

Massey, D. (2005) *For Space*. Thousand Oaks, CA: Sage.

Miller, D. (2011) *Tales from Facebook*. Cambridge: Polity.

Miller, D., Costa, E., Haynes, N., McDonald, T., Nicolescu, R., Sinanan, J., Spyer, J., Venkatraman, S. and Wang, X. (2016) 'How the World Changed Social Media.

Oxford Dictionaries (2013) *The Oxford Dictionaries Word of the Year 2013* [online] Available from: http://blog.oxforddictionaries.com/press-releases/oxford-dictionaries-word-of-the-year-2013/

Pybus, J., Coté, M. and Blanke, T. (2015) 'Hacking the social life of Big Data', *Big Data & Society*, 2(2). DOI: 10.1177/2053951715616649.

QSR (2016) *What is NCapture?* [online] Available from: www.qsrinternational.com/support/faqs/what-is-ncapture

Rogers, R. (2015) 'Digital Methods for Web Research', in J. Tainter, T. Taylor, R. Brain and J. Lobo (eds), *Emerging Trends in the Social and Behavioral*

Sciences: An Interdisciplinary, Searchable, and Linkable Resource. Hoboken, NJ: Wiley.

Selwyn, N. (2009) 'Faceworking: exploring students' education-related use of Facebook', *Learning, Media and Technology*, 34(2): 157–74.

Selwyn, N. and Grant, L. (2009) 'Researching the realities of social software use – an introduction', *Learning, Media and Technology*, 34(2): 1–9.

Selwyn, N. and Stirling, E. (2015) 'Social media and education… now the dust has settled', *Learning, Media and Technology*, pp. 1–5.

Snee, H., Hine, C., Morey, Y., Roberts, S. and Watson, H. (eds) (2015) *Digital Methods for Social Science: An Interdisciplinary Guide to Research Innovation.* London: Palgrave Macmillan.

Stirling, E. (2014) 'Why waste your time on Facebook? A temporal analysis of first-year undergraduate students and transition in UK Higher Education'. Doctoral dissertation, University of Sheffield.

Stirling, E. (2015a) '"I'm Always on Facebook!": Exploring Facebook as a Mainstream Research Tool and Ethnographic Site', *Digital Methods for Social*

Science: An Interdisciplinary Guide to Research Innovation, p. 51.

Stirling, E. (2015b) 'Technology, time and transition in higher education – two different realities of everyday Facebook use in the first year of university in the UK', *Learning, Media and Technology*, 1–19.

Thelwall, M. and Buckley, K. (2013) 'Topic-based sentiment analysis for the social web: the role of mood and issue-related words', *Journal of the American Society for Information Science and Technology*, 64(8): 1608–17.

Thelwall, M., Goriunova, O., Vis, F., Faulkner, S., Burns, A., Aulich, J., Mas-Bleda, A., Stuart, E. and D'Orazio, F. (2015) 'Chatting through pictures? A classification of images tweeted in one week in the UK and USA', *Journal of the Association for Information Science and Technology.*

Widrick, K. (2011) *Facebook Logos, Screenshots and More Rules You're Breaking.* [Online] Available from: http://katywidrick.com/2011/08/09/facebook-logos-screenshots-and-more-rules-youre-breaking/ (accessed 28 September 2016).

Documentary methods

25

Gary McCulloch

Introduction

This chapter is designed to provide an introduction to documentary methods, including the use of online archival resources, in education (see also McCulloch, 2004, 2011 and 2016 for more detailed treatments of historical and documentary research). A document may be defined briefly as a record of an event or process. Such records may be produced by individuals or groups and take many different forms.

In beginning to make use of documentary methods of research, it is important to note that there is first of all a range of published and readily accessible sources that may be used for this purpose. These include published policy reports, records of parliamentary debates, contemporary books and treatises, textbooks, autobiographies, newspapers, periodicals, novels, short stories, children's books, comics, drama, poetry, and art.

Other kinds of evidence may be more difficult to reach, especially unpublished material of different kinds, and it may be necessary to gain access to these for a full and detailed treatment of a topic. Archival documentary evidence is well established as a key source of historical data, and the chapter will investigate the uses and limitations of the archive, explaining the impact of recent technological advances in helping archival research. Archives can support the study of educational policy and administration, national and local organisations, and specific educational institutions such as schools and universities. Personal papers and records are also invaluable in biographical studies or life histories. Such unpublished evidence can have considerable advantages over published sources in that they enable the researcher to look behind the scenes to determine motivations and trace the development of arguments and conflicts that may not always become fully public in nature.

Broad distinctions may be drawn between types of documents and it is important for the researcher to observe these, although they are not always rigid typologies. One distinction that can be made, for example, is between the documents created by private individuals and family groups in their everyday lives, and the records produced by local, national and international authorities and small or large organisations (Hodder, 1998). The former class of personal or private documents might include diaries, letters, photographs, blogs, autobiographies and suicide notes (Plummer, 2001). The latter group of public and official records would include not only committee minutes, reports and memoranda, but also formal items such as birth, marriage and death certificates, driving licences and bank statements (Scott, 1990). Media documents, either printed like newspapers and magazines or visual such as television, operate at the interface of the private and public, and record aspects of both types of domain.

There are preliminary issues around ascertaining the authenticity of the document (i.e. verifying the author, place and date of its production). In some cases the document may have been forged or the authorship is in doubt. The researcher also seeks to take into account the reliability of the document, for example the credibility of the account of an event in terms of the bias of the author, the access to the event, and the interpretation of the observer. The differential survival rate of documents creates a further issue of reliability, and raises questions about how representative, typical and generalisable the surviving documents may be (Scott, 1990: 7).

A distinction may also be drawn between documents that are based on written text and other forms produced through other means. Until very recently, most written documents were produced on paper or similar materials, either by hand or mechanically. The past two decades have witnessed the exponential growth of electronic documents such as electronic mail and data communicated and stored through the Internet. This constitutes a contemporary revolution in the nature of documents, albeit that electronic documents may well retain and incorporate elements of the print culture developed over the past five centuries (McCulloch, 2004: 2). Such written, printed and electronic texts might be contrasted with visual documents such as photographs, cartoons, paintings and films (Prosser, 1998; Grosvenor, 2007), although it should be noted that texts in contemporary society have become increasingly multi-semiotic in combining and juxtaposing language and visual forms (Fairclough, 1995). They also differ from oral sources such as sound recordings of speeches. One may also distinguish textual records from material artefacts like fossils, slates, desks and buildings.

A further distinction is between documents produced independent of the researcher for a range of possible purposes outside the researcher's control, and those produced by researchers themselves as data for their research. Transcripts of interviews or completed questionnaires are examples of documents prepared by researchers for the purposes of their research (Silverman, 2001: 119). Electronic technology facilitates the rapid interchange of solicited documents in a wide variety of formats. Documentary methods generally make use of documents produced previously and by others, rather than in the process of the research or by the researcher.

There is also an established difference between primary documents and secondary documents, although this difference is more complex than it may at first appear. Primary documents are produced as a direct record of an event or process by a witness or subject involved in it. Secondary documents are formed through an analysis of primary documents to provide an account of the event or process in question, often in relation to others. However, many documents do not fit easily into this basic dichotomy. For example, autobiographies are primary documents by virtue of the author being a witness or participant in the relevant events, but are often produced years or even decades later and so may be affected by memory or selective recall. They might also be regarded as secondary documents to the extent that they seek to analyse the changing times through which the autobiographer has lived (see for instance Hobsbawm, 2002).

Moreover, some documents are edited and collected versions of diaries, letters and autobiographies. These might be described as hybrid documents. They are more widely accessible than the original primary document but have gone through an editing process that may alter some of their characteristics, whether subtly or substantially. In producing a published work of this kind, editors may tend to emphasise particular types of material to make it more interesting or more or less flattering to the authors of the document, or else to reflect specific interests (Fothergill, 1974). In such cases, one might say that some features of the primary document have been compromised by the process of being edited and presented in this way.

Virtual documents (i.e. primary documents stored electronically for access through the Internet) are available through 'the click of a mouse' (*Guardian*, 2007). These are often the most valuable for researchers, although government and other organisational websites which store documents in this way may seek to cast the government or organisation in a favourable light. On the other hand such digital documents lose the immediacy of the original paper document that they represent (McCulloch, 2004: 34–42).

Personal documents

Diaries, letters and autobiographies are generally regarded as personal documents, although they can often reveal a great deal about public issues and debates. In some cases, they may provide commentary on contemporary social developments and they often record meetings or other events in which the author has been involved. Diaries are generally produced soon after the event, although this varies, and may give detailed and intimate evidence of individuals and daily life for women no less than for men (Blodgett, 1988). In many cases, as with the published diaries of the composer Benjamin Britten, they document the tensions of adolescence and early adulthood (Britten, 2009). Political diaries, such as those of the British politician Tony Benn, can be highly revealing about policy changes, as in the case of the self-styled 'Great Debate' on education in Britain in 1976 (Benn, 1990). They also reveal much, often unintentionally, about the diarists themselves (Pimlott, 2002). School log books have an official function in that they are generally required to include specific information about the pupils, teachers and management of the school, but in some cases they may reveal the everyday life and interactions of the head teacher concerned (see, for example, McCulloch, 1989: Chapter 8).

Letter writing as a means of communication has generated a further type of documentary source, one that has been rivalled in recent times by devices such as the telephone and transformed through electronic media. They are interactive in character, explicitly forming part of a dialogue, and may again be both personal and formal in their style and substance (Earle, 1999; Dobson, 2009). Many letters relating to education, such as those from parents to a school or to a newspaper or to a Minister of Education, reflect the interaction between the personal or family domain and the concerns of an established institution (see, for instance, Heward, 1988). By contrast, autobiographies and memoirs are essentially introspective and provide an inside account of lives and relationships (see, for example, Johnson, 2013; Morgan, 2015). They often give particular emphasis to the early life and schooling. For example, David Vincent's major study of working-class autobiographies in nineteenth-century England, based on 142 accounts of this kind, demonstrates the nature of their involvement in a social network of family, friends, colleagues and acquaintances (Vincent, 1981).

Fictional works might also be classed as personal documents. Although not intended to convey the literal truth about particular events, these may represent deeper realities about social experiences. In relation to education, they can provide insights into everyday life from the imagined viewpoints of pupils and teachers, notwithstanding the dramatisation and stereotyped forms that it generally depends upon for plots and characterisation. Novels and plays have been especially useful for their depiction of teachers and teaching. James Hilton's *Goodbye, Mr Chips,* for example, is a classic account of the life story of a male veteran teacher in an elite English boarding school (Hilton, 1934), while the plays of Alan Bennett such as *Forty Years On* (1969) and *The History Boys* (2004) have evoked resilient cultural images (McCulloch, 2009). Susan Ellsmore has also explored representations of the teaching profession in films, including the film of *Goodbye, Mr Chips* produced in 1939 (Ellsmore, 2005).

The public record

The printed press embodies a further important source of primary documentary evidence. This provides a day-to-day public record very soon after the event being studied (Vella, 2009: 194), albeit one that caters for particular kinds of public taste and interest, and is by no means comprehensive in its coverage. Peter Cunningham has made interesting use of newspapers as a documentary source by examining the development of the image of the teacher in the British press from 1950 to 1990 (Cunningham, 1992). Cunningham's work compares newspaper coverage of teachers in 1950, 1970 and 1990, using *The Times* in its unofficial capacity as a newspaper of record as well as major mass-circulation newspapers of the political left and right. This has been taken further in other work that examines political cartoons involving teachers in the British press since the 1970s (Warburton and Saunders, 1996). Other particular features of newspapers also offer interesting and useful material for researchers, including leading articles, letters columns and advertisements.

School magazines have a limited circulation in and around their own institution but constitute a significant record on behalf of the institution itself, with detailed information on everyday life and interests as well as transmitting the received values of the school. J.A. Mangan's research on English public schools in the late nineteenth century demonstrated the role of school magazines as the official record of school life, reflecting in many cases an emphasis on games and sports as opposed to examinations (Mangan, 1986). Nevertheless, unofficial magazines may also provide important clues to debates and differences within the school (see, for example, McCulloch, 2007: Chapter 6).

Over the past five hundred years, books in their modern printed format have been repositories of knowledge and scholarship, besides also being a key means of challenging established orthodoxies. Tracts and treatises are important sources of documentary evidence that often embody the principal themes of debate in politics and society, although they do not always fully convey wider attitudes in a particular context, and their representative nature and influence are often exaggerated. A specific type of book that is often useful for researchers in education is the textbook, produced for schools and other educational institutions since the 1830s when the term itself appeared (Stray, 1994: 2). They are generally used to support teachers, lecturers, pupils and students to follow a syllabus, and are significant partly for the way in which they present information but also for how they project approved values and ideologies. Stuart Foster, for example, has investigated the treatment of ethnic groups in history textbooks in the United States in terms of a struggle for American identity, arguing that such works

have represented the views and interests of a white, male, Protestant middle or upper class, and have tended to support the capitalist system, traditional lifestyles and Western traditions (Foster, 1999).

Published reports are a further significant source of research evidence in this area of study. Governments as well as organisations and pressure groups produce reports in order to examine particular defined problems and propose solutions. The information that they provide is often very helpful, although it cannot be assumed that this is always accurate, and it should be checked against other sources. Policy reports are also important for revealing the kinds of assumptions that underlie policy reforms. They represent an outlook or ideology (Scott, 2000: 27) and also embody the contradictions and tensions that are inherent in state policy (Codd, 1988). Some reports are voluminous, taking up several volumes including appendices of oral and written evidence provided by witnesses, whereas in recent decades reports have tended to become shorter in length, more limited in focus and more reader-friendly in format to promote their public appeal. Again, care needs to be taken to resist assuming that such reports reflect educational practices in a straightforward manner.

The proceedings of parliamentary debates and committees provide another kind of official publication. In Britain, these are known as Hansard, after Thomas Hansard, who began publishing the debates of the House of Commons and House of Lords in 1812, and are now available online (www. parliament.the-stationery-office.co.uk; see also www.parliament.uk). In the USA, the Congressional Record provides a similar service, also available on the Internet (www.gpoaccess.gov/crecord/index. html). This was first published in 1873 and provides up-to-date and complete proceedings of debates in the House of Representatives and the Senate. Many datasets produced by governments, organisations and research project teams are also readily accessible, and these lend themselves to secondary analysis. Hakim has defined this in terms of the further analysis of existing datasets which develops the original interpretations and findings of the enquiry in a different way (Hakim, 1982). These include population census reports and datasets specially related to education, such as that of the National Child Development Study in Britain (https://discover.ukdataservice.ac.uk/series/?sn=2000032).

Much research employs one or two of these kinds of document as the principal source of data, but different combinations of personal and public documents may be applied depending on the problem being studied. For example, an education policy report may be examined through the study of the report itself, of the files of the committee that produced it, and of newspapers relating to its reception after publication. The changes in the curriculum at a university might be appraised through institutional records, lecture notes and student diaries where these exist (see, for example, Slee, 1986). The different perspectives of parents, children and teachers may also be revealed through a combination of such methods, as in the case of the Simon family and their experiences with Gresham's School in the 1930s (McCulloch and Woodin, 2010). Moreover, documentary research may frequently be allied to good effect with other research methods in education (see, for example, Saran, 1985, on combining archive and interview research). Interviews with teachers about their curriculum and pedagogic practices may be compared with documentary evidence of changing policy in these areas over the past thirty years, as in the case of research by McCulloch et al. (2000).

Archival documents

As we have seen, many documentary records are available quite readily through research libraries or the Internet. In other cases, they are stored in an organised format, usually in numbered files for identification, in archives and record offices. Archives are repositories of accumulated knowledge, in many ways the institutional memory of modern societies, and these also exist in a number of forms.

National archives preserve the official records of government departments, and local record offices those of the particular location where appropriate, and in many countries around the world these are preserved carefully and methodically to store the collective memory. In some cases they date from the nineteenth century or even earlier, and they often reflect the specific national and social characteristics (Joyce, 1999). The French Archives Nationales, set up in 1790, developed with a strong focus on the centralised state (Sheppard, 1980). Much documentary evidence has been lost for a number of reasons, whether due to being discarded by the original owners, failing to survive changes of location, or for lack of space or resources. Thus the researcher is left with only the documents, whether recent or from earlier periods of time, that remain to be examined today. There are many silences in the documents that do survive (Andrew, 1985: 156). The experience of working in an archive can also be a challenge. Beyond the costs and the time that may be involved in reaching an archive, it is often difficult to anticipate the amount and quality of documentary material that is available on a particular topic (Steedman, 2001: 29).

At the same time, the establishment and spread of online archives over the past ten years have transformed the nature of archival research. In many cases the archive catalogue or inventory of holdings is available in searchable form on the Internet so that the researcher is able to check in advance before travelling to the archive. Increasingly also the documents themselves may be researched digitally. For example, in Britain the results of the Census up to and including 1911 (www.pro.online.com/census/1911/php; see also www.uk.censusonline.gov.uk) and more than 150 years of the newspaper *The Guardian* (www.guardian.com/gnm-archive; see also *Guardian*, 2007) have been made available online. Cabinet minutes and discussions are also accessible by this means). For example, Cabinet discussion of the Conservative government on education policy in the early 1970s (Cabinet file CAB.128/50/55; see filestore.nationalarchives.gov.uk/pdfs/small/cab-128-50-cm-72-54-55.pdf) may be consulted in this way. However, there are some restrictions in terms of coverage and a subscription or other cost may often be applied.

Conclusion

Documents are a significant and often underused resource for research in education. An enormous range of primary documents is available for researchers to examine and evaluate. Diaries, letters, autobiographies and fictional writings offer many insights into both the personal and the public domains, while documents based on the media, books, reports and proceedings of debates and committees also provide extensive source material. Often, it is helpful to combine different kinds of documents to develop a fuller and more comprehensive account of specific themes. Archival documents can support research on many topics, and the scope for such research has been greatly enhanced by the online revolution of the early twenty-first century.

Questions for further investigation

1. Select one key individual or organisation and search for different types of primary documentary source that help to highlight their contributions to education. How would you seek to combine these sources in researching this topic?
2. How would you make use of the Internet to support an archive-based research study? Explain with detailed reference to one study of your choice.

Suggested further reading

McCulloch (2004) provides a detailed discussion of documentary research in relation to education, history and the social sciences, developed and updated in McCulloch (2016); Scott (1990) is dated in some respects but still useful. Analysis of a wide range of primary sources in their historical context is given in Dobson and Ziemann (2009), while Steedman (2001) reflects on the experience of archival research.

References

Andrew, A. (1985) 'In Pursuit of the Past: Some problems in the collection, analysis and use of historical documentary evidence', in R.G. Burgess (ed.), *Strategies of Educational Research*. London: Falmer, pp. 153–78.

Benn, T. (1990) *Against the Tide: Diaries 1973–76*, edited by R. Winstone. London: Arrow.

Bennett, A. (1969) *Forty Years On*. London: Faber & Faber.

Bennett, A. (2004) *The History Boys*. London: Faber & Faber.

Blodgett, H. (1988) *Centuries of Female Days: Englishwomen's Private Diaries*. Brunswick, NJ: Rutgers University Press.

Britten, B. (2009) *Journeying Boy: The Diaries of the Young Benjamin Britten, 1928–1938*, edited by J. Evans. London: Faber.

Burgess, R. (ed.) (1985) *Strategies of Educational Research: Qualitative Methods*. London: Falmer.

Codd, J. (1988) 'The construction and deconstruction of educational policy documents', *Journal of Education Policy*, 3(3): 235–47.

Cunningham, P. (1992) 'Teachers' professional image and the Press, 1950–1990', *History of Education*, 21(1): 37–56.

Dobson, M. (2009) 'Letters', in M. Dobson and B. Ziemann (eds), *Reading Primary Sources: The Interpretation of Texts from Nineteenth and Twentieth-Century History*. Abingdon: Routledge, pp. 57–73.

Dobson, M. and Ziemann, B. (eds) (2009) *Reading Primary Sources: The Interpretation of Texts from Nineteenth- and Twentieth-Century History*. Abingdon: Routledge.

Earle, R. (ed.) (1999) *Epistolary Selves: Letters and Letter-Writers, 1600–1945*. Aldershot: Ashgate.

Ellsmore, S. (2005) *Carry On, Teachers! Representations of the Teaching Profession in Screen Culture*. Stoke-on-Trent: Trentham.

Fairclough, N. (1995) *Critical Discourse Analysis: The Critical Study of Language*. London: Longman.

Foster, S. (1999) 'The struggle for American identity: treatment of ethnic groups in United States history textbooks', *History of Education*, 28(3): 251–78.

Fothergill, R. (1974) *Private Chronicles: A Study of English Diaries*. London: Oxford University Press.

Gosden, P. (1981) 'Twentieth-century archives of education as sources for the study of education policy and administration', *Archives*, 15: 86–95.

Grosvenor, I. (2007) 'From the "eye of history" to a "second gaze": the visual archive and the marginalized in the history of education', *History of Education,* 36(4–5): 607–22.

Guardian (2007) 'The Archive', 3 November.

Hakim, C. (1982) *Secondary Analysis in Social Research: A Guide to Data Sources and Methods with Examples.* London: George Allen & Unwin.

Heward, C. (1988) *Making a Man of Him: Parents and their Sons' Education at an English Public School, 1929–50.* London: Routledge.

Hilton, J. (1934) *Goodbye, Mr Chips.* London: Hodder & Stoughton.

Hobsbawm, E. (2002) *Interesting Times: A Twentieth-Century Life.* London: Allen Lane.

Hodder, I. (1998) 'The Interpretation of Documents and Material Culture', in N.K. Denzin and Y.S. Lincoln (eds), *Collecting and Interpreting Qualitative Materials.* Thousand Oaks, CA: Sage, pp. 110–29.

Johnson, A. (2013) *This Boy: A Memoir of a Childhood.* London: Bantam.

Joyce, P. (1999) 'The politics of the liberal archive', *History of the Human Sciences,* 12(2): 35–49.

McCulloch, G. (1986) '"Secondary education without selection"? School zoning policy in Auckland since 1945', *New Zealand Journal of Educational Studies,* 21(2): 98–112.

McCulloch, G. (1989) *The Secondary Technical School: A Usable Past?* London: Falmer.

McCulloch, G. (2004) *Documentary Research in Education, History and the Social Sciences.* London: Routledge.

McCulloch, G. (ed.) (2005) *The RoutledgeFalmer Reader in the History of Education.* London: RoutledgeFalmer.

McCulloch, G. (2007) *Cyril Norwood and the Ideal of Secondary Education.* New York: Palgrave Macmillan.

McCulloch, G. (2009) 'The moral universe of Mr Chips: veteran teachers in British literature and drama', *Teachers and Teaching,* 15(4): 409–20.

McCulloch, G. (2011) 'Historical and Documentary Methods', in L. Cohen, L. Manion and K. Morrison (eds), *Research Methods in Education,* 7th edn. London: Routledge.

McCulloch, G. (2016) 'Historical Research', in D. Wyse, L.E. Suter, E. Smith and N. Selwyn (eds), *The BERA/SAGE Handbook of Educational Research.* London: Sage.

McCulloch, G. and Woodin, T. (2010) 'Learning and liberal education: the case of the Simon family, 1912–1939', *Oxford Review of Education,* 36(2): 187–201.

McCulloch, G., Helsby, G. and Knight, P. (2000) *The Politics of Professionalism: Teachers and the Curriculum.* London: Continuum.

Mangan, J.A. (1986) *Athleticism in the Victorian and Edwardian Public School: The Emergence and Consolidation of an Educational Ideology.* London: Falmer.

Morgan, K. (2015) *My Histories.* Cardiff: University of Wales Press.

Pimlott, B. (2002) 'Dear diary …', *Guardian G2,* 18 October, pp. 2–3.

Plummer, K. (2001) *Documents of Life 2: An Invitation to a Critical Humanism.* London: Sage.

Prosser, J. (ed.) (1998) *Image-Based Research: A Sourcebook for Qualitative Researchers.* London: Falmer.

Saran, R. (1985) 'The Use of Archives and Interviews in Research on Education Policy', in R. Burgess (ed.), *Strategies of Educational Research: Qualitative Methods.* London: Falmer, pp. 207–41.

Scott, D. (2000) *Reading Educational Research and Policy.* London: RoutledgeFalmer.

Scott, J. (1990) *A Matter of Record: Documentary Sources in Social Research.* Cambridge: Polity.

Sheppard, J. (1980) 'Vive la différence? An outsider's view of French archives', *Archives,* 14: 151–62.

Silverman, D. (2001) *Interpreting Qualitative Data: Methods for Analysing Talk, Text and Interaction,* 2nd edn. London: Sage.

Slee, P. (1986) *Learning and a Liberal Education: The Study of Modern History in the Universities of Oxford, Cambridge and Manchester, 1800–1914.* Manchester: Manchester University Press.

Steedman, C. (2001) *Dust.* Manchester: Manchester University Press.

Stray, C. (1994) 'Paradigms regained: towards a historical sociology of the textbook', *Journal of Curriculum Studies,* 26(1): 1–29.

Travis, A. (2003) 'Online archive brings Britain's migration story to life', *Guardian,* 30 July, p. 7.

Vella, S. (2009) 'Newspapers', in M. Dobson and B. Ziemann (eds), *Reading Primary Sources: The Interpretation of Texts from Nineteenth- and Twentieth-Century History.* Abingdon: Routledge, pp. 192–208.

Vincent, D. (1981) *Bread, Knowledge and Freedom: A Study of Nineteenth-Century Working Class Autobiography*. London: Methuen.

Warburton, T. and Saunders, M. (1996) 'Representing teachers' professional culture through cartoons', *British Journal of Educational Studies*, 44(3): 307–25.

Online sources

British Cabinet (1972) Minutes of meeting, 30 November. Available at: filestore.nationalarchives. gov.uk/pdfs/small/cab-128-50-cm-72-54-55.pdf

British Census (2011) Available at: www.ons.gov. uk/2011census (accessed 1 July 2016).

British official records (2011) Available at: www. nationalarchives.gov.uk (accessed 1 July 2016).

British Parliamentary committee proceedings, evidence and reports. Available at: www.parliament.uk (accessed 1 July 2016).

British Parliamentary debates. Available at: www. parliament.uk/business/publications/hansard/ commons/ (accessed 1 July 2016).

Guardian Archive. Available at: www.theguardian. com/gnm-archive (accessed 1 July 2016).

National Child Development Study, Britain. Available at: http://discover.dataservice.ac.uk/series/?sn=z 000032 (accessed 1 July 2016)

US Congressional Record. Available at: www.congress. gov/congressional-record (accessed 1 July 2016).

Questionnaires

Peter Tymms

26

Introduction

Questionnaires are tools for collecting information and this chapter outlines the reasons for using them, the formats that are employed, administration methods, response rates, lengths of questionnaires, scale formation, and the number of items needed to create measures. Technological advances, such as those mentioned in Chapter 23, have resulted in computer delivery gradually overtaking paper-based questionnaires, and statistical techniques are advancing which can inform the development of instruments and the analysis of data. Other key issues such as research design are briefly mentioned and readers are referred to other chapters.

Purposes

The reasons for using questionnaires can be divided into four and each is outlined below.

Exploratory work

When starting an investigation the researcher may be unsure about the best way to proceed. At this stage he or she would start to read the relevant literature and talk to colleagues and perhaps some individuals from the population that is the focus of the proposed work (see Chapter 4). Then, depending on what exactly is envisaged, it might make

sense to collect some questionnaire data. At this exploratory stage collecting information from a small number of people, either using paper questionnaires or by interviews, could be helpful. This would be followed up by more serious work, but in the first instance a little information might help to start to define a problem.

Describing a population

Sometimes it is important to establish a general pattern across a population (see Chapter 15). In that case one could administer a questionnaire to a representative sample of that population – a survey (Fowler, 2013). If one wanted a breakdown of the UK population by ethnic origins, or a breakdown by age, then an exercise which collected data from a sample of the population is appropriate. Some studies try to collect data on the whole population: the UK Census does this every ten years and is based on a questionnaire to each household (Census, 2011). Other well-known examples of questionnaires which involve samples include polling for election purposes by various organisations such as Ipsos MORI (2010).

As an aside it is interesting to recall one of the most notorious mistakes made in sampling which resulted from an attempt to establish who was going to win the US election in 1936. The *Literary Digest* had correctly predicted the outcomes of the previous five elections and having polled 10 million voters confidently announced that Landon would win. In fact Roosevelt won – a sobering result for all those who would use questionnaires (Freedman et al., 2007). A correct prediction was made by George Gallup, who carefully sampled 50,000 people.

Outcomes or controls in studies

Questionnaires can also be used as part of an intervention study or a quasi-experiment which need outcome measures (see Chapter 18 on 'interventions' in this book) and, perhaps, control (baseline) measures. In such cases, the measures may be of a construct such as motivation or mental health or self-esteem. It is probable that the questionnaire would involve a series of items which are combined together to form a scale (see Chapter 28). Additionally some contextual information is usually collected.

At this point it is worth noting that tests can be very similar to questionnaires, differing mainly in style. In a test one would generally assess somebody's knowledge or understanding, whereas the word 'questionnaire' is generally reserved for something less pressured and often more diverse. Both can generate outcome measures formed from items.

Feedback

It is common for in-service and other courses to ask attendees to complete a questionnaire. These are very often intended for formative purposes, so that better experiences may be experienced next time round, although the results can also be used summatively. The formats vary dramatically, from some in which attendees are asked to rate the presenters on a scale from 1 to 5, to those that simply ask open-ended questions such as 'what was good for you?' or 'what could have been better?' Such exercises can be extended to whole conferences, where samples are sometimes asked to complete ratings on individuals or break-out sessions. In higher education courses questionnaires are often used as part of quality assurance processes. Recently the National Student Survey (2010) has assumed a position of importance among universities as they vie for ranking in league tables.

There is a growing literature surrounding students' ratings with questions over the reliability, validity and impact.

Formats

Questionnaires come in a bewildering array of formats, which can broadly be divided into those that are open-ended and those that are closed. In the former the person responding is simply given a prompt and asked to write what they feel is appropriate. These prompts allow the respondent free rein. The contrasting approach constrains the response to tick-boxes, rank ordering or writing one or just a few words. This approach can certainly facilitate the analysis of large amounts of data and should only really be used if the investigator has a clear idea of the kinds of responses that are likely to appear. It would be most appropriate to start with open-ended, qualitative work before one focuses on closed items in a questionnaire. Various formats are outlined below together with examples and the associated advantages and disadvantages. Further discussion and examples can be found in Fowler (2013) and Saris and Gallhofe, (2014).

Open-ended questions

Such questions might look like this:

What did you like about the course that you just attended?

Or it might be something which asked 'How do you feel about having attended this college?'

Short written response

Between the open-ended and closed questionnaire items comes the short response, in which the amount that someone might write is constrained. Two examples follow.

How would you describe President Trump? Use three words.

1_____2_____3_____

Use one sentence in the two lines below to describe how you feel about going into a pub.

_____

_____

Likert-type responses

This is a closed format which involves a question such as:

We have good science teachers at this school.

Tick the box which most closely matches your response to this statement.

Strongly agree ☐   Agree ☐   Not sure ☐

Disagree ☐   Strongly disagree ☐

A Likert-type question involves presenting answers on a scale where the number of possible responses can vary from three up to seven or more. As a general principle one should provide as many responses as the respondents are able to cope with, and anything beyond seven would seem to be problematic. Five is commonly used, as is three. Some writers advise researchers to use an even number of possibilities in order to force a decision from the respondents. But the job of Likert-type questions is to gauge a respondent's feeling and if they sit on the fence then the researcher should know that!

When analysing the data, it is possible to assess the extent to which the various options on the Likert scale are used. There should be some variation otherwise the item is providing no information and it is expected that all possibilities will be used to some extent. Generally a well-worded question using a five-point scale will be managed well, but younger children might have difficulty and it may also be that the use of faces, as in the example below, is better.

I like school.

    ☺

A complication arises from subjects who have no opinion or simply don't know how to respond. This can be different from a neutral response such as 'not sure'. It is possible to emphasise that respondents do not have to answer all the questions. But it can also be useful to add a response option which says 'No response'.

Multiple choice

Multiple choice is very similar to the Likert-type response, but there is no continuum. For example:

What is your country of birth?

England	☐
Wales	☐
Scotland	☐
Northern Ireland	☐
Republic of Ireland	☐
Elsewhere	☐

Please write in the present name of the country _____.

Sometimes the multiple choices will be exclusive, as above, where it is not possible to be born in more than one country. But sometimes it is possible to pick more than one.

Rank ordering

It is fairly common to see questionnaires in which people are asked to rank order a series of factors. For example:

Please rank the following in order of importance for good classroom teaching, using the numbers 1 to 7 where 1 is the most important.

	Rank
Maintaining order	
Teaching subject matter	
Motivating the students	
Getting good inspection ratings	
Getting good test marks for the pupils	
Keeping the class quiet	
Making sure there is good discussion	

As a general rule, the results from this kind of item are more difficult to analyse than from Likert-type questions or multiple-choice responses. The data do not lend themselves to the usual analyses, and it would be good to avoid this kind of question. Rank ordering can nearly always be established *post hoc* from Likert-type questions and so little is lost by their avoidance.

Semantic differentials

A really nice way to get people to respond about their feelings is to put in opposing statements or opposing words and ask to which end their views are most applicable (Osgood et al., 1957). For example:

How do you feel about ice cream?

Hate it	X Love it

The cross shows that the respondent feels more inclined towards loving rather than hating ice cream.

Your perception of work

Relaxing	X	Stressful
Enjoyable	X	Unpleasant
On top of things X		Overwhelmed

This approach can be quite motivating and interesting for respondents as well as easy to analyse. This can be done via computer or on paper. In both cases the distance of the cross from one end is the measure. The format has been used very widely in psychological research.

An interesting feature of this format is that the analyst can place a cross on the diagram to represent the average response; this has been done in the 'Your perception of work' example above for teachers of Year 2 children.

Forced choice

Q Sort, also known as Q methodology, was created by a physicist by the name of Stephenson working in the social sciences. One is given a normal distribution and a series of statements on pieces of paper which, when laid out, will just fit in under the normal distribution (Stephenson, 1952). The respondent is asked to arrange the statements in an order going from 'Statement applies extremely well' to 'Statement applies very poorly'.

Once completed, the analyst automatically has a score for each of the items derived from the position on the distribution and this is a major advantage. The process prevents an individual describing themselves or others in consistently positive terms. Because the respondent is required to put in opposing items, if one is trying to assess a trait which someone might hide this may be an approach which helps.

Wording

Anyone who has designed and used a questionnaire knows that there is considerable scope for alternative interpretations of wordings and it is therefore really important to aim to keep statements and questions brief and direct so that they are readily understood. It also means that questionnaires need to be trialled before they are used and that only a single piece of information is collected for each statement. Despite this, it is common to see questions which have two parts to them, even in some that are widely used.

It is well known that people are prepared to give opinions about things about which they have no knowledge and it is important to make sure that when we ask for information the respondent is in a position to answer. If, for example, one wants to ask about attitudes towards the content of a novel it is useful to know if they have read the book. One tactic is to ask them about other books, including non-existent books. One can expect a proportion to say that they have read the non-existent book as well as real books, and by doing this one can get a better estimate of the numbers who have read the book which is the focus of the question.

Textbooks sometimes advise questionnaire designers to make sure that some questions are worded positively and some negatively. A reason for this is to avoid respondents falling into a 'response set' whereby they will start ticking all the boxes, say on the right-hand side of the column, without thought. One has to be very careful about that advice because a negatively-worded item which should result in a 'strongly disagree' response can confuse even very bright respondents, lowering the validity of the data. It is better to word questions in different ways. Rather than reversing 'I am happy' to 'I am not happy' it is worth trying 'I am sad'. In other words, try to word items in a way which does not require the respondent to double-think their answer.

Administration

Questionnaire data can be collected in four major ways which are outlined below. Each has their strengths and weaknesses, outlined in Table 26.1 which follows the descriptions. In some cases these methods can be used simultaneously or consecutively.

Paper-based

Traditionally questionnaires have been administered on paper. They can be given out by hand or sent by post. After completion the data are usually entered into a computer and then analysed. Sometimes the results are scanned in and for large-scale exercises this makes sense, but the scanning machines tend to be uncompromising and require that the marks on the papers are accurate to an exacting degree.

Computer-delivered

It is increasingly popular to send out requests to answer questionnaires by email, directing respondents to a website, and there are numerous software packages designed for this purpose. Some, such as Survey Monkey (2010), have a basic free option. This approach has great appeal because one can reach large audiences very rapidly. It was used, for example, to survey all the Malaysian academics of six universities from the UK (Hassan et al., 2008). The major downside of the use of computer-delivered questionnaires is the extent of access to computers by the people in whom the researcher is interested.

Face-to-face

It might be that the investigator actually holds the paper-based questionnaire, perhaps on a clipboard or computer in front of him/herself, and asks a respondent what their answers are.

By phone

An alternative approach is to phone people and to administer the questionnaire verbally (Frey, 1989; Sturman and Taggart, 2008). The investigator can enter the answers straight into a computer or, possibly, write them down.

Length of questionnaires

Researchers often want to find out as much as possible when collecting data and this can result in very long questionnaires. But such instruments tend to get short shrift from respondents and, even if they do opt for completion, there are other problems with long questionnaires. Respondents may

Table 26.1 Advantages and disadvantages of the various forms of questionnaire administration

Administrative procedure	Advantages	Disadvantages
Paper-based	Easy to administer to small samples. Simple to run off copies. Well established. Tried and tested.	Cost of paper and data entry. Difficult to use over large distances such as overseas. Scanning can be troublesome. Papers can be lost in transit.
Computer-delivered	Useable on a very wide scale. Very economical. Rapid data collection. No data entry. Branching questionnaires are possible.	A major problem is the potential bias because those who don't have computers would not be able to respond.
Face-to-face	A skilled interviewer can encourage responses. He/she can flip between open and closed questions without difficulty. Additional notes can be taken relating to information that doesn't appear in a questionnaire. People can be approached in the street, in the pub or elsewhere.	An interviewer can be off-putting. An individual asked sensitive questions may be less likely to be honest. It can be expensive.
Phone	Perhaps surprisingly, phones can generate more revealing responses than face-to-face interviews. As with interviews, points of interest can be followed up. Can be recorded although by law one must ask permission and a reminder beep must be put on the line. Can be automated.	Some people may not want to respond on the phone. Phone numbers may not be readily available. It can be expensive.

lose interest in what is being asked and they may start ticking boxes without thinking or tick the same position on a page – generating a 'response set'.

The length of the questionnaire, then, is important for response rates and for validity. It is also important from an ethical point of view to avoid asking for information which the analyst is not going to use. To do so would be a waste of people's time.

Response rates

Researchers need meaningful data and low response rates threaten the validity of the information which they collect. When sending out questionnaires one wants to get back a fair proportion of those that were sent out but inevitably one very rarely gets all of them back. It is possible in a constrained situation such as a classroom to ensure nearly 100 per cent response rates, though some students may opt not to complete it. Often questionnaires are collected in a less controlled way: they are sent out, perhaps by post, and the researcher waits for responses. The *Canadian Medical Association Journal*'s medical policy states that 'Except in unusual circumstances, surveys are not considered for publication in *CMAJ* if the response rate is less than 60% of eligible participants' (Houston, 1996).

But it is common in social science to see response rates lower than that and response rates as low as 20% are sometimes published.

How to increase the response rate

There have been very clear and informative studies of how to increase the rate of response, especially when it comes to postal questionnaires, and these are well summarised in an article in which meta-analyses of the various investigations have been conducted. The recommendations are as follows (Edwards et al., 2002):

- Keep the questionnaire short or at least make it look as though it is short and easy to complete. The shorter it is, the higher the response rate. (The best response rate that the author of this chapter has had to a questionnaire is to send out a postcard with a return address and stamp on it which simply asks the respondent to tick five Likert-type questions.)
- Use coloured paper.
- Use a handwritten envelope.
- Include a first-class stamp for return.
- Use a named respondent. (If one addresses a specific person rather than the Head of Physics at Bog Standard Comprehensive, the response rate is going to be better.)
- Promise feedback.

For online questionnaires and other formats the ways to increase response rates have not been so thoroughly investigated.

Scales

As noted earlier, Likert-type responses and semantic differentials are often used to create a scale. A scale is formed to measure a construct which represents an idea that we have about a person or a place or a thing which isn't immediately apparent – a latent trait (see also Chapter 28). It is not like height which can be measured directly with a ruler, rather it might be an attitude or some aspect of personality such as introversion. We try to get at it by asking a series of questions and then aggregate those questions. Traditionally the procedure has involved checking that the items hang together well, checking the validity of items, as well as checking the scale's relationship to other measures. The process is well described in Spector (1992). More recently Item Response Theory, and more specifically Rasch measurement, have provided a modern way to approach the issue of measuring in the social sciences (Bond and Fox, 2015). This approach can help enormously when developing measures and additional advice on the analysis of questionnaire data can be found in Saris and Gallhofer (2014).

How many items are needed in a scale?

How many items are needed to get a reliable measure of a construct? Before answering this question, it is important to distinguish two things: one relates to the unit of analysis and the second to the construct being measured.

The unit of analysis

Questionnaires are usually completed by individuals; the individual is the unit of observation. But the focus of the research may not be the individual, it may a group or system to which the individual belongs. The focus is the unit of analysis, and in studying education the unit of analysis may be students or a school. Or, it could be a subgroup within a school or the educational system of a whole country. The unit of analysis is the entity which is to be measured, and we can think of measuring students, schools and countries. Consider the cognitive ability of students in a school. If the unit of analysis were the school then a variable entitled 'average ability of students in a school' might be of interest. Such a measure could be used in a multilevel analysis (see Chapter 36) of students within schools where the apparent impact of the aggregate measure, the 'average ability of students in a school', in addition to the students' individual cognitive ability, on an outcome is called a compositional effect.

The distinction between measuring individuals and measuring groups might seem obscure, but it really matters because if we are to measure a pupil, then one set of rules comes into operation, but if we are to measure a school then another set of rules is needed. We might be able to measure individual pupils well but schools not so well, and the opposite may also be true. To give a couple of examples: we can measure the height of an individual accurately and quickly, but to distinguish one school from another on the basis of the pupils' heights would not be easy. On the other hand, we don't measure a pupil's background very well by knowing if they have access to free school meals, but this poor pupil measure behaves quite well at the aggregate level in helping to characterise a school.

The construct

It is really important to be clear about what the questions in a survey are designed to measure or what the construct is that the measure is trying to assess. Such careful definition will inform the measure's development and use.

Measuring pupils

If we were interested in measuring pupils then we can reasonably ask a question such as 'How many items are needed to reliably measure pupils' emotional problems?' We can try to answer that by saying that we would be pleased if we had a valid measure with a reliability of, say, 0.9. The 0.9 figure is somewhat arbitrary but would be widely accepted by psychometricians and others as an indication of a very reliable assessment of individuals.[1] Quite often well-established instruments do not have reliabilities as high as that but are regarded as being acceptable. For example, the Strengths and Difficulties Questionnaire (SDQ; Goodman, 1997) uses five items to measure emotional problems and

has an internal reliability of about 0.7 with secondary school pupils. This is satisfactory, albeit short of the high target of 0.9. We can estimate how many items would be needed to get a reliability of 0.9 using the Spearman-Brown formula:

$$\rho_{new} = \frac{k\rho_{old}}{1 + (k-1)\rho_{old}}$$

where

- ρ_{new} is the reliability of the new measure;
- κ is how many times longer the new measure is;
- ρ_{old} is the reliability of the old measure.

This indicates that the more items we have, the more reliable the measure, and if we wanted to have a measure of reliability of 0.9 for the emotional problems measure of the SDQ we would need approximately 2.9 times as many similar items (assuming the same level of inter-item correlations). That is 14 items.

Measuring schools

How many items are needed to measure a school? Now the above formula is not appropriate. Rather the reliability[2] is given by:

$$Reliability = \frac{n\sigma_u^2}{n\sigma_u^2 + \sigma_e^2}$$

where:

- n is the number of pupils in the school;
- σ_u^2 is the school level variance;
- σ_e^2 is the pupils level variance.

In order to apply the formula Figure 26.1 can be used (Tymms, 1995). This relates the number of pupils in the school to the reliability of a school-level average for different levels of intra-school correlations.[3] The latter is a measure of how different schools are from one another. If we are looking at something like achievement on maths tests, having taken into account pupils' earlier scores, then

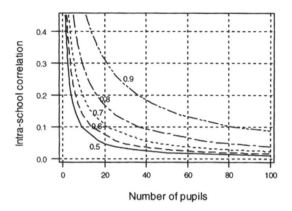

Figure 26.1   Look-up graph for indicator reliabilities

the intra-school correlation would be between 0.09 and 0.15 for a secondary school. This is sometimes stated as 'between 9 and 15% of the variance is linked to schools'.

The chart tells us that if we had a measure of maths which, controlling for prior attainment, had an intra-class correlation of 0.15, then to get a reliability of 0.9 for the school measure we would need approximately 50 pupils. It also tells us that if the intra-school correlation is 0.01 then we are going to need a very large number of pupils in order to be able to assess a school very reliably. If we have 100 pupils in a school the reliability of our estimate of that school is about 0.5. It seems unlikely that we would have enough pupils in a school to get to a point where we would have a reliability of 0.9. This is because the very low intra-school correlation indicates that school averages hardly vary at all compared to the variation in pupil scores.

A complication

The school-level section above has been set out without reference to the number of items that were used in the test. To some extent the number of items is not important provided an adequate set have been asked. An informal simulation was carried out and it indicated that after we have a few

items the intra-school correlation remains fairly constant. In other words, when we are measuring schools, we don't need large numbers of items, we simply need a few good ones. The key is the number of pupils.

Could we manage with one item? Here the validity of the measure is important (see Chapters 6, 28 and 34). A single item on a questionnaire is unlikely to capture enough of the construct that we are interested in. Ideally we would have a series of items all sampling different features of the key construct. If we are interested in emotional problems, for example, we might ask questions that relate to worries, happiness, tearfulness, nervousness and fears. Each item is designed to sample a different aspect of the construct. By assessing a range, we get a better measure.

In conclusion, in order to measure schools reliably it is important to assess an adequate number of pupils. What that number should be depends on the extent to which schools differ on the construct in question. The construct itself should be addressed using a group of items that assess the construct as broadly as possible.

Conclusion and links to other methodology

Questionnaires are one way to collect data and other sections in this book deal with interviews (see Mears, Chapter 21 in this book), which can be linked to questionnaires. In fact questionnaires can sometimes be seen as a form of interviewing. Other data such as that from tests are dealt with elsewhere in this book (see Chapter 28). Questionnaires are also relevant to experimental design (see Chapters 4 and 18) and sampling (see Chapter 6).

A further consideration when dealing with questionnaires is bias. This can come in two forms. One relates to the representativeness of those who return data and this is covered under the heading of sampling. The other relates to the wording. If questions are interpreted differently by different groups then there is a problem. This issue is discussed in Chapter 28 and elsewhere in this book.

Questions for further investigation

1. How can the response rates for online questionnaires be increased? There is a considerable amount of research suggesting how the response rates of paper-based questionnaires can be increased but the methods which have been investigated may not be relevant to online surveys and there may be other approaches which are relevant.

2. When are mobile phones suitable for collecting data? In formulating a response to this question consider the ways in which a research project might access the sample of subjects as well as the facilities available on modern mobile phones and the capacity of programmers to generate innovative approaches.

Notes

1. How high a reliability is acceptable depends on what it is to be used for. High-stakes decisions about individuals may need above 0.9; for everyday decisions 0.9 is probably adequate; if just for information, or indicative diagnosis, below this may be fine.
2. This is the 'shrinkage' formula from Goldstein (1987).
3. More generally called the intra-class correlation or ICC.

Suggested further reading

Bond, T.G. and Fox, C.M. (2015) *Applying the Rasch Model: Fundamental Measurement in the Human Sciences*, 3rd edn. Mahwah, NJ: Lawrence Erlbaum. This book is an introduction to Rasch measurement

and is very relevant to researchers who wish to measure attitudes using Likert-type response formats. It also has an interesting section about converting interviews into quantitative data linked to Piaget's work.

Edwards, P., Roberts, I., Clarke, M., DiGuiseppi, C., Pratap, S., Wentz, R. and Kwan, I. (2002) 'Increasing response rates to postal questionnaires: systematic review', *British Medical Journal*, 324: 1183–211. A key paper in synthesising the research on increasing response rates to questionnaires.

Johnson, T.P. and Wislar, J.S. (2012) 'Response rates and nonresponse errors in surveys', *JAMA*, 307(17): 1805–6. A serious issue facing all survey researchers is response rate, or rather, the extent to which the data collected are biased due to non-response. This paper provides a short authoritative summary of the issues and ways in which the issue can be tackled.

Frey, J. (1989) *Survey Research by Telephone*. London: Sage. Telephone interviews have much to be said for them and much good advice can be found in this text.

References

Bond, T.G. and Fox, C.M. (2015) *Applying the Rasch Model: Fundamental Measurement in the Human Sciences*, 3rd edn. Mahwah, NJ: Lawrence Erlbaum.

Census (2011) Available at: www.ons.gov.uk/census/index.html (accessed 24 September 2016).

Edwards, P., Roberts, I., Clarke, M., DiGuiseppi, C., Pratap, S., Wentz, R. and Kwan, I. (2002) 'Increasing response rates to postal questionnaires: systematic review', *British Medical Journal*, 324: 1183–211.

Fowler Jr, F.J. (2013) *Survey Research Methods*, 5th edn. Thousand Oaks, CA: Sage.

Freedman, D., Pisani, R. and Purves, R. (2007) *Statistics (International Student Edition)*. London: W.W. Norton and Company.

Frey, J.H. (1989) *Survey Research by Telephone*. London: Sage.

Goldstein, H. (1987) *Multi-level Models in Educational and Social Research*. London: Griffin School Effects.

Goodman, R. (1997) 'The strengths and difficulties questionnaire: a research note', *Journal of Child Psychology and Psychiatry*, 38: 581–6.

Hassan, A., Tymms, P. and Ismail, H. (2008) 'Academic productivity as perceived by Malaysian academics',

Journal of Higher Education Policy and Management, 30(3): 283–96.

Houston (1996) The *Canadian Medical Association Journal* Medical Policy. Available at: www.cmaj.ca/ (accessed 20 September 2011).

Ipsos MORI (2010) Available at: www.ipsos-mori.com/ (accessed 27 December 2010).

National Student Survey (2010) Available at: www. thestudentsurvey.com/ (accessed 27 December 2010).

Osgood, C.E., Suci, G.J. and Tannenbaum, P.H. (1957) *The Measurement of Meaning.* Urbana, IL: University of Illinois.

Saris, W.E. and Gallhofer, I.N. (2014) *Design, Evaluation, and Analysis of Questionnaires for Survey Research,* 2nd edn. Hoboken, NJ: Wiley.

Spector, P.E. (1992) *Summated Rating Scale Construction: An Introduction.* Newbury Park, CA: Sage.

Stephenson, W. (1952) 'Some observations on Q-Technique', *Psychological Bulletin,* XLIX: 483–98.

Sturman, L. and Taggart, G. (2008) 'The professional voice: comparing questionnaire and telephone methods in a national survey of teachers' perceptions', *British Educational Research Journal,* 34(1): 117–34.

Sudman, S. and Bradburn, N.M. (1982) *Asking Questions: A Practical Guide to Questionnaire Design.* San Francisco, CA: Jossey-Bass.

Survey Monkey (2010) Available at: www.survey monkey.com/ (accessed 27 September 2016).

Tymms, P. (1995) *Technical Report: Primary.* London: School Curriculum and Assessment Authority.

Measurement and validity   27

Ronald K. Hambleton

Introduction

All of the steps in the research process – from identifying a worthwhile problem to investigate and writing a research purpose, developing and validating instrumentation, through sampling, data collection and analysis, to preparing the final report – are critical, and to skip one or complete one step poorly can have a devastating impact on the overall value of that study. But some of the steps, if completed poorly, can be corrected without having to spend a lot of time or money. For example, if the statistical analyses are incomplete or carried out incorrectly, these can be fixed. If a final report is poorly written, the organisation and writing can be improved. But some steps, such as the measurement of the variables of interest in the study (e.g. reading achievement, motivation level assessment, and attitudes about sport), if done poorly, are impossible to fix without collecting more data, and often this is not possible because of time, access, and/or cost.

Of course to get the correct data, the variables of interest must be specified and clearly written. Measurement is about assigning numbers to persons or groups to represent their characteristics on these variables of interest in a research study. These variables can span the range from achievement, to aptitudes, to attitudes and personality, to psychomotor skills. These numbers often serve as the link between a researcher's purposes and the conclusions he or she wants to make.

For example, a researcher may be studying the impact of a new children's reading programme on reading comprehension. Measurements or scores provided by a reading comprehension test administered before and after the instruction provide the numbers for the researcher to analyse any gains that may have been made.

Of course not all measurements are equally useful. It is important that the measurements provided by the administration of the reading comprehension test to the participants in the study have desirable properties: there needs to be evidence that the test is in fact providing measurements that actually reflect the construct of interest (i.e. the measurements must be valid) and can be shown to be consistent, for example, to be similar to scores obtained from administering the test again or administering an equivalent form of the test (i.e. the measurements must be reliable).

Approaches to collecting data

Once the outcome variables of a study are specified, then it is possible to consider ways in which the data of interest can be collected. Researchers have many options available to them when making measurements of human characteristics in their studies, though of course all of these options are not always feasible or reasonable for a given study. What follows are some options with very brief descriptions:

- *Norm-referenced achievement and aptitude tests*. Normally, these types of tests are commercially available and there are thousands of possible choices. A good reference for these tests would be the *Buros Mental Measurement Yearbooks* found in the reference section of university libraries (also, see the website www.unl.edu/buros/) or the commercial publishers who all have websites that can be explored. The quality of these tests is generally high though the costs of these tests can often be substantial. The availability of score norms to assist in test score interpretation can be especially valuable.

- *Criterion-referenced achievement tests* (e.g. competency tests, basic skills tests, commercially available credentialing exams). Sometimes a researcher is interested in the level of accomplishment of participants in relation to a domain of content, for example high school mathematics, and the levels might be failing, basic, proficient, and advanced. Sometimes the test data will come from existing files, such as might be available from an education department, or sometimes these tests will need to be constructed by the researcher (e.g. Shrock and Coscarelli, 2007). These types of tests are prominent in the schools, training programmes, and credentialing agencies.

- *Classroom tests*. These tests may be constructed by teachers, or by researchers, and are often intended for one-time use, and rarely are the tests of the same high quality of commercial tests, but often they can be constructed to match exactly the needs of the researcher.

- *Performance tests* (e.g. writing tests, tests of psychomotor skills). These types of tests require the respondents to write something, to perform something, to construct a response to a question, etc.

- *Personality tests* (e.g. assessments of motivation, school anxiety, self-esteem, or self-concept). These tests are typically constructed by test publishers, of high quality, and with norms to aid in score interpretation.

- *Attitude scales*. Often researchers have an interest in assessing the attitudes of participants in their research, attitudes towards sports, religion, computers, etc. They can be available commercially but more often researchers will construct these types of instruments themselves so that they can assess exactly the construct of interest. In a typical attitudinal survey, respondents are presented with a series of statements (e.g. 'Watching sports on television is a big waste of my time.') to which they will provide one of five responses, 'strongly disagree', 'disagree', 'undecided', 'agree', or 'strongly agree'.

- *Interest inventories*. These types of instruments are normally available from commercial test publishers.

- *Questionnaires* (structured as well as unstructured). Questionnaires (often called 'surveys') are among the most common ways that researchers compile data for their studies. They can be tailored exactly to the needs of the researcher. The questions themselves come in two forms: structured and unstructured. Structured questions provide both a question and set of responses from which the respondent makes a choice. Sometimes the responses are unordered, such as 'What is your favourite sport? (1) hockey, (2) soccer, (3) baseball, (4) basketball, (5) other'. Other times the choices are ordered. For example, 'How often do you get to go to the movies? (1) never, (2) rarely, (3) sometimes, (4) frequently'. Other times, a question or prompt (e.g. 'Explain what you liked best about the summer programme') is presented to the respondent and they then answer in their own words. For example, 'Write 500 words or so on the similarities and differences in the educational policies of the last two Presidents of the United States: Barack Obama and Donald Trump'. Both structured and unstructured questions have their advantages and disadvantages in research studies. Often researchers will use a mix of formats to capitalise on their advantages and minimise their disadvantages (see, for example, Gay et al., 2006). What researchers seem to like most about questionnaires is the ease with which they can be constructed to meet their own research objectives. Of course, questionnaires still benefit from careful reviews and pilot-testing prior to their actual use in a study.

- *Observational methods.* Researchers conducting qualitative studies may want to collect their data through observational methods. Often this involves the development of an instrument focused on the variables of interest. For instance, a researcher may be interested in focusing on children in a classroom and their activities – listening to the teacher, talking with other children in the classroom, reading a book, looking out the window, etc. An observation form can be constructed that identifies children's possible activities, and then observers can note the time percentage for individual children engaged in those activities. Normally, training of observers or raters must be done, and multiple observers are used to check that the observations noted by one observer are replicated by others (referred to as 'inter-rater reliability studies').

- *Interviews* (structured and unstructured). Interviewing respondents is another very effective way to collect data for a research study. Questions can be structured or unstructured just as with questionnaires. The data collection method however does tend to be time-consuming and often more expensive than questionnaire research. Despite some limitations, sometimes it is the only suitable approach to collect the required data.

Research methods textbooks usually have a chapter, and often more than one chapter, on modes of data collection for research studies. Factors such as costs to purchase, required time to administer, time to development and validate, the match between an instrument and the informational needs it addresses, and expected score reliability, are the sorts of factors considered in ultimately deciding upon the mode or modes for data collection in a research study.

Scales of measurement

The measurements researchers work with (i.e. the numbers obtained from the data collection initiatives)

have different properties, and these need to be known or assumed prior to conducting any statistical analyses. When numbers are used to simply distinguish individuals or groups from each other, we say that the numbers are on a *nominal scale*. For example, we often code gender data by recording females as '1' and males as '2'. These numbers provide no information about order. They are simply labels we use to distinguish our research sample by gender. Because the numbers are simply labels, we do not use them to carry out any statistical operations other than for counting the number of objects in each category. Nominal numbers have value for helping to describe the research sample, and in conditioning the data for some analysis (e.g. splitting a sample of data into combinations of gender and ethnicity), but there is little that can be done otherwise. These nominal variables become important when there is interest in analysing a set of test scores and reporting them for, say, males and females, sorted by ethnic group.

Sometimes the numbers we use inform us about order (e.g. the order of finish of participants in a race or on a test). We may ask participants to rank order the preferences they have for their teachers, the sports they play, or the subjects they have studied. Asking participants to order lists on a questionnaire is common. Measurements that inform about order are referred to as measurements on an *ordinal scale*. Again, these numbers are limited statistically but medians can be calculated, and there are statistics that can be used to obtain score variability information. One downside to measurements on an ordinal scale is that the differences between scores of 1, 2, 3, etc. cannot be assumed to be equal. Suppose the numbers represent the placing of individuals on a test. But it should not be assumed that these differences in performance are equal. It is possible, for example, that the individual who was first may have performed substantially better than the second place participant in the study, whereas the second and third best-performing participants may have been close. These numbers (1, 2, 3, etc.) communicate the ordering of performance, but they do not communicate any information about the size of the actual performance differences.

If the numbers do communicate information about the differences, as they might on an achievement test or personality survey, we say these numbers are being reported on an *interval scale* (sometimes called an *equal-interval scale*). Now an equal interval scale for the scores on a test is probably not strictly true. For example, gaining points at the lower end of an achievement test score scale is often easy to come by whereas gaining points at the higher end is often more difficult to obtain. But it is common to assume that equal differences along an achievement, aptitude, attitude, and personality scale represent equal differences in the construct. So, on an achievement test score scale, it is common to assume that it takes the same change in achievement knowledge or skills to move from 30 to 40, 60 to 70, and 90 to 100. This surely isn't strictly true, but researchers commonly assume that it is. This assumption permits the usual array of descriptive and inferential statistics to be used on the measurements. It is common to assume that these statistical methods are robust to violations in the assumption that the measurements are being reported on an equal-interval scale. The one shortcoming with equal-interval measurements is that the zero score is arbitrary, and so ratios of scores are not acceptable. It makes no sense to say that one participant has twice the attitude of another based on scores from the administration of an attitudinal survey, because a zero score on the instrument is often quite arbitrary and rarely would it represent the absence of an attitude.

Finally, if the score scale on which measurements are made does contain a well-defined zero score, then in addition to treating the data as equal interval ratios can be carried out. This type of scale is called a *ratio scale*. Well-known examples of measurements that are reported on ratio scales include the measurement of weights, lengths, and time. In these examples, zero scores are well understood. So not only do we recognise that the numbers on these scales represent equal changes in the construct from one number to the next, we can make ratio statements too (such as one participant completed the task of interest in twice the time of another participant because a time of zero has meaning).

All four scales of measurement are valuable in social science research because they have major implications for the handling of measurements in any statistical analyses.

Criterion-referenced vs. norm-referenced measurement

Over the years, two frameworks for interpreting measurements on equal-interval scales have emerged: criterion-referenced and norm-referenced (Shrock and Cascarelli, 2007; Hambleton et al., 2016). Norm-referenced measurements are the better known of the two, and lead to a comparison of participants to a reference group of persons on the construct measured by the test of interest. For example, suppose researchers were using an intelligence test in their study. The publisher of that test has compiled 'norms' on the test which, for a fully described reference group, provide the basis for interpreting individual test scores. We might say, for example, that an individual scored about as well as a person in the reference group at the 90th percentile. Individual scores derive meaning by comparing them to a reference group. For some tests too, there may be 'norms' for multiple reference groups. This is common with some popular aptitude and personality tests.

In contrast to norm-referenced tests, criterion-referenced tests provide a basis for interpreting individual measurements in relation to a well-defined body of content (e.g. the mathematics content required for high-school graduation). Tests are constructed, a scoring scheme is developed, and performance standards (sometimes called 'cutscores') are set on the test-score scale (or perhaps on a derived-score scale) for distinguishing among failing, basic, proficient, and advanced candidates. Individual scores are used to place those individuals into performance categories. The interpretation of the individual score is made using the performance standards which were set in relation to the body of content that the test measures.

Depending on the purpose of the research study, either or both norm-referenced and criterion-referenced measurements may be of interest. Because the purposes of these two types of measurement are very different, it should come as no surprise that the approaches to constructing and evaluating each kind of test are different (Hambleton and Zenisky, 2003).

Score reliability

Books have been written about score reliability and so only a few main points can be covered here (see, for example, Thorndike and Thorndike-Christ, 2010). Score reliability is about the 'consistency' of the measurements obtained from a test administration. It is not about the test *per se*. Consistency has a meaning that shifts depending on the use of the measurements. With many achievement, aptitude and personality tests, consistency may have to do with the similarity of scores over time. With achievement tests, sometimes there is concern about the consistency of scores over parallel forms of the test. With observational data there may be concern about consistency of the measurements across observers or interviewers. In scoring performance data when judgement is involved, the concern may focus on the consistency of scores assigned to individual work across graders or raters.

There are several important points to remember about score reliability. Firstly, score reliability is measured by degree (between 0 and 1). Researchers may say that their test is reliable or not, but the reality is that it is measured from one end of a continuum (.00) to the other (1.00). Secondly, a high level of score reliability is important but does not guarantee that the resulting scores have some reasonable level of validity. Score validity is also a more important characteristic of scores than reliability. At the same time, some level of reliability of scores is required, or score validity will be very limited. Thirdly, reliability is really a function of the scores themselves, the kind of reliability being reported, and the group to which the test was administered. For example, test-retest reliability may differ from parallel-form reliability, and the results may be different for Black, White, and Hispanic students.

Why might the scores from a test be inconsistent for individual candidates? The answer is that sometimes the directions or the items may be ambiguous; or that attention, effort, or health, can fluctuate from one administration to the next; a restrictive time limit could cause guessing or quitting; observers or raters may adopt different strategies of doing their work; unforeseen interruptions can occur; and so on. Researchers must strive for high consistency or reliability in the data they are using.

Researchers have access to many designs for compiling their reliability data: test-retest (often used with standardised tests), parallel-form (often used with achievement tests), inter-rater reliability (often used with observational data or when scoring performance data), and internal consistency (e.g. coefficient alpha) are used when there is only time for a single administration of a test. Often too, reliability for standardised test scores can be found in technical manuals. With questionnaires, it would be rare to readminister these a second time. Sometimes they are completed anonymously and so it would be difficult to match up responses from the first and second administration. In addition, obtaining high response rates is difficult, and the idea of getting respondents to participate twice is difficult to imagine. Often reliability is checked by asking some similar questions in different parts of the questionnaire to check on the extent to which respondents are consistent in their answers.

Score validity

Ultimately, researchers must be concerned about the extent to which the measurements they are using are accurate representations of the constructs they want to include in their research. They can try hard to construct or select instruments for their studies, but hard work is not sufficient to defend sets of scores in a research study. Hard work and following the main steps in either selecting or constructing tests and questionnaires are important, but additional evidence for score validity is needed.

There are important features of score validity to remember. Firstly, test score validity is judged by how useful the scores are for addressing an intended purpose or use. There may be some great tests in the field for assessing the personality of adults. But these same tests would likely be completely inappropriate for children. Test score validity is very much specific to a particular group and a particular use. As with test score reliability, test score validity is very much assessed by degree, even though it is common in practice to describe a test as 'valid' or 'invalid'. There is no critical correlation or particular result that must be obtained. Test score validity is about compiling evidence, and then making a professional judgement about the worth of that evidence for supporting use of the measurements to accomplish some particular goal of a study. Finally, and again, just as with test score reliability, there are several types of evidence that can be compiled and the evidence may not always be consistent.

Historically, there are three major categories of evidence that are recognised by researchers.

Content validity evidence has to do with the extent of overlap between the content that a test or questionnaire measures and the domain of content that is of interest. Measure too little and the critics will argue that the test does not constitute a representative sample; measure too much and the critics will argue that the test measures more than was intended by the construct. Assessing content validity is a judgemental activity. With an observational instrument, questionnaire, or interview, often content validity is addressed by matching up the content of the instrument to the features or criteria that are deemed important to measure.

Criterion-related validity evidence concerns studying the relationship between the scores on the test of interest and scores measuring variables that they might be expected to predict (e.g. a study about predicting college grades from a predictor test), or variables that a test might be expected to correlate with at the present time

(e.g. a competitor to the test of interest, or perhaps high-school grades). Other names for these types of studies are 'convergent and divergent validity investigations'.

Construct validity evidence has to do with evidence that scores from a test can be interpreted in terms of the construct the test was intended to measure. For example, correlational data could be supportive, such as correlations with tests that purport to measure the same construct (here we might expect the correlations to be relatively high) or even different constructs (here we might expect the correlations to be modest or low). Content validity evidence is always valued in construct validation investigations. In addition, lots of other types of evidence may show that scores from the test or questionnaire function as they might function if they were measuring the construct of interest: they should go up and/or down (over groups perhaps and over time; testable hypotheses come from the theory associated with the construct) when expected, they should correlate with tests measuring similar constructs, and not correlate with tests measuring unrelated constructs. There is no end to the amount of evidence that can be compiled to investigate the construct validity of scores from a test. That amount surely depends on professional judgement considering the importance of the test and the resources available to researchers. But if they do too little, the credibility of the research study will be severely weakened because of questions about the validity of the measurements being used in the study.

Conclusion

So much more is known about measurement than is contained in this chapter, and many have spent their careers working solely on this single topic. They are called 'measurement specialists' or 'psychometricians' and become deeply involved in instrument development, the assessment of reliability and validity of instrument scores, the uses of measurement, the reporting of scores, and the development of professional standards for developing and using tests and questionnaires (see AERA, APA and NCME, 2014; Bartram and Hambleton, 2016). Of course they also become involved in expanding the field by developing new psychometric theories and models, for example generalisability theory (Brennan, 2001) and item response theory (Wells and Faulkner-Bond, 2016), and other types of research (e.g., the development of new modes of instrument instrumentation, new methods of collecting data from participants, and the automated scoring of participant responses) (see, for example, Brennan, 2001; Wells and Faulkner-Bond, 2016).

Questions for further investigation

1. Discuss the pros and cons of criterion-referenced and norm-referenced measurements. For which types of research are these best suited?
2. Discuss score validity and score reliability. Which do you consider more important and why?

Suggested further reading

The two references below and many others are available in their entirety on SAGE Research Methods Online (SRMO), and both are relevant for researchers wishing to follow up on the topic of measurement:

Salkind, N.J. and Rasmassen, K. (eds) (2007) *Encyclopedia of Measurement and Statistics*. Thousand Oaks, CA: Sage. The editors have compiled a highly relevant set of topics for researchers interested in learning more about measurement and related topics. Just about every topic touched on in this short chapter and many more related ones are expanded upon in this encyclopedia. Researchers can learn about many different types of assessments (ability, aptitude, and personality), specific tests, and how those tests and others might be assessed (i.e. reliability and validity).

Walford, G., Tucker, E. and Viswanathan, M. (eds) (2010) *The SAGE Handbook of Measurement*. Thousand Oaks, CA: Sage. This book spans the spectrum of approaches for collecting data and making measurements in the social sciences. The topics covered range from the very practical to the theoretical and mathematically complex.

References

American Educational Research Association (AERA), American Psychological Association (APA) and National Council on Measurement in Education (NCME) (2014) *Standards for Educational and Psychological Testing*. Washington, DC: AERA.

Bartram, D. and Hambleton, R.K. (2016) 'The ITC Guidelines: International standards and guidelines relating to tests and testing', in F. Leong et al. (eds), *International Test Commission Handbook of Testing and Assessment*. Oxford: Oxford University Press. pp. 35–48.

Brennan, R.L. (2001) *Generalizability Theory*. New York: Springer.

Gay, L.R., Mills, G.E. and Airasian, P. (2006) *Educational Research: Competencies for Analysis and Applications*, 8th edn. Upper Saddle River, NJ: Pearson Education, Inc.

Hambleton, R.K. and Zenisky, A.L. (2003) 'Issues and Practices of Performance Assessment', in C.R. Reynolds and T.W. Kamphaus (eds), *Handbook of Psychological and Educational Assessment of Children*, 2nd edn. New York: The Guilford Press. pp. 377–404.

Hambleton, R.K., Zenisky, A.L. and Popham, W.J. (2016) 'Criterion-referenced Testing: Advances over 40 years', in C.S. Wells and M. Faulkner-Bond (eds), *Educational Measurement: From Foundations to Future*. New York: Guilford, pp. 23–37.

Shrock, S.A. and Coscarelli, W.C. (2007) *Criterion-referenced Test Development: Technical and Legal Guidelines for Corporate Training*, 3rd edn. San Francisco, CA: Wiley.

Thorndike, R.M. and Thorndike-Christ, T. (2010) *Measurement and Evaluation in Psychology and Education*, 8th edn. Boston, MA: Pearson.

Wells, C.S. and Faulkner-Bond, M. (eds) (2016) *Educational Measurement: From Foundations to Future*. New York: Guilford.

Part V

Analysis methods

Using software in qualitative data analysis

Graham R. Gibbs

28

Introduction

Computer Assisted Qualitative Data Analysis (CAQDAS) programs have been developed to help manage the sheer amount of data to be analysed and their complexity and density. There are many different programs available but some are better than others at some kinds of analysis and for some purposes. If you are able to choose what software to use before you start analysis then it is important to know which is good at what. Download trial versions and try them out (see the resources section at the end of the chapter). The rest of this chapter, however, focuses on one of the most popular in the UK, NVivo, now in version 11 and available for both Mac and Widows. However, much of the advice applies to any software you might use as they all tend to cover the basic functions that I will discuss here. Many universities in the UK have a site licence for NVivo which, if you are a student, means that you will have lab access to the program and may even be able to install a copy on your own PC.

QSR, the publishers of NVivo, have created a very good set of help resources that can be accessed from their website (www.qsrinternational. com). This includes a full interactive help system that documents all the features of the program and which can be opened from the Help button in the program (top right of the screen). This is an excellent reference when you know what you are looking for, so to make good use of it you will need to understand the key things the program does to assist your qualitative analysis. That is what this chapter will do. The QSR website also has links to a good set of resources for learning the software, and that includes a Getting Started guide (a pdf) – a starter edition one for Windows (referred to below as GS11) and one for the Mac. There are also lots of videos (available on YouTube) that will show you how to use the program. These are generally quite short and are a good way of learning how to use the program, so in the rest of this chapter I will cross-reference to the appropriate video on the topic. As I write this chapter there is a mixture of videos that use version 9, version 10 and version 11 of the program. There are only minor differences between the versions for the range of functions covered here and those are mainly cosmetic (e.g. the icon design). The videos can be accessed from www.qsrinternational.com/nvivo-learning/nvivo-tutorials. Alternatively, to find a specific video, type its name into the search box in YouTube (shortened bit.ly links for these videos, correct at the time of writing, are included throughout this chapter).

Whilst there are many benefits to be gained from using CAQDAS, there are dangers too. Fielding and Lee (1998) have examined the history of the development of qualitative research and its support by computers in light of the experiences of those interviewed in their study of researchers using CAQDAS. Amongst the issues they identified was a feeling of being distant from the data. Researchers using paper-based analysis felt they were closer to the words of their respondents or their field notes than if they used computers. This is probably because many of the early programs did not make it easy to jump back to the data to examine the context of coded or retrieved text. In contrast, recent programs excel at this. A second issue, as many users and some commentators have suggested, was that much of the software seemed too influenced by grounded theory. This approach to analysis is very popular amongst both qualitative researchers and software developers. However, as Fielding and Lee point out, as programs have become more sophisticated, they have also become less connected to any one analytic approach. A related danger that some have pointed to is the over-emphasis on code and retrieve approaches. These are, indeed, core activities of CAQDAS, and some commentators have suggested that this militates against analysts who wish to use quite different techniques (such as hyperlinking) to analyse their data. However, it is clear that coding is central in the kind of analysis best supported by most CAQDAS, and although some software does have linking facilities, these are not as well developed as those that support coding.

To use CAQDAS or not

There are several considerations to examine when deciding whether to use software with your project. You might consider your project too small to justify its use. This does not simply mean a small number of participants. Interviews and observations can be long, complex and intensive and produce lots of data to analyse. On the other hand you may intend to use simple structured questionnaires, in which case the data may be quite easy to analyse without the software support.

Above all you will need to ask if the software supports your analytic approach or does it help sufficiently to make its use worthwhile. Code and retrieve or thematic coding approaches are well served by the software. These include grounded theory, interpretive phenomenological analysis, framework analysis, template analysis and many kinds of ethnographic approaches that tend to analyse data thematically. Less well served are more intensive and discursive approaches such as discourse analysis, narrative and conversation analysis. Some software does support the special mark-up needed by conversation analysis for example, and even supports the process of transcription, but these approaches are not reliant on thematic coding and thus the core function of most CAQDAS is of little use. However, many researchers using such discursive methods do use CAQDAS for part of the analysis. For example, in the early stages of data collection and identification, often referred to as the corpus construction stage, CAQDAS software is used both to manage the large amounts of data being assembled and to mark it up thematically to aid later selection for more detailed discursive analysis.

Setting up the project in NVivo

Start the program and in the welcome screen that appears select Blank Project and give it a title and description (GS11:.10). Use the Browse button to save it where you want it. The main NVivo window then opens (see Figure 28.1). When you start a new project most of this will be empty. Also, the List View and Detail View panes can be displayed at top and bottom, as in Figure 28.1, or left and right. Most of the functions of the software can be accessed from the ribbon bars, but there are keyboard shortcuts for many things and there is a right mouse button, contextual menu, which when you click on an item in the window will give you a menu of the functions that apply to that item.

Sources

The new project is just a container for your data. The next step is to introduce some data into it. These data are called sources in NVivo, and include text documents, video, audio, images and survey results, as well as a special kind of document called memos. NVivo can import a variety of types of documents including plain text (.txt), rich text format (.rtf) and Word format, both old and new (.doc and .docx), as

Figure 28.1 The NVivo main window

(Published with permission from QSR international)

well as pdfs. Watch the video 'Importing documents in NVivo 10 for Windows in 3 minutes' (http://bit.ly/2adijkh), and see the other videos on audio, images, pdfs and datasets. Once introduced, documents can be examined at any time by double clicking on their name and their contents will appear as tabs in the Detail view pane (GS11:.13).

Units of analysis

You will need to decide what are the cases in your study, because in NVivo cases can have attributes and combine together several different sources (documents, video, images etc.) This analytically separates the sources of information about the cases (e.g. the transcripts of your interviews or your video of interaction in the classroom) from the cases themselves. By the time you start using NVivo you should have a pretty good idea what these cases are. Sometimes these will reflect your sampling strategy (e.g. you may have undertaken snowball sampling of young people who played truant when at school age, in which case people

are your cases). More commonly, the cases will reflect your research questions or your research design. For instance, you may be investigating differences in classroom innovation between different teachers and different schools, and so your cases will probably be teachers (or classes) and schools. It is usually best to set these up when setting up the project, although if more appear or additional values for existing cases are discovered during the study these can be added on to the project. In NVivo cases are a kind of node and are found in the nodes list pane (GS11:.13, 22-23, video: 'Understand nodes and cases in NVivo for Windows': http://bit.ly/29Pke9G).

Attributes are variables, usually categorical variables, about the cases. For example, if the cases are people these might be the age, gender, education or work experience of the people, or if they are places they might be the population, crime rate, state, or if events they might be the date, duration, size, type etc. (video: 'Import & apply classifications & attributes in NVivo 10 for Windows in 2 mins': http://bit.ly/29XJTPR). In a mixed-methods study you might well have collected some attribute data of this kind about the cases in the quantitative part of the study. In which case you can introduce this information to the NVivo project as a spreadsheet or an SPSS data file called a casebook. Normally it is best to introduce this information before any qualitative data as it is a quick way of establishing what your cases are in the project. But you can also add attributes to cases after you have set up the project, either from data you have collected in the field or on the basis of analysis of your qualitative data. (For a discussion of how to create variables from qualitative data, see Miles et al., 2014: 140–48).

Security

As you build your project and develop your analysis, you will create files and structures you won't want to lose. Do regular saves of your data. By default, NVivo prompts every 15 minutes for you to save your data or produce back-up files, so that if the program or the computer crashes at any time, you will not lose all your work.

Most of the data you create will be very compact. Information about coding and links takes only a little space. Along with the documents you have introduced, this information is all kept together in the project file. However, you may opt to keep any very large files you may have, such as video and audio files, outside the project file. You should keep back-ups of both the project file (for NVivo this is the .nvp file) and other large data items that you are keeping outside the NVivo project file. You won't normally change primary data such as audio and video after these have been introduced into the project, so these may only need occasional back-ups. But the main project file will change every time you do some analysis so this needs regular backing up. You can do this using Copy Project in the File menu and rename the project with a version number or the date as you do so. The most convenient back-up media are flash memory – usually in the form of memory sticks – and removable hard disks. Memory sticks will be fine if you just have documents and a few pictures, but if you have lots of

video or audio files then a removable hard disk will be required. If you are working or studying at a university, you may well have access to a secure storage area which your university organises and regularly backs up. This is a good alternative, although if you have lots of large files you may need to negotiate additional space for your data.

Also keep the data confidential. Don't allow others to see your data if you have given respondents assurances that what they have told you is confidential or will be kept anonymous. Password protect your computer and your NVivo project if you can, and don't leave the program running unattended on a PC in an open office.

Coding

Coding is one of the core activities in most CAQDAS programs and NVivo is no exception. Coding means applying labels or tags (the codes) to chunks of your sources. These chunks can be passages of text, sections of video or audio, or regions of images or survey answers. Most commonly these chunks are coded as a way of indicating that their content is relevant to some theme, concept or category you have identified. Fundamentally, this tagging or coding process enables researchers to retrieve and collect together quickly all the text and other data that they have associated with a thematic idea, so that these can be examined together and the data from different cases can be compared (GS11: 18).

NVivo calls codes 'nodes'. Typically, when you first create nodes they can just be kept in a list. As you develop your coding ideas you can arrange the nodes into a hierarchy or tree shown in the node list view pane. Nodes can be re-ordered, re-named, deleted, split and combined, and nodes in a hierarchy can be re-organised by moving them from one branch of the tree to another (GS11: 20–21, video: 'Organize your Nodes in NVivo for Mac': http://bit.ly/2awXQTn – this is for the Mac version but Windows works just the same).

You can separate out the construction of a coding scheme (the nodes) from the act of coding the text and other sources. Thus you can create nodes in NVivo, perhaps with definitions and even attached memos, without any coding (i.e. without using them to tag any sources). Such nodes, often called *a priori* codes, are based on your literature review, your experience in the field or your initial hunches, and can be used later for coding (video: 'Creating nodes in NVivo 10 for Windows in 2 minutes': http://bit.ly/2awXKuV). On the other hand, a very common approach and one often combined with *a priori* codes is to read the text (or view the video) directly, and then create new nodes and code the source content to them and/or to *a priori* codes as you do so (GS11: 25-26, video: 'Coding a document in NVivo 10 in less than 3 minutes': http://bit.ly/29VRykz).

Once some sources have been coded, you can inspect what you have done in a couple of ways. With text that has been coded you can display coding stripes, to the right of the text, to show how the passages have been coded (GS11: 27) (see Figure 28.2.) Alternatively you can retrieve all the sources coded at a specific node. Just double-click the node name (in the node list pane) and a new tab will open in the Detail View pane

showing the text and other sources that have been coded at that node (GS11: 28).

This code and retrieve activity is a central one in the analytic process. First, it enables you to check that the theme you have identified makes sense, is well evidenced by the sources you have coded, and that the coding has been done consistently. It is thus a way of checking the quality of your analysis. Second, you can begin to look for patterns within the data sources coded to the same theme. For example, you can compare the results across different cases to see whether there are differences in what has been coded between groups of cases – perhaps all the older cases talk about this thematic issue in a different way from the younger ones. In this way you can build up a more sophisticated account of what is happening amongst the cases in your study.

Coding crisis

A common problem experienced by many researchers doing qualitative analysis, and especially those using software to help them, is to end up with too

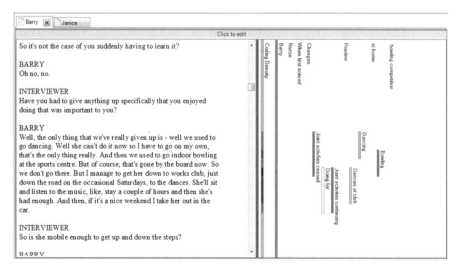

Figure 28.2 Document showing coding stripes

(Published with permission from QSR international)

many codes and/or disorganised codes. This is not necessarily a bad thing. It may simply reflect the heterogeneity of the data you are analysing and the complexity of your analysis. However, it can be a barrier to further analytic work and especially to developing a clear understanding and explanation of your data. There are several things you can do here. For example, you could print out all the codes you have (possibly with definitions and even short samples of the coded text), cut them up, and then try rearranging them. Alternatively you might cut and paste such details into a spreadsheet where you can use rows for each code and columns for things like definitions and examples and for other thoughts about the code. In both cases you are looking to re-arrange and sort the codes or sometimes to re-express them. You should look for patterns and categories amongst the codes. One reason some researchers like to move away from the software to do this is that you are attempting to re-think the analysis you are doing, and moving away from the existing project stops it interfering in the re-think. Other things that might help with this re-think are re-examining the literature for ideas or talking about your research to colleagues or your supervisor.

Some heuristics that are useful here have been suggested by supporters of grounded theory: for example, the idea of dimensions of codes (Corbin and Strauss, 2008). This is the notion that codes can be of different kinds of thing or refer to different contexts etc. of the same thing. It is quite common in the early, open stages of coding to note down all the different varieties of things without noticing that they have anything in common. Thus you might have codes for note taking, summarising, writing prompt cards, re-reading and quizzing as ways of revising for exams. In which case there can be an overall code called 'Revising' and the others can be simply ways of doing that. In NVivo this can be done easily using the hierarchical coding system (the node tree) to make 'Revising' a parent node and 'note taking', 'summarising' etc. its children nodes (GS11: 20–21, video: 'Organize your nodes in NVivo for Mac': http://bit.ly/2awXQTn).

In other cases you may find that nodes are actually about the same thing but you didn't notice you had two of them when you were coding (perhaps they relate to different cases) – in which case they can simply be combined. On the other hand when looking carefully at both the definition of a node and the text that has been coded at it, you might realise that there are two (or more) distinct analytic things represented by the coded items. In which case you can split the node by creating a new one and moving some of the coded items to the new node (and removing them from the old node).

Searching

CAQDAS programs, NVivo included, support two kinds of searching – searching for text, also called lexical searching, and searching for codes. Both can be used as ways of advancing the analytic process. In NVivo they are both types of query. Lexical searching is rather like the word-searching facility in a word processor, only more powerful. In NVivo you can search for a number of different terms (perhaps synonyms) at the same time, search for word roots (and find all the words with different endings), and even search for words spelt like the terms you are using (GS11: 32–3, video: 'Run a Text Search query with NVivo for Mac': http://bit.ly/29NNGRo) – this is for the Mac version, but Windows v.11 now uses the same display as the Mac v.10.) After the search NVivo codes all the terms it has found and you can then display these finds and look at each, in turn, in its context.

Lexical searching can help the analysis in a number of ways. First, it can be used as a way of getting familiar with the text (in addition to reading the text, of course). Search for terms that are connected with your theoretical hunches and then inspect the passages where the terms are found in the original documents. This might produce new ideas or candidates for new nodes. Second, such searching can be used as a way of looking for passages similar to those you have already coded. Passages already coded will contain terms, words or phrases that might occur elsewhere and indicate similar topic matter. Put these terms and others you can think of into the text search tool to find all the further occurrences. Of course, this won't guarantee that you find all relevant passages but it can complement your reading of the data. Beware, sometimes the search will find passages that contain the term but just aren't relevant. You need to read each in turn and decide about their relevance. Third, you can use this approach as a way of checking the validity of your analysis and in particular you can check for the occurrence of negative cases – namely instances that are inconsistent with your explanations. You may have missed these because you just weren't expecting them in the context they appear. But if they use the same terms as other instances then lexical searching will find them. However, do be aware that this approach is not infallible. Relevant passages of text might just not use the terms you are searching for and so you won't find them. In then end you will still need to read the text and inspect the other sources in a comprehensive way.

Using Query with coded text and attributes

It is quite common, even in published work, for researchers just to summarise the major thematic codes in the report on their study. This expresses what they have found and naturally tends to be quite descriptive. Sometimes that is interesting, but qualitative studies can go a lot further and offer accounts of the patterns of the occurrence of such themes and possibly suggest causes for those patterns. In CAQDAS programs this is done by running a query for differently coded text, sometimes along with attributes. In this case what is compared in the query is the actual text coded at or linked to the node or attribute. Thus in the simplest case, if your query is for sources coded at either of two nodes, what is compared is the text, image etc. coded at these nodes. The search will find all the text coded at either node, if any (including that coded at both nodes, if any).

NVivo allows two or more nodes (and sometimes attributes too) to be used in combination in a query (video: 'Explore your coding in NVivo 10 for Windows': http://bit.ly/29WWUWn). Such combinations are divided into two kinds – Boolean and proximity. Boolean queries combine codes using the logical terms like 'and', 'or' and 'not'. Proximity queries rely on the coded text being near, after or perhaps overlapping some other coded text. Commonly used proximity queries are 'followed by' (also referred to as 'sequence' or 'preceding') and 'near' (also referred to as 'co-occurrence'). Boolean queries are most useful in examining hypotheses or ideas about the data and rely on consistent and accurate coding, whereas proximity queries can be used more speculatively and to explore the data, often at an early stage of coding.

For instance, in a study of teachers' career development, you might wonder if male teachers had a different view about career development courses from female teachers. Assuming you had a node for 'career development courses' with lots of coding done and an attribute for gender, then you could run a query for text coded at the node 'career development courses' *and* in cases with the attribute female. Then repeat the query for the male cases and compare the two sets of data you have retrieved (video: 'Run a Coding query in NVivo for Mac': http://bit.ly/29VCoaR – this is for the Mac version, but Windows v.11 now uses the same display as the Mac v.10).

Teamwork

Using computers to assist with analysis is particularly useful when working in teams on projects. Partly this is because teams tend to work on larger projects, with more respondents and more settings so the database is simply larger. However, teams need to be properly coordinated and can undertake certain kinds of cross checking and the software can be of crucial help here.

When working in a team, it makes sense, very early on in the project, to create a model template for everyone to work on. This can be done in

NVivo using the Project Properties (File menu: Info). Here you can set up all the users who are entitled to use and work on the project. You should password protect the project and decide whether each researcher has read only access to the data or whether they can edit the data as well. Of course it makes sense to have a convention for how you name sources (documents, videos etc.) and cases and how you organise them in the project. One person, perhaps the senior researcher (or the NVivo expert), can set up the cases and import the documents available so far, and even establish some preliminary codes in the project along with associated definitions and linked memos about them. This project can then be shared with others in the team, and those who you decide may do so can add more sources, coding and cases as appropriate.

When several people are working on the analysis then consistency in approach becomes an issue. This may be down to simple things like how large are the chunks of text that get coded. You might decide that a minimum size might be a sentence, or that where possible and appropriate several sentences or even whole paragraphs or speeches should be coded. In other cases, it is possible to assess the reliability of coding by comparing one coder's work with that of another.

Resources

The CAQDAS Networking Project provides practical support, training and information in the use of a range of software programs designed to assist qualitative data analysis, and has links to all the manufacturers' websites (www.surrey.ac.uk/sociol ogy/research/researchcentres/caqdas/index.htm).

As I said above, QSR is the publisher of NVivo and on their website you will find links to lots of help material. For example, there are the Getting Started guides (pdfs) for both the Mac and Windows version (there are Starter, Pro and Plus editions for Windows). There are also links to the videos mentioned above and to a very useful

Forum where users can post queries about the use of the software (www.qsrinternational.com).

Other commonly used software includes:

ATLAS.ti – atlasti.com

MAXQDA – www.maxqda.com

QDA Miner – provalisresearch.com/products/qualitative-data-analysis-software/

Questions for further investigation

1. Can software help with your project's analysis? Which software will support what you need to do and which do you have access to?
2. How will you set up your data set in the software program you are using? What are the main groups of documents? What are the cases? What initial, *a priori* codes will you use?
3. How can you use the software to ensure that your analysis is of high quality and any conclusions you draw from it are justified?
4. If you are working in a team, how will you organise the analytic work? Will you share the coding and, if so, how will you compare and combine the coding you have done?

Suggested further reading

Bazeley, P. and Jackson, K. (2013) *Qualitative Data Analysis with NVivo*, 2nd edn. London: Sage. This works through all the stages of undertaking an analysis using one program, NVivo. There are detailed instructions on how to use the software at each step of your research.

Lewins, A. and Silver, C. (2014) *Using Software in Qualitative Research: A Step-by-Step Guide*, 2nd edn. London: Sage. Written by two experts from the CAQDAS Networking Project, this covers in detail the three most popular programs (NVivo, MAXQDA and ATLAS.ti) as well as some discussion of other programs (such as Transana, QDA Miner and Dedoose). There is good advice on how to choose which program is right for your analysis and how to set up and use the programs for your project.

References

Corbin, J.M. and Strauss, A.L. (2008) *Basics of Qualitative Research: Techniques and Procedures for Developing Grounded Theory*, 3rd edn. Thousand Oaks, CA: Sage.

Fielding, N.G. and Lee, R.M. (1998) *Computer Analysis and Qualitative Research*. London: Sage.

Miles, M.B., Huberman, A.M. and Saldaña, J. (2014) *Qualitative Data Analysis: A Sourcebook of New Methods*, 2nd edn. Thousand Oaks, CA: Sage.

Statistical analysis tools

Paul Connolly

29

Introduction

The purpose of this chapter is to provide you with a brief overview of a number of software packages available for statistical analysis. Having been introduced to a wide range of statistical techniques in previous chapters, this chapter takes a much more practical look at how you would go about performing some of these techniques. To do this we will take some real data and explore how they can be analysed with four statistical software packages: Excel, IBM® SPSS Statistics software (SPSS®), Stata, and MLwiN. The data are taken from a cluster randomised controlled trial that sought to evaluate the effects of a pre-school programme on improving young children's socio-emotional development, respect for cultural diversity, and willingness to be inclusive of others.

Given the limited space available, this chapter is not intended to provide detailed guidance on how to use each of the four packages being featured. There already exist excellent introductory and advanced texts that can do this for each of these packages, and some suggested reading in this regard is provided at the end of the chapter. Rather, the purpose of this chapter is just to give you an overall sense of how researchers actually handle quantitative data, and how they go about running the types of statistical analyses covered in previous chapters. In organising the chapter around an analysis of some real data, the aim is to enable some comparisons to be made between the different software packages and their respective strengths and limitations. It is assumed that you already have some familiarity with the statistical techniques that will be used here (summary statistics, independent samples t-test, linear regression, and multilevel analysis), and if not you are encouraged to refer back to the relevant chapters that feature these techniques before continuing with this one.

The quantitative dataset

The first thing we need to do is to input our quantitative data into a file and prepare them ready for analysis. The data we will be analysing in this chapter form just a small part of a much larger cluster randomised controlled trial. The trial itself took place over a whole academic year (October 2008 to May 2009) and involved 1,081 children aged 3–4 years attending 74 pre-school settings. The settings were initially recruited to the trial and then randomly assigned either to be trained in and then undertake the pre-school programme for the year (the intervention group) or to continue with their normal activities (the control group). The programme itself – the *Media Initiative for Children Respecting Difference Programme* – is aimed at 3–4-year-olds and seeks to increase their socio-emotional understanding, respect for cultural diversity, and willingness to be inclusive of others. For this chapter we will focus on just three outcomes relating to their socio-emotional understanding, which were:

- children's ability to recognise emotions in others;
- children's ability to recognise instances of exclusion;
- children's ability to recognise how being excluded makes someone feel.

The first outcome, emotional recognition, was measured on a continuous scale with a range of 0 to 8, while the other two outcomes were simple binary measures indicating whether a child was able to demonstrate their awareness of exclusion (or of how being excluded made someone feel) or not. Data were collected through interviews with each of the children individually prior to the commencement of the programme in September 2008 and then again at the end of the programme in June 2009. More details on each of these measures, together with further information on the programme and full details of the research instrument and data collection methods, are provided in the main report of this trial that is available to download online (see Connolly et al., 2010).

The data relating to these variables had been entered into a simple Excel spreadsheet as shown in Figure 29.1. This is the typical format of a quantitative dataset and one recognised and used by nearly all statistical software packages. As can be seen, the dataset comprise an array of numbers organised into rows and columns. Each row (running horizontally) represents an individual case (in this instance a child) and each column (running vertically) represents a variable. It can be seen that, barring the first row of variable names, data for the first 25 children are visible. This is just a small fraction of the dataset, however, and it is possible in Excel to use the right-hand scrollbar to move right down the dataset to view the final 1,081st child.

In relation to the columns, it can be seen that there are nine variables in total, with the final six variables representing each child's pre-test and post-test scores for the three outcome variables described above (indicated with the suffixes '1' and '2' respectively). If you look at the numbers in each column, then you can see that they range from '0' to '8' for the two expression variables and take on the values of '0' or '1' for the exclusion and feelings variables. The first three variables in the dataset represent a child's unique identifying number, a

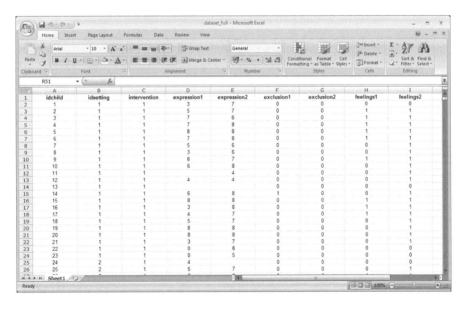

	A	B	C	D	E	F	G	H	I
1	idchild	idsetting	intervention	expression1	expression2	exclusion1	exclusion2	feelings1	feelings2
2	1	1	1	3	7	0	0	0	0
3	2	1	1	5	7	0	0	1	1
4	3	1	1	7	6	0	0	1	1
5	4	1	1	7	8	0	0	1	1
6	5	1	1	8	8	0	0	1	1
7	6	1	1	7	8	0	0	1	1
8	7	1	1	5	6	0	0	0	1
9	8	1	1	3	6	0	0	0	1
10	9	1	1	6	7	0	0	1	1
11	10	1	1	6	8	0	0	1	1
12	11	1	1		4	0	0	0	1
13	12	1	1	4	4	0	0	0	1
14	13	1	1			0	0	0	0
15	14	1	1	6	8	1	0	0	1
16	15	1	1	8	8	0	0	1	1
17	16	1	1	3	8	0	0	1	1
18	17	1	1	4	7	0	0	1	1
19	18	1	1	5	7	0	0	0	1
20	19	1	1	8	8	0	0	0	1
21	20	1	1	8	8	0	0	0	1
22	21	1	1	3	7	0	0	0	1
23	22	1	1	0	8	0	0	0	0
24	23	1	1	0	5	0	0	0	0
25	24	2	1	4		0	0	0	0
26	25	2	1	5	7	0	0	0	1

Figure 29.1 The first 25 cases of the dataset as they appear in Excel

unique identifying number for the pre-school setting they attended, and a dichotomous variable
coded '1' if that setting was part of the intervention
group and '0' if it was part of the control group. It
can also be seen that some of the individual boxes
(called 'cells') are empty, indicating that some data
are missing.[1]

By way of illustration let us take the first child in
the dataset (with the unique identifying number
'1'). It can be seen from Figure 29.1 that this child
attended setting number '1' that was, in turn, part
of the intervention group, and that his/her emotional recognition score changed from '3' at pre-test
to '7' at post-test. Interestingly, this child failed to
demonstrate recognition of an instance of exclusion or of understanding how it feels to be
excluded at pre-test, and this did not change at
post-test (with all four variables coded '0').

Statistical analysis with Excel

We have begun with Excel as this is likely to be the
software package that students are most familiar

with and the one they are also likely to have used
the most. While you may well have used it previously as a simple spreadsheet, it is easy to overlook
the fact that Excel is also capable of performing
most of the common forms of statistical analysis
that you are likely to wish to undertake for a simple
quantitative education research project. To illustrate
this, Figure 29.2 shows how Excel can be used to
perform an initial analysis of the present data.
Simply for the purposes of fitting all of the relevant
information onto one screen, I have removed all
but three of the original variables.

The first piece of analysis we can perform is to
compare the two groups of children at post-test to
see if their scores in relation to the first outcome
variable – emotional recognition – differ. As the
two groups of children have been allocated randomly then we would expect them to be broadly
similar (although we should never assume this),
and so a simple comparison of their post-test
scores should provide the first indication of
whether the programme has been more effective in
improving the children's ability to recognise emotions in comparison with what pre-schools will
have normally done.

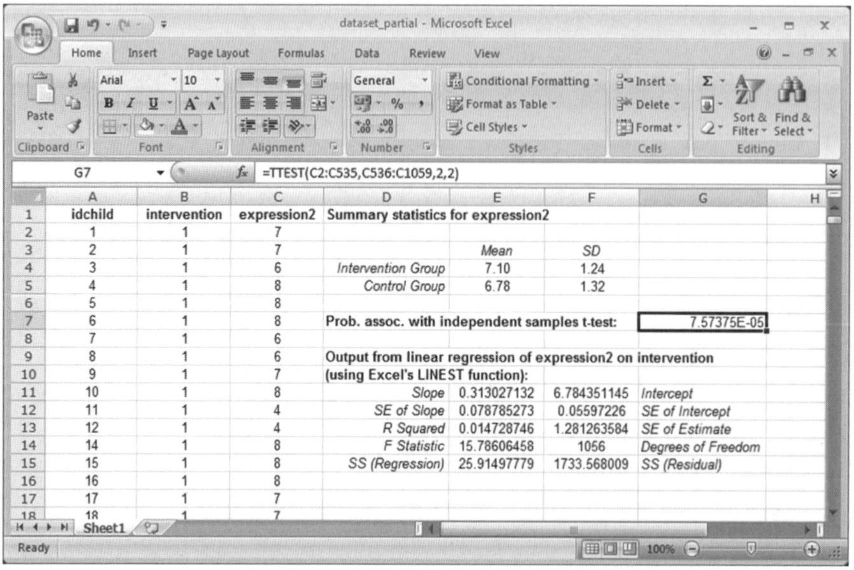

Figure 29.2   Statistical analysis in Excel

To calculate the mean post-test emotional recognition score for children in the intervention group, you begin by clicking in any empty cell (I chose cell E5), and then typing in the formula '=AVERAGE(C2:C535)' before pressing the return key. This formula tells Excel to calculate the average (in this case the mean score) for all of the numbers in cells C2 through to C535 inclusive (i.e. all of those in the intervention group) and then display the resultant score in this cell. The dataset has been sorted so that all of the children in the intervention group come first, followed by all those in the control group.

In a similar vein, the mean score for those in the control group is calculated by clicking in another cell (in this case I chose E4) and typing in the formula '=AVERAGE(C536:C1059)' and pressing return.[2]

The standard deviations associated with both these mean scores are also calculated in a similar way by clicking in empty cells (F5 and F4 respectively) and typing in the formulae 'STDEV(C2:C535)' and 'STDEV(C536:C1059)' respectively. It can be seen from Figure 29.2 that, in addition to entering these four formulae, I have also just added some text in the accompanying cells to label each of the scores generated. Also, and for completeness, I should say that I have formatted these cells (by selecting the 'Format' option from the menu above the spreadsheet) so that the figures are only reported to two decimal places.

As can be seen, at first sight there does seem to be a positive effect associated with the programme, with the children in the intervention group having a mean emotional recognition score of 7.10 (sd = 1.24) compared to 6.78 (sd = 1.32) among those in the control group. Of course there is the possibility that this difference could have occurred randomly, with the original process of random allocation possibly creating two slightly different groups of children. We can assess what evidence there is for this by conducting an independent samples t-test. To do this, we simply select any empty cell (cell G7 in my case) and type in the following formula before clicking return: '=TTEST(C2:C535,C536:C1059,2,2)' It can be seen in Figure 29.2 that as cell G7 has been selected, then the reference 'G7' appears in the window immediately above the column headers and this is followed, to the right, by the formula that has been entered into that cell.

This TTEST function returns the probability associated with an independent samples t-test that compares the mean scores of the two groups of cases 'C2:C535' and 'C536:C1059' against a two-tailed test, assuming that the variances of the two groups of cases are similar (the last two digits in the formula – '2' and '2' respectively – specify these two options). The figure that is produced, 7.57375E-05, is interpreted as 7.57375×10^{-5} or 0.0000757375. As such, with p = 0.000076 we can conclude that the difference in mean scores between the children in the intervention and control groups is highly unlikely to have occurred by chance.

Another way of conducting the same test for statistical significance is by using linear regression. This can also be undertaken in Excel by selecting ten empty available cells (organised in five rows and two columns) and entering the following formula into the top left cell of those selected: '=LINEST(C2:C1059,B2:B1059,TRUE,TRUE)'. This formula tells Excel to regress the variable found in cells 'C2:C1059' (the response or dependent variable, 'expression2' in this case) on those found in cells 'B2:B1059' (the predictor or independent variable, 'intervention' in this case), and then to display various statistics associated with the resultant model in the ten cells selected. It can be seen from Figure 29.2 that the ten cells selected in this case were E11:F15 and the formula was therefore entered into cell E11. Unfortunately, Excel simply returns the statistics without any labels. To help interpretation I have therefore typed in labels for each of the statistics produced.

For now, we shall just concern ourselves with the estimates produced through the linear regression for the intercept and slope. These, in turn, give us the following formula for a child's predicted post-test emotional recognition score, based on whether they were a member of the control or intervention group:

expression2 = 6.78435 + 0.31303*intervention

As the variable 'intervention' was coded '0' for those in the control group, we can use this formula to predict that the mean emotional recognition score for a child in the control group at post-test will be: 6.78435 + 0.31303*(0) = 6.78435, or 6.78 if we round it up to two decimal places. Similarly, as those in the intervention group were coded '1', we can use the formula to predict their mean post-test score as 6.78435 + 0.31303*(1) = 7.09738, or 7.10 if we again round this up to two decimal places. Not surprisingly, these two mean scores tally with those calculated earlier. It can be seen that the coefficient for 'intervention' (0.31303) therefore represents the average increase in a child's emotional recognition score for those in the intervention group compared to those in the control group. Unfortunately, Excel does not report whether this coefficient is significant as part of the output it produces for the LINEST function. However, this can be calculated using some of the other information provided and this would give us the same significance value of p = 0.000076.[3]

Whichever way we test the difference in mean emotional recognition scores between the intervention and control group, we thus arrive at the same result, which is that the difference is highly statistically significant. This, then, is where we can draw our first tentative conclusion based upon the logic of randomised controlled trials. In essence we can assume that if our sample is large enough then the random allocation of the children will have produced two well-matched groups who are only likely to differ due to random variation. The significance test reported above tells us that such random variation is unlikely to be the cause of the difference in the post-test scores that we have found. Thus, as the only other difference between the children is that one has participated in the Media Initiative programme for the last year while the other has not, we can therefore conclude with a degree of confidence that the higher emotional recognition scores found among those children in the intervention group must be due to the effects of the programme.

Statistical analysis with SPSS

There are, however, two limitations with the logic outlined above. The first is that the random allocation procedure may still have created two groups that are different at pre-test and so, at the very least, simply comparing post-test scores like this may give inaccurate estimates of the size of the differences found between the groups. The second is that this particular trial was actually a *cluster* randomised trial, meaning that the units of randomisation were the 74 pre-school settings rather than individual children. While this could increase the risk of producing two groups that may differ at pre-test, a more serious concern is that unless the clustered nature of the data is accounted for in the analysis then this is likely to produce findings that can be misleading (most simply, findings that may be statistically significant when they should not be).

One way to address the first issue is to control for any pre-test differences in the analysis. This can be done very simply by extending the linear regression model described above to include an additional independent variable representing the children's pre-test scores. While we can perform this analysis in Excel, we will use the opportunity to illustrate the second software package, SPSS. The main SPSS environment is shown in Figure 29.3. Ignoring the drop-down menus for the moment, it can be seen that the dataset is essentially in the same format as that for Excel. Each row represents one case and the names of the nine variables can be seen running across the top of the first nine columns. When you open SPSS for the first time, it is possible to select the option of just typing in data into the cells just as you would in Excel. However, one useful feature of SPSS is that you can import existing datasets, including those created in Excel. In addition, and in this present case, it is as easy just to select and copy all of the data in the Excel worksheet and then simply paste them into SPSS.

If you look to the bottom left of the SPSS window shown in Figure 29.3, you can see two tabs. The one currently selected is 'Data View' and this is why the data are currently being displayed in the main area of the window. However, if you selected 'Variable View' you would see a list of the variables instead. It is in Variable View where you would create or edit

the names of your variables ('idchild', 'idschool' and so on) and also where you can set labels for the particular values of a variable (i.e. in relation to 'exclusion1' we could label '0' as 'Did not recognize exclusion' and '1' as 'Recognized exclusion').

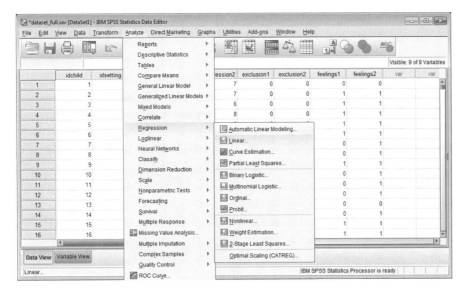

Figure 29.3 Undertaking linear regression in SPSS

(Reprint courtesy of International Business Machines Corporation, © International Business Machines Corporation)

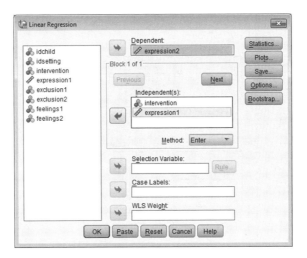

Figure 29.4 The Linear Regression window in SPSS

(Reprint courtesy of International Business Machines Corporation, © International Business Machines Corporation)

One of the benefits of SPSS over software packages like Excel is the drop-down menu system that tends to make performing statistical analysis much simpler. In relation to the present case where we wish to undertake a linear regression, it can be seen from Figure 29.3 that we just need to select 'Analyze → Regression → Linear … '. This opens up the second window shown in Figure 29.4. As can be seen, all of the variable names are listed to the left and all we need do is select the relevant variables and use the arrow buttons to move them across to the windows to the right to designate them either as dependent or independent variables. For the default model and output we then just need to click the 'OK' button and the results will appear in a separate SPSS Output Window as is shown in Figure 29.5.

As can be seen, SPSS presents the output from the linear regression in a very clear way. For the purposes of the present analysis, our main interest is the coefficients table, and particularly the unstandardised coefficient for the independent variable 'intervention' (0.453) that now represents the difference in mean scores between the control and intervention groups once any variations in the children's pre-test scores ('expression1') have been controlled for. As can be seen, this difference is now greater than the raw difference between the mean post-test scores for the two groups (which was 0.313 from the earlier analysis in Excel). Moreover, we can calculate the standardised effect size for this difference of 0.453 simply by dividing it by the standard deviation of the post-test variable 'expression2' for the sample as a whole.[4] Thus as

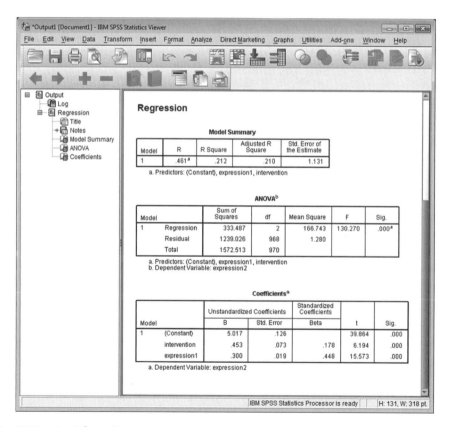

Figure 29.5 SPSS output for a linear regression

the standard deviation for the sample as a whole is 1.290 then this gives us an estimated effect size of d = 0.453/1.290 = 0.351. Hence we can use this to conclude that participating in the Media Initiative programme is likely to lead to an increase in children's emotional recognition scores by 0.351 of a standard deviation. Interestingly, had we not controlled for differences in pre-test scores then this would have resulted in an under-estimated effect size of d = 0.313/1.290 = 0.243.

Statistical analysis in Stata

Another specialist software package for statistical analysis is Stata. The main Stata environment is shown in Figure 29.6. As can be seen, the Stata environment comprises four main windows: the Variables Window (bottom left) where all of the variables included in the dataset are listed; the Command Window (bottom right) where specific commands can be entered directly; the main

Output Window (top right) where the output generated by the commands appears; and the Command Window (top left) which keeps a running record of each command. The actual dataset can be viewed by clicking on the view dataset icon (third from the right in the row of icons immediately above the four main windows). The format of the dataset is just the same as it is in Excel and SPSS, and data can either be typed directly into the separate dataset window once it is opened or copied and pasted into it. Stata also has the facility to import datasets in a variety of formats.

Just as with SPSS, Stata also has a simple to use drop-down menu system that can be used to perform statistical analyses. However, one of the strengths of Stata is its simple and intuitive command language that often makes it much quicker to run analyses by typing commands directly into the Command Window. Thus to run the simple linear regression we conducted earlier in Excel, where the variable 'expression2' was regressed on 'intervention', we simply type in the command: 'regress

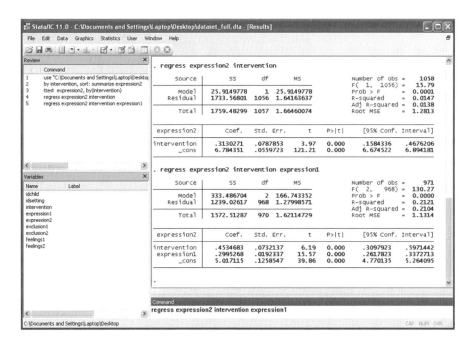

Figure 29.6 Linear regression in Stata

Source: StataCorp. 2009. Stata: Release 11. Statistical Software. College Station, TX: StataCorp LP

expression2 intervention' (i.e. the command 'regress' followed by the dependent variable and then any independent variables in the model). In a similar vein, to run the extended regression model we illustrated with SPSS we simply type in 'regress expression2 intervention expression1'. As can be seen, each of these commands appears in the Output Window followed by the relevant output. (For the interested reader, the output for both of these models can be compared with the same models generated in Excel and SPSS respectively. Fortunately, the results are all the same!)

One of the benefits of Stata over SPSS is that it is better able to handle and run a range of multilevel models. This takes us on to the second concern raised earlier regarding the simple analysis of post-test scores undertaken in Excel: the need to address the effects of clustering. One way of doing this is to run the same extended linear regression model but as a multilevel model with children (level one) nested within preschool settings (level two). The command for doing this in Stata and the resultant output are shown in Figure 29.7. It can be seen that the first part of the command is similar to

```
. xtmixed expression2 intervention expression1, || idsetting:, mle variance

Performing EM optimization:

Performing gradient-based optimization:

Iteration 0:    log likelihood = -1486.6935
Iteration 1:    log likelihood =  -1486.693
Iteration 2:    log likelihood =  -1486.693

Computing standard errors:

Mixed-effects ML regression              Number of obs      =       971
Group variable: idsetting                Number of groups   =        73

                                         Obs per group: min =         1
                                                        avg =      13.3
                                                        max =        48

                                         Wald chi2(2)       =    255.21
Log likelihood =  -1486.693              Prob > chi2        =    0.0000

------------------------------------------------------------------------------
 expression2 |     Coef.   Std. Err.     z    P>|z|    [95% Conf. Interval]
-------------+----------------------------------------------------------------
intervention |  .4323839   .1024158    4.22   0.000    .2316525    .6331152
 expression1 |  .3034466   .0192968   15.73   0.000    .2656255    .3412677
       _cons |   4.97564    .136818   36.37   0.000    4.707482    5.243798
------------------------------------------------------------------------------


------------------------------------------------------------------------------
  Random-effects Parameters  |   Estimate   Std. Err.    [95% Conf. Interval]
-----------------------------+------------------------------------------------
idsetting: Identity          |
                  var(_cons) |   .0807659   .0303175    .0386997    .1685575
-----------------------------+------------------------------------------------
               var(Residual) |   1.196758   .0562816     1.09138    1.312312
------------------------------------------------------------------------------
LR test vs. linear regression: chibar2(01) =   18.88 Prob >= chibar2 = 0.0000
```

Figure 29.7   Output of multilevel linear regression model in Stata

Source: StataCorp. 2009. Stata: Release 11. Statistical Software. College Station, TX: StataCorp LP

that for a single-level linear regression, but just starting with the command name 'xtmixed'. What follows is the name of the level two variable ('idsetting') and then, after the final comma, any options that you wish to specify (in this case we have just asked Stata to use maximum likelihood estimation, 'mle', and to report variances and covariances for the random parts of the model). It does not take long to learn the format of commands like this. However, for those new to Stata it is always possible to run the first model using the drop-down menu and then to cut and paste the resultant commands into the Command Window and adapt them when wishing to run further models.

The model reported in Figure 29.7 now represents the appropriate way of analysing a cluster randomised controlled trial as it not only controls for any pre-test differences but also properly takes into account the clustered nature of the data. As can be seen, there is a slight change in the coefficient for 'intervention' (changing from 0.453 to 0.432) and also, as expected, the standard error of this estimate has increased (from 0.073 for the single level model to 0.102 for this multilevel model). As it happens, given that the original difference was highly statistically significant then this increase in the standard error has had little effect on the findings. However, for effects that are smaller and/or that are only marginally statistically significant, then appropriately accounting for the clustering of the data in this way can change the findings notably (see Bland, 2010).

Statistical analysis with MLwiN

Finally, it is worth briefly introducing the more specialist multilevel software package MLwiN just to illustrate another type of user interface. The

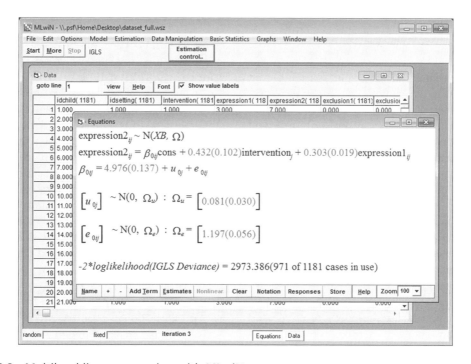

Figure 29.8   Multilevel linear regression with MLwiN

Source: Rasbash, J., Charlton, C., Browne, W. J., Healy, M. and Cameron, B. (2005) MLwiN Version 2.02. Centre for Multilevel Modelling, University of Bristol

main MLwiN environment is shown in Figure 29.8. As can be seen, MLwiN uses a windows-based system. In Figure 29.8 there are currently two windows open within the main MLwiN environment: the Data Window and the Equations Window. The former simply displays the dataset in exactly the same format as with the other software packages covered in this chapter. This is the window that one would open to type in data directly and/or copy and paste data. There is also a separate Names Window (similar to the Variable View feature in SPSS) which includes a list of variables in the dataset and that can be used to rename variables and assign labels to particular values within variables.

Perhaps the most notable difference between MLwiN and the other packages featured in this chapter is the Equations Window. This is, in essence, where the statistical models are generated and then estimated. When this window is first opened it simply has the following information:

$$y \sim \mathrm{N}(XB, \Omega)$$

$$y = \beta_0 x_0$$

This is the default starting point based on an assumption that the response variable, y, is normally distributed. If the variable follows a different distribution (i.e. binomial or poisson) then you simply click anywhere on 'N(XB, Ω)' and a pop-up window appears allowing you to set a different distribution ('binomial', for example, if you wished to undertake a logistic regression). The model is then built up in a similar interactive way. Thus to set the response variable you simply click on 'y' and a pop-up window opens that allows you to select the variable you require from a list of all variables in the dataset. It also asks you to specify how many levels are in the model and which variables represent which levels (in our case there are two levels with 'idchild' representing level one and 'idsetting' representing level two). You then build up the right-hand side of the model in the same way. You can click on the 'Add Term' button at the bottom of the Equations Window to add additional new terms and then clicking on each term will

open a pop-up menu to allow you to select which variable you wish to include.

As you build the model in the first instance each term will be preceded by the numbers '1.000(1.000)' that will appear in blue. These represent the estimated coefficient and associated standard error for that term. When they are coloured blue this indicates that the model has yet to be estimated. Once the model has been built up as required the last step in the process is to run the algorithm to estimate the model parameters and this is done by clicking the 'Start' button at the top of the main MLwiN Window. Once the model has been estimated, all of the parameters turn green in colour. Figure 29.8 illustrates this by showing the estimated multilevel model that we generated earlier in Stata. You can compare the parameters estimated here with those in the same model estimated with Stata. Reassuringly the figures are once more all the same!

Conclusion

Given the limits of space it has only been possible to provide the very briefest of overviews of software packages that can be used to undertake statistical analysis. As has been seen, at the heart of all of the packages featured here is the dataset, which takes the same format each time of individual cases organised into rows and variables into columns. Once you have a dataset ready to analyse you are faced with the decision of which statistical software package to use. In this chapter we have looked at four of them – Excel, SPSS, Stata and MLwiN – and shown that each has its particular strengths and limitations. Perhaps the main strength of Excel is its wide availability and the likelihood that many people reading this book will already have it on their laptop or PC, or have something very similar (like 'Numbers' for Macs). As shown in this chapter, for simple statistical analysis it has much to commend it. However, if you are planning to undertake a fair amount of statistical analysis, and/or analysis that is more advanced, then a dedicated statistics software package with a simple graphical user interface like SPSS or Stata (or other packages such as Minitab) will be more appropriate. Given the types of analysis most students in education are likely to perform – such as standard hypothesis testing and common multivariate techniques such as multiple regression, factor analysis and cluster analysis – then there is little to distinguish between packages like these. However, it is also likely that there will be occasions when some students may need to supplement one of these generic statistics packages should they wish to undertake more specialist statistical analysis. While Stata can handle much multilevel modelling, it is arguably the case that more specialist multilevel modelling packages such as MLwiN and HLM have a greater degree of flexibility and range of options available. Moreover, there are also specialist statistics packages for other advanced statistics techniques, such as Amos or Lisrel for structural equation modelling.

If you are a student you are likely to already have access through your university or college to a particular software package. However, and if not, perhaps the main advice is for you to 'shop around' and try out some of these packages for yourself to see what suits your own style and requirements the most. Fortunately, trial versions of most of the statistics packages available can be downloaded free of charge in order for you to try these for yourself. Prior to doing this, you should consult some of the many reference books out there that will provide you with a practical orientation to the software you are interested in trying out, whether that be Excel (Schmuller, 2013), SPSS (Muijs, 2011; Field, 2013) or Stata (Kohler and Kreuter, 2012; Acock, 2016). For MLwiN there is a dedicated website (www.cmm.bristol.ac.uk) where a trial version of the package can be downloaded and also where the User Manual is available for free, as well as a wide range of online resources provided to guide you through your first analyses with MLwiN. Also, and especially if you do not have access to a software package through your college or university, it is worth considering R, which is an open source, and thus a free, statistical software package that can be downloaded directly from the web (see www.r-project.org). Whilst there is a fairly steep learning curve in relation to using the main software package as it

requires the use of commands and thus knowledge of R commands, there now exist several plug-ins that are also freely available to download that provide much more user-friendly graphical user interfaces to run R (see, for example, RStudio, Deducer or R Commander).

Questions for further investigation

1. Try using the statistics software packages mentioned above (Excel, SPSS, Stata, etc.). Which do you find easiest to use, and for what purposes? List the pros and cons of each package.

Notes

1. While there are various options available in relation to how best to deal with missing data like these, including inputting values, these are beyond the scope of this present chapter. As such, and for the purposes of the analyses to follow, all missing data are simply left as they are.

2. You may have noticed that there are now just 1,058 cases whereas the original sample comprises 1,081 children. The reason for this is that I have deleted all cases where there is a missing value for the variable 'expression2'. If you compare Figures 29.1 and 29.2, for example, you will see that child '13' has been deleted. It is not necessary to do this before using the AVERAGE function in Excel; however, it is necessary before the LINEST function can be used that will be discussed shortly.

3. In this case, the test statistic for calculating the significance of the slope term is calculated by dividing the value of the slope by its standard error, which is 0.07879 in this case as shown in Figure 29.2. The test statistic, t, is therefore $0.31303/0.07879 = 3.973$. This, in turn, can then be used to calculate the probability associated with this statistic for 1,056 degrees of freedom which is $p = 0.000076$.

4. This effect size measure is Cohen's d that represents the difference between two mean scores divided by their pooled standard deviation.

Suggested further reading

Field, A. (2013) *Discovering Statistics Using IBM SPSS Statistics*, 4th edn. London: Sage. This text provides comprehensive illustrated step-by-step guides showing how to use SPSS, with plenty of exercises to encourage the reader to practise and consolidate their new skills.

Schmuller, J. (2013) *Statistical Analysis with Excel for Dummies*, 3rd edn. Hoboken, NJ: Wiley. This book makes it easy to crunch numbers and interpret statistics with Excel – information that will help readers improve their performance on the job or in the classroom.

References

Acock, A.C. (2016) *A Gentle Introduction to Stata*, 5th edn. College Station, TX: Stata.

Bland, J.M. (2010) 'Analysing cluster randomized controlled trials in education', *Effective Education*, 2: 165–80.

Connolly, P., Miller, S. and Eakin, A. (2010) *A Cluster Randomised Trial Evaluation of the Media Initiative for Children: Respecting Difference Programme*. Belfast: Centre for Effective Education, Queen's University Belfast. Available at: www.paulconnolly.net/publications/ (accessed 6 July 2016).

Field, A. (2013) *Discovering Statistics Using IBM SPSS Statistics*, 4th edn. London: Sage.

Kohler, U. and Kreuter, F. (2012) *Data Analysis Using Stata*, 3rd edn. College Station, TX: Stata.

Muijs, D. (2011) *Doing Quantitative Research in Education with SPSS*, 2nd edn. London: Sage.

Rasbash, J., Steele, F., Browne, W.J. and Goldstein, H. (2012) 'A User's Guide to MLwiN', Centre for Multilevel Modelling, University of Bristol.

Schmuller, J. (2013) *Statistical Analysis with Excel for Dummies*, 3rd edn. Hoboken, NJ: Wiley.

Discourse analysis

Elaine Vaughan

30

Introduction

As McCarthy et al. (2002: 55) so succinctly put it, 'Life is a constant flow of discourse – of language functioning in one of the many contexts that together make up a culture'. In an obvious, though nevertheless taken-for-granted, way, language is intrinsic to the creation and maintenance of the institutions and practices that we may wish to investigate as educational researchers; hence the importance of discourse analysis, and its critical contribution to our analytical toolkit. But discourse analysis is a teeming field as anyone who has attempted a literature search on the topic will attest (Taylor, 2001: 10). It is made up of a variety of disciplinary fields, all of which take a specific view of what *discourse* and *discourse analysis* means. In this chapter, an overview of the provenance of what has come to be termed 'discourse analysis' will be outlined. As it is not possible to deal with all of these in detail, a selection of fields, their theoretical backgrounds and methodological concerns will be discussed. Research methods are rarely, if ever, independent of some epistemological stance (Gee, 2014), and so this direction is taken in order to illustrate how the findings a researcher might arrive at by using a particular discourse analytic approach are inextricably linked to the theory that underlies their method.

If we start with what is meant by the term *discourse analysis,* we will find that it has been defined in textually as well as soically orientated terms (Paltridge, 2012). For Stubbs (1983: 1) discourse analysis refers to the study of ' … the organisation of language above the sentence'; Brown and Yule (1983: 1) see the analysis of discourse as ' … necessarily, the analysis of language in use', while for Fairclough (1992: 28), discourse itself is ' … more than just language use: it is language use, whether speech or writing, seen as a type of social practice'. Schiffrin (1994: viii) provides a useful way of conceptualising what discourse analysis is about in her identification of some of the questions that discourse analysts, whatever their disciplinary origin or theoretical bent, attempt to answer: 'How do we organise language into units that are larger than the sentence? How do we use language to convey information about the world, ourselves, and our social relationships?' Jaworski and Coupland (2014: 3) state that the reason that discourse 'falls squarely within the interests not only of linguists, literary critics, critical theorists and communication scientists, but also of geographers, philosophers, political scientists, sociologists, anthropologists, social psychologists and many others' (we might add here 'and educational researchers') is because 'despite important differences of emphasis, discourse is an inescapably important concept for understanding society and human responses to it, as well as for understanding language itself'. Therefore, for linguists and those interested in how language works, and for those whose research agenda foregrounds how language is implicated in social processes, discourse analytic methods are relevant.

Approaches to discourse analysis

As previously mentioned, the ways in which discourse is conceptualised and studied have emerged from the theoretical viewpoint of many different disciplines, and though the approaches that have spread tentacle-like from these disciplines may differ, they are united in that now, on the whole, they prioritise naturally occurring language, as opposed to abstract formulations. The fact that there is such a range of theoretical stances on discourse, situated in sometimes quite distinct perspectives which influence how discourse is defined, viewed and analysed, raises a very practical issue for the researcher: it can be difficult to ascertain *where* in the discourse analytic literature to start. As Gee has pointed out, just as discourse analysis has no single body of content, there is also no theory that can be said to be 'universally right or universally applicable' (2014: 1–2). In addition, different approaches sometimes reach similar conclusions though using different tools and terminologies connected to different 'microcommunities' of researchers' (ibid.) There is a lot to be said, in fact, for taking an eclectic approach to discourse-based analysis (see Cole and Zuengler (eds) 2008, for example, for educational settings). Eggins and Slade (1997: 24) present a useful schematic which positions their own eclectic approach to the analysis of casual conversation in relation to the theoretical origins of each discourse analytic approach they consider relevant to it, and this contributes to creating a coherent picture of discourse-focused research studies and the theoretical foundations they are built on (see also McCarthy et al., 2002: 60). Briefly then, and in very broad strokes, they describe the field of discourse analysis as being populated by work in:

- ethnomethodology (Garfinkel, 1967), a movement within the discipline of sociology, via *conversation analysis* (dealt with in more detail below);
- sociology and anthropology, via *interactional sociolinguistics* (concerned generally with how language is affected by the social context in which it takes place) and *variation theory* (which in its early stages, for example, was characterised by work which focused on the relationship between social and geographical factors and phonological patterns, e.g. Labov, 1972);
- the philosophy of language, via *Speech Act Theory* (which centres around the fact that we can 'do' things with words, like apologise, criticise or compliment) and *pragmatics* (a branch of analysis interested in the relationship between what is said and what is meant);
- linguistics, via structural-functional approaches to the analysis of language, such as the Birmingham School (see below for a more detailed view) and a research agenda which has come to be known as Critical Discourse Analysis, now quite distinct from, but originating in, critical linguistics.

For a more detailed and comprehensive overview of each of these discourse analytic areas, see the suggested readings at the end of this chapter, and overviews in Gee and Handford (eds) (2012), Hyland and Paltridge (2012), Jaworski and Coupland (2014), and Schiffrin et al. (2015); for an excellent guide which situates discourse analysis for language teachers, see McCarthy (1991). The areas that will be discussed in greater detail here, along with a focus on how discourse is approached theoretically and methodologically, and in terms of data collection and analysis, are Birmingham School discourse analysis and conversation analysis. This selection of approaches may seem quite random; however, one of the critical touchstones for any researcher seeking to explore discourse analysis in relation to educational research is Sinclair and Coulthard's pioneering (1975) work on discourse structures in the classroom (this approach is frequently glossed as the Birmingham School of discourse analysis, the driving force having been a group of researchers at the University of Birmingham). Conversation analysis has contributed enormously to what has been described as 'institutional talk', what any educational researcher will be dealing with as data may well be broadly categorised thus. The overview that follows presents canonical work in discourse analysis, provides samples of naturally occurring discourse in specific educational contexts, and suggests further reading to guide educational researchers entering the field of discourse analysis.

Birmingham School

In 1975, Sinclair and Coulthard published a seminal paper describing a structural approach to the description of classroom discourse (Sinclair and Coulthard, 1975). The aim of this work was to investigate the structure of verbal interaction in the classroom and, crucially, anchor it to the discipline of linguistics (Coulthard, 1985: 120). The data they analysed were from traditional teacher-fronted, primary-level lessons in England, with the teacher asking 'display' questions (i.e. questions to which they know the answer) and the pupils answering those questions when nominated by the teacher. Below is an extract typical of the data they analysed (Extract 1):

Extract 1

T = Teacher; P = any pupil who answers

> **T:** Now then. I've got some things here too. Hands up. <u>What's that? What is it?</u>
> **P:** <u>Saw.</u>
> **T:** <u>It's a saw. Yes this is a saw.</u> What do we do with a saw?
> **P:** Cut wood.
> **T:** Yes, you're shouting though. <u>What do we do with a saw? Marvelette?</u>
> **P:** <u>Cut wood.</u>
> **T:** <u>We cut wood</u>.

> (Sinclair and Coulthard, 1975: 93–4)

The boundary of the lesson is realised in 'Now then' and these boundaries are categorised within a larger category of *transactions*. Sinclair and Coulthard called the question-answer-feedback sequences (underlined in the extract) *exchanges*. These exchanges are made up of different *moves* – a

questioning move, an answering move and a feedback move. Finally, within these moves, we can see individual actions, such as the nomination of a student to answer a question, or an instruction to the students to raise their hands, even an admonishment to the pupil who shouts their answer – these they classified as *acts*. The status and relationship of moves and acts in discourse are very similar to that of words and morphemes in grammar (Coulthard, 1985: 125) 'whereby words combine to make groups, groups combine to make clauses and clauses combine to make sentences' (Hoey, 1993: 115). In this respect, Sinclair and Coulthard draw heavily on the early descriptive work of Halliday (1961; the Hallidayan approach to discourse has been very influential, and is strongly connected to an approach to discourse analysis termed *Systemic-Functional Linguistics*). This is very clearly evidenced in the model they developed to describe how smaller units combine with other units of the same size to form larger units; *lesson* is at the 'top' of their rank-scale model for classroom discourse. In descending order of size, their analytical units are *transaction*, *exchange*, *move* and *act: acts* combine to form *moves* which in turn combine to form *exchanges*, and so on.

Sinclair and Coulthard see the exchange as the heart of classroom discourse (Hoey, 1993: 116). A three-move structure was proposed for exchanges – *Initiation*, *Response* and *Feedback* (IRF). They posited that all exchanges will feature Initiation and Response but not necessarily Feedback, later glossed as *Follow-up*. As Hoey observes (1993: 118), 'Feedback is uncommon in some interactive genres, while in others, like classroom discourse and quiz shows, it is virtually compulsory'. Sinclair and Coulthard distinguish between free and bound exchanges and teaching and boundary exchanges, which mark the boundaries of the major sections of the lesson. Stubbs (1983: 146) suggests that Sinclair and Coulthard's model is most suited to what he calls 'relatively formal situations in which a central aim is to formulate and transmit pieces of information', and so is suitable when analysing the structure of classroom discourse, a doctor–patient interaction or service encounters (such as the interaction which occurs when we buy something in a shop or go to a hairdresser's, etc.). Casual conversation, however, does not necessarily lend itself to this type of analysis, given that its general aim could be said to be 'a phatic or social one rather than the transmission of information' (Clancy, 2004: 138). Stubbs (1983) and Hoey (1991 and 1993) have adapted Sinclair and Coulthard's model in order to analyse conversation in more informal settings. What they suggest is that exchange structure in everyday, naturally occurring spoken discourse is more complicated than the simple three-part exchange of Initiation–Response–Feedback. Hoey (1991: 74) states that:

> Just as most naturally occurring sentences are complex, that is, constructed out of one or more clause, so also most naturally occurring exchanges are complex – the result of combining two or more simple exchanges. The simple exchange is characterised by having a single initiation and response, while complex exchanges have one or more of each.

Hoey claims that speakers combine exchanges and in doing so make discourse more complex and flexible. The example from a study of family discourse (Clancy, 2004: 139) given in Extract 2 illustrates this complexity. In this extract, two family members, Susan and Tom, are discussing whether or not you can use a steam cleaner to clean a car.

Extract 2

S = Susan; T = Tom

T: Handy now if you had a what d'you ma call it? You know if you got a second *Initiation* hand car or anything like that.

S: You're not supposed to be able to use it on a car on the outside of a car. *Response*

T: I mean on the inside of it. *Feedback treated as Initiation*

S: Oh yeah. It'd | it would clean the inside of a car no bother. But it's supposed *Response* to be too hot for the outside of a car.

Here, *Feedback* is treated as *Initiation* in that the listener treats the *Feedback* as if a new exchange has been started. The discrepancy between the ad hoc nature of this tiny sliver of casual conversation and the excerpt from Sinclair and Coulthard's data is conspicuous. As Walsh (2006: 47) points out there is, furthermore, a major discrepancy between the context of the 1960s' primary school classroom and the contemporary, in Walsh's context, language classroom, which displays far more 'equity and partnership in the teaching-learning process' (2006: 47). Despite the fact that it has been shown to be perhaps too rigid for modern classroom discourse, Sinclair and Coulthard's model still has resonance for discourse analysts looking at interaction in classrooms. Their theorising of the components of the exchange has been highly influential, and no discussion of discourse analysis, particularly as it relates to educational discourse, would be complete without it.

Conversation analysis

Conversation analysis (CA) has its theoretical roots in ethnomethodology, which itself is a hybrid research approach. The originator of the approach, sociologist Harold Garfinkel, modelled this hybrid label after existing terms in research concerned with cross-cultural analyses of 'doing' and 'knowing'. Essentially, it presupposes people have a reserve of common-sense knowledge regarding their activities and how those activities are organised within enterprises. It is this fundamental reserve which makes the knowledge orderable. Ethnomethodological research is thus concerned with revealing what it is that we know. Another suggestion within this area is that 'knowledge is neither autonomous nor decontextualised; rather, knowledge and action are deeply linked and mutually constitutive' (Schiffrin, 1994: 233). Furthermore, participants continuously engage in interpretive activity, negotiating and creating knowledge during the course of their social action; this action and interaction in turn generate the knowledge by which further activity can be created and sustained. Therefore, 'social action not only displays knowledge, it is also critical to the creation of knowledge' (Schiffrin, 1994: 233).

These precepts were then applied specifically to conversation, most significantly by Harvey Sacks, Emmanuel Schegloff and Gail Jefferson. To connect the principal ideological tenets of ethnomethodology and CA, let us assume that our knowledge manifests itself publicly in our utterances. These utterances are designed to occur in particular sequential orders and in particular ways depending on social contexts. Here, CA and ethnomethodology converge: conversation is how our sense of the world in general, and social order in particular, are both constructed and negotiated – we create our world with words. CA at this point diverges in its theoretical construction of underlying 'patterns' of conversation and its methods of analysis. It employs its own esoteric transcriptions, and notation of relevant features and ' … its broader provenance extends to … the disposition of the body in gesture, posture, facial expression, and ongoing activities in the setting … ' (Schegloff, 2002: 3).

Its catholic concerns mean there is much to interest the discourse analyst. Where it is most obviously at variance with other methods of discourse analysis is in the fact that it has been wary of linguistic categorisation, namely in the categorisation of the linguistic function of specific items or phrases, believing categorisations may be over-generalised, indeed may not at all reflect the actual uses of the items or phrases. Conversation analysts also avoid making generalisations about what interactants (or participants) 'know', and contest social 'identity' as necessarily a factor, insofar as 'social identity' is a problematic construct; more cautiously again, as Schegloff (1987: 219) asserts, ' … the fact that they [social interactants] are "in fact" respectively a doctor and a patient does not make these characterisations *ipso facto* relevant'.

Heritage (1984: 241) lists three assumptions of CA:

- Interaction is structurally organised.
- Contributions to interaction are contextually oriented.
- These two properties inhere in the details of interaction so that no order of detail can be dismissed a priori as disorderly, accidental or irrelevant.

What is said constitutes not only data for analysis but also the basis of the development of hypotheses and conclusions for CA as a discipline. CA believes that interaction (conversational or otherwise) is 'structurally organised'. It articulates this *structure* through the isolation and analysis of certain features of conversation, for example, adjacency pairs. Schegloff and Sacks' (1973: 295–6) work on adjacency pairs defines them as two-part sequences, ordered as first part and second part. The presence of a first part requires the corollary presence of a second part, or one of an appropriate range of second parts. In other words, the first part of a pair *predicts* the occurrence of the second: 'Given a question, regularly enough an answer will follow' (Sacks, 1967, cited in Coulthard, 1985: 69). Adjacency pairs are integral to the turn-taking system in conversation (discussed below) and the absence of a second part is noticeable in conversation, if only for practical reasons (an unanswered question may stall the development of the conversation). Further work in analysing adjacency pairs (Atkinson and Drew, 1979; Levinson, 1983; Pomerantz, 1984) has developed the notion of preferred and dispreferred second parts. For example, an invitation first part 'prefers' an acceptance second part, as opposed to a refusal (even when this refusal is not a 'flat' refusal but tempered with an 'account' of the refusal). Hoey (1993) has also mentioned 'adjacency pairs' such as 'hi/hi' and 'how are you/ fine' and defines them as 'frozen exchanges' – there is no need to actively process this type of interaction, though they are necessary procedural preambles to the development of the exchange (see the section above for more on exchange structure analysis).

The most fundamental aspects of the *organisation* of conversation are, according to Schegloff (2002: 4–5):

(a) turn-taking (the organisation of participation);
(b) turn organisation (forming talk so that it is recognisable as a unit of participation);
(c) action formation (forming talk so that it accomplishes one or more recognisable actions);

(d) sequence organisation (deploying resources for making contributions cohere, for example, topically);

(e) organisation of repair (dealing practically with problems in interaction, for example problems in hearing and/or understanding);

(f) word/usage selection (selection, usage and understanding of words used to compose the interaction);

(g) recipient design (all of the above as they relate to our co-participants in talk-in-interaction).

To extrapolate from these, the turn-taking system is of immediate concern to any analysis of talk in general, and of course institutional talk in particular. CA attempts to explain how participants in talk decide who talks, how the flow of conversation is maintained, and how gaps and overlaps are avoided. It has posited ' … a basic set of rules governing turn construction, providing for the allocation of a next turn to one party, and co-ordinating transfer so as to minimise gap and overlap' (Sacks et al., 1974: 12). A full discussion of these rules is not possible here. Probably the most salient aspect of the discussion of these turn-taking rules ('taking' in its literal sense) is the ability of participants to identify and seize upon 'transition-relevance places' (i.e. points in the interaction where it is possible and/or appropriate to take or resume a turn so that the interaction runs smoothly).

Another of the above aspects that is particularly interesting is the idea of recipient design – the design of utterances or turns with a view to our co-participants. Tannen and Wallat, for example, have studied how a paediatrician selects and switches between different linguistic registers according to whether she is addressing the mother or the child during the consultation (Tannen and Wallat, 1987, cited in Drew and Heritage, 1992: 9). In institutional talk, recipient design may not only be an asymmetrical phenomenon (where we, consciously or unconsciously, consider what the effect of our contributions on our superiors will be), but also of consideration in maintaining and enhancing our institutional and social profiles with regard to our colleagues. In terms of institutional talk, Heritage (2004: 225) suggests a number of dimensions of

analysis that can reveal the 'fingerprint' (cf. Heritage and Greatbatch, 1991: 95–6) of the institutional situation under analysis. These are:

- its turn-taking system;
- the overall structure of the interaction;
- sequence organisation;
- turn design;
- lexical choice; and
- epistemological and other forms of asymmetry.

As an example of how CA-type analysis can be applied to real data, consider this extract from a staff meeting in the English language department of a public university. The meeting is drawing to a close, and the chair of the meeting is Peter, the head of department. Rita, Olivia, Harry and Julia are teachers in the department who are present at the meeting.

Extract 3

[Note: <$O> marks the beginning of an overlapped utterance; <\$O> marks the end of an overlapped utterance]

(1) **Peter: I'm teaching this after** I'll write that down chapter four done. Eh I think maybe should we

I think we should meet maybe a little bit regularly. <$O1> When could we meet again? <\$O1>. **Is a weekly meeting maybe a little bit too maybe once a fortnight at least?**

(2) **Rita:** <$O1> I think that would be a good idea. <\$O1>.

(3) **Olivia:** Yeah. Once a fortnight.

(4) **Peter:** Once a fortnight **okay.**

(5) **Harry:** Yeah we should try to start preparing for that PET exam like we need.

(6) **Julia:** We need to get all the resources.

(7) **Peter:** And resources for that as well. **Okay.**

(8) **Rita: Okay. Thank you.**

(Vaughan, 2009)

We can note a number of features of this closing phase. From the point that we pick up the interaction, there are eight turns which accomplish the closing of the meeting. Researchers have identified making arrangements as one of the sequence types regularly used to move out of closings along with back-references, topic initial elicitors (e.g. *yeah, okay*), in-conversation objects (e.g. minimal response tokens), solicitudes (*drive carefully, take care*), re-iterating the reason for a phone call and appreciations (*thank you*). At the end of the meeting, Peter (the head of department) moves to close by making an arrangement for the next meeting (*when could we meet again? Is a weekly meeting maybe a little bit too maybe once a fortnight at least?*). When two of the participants answer his question – Rita (3) and Olivia (4) – Peter summarises the response and this is bounded by *okay* suggesting a final turn. Harry, however, initiates a new topic (6) and this is supported by Julia (7); Peter moves to shut this topic down fairly decisively by summarising it and again bounding the move with *okay*. The meeting closes when Rita echoes the boundary marker and thanks Peter. The hierarchical, institutional nature of the talk is evident in the way that Peter, as head of department, takes control of the closing phase of the meeting (for more on meetings as interactional events and phases within them, see Bargiela-Chiappini and Harris, 1997). The relationship between language and power, both at the micro- and macro-level, is very much a concern of Critical Discourse Analysis (see for example Fairclough, 2010; for an extensive overview of Critical Discourse Analysis in educational research see Rogers, 2011).

Discourse analysis and teacher language: data and analysis

Turning our attention briefly to research on the topic of how teachers use language is helpful in terms of conceptualising what type of research is being done, how discourse analytic data are collected and analysed, and the ethical concerns that are implicated in accessing and using this type of data. Frequently, discourse analysis is categorised as an exclusively qualitative method, however

this is not always the case (as will be seen below). In addition, this sphere of research highlights how central understanding teacher language is in connection to how classrooms work, and how the profession considers its practices within them reflexively. Walsh (2006), in relation to English language teaching, suggests that teachers' classroom language is characterised in the following ways:

- Teachers control patterns of communication in the classroom.
- The classroom is dominated by question-and-answer routines.
- 'Repair' or correction of learner errors is a prerogative of the teacher.
- Teachers typically modify their speech to accommodate learners.

Walsh's own research proposes a framework (Self-Evaluation of Teacher Talk, or SETT) to aid teachers in their description of language used in this classroom context and as a conduit for understanding the complex interactional processes that occur within it (Walsh, 2006: 62–92). SETT is a very useful framework for educators with an interest in researching teacher language in the classroom context. Walsh's focus is second language teaching and learning contexts, although as a robust framework for reflecting on classroom interaction it is adaptable to other classroom contexts (see also Walsh, 2013 in the further reading suggestions at the end of this chapter).

More findings from the field of language teacher education (LTE) are also illuminating in terms of the professional concerns of language teachers. In the initial stages of LTE, the development of trainees' language awareness is obviously a priority. Trappes-Lomax and Ferguson (2002) highlight practical concerns in language education for trainees, such as meta-linguistic awareness, target language proficiency, and pedagogical skills with regard to teaching language. While these concerns take centre stage, concepts such as language as a social institution, as verbal and reflexive practice and its position as the medium of classroom communication are considered neglected, though essential, aspects of teachers' language awareness. An example of the extent to which trainee teachers are required to be reflexive in their awareness of language and its use in the classroom is evident in Extract 4, which is taken from Farr's (2005) analyses of trainer–trainee interaction in LTE in the Irish context (see also Farr, 2010).

Extract 4

Tr = Trainer; Tee = Trainee

Tr:　… now one area that I want you to try a difficult area to work on+

Tee:　My voice is it? I noticed.

Tr:　The sounds you know the pronunciation of the T H sounds+

Tee:　Mmhm.

Tr:　+ah don't don't do you ever use them correctly? You're from Cork are you?

Tee:　Killarney.

Tr:　Killarney.

(Farr, 2005: 198)

The discourse of teacher training has huge potential as a route for investigation in educational research. Farr's work is focused on a specific event, feedback meetings on trainees' observed classes, an event within the initial training of teachers which is inherently face-threatening (Reppen and Vásquez, 2007: 16). This is manifestly evident in the extract from Farr's data above: here the trainer is required to criticise the trainee's regional accent and contrast it with the 'correct' pronunciation they should be modelling for their students. Also in the teacher-training context, Vásquez and Reppen (2007) report on collecting recordings of post-observation meetings. Both researchers were teaching on an MA in TESL (Teaching English as a Second Language) as part of which students gain practical teaching experience. The post-observation meetings conducted by them, as supervisors, were intended to engender a reflective rather than evaluative model of feedback, and so as supervisors/mentors they wished to

create an open, discursive space to facilitate this (Vásquez and Reppen, 2007: 159). However, an analysis of the participation patterns in the meetings indicated that, in fact, the supervisors/mentors did more of the talking than the trainees. This empirical insight led to an actual change in practices for the supervisors/mentors involved. They increased the number of questions they asked the trainees, and thus they were able to turn the floor over to the trainees by creating more effective discursive conditions for reflection.

All discourse analysts use texts – whether spoken or written. Many of the spoken texts have been, in the past, transcriptions of interviews or more naturally occurring events and interactions. The act of transcribing these spoken interactions represents the final stage in data collection for analysts, the initial stages being the negotiation of access to the situation that will yield the desired spoken data and obtaining consent to record from potential participants. All academic institutions will have their own ethical guidelines and procedures, but the fundamentals of ethical access to and use of data require that participants are guaranteed anonymity – in transcribing the event participants should naturally be given pseudonyms; however, any other references within the transcript that could potentially identify the speakers should also be removed, such as institutional names, geographical references and so on. Transcription itself is, as Roberts (2016) points out, a great deal more and a great deal less than talk written down. The way in which an event is transcribed can bias how it is read and interpreted, and any transcription represents an event that has been reduced in two ways: firstly, the recording removes it from its original context (live, online production of talk), and secondly, it is further reduced by being orthographically transcribed. In addition, transcriptions that attempt to be faithful to the original event by including pauses, hesitations, false starts, ellipses and contractions, to name but a few, run the risk of appearing 'messy' or 'incoherent'; however, as Cameron (2000: 33) argues, we frequently think transcribed talk is 'incoherent' and not communicatively efficient because the written form is our model of coherence and this is a bias we need to 'unlearn':

> Analysts of talk must work from the assumption that if communication is not breaking down in a given instance then participants must be able to make sense of it, no matter how incoherent it must seem; and if certain features recur in spoken language data, they must serve some purpose, however obscure we find it.

For example, in an investigation of the workplace meetings of English language teachers, the present author found laughter to be a frequent feature within the transcripts (Vaughan, 2007, 2008). This prompted a focus on the interactional implications of humour and laughter in the meetings in terms of when they occur and who produces them. This study, and also the studies carried out by Vásquez and Reppen, and Farr, mentioned above, share a common characteristic. They synthesise quantitative methodologies derived from the area of corpus linguistics with discourse analytic methods. As mentioned, discourse analysis has frequently been referred to as a qualitative method; however, many discourse analysts have always integrated some form of quantitative analysis to complement the qualitative insights that the data they collect yield. Corpus-based studies store the transcriptions of spoken text, or selections of written text, as text files and use specialised software such as WordSmith Tools (Scott, 2008). Previously, corpora, or 'computerised collections of authentic texts, amenable to automatic or semi-automatic processing or analysis … selected according to specific criteria in order to capture the regularities of a language, a language variety or sublanguage' (Tognini-Bonelli, 2001: 55), were by definition large, expensive to compile (particularly spoken components), and the preserve of researchers working at the level of word or clause. However, in recent times more researchers have been fruitfully using corpora

large and small to investigate discourse-level phenomena (Ädel and Reppen, 2008). For an overview of how to build spoken and written corpora, and using corpus analysis tools to retrieve information about linguistic patterns from computerised collections of texts, see O'Keeffe and McCarthy (2010). For an overview and discussion of how teachers can use corpora for their own research, see Vaughan (2010).

Discourse analysis is not, therefore, a discrete research 'tool' as such, but a label that glosses a teeming and heterogeneous field of research. What the various approaches to language now have in common is a focus on naturally occurring language-in-use. The two approaches summarised here – Birmingham School discourse analysis and conversation analysis – derive from a broadly linguistic and broadly sociological theoretical basis respectively, and the approaches produce different ways of understanding how language is organised above the sentence. While discourse analysts of the Birmingham School are interested in how language is structured according to the genre in which it occurs (owing much to the Systemic Functional Linguistics that underpins it), conversation analysts have concerned themselves much more with how speakers naturally and instinctively navigate interaction, the careful observation and consideration of which reveal an order to the ostensible chaos of conversation. Both approaches are descriptive in this way. Research into the language used in educational contexts has also been exemplified, in terms of initial teacher training, the post-observational meeting, with teachers analysing their own use of language in the classroom (Walsh's SETT approach) in addition to data from outside the classroom, e.g. teacher interaction in meetings, and teacher meetings as a site for investigating communities of practice (cf. Wenger, 1998; Vaughan, 2007, 2008).

Language is never neutral, and as researchers using language we strive to acknowledge and mitigate our biases in analysing it – it is, however, fundamental to social life and the institutions that it permeates.

Questions for further investigation

1. In the context that you are researching, what types of talk or written text are embedded in it (e.g. policy documents, textbooks, meetings, informal situations of talk within an institution)?
2. How might you 'capture' some of this spoken or written discourse? What might a sufficient sample of it be?
3. If you are recording spoken discourse, how will you present your aims to participants in order to gain consent to record? How much input will your participants have into the research? Will they have access to the transcriptions? Will you follow up with them in terms of interviews or questionnaires?
4. As you read your transcriptions/collections of written discourse, what are the first things that strike you about them? Can you identify any particular lexical items (particular words or phrases) or linguistic strategies (such as indirectness or questions) that appear to be frequent?
5. How will you code and investigate those items? When you do a literature search on the item/strategy, what tradition or approach to discourse analysis does research on this particular item seem to 'fit' into, if any?

Suggested further reading

Gee, J.P. (2014) *An Introduction to Discourse Analysis: Theory and Method*, 4th edn. London: Routledge. Gee distinguishes between Discourse ('big D Discourse') and discourse ('little d') in this introductory text – a useful distinction for newcomers to discourse analysis and its quite broad field of literature. Gee's work more generally will be of interest to educational researchers.

Van Dijk, T. (ed.) (2011) *Discourse Studies: A Multidisciplinary Introduction*, 2nd edn. London: Sage. This is a fully updated edition of the classic introductory textbook, which is designed for use by researchers new to the field of discourse analysis. It comprises contributions by leading scholars and multiple perspectives on discourse analysis. The introduction is a comprehensive overview of the history and contemporary issues in discourse analysis, and is particularly useful for situating the sheer scope of what is entailed in looking at language as discourse.

Walsh, S. (2013) *Classroom Discourse and Teacher Development*. Edinburgh: Edinburgh University Press. Walsh's work as a whole will be useful for educational researchers who wish to focus on interaction in classroom contexts. Here, Walsh also argues for an evidence-based orientation to re-energising the area of reflective practice, using interactional data sourced in classrooms with the individual research agendas of teacher-researchers at the centre of the process. Walsh argues for attending to dialogic forms of reflection and empirical interactional research to support a tangible unification of pedagogical theory and practice.

References

Ädel, A. and Reppen, R. (eds) (2008) *Corpora and Discourse: The Challenges of Different Settings*. Amsterdam: John Benjamins.

Atkinson, J. and Drew, P. (1979) *Order in Court: The Organisation of Verbal Interaction in Judicial Settings*. London: Macmillan.

Bargiela-Chiappini, F. and Harris, S. (1997) *Managing Language: The Discourse of Corporate Meetings*. Amsterdam: John Benjamins.

Brown, G. and Yule, G. (1983) *Discourse Analysis*. Cambridge: Cambridge University Press.

Cameron, D. (2000) *Working with Spoken Discourse*. London: Sage.

Clancy, B. (2004) 'The exchange system in family discourse', *Teanga*, 21: 134–50.

Cole, K. and Zuengler, J. (eds) (2008) *The Research Process in Classroom Discourse Analysis: Current Perspectives*. London: Routledge.

Coulthard, M. (1985) *An Introduction to Discourse Analysis*, 2nd edn. London: Longman.

Drew, P. and Heritage, J. (1992) *Talk at Work: Interaction in Institutional Settings*. Cambridge: Cambridge University Press.

Eggins, S. and Slade, D. (1997) *Analysing Casual Conversation*. London: Continuum.

Fairclough, N. (1992) 'Introduction', in N. Fairclough (ed.), *Critical Language Awareness*. London: Longman.

Fairclough, N. (2010) *Critical Discourse Analysis: The Critical Study of Language*. New York: Routledge.

Farr, F. (2005) 'Reflecting on Reflections: The spoken word as a professional development tool in language teacher education', in R. Hughes (ed.), *Spoken English, Applied Linguistics and TESOL: Challenges for Theory and Practice*. Hampshire: Palgrave Macmillan, pp. 182–215.

Farr, F. (2010) *The Discourse of Teaching Practice Feedback*. London: Routledge.

Garfinkel, H. (1967) *Studies in Ethnomethodology*. Englewood Cliffs, NJ: Prentice Hall.

Gee, J.P. (2014) *How to do Discourse Analysis: A Toolkit*, 2nd edn. London: Routledge.

Gee, J.P. and Handford, M. (2012) *The Routledge Handbook of Discourse Analysis*. London: Routledge.

Halliday, M.A.K. (1961) 'Categories of the theory of grammar', *Word*, 17: 241–92.

Heritage, J. (1984) *Garfinkel and Ethnomethodology*. Cambridge: Polity.

Heritage, J. (2004) 'Conversation Analysis and Institutional Talk: Analysing data', in D. Silverman (ed.), *Qualitative Research: Theory, Method and Practice*, 2nd edn. London: Sage, pp. 222–45.

Heritage, J. and Greatbatch, D. (1991) 'On the Institutional Character of Institutional Talk: The case of news interviews', in D. Boden and D.H. Zimmerman (eds), *Talk and Social Structure: Studies in Ethnomethodology and Conversation Analysis*. Cambridge: Polity, pp. 93–137.

Hoey, M. (1991) 'Some Properties of Spoken Discourses', in R. Bowers and C. Brumfit (eds), *Applied Linguistics and English Language Teaching*. London: Modern English Publications in association with the British Council, pp. 65–84.

Hoey, M. (1993) 'The Case for the Exchange Complex', in M. Hoey (ed.), *Data, Description, Discourse: Papers on the English Language in Honour of John McH Sinclair*. London: Harper-Collins, pp. 115–38.

Hyland, K. and Paltridge, B. (eds) (2012) *The Continuum Companion to Discourse Analysis*. London: Continuum.

Jaworski, A. and Coupland, N. (2014) *The Discourse Reader*, 3rd edn. London: Routledge.

Labov, W. (1972) *Sociolinguistic Patterns*. Oxford: Blackwell.

Levinson, S. (1983) *Pragmatics*. Cambridge: Cambridge University Press.

McCarthy, M. (1991) *Discourse Analysis for Language Teachers*. Cambridge: Cambridge University Press.

McCarthy, M., Matthiessen, C. and Slade, D. (2002) 'Discourse Analysis', in N. Schmitt (ed.), *An Introduction to Applied Linguistics*. New York: Arnold, pp. 55–73.

O'Keeffe, A. and McCarthy, M. (2010) *The Routledge Handbook of Corpus Linguistics*. London: Routledge.

Paltridge, B. (2012) *Discourse Analysis*, 2nd edn. London: Bloomsbury.

Pomerantz, A. (1984) 'Agreeing and Disagreeing with Assessments: Some features of preferred/dispreferred turn shapes', in J.M. Atkinson and J.C. Heritage (eds), *Structures of Social Action: Studies in Conversation Analysis*. Cambridge: Cambridge University Press, pp. 57–101.

Reppen, R. and Vásquez, C. (2007) 'Using Corpus Linguistics to Investigate the Language of Teacher Training', in J. Waliński, K. Kredens and S. Goźdź-Roszkowski (eds), *Corpora and ICT in Language Studies*, PALC 2005. Frankfurt am Main: Peter Lang, pp. 13–29.

Roberts, C. (2016) 'Issues in transcribing spoken discourse'. Available at: www.kcl.ac.uk/sspp/departments/education/research/ldc/knowledge-transfer/DATA/part1.pdf (accessed 11 May 2016).

Rogers, R. (2011) *An Introduction to Critical Discourse Analysis in Education*, 2nd edn. London: Routledge.

Sacks, H., Schegloff, E.A. and Jefferson, G. (1974) 'A simplest systematics for the organisation of turn-taking for conversation', *Language*, 50(4): 696–735.

Schegloff, E.A. (1987) 'Between Macro and Micro: Contexts and Other Connections', in J. Alexander, B. Giesen, R. Munch and N. Smelser (eds), *The Micro-Macro Link*. Berkeley and Los Angeles, CA: University of California Press, pp. 207–34.

Schegloff, E.A. (2002) 'Conversation analysis and applied linguistics', *Annual Review of Applied Linguistics*, 22: 3–31.

Schegloff, E.A. and Sacks, H. (1973) 'Opening up closings', *Semiotica*, 8(4): 289–327.

Schiffrin, D. (1994) *Approaches to Discourse*. Oxford: Blackwell.

Schiffrin, D., Tannen, D. and Hamilton, H.E. (eds) (2015) *The Handbook of Discourse Analysis*, 2nd edn. Oxford: Wiley Blackwell.

Scott, M. (2008) *WordSmith Tools Version 5*. Liverpool: Lexical Analysis Software Ltd.

Sinclair, J. McH. and Coulthard, M. (1975) *Towards an Analysis of Discourse*. Oxford: Oxford University Press.

Stubbs, M. (1983) *Discourse Analysis: The Sociolinguistic Analysis of Natural Language*. Oxford: Blackwell.

Taylor, S. (2001) 'Locating and Conducting Discourse Analytic Research', in M. Wetherell, S. Taylor and S.J. Yates (eds), *Discourse as Data*. London: Sage/Open University Press, pp. 5–48.

Tognini-Bonelli, E. (2001) *Corpus Linguistics at Work*. Amsterdam: John Benjamins.

Trappes-Lomax, H. and Ferguson, G. (2002) *Language in Language Teacher Education*. Amsterdam: John Benjamins.

Vásquez, C. and Reppen, R. (2007) 'Transforming practice: changing patterns of interaction in post-observation meetings', *Language Awareness*, 16(3): 153–72.

Vaughan, E. (2007) '"I think we should just accept our horrible lowly status": analysing teacher–teacher talk in the context of community of practice', *Language Awareness*, 16(3): 173–89.

Vaughan, E. (2008) '"Got a Date or Something?" An analysis of the role of humour and laughter in the workplace', in A. Ädel and R. Reppen (eds), *Corpora and Discourse: The Challenges of Different Settings*. Amsterdam: John Benjamins, pp. 95–115.

Vaughan, E. (2009) 'Just Say Something and We Can All Argue Then: Community and Identity in the Workplace Talk of English Language Teachers', PhD thesis, Limerick, Ireland: Mary Immaculate College, University of Limerick.

Vaughan, E. (2010) 'How Can Teachers use Corpora for their Own Research?', in A. O'Keeffe and M. McCarthy (eds), *The Routledge Handbook of Corpus Linguistics*. London: Routledge, pp. 471–84.

Walsh, S. (2006) *Investigating Classroom Discourse*. London: Routledge.

Wenger, E. (1998) *Communities of Practice: Learning, Meaning and Identity*. Cambridge: Cambridge University Press.

Media analysis

Michael Atkinson

31

Introduction

The analysis of (mass) media production, the meaning of its content and its varied effects on audiences as 'interpretive communities' (Fish, 1980) has mushroomed in popularity within the academy over the last three decades. The burgeoning interest is due, in part, to the growth and proliferation of media technology, the shrinking of cultural space between groups through ongoing globalisation processes, and the nature of everyday life within information-obsessed and consumer-driven late market capitalist societies. Quite some time ago, Stuart Hall (1980) pointed to the power of the media in constructing and disseminating social knowledge in late modern societies, commenting on how the media deliberately assemble (or, *encode*) information and then on how audiences are encouraged to receive (*decode*) the information in a narrow range of manners. Today, the media function as more than a one-way assemblage of cultural information distribution and education portals in our societies. Sociologist Pierre Bourdieu (1993) notes that the media constitute, to all intents and purposes, an 'autonomous [popular] cultural' field; endowed with the ability to entertain, provoke, distract, produce, connect, and of course educate people in unique manners.

Debates concerning the media as a primary definer or director of culture or central educator about a broad range of social issues continue (Kennedy and Hills, 2015). Media critics cite how theorists including Louis Althusser, Jean Baudrillard and Guy DeBord cleverly exposed the media's overarching, coercively ideological, and top-down impact on public behaviours and attitudes, whilst others call attention to theorists including Marshall McLuhan, Manuel Castells, Douglas Kellner, who respectively heralded the growth of 'new media' as a watershed moment in the extension of human agency and cultural self-determination. Some researchers view television, radio, popular music, print media, the Internet and other mass mediators of culture as sites of suffocating and hegemonic social reproduction, and yet others see the possibility for many cultures and ideological positions and possibilities to be represented, negotiated, contested and resisted in increasingly democratic (or at least more 'open' and accessible) media spaces. Cutting across differences of opinion regarding the social functions and impacts of the media are, nevertheless, a series of core questions or substantive concerns driving most research:

- What are people exposed to by the media (i.e. the *encoded* messages)?
- How do audiences actively interpret media content (i.e. how are interpretive communities constituted)?
- How are media messages actively used by people and when do they become incorporated into (popular) cultural practice?
- Are cultural differences and spaces eroding between groups as a result of the mass mediation of cultures in an increasing global society?

- What systems of representation, ideology or discourse dominate in the media?
- How and why are people (especially youth) producing their own media, and exploring the link between new social media and human agency?

From the outset, we must be mindful that the systematic analysis of media forms, their content and impacts is not one methodology but rather a house of interrelated techniques. Whilst researchers grant, in varying degrees and forms, baseline attention to the encoding-decoding-usage process in most active research on media, no one style of, or approach to, media analysis reigns supreme as proto-typical. There are quantitative, qualitative, historical, semiotic, structural, post-structural, feminist, critical realist, post-positivist, existential, and a full range of other ways of performing media research. Whatever the orientation, those conducting media research strive to better understand how the mass circulation of images, messages, discourses and symbols through societies creates, disrupts, reflects, reproduces, distributes and aligns collective definitions of reality (or simply, knowledge) for people. In this pursuit, media research ranges from very politically and ideologically passionate efforts to quasi-neutral and purely descriptive reports. Students often complain that media research is densely theoretical and conceptually labyrinth-like at times. Such is unfortunate, as much media research sheds considerable light on the real-world influence of media on human groups, cultural practices and social structures.

The remainder of this chapter addresses several of the most common methods employed in/as media research, and their strengths and limitations. The aim is to illustrate a cross-section of the broader panorama of media analysis methods and techniques available, and their widespread applicability to a host of substantive areas of investigation.

Conducting media analysis

Students are immediately drawn to media analysis as many of them have practised it informally for

years as voracious media consumers in their own right. However, they quickly realise that the systematic analysis of the media is much more murky, complicated and conceptually taxing than lay interpretations of the relative palatability of selected popular media content. Most research projects drawing upon media analysis commence in a relatively common manner: one determines the explicit substantive focus of the project and the parameters of the case study in question (for example, is it a project focusing on media encoding, distribution, or reception?) and then chooses representative or at least conceptually appropriate units/texts to sample. The arduous methodological trench work begins when researchers are forced to address how they will analyse media data!

Among the most straightforward media analytic designs is *manifest content analysis*. Here, the goal of the research is to examine the overt or surface-level characteristics of media texts. For example, one might be interested in studying whether patriarchal ideologies still dominate in media representations of amateur or professional sport. To investigate the question further, a researcher could sample ten years of Summer and Winter Olympic Games' television coverage in Britain as the case study data. Before analysing any of the television content, the researcher would have to decide what would be examined in the broadcasts, and how to 'count' the presence of patriarchy. One might suggest that the percentage of men's versus women's sports coverage, the gender of athletes interviewed or showcased in special stories, whether one gender is featured in more 'primetime' events than the other are all empirical indicators of patriarchal attitudes. These are easily recognised by a researcher, and could be tallied quite quickly across the broadcasts. At the end of the study, basic descriptive statistical and impressionistic analysis could be offered to conclude whether, on the surface, Olympic television broadcasts in Britain seemed to privilege men over women, potentially indicating the enduring face of patriarchy in the representation of Olympic sport. A number of studies have conducted such an analysis of patriarchy and sport media, and found vast discrepancies in the media coverage of men and women in organised sport (see Cooky et al., 2013).

Discourse analysis

Discourse analysis is a technique inspired by French structuralists including Ferdinand de Saussure, Jacques Lacan and Roland Barthes, and critical post-structuralists including Judith Butler, Julia Kritseva and Michel Foucault. Discourse analysis is not a single method, but instead a series of complementary techniques focusing on the interpretive 'reading' of a sample of media texts in order to expose the dominant *episteme* (knowledge), assumptions, ideologies or values underwriting them. Another way of describing discourse analysis is to call it the study of the 'dominant languages' or ideologies in media texts that frame how audiences are supposed to understand and use them. Hall (1980) refers to this process as the encoding of 'preferred' meanings in a text that limit alternative (or 'resistive') readings and understandings of a represented subject. For discourse analysts, the exposure of dominant discourses in texts is critically important, as those who tend to control how something is spoken about (and thus thought about and known) have immense social power to frame reality and dictate policy. Discourse analysts see mass-circulated media texts as connected through and composed by socially diffuse, what Deleuze and Guattati (1987) call 'rhizomatically' creeping, systems of language encoded with dominant ideologies. Discourse analysts assert that no media text is ever 'neutral' or outside the trappings of language or ideology. Rich and Miah's (2009) research on the medicalisation of cyberspace illustrates how governmental ideologies of self-surveillance and associated neo-liberal discourses of healthism abound on-line. Rich and Miah (2009) highlight how the Internet has become a zone for spreading dominant, conservative and self-blaming health messages, and as such, how they systematically blur and eschew the real material differences in people's access to quality, state-provided healthcare schemes and styles of healthy living. Giroux's (2014) work on discourses of neo-liberalism in stories about education cutbacks in the United States and Canada exposes how the slashing of public school budgets is largely framed by late modern, supply-side economics mantras and principles. Giroux illustrates how stories are embedded with neo-liberal understandings of the role of 'waste and fat cutting' in the school system as something positive, while obfuscating the real-world impact of the erosion of the social safety net on children's futures. To be sure, discourse analysis is the most commonly cited technique of media analysis in much of the social science and education literature today.

Narrative analysis

Narrative analysis is similar to, and yet importantly different from, discourse analysis. Narrative analysis, the examination of how stories are told through the media or a specific set of media texts, looks and feels like discourse analysis, but their respective emphases on how power is related to discourse/narrations in the media are quite different. Narrative analysis tends to focus on how and why individuals, groups, organisations, or others, choose specific language and symbols to represent something about themselves. Whereas the approach in discourse analysis tends to be rather top-down (that is, focusing how discourses wrapped in ideologies are spread throughout society by powerful or elite groups), narrative analysis tends to home in on how the media may be used to create and disseminate a wide range of cultural identities, images and opportunities for social storytelling. Gillett (2003), for example, argues that the media are a critical cultural context where gay men are able to write their social selves in empowering manners, especially in the case of telling different (i.e. non-medically pathological) stories about life with HIV/AIDS. Gillett's (2003) examination of how men narrate gay identities through magazines and websites attests to the emancipatory potential of public storytelling as a form of claims-making and knowledge production for socially marginalised communities. Gillett (2003) calls attention to how narrative work serves as a vital technique for publicly distancing gay sexualities and identities from medicalised understandings of the 'diseased' body. As the narrations show the human, mundane, emotional and 'everyday' aspects of being HIV+, different realities about being gay in society are offered.

While the techniques of media analysis listed above, by and large, emphasise how to mediate, produce or shape cultural meaning and social practices, *audience ethnography* strives to understand how people actively receive, decode and use media texts. An audience ethnography might be designed as a one-shot case study, or structured as a long-term panel study of how a group interprets media over the course of time. In the typical scenario, participants in an audience ethnographic project are asked to collectively or individually watch, read or listen to select media and then respond to their content. A researcher acts as a facilitator in these scenarios, prompting questions among respondents about what the messages or symbols in the media might mean to them and how they can actively decode them from a variety of cultural standpoints (such as, age, race, sexuality, gender, class). The underpinning logic of doing audience ethnography is that by observing and questioning how people make sense of media data 'live' and *in situ*, researchers compile a more valid understanding of the process of immediate reception and the cognitive processing of media content. Wilson and Sparkes (1996), for example, illustrate how African-Canadian teenage boys fashion their own constructions of, and lived experiences with, Black masculinity to interpret mass mediations of 'Blackness' in basketball shoe advertisements. Wilson and Sparkes (1996) discuss how the boys find humour, reality, and frequent inferential racism in the depictions of Black masculinity in the advertisements. They also attest to how young people selectively take from the commercials what makes sense to them culturally, and how they negate or resist supposedly preferred images and constructions of 'Blackness' in the commercials. Through Wilson and Sparkes' audience ethnographic analysis, an understanding of people's creative capacities to make sense of

media in complex and nuanced ways results, thus challenging simplistic readings and portrayals of people as merely the unreflexive cultural dupes of dominant media discourses and images. Still, what is especially curious about audience ethnography is that media and visual culture methodologists have championed the approach for well over two decades, but very few have actively pursued audience ethnographic methods.

Photo elicitation

Photo elicitation, like audience ethnography, is designed to stimulate conversation about how the media are actively received and decoded by people. Here, a researcher will show a subject a series of pictures and ask them what they see in the pictures, what the images mean to them, or to provide an account of what is happening in the picture. Rather than ask a question, then, the researcher asks a person to respond to something visual in the hope it will stir alternative ways of thinking about the subject at hand. *Photovoice* is a similar method to photo elicitation, by which researchers encourage or ask participants in a project to take their own pictures of, video record or draw people, places, events or images which mean something to them (i.e. related to a well-specified and overarching research project). For example, I have conducted research with chronically ill athletes, and people living with cancer, liver disease, HIV and other conditions. At one stage of the research process I asked several participants to take one of my video cameras and film their own mini-documentaries of a week in their lives. The participants did so with much enthusiasm and produced amazing short features of their lives as wounded athletes. By having the subjects highlight what they understood to be the relevant day-to-day structures and meanings of their lives as wounded athletes, I gained a deeper understanding of how illness and sport identities must be negotiated daily (Atkinson and Young, 2008). Other studies have focused on how young people come to terms with and learn about their embodied identities through pictures. For example,

McHugh et al. (2013) have studied how Aboriginal youth in western Canada may express their physical cultural experiences through visual means. These young students, like most others, might not be able to verbally articulate how they understand their experiences as well as they may be able to represent them graphically through a series of visual maps. In such cases, the methodological point of photovoice or drawing is to access subjects' ways of knowing a topic.

With the rise of new on-line media the practice of *netnography* is gaining popularity as a technique of analysis. Netnography is literally an on-line ethnography of Internet sites, wherein a research does not simply observe the content of websites, but also actively contributes to them as a registered or recognised member. Wilson and Atkinson (2005), for example, studied the online recruiting and social connecting mechanisms provided by rave and straightedge blogs, forums and chatrooms. In both subcultures, young people use Internet sites as a technique for performing community and fostering the bonds between members across great spaces. Both of the researchers participated and chatted with members online as a means of conducting quasi-interviews, but more importantly, in gaining a first-hand understanding of how new media space is produced by groups in 'real time' as a vehicle for developing a sense of mutual identification and commitment. Bennett's (2008) book, *Civic Life Online*, presents a series of chapters detailing the emancipatory potential of new media forms such as personal websites, blogs, social networking sites and other forms of computer-mediated communication (CMC) for youth in particular. The separate chapters in the book attest to how the development on online space provides an opportunity for people to be their own media producers, and thus become public knowledge producers and cultural claims-makers. To date, very few inside the academy have rigorously attended to the study of how, why, and when youth choose to become media encoders, and how this may impact systems of ideological production and dissemination within popular culture. Ohler (2007) has extended the study of new media into the classroom. His work advocates the use of computer programs and Internet space as a means of teaching students how to create and publish avant-garde digital stories. Ohler's (2007) emphasis is on the creation of dynamic texts, embedded with movies, images, digital interviews, and other visual-spoken forms of knowing. Ohler (2007) further emphasises the creative and knowledge-production capabilities of new, digital stories in that they allow for the producers to play around with sound, speed, camera angles and other cinematic techniques in order to create desired feels, moods or atmospheres in stories. New media analytic methods advocated by Bennett (2008) and Pink (2013) establish exciting ways of knowing and seeing subjects of interest, and illustrate the potential for knowledge production and translation once representations of lived experience and human condition are liberated from one-dimensional written/textual ways of knowing.

A final series of comments about the role of theory in conducting media analysis is warranted. The lion's share of media analytic research is interpretive and qualitative in orientation; that is to say, researchers are not so concerned with testing formal hypotheses derived from theory against media data in most cases. So, it is fair to suggest that media analysis is based more on the use of media research to explore, probe and extend the empirical applicability of particular concepts, axioms or ideas from extant theories. More often than not, researchers have particular penchants for the proscribed theoretical ideas they regularly employ in order to make sense of emergent data. For instance, post-structural, neo-Marxist and neo-Gramscian, cultural studies, feminist, queer and post-colonial/critical race theories are used quite extensively to wade through and interpret the potential significance of media texts. The vast majority of projects are not, despite internal claims otherwise, 'grounded theoretical' examinations of media production and dissemination. Grounded theory is a very special data analytic procedure (Charmaz, 2006), and it has come to be lazily used among qualitative researchers and conflated with interpretive analysis or hermeneutics in general. When a set of theoretical decisions about how to read and report media data is sorted *a priori* to the data collection process, or a pre-existing theoretical schema is applied to emergent media data in a project, such is not in the spirit of grounded theoretical development.

Critiques

Media analysis receives substantial criticism from academics who consider themselves dyed-in-the-wool scientists. Due in large part to the extensive amount of reflexively interpretive analysis in most media studies projects, the overall methodology is prone to contestation from researchers searching robustly objective, reliable and generalisable data. Whilst there are many criticisms of media analysis studies, five are especially common. *First*, quarrels about the rigours of sampling in media projects are practically inevitable. The sampling approach underpinning many media-based projects is almost always non-probability based, but researchers nevertheless tend to make grand claims about the generalisability of their data and theoretical conclusions. Further, very little theoretical or conceptual rationale is offered as to why the sample data have been collected, or why they may be representative of 'something' at all. *Second*, the question of how theory guides media research looms large. Even though many researchers purport to conduct 'grounded theory' through the data analysis process, their studies read as if the theoretical reading had been determined well in advance (see above). In this instance, one is led to question whether or not media studies are simply vehicles for reifying, rather than testing, expanding or amending, extant theories of cultures, individuals and societies.

Third, questions of the internal validity and reliability of researchers' readings of media texts, or interpretations of audience interpretations of texts, chase practically all media-based studies. If, as semioticians instruct, media texts are indeed polysemic or 'floating' and thus open for countless cultural interpretations, then how is one researcher's set of conclusions any more reality-congruent than another's? If a thousand media researchers might decode the significance of, say, media accounts of the obesity epidemic in the London broadsheets in a thousand different ways, what is the legitimate role of media analysis in the academy? What trustworthy, usable, intersubjectively agreed upon or definitive knowledge does it generate? *Fourth*, new questions of best ethical practice (especially around participant anonymity and confidentiality) surround the media project in which photographs, film, blogs, websites, and other Internet spaces are employed as data. While the use of new media and their forms of representation well and truly opens up representational practice in our research efforts, the 'public' nature (and therefore 'free to use' nature) of online material, and our ability to 'invade' personal webspace for our research purposes, remain grey areas in research ethics debates. *Fifth*, even the most ardent defenders of media analysis struggle with how to best represent visual, spoken, moving, ambiguous and mass distributed media texts into academic papers. Thrift (2007), like Richardson (1999), challenges all qualitative researchers to seek new forms of moving, emotional, aesthetic and personally compelling forms of academic writing and representation that bring audiences 'closer' to that which has been studied in the here and now of everyday life. Their criticism is based on the idea that researchers take very complex, visceral and sensual practices like media reception and usage, and then transform or represent it, as a theoretically obtuse, written, textual analysis. Atkinson (2010), for example, has explored the role of 'infographics' (using pictures and selected field notes as the main body of a research report) in the effort of reducing of the author's own theoretical voice in the academic text.

Conclusion

In sum, media analysis continues to develop and flourish within universities, drawing more practitioners on a yearly basis across a swathe of academic departments. Advocates call attention to the insights offered by such research in societies obsessed with and saturated by the mass mediation of culture, whilst critics continue to question the scientific legitimacy and rigour of much media-focused research.

Questions for further investigation

1. Do you think media producers actually encode and communicate preferred meaning into texts, or are audiences simply able to read media freely?
2. Select any edition of a popular magazine for teenage boys, and one for teenage girls. Examine the advertisements in each of the magazines and 'read' any messages or discourses about gender in the ads. Compare and contrast between the boys' magazine ads and the girls' magazine ads.
3. If you were asked to conduct an audience ethnography of popular movies, how would you design and implement the project?
4. Select a subject of interest to you, and think of how you might use either photovoice or photo elicitation to produce data for a study on the subject.
5. How do you think the rise and popularity of new media creates both challenges and possibilities for enhanced learning in the classroom?

Suggested further reading

Banks, M. and Zeitlyn, D. (2015) *Visual Methods in Social Research*, 2nd edn. London: Sage. This text is a fine instructional reader on how to approach the visual field in active social research. It presents a concise and yet broad review of the nature of the visual, and how to conceptualise the visual actively.

Black, J., Castro, J. and Lin, C. (2016) *Youth Practices in Digital Arts and New Media*. New York: Springer. This edited volume presents cutting edge research and theory in youth uses of, and engagements with new media in both building communities and in pedagogical contexts. It focuses more on how youth are active producers in media/learning contexts rather than passive receptors of media.

Hall, S. (1980) 'Encoding/decoding', in *Culture, Media, Language: Working Papers in Cultural Studies, 1972-79*, Centre for Contemporary Cultural Studies. London: Hutchinson. pp. 128-38. This essay is a must-read for students as they first encounter mass media research. Among other contributions to the field of media research, this article carefully and thoughtfully outlines the ways in which media messages are produced and received in the transmission process.

Pink, S. (2013) *Doing Visual Ethnography*, 3rd edn. London: Sage. This book is absolutely essential reading for any researcher wishing to engage with images, technologies and society. It includes chapters on web-based practices for conducting visual analysis of images presented online, and the issues surrounding the representation, interpretation and authoring of knowledge with the rise of digital media.

Ruddock, A. (2007) *Investigating Audiences*. London: Sage. Ruddock's book is a standout within publications that tackle the thorny issue of how audiences receive, use and rearrange media messages. While much is written about 'media effects' on audiences, this book pauses to ask whether or not we actually (empirically) know how various media are interpreted by audiences.

References

Atkinson, M. (2010) 'Fell running in post-sport territories', *Qualitative Research in Sport & Exercise*, 2: 109–32.

Atkinson, M. and Young, K. (2008) *Sport, Deviance and Social Control*. Champaign, IL: Human Kinetics.

Bennett, W.L. (2008) *Civic Life Online: Learning How Digital Media Can Engage Youth*. Cambridge, MA: MIT Press.

Bourdieu, P. (1993) *The Field of Cultural Production*. New York: Columbia University Press.

Charmaz, K. (2006) *Constructing Grounded Theory: A Practical Guide Through Qualitative Analysis*. London: Sage.

Cooky, C., Messner, M. and Hextrum, R. (2013) 'Women play sport, but not on TV. a longitudinal study of televised news media', *Communication & Sport*, 1: 203–30.

Deleuze, G. and Guattari, F. (1987) *A Thousand Plateaus*. Minneapolis, MN: University of Minnesota Press.

Fish, S. (1980) *Is There a Text in This Class? The Authority of Interpretive Communities*. Cambridge, MA: Harvard University Press.

Gillett, J. (2003) 'Media activism and Internet use by people with HIV/AIDS', *Sociology of Health and Illness*, 25: 608–24.

Giroux, H. (2014) *Neoliberalism's War on Higher Education*. Chicago, IL: Haymarket Books.

Hall, S. (1980) 'Encoding/decoding', in *Culture, Media, Language: Working Papers in Cultural Studies, 1972–79*, Centre for Contemporary Cultural Studies. London: Hutchinson. pp. 128-38.

Kennedy, E. and Hills, L. (2015) *Sport, Media & Society*. London: Bloomsbury.

McHugh, T., Coppola, A. and Sinclair, S. (2013) 'An exploration of the meanings of sport to urban Aboriginal youth', *Qualitative Research in Sport, Exercise and Health*, 5: 291–311.

Ohler, J. (2007) *Digital Storytelling in the Classroom*. Thousand Oaks, CA: Corwin.

Pink, S. (2013) *Doing Visual Ethnography*. London: Sage.

Rich, E. and Miah, A (2009) 'Prosthetic surveillance: The medical governance of health bodies in cyberspace', *Surveillance and Society*, 6(2): 163–77.

Richardson, L. (1999) 'Feathers in our CAP', *Journal of Contemporary Ethnography*, 28: 660–8.

Thrift, N. (2007) *Non-Representational Theory: Space, Politics, Affect*. London: Routledge.

Wilson, B. and Atkinson, M. (2005) 'Rave and straight-edge, the virtual and the real: exploring on-line and off-line experiences in Canadian youth subcultures', *Youth & Society*, 36: 276–311.

Wilson, B. and Sparkes, R. (1996) 'It's Gotta Be the Shoes: youth, race, and sneaker commercials', *Sociology of Sport Journal*, 13: 398–427.

Biographical research

32

Michael Tedder

Introduction

Researchers who consider using biographical methods as part of an enquiry in education are quickly confronted with some fundamental research issues: the intrinsic subjectivity of biography means that they need to decide whether and how they think it possible to be 'objective', or whether the process of undertaking their enquiry is inevitably 'subjective'. They have to consider what tests for 'truth' may be possible given the nature of the data they are collecting. Biographical research does not usually claim to achieve the objectivity or replicability of much conventional research; rather the quest is for insight and understanding using theoretical framings from a range of academic disciplines and sub-disciplines. Researchers may follow sociological and anthropological traditions or they may draw on the possibilities opened by psychological and psychoanalytical theories. There is extensive related work in oral history, in literature and linguistics, in cultural studies. This interdisciplinary context means that the educational researcher has numerous practical and theoretical issues to resolve if biography is to be the data source.

The distinctive feature of biographical research is that it enquires into the way that people make sense of their lives through the collection, analysis and representation of data about individual experiences of life. Such research can be regarded as a kind of ethnography if we take that as signifying that the main concern is with *meaning*, that the

enquiry is interested in the ways that people describe and understand themselves and their actions and their interactions with others. It is not necessarily the factual accuracy of descriptions and explanations that interests biographical researchers, but instead the expressions of understanding that research participants make and the forms such expressions take. The research challenge is to decide how to use such data in suitably systematic and rigorous ways.

There are no data collection methods that are peculiar to biographical research. The most common method is the personal interview, an invitation to someone to tell stories about their life, that might be a singular event or one of a series of interviews in a longitudinal study. Other documentary sources might also be used, such as personal diaries, letters and autobiographies or, in this digital age, blogs, tweets and social media exchanges. Collecting data from focus group interviews and observation may also have a role to play. In his introduction to the field, Norman Denzin (1989) outlined a comprehensive listing of artefacts, methods and key concepts in the traditions of collecting and representing biographical data: included in his list are biography and autobiography, life story and life history, narrative as well as oral history and personal history, case history and case study. Each of these means something subtly different – and would signify different approaches to different researchers – but they are all processes and products within biographical research.

The appeal of biographical research

Historians of social science research comment on the ebb and flow of research focused on biography. In the early twentieth century, a study of Polish migrants by Thomas and Znaniecka and of a juvenile delinquent called Stanley by Clifford R. Shaw are often quoted as milestones in the development of the Chicago School of sociology. The writings of George Herbert Mead are cited for the importance they place on understanding individuals through their participation in social acts. There was a reaction against forms of research based on individuals and their personal experience in the latter half of the twentieth century, but constructing biography for research has undergone a resurgence in recent decades to the extent that some writers (such as Chamberlayne et al., 2000) have observed a 'biographical turn' in the social sciences.

This 'biographical turn' can be understood in several ways. Some commentators characterise interest in the personal as a feature of the individualisation and commodification of modern life. The preoccupation of popular media with celebrity and the public appetite for disclosure of emotion and interpersonal conflict might be regarded as facets of these trends. Social networking has opened new avenues for personal disclosure and inter-personal exchange. The growing popularity throughout the UK of oral history projects and tracing family genealogies suggests that there is greater valuing of individual stories within British culture. That popularity is evident also in the USA in the operation of an organisation like StoryCorps that records discussions between two people who are relations or friends. Participants each receive a CD copy of their discussion while a second copy is archived in the Library of Congress. Since 2003, more than 60,000 such recordings have been archived. StoryCorps has a commitment to social justice and strives to articulate the diverse community voices that can be heard in modern America.

For social scientists, biographical methods offer a means of exploring questions about identity and sense of self in a fragmented and rapidly changing world. Giddens (1991) famously wrote of the 'reflexive project of the self' that he sees as characterising individuals and their moulding of lifestyles in late-modern society. Bauman (2004) has written extensively on the 'liquid' qualities of late modernity and offers a critical perspective on the personalisation of modern society. Biographical research offers empirical means for enquiry into such issues; it provides an approach to understanding how people come to terms with uncertainties about identity and change in contemporary society. It generates data about whether and how far people have, or think they have, influence and control over the kinds of change they experience.

This brings us to an important proposition that interests many biographical researchers: that the narration of a life story not only enables people to articulate their identity but also offers the possibility of learning from their life and the potential to effect change as a consequence. Among the leading contributors to the field is Peter Alheit whose work explores the relationship of biography to learning in the workplace and across the life-course (see Alheit, 1994, 2005; Alheit and Dausien, 2002). Pierre Dominicé (2000) has worked particularly with teachers in Switzerland in the development of 'educational biographies', and he also argues that the practice of telling stories about life and experience enables adult learners to effect change. Biographical research and the notion that developing life stories may have agentic possibilities appeals to adult educators who are committed to ideals of emancipatory and transformative education. (For further discussion of the relationship of agency and learning, see Biesta and Tedder, 2007.)

For Chamberlayne et al. (2000), the concern of social scientists to link micro and macro levels of socio-political analysis explains the recent burgeoning of interest in biographical research methods. It is part of a long-established concern of sociologists, evident in writers like C. Wright Mills who is often quoted for emphasising the interconnection of the private and public domains of human life:

… many personal troubles cannot be solved merely as troubles but must be understood in terms of public issues – and in terms of the problems of history making. Know that the human meaning of public issues must be revealed by relating them to personal troubles and to the problems of individual life. (Wright Mills, 1970: 248)

Another reason that biographical research appeals to some researchers is that it appears easy. What could be more straightforward in carrying out a research project than asking people to tell you stories about themselves? However, as Harry Wolcott wryly observes:

> Qualitative approaches beckon because they appear easy or natural. And were it not for the complexity of conceptualising qualitative studies, conducting the research, analysing it, and writing it up, perhaps they would be. (Wolcott, 1990: 11)

It may seem 'easy and natural' to collect biographical data but no one who engages seriously in such research should underestimate the challenge of collecting data in a sensitive and ethical manner, of managing and archiving large quantities of recordings and transcriptions, of discerning analytical sense in disparate data sources, or of interpreting and writing with meaning and rigour for different audiences.

Conducting biographical research

In collecting data for an oral history or a life story, interviewing is the central – though not the only – method of generating data, and an interviewer needs to be familiar with the strengths, possibilities and limitations of interviewing. Introductory literature on research methods tends to suggest that conducting an interview is essentially a technical procedure: interviewing is portrayed as managing a kind of oral questionnaire for which the requisite skills are structuring questions and developing codes for analysing responses. However, experienced interviewers usually develop an awareness of the complexity of such meetings. Ellis and Berger (2002) said:

> The interviewing process becomes less a conduit of information from informant to researchers that represent how things are, and more a sea swell of meaning making in which researchers connect their own experiences to those of others. (Ellis and Berger, 2002: 853)

The meaning and significance of what is said at a particular time and place between different individuals reach far beyond the moment. There is great diversity in what interviewees bring to an interview: responses to questions about past, current or anticipated experiences may be tentative or speculative, particularly if the interview offers an unprecedented opportunity for the interviewee to discern and construct coherence within a life story. Alternatively, an interviewee may have stories that have been reviewed and rehearsed, introspectively or with others, and those stories may have achieved a degree of coherence through reflection and repetition. Whether a narrative is newly minted or recycled, the teller engages in processes of selection and interpretation that are structured by the norms and values of the culture of which he or she is part. What a researcher brings to the encounter will be just as significant in discerning meaning in what the participant says or does not say.

Some scholars use different terms to distinguish between different stages of biographical research. Denzin (1989) makes a distinction between an 'oral history', which he said can be obtained through conversations and interviews, and a 'life history' or 'personal history' that builds on such conversations and interviews to construct a written account of a person's life. A similar distinction is made between a 'life story' and 'life history' by Goodson and Sikes (2001). They propose that a 'life story' might be conceived as a simple narrative, a personal reconstruction of what an individual considers significant about his or her life. A 'life history', however, moves through stages of interpretation: it may be co-constructed by the researcher and project participant or it may be that the researcher uses a range of data sources. The outcome is a narrative that becomes contextualised and theorised and in the process becomes a history rather than a story.

Biographical research projects are often interested in the way that human experience is temporally situated, that our experiences happen in time (Biesta et al., 2010). Scholars tend to assume that everyone shares interior thought processes through which each person makes sense or constructs meaning from 'real-life' experiences, so people are invited to talk about how they see their lives progressing and changing over time. Listening to the interweaving of stories about the past, the present and the future offers a means of unravelling how change is perceived and understood. As West writes, 'The stories people tell are always a reconstruction of events, afterthoughts, rather than the events themselves, while the powerful discourses of a culture and unconscious processes of wanting to please or appease circulate in stories' (West, 2016). Some biographical research has focused on the nature of memory and the manner in which individuals when telling their stories adapt them over time to accommodate changing social and cultural conditions. Some will see the unreliability or variability of individual memory as a problem, a factor of unreliability in research data, but others will argue that biographical research gives us a vital tool to explore the meaning and significance of such change.

There are always important ethical issues to be considered in biographical research. Clearly, the researcher needs to observe the relevant codes of the organisation undertaking the research. However, while a code provides rules to follow, the real challenge is to have the sensitivity and skill to ensure such guidance becomes operational.

Analysing and writing up biographical research

Part of the researcher's task in the analysis of biographical data is to construct a narrative that renders as clearly as possible what participants have said in the stories collected. However, there are processes of selection and decisions about meaning at every stage in the development of such narratives. Life stories cannot be treated as an objective account of the facts of a life, rather they are 'lives interpreted and made textual' and represent 'a partial, selective commentary on lived experience' (Goodson and Sikes, 2001).

It is standard practice to transcribe interviews and a transcriber undertakes analysis when making decisions about possible meanings to include in transcription. Matters such as the level of detail to include, what to do about non-grammatical structures, whether to indicate pauses and non-verbal signifiers, all have a bearing on interpreting meaning. There is always a challenge in transcribing silence.

Once there is an artefact – whether a transcribed text, or audio or video recording – it becomes possible to undertake coding, to identify what the researcher finds are significant themes and patterns within the data. Some researchers will delay coding on the grounds that they want to avoid reorganising and probably distorting the participant's voice. Many are attracted to grounded theory (Glaser and Strauss, 1967; Strauss and Corbin, 1998) for the notion that analysis and interpretation can be inducted from the data of a research project, that the data should 'speak for itself'. Grounded theory offers an approach in which substantive theory is constructed from immersion in the data: by repeated listening to audio tapes, viewing of videos and reading of transcripts, themes and patterns emerge as potential categories for organising the data. Additional appropriate cases may be sought to 'saturate' the categories and it might be possible to use processes, such as the 'constant comparative method', for more general analysis. Computer programs are available that have been specifically designed to facilitate such analysis.

While some researchers claim they use adapted versions of 'grounded theory', others say it is impossible for a researcher not to have a framework of pre-formed ideas, values and beliefs that will influence what she or he thinks is significant in the data and therefore what categories emerge. Some researchers have adopted the term 'Auto/biography' (with a forward slash) to communicate the idea that the researcher is aware of the reflective and self-reflexive nature of their role, that she or he is a dynamic and interactive part of the research process.

Important questions are raised by Marxist, feminist and postmodern researchers about the power relationship between researcher and researched in deciding what meanings are significant and need to be included in a research narrative and what meanings can be excluded. Marxists tend to question how far research participants can articulate the social divisions of which they are part. For feminists, it has been crucial to give greater prominence to women's stories about domestic life, about maternity or about female labour, matters that have been excluded from most accounts of social history. Postmodern critics draw attention to the way practices of storytelling are deeply embedded within our culture and referential to particular cultural narratives. Researchers from critical perspectives tend to argue for social justice, for the importance of hearing the voice of 'the other', of people on the margins of society, of giving proper attention to the excluded and unheard. All would argue the importance of researchers being aware of their role in what becomes articulated, conscious that they are part of the social matrix that permits some forms of expression and denies others.

Exemplary studies

Distress in the City

Linden West and colleagues have used auto/biographical methods over the years to research the experiences of adults in higher education, the lives of GPs working in inner-city communities, and the perceptions of families and professional workers of a Sure Start project in Kent. West's approach to interviewing explores the emotional dimensions of his participants' lives and his analysis of data is framed by a psychoanalytical understanding of biographical interviews. West is a

researcher conscious of the way that responses are shaped auto/biographically, of how unconscious, intersubjective and power dynamics work. He asserts that we are all storied as well as storytellers, capable of being constrained as well as liberated by our stories.

In 2016 West published an ambitious study grounded in his own autobiography (West, 2016). He was troubled by reports of racism and of the success of right-wing political activists in the town where he was brought up, and disturbed by reports that young men from families of South Asian origin were attracted to Islamic fundamentalism. A picture had emerged of a 'distressed' or 'failed' city undermined by the abandonment of regeneration projects, corroded by declining industry and growing unemployment. There were statistical surveys of poverty, of the increasing incidence of mental illness and reports of underachievement in schools, but West sought to understand the human experiences that were embodied in such data. He wanted to ask questions about why the culture and educational structures that he remembered from his formative years had decayed.

In five years of fieldwork, West conducted interviews with more than 50 people, some being interviewed three times. Stories are constructed from interviews with white working-class people and with people from ethnic minorities, and West illuminates the complexities of individual lives in contemporary housing estates where there are few jobs and many idle young people. Among the emergent themes is the appeal of fundamentalism and how, in some ways, the appeal of Islamic fundamentalism to some young men from ethnic minorities mirrors the appeal of far-right groups to the white population. West observes psychoanalytical and social patterns in fundamentalism, whether political, religious or economic, and suggests that, for some individuals, extreme groups provide meaning, purpose, identity and recognition through their compelling narratives about life's problems.

A recurring theme in the study is of the decline of adult education through organisations like the Workers Education Association (WEA) and local universities and the consequent loss of opportunities for working-class people. Routes that once existed for the education of leaders in the community have been eroded. Nonetheless, West strives to identify new resources of hope. He discusses new forms of citizenship education and references the critical theorist Axel Honneth (2007, 2009) to argue that processes of mutual recognition and respect are essential for the development of positive human relationships, both for individuals and for society. There are significant implications for teaching and education if they were to emphasise qualities of human interaction and mutual recognition rather than technique and teaching technologies. For a society with potentially antagonistic groups, the operation of dialogue and thought across difference is a vital concern for democratic education.

Thus West strives to explore connections between the 'macro'-level processes of history, globalisation, ideology, the 'meso' level of civil authorities and educational institutions, and the 'micro'-level accounts of well-being and distress of people in relationships.

Learning in the life-course

The project 'Learning Lives: Learning, Identity and Agency' was a substantial mixed-methods study of adult learning undertaken between 2004 and 2008 by a team of researchers from four UK universities (Biesta et al., 2011). The qualitative dimension of the project comprised a longitudinal study of adult learning biographies: a total of 528 interviews were carried out with 117 people, 59 male and 58 female, aged between 25 and 84. Some participants were interviewed as many as nine times. The official aim of the project was to deepen understanding of the complexities of learning in the life-course and to investigate what learning 'means' and 'does' in the lives of adults. Such a project was timely when 'lifelong learning' had become part of the rhetoric of government policy and education management.

The interviewers used a combination of life-history and life-course approaches. The first interview with each participant focused on the life story ('Tell me about your life …'); subsequent interviews invited reflection on issues that had emerged

in the transcripts, but increasingly focused on ongoing events in the life-course of interviewees. Sometimes the events were structured transitions within life and sometimes they were changes of a more incidental and possibly critical nature, such as redeployment or illness. Such events offer opportunities for learning, both formal and informal, and longitudinal interviews monitored the stories that people told about such opportunities.

One of the central themes explored in the project concerned the nature of narrative and its significance for learning (Goodson et al., 2010). Unsurprisingly, the researchers found that some people are more adept at telling stories about their lives than others, but this suggested that the potential for learning from narrative also varies. They propose that a life story can be conceived as a 'site for learning' within which learning can take place both during the creation of a story (i.e. within the *narration* of a life story) and in the telling and retelling of such stories with others (i.e. in having a *narrative* to tell). Two analytical tools were developed by the researchers, one for the analysis of the *narrative quality* of narration and narrative and the other for the analysis of the *efficacy* of narrative and narration. Within the latter a distinction was made between the *learning potential* and the *action potential* of narrative and narration (Tedder and Biesta, 2009). The writers suggest that narration is not only about the construction of a particular version of one's life, it is at the same time a construction of a particular version of the self.

Goodson et al. (2010) state that the 'Learning Lives' project found only a small number of participants actually identified their storying as a learning process, although the stories they told contained abundant evidence of learning and of the impact of this learning on people's lives. It was also evident that having a narrative in the form of sophisticated, well-developed stories was no guarantee of effective learning: some people were found to be 'caught' in their stories, unable to use them to generate new perspectives and insights, and there was thus little 'action potential' from such storying. Equally, not providing a narration or narrative did not prevent people from being able to learn or from being effective and influential members of their community. Goodson (2013) has subsequently sought to devise a classification for patterns of story telling in life histories.

Conclusion

Biographical research can produce vivid research data in the form of stories that are engaging and that resonate strongly with contemporary social and cultural mores. For social science and education researchers, such stories can provide insights into individual experiences of change, whether the change is personal, psychological and educational, or social, political and cultural. No other form of research focuses so explicitly on the relationship between the personal and the social, on exploring the way that social 'context' permeates the way people construct meaning from their individual experience and the way that social norms find expression through individual sense-making and action-taking.

Biographical research tends to be theoretically eclectic, drawing from multidisciplinary sources, from sociology and anthropology, overlapping with psychology and psychotherapy, history, literature and cultural studies. The inherent appeal of narrative and the eclectic theoretical framing can give to biographical research qualities of narrative richness and a depth of insight that will help persuade a reader of the authenticity and credibility of its depiction of the complexities of the 'real world'. Biographical research challenges epistemological reductionism and superficiality.

The very appeal of narrative, however, makes biographical research susceptible to a reliance on description and vulnerable to being dismissed as merely anecdotal. For some academics and many policy makers a biographical approach scarcely registers as legitimate research. At a time when much official research effort is directed towards securing straightforward solutions to difficult problems, research that actively seeks to portray complexity will hold little appeal for some research funders. A researcher in education using biographical methods needs to be prepared to argue for the legitimacy of individual stories and for the significance in research narratives of the personal domain.

A tradition is becoming established of biographical research in education. For reasons of accessibility, much of the work to date has been with students, teachers and educational professionals. There has been some significant international collaboration between European researchers (see West et al., 2007; Merrill and Tett, 2013). The work of Andrew Sparkes and Brett Smith (Sparkes and Smith, 2003; Smith and Sparkes, 2008) uses narrative and life storytelling centred on sports injury, disability and gender to offer significant insights into the learning lives of individuals from some rather different groups. There has been limited research among the general population that addresses questions of learning and education even though existing research shows how biographical narratives can contribute to certain forms of learning. While we recognise that life-storying is a genre that can be practised, we also know little about how far it may have importance for different forms of learning. We have yet to address what the implications might be for the organisation of the curriculum and for formal education. The task of undertaking biographical research that is carefully analysed and critically theorised in order to address educational questions has scarcely begun.

Questions for further investigation

1. What are the strengths and limitations of interviewing for the life story of someone who is different from you in terms of (a) age; (b) gender; (c) ethnicity; (d) social group?
2. How would you address the ethical issues of interviewing someone in

(Continued)

(Continued)

terms of (a) ensuring the confidentiality of their part in data collection; (b) respecting their rights in data analysis and interpretation?

3. How far would you say your life is influenced by social forces? How far do you have influence over such forces and how might biographical research help with the recognition of such processes?

4. What educational issues or research questions can be usefully addressed through collecting biographical interviews and constructing life histories?

Suggested further reading

For further reading, I commend firstly the publications that informed the exemplary studies:

Goodson, I., Biesta, G.J.J., Tedder, M. and Adair, N. (2010) *Narrative Learning*. London: Routledge.

West, L. (2016) *Distress in the City: Racism, Fundamentalism and a Democratic Education*. London: UCL Institute of Education Press.

For general purpose texts on 'How to do biographical research', I would recommend:

Merrill, B. and West, L. (2009) *Using Biographical Methods in Social Research*. London: Sage.

Roberts, B. (2002) *Biographical Research*. Buckingham: Open University Press.

For a more robust and comprehensive consideration of biographical research in its academic context, the following offers a huge compendium of relevant and thought-provoking material.

Harrison, B. (ed.) (2009) *Life Story Research*. London: Sage.

Other publications on practices and issues in qualitative research have proved invaluable to the author, including:

Denzin, N.K. and Lincoln, Y.S. (eds) (1998) *Strategies of Qualitative Inquiry*. Thousand Oaks, CA: Sage.

Gubrium, F.G. and Holstein, J.A. (eds) (2002) *The SAGE Handbook of Interview Research*. Thousand Oaks, CA: Sage.

References

Alheit, P. (1994) *Taking the Knocks: Youth Unemployment and Biography – A Qualitative Analysis*. London: Cassell.

Alheit, P. (2005) 'Challenges of the Postmodern "Learning Society": A critical approach', in A. Bron, E. Kurantowicz, H.S. Olesen and L. West (eds), *'Old' and 'New' Worlds of Adult Learning*. Wroclaw: Dolnoslaskiej Szkoly Wyzszej Edukacji.

Alheit, P. and Dausien, B. (2002) 'The "double face" of lifelong learning: two analytical perspectives on a "silent revolution"', *Studies in the Education of Adults*, 34(1): 1–20.

Bauman, Z. (2004) *Identity*. Cambridge: Polity.

Biesta, G. and Tedder, M. (2007) 'Agency and learning in the lifecourse: towards an ecological perspective', *Studies in the Education of Adults*, 39(2): 132–49.

Biesta, G., Field, J., Hodkinson, P., Macleod, F. and Goodson, I.F. (2011) *Improving Learning Through the Life Course: Learning Lives*. London: Routledge.

Biesta, G., Field, J. and Tedder, M. (2010) 'A time for learning: representations of time and the temporal dimensions of learning through the lifecourse', *Zeitschrift für Pädagogik*, 56(3): 317–27.

Chamberlayne, P., Bornat, J. and Wengraf, T. (eds) (2000) *The Turn to Biographical Methods in Social Science*. London: Routledge.

Denzin, N. (1989) *Interpretive Biography*. London: Sage.

Denzin, N.K. and Lincoln, Y.S. (eds) (1998) *Strategies of Qualitative Inquiry*. Thousand Oaks, CA: Sage.

Dominicé, P. (2000) *Learning from Our Lives*. San Francisco, CA: Jossey-Bass.

Ellis, C. and Berger, L. (2002) 'Their Story/My Story/Our Story', in F.G. Gubrium and J.A. Holstein (eds), *The Sage Handbook of Interview Research*. Thousand Oaks, CA: Sage.

Giddens, A. (1991) *Modernity and Self-Identity*. Oxford: Blackwell.

Glaser, B. and Strauss, A. (1967) *The Discovery of Grounded Theory*. London: Weidenfield & Nicolson.

Goodson, I. (2013) *Developing Narrative Theory: Life Histories and Personal Representation*. London: Routledge.

Goodson, I. and Sikes, P. (2001) *Life History Research in Educational Settings*. Buckingham: Open University Press.

Goodson, I., Biesta, G.J.J., Tedder, M. and Adair, N. (2010) *Narrative Learning*. London: Routledge.

Honneth, A. (2007) *Disrespect: The Normative Foundations of Critical Theory*. Cambridge: Polity.

Honneth, A. (2009) *Pathologies of Reason: On the Legacy of Critical Theory*. New York: Columbia University Press.

Merrill, B. and Tett, L. (2013) 'Access retention and withdrawal: a European perspective', *Studies in the Education of Adults*, 45(2):115–18.

Smith, B. and Sparkes, A.C. (2008) 'Narrative and its potential contribution to disability studies', *Disability and Society,* 23(1):17–28.

Sparkes, A.C. and Smith, B. (2003) 'Men, sport, spinal cord injury and narrative time', *Qualitative Research,* 3: 295–320.

Strauss, A.L. and Corbin, J. (1998) 'Grounded Theory Methodology: An overview', in N.K. Denzin and Y.S. Lincoln (eds), *Strategies of Qualitative Inquiry*. Thousand Oaks, CA: Sage.

Tedder, M. and Biesta, G. (2009) 'Biography, Transition and Learning in the Lifecourse: The role of narrative', in J. Field, J. Gallacher. and R. Ingram (eds), *Researching Transitions in Lifelong Learning*. London: Routledge.

West, L. (2016) *Distress in the City: Racism, Fundamentalism and a Democratic Education*. London: UCL Institute of Education Press.

West, L., Alheit, P., Andersen, A.S. and Merrill, B. (eds) (2007) *Using Biographical and Life History Approaches in the Study of Adult and Lifelong Learning: European Perspectives*. Frankfurt am Main: Peter Lang.

Wolcott, H.F. (1990) *Writing up Qualitative Research*. Thousand Oaks, CA: Sage.

Wright Mills, C. (1970) *The Sociological Imagination*. (Originally 1959.) Harmondsworth: Penguin.

Statistical hypothesis tests

33

Michael Borenstein

Introduction

Statistical analysis in educational research is usually conducted within either of two frameworks. One is significance testing, where the researcher poses a null hypothesis and then attempts to reject that hypothesis. The other is effect size estimation, where the researcher reports the magnitude of the treatment effect and its confidence interval. My first goal in this chapter is to introduce the two frameworks. My second goal is to explain why researchers in the field of education (as well as many other fields) should focus primarily on effect size estimation rather than tests of significance.

Motivational example

Suppose that students enrolled in a SAT preparatory course currently use one curriculum and we anticipate that a modified curriculum will yield higher test scores. We draw a sample of students, assign the students randomly to either of the two curricula, and then compare the SAT scores for the two groups at the conclusion of the course. There are 100 students in each group, the standard deviation within groups is known to be 100, and the mean SAT scores for the two groups are 420 vs 400, for a difference of 20 points.

As always, our goal is to make inferences from this sample to the larger population from which the sample was drawn. To distinguish between the sample and the population I will follow the convention of using Greek letters for population parameters and Roman letters for the sample statistics. The mean difference in the population is denoted Δ (delta), while the mean difference in the sample is denoted D.

Significance tests

One approach to the analysis is the significance testing framework (formally, the null hypothesis significance test, or NHST). Under this paradigm we pose the null hypothesis that the effect size (here the mean difference in SAT scores for the two curricula) is zero, and then attempt to disprove this hypothesis.

The fact that the mean difference in the sample (D) is not zero does not, in itself, tell us that the mean difference in the population (Δ) is not zero. This is because even if Δ is zero, in any given sample D will be lower or higher than zero due to random sampling error. Rather, to establish that Δ is not zero, we need to assess D in relation to its sampling error.

Concretely, if we were to draw an infinite number of samples from a population where Δ is zero, we can anticipate how the sample Ds would be distributed, and identify the range within which (for example) 95% of all Ds would fall, and define this as the 'acceptable' range. If D in our study falls inside this range we will conclude that there is no reason to reject the null (the result is not statistically significant). If D in our study falls outside of this range, there are two possible reasons. Either the null hypothesis is true and our study is among the 5% that happen to fall at the extreme, or the null hypothesis is false – one curriculum really does yield a higher mean score than the other, and this is the reason that our study yielded a mean difference so far from zero. We reject the first option in favour of the second (the result is statistically significant).

To implement this strategy we need to identify the acceptable range, and we do so using:

$$\Delta \pm SE_D \times Z_{1-\alpha}$$

The first element in this formula, Δ, is the mean difference under the null hypothesis (that is, zero). The sample Ds will be distributed about this value.

The second element, SE_D, is the standard error of D, and reflects the width of the distribution of D. The standard error, SE_D, is defined as:

$$SE_D = SD_W \sqrt{\frac{1}{n_T} + \frac{1}{n_c}}$$

where SD_W is the standard deviation of scores within groups, while n_T and n_c are the sample size within each group. If the standard deviation of scores within each group is relatively small, and/or the sample size within each group is relatively high, then the estimate of the group means (and of D) will tend to be relatively precise, leading to a smaller SE_D and relatively narrow width for the acceptable range.

The third element in the formula is $Z_{1-\alpha}$, where Z is the standard normal deviate corresponding to $1-\alpha$ (one minus alpha) and α is the criterion for significance. If we set α at 0.05, then the acceptable range includes $(1-\alpha$, or$)$ 95% of the distribution of Ds, and the corresponding Z-value is 1.96. If we set α closer to zero (for example 0.01 rather than 0.05) the Z-value increases (for $\alpha = 0.01$, $Z = 2.58$), the acceptable range gets wider, and we require a higher (absolute) value of D to reject the null hypothesis.

In the SAT example:

$$SE_D = 100\sqrt{\frac{1}{100} + \frac{1}{100}} = 14.14$$

If we set α at 0.05, then $Z_{1-\alpha}$ is 1.96, and the limits for the acceptable range are

Lower = $0.00 - 1.96 \times 14.14 = -27.72$

and

Upper = $0.00 - 1.96 \times 14.14 = +27.72$

In words, if the null hypothesis is true ($\Delta = 0$) and we were to perform an infinite number of studies, in 95% of those studies D would fall in the range of -27.72 to $+27.72$. In our example D is 20 points, and so we do not reject the null hypothesis – we conclude that Δ might (or might not) be zero. If D had been a difference of 30 points, then we would have rejected the null hypothesis – we would have concluded that Δ is probably not zero.

The NHST framework is sometimes presented using a 2×2 format (see Table 33.1). The row labelled $\Delta = 0$ addresses the case where the null hypothesis is true. We hope that when Δ is zero, D will fall within the acceptable range (Cell B) and yield a non-significant result. However, we recognise that it may fall outside that range, leading to us to reject the null hypothesis (Cell A), which is called a Type I error. If the null hypothesis is true and a is set at 0.05, then 5% of studies will result in a Type I error. If the null hypothesis is false, then the Type I error rate is zero by definition.

The row labelled $\Delta \neq 0$ addresses the case where the null hypothesis is false. We hope that when Δ is not zero, D will fall outside the acceptable range (Cell C) and yield a significant result. However, we recognise that it may fall inside that range (Cell D). In this case we do not reject the null, and this is called a Type II error. The proportion of studies that will yield a significant result (and fall into Cell C rather than Cell D) is the power of the test, while 1-power, the type II error rate, is called β (beta).

Table 33.1 Table of possible outcomes under NHST

	Result	
	Significant	**Not significant**
$\Delta = 0$	(A) Type I error	(B) Correct
$\Delta \neq 0$	(C) Correct	(D) Type II error

Power depends on the true mean difference (the larger the value of Δ, the larger the expected value of D and the greater the likelihood that it will fall outside the acceptable range), on the sample size (the larger the sample size, the narrower the acceptable region and the more likely that D will fall outside its bounds) and the value of α (when α is set at 0.05 rather than 0.01, the narrower the acceptable region and the more likely that D will fall outside its bounds). If a study has a power of 90% to reject the null then 90% of studies will yield effects outside the acceptable range and result in a correct conclusion, while 10% will yield effects within the acceptable range and result in a type II error.

I have presented the logic of the significance test by showing how we define an acceptable range based on SE_D and Z, and then see where D falls relative to this range. This approach lends itself to a clear explication of the significance test framework. In practice, one would typically reverse the process, computing a test statistic Z based on D and SE_D and then comparing this with the Z distribution. The two approaches are mathematically identical to each other.

To apply the traditional approach, we compute the test statistic Z, defined as:

$$Z = \frac{D}{SE_D}$$

where D and SE_D have the same definitions as before. If the test statistic Z is greater than the Z-value corresponding to $1-\alpha$ (or equivalently, if the p-value corresponding to Z is less than α) the result is statistically significant.

In the SAT example,

$$Z = \frac{20}{14.14} = 1.41$$

The test statistic Z is 1.41, which does not meet the threshold of $Z = 1.96$ (equivalently, the corresponding p-value is 0.157, which is greater than 0.05) and therefore the result is not statistically significant.

In sum, under the NHST framework we focus on the question of whether or not the difference in means is precisely zero. A non-significant result leads us to conclude that the true difference may be zero. A significant result leads us to conclude that the true difference is probably not zero.

NHST: the wrong framework for educational research

I have dedicated this much space to NHST because it is ubiquitous in social science research and is therefore important to understand. However, NHST is a very poor framework for the vast majority of analyses in this field, for the following reason. The null hypothesis significance test addresses a question that we typically don't care about and neglects the question that we do care about.

The only question addressed by NHST is the question of whether or not the effect size is precisely zero. For some studies, this is indeed the question of interest. For example, if the null hypothesis is that people who purport to have paranormal abilities will have the same accuracy in reading minds as 'normal' people, or that people treated with homeopathic medicine will have the same outcomes as people treated with a placebo, then the question of interest really is whether or not the effect is precisely zero. In these cases NHST is the appropriate framework.

However, in the vast majority of social science research, the researcher has little (if any) interest in whether or not the effect size is precisely zero. Rather, the goal of the research is to estimate the actual size of the effect, since this is the issue that tells us whether or not the intervention's impact is of substantive importance. In the SAT study, for example, the p-value can only tell us that the impact of the intervention is (probably) not zero. Simply knowing that the effect is not zero does not tell us whether or not we should go to the expense of implementing the new curriculum. Rather, we want to know if the new curriculum increases the mean SAT score by zero points, 20 points, 50 points or 80 points. This is the issue addressed by effect size estimation.

Effect size estimation

An effect size is a value that reflects the magnitude of the relationship between two variables. It captures the substantive finding that the research is intended to address, and it does so using a metric that is meaningful and intuitive. In the SAT example we can use D, the difference in means, as the effect size. Other common effect sizes include the standardised difference in means, the risk difference and the correlation coefficient.

Recall that under the NHST framework we built a distribution of Ds (the acceptable region) around the null hypothesis – thus focusing on a specific effect size (zero) that is usually of little interest. By contrast, under the framework of effect size estimation we build a distribution of Ds (a confidence interval) around the observed effect size – thus focusing on the actual effect, which is what we care

about. The lower and upper limits for the interval (D_{LL} and D_{UL}) are given by:

$$D_{LL} = D - SE_D \times Z_{CI\,Level}$$

$$D_{UL} = D + SE_D \times Z_{CI\,Level}$$

where SE_D is the same as before and $Z_{CI\,Level}$ is the Z value corresponding to the confidence level (for example, 1.96 for the 95% confidence interval).

In the SAT example, where D is 20 points and SE_D is 14.14, the 95% confidence interval is given by:

$$D_{LL} = 20 - 14.14 \times 1.96 = -7.72$$

$$D_{UL} = 20 + 14.14 \times 1.96 = 47.72$$

This means that the true effect probably falls in the range of –7.72 (in favour of the old curriculum) to 47.72 (in favour of the new curriculum). Formally, it means that in 95% of all possible studies, the confidence interval computed in this way will include the true effect, Δ.

These two approaches, NHST on the one hand, and effect size estimation on the other, are in many ways the same. In one case we focus on the null, identify a range of likely D values under the null, and then ask whether or not the observed D falls inside that range. In the other we focus on D, and identify a range of likely Δ values given D.

Importantly, since SE_D is identical in the two approaches, the 95% distribution about the null will include D if and only if the 95% distribution about

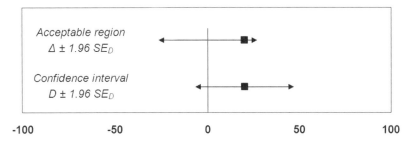

Figure 33.1 NHST (acceptable region) versus effect size estimation (conference interval)

D includes the null. Put another way, the p-value will be less than 0.05 if and only if the 95% confidence interval for D does not include zero. As such, the two approaches are completely congruent with each other mathematically, and the difference between them is one of form rather than substance (see Figure 33.1).

Nevertheless, this difference in form – whether to focus on the viability of the null hypothesis or to focus on the estimate of the effect size – turns out to be critically important for two reasons.

Effect size estimation addresses the question of interest

First, effect size estimation addresses the question that we intend to address ('What is the magnitude of the effect?'), while the NHST does not. The only information provided by the NHST (that we can or cannot rule out an effect size of precisely zero) is of little practical use.

Consider the four SAT studies in Figure 33.2, and assume that a 25-point difference in means would have practical importance. Using the effect size framework, two studies (A and D) show that the intervention may (or may not) be useful while two (B and C) show clearly that it is not useful. This speaks to the question of interest.

By contrast, under the NHST framework two studies (A and B) allow us to reject the null hypothesis while two (C and D) do not. As such, we are grouping studies A and B together despite the fact that the substantive implications of the two are very different (one tells us that the effect size is trivial while the other tells us that it could be as large as 94 points). Similarly, we are grouping studies C and D despite the fact that the substantive implications of the two are very different (again, one tells us that the effect is trivial and the other tells us that it could be as large as 74 points).

NHST lends itself to mistakes of interpretation

The second reason that the difference in format (effect size estimation rather than NHST) is important is because the NHST lends itself to mistakes of interpretation and these mistakes are common.

The NHST, when interpreted properly (that we can or cannot rule out a zero effect), often tells us nothing of practical importance. Since this would imply that the study provides nothing of real value, researchers often assume that the results must be telling us something about the magnitude of the effect and press the results into service as an indicator of effect size. If the effect is (or is not) statistically significant, this information is interpreted as

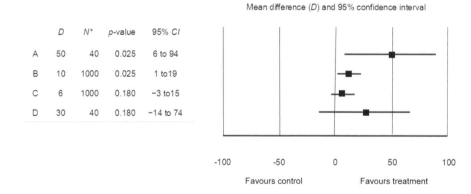

Figure 33.2 Four fictional studies to assess the impact of curricula on SAT scores

meaning that the effect is (or is not) of substantive significance. Similarly, the *p*-value is often pressed into service as an index of effect size, with a *p*-value of 0.05 taken to reflect a moderate effect, 0.01 a strong effect, and 0.001 a very strong effect.

However, these interpretations are not justified. The *p*-value depends on both the size of the effect and the size of the sample. This is appropriate (indeed necessary) when the *p*-value is used in the context of NHST, since it is the combination of these factors that tells us that the null hypothesis is (or is not) probably false. By contrast, the fact that the *p*-value depends on both the size of the effect and the size of the sample makes it a poor choice as an index of effect size since it makes it difficult for us to distinguish between the two factors. While a *p*-value of 0.02 could reflect a large effect size, it could also reflect a small (or even trivial) effect size in a large study.

Again, consider the four studies in Figure 33.2. Suppose you were told that a study yielded a *p*-value of 0.02. Many people would envision the results as looking like Study A, where the difference in means is substantial. But the results might also look like Study B, where the difference in means is trivial. Similarly, suppose you were told that a study yielded a *p*-value of 0.18. Many people would envision the results as looking like Study C, where the treatment effect is shown to be small. But the results might also look like Study D, where the observed effect is substantial, and the true effect could be as high as 74 points.

By contrast, when we use the effect size approach, we report the effect size and its precision (or confidence interval) as two distinct values, and thus avoid these mistakes of interpretation. In A and D the effect is large whereas in B and C the effect is small. In B and C the effect size is known precisely, whereas in A and D it is not known precisely.

In context

Readers who have been trained to work exclusively within the NHST framework may find the previous sections surprising. In fact, though, these ideas have been expressed many times by scores of researchers over a period of decades. At the end of this chapter I have listed a few of the papers and books that deal with this subject.

Why does it work at all?

Given that NHST focuses on a question with little (if any) relevance to practical issues in education and that the *p*-values reported by studies are often misinterpreted, one might wonder how educational research has managed to make any progress at all over the past decades.

David Rindskopf (1970) argues that when the system works, it works because of a set of happy coincidences. Recall that the power of a study depends on the sample size, on alpha and on the true effect size. In educational research, many studies tend to have comparable sample sizes and α is usually set at 0.05. Once these two factors are set, power tends to be poor (say, 20%) when the true effect is small, somewhat better (50%) when the true effect is moderate, and better (80%) when the true effect is large. As such, the system will tend to weed out the less effective interventions while identifying those with real potential.

When this set of coincidences allows NHST to work at all, it does work very well. If an intervention is moderately effective, so that power is around 50%, then half the studies will yield a significant result while half will not. The correct interpretation, of course, is that some studies will allow us to reject the null while others do not (presumably because of low power). In practice, researchers often see the results as 'conflicting', with some studies rejecting the null and others (making the mistakes outlined above) suggesting that the null is true. Even when the results are interpreted properly, focusing on the *p*-value rather than the size of the effect is a poor practice. Decisions about the utility of an intervention should be based on the magnitude of the effect size, not on evidence that the effect is (or is not) zero.

Effect sizes and research synthesis

While there has been only modest progress over the past few decades in moving from NHST to effect size estimation, there is reason to expect that this trend will accelerate. Over the past two decades researchers have embraced the importance of research synthesis (or systematic reviews) which serve as the basis for evidence-based practice. The goal of research synthesis is to study the pattern of effects – if the treatment effect is consistent across studies, then we can report that the effect is robust across the kinds of studies included in the analysis. If the treatment effect varies, then we can report that the effect varies, and possibly identify factors associated with this variation. In order to perform a research synthesis of this kind we need to start with the effect size for each study, and so the importance of presenting this information is becoming more widely recognised (see, for example, Schmidt, 1996; Harlow et al., 1997; Stang and Rothman, 2011; Greenland and Poole, 2011; Gelman, 2013; Greenland et al., 2016; Wasserstein and Lazar, 2016).

Statistical notes

In this chapter I focused on the effect size D, which is a raw difference in means. There are many other effect sizes (see Chapter 37 by Robert Coe in this volume; Borenstein, 2009; Borenstein et al., 2011) but the issues raised in this chapter apply to those as well.

My goal in this chapter has been to introduce NHST and effect size estimation, and to show why the latter is a better match for most social science research. To keep the focus on these goals I used an example (the SAT study) where the effect size is the raw mean difference, D. The formula for the standard error of D does not depend on D (only on the standard deviation and the sample size) and therefore the standard error is identical for NHST (where Δ is zero) and for effect size estimation (where D is the observed effect). By contrast, for many effect sizes (including the standardised mean difference and effect sizes for binary data) the standard error does depend on the effect size (though the impact is usually small). Therefore it is possible to have a case where the 95% confidence interval includes zero while the p-value is less than 0.05. For this reason, if one needs to report a p-value, then the p-value should be based on NHST formulas. This is a technical statistical matter and does not detract from the basic theme of this chapter.

I also made the assumption that the standard deviation of SAT scores within groups is known (rather than estimated from the sample), which allowed me to use the Z-distribution rather than the t-distribution for computing the acceptable range and the confidence interval. Typically, we do need to estimate the standard deviation from the sample and therefore use the t-distribution for both.

Conclusion

The question addressed by NHST – 'Is the effect size precisely zero?' – is of little relevance to most education research. When interpreted properly, NHST tells nothing about the substantive import of an intervention or relationship. When interpreted improperly (as is often the case) NHST can lead to incorrect conclusions. In particular, because the p-value reported for the significance test combines information about the effect size with information about the sample size, people often equate a significant p-value with a large effect size and a non-significant p-value with a small effect size, when these conclusions may not be justified.

By contrast, when we report an effect size with its confidence interval we focus on the question of interest – 'What is the magnitude of the effect?' Additionally, we report a confidence interval that speaks to the precision of the estimate. Because the effect size and the precision are reported as distinct values, the mistakes of interpretation that are common for NHST are less likely for effect size estimation.

NHST and effect size estimation are congruent with each other. The key difference is not in the mathematics, but rather in the focus of the report. However, this change in focus, because it directs attention to the relevant question and helps avoid mistakes of interpretation, is critically important.

Questions for further investigation

1. What are the fundamental differences between a statistical significance and a practical significance?
2. See the suggested readings below. View the papers by Jacob Cohen and discuss the effects of the misapplication of *p*-values.

Suggested further reading

Two of my favourite readings on NHST are papers written by my mentor, Jacob Cohen, entitled 'Things I have learned (so far)' (1990) and 'The Earth is round' (1994). Jack shows how *p*-values have been misapplied over a period of decades and how this has served to undermine science and confuse generations of researchers.

The next two readings are collections of essays on the use (and misuse) of significance tests. *The Significance Test Controversy – A Reader* (Morrison and Henkel, 1970) is a collection of early essays that expand on the issues raised in this chapter and also provide some historical context. *What If There Were No Significance Tests?* (Harlow et al., 1997) is a similar collection of essays published thirty years later.

Recently, some influential organisations have published papers and guidelines that discourage the inappropriate use of significance tests. The American Statistical Association published *The ASA's Statement on Statistical Significance and P-Values* (Wasserstein and Lazar, 2016), which makes many of the points that I discussed in this chapter. The online version of the statement also includes links to commentaries by many of the people who were involved in the discussion that led to the statement. *The European Journal of Epidemiology* published a paper entitled 'Statistical tests, P-values, confidence intervals, and power: a guide to misinterpretations' (Greenland et al., 2016). The individual authors have been writing about the mis-use of *p*-values for decades, and it is good to see their work synthesised in this collaborative paper. What makes this paper especially valuable is a list of 25 common mistakes that people make when using *p*-values.

The final two readings are books on research synthesis and meta-analysis. In this chapter I have discussed why we need to report an effect size for each study. These books show how we can use that effect size, in concert with effect sizes from other studies, to get a more appropriate picture of an intervention's effect. The books are *The Handbook of Research Synthesis* (2nd edn) (Cooper et al., 2009) and *Introduction to Meta-analysis* (Borenstein et al., 2009).

References

Borenstein, M. (1994) 'The case for confidence intervals in controlled clinical trials', *Controlled Clinical Trials*, 15: 411–28.

Borenstein, M. (2009) 'Effect Sizes for Continuous Data', in H. Cooper, L.V. Hedges and J.C. Valentine (eds), *The Handbook of Research Synthesis and Meta-Analysis*, 2nd edn. New York: Russell Sage Foundation, pp. 221–35.

Borenstein, M., Hedges, L.V., Higgins, J. and Rothstein, H.R. (2009) *Introduction to Meta-analysis*. Chichester: Wiley.

Borenstein, M., Hedges, L.V., Higgins, J. and Rothstein, H.R. (2011) *Computing Effect Sizes for Meta-analysis*. Chichester: Wiley.

Cohen, J. (1990) 'Things I have learned (so far)', *American Psychologist*, 45: 1304–12.

Cohen, J. (1994) 'The earth is round (p < .05)', *American Psychologist*, 49: 997–1003.

Cooper, H.M., Hedges, L.V. and Valentine, J.C. (2009) *The Handbook of Research Synthesis and Meta-Analysis*, 2nd edn. New York: Russell Sage Foundation.

Gelman, A. (2013) 'P-values and statistical practice', *Epidemiology*, 24: 69–72.

Greenland, S. and Poole, C. (2011) 'Problems in common interpretations of statistics in scientific articles, expert reports, and testimony', *Jurimetrics*, 51: 113–29.

Greenland, S., Senn, S.J., Rothman, K.J., Carlin, J.B., Poole, C., Goodman, S.N. and Altman, D.G. (2016) 'Statistical tests, *P* values, confidence intervals, and power: a guide to misinterpretations', *European Journal of Epidemiology*, 31: 337–50.

Harlow, L.L., Mulaik, S.A. and Steiger, J.H. (1997) *What If There Were No Significance Tests?* Mahwah, NJ: Lawrence Erlbaum.

Morrison, D.E. and Henkel, R. (eds) (1970) *The Significance Test Controversy – A Reader*. Chicago, IL: Aldine.

Rindskopf, D. (1970) 'Testing "Small" not Null Hypotheses: Classical and Bayesian approaches', in D.E. Morrison and R. Henkel (eds), *The Significance Test Controversy: A Reader*. Chicago, IL: Aldine.

Schmidt, F.L. (1996) 'Statistical significance testing and cumulative knowledge in psychology: implications for training of researchers', *Psychological Methods*, 1: 115–29.

Stang, A. and Rothman, K.J. (2011) 'That confounded P-value revisited', *Journal of Clinical Epidemiology*, 64: 1047–8.

Wasserstein, R.L. and Lazar, N.A. (2016) 'The ASA's Statement on p-values: context, process, and purpose', *The American Statistician*, 70(2): 129–33.

Analysis of variance (ANOVA)

34

Harvey J. Keselman and Lisa M. Lix

Introduction

Assessing whether treatment groups are equivalent on some measure of central tendency is a common problem for researchers in many fields. The classical method for examining this question has been the analysis of variance (ANOVA) F-test.

Consider a study in which a randomised trial is undertaken to compare a control group, an intervention group receiving a standard treatment, and an intervention group receiving a new treatment on a single continuous outcome measure such as health status. How can we determine whether there is a statistically significant difference in the mean outcome score among the three groups? The conventional method of analysis for these data is ANOVA. ANOVA encompasses a broad collection of statistical procedures used to partition variation in a dataset into components due to one or more categorical explanatory variables (i.e. factors). The topics covered in this chapter are: (1) a description of the applications of ANOVA in research; (2) considerations in applying ANOVA to a dataset; (3) the basic computations that underlie ANOVA along with ancillary procedures; (4) criteria to assess the reporting of ANOVA results in the education literature; and (5) discussing the robustness of ANOVA to violations of its normality assumption and possible alternative procedures that researchers can use.

Applications of ANOVA

Data arising from many different types of studies can be analysed using ANOVA, including the following:

- *One-way independent groups design,* in which three or more groups of study participants are to be compared on a single outcome measure (or dependent variable). This is the simplest type of design in which ANOVA is applied.
- *Factorial independent groups design,* in which two or more factors (or independent variables) are crossed so that each combination of categories, or cell of the design, comprises an independent group of study participants. Interaction and main effects will usually be tested in factorial designs. A statistically significant two-way interaction implies that the effect of one factor is not constant at each level of a second factor.
- *One-sample repeated measures design,* in which a single group of study participants is observed on two or more measurement occasions. The measurements for each participant are typically correlated.
- *Mixed design,* which contains both independent groups and repeated measures factors. Within-subjects interaction and main effects as well as the between-subjects main effect may be tested in a mixed design. A significant within-subjects two-way interaction effect implies that the repeated measures effect is not constant across groups of study participants.

Considerations in applying ANOVA

The assumptions that underlie validity of inference for the ANOVA F-test in independent groups designs are as follow:

- The outcome variable follows a normal distribution in each population from which the data are sampled. More will be said about this later in the chapter.
- Variances are equal (i.e. homogeneous) across the populations.
- The observations which comprise each sample are independent.

In one-sample repeated measures and mixed designs, measurements obtained from the same study participant are usually correlated, but it is assumed that measurements from different study participants are independent. In these designs it is also assumed that the data:

- follow a multivariate normal distribution;
- conform to the assumption of multisample sphericity.

Multivariate normality is satisfied when the marginal distribution for each measurement occasion is normal and the joint distributions of the measurement occasions are normal. For multisample sphericity to be satisfied, pairs of repeated measurements are assumed to exhibit a common variance. Furthermore, this variance is assumed to be constant across independent groups of study participants.

How it works/the basics

Variability in the outcome variable scores is used to determine whether there is an effect due to one or more independent variables (e.g. Method of Teaching Instruction: Method 1, Method 2, Method 3) and/or the combined effects of multiple independent variables (i.e. Method of Teaching Instruction *and* Hours Studied per Week: less than or equal to 10, greater than 10). In other words, the null hypothesis of equality of the population means (e.g. $H_0 : \mu_1 = \mu_2 = ... = \mu_A$) is tested by examining variation in the data.

We begin by focusing on the one-way independent groups design that contains a single independent variable denoted by A with A groups or levels. The ANOVA F-test compares a variance (i.e. MS_{BG}) whose magnitude is due to the (systematic) treatment effect (*when it exists*) as well as uncontrolled non-systematic effects (i.e. error) to a variance (MS_{WG}) whose size is only a function of non-systematic effects (i.e. error). The former, between-groups variance, is calculated from the variability that exists between the means of the treatment groups, while the latter, within groups variance, is calculated from the variability that exists among the scores within each of the groups. These variances, in the ANOVA context, are denoted as mean squares (MS) because the sums of the squared deviation scores are divided by the degrees of freedom (df; i.e. MS = SS/df). The between-groups MS, whose magnitude is a function of treatment variance and error variance, equals SS_{BG}/df_{BG}, while the within-groups MS, whose magnitude is only due to error variance, equals SS_{WG}/df_{WG}. In the population, treatment variance and error variance are denoted as σ_A^2, and σ_e^2 respectively. The df for MS_{BG} is equal to the number of levels of variable A minus one. The df for MS_{WG} equals the total number of observations in the study, N, minus the number of levels of the independent variable. The statistic to test the null hypothesis of mean equality is the ratio of MS_{BG} to MS_{WG}. This ratio will be approximately equal to one when there are no effects due to the independent variable, because each MS will be estimating error variance. This ratio will be greater than one when a treatment effect exists, that is when the null hypothesis is false.

How does one answer the following question 'Is the value of the F-test greater than one merely by chance (for example, because of sampling variation) or because a treatment effect really exists in the population?' One does so by calculating the probability of observing the test statistic by chance assuming the null hypothesis of no treatment effect is true. If this probability is less than the criterion of significance, denoted by the Greek letter alpha (α), then one concludes there is sufficient evidence of a treatment effect and the null hypothesis is rejected in favour of the alternative hypothesis (H_A) that not all population means are equivalent. Typically, α is set equal to 0.05.

Having laid out the mechanics of an ANOVA F-test, the results of the analysis are typically reported in a tabular format that includes information about the sources of variation in the data and their associated df, MS and the F-test value (see Table 34.1). For completeness, we have included the population variances that contribute to each MS so that readers can see how the rule for forming the test statistic applies to our exemplar designs; the column containing this information is denoted E(MS). The expectation operator (i.e. E) indicates what we 'expect' the value of the MS to be in the long run.

Now consider the factorial independent groups design containing independent variables, A (e.g. method of instruction) and B (e.g. hours studied per week). Prior to the time of the well-known statistician Ronald Fisher, experimenters would manipulate only one variable at a time. Fisher proved that two or more variables could be examined simultaneously, without the effects of one variable confounding the other. Furthermore, in addition to examining the effect of each variable (i.e. each *main effect*) on the variability in the dependent scores, Fisher noted

that researchers could also determine whether the variables interact to produce a unique effect on the scores above and beyond what one would predict from knowing the main effects.

To illustrate, consider the schematic in Figure 34.1. To test whether there is an effect due to variable A, the marginal means for this variable are used to compute the ANOVA F-test. (*Note*: Sample means are depicted with a caret ($\wedge$) over the population mean (μ).) Likewise, to test whether there is a B main effect, the marginal means for this variable are used to compute the ANOVA F-test. To test if there is an AxB interaction, the cell means are used to compute the ANOVA F-test; this is done by examining whether the simple effects (differences between the means of one variable at a fixed level of the other variable, e.g. the differences between the A means at a fixed level of, say, B_1 – in other words comparing $\hat{\mu}_{11}$ and $\hat{\mu}_{21}$) of one variable are constant across the levels of the other variable. The three null hypotheses tested in a two-way independent groups factorial design are: (a) $H_A : \mu_{1.} = \mu_{2.} \ldots = \mu_{A.}$, (b) $H_B : \mu_{.1} = \mu_{.2} = \ldots = \mu_{.B}$, and (c) $H_{AB} : \mu_{jk} - \mu_{j.} - \mu_{.k} + \mu_{jk}$, (for all j and k) where $j = 1, \ldots, A$ and $k = 1, \ldots, B$. A dot notation replacing a subscript indicates that that variable has been summed over; thus $\mu_{1.}$ is the A_1 population marginal mean. The null hypothesis for the interaction effect is not intuitively obvious but, needless to say, it tests, as we have stated previously, whether the simple effects of one variable are constant across the levels of the other variable. Also note from the

Table 34.1   ANOVA summary table for a one-way independent groups design containing Factor A

Source of variation	Sums of squares (SS)	df	Mean square (MS)	E(MS)	F-test
Between groups	SS_{BG}	$A-1$	SS_{BG}/df_{BG}	$\sigma_e^2 + \sigma_A^2$	MS_{BG}/MS_{WG}
Within groups	SS_{WG}	$N-A$	SS_{WG}/df_{WG}	σ_e^2	

Note: It is assumed that Factor A is a fixed-effect variable, which means that levels of the variable have not been sampled from a larger pool of levels, and consequently all levels of interest are contained in the study. df = degrees of freedom. N = total sample size. In the df column, A = number of levels of Factor A.

ANOVA summary table (Table 34.2) that the df and F-tests are formed in the manner previously described for the one-way independent groups design. That is, the main effect df are the number of treatment levels minus one, i.e. $(A–1)$ and $(B–1)$. The interaction df is equal to the product of the df for the effects that comprise the interaction, i.e. $(A–1)(B–1)$. The df for the denominator MS (no longer called the within-groups ms but now the within-*cells* MS) for the F-tests are arrived at in a manner that is consistent with what we stated for the one-way independent groups design, i.e. $N–AB$, that is the df are the total number of observations (N) minus the total number of treatment combination cells (AB).

This approach to assessing effects generalises to higher-order factorial ANOVA designs. For a three-way independent groups design containing independent variables A, B, and C, there are three two-way interaction effects: A × B, A × C and B × C, and one three-way interaction effect: A × B × C.

ANOVA summary tables for a two-way independent groups factorial design, a one-way repeated measures design and a mixed design containing one between-subjects variable and one repeated measures variable are presented in Tables 34.2 to 34.4, respectively.

For mixed designs (i.e. Table 34.4), all other things constant, within-subjects effects are typically easier to detect than between-subjects effects because differences between individuals do not contribute to a repeated measures error term. Both the B main effect and the A × B interaction effect are within-subjects effects and are easier to detect than if both A and B were between-subjects variables (see Maxwell and Delaney, 2004). For this design two different MSs are used as denominator values to calculate the F-tests because the mixed design is a combination of a one-way independent groups design [MS_A and ($MS_{S/A}$ = MS_{WG})] and a one-way repeated measures design (MS_A and MS_{AxS}). Accordingly, the between-subjects effect (A) has a between-subjects error term ($MS_{S/A}$) and the within-subjects effects (B and AxB) have a within-subjects error term ($MS_{BxS/A}$). The df for $MS_{BxS/A}$ is the product of the df for the effects that comprise the interaction, namely $(B–1)$ and $(N–A)$.

As we indicated previously, ANOVA F-tests require that certain characteristics (e.g. normality, homogeneity of variances, etc.) prevail in the population in order to obtain valid results. Prior to adopting the ANOVA F-test, the researcher should carefully evaluate whether the study data satisfy these assumptions. For example, within the context of a one-way independent groups design, the normality and homogeneity of variance assumptions should be examined. A prevalently used statistical package for obtaining numerical results is PASW (formerly known as SPSS). This package

		Variable B		Marginal A means
	Variable values	B_1	B_2	
Variable A	A_1	$\hat{\mu}_{11}$	$\hat{\mu}_{12}$	$\hat{\mu}_{1\cdot}$
	A_2	$\hat{\mu}_{21}$	$\hat{\mu}_{22}$	$\hat{\mu}_{2\cdot}$
Marginal B means		$\hat{\mu}_{\cdot 1}$	$\hat{\mu}_{\cdot 2}$	

Figure 34.1   Schematic of cell and marginal means for a factorial independent groups design with independent variables A and B

Note: Dot notation is used to indicate that the variable that the dot replaced has been summed over, e.g. a dot in the first subscript indicates that A has been summed over to get the B marginal value.

Table 34.2 ANOVA summary table for a factorial independent groups design containing Factors A and B

Source of variation	Sums of squares (SS)	df	Mean square (MS)	E(MS)	F-test
A	SS_A	$A-1$	SS_A/df_A	$\sigma_e^2 + \sigma_A^2$	MS_A/MS_{WG}
B	SS_B	$B-1$	SS_B/df_B	$\sigma_e^2 + \sigma_B^2$	MS_B/MS_{WG}
A × B	SS_{AB}	$(A-1)(B-1)$	SS_{AB}/df_{AB}	$\sigma_e^2 + \sigma_{A\times B}^2$	MS_{AB}/MS_{WG}
Within groups	SS_{WG}	$N-AB$	SS_{WG}/df_{WG}	σ_e^2	

Note: See Table 34.1 note. In the df column, A = number of levels of Factor A, B = number of levels of Factor B.

Table 34.3 ANOVA summary table for a one-sample repeated measures design containing the within-subjects Factor A

Source of variation	Sums of squares (SS)	df	Mean square (MS)	E(MS)	F-test
A	SS_A	$A-1$	SS_A/df_A	$\sigma_e^2 + \sigma_A^2 + \sigma_{A\times S}^2$	$MS_A/MS_{A\times S}$
S	SS_S	$N-1$	SS_S/df_S	$\sigma_e^2 + \sigma_S^2$	*
A × S	$SS_{A\times S}$	$(A-1)(N-1)$	$SS_{A\times S}/df_{A\times S}$	$\sigma_e^2 + \sigma_{A\times S}^2$	

Note: There is no proper test for the Subject (S) effect. However, we expect study participants to differ from one another – one reason why a simple repeated measures design was likely selected by the experimenter. Thus researchers would not typically be interested in testing this effect. The Subjects factor is a random-effects variable since study participants are sampled from a larger pool of participants. See Table 34.1 note.

Table 34.4 ANOVA summary table for a two-way mixed design containing between-subjects (A) and within-subjects (B) factors

Source of variation	Sums of squares (SS)	df	Mean square (MS)	E(MS)	F-test
Between subjects					
A	SS_A	$A-1$	SS_A/df_A	$\sigma_e^2 + \sigma_A^2$	$MS_A/MS_{S/A}$
S/A	$SS_{S/A}$	$N-A$	$SS_{S/A}/df_{S/A}$	σ_e^2	
Within subjects					
B	SS_B	$B-1$	SS_B/df_B	$\sigma_e^2 + \sigma_{B\times S/A}^2 + \sigma_A^2$	$MS_B/MS_{B\times S/A}$
A × B	SS_{AB}	$(A-1)(B-1)$	SS_{AB}/df_{AB}	$\sigma_e^2 + \sigma_{B\times S/A}^2 + \sigma_{A\times B}^2$	$MS_{AB}/MS_{B\times S/A}$
B × S/A	$SS_{B\times S/A}$	$(N-A)(B-1)$	$SS_{B\times S/A}/df_{B\times S/A}$	$\sigma_e^2 + \sigma_{B\times S/A}^2$	

Note: S/A is read as S 'within' A, meaning subjects are nested within groups, and this value is equivalent to MS_{WG}. See the notes from Table 34.1 and 34.3.

provides tests of normality (Komolgorov-Smirnov and Shapiro-Wilk) through its Descriptive Statistics/Explore program and a test for variance homogeneity (i.e. Levin) is obtained from its programs which compute ANOVAs (Compare Means/Oneway or General Linear Model/Univariate programs) (see Norusis, 2008). Similar diagnostic procedures are available in other software packages (e.g., SAS, 2010a). Descriptive tools such as box plots, normal probability plots and histograms can also provide valuable insights into the characteristics of the study data.

Ancillary procedures

Effect size (ES) and proportion of variance accounted for statistics

Researchers are encouraged to supplement tests of significance with statistics that quantify the magnitude of effect associated with an independent variable. According to *The Publication Manual of the American Psychological Association* (2009) 'it is almost always necessary to include some measure of the effect size in the Results section' (APA, 2009: 34). The practice of reporting ESs has also received support from the APA Task Force on Statistical Inference (Wilkinson and the Task Force on Statistical Inference, 1999).

Cohen (1965) defined one well-known test statistic that quantifies mean differences (e.g. $\bar{A}_1 - \bar{A}_2$ --a difference between the A_1 and A_2 marginal means) in standard deviation units (typically called Cohen's *d*). If the measurement scale is meaningful (i.e. not arbitrary), the mean difference need not be standardised. Other ES measures include omega squared (ω^2) and eta squared (η^2), which quantify the proportion of variation explained by an independent variable (see Howell, 2008: 402–6).

ES measures are important to report alongside tests of statistical significance. The latter are sensitive to sample size. Even a small treatment effect may be statistically significant if the sample size is sufficiently large. Thus we want to know that the effect is not only statistically significant,

but also that the magnitude of the effect is noteworthy. Guidelines are given by numerous authors for interpreting the magnitude of treatment effects (i.e. small, medium, large ESs) for social science data (Howell, 2008). Also see Chapters 33 and 37.

Confidence intervals (CIs)

The American Psychological Association's Task Force (Wilkinson and the Task Force on Statistical Inference, 1999) also recommends that tests of significance be supplemented with CIs for various statistics. For example, a 95% CI may be estimated for the difference statistic $\bar{A}_1 - \bar{A}_2$. A CI establishes an upper and lower limit for the population value of interest, such as the mean difference (e.g. $\mu_1 - \mu_2$). CIs assume a common form: the statistic (e.g. $\bar{A}_1 - \bar{A}_2$), plus and minus a critical value from the appropriate sampling distribution of the statistic, times the standard error. (Standard deviations of statistics are referred to as standard errors.) For example, assume one wants to set an interval around $\bar{A}_1 - \bar{A}_2$. The 95% CI would be:

$$(\bar{A}_1 - \bar{A}_2) \pm \sqrt{F_{\dot{a};1,N-A}} \sqrt{MS_{WG} \Sigma(c_j^2 / n_j)}$$

Because $(\bar{A}_1 - \bar{A}_2)$ is a contrast (i.e. comparison) among means having one numerator df, where the c_j s and n_j s are the contrast coefficients (+1 and −1) and group sizes, respectively, the standard error of the contrast equals $\sqrt{MS_{WG}\Sigma(c_j^2 / n_j)}$ (see Maxwell and Delaney, 2004: 170).

Power to detect treatment effects

The power of a statistical test is the probability of detecting the effect of an independent variable(s) when it is present in the population. In other words, statistical power is the probability of rejecting the null hypothesis of no treatment effects in favour of a true alternative hypothesis that states there are treatment effects. When designing their experiments, researchers should determine the conditions of the experiment so that if there is an effect due to their independent variable(s) it/they would be detected. That is, why put time and effort into designing and running an experiment if you do not have a high chance of detecting a true population effect? In particular, after diligently making sure that extraneous variables are controlled through appropriate experimental design procedures, so that variability in the dependent scores can only be due to the independent variable(s), researchers must decide on their criterion of significance (i.e. α) and how many subjects they need in order to detect the effect some percentage of the time when it exists. Because it is customary to set the criterion of falsely rejecting the null hypothesis at 0.05, and because researchers typically believe that the probability (Pr) of falsely rejecting the null hypothesis (a type I error $=\alpha$) is a mistake that is four times as serious as falsely accepting the null hypothesis when an alternative hypothesis is indeed true (i.e. a type II error $=\beta$), the power $1-Pr(\beta)$ that researchers typically strive to achieve is 0.80 (or greater). Researchers can postulate the magnitude of the effect that they believe exists (from prior research or a pilot study) with effect size/proportion of variance accounted for statistics (e.g. d, ω^2 or η^2), and then refer the value to an appropriate table or graph to determine how many subjects are required to detect the effect with the specified probability (Howell, 2008: 545; Maxwell and Delaney, 2004: Table A.11). Software programs that calculate power for popular statistical tests, including ANOVA F-tests, are readily available. For example, GPOWER can be freely obtained from www.psycho.uni-duesseldorf.de/aap/projects/gpower/.

Robust analogues to ANOVA *F*-tests

Many studies have demonstrated that the F-test and associated procedures (i.e. ES statistics, contrasts on means, CIs) are not robust to assumption violations, meaning that they are sensitive to changes in those factors that are extraneous to the hypothesis of interest. The F-test may become seriously biased when assumptions are not satisfied, resulting in spurious decisions about the hypothesis under consideration (see Erceg-Hurn et al., 2011; Keselman et al., 2008a, 2008b; Wilcox, 2003).

The assumptions which underlie the ANOVA F-test are unlikely to be satisfied in many studies. Outliers or extreme observations are often a significant concern because they can result in a substantial loss of power to detect a treatment effect. For example, in studies about reaction times, a few very large or small values may be observed. Furthermore, study participants who are exposed to a particular treatment or intervention may exhibit greater (or lesser) variability on the outcome measure than study participants who are not exposed to it. Heterogeneity of variance can have serious consequences for control of the type I error rate.

Researchers who rely on the ANOVA F-test (and ancillary procedures) to test hypotheses about equality of means may therefore unwittingly fill the literature with non-replicable results or at other times may fail to detect effects when they are present. In this era of evidence-informed decision making, it is crucial that the statistical procedures applied to a set of data produce valid results.

Applied researchers often regard non-parametric procedures based on rank scores, such as the Kruskal-Wallis test or Friedman's test, as appealing alternatives to the ANOVA F-test when the assumption of normality is suspect. However, non-parametric procedures test hypotheses about equality of distributions rather than equality of means. They are therefore sensitive to variance heterogeneity, because distributions with unequal variances will necessarily result in rejection of the null hypothesis. Rank-transform test procedures are also appealing because they can be implemented using existing statistical software. A rank-transform ANOVA F-test is obtained by converting the original scores to ranks prior to applying the conventional ANOVA F-test to the data. One limitation of rank-transform procedures is that they cannot be applied to tests of interaction effects in factorial designs. The ranks are not a linear function of the original observations, therefore ranking the data may introduce additional effects into the statistical model. Furthermore, ranking may alter the pattern of the correlations among the measurement occasions in repeated measurement designs. Rank-transform tests, while insensitive to departures from normality, must therefore be used with caution.

Non-rank transformations of the data, to stabilise the variance or reduce the influence of extreme observations on estimation and inference, are another popular choice. Common transformations include logarithmic, square root and reciprocal transformations. The primary difficulty with applying a transformation to one's data is that it may be difficult to interpret the null hypothesis when the data are no longer in the original scale of measurement.

When variance equality cannot be assumed, robust parametric procedures such as the Welch test (Erceg-Hurn et al., 2013) for the one-way independent groups design are recommended as alternatives to the ANOVA *F*-test. Welch's test does not pool the group variances in the computation of the test statistic error term, and modifies the degrees of freedom using a function based on the sample sizes and the variances. However, Welch's test assumes that the data satisfy the assumption of normality. If normality is not tenable, then a modification of the Welch test should be considered. One alternative involves substituting robust measures of location and scale for the usual mean and variance in the computation of the test statistic. Robust measures are less affected by the presence of outlying scores or skewed distributions than traditional measures of location and scale. There are a number of robust estimators that have been proposed in the literature; among these, the trimmed mean has received substantial attention because of its good theoretical properties, ease of computation and ease of interpretation. The trimmed mean is obtained by removing (i.e. censoring) the most extreme scores in the distribution, which have a tendency to 'shift' the mean in their direction (Erceg-Hurn et al., 2013). Current recommendations are to remove between 10 and 20% of the observations in *each* tail of the distribution. A consistent robust estimator of variability for the trimmed mean is the Winsorised variance, which is

computed by replacing the most extreme scores in the distribution with the next most extreme observations. While robust estimators are insensitive to departures from a normal distribution, they test a different null hypothesis from traditional estimators. *The null hypothesis is about equality of trimmed population means.* Many researchers subscribe to the position that inferences pertaining to robust parameters (i.e. population trimmed means) are more valid than inferences pertaining to the usual least squares parameters (the (μs) when they are dealing with populations that are non-normal in form (e.g. Huber, 1981; Wilcox and Keselman, 2004). Thus one is testing a hypothesis that focuses on the majority (i.e. central part) of the population rather than the entire population.

Computationally intensive methods, such as the bootstrap, have also been used to develop alternatives to the ANOVA *F*-test (and ancillary procedures). Under a bootstrap methodology, the usual ANOVA *F*-test is computed on the original observations, but statistical significance is assessed using the empirical distribution of the test statistic rather than the theoretical sampling distribution (i.e. *F* distribution) of the statistic. The empirical distribution is obtained by generating a large number (e.g. 1,000) of bootstrap datasets; each dataset is a random sample (sampling with replacement) from the original observations. The *F*-test is computed for each bootstrap dataset. The resulting bootstrapped test statistics are ranked in ascending order; the critical value for assessing statistical significance corresponds to a pre-selected percentile of the empirical distribution, such as the 95th percentile. Research has shown that bootstrap test procedures have good properties in the presence of assumption violations. For example, the bootstrapped ANOVA *F*-test for repeated measures designs will effectively control the rate of Type I errors to α, the nominal level of significance, under departures from both normality and sphericity.

Researchers in the behavioural, biological, and health sciences are routinely encouraged to assess whether derivational assumptions hold prior to using a test (ANOVA *F*-test) of significance (Lix and Keselman, 2004, 2009; Kirk, 2013). Indeed, it is well known that psychological, biological and medical data rarely are normal in form (Lix and Keselman, 2005; Micceri, 1989). For example, many psychologists collect reaction time data; these data typically will be positively skewed (not symmetric as would be the case with a normal distribution), because of large outlying values in the right tail of the distribution: this distribution reflects the fact that some individuals will have very long reaction times, while the vast majority of individuals will have short or moderate reaction times. With regard to the assumption that the data in the treatment populations are normal in shape, researchers as we indicated previously can use a test for normality (for example Shapiro-Wilkes, Kolmogorov-Smirnov — see D'Agostino and Stephens, 1986; SAS, 2010b: 357). If the results of the preliminary test indicate that the empirical data in each treatment group conform to a theoretical normal distribution, researchers can go on to test for mean equality with the ANOVA F-test (assuming that the other assumptions are examined and believed to be true as well). However, if the result of the test for normality indicates the empirical data are not normally distributed within each treatment group, researchers must take remedial action. As previously discussed, the choices available to researchers for dealing with non-normal data are to: (1) transform their data to achieve normality (Box and Cox, 1964); (2) use a procedure that does not require the data to be normally distributed (a rank transformation test; see Akritas et al., 1997); or (3) use a procedure (Welch-James-WJ) that can perform accurately in the presence of non-normality, for example procedures that use robust estimators such as trimmed means and Winsorised variances rather than the usual least squares estimators in the test statistic (Erceg-Hum et al., 2013; Keselman et al., 2008a). Prior empirical research indicates that these alternative methods can be quite successful in controlling Type I and Type II errors when data are non-normal in the treatment populations (see Lix and Keselman, 1998). Nonetheless, some of the better approaches, such as alternative (3) above, are not available in the major statistical packages and therefore are not typically used by researchers; Keselman et al. (2008) have provided a software program to implement the WJ procedure.

However, now researchers have available methods that incorporate the fact that data are non-normal into their testing procedures for mean equality, i.e generalised linear models. In particular, as previously noted, the SAS (2010a, 2010b) and PASW (SPSS, Inc., 2009) systems of statistical programs allow users to conduct tests for mean equality where the data need not be presumed to be normal in form (see for example the SAS GLIMMIX procedure) through generalised linear models (Breslow and Clayton, 1993; Fox, 2009; Nelder and Wedderburn, 1972). Indeed, generalised linear models allow users to perform tests for mean equality for data that can be lognormal, exponential, beta, or gamma distributed. Furthermore, researchers can even adopt a generalised linear model that specifies that data in the treatment groups have varied forms; for example in some groups the data are normally distributed while in others they are exponentially distributed. Clearly, this approach for dealing with non-normal data *could* provide researchers with a remarkably reliable and valid way of testing for treatment group equality where data are not normal in form. However, researchers in psychology, biology, and other behavioural and social sciences, typically do not know how their data will be distributed in the populations and accordingly must rely on statistical methods to determine the appropriate shape to assume for their data. The two most popular statistical packages employed by behavioural sciences and biological researchers (SAS and SPSS), in addition to providing appropriate plots of the empirical data (including normality probability plots, box plots, and so forth), provide users with statistics that can be used to test for normality and tests that examine the fit of the data to various theoretical distributions.

Accordingly, whether generalised linear model analyses will work well depends on how good these preliminary tests for normality and fit perform. Evidence regarding the accuracy of these tests in related areas of analyses is not encouraging (Dufour et al., 2010; Keselman et al., 2006). That is, will this approach to handling non-normal data result in better tests for mean equality across groups compared to the previously enumerated methods (including the ANOVA *F*-test) that are available to researchers?

This problem was investigated by Keselman, Othman and Wilcox (2016). They sampled data from various non-normal distributions (skewed distributions having different degrees of skewness and kurtosis, multinomial Likert type distributions, and mixed-normal distributions) either having equal variances or having unequal variances and unequal group sizes that were either positively or negatively paired with one another. The ANOVA *F*-test was then compared with GLIMMIX (SAS's generalised linear model program) results when the GLIMMIX test was adopted following a significant test for non-normalitity with the Anderson-Darling test statistic or based on the results from applying the Akaike (1974) goodness of fit statistic.

It is apparent from their empirical findings that adopting a generalised linear model approach (such as GLIMMIX) procedure to assess treatment group equality across groups does not work when the link function of the data is based on the Anderson-Darling test for distribution shape, the smallest Akaike fit-statistic value, or always assuming a log-normal distribution. They reported that the generalised linear model solutions were not better at controlling the number of Type I errors as compared to the traditional ANOVA *F*-test. Indeed, for the cases investigated, the ANOVA *F*-test resulted in an inflated (liberal) or deflated (conservative) rate of Type I error 62 percent of the time, while the rate for the GLIMMIX solutions varied from 56 to 61 percent.

Therefore, researchers should adopt a generalised linear model analysis with caution as it will not necessarily provide better Type I error control when the data are non-normal. As was indicated by Cerrito (2005), GLIMMIX is a difficult procedure to adopt, and much thought should be given to choosing this method of analysis. As he stated, 'While it is possible to use PROC GLIMMIX as the most complex of the models, it is not advisable. Even so, choices as to random versus fixed effects, link function, and covariance matrix still have to be made. Therefore, the investigator should use the simplest procedure that will accommodate the variable choices' (Cerrito, 2005: 7) (see also Stroup, 2013, Chapter 3).

All, however, is not lost. As previously indicated, one can successfully test for equality of central tendency across groups when data are non-normal and variances are heterogeneous by adopting the non-pooled Welch-James statistic (WJ*t*) with robust estimators of central tendency and variability. This is a finding that has been established in many research investigations (e.g. Keselman et al., 2002; Keselman et al., 2003; Keselman et al., 2007; Keselman et al., 2008a, 2008b). As well, the WJ*t* statistic can be applied with bootstrapping methodology (Erceg-Hurn et al., 2013; Keselman et al., 2002) resulting in very good Type I error control.

Assessing ANOVA results reported in empirical research

For decision makers to have confidence in ANOVA results reported in the empirical literature, it is *important* that the choice of test procedures is justified and the analytic strategy is accurately and completely described. The reader should be provided with a clear understanding of the characteristics of the data under investigation. This can be accomplished by reporting exploratory descriptive analysis results, including standard deviations (or variances), sample sizes, skewness (a measure of symmetry of the distribution) and kurtosis (a measure of peakedness of the distribution), and normal probability plots. As a general rule of thumb, skewness and kurtosis measures should be within the range from +1 to −1 in order to assume that the data follow a normal distribution. The normal probability plot is a graphic technique in which the observations are plotted against a theoretical normal distribution; if all of the points fall on an approximate diagonal line, then normality is likely to be a tenable assumption.

While preliminary tests of variance equality, such as Levene's test, or tests of sphericity, such as Mauchly's test, are available in statistical software packages, their use is not always recommended. Many tests about variances are sensitive to departures from a normal distribution, and those that are insensitive to non-normality may lack statistical power to detect departures from the null hypothesis of equal variances which can result in erroneous decisions about the choice of follow-up tests.

For factorial designs, unless there is theoretical evidence that clearly supports the testing of main effects only, the analysis should begin with tests of interactions among the study factors. Graphic presentations of the cell means may be useful to characterise the nature of the interaction for readers.

Tests of main and interaction effects should be completely described. This includes reporting the value of the test statistic, degrees of freedom and the p-value or critical value for each effect that is tested.

A statistically significant ANOVA F-test is routinely followed by multiple comparisons to identify the localised source of an effect. The choice of a multiple comparison test statistic and procedure for controlling the familywise error rate, the probability of making at least one Type I error for the entire set of comparisons, should be explicitly identified in the reporting of results. A simple Bonferroni approach may suffice, in which each of p comparisons is tested at the α/p level of significance. However, this multiple comparison procedure is less powerful than stepwise Bonferroni procedures, such as Hochberg's (1988) procedure (see also Keselman et al., 2011; Keselman and Miller, 2012).

Conclusion

The ANOVA F-test (and its ancillary procedures) is one of the most popular test procedures for analysing behavioural and social science data because it can be used in a wide variety of research applications. Researchers may be reluctant to bypass the conventional ANOVA F-test in favour of an alternative approach. This reluctance may stem, in part, from the belief that the F-test is robust to departures from derivational assumptions (see, for example, Aron et al., 2009). While the Type I error rate, the probability of erroneously rejecting a true null hypothesis, *may* be relatively insensitive to the presence of non-normal distributions, power rates can be substantially affected. This is a critical issue, particularly for small-sample designs which are common in behavioural and social science research. Departures from variance homogeneity and multi-sample sphericity can result in seriously biased tests of between-subjects and within-subjects effects, respectively. Statistical procedures that are robust to assumption violations have been developed for both simple and complex factorial designs, and are now routinely available in many statistical software packages (Erceg-Hurn et al., 2013; Keselman et al., 2008a, 2008b; Wilcox and Keselman, 2004).

In conclusion, we wish to note that the ANOVA layout, effect size measures, confidence intervals and statistical power analyses which were the focus of this chapter provide the basic schemata for a variety of analyses, whether one adopts the classical ANOVA F-test or one of its robust counterparts. As we stated previously, there are different perspectives as to whether the ANOVA F-test and its ancillary procedures are robust to derivational assumptions. Applied researchers must be able to make an appropriate justification for the choice of testing procedures based on a careful examination of the study data. We recommend that researchers consider adopting *both* classical and robust procedures. When the results of the two approaches agree, researchers can be more confident in their conclusions.

Questions for further investigation

1. Discuss the different types of testing procedures detailed in this article. List the pros and cons of the robust and classical procedures. When would one be prevalent over the other and what are the benefits of using both techniques in data analysis?

Suggested further reading

There is a wealth of reading available if you are interested in furthering your studies in this area. Please see the papers and texts referenced below, as well as Chapter 37 by Robert Coe, 'Effect Size', in this volume, which will prove a sound starting point.

It would be worthwhile for the reader of this chapter to also read the article by Keselman, H.J., Othman, A.R. and Wilcox, R. (2016) 'Generalized linear model analyses for treatment group equality when data are non-normal', *Journal of Modern Applied Statistical Methods*, 15: 32–61.

A good introduction to robust estimation and testing can be found in the paper by Erceg-Hurn, D.M., Wilcox, R.R. and Keselman, H.J. (2013) 'Robust statistical estimation', in T. Little (ed.), *The Oxford Handbook of Quantitative Methods*. New York: Oxford University Press.

Additional reading regarding generalised linear models can be obtained from Fox, J. (2015) *Applied Regression Analysis and Generalized Linear Models*, 3rd edn. London: Sage.

References

Akaike, H. (1974) 'A new look at the statistical model identification', *IEEE Transaction on Automatic Control*, 19(6): 716–23.

Akritas, M.G., Arnold, S.F. and Brunner, E. (1997) 'Nonparametric hypotheses and rank statistics for unbalanced factorial designs', *Journal of the American Statistical Association*, 92(437): 258–65. doi: 10.1080/01621459.1997.10473623

American Psychological Association (APA) (2009) *Publication Manual of the American Psychological Association*, 6th edn. Washington, DC: American Psychological Association.

Aron, A., Aron, E.N. and Coups, E.J. (2009) *Statistics for Psychology*, 5th edn. Upper Saddle River, NJ: Pearson.

Box, G.E.P. and Cox, D.R. (1964) 'An analysis of transformations', *Journal of the Royal Statistical Society: Series B (Methodological)*, 26(2): 211–52. Available from www.jstor.org/stable/2984418

Breslow, N.R. and Clayton, D.G. (1993) 'Approximate inference in generalized linear mixed models', *Journal of the American Statistical Association*, 88(421): 9–25. doi: 10.1080/01621459.1993.10594284

Cerrito, P.B. (2005, October) 'From GLM to GLIMMIX – Which model to choose?' Paper presented at the 13th Annual Conference of the Southeast SAS Users Group, Portsmouth, VA.

Cohen, J. (1965) 'Some statistical issues in psychological research', in B.B. Wolman (ed.), *Handbook of Clinical Psychology*. New York: McGraw-Hill, pp. 95–121.

Conover, W.J. and Iman, R.L. (1981) 'Rank transformation as a bridge between parametric and nonparametric statistics', *American Statistician*, 35: 124–9.

D'Agostino, R.B. and Stephens, M.I.A. (eds) (1986) *Goodness-of-fit Techniques*. New York: Marcel Dekker.

Dufour, J., Farhat, A., Gardiol, L. and Khalaf, I. (2010) 'Simulation-based finite-sample normality tests in linear regressions' (unpublished paper). Université de Montreal, Montreal, Québec.

Erceg-Hurn, D.M., Wilcox, R.R. and Keselman, H.J. (2013) 'Robust statistical estimation', in T. Little (ed.), *The Oxford Handbook of Quantitative Methods*. New York: Oxford University Press.

Fox, J. (2009) *A Mathematical Primer for Social Statistics*. Thousand Oaks, CA: Sage.

Fox, J. (2015) *Applied Regression Analysis and Generalized Linear Models*, 3rd edn. London: Sage.

Hill, M.A. and Dixon, W. J. (1982) 'Robustness in real life: a study of clinical laboratory data', *Biometrics*, 38: 377–96.

Hochberg, Y. (1988) 'A sharper Bonferroni procedure for multiple tests of significance', *Biometrika*, 75: 800–2.

Howell, D.C. (2008) *Fundamental Statistics for the Behavioral Sciences*, 6th edn. San Francisco, CA: Thomson Wadsworth.

Huber, P.J. (1981) *Robust Statistics*. New York: Wiley.

Keselman, H.J. (2005) 'Multivariate normality tests', in B.S. Everitt and D.C. Howell (eds), *Encyclopedia of Statistics in Behavioural Science* (Vol. 3). London: Wiley, pp. 1373–79.

Keselman, H.J., Algina, J., Kowalchuk, R.K. and Wolfinger, R.D. (2006) 'Model selection criteria in the analysis of repeated measurements', *The American Statistician*, 60(3): 210–11. doi: 10.1080/03610919808813497

Keselman, H.J., Algina, J., Lix, L.M., Wilcox, R.R. and Deering, K. (2008a) 'A generally robust approach for testing hypotheses and setting confidence intervals for effect sizes', *Psychological Methods*, 13: 110–29.

Keselman, H.J., Algina, J., Lix, L.M., Wilcox, R.R., and Deering, K. (2008b) 'Supplemental material for: A generally robust approach for testing hypotheses and setting confidence intervals for effect sizes'. Available from: http://supp.apa.org/psycarticles/supplemental/met_13_2_110/met_13_2_110_supp.html (last accessed 1 December 2016).

Keselman, J.C., Lix, L.M. and Keselman, H.J. (1996) 'The analysis of repeated measurements: a quantitative research synthesis', British Journal of Mathematical and Statistical Psychology, 49: 275–98.

Keselman, H.J., Othman, A.R. and Wilcox, R. (2016) 'Generalized linear model analyses for treatment group equality when data are non-normal', Journal of Modern Applied Statistical Methods, 15: 32–61.

Keselman, H.J. and Miller, C.E. (2012) 'Correction to many tests of significance: new methods for controlling Type I errors', Psychological Methods, 17(4): 679.

Keselman, H.J., Miller, C.E. and Holland, B. (2011) 'Many tests of significance: new methods for controlling Type I errors', Psychological Methods, 16: 420–31.

Keselman, H.J., Wilcox, R.R. and Lix, L.M. (2003) 'A generally robust approach to hypothesis testing in independent and correlated groups designs', Psychophysiology, 40: 586–96. doi: 10.1111/1469-8986.00060

Keselman, H. J., Wilcox, R. R., Lix, L. M., Algina, J. and Fradette, K. (2007) 'Adaptive robust estimation and testing', British Journal of Mathematical and Statistical Psychology, 60(2): 267–93. doi: 10.1348/000711005X63755

Keselman, H.J., Wilcox, R.R., Othman, A.R. and Fradette, K. (2002) 'Trimming, transforming statistics, and bootstrapping: circumventing the biasing effects of heteroscedasticity and nonnormality', Journal of Modern Applied Statistical Methods, 1(2): 288–309. Retrieved from http://digitalcommons.wayne.edu/jmasm/vol1/iss2/38/

Kirk, R.E. (2013) Experimental Design: Procedures for the Behavioral Sciences, 4th edn. Thousand Oaks, CA: Sage.

Lix, L.M. and Keselman, H.J. (1998) 'To trim or not to trim: tests of mean equality under heteroscedasticity and non-normality', Educational and Psychological Measurement, 58: 409–29.

Lix, L.M. and Keselman, H.J. (2004) 'Multivariate tests of means in independent groups designs: Effects of covariance heterogeneity and non-normality', Evaluation & The Health Professions, 27: 45–69.

Lix, L.M. and Keselman, H.J. (2005) 'Within-case designs: Distribution-free methods', in B.S. Everitt and D.C. Howell (eds), Encyclopedia of Behavioral Statistics. New York: Wiley, pp. 2122–6.

Lix, L.M. and Keselman, H.J. (2009) 'Analysis of variance', in M. Kattan and M.E. Cowen (eds), Encyclopedia of Medical Decision Making. Thousand Oaks, CA: Sage.

Lix, L.M., Keselman, J.C. and Keselman, H.J. (1996) 'Consequences of assumption violations revisited: a quantitative review of alternatives to the one-way analysis of variance F test', Review of Educational Research, 66: 579–619.

Maxwell, S.E. and Delaney, H.D. (2004) Designing Experiments and Analyzing Data, 2nd edn. Mahwah, NJ: Lawrence Erlbaum.

Micceri, T. (1989) 'The unicorn, the normal curve, and other improbable creatures', Psychological Bulletin, 105(1): 156–66.

Nelder, J.A. and Wedderburn, W.M. (1972) 'Generalized linear models', Journal of the Royal Statistical Society: Series A (General), 135(3): 370–84. doi:10.2307/2344614

Norusis, M.J. (2008) SPSS Statistics 17.0: Guide to Data Analysis. Upper Saddle River, NJ: Prentice Hall.

SAS Institute, Inc. (2010a) SAS/STAT 9.22 User's Guide. Cary, NC: SAS Institute, Inc.

SAS Institute, Inc. (2010b) Base SAS 9.2 Procedures Guide: Statistical Procedures, 3rd edn. Cary, NC: SAS Institute, Inc.

Scariano, S.M. and Davenport, J.M. (1987) 'The effects of violations of independence assumptions in the one-way ANOVA', American Statistician, 41: 123–9.

SPSS, Inc. (2009) PASW Statistics for Windows, version 18.0. Chicago, IL: SPSS, Inc.

Stroup, W.W. (2013) Generalized Linear Mixed Models: Modern Concepts, Methods and Applications. Boca Raton, FL: CRC Press.

Toothaker, L.E. (1991) Multiple Comparisons for Researchers. Newbury Park, CA: Sage.

Wasserman, S. and Bockenholt, U. (1989) 'Bootstrapping: applications to psychophysiology', Psychophysiology, 26: 208–21.

Wilcox, R.R. (1995) 'ANOVA: a paradigm for low power and misleading measures of effect size?', *Review of Educational Research,* 65: 51–77.

Wilcox, R.R. (2003) *Applying Contemporary Statistical Techniques.* New York: Academic.

Wilcox, R.R. and Keselman, H.J. (2003) 'Modern robust data analysis methods: measures of central tendency', *Psychological Methods,* 8: 254–74.

Wilcox, R.R. and Keselman, H.J. (2004) 'Multivariate location: robust estimators and inferences', *Journal of Modern Applied Statistical Methods,* 3: 2–12.

Wilkinson, L. and the Task Force on Statistical Inference (1999) 'Statistical methods in psychology journals', *American Psychologist,* 54: 594–604.

Zimmerman, D.W. (2004) 'A note on preliminary tests of equality of variances', *British Journal of Mathematical and Statistical Psychology,* 57: 173–81.

Multiple linear regression

Stephen Gorard

35

Introduction

This chapter provides a brief and basic introduction to regression techniques and the use of several variables in one consolidated analysis, focusing here on multiple linear regression. There are, of course, many other kinds of regression and even more ways of conducting multiple variable analysis, and some of these are referenced later in the chapter. However, most of the advice given in this chapter, about interpretation and judgement for example, would apply equally to all of these other techniques of analysis as well. For the benefit of some readers the chapter starts with a reprise of the ideas of correlation and two-variable regression (see examples in Chapter 16). The next section describes a basic multiple linear regression, and ensuing sections look at the interpretation of results and some of the potential dangers of being misled.

Correlation and simple regression

There is a correlation between people's height and their foot length. In general, taller people tend to have bigger feet (and vice versa). This correlation is not perfect, and some tall people have quite dainty feet for example. But imagine you were told that three people have heights of 2m, 1.7m and 1.2m, and that the same three people have foot lengths of 0.2m, 0.25m and 0.3m. You are asked to guess which foot size matches which height. In the absence of any other evidence you would be wise to place the smallest foot size with the shortest person and so on. Imagine that this is correct, and that a fourth person has a foot size of 0.3m. You are asked to estimate how tall they would be. In the absence of any other evidence, you would be wise to imagine them as near the height of 2m. This, in essence, is a simple regression. You use an existing correlation between two measures to estimate an unknown value of one measure from a known value of the other measure for the same case or individual.

Several things should be clear from this example. First, regression is rather easy and intuitive in nature. Second, it can easily yield an incorrect answer. How likely it is that the fourth person is near 2m in height depends upon the representativeness of the first three cases, the accuracy of all of the measurements involved, the variability of all measures involved, and the strength of the correlation. Third, regression is not a definitive test of anything, and it does not prove anything. It is only of use for estimating, or a best guess in the absence of any other evidence. Fourth, it is impossible to demonstrate causes using regression alone. An individual's height does not cause their foot size or vice versa. However elaborate a regression model is, it is merely an expression of association between the two variables. We may imagine in some regression models that the link is a causal one, but the indications of this causality come from our knowledge of the real world outside the regression model, not from the model itself. For example, imagine that a pupil's repeated absence from school is correlated with their examination performance. This might be a negative correlation, meaning that the two measures are related inversely, so that an individual with higher recorded absence from school would tend to attain fewer GCSE passes (the GCSE is a standard national examination in each curriculum subject for 16-year-olds in England). We might imagine that absence from school therefore impairs examination performance. But that explanation must be based on our wider knowledge of the mechanisms involved, not on the regression pattern alone. Otherwise, it could be that failure at school leads to school avoidance, or the two measures could be mutually reinforcing, or there might be any number of other things affecting both measures (poverty, illness and so on).

The most commonly used technique for correlation/regression is based on the Pearson's R correlation coefficient. An R score of 1 means a perfect correlation or even identity, an R of −1 means a perfect inverse, and an R of 0 means no correlation at all between the two variables. Usually you will uncover R values between these extremes. For example, using data from an imaginary 400 pupils, the correlation between the precise age of a pupil in months and their examination score (measured as number of GCSEs passed, as above) might appear as Table 35.1 (using SPSS). The correlation between the two measures is 0.643, meaning that any relationship is positive (a higher age is linked to better GCSE scores). It also

means that any relationship is imperfect. If we square the R value of 0.643 we get an R^2 value of just over 0.4. This 'effect size' tells us that around 40 per cent of the variation in the two measures is common to both, and that around 60 per cent is independent. Even if higher age were assumed to *cause* better performance, the R^2 tells us that there are other factors involved as well, including errors in measurement and recording (Gorard, 2010a).

Table 35.1 also reports 'Sig.' or significance; it marks significant values with ** and includes an explanatory footnote that this means significant at the 0.01 level. SPSS generates these items automatically, and there is no way of switching them off at present, so you must just ignore them when they are not relevant. They could only be relevant when the measures are very accurate, come from a sample drawn randomly with full response from a known population, and you want to estimate the likelihood that *if* there is no sizeable correlation in the population you would obtain an R value at least as large as the one in the table. Why anyone should want to know the latter is inconceivable, and I have never encountered such a situation in real life – my advice is that you should usually ignore these items to focus on judgement based on the values of N and R and the accuracy and distribution of your two measures. The key point is that you must not mistake the Sig. as being any indication of the importance of your results (Gorard, 2010b). It also means that you do not need to repeat a table like this in any report. The R (0.64) and N (400) figures will suffice.

Table 35.1   Correlation between age in months and number of GCSEs passed

		Age	GCSEs
Age	Pearson Correlation	1	.643(**)
	Sig. (2-tailed)		.000
	N	400	400
GCSEs	Pearson Correlation	.643(**)	1
	Sig. (2-tailed)	.000	
	N	400	400

**Correlation is significant at the 0.01 level (2-tailed).

The calculation of R is based on two key assumptions. The two sets of values used for the correlation/regression must be real measures, in the way that height or number of days missing from school are real numbers, and that the ethnic origin of an individual or the number on their national identity card is not. And the two sets of values must cross plot to form an approximate straight line. Figure 35.1 shows a cross plot of our imaginary data on pupil age and GCSE passes. Although there is variation in the number of passes for each age value, and a cluster of pupils with zero passes, the graph shows a small near linear positive relationship between age and GCSE passes (as we would expect from the correlation coefficient of 0.643). Note that a very low or zero value of R does not mean that the two measures are not related, merely that they are not obviously linearly related. In situations where the two measures form a curve when cross plotted, it is sometimes possible to transform the variables (e.g. by conversion to logarithms) to make a better line of fit, although this can introduce further problems (Harwell and Gatti, 2001). In addition, there are correlation and regression techniques available for use with categorical variables (Siegel, 1956).

There is a line of best fit that is usually seen as the line on a graph like Figure 35.1 that minimises the mean deviation of all points from the line. Once this line has been calculated as part of the regression analysis, it is possible to use it to read off the values of one variable (such as height, the dependent variable in our example) from the values of the other (such as foot length, the independent variable). The words dependent and independent are traditional, but do not be confused into thinking that they mean one measure is caused by the other or that the other measure could not equally well be the dependent one. The key output from SPSS when conducting a simple bivariate linear regression, using the same data as Table 35.1 but shorn of items relating to significance and standard errors, could appear like Table 35.2. The dependent (predicted) variable is

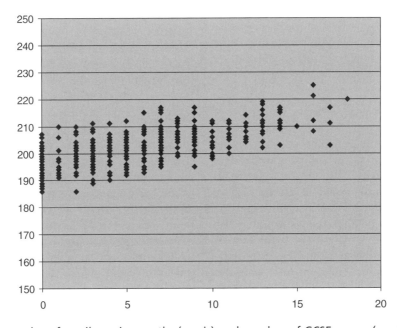

Figure 35.1 Cross plot of pupil age in months (y axis) and number of GCSE passes (x axis)

N = 400

Source: Hypothetical data

the number of GCSE passes per individual, and the independent (predictor) variable is the number of half days absent from school. In this example the model R value is 0.643, also shown as beta in Table 35.2.

Table 35.2 Regression analysis, predicting GCSE passes from school absence

Model		B	Beta
1	Constant	−78.185	
	Age	.414	.643

Dependent variable: GCSEs.

The R value, identical to that in Table 35.1, is an estimate of how closely correlated the two measures are. What is new in this regression analysis is the B column. This gives a theoretical coefficient (or multiplier) for the pupil age to yield the best estimate of the number of GCSE passes for all cases. The constant yields the intercept on the graph (see below). So our best estimate for any pupil, ignoring measurement and other errors that we cannot estimate, is:

$$\text{Number of GCSE passes} = -78.185 + (0.414 * Age)$$

Using this equation we can estimate the number of GCSE passes for individuals whose results we do not know but whose ages we do know. Someone who is 189 months old would be predicted to achieve −78.185 + (0.414 * 189) GCSE passes. This is very near zero, as we would expect from Figure 35.1, since the imagined line of best fit crosses the y axis (a value of zero GCSE passes) at around 189. On the other hand, someone aged 210 months would be predicted to gain around 9 GCSE passes, since −78.185 + (0.414 * 210) is near 9. Again this makes sense looking at the data in Figure 35.1. However, age is not the only thing related to examination outcomes. Even if it is a contributory factor, there may be many other measures which could help to make our estimate even more accurate. This leads us to consider multiple linear regression.

Multiple regression

Going back to the very first illustration, imagine you were told that four people have heights of 2 m, 2 m, 1.7 m and 1.2 m, and that the same four people have foot lengths of 0.2 m, 0.25 m, 0.27 m and 0.3 m. You are asked to guess which foot length matches which height. Here you have two individuals with the same height who must have different foot lengths. How do you decide which matches which? What you really need is more information. Knowing the individual's sex or ethnicity may help here. Factoring a third, fourth or fifth variable into your calculation at the same time as the original two measures is what multiple regression does. Using the same approach as simple regression, the model could calculate the best single predictor, and then keep adding the next best predictor to the model to make the estimates more accurate, until either we run out of possible predictors or the model cannot improve (its R^2) any further with the available predictors.

For example, we might improve our estimate of GCSE passes by adding more independent variables to our main predictor of pupil age in months. Perhaps, as suggested earlier, a pupil's pattern of absences from school makes a difference to their GCSE attainment. A practical problem is that this new variable might be correlated with pupil age as well as with GCSE passes. We cannot therefore simply total the correlations of each independent variable with the GCSE passes. For example, if pupil absence is negatively correlated with their GCSE passes, we cannot simply add this to the correlation for pupil age. If age and absences have some correlation between themselves, then using both together means we end up using their common variance twice. The real multiple correlation between age and absence on the one hand and GCSE passes on the other is likely to be less than the sum of the two correlations. This is one key reason for using multiple linear regression, since it takes into account the correlations between multiple independent variables when combining them to predict/explain the variance in the dependent variable. In fact the number of days absent from school correlates with GCSE passes at R of −0.455, and it correlates with pupil age at R of −0.321. So, multiple regression is clearly indicated if we wish to use both predictors at once.

Multiple regression is done in the same way as simple regression (using SPSS) but with more than one independent variable. The output, continuing the GCSE passes example, could look like Tables 35.3 and 35.4 (as above, shorn of items relating to standard errors and significance). Table 35.3 shows the value of R (0.712), which means the same as it does in simple regression, except that it now expresses the multiple correlation between GCSE passes on the one hand, and all independent variables in combination on the other. Note that adding the second predictor variable leads to a better model (R), 0.712 rather than 0.643, with more accurate estimates of the dependent variable, but does not increase R by as much as its simple correlation with the dependent variable.

Table 35.3 Summary model for multiple regression analysis

Model	R	R square
1	.712	.506

Predictors: (Constant), Absences, Age.

Table 35.4 is like Table 35.2, but here shows the coefficients (or multipliers) for more than one predictor variable. Given the values in Table 35.4, you can therefore calculate (or use the computer to calculate) expected GCSE passes for any pupil, as long as you know their precise age and number of absences from school. And you can do so more accurately than you could using either age or absences alone.

The multiple regression equation would be of the form:

$$\text{GCSE passes} = -66.845 + (0.364 * \text{Age}) - (0.244 * \text{Absences})$$

If more explanatory variables are available you can simply add them to this analysis. Each will yield a further row in Table 35.4 and a B coefficient that

can be added to the equation and used to help predict the dependent value for any case. Each explanatory variable added should substantially increase the R value in Table 35.3. If it does not, then that variable is not really 'explanatory' (but see below for a discussion about the order of entering variables into your model).

Table 35.4 Coefficients for multiple regression analysis

Value	B	Beta
Constant	−66.845	
Age	.364	.566
Absences	−.244	−.315

Dependent variable: GCSEs.

Basic assumptions

The underlying assumptions for an analysis are the things that the analytical software needs to be true in order for the calculated result to be correct. Most basic assumptions for multiple linear regression are the same as for correlation and simple regression (Maxwell, 1977; Achen, 1982).

- All variables used should be real numbers.
- All variables are measured as far as possible without error.
- There should be an approximate linear relationship between the dependent variable and the independent variables (both individually and grouped).

To these is added one more basic one.

- No independent variable is a perfect linear combination of another (not perfect 'multi-collinearity').

If the basic assumptions are not true, or at least nearly so, then the regression results can be very misleading. Regression does not work well with categorical independent variables having more than two values (Hagenaars, 1990), but if a variable (such as sex) has only two possible values it can be treated as an equal interval variable (since there is only one interval). Further, even variables with more than two categories can be used by converting them to a series of dummy variables. A social class scale with three categories, for example, could be treated as two dummy variables. The first dummy is a yes/no (or rather 0/1) variable representing being in the 'Professional' class or not, and the second dummy represents being in the 'Intermediate' class or not. 'Working' class is therefore defined as being not Professional and not Intermediate class. Some writers have argued that this treatment is a distortion and not really appropriate, especially now that newer methods have been developed specifically to deal with categorical variables (such as logistic regression – see the example in Selwyn and Gorard, 2016). Since it is assumed in regression that the variables are normally distributed (Lee et al., 1989), and dummy variables cannot have such a distribution, then simply converting a categorical variable into a set of dummies is not the solution. These dummy variables add to the measurement error (Blalock, 1964). For more on this, and other potential flaws in regression analysis such as omitted variable bias, heteroscedasticity and multicollinearity, see Maddala (1992).

The full set of assumptions underlying regression techniques is large and therefore can be rather off-putting. But unless the standard error or significance is an issue for you most of these further assumptions are less important, or indeed completely irrelevant, like the first one below.

- The measurements are from a random sample (or at least a probability-based one).
- There are no extreme outliers.
- The dependent variable is approximately normally distributed (or at least the next assumption is true).
- The residuals for the dependent variable (the differences between calculated and observed scores) are approximately normally distributed.
- The variance of each variable is consistent across the range of values for all other variables (or at least the next assumption is true).

- The residuals for the dependent variable at each value of the independent variables have equal and constant variance.
- The residuals are not correlated with the independent variables.
- The residuals for the dependent variable at each value of the independent variables have a mean of zero (or they are approximately linearly related to the dependent variable).
- For any two cases the correlation between the residuals should be zero (each case is independent of the others).

However, these assumptions are the subject of some dispute, both over what the assumptions really are and the implications for running an analysis that does not meet them (Menard, 1995; Miles and Shevlin, 2001; de Vaus, 2002). In any real research project involving multiple regression, at least some of the assumptions are likely to be violated (Berry and Feldman, 1985). This, in itself, may not be fatal to the validity of the work, and even where the regression is flawed it is sometimes only the intercept (or constant) that is affected while the derived coefficients may still be used with care. On the other hand, some commentators insist that regression analysis only makes sense when the variables are precisely measured, otherwise the coefficient values will be misleading. As with almost any technique, the best defence against any such problems is a large high-quality sample and using only the best measurements possible. In general, if any assumptions are not true for any analysis, the impact is to reduce the apparent size of any relationship uncovered. Therefore, and in general, if you obtain a powerful result it is still relatively safe to proceed to investigate it.

Cautions and interpretations

Multiple regression is powerful, easy to use and reasonably tolerant in its assumptions (or relatively unaffected by violation of them). Nevertheless, it is still often used poorly, with incorrect conclusions drawn from weak findings. This section raises some cautions for the interpretation of regression data. Three of these have been outlined before. A zero or weak correlation coefficient does not mean that there is no interrelationship between the variables involved. It might just mean that the interrelationship is more complex than a simple linear correlation. Also, regression does not test anything. It merely models a relationship that we prescribe as analysts. The fact that there is such a model is therefore weak evidence in itself. It is certainly not evidence of a specific, or indeed any, causal relationship between the variables involved. For any study, the regression model explaining the greatest variance in the dependent variable (e.g. exam score) will use all available independent variables. This is the model you get if you simply enter all of the variables at once. However, it is possible to create simpler models containing fewer variables but still explaining a large proportion of the variance. These models are easier to use and understand, and so more practical. In several forms of multivariate analysis, the order in which independent variables are entered into the explanatory model can also make a very substantial difference to the results obtained. It is always worth changing the order of entry of your variables to see how robust the findings are.

Another problem is that because regression models are fitted to the data after collection, it is possible to use the natural but often meaningless variation in the independent variables to match individual scores in the purportedly dependent variables. The ensuing model is completely irrelevant but can have a very high R-value (and of course misleading probabilities). For example, a dataset with as many independent variables as cases will *always* yield an R of 1, even if the scores are randomly generated (Gorard, 2006a). This is why reputable texts emphasise that the number of cases in any study must outnumber the number of variables by at least an order of magnitude. If we vary the analysis to use 'backward' elimination of any redundant variables, it is possible to reduce the number of independent variables in the model without substantially reducing the R-square value. In other words, we can still create a perfect prediction/explanation for the dependent variable, but this time using fewer variables than cases. If we are happy to allow the R-squared value to dip below 1.0 then the number of variables needed to predict the values of the dependent variable can be reduced dramatically. It is easily possible, in this way, to produce a model with an R-value of 0.6 or higher using only 10 or fewer variables for 100 cases, even where all of the values are nonsensical random numbers. This R-value is higher than many of those that are published in journals and that have been allowed to affect policy or practice. Many of these remaining variables will be labelled 'significant' by the software. And the ratio of cases to variables is 10:1, which can be considered reasonably healthy.

This is part of the reason for being very cautious about small values of R^2. Unfortunately, there is no standard scale of substantive importance for effect sizes like R^2 (Gorard, 2006b), and things like significance tests are no use here even if the data meet the requirements, such as being based on a good random sample (Gorard, 2010b). That is why the judgement to publish a regression model needs to be justified in terms of N, R^2, the quality of the measures, the theoretical explanation, its practical importance or the steps taken to test the association more rigorously via a randomised controlled trial or similar.

Conclusion

I have used simple linear regression in this explanation for clarity and familiarity, but the danger of spurious findings is a general one and cannot be overcome by using alternative forms of regression. Similar arguments apply to logistic regression or to multilevel modelling. In fact, more complex methods can make the situation worse, because they make it harder to establish how many cases (sampling units) there are. Complex statistical methods cannot be used *post hoc* to overcome design problems or deficiencies in datasets. It is worth stating this precisely because of the 'capture' of funders by those pushing for more complex methods of probability-based traditional analysis, whereas of course 'in general, the best designs require the *simplest* statistics' (Wright, 2003: 130). A good defence is, as always, to increase the number of cases and minimise the number of variables. Another defence is to look at the same variables in another way, using a complementary method. This is one of the strengths of mixed-methods work, wherein a tentative, theoretical or statistical result can be tested by a field trial and/or in-depth observation, for example.

Multiple regression is an easy to use and powerful method for summarising patterns in large datasets. It is also a fascinating entry into the world of modelling and complex multivariate analysis. I recommend it as a useful tool to help you think about your data and form judgements about what the data might mean (Gorard, 2001). However, despite talk of predictions, regression has rarely if ever been used to predict real-life events such as stock market crashes, eclipses or even a thunderstorm (Brighton, 2000). This limited practical success in isolation is to be expected if you understand what regression is and is not. Imagine it as like drawing a graph. The graph does not really tell you anything new, and it is not a test of anything. But it can help you think about the meaning of your results. Regression can do the same with more variables than a graph usually can, and it can encourage you to consider interactions between variables. No more, no less. It is more likely to be the start of your investigation trying to explain the pattern uncovered than an end in itself (Phillips, 2014).

Questions for further investigation

1. Find a dataset in your own area of interest that contains a large number of cases and at least three real-number variables. Select three such variables, and draw a cross-plot graph of each pair. Note any near linear patterns. Run a correlation analysis for each pair. Run a regression analysis with one variable as the imagined dependent variable and one as the predictor. Note the relationship to correlation. Now run a regression with two predictors. Note the differences to bivariate regression results.

2. Find an article in your area of interest that uses regression. Prepare a critique, noting how well and fully the paper presents the methods, whether the paper includes undigested computer output or whether the tables are made easy to read, whether the paper uses significance incorrectly (with population data or a convenience sample) and whether the paper uses causal words like 'influence' or 'impact' without justification.

Suggested further reading

Gorard, S. (2006) *Using Everyday Numbers Effectively in Research*. London: Continuum. This book illustrates how numbers can be used routinely and successfully for research purposes – without your ever having to consider confidence intervals, probability densities, Gaussian distributions, or indeed any of those complicated and generally useless things that appear in treatises on statistics. This no-nonsense guide should prove essential reading for all educational and social science researchers.

Hancock, G. and Mueller, R. (2010) *The Reviewer's Guide to Quantitative Methods in the Social Sciences*. London: Routledge. Designed for evaluators of research manuscripts and proposals in the social and behavioural sciences and beyond. Covering virtually all of the popular classic and emerging quantitative techniques, thus helping reviewers to evaluate a manuscript's methodological approach and its data analysis.

References

Gorard, S. (2013) *Research Design: Robust Approaches for the Social Sciences*. London: Sage. Explains in detail how the nature of any analysis such as regression modelling is dependent upon prior research design decisions. The model must fit into a chain of reasoning from initial research question to the conclusions drawn.

Achen, C. (1982) *Interpreting and Using Regression*. London: Sage.

Berry, W. and Feldman, S. (1985) *Multiple Regression in Practice*. London: Sage.

Blalock, H. (1964) *Causal Inferences in Nonexperimental Research*. Chapel Hill, NC: University of North Carolina Press.

Brighton, M. (2000) 'Making our measurements count', *Evaluation and Research in Education,* 14(3 & 4): 124–35.

de Vaus, D. (2002) *Analyzing Social Science Data: 50 Key Problems in Data Analysis*. London: Sage.

Gorard, S. (2001) *Quantitative Methods in Educational Research: The Role of Numbers Made Easy*. London: Continuum.

Gorard, S. (2006a) *Using Everyday Numbers Effectively in Research:* Not *a Book About Statistics*. London: Continuum.

Gorard, S. (2006b) 'Towards a judgement-based statistical analysis', *British Journal of Sociology of Education,* 27(1): 67–80.

Gorard, S. (2010a) 'Measuring is More Than Assigning Numbers', in G. Walford, E. Tucker and M. Viswanathan (eds), *The SAGE Handbook of Measurement*. Los Angeles: Sage, pp. 389–408.

Gorard, S. (2010b) 'All evidence is equal: the flaw in statistical reasoning', *Oxford Review of Education,* 36(1): 63–77.

Hagenaars, J. (1990) *Categorical Longitudinal Data: Log-linear, Panel, Trend and Cohort Analysis*. London: Sage.

Harwell, M. and Gatti, G. (2001) *Review of Educational Research,* 71(1): 105–31.

Lee, E., Forthofer R. and Lorimor, R. (1989) *Analyzing Complex Survey Data*. London: Sage.

Maddala, G. (1992) *Introduction to Econometrics*. New York: Macmillan.

Maxwell, A. (1977) *Multivariate Analysis in Behavioural Research*. New York: Chapman & Hall.

Menard, S. (1995) *Applied Logistic Regression Analysis*. London: Sage.

Miles, J. and Shevlin, M. (2001) *Applying Regression and Correlation*. London: Sage.

Phillips, D. (2014) 'Research in the grad sciences, and in the very hard "softer" sciences', *Educational Researcher*, 43(1): 9–11.

Selwyn, N. and Gorard, S. (2016) 'Students' use of Wikipedia as an academic resource', *The Internet and Higher Education*, 28: 28–34.

Siegel, S. (1956) *Nonparametric Statistics*. Tokyo: McGraw-Hill.

Wright, D. (2003) 'Making friends with your data: improving how statistics are conducted and reported', *British Journal of Educational Psychology,* 73: 123–36.

Multilevel analysis

36

Michael Seltzer and Jordan Rickles

Introduction

The data that we encounter in educational research often have what is termed a 'multilevel', 'nested' or 'hierarchical' structure. One source of multilevel data structures is the kinds of sampling and data collection designs employed in educational surveys such as High School and Beyond (HSB) and the Early Childhood Longitudinal Study (ECLS) (e.g. cluster sampling designs). For example, in their study of the effects of teachers' literacy instructional practices on kindergarten students' language and literacy skills, Xue and Meisels (2004) conducted analyses using a sample from ECLS consisting of over 13,000 kindergarten students nested within 2,690 classrooms, which in turn were nested in 788 schools.

A multilevel structure can also arise from an experimental or quasi-experimental research design that involves, for example, assigning intact classrooms or schools to treatment and comparison conditions and assessing student-level outcomes. For example, to study the effectiveness of Comer's School Development Program (CSDP), Cook et al. (1999) randomly assigned 23 middle schools to treatment (CSDP) or control conditions. The sample for this study comprised of approximately 12,000 students and 2,000 staff members nested within these 23 schools. (See Chapter 18 in this book for a discussion of these types of designs, which are termed 'cluster randomised designs'.)

Similarly, many studies in education – surveys as well as experimental studies – entail collecting measures of key constructs at multiple points in time for each student in a sample (e.g. measures of student achievement in reading or mathematics across a series of grades). This gives rise to a multilevel structure in which longitudinal data are nested within each student.

In many studies in which students are nested within a sample of different groups (e.g. classes or schools), we often find that there are appreciable differences across groups in students' prior educational experiences and background characteristics, in contextual factors such as normative climate, and in the quality of the curricula and instructional practices that students in these different groups encounter. Such factors give rise to a certain degree of similarity among the outcome scores for the students nested within a given group, i.e. student outcome scores are dependent to some extent on group membership. This is referred to by statisticians as intra-class correlation. When we ignore such dependencies in our analyses – that is, when we use standard regression methods to analyse the student-level data in a sample and ignore the fact that students are nested within different groups – we run the risk of obtaining standard errors for estimates of key parameters (e.g. programme effects) that are too small. That is, we underestimate the statistical uncertainty. This, in turn, can give rise to spuriously significant results.

A second problem that arises when we ignore the nested structure of our data – one that we emphasise in this chapter – is connected with Cronbach et al.'s (1976: 1) concern that the analyses we conduct in educational research might often conceal more than they reveal. For example, minority gaps in achievement, and gender gaps in mathematics and science achievement, are important educational policy issues in the United States. Often overall estimates of minority or gender gaps based on large-scale survey data sets receive appreciable attention. However, such single-number summaries conceal the fact that differences in achievement between minority and non-minority students, for example, may vary extensively across schools; in some schools the difference may be substantial, but in others there may be no gap at all. Approaching such policy issues from a multilevel perspective encourages us to attend to differences in the magnitude of minority gaps across schools, and to try to identify those school policies and practices that are systematically related to differences in the magnitude of minority gaps (e.g. Lee and Bryk, 1989). Along these lines, interest might also centre on the relationship between student socio-economic status (SES) and achievement, and why differences in SES might be associated with large differences in achievement between students in some schools, but negligible differences in achievement in others.

Thus multilevel modelling enables us to study differences across groups in how equitably outcomes of interest are distributed with respect to various demographic characteristics. In the following section, in an extended example of the logic and application of multilevel modelling, we show how such models enable us to investigate the extent to which the effects of programmes vary across sites, and identify key factors that might underlie such variability. We then briefly discuss several other types of applications, including a school effects application from work by Lee and Bryk (1989) and Raudenbush and Bryk (1986) that investigated whether 12th grade mathematics achievement is higher in Catholic high schools than in public high schools, and whether differences in student SES are less consequential with regard to student achievement in Catholic versus public high schools. At the end of the chapter, questions to follow up this introduction to multilevel modelling are asked and a variety of further reading sources are provided.

Before turning to our extended example, we wish to point out that multilevel models are also often referred to as hierarchical models and mixed models. The term 'mixed models' helps convey the idea that multilevel models combine key elements of standard regression models (i.e. fixed effects regression models) with key elements of ANOVA models with random effects (see Raudenbush, 1993).

Two key papers that helped lay the conceptual groundwork and initial analysis strategies for multilevel modelling are papers by Cronbach et al. (1976) and Burstein (1980). Also, see Raudenbush and Bryk (2002: Chapter 1) for a discussion of important technical work connected with the development and implementation of more comprehensive multilevel modelling frameworks.

In the example that follows we employ a software program developed by Raudenbush et al. (2004) called HLM. A list of several other available programs is provided later in the chapter.

An illustration of multilevel modelling via analyses of the data from a multi-site evaluation of the Transition Mathematics curriculum

In this example, we focus on a subset of the data from an evaluation of an innovative pre-algebra curriculum called Transition Mathematics (TM). Specifically we present a series of analyses using a sample of 19 carefully matched pairs of classrooms located in various school districts throughout the United States.[1] (Note that in this section we use the terms 'sites' and 'matched pairs of classes' interchangeably.) Within each pair, one class was taught by a teacher who implementcd TM and the other was taught by a teacher who used the pre-algebra curriculum already in place at that site. In the case of ten pairs, the decision as to which teacher would use TM with his or her class was based on random assignment; various logistical factors precluded random assignment in the case of nine pairs. One question we will explore later is whether the effects of TM in sites in which assignment was random are similar to the effects in sites where random assignment was not feasible.

We begin by focusing on the following question: 'On a 19-item post-test assessing student readiness for geometry, what is the expected difference in outcomes when students work with TM materials versus when they work with more traditional materials?'

We first conduct an analysis that ignores the nested structure of the data. Specifically, to compare the mean geometry readiness scores for the 273 students in the sample who worked with TM materials and the 276 students who did not, we fit the following simple regression model to the sample of 549 student-level observations:

$$Y_i = \beta_0 + \beta_1 X_i + r_i \quad r_i \sim N(0, \sigma^2) \qquad (36.1)$$

where Y_i is the geometry readiness score for student i; X_i is a treatment indicator variable that takes on a value of 1 if student i is a TM student or a value of 0 if student i is a comparison group student; β_0 is the intercept parameter in the model, representing the expected geometry score when students work with traditional materials, i.e. when $X_i = 0$. β_1 is the parameter of primary interest and captures the expected difference in geometry readiness scores when students work with TM materials ($X_i = 1$) vs. using more traditional materials. Note that the r_i are residuals assumed independent and normally distributed with mean 0 and variance σ^2, where σ^2 represents the amount of variance in student outcome scores that remains after taking into account TM/comparison group membership. When we fit this model to the data, the resulting estimate of β_1 and its standard error are: $\beta_1 = 1.39$ and SE = 0.36 ($t = 1.39 / 0.36 = 3.56$, $df = 547$, $p < 0.001$). Note that these results are identical to what we would obtain conducting a standard two-group comparison of the mean geometry readiness score for the 273 students who worked with TM materials ($\overline{Y}_{TM} = 10.1$) and the mean geometry readiness score for the 276 students who worked with more traditional materials ($\overline{Y}_c = 8.7$).

In the above analysis, it is assumed that the outcome scores for students in the sample, after taking into account whether students worked with TM or more conventional curricular materials, are independent. But since the 549 students in our sample are nested in different pairs, we might very well suspect that how well TM or comparison group students perform on the post-test may depend on pair or site membership. Thus we now fit the above regression model in equation 36.1 to each site's data to obtain an estimate of the TM effect for each site and its SE. These results appear in Table 36.1. As can be seen, the site TM effect estimates vary substantially, ranging from a negative value of −2.21 points for site 10 to a positive value of 4.56 points for site 19. (Note that the negative estimate for site 10 indicates that the TM students in that site scored approximately 2.21 points lower on the geometry readiness post-test.)

The TM effect estimate for a given site ($\hat{\beta}_{1j}$) provides us with an estimate of the true TM effect for that site. The standard error for ($\hat{\beta}_{1j}$) conveys how precise the estimate is (i.e. how much the estimate might differ from the true effect for that site).

Importantly, the standard error provides the basis for forming a confidence interval that gives us a sense of how big or little a site's true TM effect might be. For example, if we take the TM effect estimate for site 8 (4.25 points), and add and subtract 2 standard errors (i.e. 2 × 0.85), this yields an approximate 95% interval with lower and upper boundaries of 2.58 points and 5.92 points, respectively. On the basis of this confidence interval, the idea that the true TM effect for site 8 equals 0, for example, is highly doubtful. As can be seen in Figure 36.1, all six sites with TM effect estimates greater than 2 points have intervals that lie above a value of 0, and the intervals for two of those sites lie completely above a value of 1.39 (i.e. the estimate of the overall effect of TM obtained in the traditional analysis). For the other sites in the sample, the 95% intervals include a value of 0, and the intervals for two of those sites lie completely below a value of 1.39. (See Denson and Seltzer, 2011: 221, for a discussion of these concepts in the context of meta-analysis; see also

Table 36.1 Site-by-site analysis: OLS estimates of means and TM effects

Site (j)[a]	Size (n_j)	Site mean ($\hat{\beta}_{0j}$)	SE ($\hat{\beta}_{0j}$)	TM effect ($\hat{\beta}_{1j}$)	SE ($\hat{\beta}_{1j}$)	95% CI ($\hat{\beta}_{1j}$)	Implementation of reading (0 = low, 1 = high)
1	31	13.52	0.48	−0.23	0.96	(−2.10, 1.65)	0
2	27	6.59	0.46	2.12*	0.93	(0.31, 3.93)	1
3	34	5.15	0.38	0.33	0.77	(−1.18, 1.84)	0
4	44	7.86	0.49	−0.24	0.99	(−2.18, 1.70)	0
5	17	8.47	0.61	0.29	1.22	(−2.09, 2.67)	0
6	35	11.54	0.57	1.50	1.15	(−0.76, 3.76)	1
7	37	13.97	0.39	1.27	0.79	(−0.27, 2.81)	1
8	42	6.98	0.43	4.25*	0.85	(2.58, 5.92)	1
9	17	8.71	0.73	4.06*	1.54	(1.05, 7.07)	1
10	28	6.68	0.56	−2.21	1.13	(−4.43, 0.01)	0
11	31	14.42	0.50	1.20	1.00	(−0.75, 3.15)	1
12	31	10.87	0.76	1.15	1.52	(−1.83, 4.12)	0
13	25	10.12	0.58	4.20*	1.29	(1.66, 6.73)	1
14	23	10.83	0.71	1.11	1.43	(−1.70, 3.92)	0
15	33	11.45	0.64	−1.61	1.28	(−4.12, 0.90)	0
16	33	8.70	0.56	1.90	1.13	(−0.31, 4.11)	0
17	27	6.81	0.56	0.93	1.14	(−1.30, 3.15)	1
18	17	5.29	0.53	2.69*	1.08	(0.57, 4.80)	0
19	17	7.12	0.82	4.56*	1.72	(1.18, 7.94)	1

a. The subscript j is used to reference each of the sites in the sample.

* Denotes a TM effect estimate that is more than twice its standard error.

Adapted from Seltzer (1994)

Chapter 38 by Hedges in this volume for an example of the use of plots similar to Figure 36.1 in meta-analysis.)

Thus the above results indicate that there is likely substantial variability in the true effects of TM across sites. Given, for example, that teachers may vary substantially in their patterns of implementation, and that the quality of students' prior educational experiences might differ appreciably across sites, the results that we see in Table 36.1 and Figure 36.1 are in some respects not very surprising.

But note that the single-number summary based on the traditional analysis concealed this heterogeneity. On the basis of that analysis, decision makers might mistakenly conclude that the effects of TM are uniform across sites. Furthermore, the results from such an analysis do not encourage us to ask whether, and if so why, TM may be more successful in some sites than others.

We now show how multilevel models enable us to represent the location (nesting) of students in different sites, and investigate the variability in programme effects across sites. We begin by specifying a within-site (level-1) model. The regression model that we fitted to each site's data in the previous analysis provides the basis of our level-1 model. In addition to a subscript (i) that indexes students,

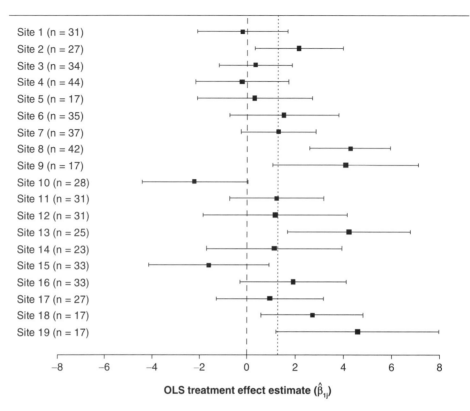

Figure 36.1   OLS estimate and 95% confidence interval for the TM treatment effect in each site (the vertical dark dashed line marks the treatment effect grand mean (1.39))

we also need to include a subscript (*j*) denoting the site membership of students. Thus:

$$Y_{ij} = \beta_{0j} + \beta_{1j} (X_{ij} - \overline{X}_{.j}) + r_{ij} \quad r_{ij} \sim N(0, \sigma^2) \qquad (36.2)$$

where Y_{ij} is the geometry readiness score for student *i* in site j; since there are 19 sites in our sample, our subscript or index for sites takes on values from 1 to 19 (*j* = 1, …, 19) and X_{ij} is a treatment indicator that takes on a value of 1 if student *i* in site *j* is a TM student (0 otherwise). β_{1j}, which is the parameter of primary interest in the level-1 model, represents the true TM effect for site *j*. Note that the predictor X_{ij}, is centred around its site mean $(\overline{X}_{.j})$. This type of centring, which is termed 'group-mean centring', is widely used in HLM analyses. As Raudenbush and Bryk (2002) note, group-mean centring of predictors

at level-1 gives the intercept term β_{0j} a useful interpretation (i.e. β_{0j} represents the mean outcome score for site *j*). While β_{1j} is of primary interest in our application, as will be seen later, in some applications group mean outcome scores as well as slopes are of substantive interest. Finally, in the above model σ^2 represents within-site variance of geometry readiness score.

If we fit the above model to each site's data using a standard regression program, we obtain the OLS estimates of the site TM effects shown in Table 36.1 and, furthermore, the resulting OLS estimate of β_{0j} for a given site will simply be equal to the mean geometry readiness outcome score for the sample of students in that site.

As discussed above, each site's TM effect estimate contains a certain degree of error (see Table 36.1).

Table 36.2 Multilevel Model A for the TM evaluation data

Fixed effects	Estimate	SE	t-ratio	Approx. df	p-value
Grand mean (γ_{00})	9.22	0.66	13.97	18	0.000
Overall TM effect (γ_{10})	1.34	0.43	3.14	18	0.006

Variance components	Estimate	df	Chi-square	p-value
Between-site:				
Site mean geometry readiness (τ_{00})	7.94	18	494.8	0.000
Site TM effects (τ_{11})	2.12	18	47.5	0.000
Within-site:				
Residual variance (σ^2)	9.09			

A key question is 'To what extent is the variation in TM effect estimates across sites due to such error, and how much is connected with differences in the true effects of TM across sites?' Raudenbush and Bryk term the latter type of variability 'parameter variance' (e.g. heterogeneity in the true effects of TM). How might we obtain an estimate of the amount of parameter variance in TM effects?

A key feature of multilevel models is that they enable us to represent the fact that level-1 parameters (e.g. site TM effects (β_{1j}) and site means (β_{0j})) may vary across groups (e.g. sites). In particular, level-1 parameters are treated as outcomes in a between-group (level-2) model. We first specify a between-site model in which level-1 parameters (e.g. site TM effects) are viewed as varying around a corresponding grand mean (e.g. a mean TM effect):

$$\beta_{0j} = \gamma_{00} + u_{0j} \qquad u_{0j} \sim N(0, \tau_{00}) \qquad (36.3)$$

$$\beta_{1j} = \gamma_{10} + u_{0j} \qquad u_{1j} \sim N(0, \tau_{11}) \qquad (36.4)$$

In Equation 36.4, for example, γ_{10} represents an overall, average TM effect, and u_{1j} is a level-2 residual that captures the deviation of the true TM effect for site j from the average TM effect; the level-2 residuals allow for the possibility that the true TM effect for some sites may lie close to the average effect, but may be substantially larger

or smaller than the average effect in the case of other sites. The variance term in this equation (τ_{11}) represents the amount of heterogeneity in the true effects of TM across sites. As noted above, the variability in TM effect estimates that we see across sites in Table 36.1 is attributable in part to estimation error (error variance) connected with each of the estimates and to differences in the true effects of TM termed 'parameter variance'. τ_{11} represents the latter source. Similarly, γ_{00} in equation 36.3 is the grand mean for geometry readiness scores, u_{0j} is a residual term representing the deviation of the true mean outcome score for a given site (β_{0j}) from the grand mean, and τ_{00} represents the amount of variance connected with underlying differences in mean outcome scores across sites (i.e. it is the parameter variance in site mean outcome scores).

The above level-1 and level-2 models comprise the first multilevel model that we will fit to the data; we term this Model A. In the parlance of multilevel modelling, γ_{00} and γ_{10} are referred to as fixed effects, u_{0j} and u_{1j} are termed random effects, and σ^2, τ_{00} and τ_{11} are termed variance components. The key level-2 parameters in our model are γ_{10} (i.e. the average TM effect) and τ_{11} (i.e. the parameter variance in site TM effects).

In Table 36.2 we see that the resulting estimate of γ_{10} is 1.34 points (SE = 0.43; t = 3.14, approx. df = 18, p. = 0.006). To help grasp how this average effect was computed, note that the HLM program

Table 36.3   Multilevel Model B for the TM evaluation data

Fixed effects	Estimate	SE	t-ratio	Approx. df	p-value
Model for site mean readiness:					
Grand mean (γ_{00})	9.21	0.29	31.90	17	.000
Between-site pre-test/post-test slope (γ_{01})	0.60	0.07	8.99	17	.000
Model for site TM effects:					
Expected TM effect at low impl. sites (γ_{10})	0.23	0.46	0.50	17	0.620
Expected increase in effect of TM at high impl. sites (γ_{11})	2.29	0.65	3.52	17	0.003

Variance components	Estimate	df	Chi-square	p-value	
Between-site:					
Site mean geometry readiness (τ_{00})	1.24	17	81.83	.000	
Site TM effects (τ_{11})	0.87	17	28.13	.000	
Within-site:					
Residual variance (σ^2)	9.10				

essentially used the TM effect estimates for the 19 sites shown in Table 36.1 to compute a weighted average, where those sites whose TM effects were estimated with more precision received more weight.[2]

While this estimate of the average TM effect is similar to the one obtained in the analysis in which we ignored the nested structure of the data, note that the standard error of HLM's estimate is approximately 20% larger. To help understand this difference, we first turn to HLM's estimate of the heterogeneity in site TM effects, i.e. $\hat{\tau}_{11} = 2.12$. A chi-square test of the hypothesis that τ_{11} is equal to 0 (i.e. the hypothesis of no variability in the true effects of TM across sites) yields a p-value less than 0.001, which points to strong evidence against this hypothesis.

Since it is easier to interpret standard deviations rather than variances, we take the square root of our estimate of τ_{11} (2.12), which yields a value of 1.46. This standard deviation, combined with our estimate of the average TM effect, provides a 'best guess' regarding the distribution of site TM effects. For example, based on our results, a site whose true TM effect is 2 standard deviations above the average would be equal to 1.34 + (2 × 1.46) = 4.26

points; similarly a site whose true effect is 2 standard deviations below the average effect would be equal to 1.34 − (2 × 1.46) = −1.58 points. This suggests that a substantial amount of the variability that we see in the TM effect estimates in Table 36.1 is connected with parameter variance, i.e. heterogeneity in the true effects of TM across sites.

In contrast to the analysis that ignores the nesting of individuals in different sites, the standard error for the average TM effect based on the above HLM analysis reflects the fact that how well TM students fare relative to comparison group students depends substantially on site membership. Specifically, HLM's estimate of τ_{11} is a key component of the standard error. Furthermore, when this component is large, the magnitude of the standard error – the precision with which we are able to estimate the average effect – depends not only on how many students there are in our sample but also, crucially, on how many sites there are in our sample as well. In this connection, the *df* for hypothesis tests regarding γ_{10} is equal to the number of sites minus 1 (i.e. 18).

The results based on Model A, along with the exploratory analyses that we conducted, point to substantial variability in the effectiveness of TM across sites. This variability encourages us to ask 'Why might TM be appreciably more effective at some sites than others? What factor(s) might be critical with respect to the success of the programme?' We now show how such questions can be addressed by adding predictors to the level-2 (between-site) model.

The reading material contained in the TM text is viewed as a key component of TM by its programme developers. We now model differences in the effects of TM as a function of a measure of implementation that takes on a value of 1 if the TM teacher at a site indicated that they discussed the reading in the text on a daily basis (IMPLRDG$_j$ = 1, i.e. high implementation), and a value of 0 if the reading was discussed frequently but was not part of the daily routine (IMPLRDG$_j$ = 0, i.e. low implementation).

As can be seen in Table 36.3, TM effect estimates tend to be higher in those sites in which the reading

in the text is discussed on a daily basis. This pattern is also evident in the plot of TM effect estimates versus level of implementation in Figure 36.2. We now investigate more formally whether increases in the level of implementation are systematically related to increases in the effectiveness of TM by including IMPLRDG$_j$ as a predictor in the level-2 equation for site TM effects (β_{01}):

$$\beta_{0j} = \gamma_{00} + \gamma_{01}\overline{PRE}_j + u_{0j}\ u_{0j} \sim N(0, \tau_{00}) \quad (36.5)$$

$$\beta_{1j} = \gamma_{10} + \gamma_{11}\overline{IMPLRDG}_j + u_{1j}\ u_{1j} \sim N(0, \tau_{11}) \quad (36.6)$$

Based on the 0/1 coding scheme for IMPLRDG$_j$, γ_{10} is the expected effect of TM at low implementation sites and γ_{11} is the expected increment in the effect of TM at high implementation sites. Similar to a regression model, u_{1j} is a residual capturing the deviation of the site TM effect for site j from an

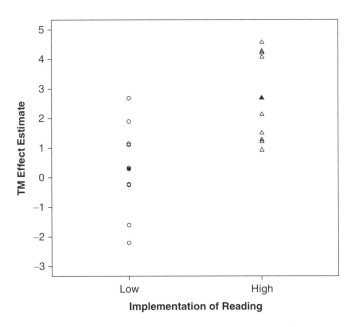

Figure 36.2 Site TM effect estimates by level of implementation of reading

Circles and triangles are used to represent low- and high-implementation sites, respectively. The mean of the TM effect estimates for the ten low-implementing sites is represented by a dark circle, and the mean of the TM effect estimates for the nine high-implementing sites is represented by a dark triangle.

Adapted from Seltzer and Rose (2011)

expected value based on IMPLRDG_j. Thus τ_{11} now represents the remaining parameter variance in site TM effects after taking into account IMPLRDG_j.

While the level-2 equation for site TM effects is of primary interest in this analysis, there are many applications, as will be seen in the rest of this chapter, where interest might centre on mean outcome scores (β_{0j}) and modelling them as a function of various group characteristics. To help illustrate such possibilities, we model β_{0j} as a function of site mean pre-test scores on a 40-item general mathematics test ($\overline{\text{PRE}}_j$). Thus, as in a regression analysis, the coefficient γ_{01} captures the expected change in site-mean readiness scores when site pre-test means increase 1 unit, and τ_{00} now represents the parameter variance in site mean readiness scores that remains after taking into account site mean pre-test scores.[3]

We term the multilevel model defined by equation 36.2 (level-1) and equations 36.5 and 36.6 (level-2) 'Model B'. In Table 36.3, we see that the estimate of the expected effect of TM in low implementation sites (γ_{10}) is extremely small (i.e. 0.23 points; SE = 0.46), and is clearly not statistically significant; this suggests that given a low level of implementation, TM and more traditional curricula may, on average, be equally effective. In contrast, the estimate for the expected increase in TM given a high level of implementation (γ_{11}) is 2.29 points (SE = 0.65). Thus while the results based on Model A point to an overall average effect of 1.34 points, the results based on Model B point to an expected effect that is negligible when implementation is low, and an effect of approximately two and a half points given a high level of implementation (i.e. 0.23 + 2.29 = 2.52 points).

We also see that the inclusion of IMPLRDG_j in the model results in a substantial reduction of parameter variance in site TM effects (i.e. while the estimate of τ_{11} based on Model A is 2.12, the estimate based on Model B is 0.87, which represents a reduction of nearly 60%).

From a substantive standpoint, the amount of parameter variance in site TM effects that remains is appreciable. Some of the remaining variance may be due to unique site characteristics or events

(e.g. perhaps the principals at one or two sites were extremely supportive of the TM programme). However, some may be due to factors that are systematically related to differences in the effect of TM. Thus, akin to multiple regression analyses, we can specify multiple predictors in level-2 models. This is especially important. For example, if we are concerned that a particular factor may be confounding the relationship between a key level-2 predictor (e.g. IMPLRDG_j) and the magnitude of within-group relationships of interest (e.g. site TM effects), we can attempt to control for that factor by including it as a predictor in the model. Thus, for example, as noted earlier, the assignment of teachers to TM comparison conditions was random in some sites but not in others. In an analysis controlling for type of assignment, Seltzer (2004) found that the results concerning the relationship between implementation of reading and the magnitude of site TM effects remained virtually unchanged.

Note that we can also specify multiple predictors in level-1 models. For example, as in an analysis of covariance (ANCOVA), we could expand the level-1 model specified in equation 36.2 to include student scores on a pre-test as a covariate; thus β_{1j} would represent the TM effect for site j holding constant student pre-test scores.

Before moving to the next section of this chapter, we wish to refer the reader to a recent article by Raudenbush and Bloom (2015) on the analysis of data from multi-site randomised trials, in which they present a cutting-edge strategy for investigating theories concerning why a program works and for whom it works. Their framework draws on key concepts and techniques in the causal inference literature (see for instance Morgan and Winship, 2015).

Additional applications and examples

School effects research

The kinds of two-level multilevel models that we employed in the analyses of the TM data can be directly used in various school effects research applications. In particular, we can employ these models in investigating the extent to which minority gaps, gender gaps and/or SES-achievement slopes vary across schools, and in attempting to identify those school policies and practices that underlie this variability. Thus, for example, in an analysis based on a sample from the HSB study consisting of over 7,000 students nested within 90 public and 70 Catholic high schools, Raudenbush and Bryk (1986, 2002) specified a level-1 (within-school) model in which student 12th grade mathematics achievement scores were modelled as a function of student SES:

$$Y_{ij} = \beta_{0j} + \beta_{1j}(SES_{1j} - \overline{SES}_{\cdot j}) + r_{ij} \quad r_{ij} \sim N(0,\sigma^2) \quad (36.7)$$

where Y_{ij} and SES_{ij} represent, respectively, the 12th grade mathematics achievement score and SES value for student i in school j. This model is formally identical to the level-1 (within-site) model employed in the multilevel analyses of the TM data. In equation 36.7, β_{1j} is the SES-achievement slope for school j capturing the expected increase in student achievement when SES increases 1 unit and, by virtue of centring SES around its group mean, β_{0j} is the school mean achievement score for school j. Note that a relatively flat SES-achievement slope for a given school would suggest that the differences in SES are fairly inconsequential with respect to student achievement. To investigate whether school mean achievement tends to be higher and SES-achievement slopes flatter in Catholic schools, Raudenbush and Bryk posed level-2 (between-school) equations in which school mean achievement (β_{0j}) and SES-achievement slopes (β_{1j}) were modelled as a function of sector (i.e. SECTOR, where SECTOR$_j$ = 1 if school j was a Catholic school and 0 otherwise). Since Catholic schools tend to serve students with higher SES values, Raudenbush and Bryk controlled for differences among schools in their mean SES values ($\overline{SES}_{\cdot j}$) by also including ($\overline{SES}_{\cdot j}$) as a predictor in each level-2 equation. The results based on their analysis pointed to higher school mean achievement in Catholic schools as well as a more equitable distribution of achievement within Catholic schools (i.e. flatter slopes). Note that such models can be expanded by including additional predictors in the within-school and between-school models (see, for example, Lee and Bryk, 1989).

A recent valuable application of multilevel models in the area of school effects research is a study conducted by Palardy (2013). The study uses multilevel models to describe the connection between school factors, particularly access to key educational resources and experiences, and student high-school graduation rates and rates of four-year college attendance in the United States.

Standard errors for estimates of fixed effects

As noted earlier, when we ignore the fact that students are nested within different groups, we run the risk of obtaining standard errors for estimates of fixed effects (e.g. sector effects) that are too small. This is especially so when interest centres on drawing inferences concerning the coefficients for predictors in level-2 equations for group-mean outcome scores (β_{0j}) (e.g. the fixed effect relating differences in sector to differences in school-mean achievement). For an example, see Seltzer's (2004) analyses of the data from a study of reform-minded mathematics instruction.

Longitudinal analysis

The kinds of multilevel models discussed above can also be used in studies of change. Consider, for example, one of the cohorts in the LSAY sample that Seltzer et al. (2003) focused on in their analyses of patterns of student change in mathematics achievement across grades 7 through 10. In this cohort, mathematics achievement scores collected in grades 7–10 are nested within each student. In a level-1 (within-student) model, we can model each student's time series as a function of grade, capturing, for example, a rate of change for each student (i.e. a slope relating mathematics achievement to grade). In a level-2 (between-student) model, we can model differences among students in their rates of change as a function of differences in their home environments and educational experiences. (See Singer and Willett, 2003, and Rojas and Iglesias, 2013, for accessible treatments of the use of multilevel models in investigating patterns of change.)

Three-level models

Multilevel models can be expanded to accommodate three or more levels of nesting. For example, in the case of the NELS sample where we have time-series data nested within students who, in turn, are nested in different high schools, we can pose three-level models consisting of a level-1 (within-person) model, which enables us to estimate a rate of change for each student, a level-2 (within-school) model that captures variability in student growth rates within schools, and a level-3 (between-school) model that enables us to investigate factors associated with differences across schools in their mean rates of change.

Note also that various commonly employed experimental designs in studies of instruction yield data that necessitate the use of three-level models. Consider, for example, a study in which schools are randomly assigned to an innovative or traditional first-grade reading programme, yielding a three-level data structure (i.e. students nested within different first-grade classrooms which, in turn, are nested within schools that have been assigned to treatment or comparison conditions; see Nye et al., 2004; Spybrook et al., 2011).

Data structures consisting of students nested within classrooms, which, in turn, are nested in different schools can also arise in the case of large-scale surveys such as ECLS. Palardy (2015), in a set of multilevel analyses of the ECLS data, found that achievement gaps between underrepresented minority and white students increased appreciably between the start and end of first grade, and that inequalities in the distribution of key educational resources within-schools and particularly between-schools were strongly associated with these widening gaps.

Conclusion

Multilevel modelling encourages us to attend to differences in relationships of interest across groups, and thus opens up possibilities for investigating why programs of interest are more successful in some sites than others, and why student achievement is more equitably distributed with respect to student background characteristics in some schools than in others. Multilevel modelling also provides us with more appropriate standard errors for estimates of various between-group effects of interest.

Questions for further investigation

1. Think about an issue or set of questions in education that you are interested in studying. How might what you have learned about multilevel modelling help to broaden the questions you wish to investigate and design a study to investigate these questions?
2. How might you proceed in analysing the data from your study?

Notes

1. Note that this is the same data set used in Seltzer (1994, 2004), but for the analyses in this chapter we have omitted an outlying site.
2. Note that the weights used in estimating fixed effects are based on HLM's estimates of the variance components in the model; for details, see Raudenbush and Bryk (2002: Chapter 3).
3. As in the case of level-1 equations, we can choose various centrings for predictors in the level-2 equations. Though not shown in Equation 36.6, we centered $\overline{PRE_j}$ around the grand mean pretest score $(\overline{PRE})$. By virtue of this centring, γ_{00} retains its meaning as the grand mean for geometry readiness scores. See Raudenbush and Bryk (2002) for further details regarding centring level-2 predictors.

Support for Jordan Rickles' work on this chapter was provided through an Institute of Education Sciences training grant fellowship.

Suggested further reading

Raudenbush and Bryk (2002) provide a detailed, comprehensive discussion of the logic of multilevel modelling and present an array of applications. In addition they provide coverage of various advanced topics, including multilevel modelling for categorical (e.g. binary) outcomes, and estimation theory for multilevel models. Snijders and Bosker (2012) also provide a comprehensive and accessible treatment of multilevel models that covers a range of applications; particularly valuable is a section of their book that focuses on strategies for handling missing data in multilevel analysis. For a very clear book-length introduction to multilevel modelling see Kreft and DeLeeuw (1998).

In addition to the HLM program, there are many other available programs for multilevel analysis, including MLwiN developed by Goldstein and his associates, SuperMix developed by Hedeker and Gibbons, SAS Proc Mixed, the *xtmixed* module in Stata, the *mixed* procedure in SPSS and the *lme4* package in R developed by Bates and Maechler. (See Chapter 29, 'Statistical Analysis Tools', in this book for a brief introduction to xtmixed and MLwiN.)

There are several websites that provide very useful, freely available materials and on-line courses on multilevel modelling and the use of various software packages in estimating multilevel models:

Academic Technology Services at UCLA: www.ats. ucla.edu/stat/seminars/
Centre for Multilevel Modelling: www.cmm.bristol. ac.uk/
Stat/Math Center at Indiana University: www.indiana. edu/~statmath/stat/all/hlm/

References

Burstein, L. (1980) 'The analysis of multi-level data in education research and evaluation', *Review of Research in Education*, 8: 158–233.

Cook, T., Habib, F., Phillips, M., Settersten, R., Shagle, S. and Degirmencioglu, S. (1999) 'Comer's school development program in Prince George's County, Maryland: a theory-based evaluation', *American Educational Research Journal*, 36: 543–97.

Cronbach, L., Deken, J. and Webb, N. (1976) *Research on Classrooms and Schools: Formulations of Questions, Design, and Analysis* (Occasional Paper). Stanford, CA: Stanford Evaluation Consortium.

Denson, N. and Seltzer, M. (2011) 'Meta-analysis in higher education: an illustrative example using hierarchical linear modeling', *Research in Higher Education*, 52: 215–44.

Kreft, I. and DeLeeuw, J. (1998) *Introducing Multilevel Modeling*. Thousand Oaks, CA: Sage.

Lee, V. and Bryk, A. (1989) 'A multilevel model of the social distribution of educational achievement', *Sociology of Education*, 62: 172–92.

Morgan, S. and Winship, C. (2015) *Counterfactuals and Causal Inference: Methods and Principles for Social Research,* 2nd edn. New York: Cambridge University Press.

Nye, B., Konstantopoulos, S. and Hedges, L. (2004) 'How large are teacher effects?', *Educational Evaluation and Policy Analysis*, 26: 237–57.

Palardy, G. (2013) 'High school socioeconomic segregation and student attainment', *American Educational Research Journal,* 50: 714–54.

Palardy, G. (2015) 'Classroom-based inequalities and achievement gaps in first grade: the role of classroom context and access to qualified and effective teachers', *Teachers College Record*, 117: 1–48.

Raudenbush, S. (1993) 'Hierarchical Linear Models and Experimental Design', in L. Edwards (ed.) *Applied Analysis of Variance in Behavioral Science*. New York: Marcel Dekker, pp. 459–96.

Raudenbush, S., and Bloom, H. (2015). 'Learning about and from a distribution of program impacts using multisite trials', *American Journal of Evaluation,* 36: 475–99.

Raudenbush, S. and Bryk, A. (1986) 'A hierarchical model for studying school effects', *Sociology of Education*, 59: 1–17.

Raudenbush, S. and Bryk, A. (2002) *Hierarchical Linear Models: Applications and Data Analysis Methods*. Thousand Oaks, CA: Sage.

Raudenbush, S., Bryk, A., Cheong, Y. and Congdon, R. (2004) *HLM 6: Hierarchical Linear and Nonlinear Modeling*. Lincolnwood, IL: Scientific Software International.

Rojas, R., and Iglesias, A. (2013) 'The language growth of Spanish-speaking English language learners', *Child Development*, 84: 630–46.

Seltzer, M. (1994) 'Studying variation in program success: a multilevel modeling approach', *Evaluation Review,* 18: 342–61.

Seltzer, M. (2004) 'The Use of Hierarchical Models in Analyzing Data from Experiments and Quasi-experiments Conducted in Field Settings', in D. Kaplan (ed.), *The Handbook of Quantitative Methods for the Social Sciences*. Thousand Oaks, CA: Sage, pp. 259–80.

Seltzer, M. and Rose, M. (2011) 'Constructing Analyses: The development of thoughtfulness in working with quantitative methods', in C. Conrad and R. Serlin (eds), *Handbook for Research in Education: Engaging Ideas and Enriching Inquiry*, 2nd edn. Thousand Oaks, CA: Sage Publications, pp. 245–62.

Seltzer, M., Choi, K. and Thum, Y.M. (2003) 'Examining relationships between where students start and how rapidly they progress: using new developments in growth modeling to gain insight into the distribution of achievement within schools', *Educational Evaluation and Policy Analysis*, 25: 263–86.

Singer, J. and Willett, J. (2003) *Applied Longitudinal Analysis: Modeling Change and Event Occurrence.* New York: Oxford University Press.

Snijders, T. and Bosker, R. (2012) *Multilevel Analysis: An Introduction to Basic and Advanced Multilevel Modeling,* 2nd edn. Thousand Oaks, CA: Sage.

Spybrook, J., Bloom, H., Congdon, R., Hill, C., Martinez, A. and Raudenbush, S. (2011) *Optimal Design Plus Empirical Evidence: Documentation for the "Optimal Design" Software*. New York: William T. Grant Foundation.

Xue, Y. and Meisels, S. (2004) 'Early literacy instruction and learning in kindergarten: evidence from the Early Childhood Longitudinal Study – kindergarten class of 1998–1999', *American Educational Research Journal*, 41: 191–229.

Effect size

Robert J. Coe

37

Introduction

'Effect size' is simply a way of quantifying the size of the difference between two groups. It is easy to calculate, readily understood, and can be applied to any measured outcome in education or social science. It is particularly valuable for quantifying the effectiveness of a particular intervention relative to some comparison. It allows us to move beyond the simplistic 'Does it work or not?', to the far more sophisticated 'How well does it work in a range of contexts?' Moreover, by placing the emphasis on the most important aspect of an intervention – the size of the effect – rather than its statistical significance (which conflates effect size and sample size), it promotes a more scientific approach to the accumulation of knowledge. For these reasons, effect size is an important tool in reporting and interpreting effectiveness.

The routine use of effect sizes, however, has until recently been limited to meta-analysis – for combining and comparing estimates from different studies – and has been all too rare in original reports of educational research (Keselman et al., 1998). This is despite the fact that measures of effect size have been available for at least seventy-five years (Huberty, 2002) and the American Psychological Association has been officially encouraging authors to report effect sizes since 1994 – but with limited success (Wilkinson et al., 1999; Fritz et al., 2012). In recent years the use and interpretation of effect sizes in education have risen in prominence with their implementation in high-profile summaries of the relative impact of different educational interventions, such as those by Hattie (2009), Marzano et al. (2001) and the Education Endowment Foundation (Higgins et al., 2013). (See Chapter 38 by Hedges in this volume for discussion of the use of effect sizes in meta-analysis.) This chapter is written for non-statisticians and is intended to be introductory, although it does assume some familiarity with the statistical ideas of the mean and standard deviation. It describes what effect size is, what it means and how it can be used, and outlines some potential problems associated with using it.

Why do we need 'effect size'?

Perhaps the most obvious motivation for the use of effect size is that it allows meaning to be given to a difference recorded by an unfamiliar instrument and reported on an unknown scale. By using the familiar concept of the standard deviation, it allows the difference to be calibrated in terms of the amount of variation within the overall population.

To illustrate this, consider a hypothetical experiment to evaluate a new reading scheme. Children in each school were randomly allocated to use the new scheme (treatment) or continue with the old (control). The main outcome was an overall measure of reading, which included a reading comprehension subtest. The researchers also wanted to know whether the effects varied in different schools. Results are shown in Table 37.1.

Table 37.1   Reading comprehension and effect

Outcome measure	Treatment group			Control group			Significance
	Mean	n	SD	Mean	n	SD	
Overall reading score	26.9	104	6.9	24.8	105	7.6	$p < 0.05$
Reading comprehension subscore	7.5	105	3.1	5.6	105	3.5	$p < 0.01$
Reading comprehension subscore (school 1)	8.1	59	3.2	5.6	59	3.0	$p < 0.01$
Reading comprehension subscore (school 2)	6.7	46	3.6	5.6	46	3.5	ns

On both the overall score and the comprehension subtest the difference between the means for the two groups is about 2 points, but these points are hard to interpret. If we use the standard deviation as a reference, we see that the former is about 0.3 of a standard deviation, the latter about 0.6 – the effect is around twice as big on the comprehension subtest when calibrated against the spread of scores on each test.

A second reason for using effect size is that it emphasises amounts, not just statistical significance. It is often more useful to know how big a difference is between two groups rather than just whether it is beyond what might reasonably occur by chance. An example can be seen in Figure 37.1, which shows the effect sizes for the comparisons in Table 37.1, together with their confidence intervals (see below for an explanation of confidence intervals).

It is immediately clear that the effect on comprehension is bigger than on overall reading, although their confidence intervals do overlap. It is also clear that the overall effect on reading was about the same as the effect on reading comprehension in school 2 (both around 0.3). The traditional interpretation of these comparisons might be that the former showed an effect ($p < 0.05$) while the latter did not (see the significance column in Table 37.1). In fact, the effect was about the same in both cases – only the smaller sample size in the latter case increased the margin of error to the point where the range of plausible values for the effect includes zero.

Further reasons for using effect sizes include that they draw attention to statistical power (Cohen, 1969), that they may reduce the risk of pure sampling variation being misinterpreted as a real difference (Cumming, 2014), that they may help to reduce the under-reporting of 'non-significant' results (Rosenthal, 1979; Ioannidis, 2005) and that they allow a ready accumulation of knowledge from multiple studies using meta-analysis (see Chapter 38 in this book). Effect sizes are also generally required for a power calculation (i.e. to estimate the sample size required to have a reasonable probability of finding an effect that is both practically important and statistically significant).

How is it calculated?

The most common measure of effect size is the *standardised mean difference* between the two groups – in other words, the difference between the means for each group divided by the standard deviation. Algebraically:

$$d = \frac{m_1 - m_2}{s}$$

The *standard deviation* is a measure of the spread of a set of values. In the context of an experiment in which the effect size is the difference between treated and control groups it might be thought that the control group would provide the best estimate of standard deviation, since it consists of

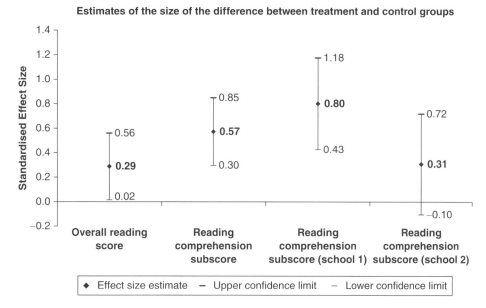

Figure 37.1   Effect sizes for the comparisons of Table 37.1

a representative sample of the population who have not been affected by the experimental intervention. This is the approach used by Glass et al. (1981), sometimes referred to as *Glass' Δ (delta)*.

However, unless the control group is very large, the estimate of the 'true' population standard deviation derived from only the control group is likely to be appreciably less accurate than an estimate derived from both the control and experimental groups. Moreover, in studies where there is not a true 'control' group (for example when two different treatments are compared) then it may be an arbitrary decision which group's standard deviation to use and it might make an appreciable difference to the estimate of effect size.

For these reasons, it is often better to use a 'pooled' estimate of standard deviation. The pooled estimate is essentially an average of the standard deviations of the experimental and control groups. If the two groups are not the same size this average is weighted to reflect the imbalance. If more than two groups are compared, there is a further choice about which ones to use in the pooled estimate. Slight differences in this choice and in the choice

of weightings give rise to *Cohen's d* (Cohen, 1969) or *Hedges' g* (Hedges and Olkin, 1985), though different sources differ in the precise definitions of each. The latter is given by taking:

$$S = \sqrt{\frac{(n_1 - 1)s_1^2 + (n_2 - 1)s_2^2}{(n_1 - 1) + (n_2 - 1)}}$$

Note that a pooled standard deviation is not the same as the standard deviation of all the values in both groups 'pooled' together. If, for example, each group had a low standard deviation but the two means were substantially different, the true pooled estimate would be much lower than the value obtained by pooling all the values together and calculating the standard deviation. The implications of choices about which standard deviation to use are discussed by Olejnik and Algina (2000).

The use of a pooled estimate of standard deviation depends on the assumption that the two calculated standard deviations are estimates of *the same* population value. In other words, that the experimental and control group standard deviations differ only as a result of sampling variation. Where this assumption cannot be made (either because there is some reason to believe that the two standard deviations are likely to be systematically different or if the actual measured values are very different), then a pooled estimate should not be used.

How can effect sizes be interpreted?

One feature of an effect size is that it can be directly converted into statements about the overlap between the two samples in terms of a comparison of percentiles.

An effect size is exactly equivalent to a 'Z-score' of a standard normal distribution. For example, an effect size of 0.8 means that the score of the average person in the experimental group is 0.8 standard deviations above the average person in the control group, and hence exceeds the scores of 79% of the control group.

Figure 37.2 illustrates how effect sizes correspond to percentiles of a normal distribution and the equivalent change in rank order for a group of 25. For example, for an effect size of 0.6, the value of 73% indicates that the average person in the

experimental group would score higher than 73% of a control group that was initially equivalent. If the group consisted of 25 people, this is the same as saying that the average person (i.e. ranked 13th in the group) would now be on a par with the person ranked 7th in the control group. It should be noted that these values depend on the assumption of a normal distribution. The interpretation of effect sizes in terms of percentiles is very sensitive to violations of this assumption (see below).

Another way to interpret effect sizes is to compare them to the effect sizes of differences that are familiar. For example, Cohen (1969: 23) describes an effect size of 0.2 as 'small' and gives to illustrate it the example that the difference between the heights of 15-year-old and 16-year-old girls in the United States corresponds to an effect of this size. An effect size of 0.5 is described as 'medium' and is 'large enough to be visible to the naked eye'. A 0.5 effect size corresponds to the difference between the heights of 14-year-old and 18-year-old girls. Cohen describes an effect size of 0.8 as 'grossly perceptible and therefore large' and equates it to the difference between the heights of 13-year-old and 18-year-old girls. As a further example he states that the difference in IQ between holders of the PhD degree and 'typical college freshmen' is comparable to an effect size of 0.8.

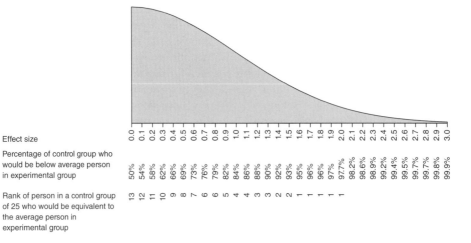

Effect size	0.0	0.1	0.2	0.3	0.4	0.5	0.6	0.7	0.8	0.9	1.0	1.1	1.2	1.3	1.4	1.5	1.6	1.7	1.8	1.9	2.0	2.1	2.2	2.3	2.4	2.5	2.6	2.7	2.8	2.9	3.0
Percentage of control group who would be below average person in experimental group	50%	54%	58%	62%	66%	69%	73%	76%	79%	82%	84%	86%	88%	90%	92%	93%	95%	96%	96%	97%	97.7%	98.2%	98.6%	98.9%	99.2%	99.4%	99.5%	99.7%	99.7%	99.8%	99.9%
Rank of person in a control group of 25 who would be equivalent to the average person in experimental group	13	12	11	10	9	8	7	6	6	5	4	4	3	3	2	2	1	1	1	1	1										

Figure 37.2   How effect sizes correspond to percentiles of a normal distribution

Cohen does acknowledge the danger of using terms like 'small', 'medium' and 'large' out of context, but this categorisation is one of the most frequently cited rules of thumb in interpreting effect sizes. Glass et al. (1981: 104) are particularly critical of this approach, arguing that the effectiveness of a particular intervention can only be interpreted in relation to other interventions that seek to produce the same effect. They also point out that the practical importance of an effect depends entirely on its relative costs and benefits. In education, if it could be shown that making a small and inexpensive change would raise academic achievement by an effect size of even as little as 0.1, then this could be a very significant improvement, particularly if the improvement applied uniformly to all students, and even more so if the effect were cumulative over time.

Glass et al. (1981: 102) give the example that an effect size of 1 corresponds to the difference of about a year of schooling on the performance in achievement tests of pupils in elementary (i.e.

primary) schools. However, analyses of scores on a range of different tests with children of different ages (Hill et al., 2007; Lipsey et al., 2012) suggest that this changes significantly with the age of the child and the type of test being used. For children in grades 8–11, for example, a year's schooling probably corresponds to about 0.2 of a standard deviation on most measures.

In England, the distribution of GCSE grades in compulsory subjects (i.e. Maths and English) has standard deviations of between 1.5 and 1.8 grades, so an improvement of one GCSE grade represents an effect size of 0.5–0.7. In the context of secondary schools therefore introducing a change in practice whose effect size was known to be 0.6 would result in an improvement of about a GCSE grade for each pupil in each subject. For a school in which 50% of pupils were previously gaining five or more A*–C grades, this percentage (other things being equal and assuming that the effect applied equally across the whole curriculum) would rise to 73%.[1] Even Cohen's 'small'

Table 37.2 Examples of average effect sizes for different interventions on learning

Intervention	Effect size	Comments
Ability grouping: dividing teaching groups by ability or attainment	0.09	Extensive evidence shows small or even negative effects on learning and other outcomes, but cost is low
Learning styles: matching teaching approaches to individual learning style	0.14	Good evidence shows small effects which may be due to the range of approaches rather than the matching per se, but cost is low
Reducing class size: from 30 to 15	0.21	Good evidence shows modest effects, but cost is extremely high
Assessment for learning: using formative assessment and feedback to inform teaching and learning	0.32	Limited evidence shows moderate impact for moderate cost
ICT: using technology (e.g. computers) in teaching	0.37	Extensive evidence of moderate overall effects, but a wide diversity of interventions and effects is present here. Overall, moderate impact for high cost
One-to-one tutoring: one teacher giving remedial support to one pupil	0.41	Good evidence shows moderate impact for very high cost
Peer tutoring: learners teach each other	0.55	Extensive evidence shows high impact for low cost
Meta-cognitive strategies: teaching learners to think explicitly about learning	0.66	Extensive evidence shows high impact for low cost

Adapted from Higgins et al. (2013)

effect of 0.2 would produce an increase from 50% to 58% – a difference that most schools would probably categorise as quite substantial. Olejnik and Algina (2000) give a similar example based on the Iowa Test of Basic Skills.

Finally, the interpretation of effect sizes can be greatly helped by a few examples from existing research. Table 37.2 lists a selection of these, adapted from Higgins et al. (2013). The examples cited are given to illustrate the use of effect size measures; they are not intended to be the definitive judgement on the relative efficacy of different interventions. In interpreting them, therefore, one should bear in mind that most of the meta-analyses from which they are derived can be (and often have been) criticised for a variety of weaknesses, that the range of circumstances in which the effects have been found may be limited, and that the effect size quoted is an average which is often based on quite widely differing values.

It seems to be a feature of educational interventions that very few of them have effects that would be described in Cohen's classification as anything other than 'small'. This appears particularly so for effects on student achievement. No doubt this is partly a result of the wide variation found in the population as a whole, against which the measure of effect size is calculated. One might also speculate that achievement is harder to influence than other outcomes, perhaps because most schools are already using optimal strategies, or because different strategies are likely to be effective in different situations – a complexity that is not well captured by a single average effect size.

A number of other features of study design seem to be systematically related to the size of the effects they report and should therefore be considered in interpreting effect sizes, particularly if estimates from different types of study are to be compared fairly. In an empirical analysis, Cheung and Slavin (2015) found that 'effect sizes are roughly twice as large for published articles, small-scale trials, and experimenter-made measures, than for unpublished documents, large-scale studies, and independent measures, respectively. In addition, effect sizes are significantly higher in quasi-experiments than in randomized experiments'.

What is the margin for error in estimating effect sizes?

Clearly, if an effect size is calculated from a very large sample it is likely to be more accurate than one calculated from a small sample. This 'margin of error' can be quantified using the idea of a 'confidence interval', which provides the same information as is usually contained in a significance test: using a '95% confidence interval' is equivalent to taking a '5% significance level'. To calculate a 95% confidence interval, you assume that the value you have (e.g. the effect size estimate of 0.8) is the 'true' value, but calculate the amount of variation in this estimate you would get if you repeatedly took new samples of the same size (i.e. different samples of 38 children). For every 100 of these hypothetical new samples, by definition, 95 would give estimates of the effect size within the '95% confidence interval'. If this confidence interval includes zero, then that is the same as saying that the result is not statistically significant. If, on the other hand, zero is outside the range, then it is 'statistically significant at the 5% level'. Using a confidence interval is a better way of conveying this information since it keeps the emphasis on the effect size – which is the important information – rather than the p-value. It is important to remember that this statistical confidence interval captures the variation in the effect size estimate that would arise purely as a result of re-sampling, assuming that every other aspect of the study were unchanged (and this limitation applies to the traditional significance test as well). A sensible estimate of the amount of variation in the effect that should be expected if we were to implement or replicate the intervention would therefore probably be quite a bit larger, given inevitable variations in context, population, implementation, etc.

Technically, estimating confidence intervals for effect sizes requires the use of a non-central t-distribution which is quite complex to calculate.

Fortunately, however, a simple formula given by Hedges and Olkin (1985: 86) provides an excellent approximation to the standard error of the effect size, d:

$$S_d \cong \sqrt{\frac{n_1 + n_2}{n_1 n_2} + \frac{d^2}{2(n_1 + n_2)}}$$

Hence a 95% confidence interval for d would be from

$$d - 1.96\ S_d \text{ to } d + 1.96\ S_d$$

Figure 37.3 shows the size of the margin of error with different sample sizes. For example, with two groups of 50 each (total 100) the margin of error is 0.4. Hence an effect size estimate of, say, 0.5 would have a 95% CI from 0.1 (i.e. 0.5 − 0.4) to 0.9 (0.5 + 0.4).

What other factors can influence effect size?

Although effect size is a simple and readily interpreted measure of difference, it can also be sensitive to a number of spurious influences, so some care needs to be taken in its use. Some of these issues are briefly outlined here.

Restricted range

If the samples being compared have too narrow a range of values, the estimate of the standard deviation will be too low. The standardised mean difference, calculated by dividing by this standard deviation, will therefore be inflated. For example, in considering the effect of an intervention with university students, or with pupils with reading difficulties, one must remember that these are restricted populations: an effect size calculated from an intervention using these 'restricted range' groups will be larger than would be seen for the same intervention with a fully representative sample.

Ideally, in calculating effect size one should use the standard deviation of the full population in order to make comparisons fair. However, there will be many cases in which unrestricted values are not available, either in practice or in principle. In reporting the effect size, one should draw attention to this fact; if the amount of restriction can be quantified it may be possible to make allowance for it. Any comparison with effect sizes calculated from a full-range population must be made with great caution, if at all. One particular case where this issue arises is when a regression or ANCOVA model has been used to estimate effects after adjusting for covariates. Here the standard deviation to use in calculating an effect size should normally be from the unadjusted outcome, not the residuals.

Non-normal distributions

The interpretations of effect sizes given in Table 37.1 depend on the assumption that both control and experimental groups have a 'normal' or Gaussian distribution – the familiar 'bell-shaped' curve. Needless to say, if this assumption is not true then the interpretation may be altered, and in particular it may be difficult to make a fair comparison between an effect size based on normal distributions and one based on non-normal distributions.

Measurement reliability

A third factor that can spuriously affect an effect size is the reliability of the measurement on which it is based. According to classical measurement theory, any measure of a particular outcome may be considered to consist of the 'true' underlying value together with a component of 'error'. The problem is that the amount of variation in measured scores for a particular sample (i.e. its standard deviation) will depend on both the variation in underlying scores and the amount of error in their measurement. With an unreliable measure, the standard deviation is inflated, thereby reducing the effect size.

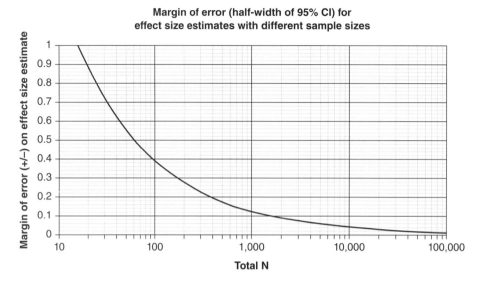

Figure 37.3 Approximate half-width of 95% confidence intervals with sample size, assuming equal numbers in each group, for small effect sizes (<1)

In interpreting an effect size, it is therefore important to know the reliability of the measurement from which it was calculated. This is one reason why the reliability of any outcome measure used should be reported. It is theoretically possible to make a correction for unreliability (sometimes called 'attenuation'), which gives an estimate of what the effect size would have been had the reliability of the test been perfect. However, in practice the effect of this is rather alarming, since the worse the test was, the more you increase the estimate of the effect size. Moreover, estimates of reliability are dependent on the particular population in which the test was used, and are themselves anyway subject to sampling error. For a further discussion of the impact of reliability on effect sizes, see Baugh (2002).

Are there alternative measures of effect size?

A number of statistics are sometimes proposed as alternative measures of effect size, other than the 'standardised mean difference'. Some of these will be considered here.

Perhaps the most widely used is the proportion of variance accounted for: R^2. If the correlation between two variables is 'r', the square of this value (usually denoted with a capital letter: R^2) represents the proportion of the variance in each that is 'accounted for' by the other. In other words, this is the proportion by which the variance of the outcome measure is reduced when it is replaced by the variance of the residuals from a regression equation. This idea can be extended to multiple regression (where it represents the proportion of the variance accounted for by all the independent variables together) or ANOVA (e.g. 'eta-squared', η^2). Keselman and Lix discuss the use of effect sizes in Chapter 34 on ANOVA in this volume.

A simple formula (for example, see Cohen, 1969) can be used to convert between d and R^2. Because R^2 has this ready convertibility, it (or alternative measures of variance accounted for) is sometimes advocated as a universal measure of effect size (e.g. Thompson, 1999). One disadvantage of such an approach is that effect size measures based on variance accounted for suffer from a number of technical limitations, such as sensitivity to violation of assumptions (heterogeneity of variance, balanced designs) and their standard errors can be large (Olejnik and Algina, 2000). They are also generally more statistically complex and hence perhaps less easily understood. Further, they are non-directional; two studies with precisely opposite results would report exactly the same variance accounted for. There is also scope for confusion in the use of the word 'effect' to describe a relationship that is essentially correlational.

It has been shown that the interpretation of the 'standardised mean difference' measure of effect size is very sensitive to violations of the assumption of normality. For this reason, a number of more robust and non-parametric alternatives have been suggested. An example of a simple, non-parametric effect size statistic, based on dominance, is given by Cliff (1993). In recent years, interest in and advocacy for the use of robust statistics have grown (Wilcox, 1998). These allow many of the advantages of using classical parametric statistics to be maintained while reducing their sensitivity to common violations of their assumptions. Algina et al. (2005) describe a robust equivalent to Cohen's *d*, which uses trimmed means with a Winsorised standard deviation, rescaled to make it comparable with the more familiar Cohen's *d* and confidence intervals estimated by bootstrapping.

There are also effect size measures for multivariate outcomes. A detailed explanation can be found in Olejnik and Algina (2000). A method for calculating effect sizes within multilevel models has been proposed by Tymms et al. (1997). Good summaries of many of the different kinds of effect size measures that can be used and the relationships among them can be found in Snyder and Lawson (1993), Rosenthal (1994) and Kirk (1996).

Finally, a common effect size measure widely used in medicine is the 'odds ratio'. This is appropriate where an outcome is dichotomous: success or failure, a patient survives or does not. Explanations of the odds ratio can be found in a number of medical statistics texts, including Altman (1991) and Fleiss (1994).

Conclusion

Effect size is not a panacea for all statistical ills. It is complex and can easily be misinterpreted – and often is. However, it does provide a scale-free way of representing how big a difference on an unfamiliar measure is, and arguably a more intuitive way than in traditional significance testing of drawing attention to what really matters in statistical analysis. Although effect size is probably still not mainstream in textbooks and statistical courses, its use seems to be growing, so researchers need to understand this and use it where appropriate.

Questions for further investigation

1. To what extent does the use of effect sizes avoid the problems associated with the misuses and misunderstandings of statistical hypothesis tests and p-values (see Cumming, 2014)?
2. Find an example in a report of a study in education where an effect size provides a useful way of presenting and interpreting the results; then find another where an effect size is misused, oversimplified or misrepresented.

Note

1. This calculation is derived from a probit transformation (Glass et al., 1981: 136), based on the assumption of an underlying normally distributed variable measuring academic attainment, some threshold of which is equivalent to a student achieving 5+ A*–Cs. If $\Phi(z)$ is the standard normal cumulative distribution function, p_1 is the proportion achieving a given threshold and p_2 the proportion to be expected after a change with effect size, *d,* then:

$$p_2 = \Phi\{\Phi^{-1}(p_1) + d\}$$

Suggested further reading

There is an abundance of additional reading on the areas suggested in this chapter. Please see the papers and texts listed below, as well as Chapter 34 in this book.

Ellis (2010) *The Essential Guide to Effect Sizes* is a detailed, yet accessible, introduction that outlines a range of different effect size measures, why they are important, how they can be interpreted, and how they are sometimes misused. It also covers statistical power and meta-analysis.

Lipsey et al.'s (2012) report for the Institute of Education Sciences ('Translating the Statistical Representation of the Effects of Education Interventions into More Readily Interpretable Forms') gives a good overview of how effect sizes can and should be interpreted.

Bibliography

Algina, J., Keselman, H.J. and Penfield, R.D. (2005) 'An alternative to Cohen's standardized mean difference effect size: a robust parameter and confidence interval in the two independent group case', *Psychological Methods,* 10(3): 317–28.

Altman, D.G. (1991) *Practical Statistics for Medical Research*. London: Chapman & Hall.

Baugh, F. (2002) 'Correcting effect sizes for score reliability: a reminder that measurement and substantive issues are linked inextricably', *Educational and Psychological Measurement,* 62(2): 254–63.

Carpenter, J. and Bithell, J. (2000) 'Bootstrap confidence intervals: when, which, what? A practical guide for medical statisticians', *Statistics in Medicine,* 19: 1141–64.

Cheung, A. and Slavin, R.E. (2015) 'How methodological features affect effect sizes in education'. *Best Evidence Encyclopedia*, Johns Hopkins University, Baltimore, MD. Available online at: www.bestevidence.org/word/methodological_Sept_21_2015.pdf

Cliff, N. (1993) 'Dominance statistics – ordinal analyses to answer ordinal questions', *Psychological Bulletin,* 114(3): 494–509.

Cohen, J. (1969) *Statistical Power Analysis for the Behavioral Sciences*. New York: Academic.

Cumming, G. (2014) 'The New Statistics: why and how', *Psychological Science,* 25(1): 7–29.

Cumming, G. and Finch, S. (2001) 'A primer on the understanding, use, and calculation of confidence intervals that are based on central and noncentral distributions', *Educational and Psychological Measurement,* 61: 532–74.

Ellis, P.D. (2010) *The Essential Guide to Effect Sizes: Statistical Power, Meta-Analysis and the Interpretation of Research Results*. Cambridge: Cambridge University Press.

Fleiss, J.L.(1994) 'Measures of Effect Size for Categorical Data', in H. Cooper and L.V. Hedges (eds), *The Handbook of Research Synthesis*. New York: Russell Sage Foundation.

Fritz, C.O., Morris, P.E. and Richler, J.J. (2012) 'Effect size estimates: current use, calculations, and interpretation', *Journal of Experimental Psychology: General,* 141(1): 2–18.

Glass, G.V., McGaw, B. and Smith, M.L. (1981) *Meta-Analysis in Social Research*. London: Sage.

Grissom, R.J. (1994) 'Probability of the superior outcome of one treatment over another', *Journal of Applied Psychology,* 79(2): 314–16.

Grissom, R.J. and Kim, J.J. (2001) 'Review of assumptions and problems in the appropriate conceptualization of effect size', *Psychological Methods,* 6: 135–46.

Grissom, R.J. and Kim, J.J. (2005) *Effect Sizes for Research: A Broad Practical Approach*. Mahwah, NJ: Erlbaum.

Hattie, J. (2009) *Visible Learning: A Synthesis of Over 800 Meta-analyses Relating to Achievement*. Abingdon: Routledge.

Hedges, L.V. and Olkin, I. (1985) *Statistical Methods for Meta-Analysis*. New York: Academic.

Higgins, S., Katsipataki, M., Kokotsaki, D., Coleman, R., Major, L.E. and Coe, R. (2013) The Sutton Trust-Education Endowment Foundation Teaching and Learning Toolkit. London: Education Endowment Foundation. Available at: www.educationendowmentfoundation.org.uk/toolkit.

Hill, C.J., Bloom, H.S., Black, A.R. and Lipsey, M.W. (2007) *Empirical Benchmarks for Interpreting Effect Sizes in Research MDRC Working Papers on Research Methodology*. New York: MDRC. Available at: www.mdrc.org/publication/empirical-benchmarks-interpreting-effect-sizes-research (last accessed 15 November 2016).

Huberty, C.J. (2002) 'A history of effect size indices', *Educational and Psychological Measurement,* 62(2): 227–40.

Ioannidis, J.P.A. (2005) 'Why most published research findings are false', *PLoS Medicine*, 2: 8. Available at: www.plosmedicine.org/article/info:doi/10.1371/journal. pmed.0020124 (accessed 26 September 2016).

Keselman, H.J., Huberty, C.J., Lix, L.M., Olejnik, S. et al. (1998) 'Statistical practices of educational researchers: an analysis of their ANOVA, MANOVA, and ANCOVA analyses', *Review of Educational Research*, 68(3): 350–86.

Kirk, R.E. (1996) 'Practical significance: a concept whose time has come', *Educational and Psychological Measurement*, 56(5): 746–59.

Kulik, J.A. and Kulik, C.C. (1982) 'Educational outcomes of tutoring: a meta-analysis of findings,' *American Educational Research Journal*, 19: 237–48.

Lipsey, M.W., Puzio, K., Yun, C., Hebert, M.A., Steinka-Fry, K., Cole, M.W., Roberts, M., Anthony, K.S. and Busick, M.D. (2012) 'Translating the Statistical Representation of the Effects of Education Interventions into More Readily Interpretable Forms. (NCSER 2013-3000)'. Washington, DC: National Center for Special Education Research, Institute of Education Sciences, U.S. Department of Education. (This report is available on the IES website at http://ies.ed.gov/ncser/.)

Marzano, R.J., Pickering, D. and Pollock, J.E. (2001) *Classroom Instruction that Works: Research-based Strategies for Increasing Student Achievement*. Alexandria, VA: ASCD.

Olejnik, S. and Algina, J. (2000) 'Measures of effect size for comparative studies: applications, interpretations and limitations', *Contemporary Educational Psychology*, 25: 241–86.

Rosenthal, R. (1979) 'The file drawer problem and tolerance for null results', *Psychological Bulletin*, 86(3): 638–41.

Rosenthal, R. (1994) 'Parametric Measures of Effect Size', in H. Cooper and L.V. Hedges (eds), *The Handbook of Research Synthesis*. New York: Russell Sage Foundation.

Smith, M.L. and Glass, G.V. (1980) 'Meta-analysis of research on class size and its relationship to attitudes and instruction', *American Educational Research Journal*, 17: 419–33.

Snyder, P. and Lawson, S. (1993) 'Evaluating results using corrected and uncorrected effect size estimates', *Journal of Experimental Education*, 61(4): 334–49.

Thompson, B. (1999) 'Common Methodology Mistakes in Educational Research, Revisited, Along with a Primer on Both Effect Sizes and the Bootstrap'. Invited address presented at the annual meeting of the American Educational Research Association, Montreal.

Tymms, P., Merrell, C. and Henderson, B. (1997) 'The first year at school: a quantitative investigation of the attainment and progress of pupils', *Educational Research and Evaluation*, 3(2): 101–18.

Vincent, D. and Crumpler, M. (1997) *British Spelling Test Series Manual 3X/Y*. Windsor: NFER-Nelson.

Wilcox, R.R. (1998) 'How many discoveries have been lost by ignoring modern statistical methods?', *American Psychologist*, 53(3): 300–14.

Wilkinson, L. and Task Force on Statistical Inference, APA Board of Scientific Affairs (1999) 'Statistical methods in psychology journals: guidelines and explanations', *American Psychologist*, 54(8): 594–604.

Meta-analysis

Larry V. Hedges

Introduction

Independent replication of results has long been considered a central feature of scientific enquiry. A body of replicated results presents the question of how best to interpret those results. Standard statistical methods focus on the results of single studies in isolation. For example, standard statistical methods might be suitable for testing hypotheses about the existence of treatment effects in each study but do not provide methods for dealing with multiple studies. To deal with statistical evidence from several independent studies, special statistical methods are needed. Meta-analysis is the use of statistical methods to combine the results of a set of research studies that examine the same question. Meta-analysis is often used for carrying out the synthesis of results in systematic reviews and the term has sometimes been used to encompass the entire process of carrying out a research review using statistical methods. However, we use the term 'meta-analysis' to refer only to the statistical aspects of systematic reviews: combining evidence across independent studies using statistical methods.

The term 'meta-analysis' was suggested by Glass (1976) to describe the process of combining the results of statistical analyses in different studies for the purpose of drawing general conclusions. Although it dates from 1976, the process of using statistical methods for combining evidence across studies has a much longer history. Early examples of published meta-analysis (described not as meta-analysis but as combining information across studies) include Pearson (1904) in medicine, Tippett (1931) and Fisher (1932) in statistics, Birge (1932) in physics, and Cochran (1937) in agriculture.

Why is meta-analysis necessary?

Statistical significance tests are often used to help interpret the results of individual research studies. It therefore seems quite intuitive to use the outcomes of significance tests in each study to assess results across studies. Consider a series of studies all of which evaluate the effect of the same treatment via a hypothesis test. Intuitively, if a large proportion of studies obtain statistically significant results, then this should be evidence that there is a (non-zero) effect in these studies. Conversely, if few studies find significant results, then the combined evidence for a non-zero effect would seem to be weak. In spite of the intuitive appeal of this logic, it has very undesirable properties as a method of drawing inferences about treatment effects from a collection of studies. Not only does this strategy have exceptionally low sensitivity (low power in the statistical sense), its sensitivity can also actually decline as the amount of evidence (the number of studies) increases (Hedges and Olkin, 1980).

Similarly, it seems intuitively sensible to say that if both study A and study B find statistically significant effects of a treatment, then study B has replicated the finding of study A. Similarly, it seems intuitive to say that if study A finds a statistically significant effect of a treatment and study B does not, then study B has failed to replicate. This intuition is also faulty. Significance tests compare an observed effect with a null (typically zero) effect. However, it is easy to find examples where two studies both have significant treatment effects (meaning that they are both reliably different from zero) but these two effects are themselves significantly different (meaning that they are reliably different from each other). Moreover, the fact that one effect is statistically significant (reliably different from zero) and the other is not does *not* imply that they are significantly different from each other.

More fundamentally, the use of statistical significance to represent the outcomes of studies is problematic in this context because statistical significance values (p-values) confound information about two aspects of a study: features of the design (principally the sample size) and a feature of the outcome that is independent of the design (the effect size). Highly statistically significant results can occur because the sample size is large (even if the effect size is small) or because the effect size is large (even if the sample size is small). Meta-analysis attempts to combine the information about study outcomes that is independent of the particular design used (and in particular is independent of sample sizes) by explicitly focusing on effect size.

Effect sizes

In order to use statistical methods to combine the results of studies, it is essential that the results of each study be described by a numerical index and that these indexes have the same meaning across studies. In education and the social sciences, these numerical indexes of study outcomes are called effect sizes. Simple effect sizes include the correlation coefficient and the difference between treatment and control group means divided by the standard deviation (often called the standardised mean difference or the *d*-index). Effect sizes are discussed more extensively in Chapter 37 of this book.

An important distinction is the difference between the observed effect size (the sample effect size) and the underlying parameter that it estimates. For example, consider a study that estimates the correlation between two variables (such as socio-economic status and achievement). Such a study, with a particular sample of individuals, would compute a value of the correlation. If that study were replicated with a different sample of individuals (sampled from the same population as the first sample), it is unlikely that the value of the correlation computed in the replication would be the same as with the original sample. In fact, if we replicated the study a very large number of times (each time using a different sample from the same population), we would get a range of values of the correlation. This range of values is what statisticians call the sampling distribution of the estimate. The average of all these correlation values is what we call the effect size parameter, and any one of the correlations computed from a particular sample is an effect size estimate. The standard deviation of the collection of estimates is called the standard error of the estimate and is used to quantify the variation of the observed effect sizes from sample to sample. (Another way to define the effect size parameter is as the correlation that would be obtained from an indefinitely large sample.)

One way of thinking about the distinction between the effect size estimate and the effect size parameter is that the difference between the effect size estimate and the corresponding parameter is an estimation error. Thus if d is the effect size estimate, δ is the effect size parameter, and ε is the estimation error, then $\varepsilon = d - \delta$ or $d = \delta + \varepsilon$. In this framework, the standard error of the estimate describes the variation in the estimation errors.

Typically, we will have only one effect size estimate from a study but the thought experiment above is meant to clarify the distinction between the effect size parameter and the observed effect size and to define the standard error. It may not be obvious therefore how one might obtain the standard error of an effect size estimate. As it turns out, statisticians have been able to deduce formulae for these standard errors (or more typically the variance which is the square of the standard error) in terms of sample sizes and effect sizes. For example, the variance of the correlation is $(1 - r^2)^2/(n - 1)$, where n is the sample size and the variance of the standardised mean difference is $2(1 + d^2/8)/n$, where n is the sample size in each group. For a more extensive discussion of computing effect sizes and their variances see Borenstein et al. (2009) or Cumming (2012).

We emphasise the difference between an effect size estimate and the corresponding effect size parameter by using Roman letters for the effect size estimates and the corresponding Greek letters for the effect size parameter (r and ρ or d and δ).

In meta-analysis, the results of each study are summarised by its effect size. The data provided by each study are then an effect size estimate and its standard error.

Procedures in meta-analysis

The typical meta-analysis starts by assembling the effect size estimates from each study and their standard errors (or the square of the standard error, also known as the variance of the effect size).

Sometimes additional information about each study is collected in the form of study characteristics that are potential moderators of the effect size.

The first analytic step in many meta-analyses is to examine the effect sizes descriptively. Effect size estimates will typically differ somewhat across studies. Because most meta-analyses involve collections of studies with (somewhat to profoundly) different sample sizes, and because standard errors depend on the sample size, the standard errors of the effect sizes will also typically differ. One way to characterise the range in which the effect size parameter for a study is likely to lie is by computing a (95%) confidence interval for the effect size parameter based on the estimate and its standard error. If d is the effect size estimate, and v is its variance, so that $S = \sqrt{v}$ is its standard error, then the 95% confidence interval for the effect size parameter δ is

$$d - 2S \leq \delta \leq d + 2S$$

Often the effect sizes and their confidence intervals are displayed together in a graphic called a forest plot.

Because the confidence intervals reflect a range of uncertainty of the estimates, the forest plot permits the analyst to see how similar the

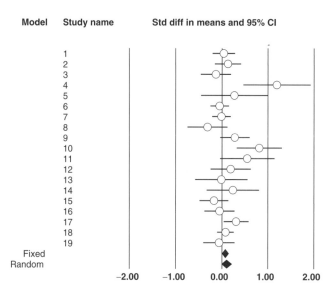

Figure 38.1   Forest plot of teacher expectancy data

effect size estimates are and to also see the range of uncertainty of each estimate. Figure 38.1 is an example of a forest plot.

Combining effect size estimates across studies

Effect size estimates are usually combined across studies by taking an average. However, the estimates from different studies have quite different uncertainties (that is, have different standard errors) which is indicated by confidence intervals having different widths on the forest plot. Therefore in combining (averaging) estimates across studies, it makes sense to give more weight to the effect size estimates that have less uncertainty (smaller standard errors). The weights that produce the most precise weighted estimate are inversely proportional to the variance (the square of the standard error) of the effect size estimates. This is why meta-analyses use inverse variance weights to compute a weighted average of the effect size estimates.

The weighted average estimate of k effect size estimates $d_1, \ldots, d_k$ that have variances $v_1, \ldots, v_k$ is given by:

$$d. = \frac{\sum_{i=1}^{k} w_i d_i}{\sum_{i=1}^{k} w_i}$$

and the variance of this weighted average is:

$$v. = \frac{1}{\sum_{i=1}^{k} w_i}$$

where the weights are given by $w_i = 1/v_i$. and the standard error is $S. = \sqrt{v}$. The standard error $S.$ can be used to construct a confidence interval for $d.$ or to test hypotheses about the average effect size parameter (e.g. that the average effect size is zero). The 95% confidence interval for the average effect size is:

$$d. - 2S. \leq \delta \leq d. + 2S,$$

(see, for example, Pigott, 2012).

Assessing heterogeneity

A logical question that arises in carrying out meta-analyses is whether the effect sizes are consistent across studies (this corresponds to the question, for example, of whether the treatment effect sizes are consistent across studies). However, even if the effect size parameters in every study were identical, the observed effect size estimates would be expected to differ due to estimation error. Therefore it is not always obvious whether a set of effect size estimates indicates that the underlying effect size parameters are likely to be different or if the values of the effect size estimates are likely to have occurred because of estimation errors.

One approach to this problem is to use a statistical test of heterogeneity of effect sizes (see Hedges and Olkin, 1985). This test computes a statistic that is a weighted sum of squared deviations from the weighted mean effect size:

$$Q = \sum_{i=1}^{k} (d_i - d.)^2$$

When the effect size *parameters* are identical across studies, the Q-statistic has a chi-square distribution with $(k-1)$ degrees of freedom, which is used to get critical values to determine when an obtained value of Q is large enough to indicate heterogeneity at a particular significance level.

The statistical test based on the Q-statistic can give an indication that the effect size parameters are not identical, but it does not describe *how different* the effect size parameters might be across studies. To describe the amount of heterogeneity in effect size parameters in meta-analysis, one can estimate the actual variation of the underlying effect size parameters, often called the between-studies (effect size) variance component and symbolised by τ^2. One use for the variance component (or rather its square root τ) is to characterise the plausible range in which the effect size parameters might lie. Approximately 95% of the effect size parameters might be expected to lie in the range from $d. - 2\tau$ to $d. + 2\tau$ (note the use of τ not τ^2).

Quantifying the variation of the effect size parameters via τ^2 leaves open the question of how much of the variation in the observed effect size estimates is real variation (variation in effect size parameters) and how much is due to estimation error. One way to quantify the proportion of real variation is the index I^2, which is an estimate of τ^2 divided by the total variation of the effect size estimates. It can be computed very simply as:

$$I^2 = \frac{Q - (k - 1)}{Q}$$

Fixed versus random effects

Practitioners of meta-analysis sometimes take different perspectives on whether the heterogeneity of effect size parameters should be counted as random variation in meta-analysis. One perspective is that heterogeneity is due to real differences between studies that are consequences of the study design, even if we do not understand exactly what these were. A different perspective is that if we do not understand the sources of these differences, it is safer to treat them as if they were random disturbances. The first perspective (between-study differences are systematic) implies that any heterogeneity of effect size parameters is not a random phenomenon and therefore does not add statistical uncertainty to the analysis. This is sometimes called the *fixed effects* analysis strategy and was described above.

The second perspective (between-study differences need to be treated as unsystematic) implies that heterogeneity of effect sizes is a random phenomenon that must add to the statistical uncertainty of the analysis. This is called the *random effects* analysis. The random effects analysis is analogous to the fixed effects analysis in every way except the weights used. In the random effects analysis, the variance of the effect size estimate is defined as $v_i + \tau^2$ (as opposed to just v_i in the fixed effects analysis). Therefore the weights used in the random effects analysis are $w_i = 1/(v_i + \tau^2)$ (as opposed to just $w_i = 1/v_i$ in the fixed effects analysis). The process of computing the weighted mean,

its standard error, confidence intervals for the mean and tests for the mean effect size is exactly the same as in the fixed effects analysis.

The fixed and random effects analyses yield identical results if $\tau^2 = 0$, because then the weights are identical in the two analyses. If $\tau^2 > 0$, then the random effects weights are each larger and tend to be more equal than the fixed effects weights. More equal weights often lead to slightly different weighted means in the random effects analysis than in the fixed effects analysis, but they may be either smaller or larger. The generally larger weights imply that the variance of the weighted average (and its square root, the standard error) will be larger in the random effects analysis than in the fixed effects analysis. This reflects the fact that there is an additional source of uncertainty for each estimate in the random effects analysis (quantified by τ^2) and therefore the uncertainty of the weighted mean is larger.

While researchers who use meta-analysis disagree about whether random effects analyses are preferable, there is general agreement that meta-analyses are more interpretable when there is less unexplained heterogeneity. Many specialists in meta-analysis recommend generally using random effects analyses because they are generally more conservative. For a broad discussion, see for example Borenstein et al. (2010).

Analysis of variance and regression analyses in meta-analysis

One approach to dealing with heterogeneity of effect sizes in meta-analysis is to use statistical models to explain this variation as attributable to differences in study characteristics, such as type of sample, intensity or duration of the treatment, characteristics of the measurement of the outcome, or features of the study design. While standard analysis of variance and multiple regression analyses are not directly applicable in meta-analysis, generalisations of these methods are available that are designed for meta-analysis (see, for example, Cooper et al., 2009). These methods make it possible to determine whether variables describing studies are related to effect size and to estimate the remaining level of heterogeneity after the effects of study-level variables have been accounted for.

Both fixed effects and random effects analogues to analysis of variance and regression analysis are available and differ in whether or not they treat the heterogeneity in effect sizes as a random phenomenon that contributes uncertainty to the analysis. If the remaining level of heterogeneity is large, then many researchers would argue for the use of random effects analyses that are more conservative (see, for example, Borenstein et al., 2010).

Publication bias

A challenge to the interpretation of published scientific findings is that they may not be representative of the studies actually conducted. This challenge obviously applies to summaries of such findings, including meta-analyses. For example, if studies with positive findings are more likely to be published and therefore available for inclusion in meta-analyses, the findings of individual published studies and any summaries of them will tend to be positively biased. Often publication bias is tied to statistical significance testing: studies that do not obtain statistically significant results are less likely to be published (or even submitted for publication). Unfortunately there is evidence of such bias in many areas of scientific work, including education and the social sciences (see Rothstein et al., 2005). However, while it is difficult to understand whether publication bias may be operating when interpreting a single study, there are methods for detecting and even adjusting for the effects of publication bias in meta-analysis.

One of the most useful tools for detecting publication bias is the funnel plot. A funnel plot is a plot of each study's effect size versus its standard error (or its sample size). If there is no publication bias, the plot should look like a funnel, because the studies whose effect sizes have larger standard errors should exhibit more variation and those effects have smaller standard errors. If there is publication bias in which statistically insignificant effects are less likely to be observed, effect sizes with large standard errors and small effect sizes (which will tend to be statistically insignificant) will be less likely to be observed. Thus part of the funnel plot will be missing (the part of the upper corner nearest to the vertical line representing zero effect size). Consequently this plot can be used for a visual indicator of possible publication bias. There are also statistical tests for publication bias based on funnel plots (e.g. Begg, 1994).

A great deal of work has been devoted to adjustment for the effects of publication bias in meta-analysis. The simplest of such methods is called the trim and fill procedure (Duval, 2005). The idea of trim and fill is to use the funnel plot to estimate the number of effect sizes that are missing due to publication bias, then fill them in (impute the missing values) using values on the opposite side of the funnel plot (and presumably not subject to publication selection). There are also more sophisticated methods involving estimation based on non-parametric selection models that are more persuasive but also more complex (see, for example, Hedges and Vevea, 2005).

Example

Raudenbush (1984) reported a meta-analysis of 19 experimental studies of teacher expectancy effects on pupil IQ. Using the fixed effects analysis of these standardised mean difference effect sizes, the weighted mean was $d. = 0.06$, with a standard error of $S. = 0.036$, which corresponded to a confidence interval for the mean effect size of –0.01 to 0.13. This analysis would suggest that the average effect size was not significantly different from zero. The random effects analysis yielded a similar conclusion with a weighted mean effect size of 0.11 with a standard error of 0.079, and a 95% confidence interval for the weighted mean effect size of –0.04 to 0.27. The standard error was more than twice as large in the random effects analysis because there was considerable heterogeneity in the results. The Q-statistic was $Q = 35.83$, which was large enough to indicate heterogeneity at the 0.001 level of statistical significance. The value of the variance component was $\tau^2 = 0.082$, so that the standard deviation of the distribution of effect size parameters across studies was $\tau = 0.286$. The value of I^2 was $I^2 = 49.8\%$, meaning that about half the total variation of the observed effect sizes was due to variation in the effect size parameters across studies.

Conclusion

Raudenbush showed that a crucial variable in explaining the variation in effect sizes across studies was the amount of prior contact that the teachers had had with the students before the expectancy effect was experimentally induced. Producing an effect on students required that teachers believed the information the experimenters gave them to try to change their expectations about the students. Consequently, teachers who had had enough experience with students to form expectations before the experimenters tried to change them were not influenced by what the experimenters told them. For students of these teachers, there were essentially no effects. For students of teachers who had been with their class for a week or less, analysis of variance methods showed that there was a substantial and consistent positive effect size. In this analysis there was essentially no heterogeneity of effects once the amount of prior teacher contact with their class was taken into account.

Questions for further investigation

1. Discuss your understanding of the usefulness of meta-analysis in statistical testing and analysis. Has it improved in light of the information in this chapter and elsewhere in this volume?

2. Discuss the benefits of employing meta-analysis to a study over a traditional literature review.
3. How might a meta-analysis reach different conclusions from a conventional literature review?

Suggested further reading

Borenstein, M., Hedges, L.V., Higgins, J.P.T. and Rothstein, H. (2009) *Introduction to Meta-analysis.* London: Wiley. This book provides a clear and thorough introduction to meta-analysis, the process of synthesising data from a series of separate studies.

Cooper, H. (2010) *Research Synthesis and Meta-analysis: A Step by Step Approach*, 5th edn. Thousand Oaks, CA: Sage. An invaluable tool for learning the techniques of researching, reviewing and analysing research literature. Applying basic tenets of sound data gathering to a comprehensive synthesis of past research on a topic, from conceptualisation of the research problem to the concise summary of the research review.

Higgins, J.P.T. and Green, S. (eds) *Cochrane Handbook for Systematic Reviews of Interventions* Version 5.1.0 [updated March 2011] [www.cochrane-handbook.org]. The Cochrane Collaboration, 2011. Designed to support Cochrane Collaboration systematic reviews in medicine, but has much useful content for education researchers and social scientists. The primary focus is on meta-analyses of randomised controlled trials, but is useful when considering meta-analyses of non-randomised studies.

Lipsey, M. and Wilson, D. (2001) *Practical Meta-analysis.* Thousand Oaks, CA: Sage. By integrating and translating the current methodological and statistical work into a practical guide, the authors provide readers with a state-of-the-art introduction to the various approaches to doing meta-analysis.

Rothstein, H., Sutton, A. and Borenstein, M. (eds) (2005) *Publication Bias in Meta-analysis.* New York: John Wiley. Adopts an inter-disciplinary approach and makes an excellent reference volume for any researchers and graduate students who conduct systematic reviews or meta-analyses.

References

Begg, C.B. (1994) 'Publication Bias', in H. Cooper and L.V. Hedges (eds), *The Handbook of Research Synthesis*. New York: Russell Sage Foundation, pp. 399–410.

Birge, R.T. (1932) 'The calculation of errors by the method of least squares', *Physical Review*, 40: 207–27.

Borenstein, M., Hedges, L.V., Higgins, J.P.T. and Rothstein, H. (2009) *Introduction to Meta-Analysis*. London: Wiley.

Borenstein, M., Hedges, L.V., Higgins, J.P.T. and Rothstein, H. (2010) 'A basic introduction to fixed-effect and random-effects models for meta-analysis', *Journal of Research Synthesis Methods*, 1: 97–111.

Cochran, W.G. (1937) 'Problems arising in the analysis of a series of similar experiments', *Journal of the Royal Statistical Society (Suppl.)*, 4: 102–18.

Cooper, H., Hedges, L.V. and Valentine, J. (2009) *The Handbook of Research Synthesis and Meta-analysis*, 2nd edn. New York: Russell Sage Foundation.

Cumming, G. (2012) *Understanding the New Statistics: Effect Sizes, Confidence Intervals and Meta-analysis*. New York: Routledge.

Duval, S. (2005) 'The Trim and Fill Method', in H. Rothstein, A. Sutton and M. Borenstein (eds), *Publication Bias in Meta-analysis*. New York: John Wiley, pp. 127–44.

Fisher, R.A. (1932) *Statistical Methods for Research Workers*, 4th edn. London: Oliver & Boyd.

Glass, G.V. (1976) 'Primary, secondary, and meta-analysis of research', *Educational Researcher*, 5: 3–8.

Hedges, L.V. and Olkin, I. (1980) 'Vote counting methods in research synthesis', *Psychological Bulletin*, 88: 359–69.

Hedges, L.V. and Olkin, I. (1985) *Statistical Methods for Metaanalysis*. New York: Academic.

Hedges, L.V. and Vevea, J.L. (2005) 'Selection Model Approaches to Publication Bias', in H. Rothstein, A. Sutton and M. Borenstein (eds), *Publication Bias in Meta-analysis*. New York: John Wiley, pp. 145–74.

Pearson, K. (1904) 'Report on certain enteric fever inoculations', *British Medical Journal*, 2: 1243–6.

Pigott, T. (2012) *Advances in Meta-analysis*. New York: Springer Science & Business Media.

Raudenbush, S.W. (1984) 'Magnitude of teacher expectancy effects on pupil IQ as a function of the credibility of expectancy induction: a synthesis of findings from 18 studies', *Journal of Educational Psychology*, 76: 85–97.

Rothstein, H., Sutton, A. and Borenstein, M. (eds) (2005) *Publication Bias in Meta-analysis*. New York: John Wiley.

Tippett, L.H.C. (1931) *The Method of Statistics*. London: Williams & Norgate.

Software for meta-analysis

Comprehensive Meta-Analysis (CMA), developed by Borenstein, Hedges, Higgins and Rothstein – see www.Meta-Analysis.com

Metawin Version 2.0, developed by Rosenberg, Adams and Gurevitch – see www.metawinsoft.com RevMan, developed by the the Cochrane Collaboration – see www.cc-ims.net/RevMan

Index

Page numbers followed by f are figures; those followed by t are tables.